Social Studies in a Global Society

Social Studies in a Global Society

Fred Stopsky
Sharon Shockley Lee
with the assistance of Roy Tamashiro

Delmar Publishers Inc. ™

Cover: Design M Design W
Delmar Staff

Associate Editor: Erin J. O'Connor
Senior Project Editor: Andrea Edwards Myers
Production Coordinator: James Zayicek
Art and Design Coordinator: Karen Kunz Kemp

For information, address Delmar Publishers Inc.
3 Columbia Circle, Box 15-015
Albany, New York 12212-5015

Copyright © 1994 by Delmar Publishers Inc.

The Trademark ITP is used under license.

Printed in the United States of America
Published simultaneously in Canada
by Nelson Canada,
a division of The Thomson Corporation

1 2 3 4 5 6 7 8 9 10 XXX 00 99 98 97 96 95 94

Library of Congress Cataloging-in-Publication Data
Stopsky, Fred.
    Social studies in a global society / Fred Stopsky, Sharon Shockley Lee,
Roy Tamashiro—1st ed.
        p.   cm.
    Includes bibliographical references (p.) and index.
    ISBN 0-8273-5655-2
    1. Social sciences—Study and teaching (Elementary)—United
States.   2. Curriculum planning—United States.   3. International
education—United States.   4. Social sciences—Study and teaching
(Elementary)—United States—Case studies.   I. Sharon Shockley Lee.
II. Roy Tamashiro, 1955– .   III. Title.
LB1584.S696   1994
372.83′044—dc20   93-25149
                                                              CIP

Contents

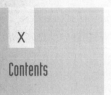

X

Contents

Preface

This book is written for the new generation of elementary and middle school teachers who will assume leadership in educating America's youth for the new century that dawns in a few short years. They face an awesome task to prepare children for life in a world undergoing the most rapid change in human history. The end of the Cold War, dramatic changes in economic interrelations, and fundamental alterations in the way people work and live place increased responsibility upon educators to make learning meaningful and relevant. Global understanding is more vital than ever before, and global collaboration is essential for humanity to resolve human and ecological issues that threaten world peace and survival. We realize no single book is capable of changing the educational system, but we hope our endeavors to demonstrate the active role youth can play within and outside school to improve the quality of life will make social studies the foundation of school programs upon which we can create a society that respects multiculturalism, diversity, and the uniqueness of each individual citizen.

Audience and Purpose

This book is primarily written for undergraduates taking a course in methods of teaching social studies for elementary or middle school. Graduate students or classroom teachers will also find the book beneficial in providing practical ideas that can be implemented within the elementary or middle school classroom.

Social studies has long been devalued among students because of its failure to be relevant to their lives. Our text offers a fresh perspective, combining theory with practical elements to make social studies a vibrant and exciting program that challenges students upon both intellectual and emotional levels. We emphasize that social studies is the study of how humans think, behave, feel, and act. Our text is a story about people and events because our past, present, and future are interesting stories about roads taken or not taken, about visions and dreams, about hopes and expectations.

The authors are teachers who taught in elementary, middle school, and high school. Our book is written for students who will one day teach students. The text offers a rich variety of concrete suggestions about making social studies interesting, and numerous examples drawn from the files of outstanding classroom teachers. These materials emphasize the importance of active student involvement in the learning process. Theory *is* important, but theory without engagement of the learner is empty.

Our text continually reinforces the concept that social studies is an active process in which learner and teacher collaborate to shape what is to be learned. The text demonstrates how to apply knowledge to the lives and interests of young people in ways that enable them to assume authorship of the learning process. Social studies is a never-ending story. The imagination of youth is best served by presenting them with the human drama that has and will continue to shape our ways of thought and behavior.

Coverage and Features

The text is organized around two basic ideas: integration of information with application, and models of successful practices. Throughout each chapter, the reader is provided numerous examples of how to apply information being learned to actual classroom situations, and at the conclusion is given examples drawn from lesson plans of outstanding elementary and middle school teachers. In addition, at the end of most chapters is a provocative reading selection related to material covered in the chapter.

The text offers several unusual features in addition to the normal range of material offered in elementary and middle school works. The information and lesson plans offered concerning global education are more far-reaching than previous texts, and action research, a way of engaging youth in the reconstruction of society, has not previously been presented. The chapter on creative thinking, which includes a segment on humor in education as well as practical memory strategies to enhance learning, offers the prospective teacher concrete ways to implement an exciting social studies program.

Our emphasis upon multiculturalism is demonstrated by focusing an entire chapter on this issue, and our endeavor to offer a path that links diversity with commonality should assist the novice in grasping the key elements in a multiethnic program of action. We emphasize the importance of a whole-language approach in teaching social studies and have paid particular attention to ways of providing an interdisciplinary approach to teaching about current events. The chapter on technology offers several examples of using technology within the framework of a social studies program.

At the end of each chapter are key questions and activities to stimulate dialogue within the class and engage students as active participants in social studies education. We seek to model in the textbook the same attitude toward social studies that teachers should model in the elementary and middle school classroom. There is also a list of suggested readings for further investigation of topics presented in the chapter.

Acknowledgments

It is ordinary in a textbook for authors to acknowledge their professional peers who have provided assistance in development of the project. We have been aided by professional colleagues, but our greater debt is to the thousands of elementary and middle school teachers we have been fortunate to teach in our combined forty years of sharing with students attending Webster University's graduate and undergraduate programs for classroom teachers. Their contribution to our knowledge is enormous; their practical advice cannot be replicated in any book ever written; and their continual dialogue about the "real world of teaching" has kept us from being divorced from reality.

The authors and Delmar Publishers would also like to thank those individuals who reviewed the manuscript and offered valuable suggestions and insight.

John A. Lutjemeier, Houston Baptist College
Kenneth Murray, West Virginia University
Robert D. Price, University of Colorado
Ben Smith, Kansas State University
Lloyd A. Stjernberg, Drake University
James Stockard, Auburn University
Kay Terry, Western Kentucky University

Our hope is that readers of this text will one day be able to share with their college educators a similar concern with meeting the needs of children, and a commitment to creating schools in which the integrity of each child is respected and diversity is recognized as a human right. The success of a text is not in number of copies sold, but in the impact it has upon readers to become participants in the reconstruction of society.

Prologue

The Animal School

Once upon a time, the animals decided they must do something heroic to meet the problem of a "new world." So, they organized a school. They adopted an activity curriculum consisting of running, climbing, swimming, and flying. To make it easier to administer the curriculum, all the animals took all the subjects.

The duck was excellent in swimming, in fact, better than his instructors, but he made only a passing grade in flying and was poor in running. Since he was failing running, he had to stay after school and also drop swimming in order to practice running. This was kept up until his web feet were badly torn and he was only average in swimming. But, average was acceptable in school, so nobody worried about that, except the duck.

The rabbit started at the top of class in running, but had a nervous breakdown because of so much make-up work in swimming. The squirrel was excellent in climbing until he became frustrated in the flying class when his teacher made him start from the ground up instead of from the tree down. He also developed a charley horse from overexertion and then got a "C" in climbing and a "D" in running.

The eagle was a problem child and was disciplined severely. In the climbing class he beat all the others to the top of the tree but insisted on using his own way to get there. At the end of the year an abnormal eel that could swim exceedingly well, and also run, climb, and fly a little, had the highest average and was valedictorian.

The prairie dogs stayed out of school and fought the tax levy because the administration would not add digging and burrowing to the curriculum. They apprenticed their child to a badger and later joined the groundhogs and gophers to start their own private school.

Introduction

This book is written for people who believe in the importance of human (and animal) diversity, and the right of each child to fulfill her or his unique capacities. Our introductory metaphor about the animal school contains the philosophy of this book: Curriculum must be relevant to the lives, interests, and needs of students. We believe the best vehicle to achieve this goal is creating exciting and meaningful social studies programs that engage students with the drama of human existence. Social studies is not about facts, but about the ongoing creation of today, and the re-creation of yesterday.

How can one re-create the past? We do it everyday when we reflect upon a past incident. The argument with a loved one is altered when flowers or a note appear, and our minds recast what happened in light of new events. Social studies is an active process, an ever-changing one in which each student has a role and function. The authors are aware that many students regard social studies as dealing with "dead events" or with the compilation of names, dates, and facts. Perhaps reviewing the common myths concerning social studies will enable the reader to gather a fresh perspective as she or he reads this book.

Myth: *Social studies is about names, dates, and facts.* This book emphasizes that social studies contains the diverse stories of human beings from every society on the face of this planet. The fact of one nation is the opinion of another. Americans refer to "World War II," but Russians call it "The Great Patriotic War." The authors agree that students need information, but that data should always be presented in a cultural context, not as a given. Native Americans were not discovered by Columbus; they were here in the western hemisphere and could logically argue that they discovered Columbus.

Myth: *Social studies is boring.* There are numerous studies indicating most students regard social studies as a boring subject. This book provides hundreds of practical suggestions to make social studies exciting and interesting. Social studies should be fun because it is about life, and social studies should be serious, because that is another aspect of everyday existence.

Myth: *Social studies is not practical.* Social studies is the most practical subject in the curriculum because it deals with understanding human behavior. Young people attempt to grasp how and why they behave as well as the more complex problem of understanding adult behavior. Social studies is the one subject area in the curriculum that is concerned with those everyday topics. In this book you will learn about successful social studies programs that train students to be "peer mediators" and how students work with their peers in resolving school conflict.

Myth: *Social studies covers too much material.* There is little doubt many teachers attempt to cover every aspect of a textbook and in so doing give equal treatment to the unimportant as well as the important. Our book emphasizes the need to focus in-depth upon fewer topics and separate trivia from importance. Great historians or social scientists concentrate to bring into clear perspective the ideas they are discussing. Social studies cannot "cover" everything; it is always selective and teachers must make choices about what is most relevant to the lives of students in their classrooms.

Myth: *Social studies has nothing to do with the community since it is about the past.* Social studies as conceived in our approach is vitally concerned about issues of local and national communities. You will read about successful programs in which students engage in Action Research to study local community issues and then take action to improve the quality of life within their own geographic environment. Unless students grasp the connection between the world of the classroom and the world outside, they will avoid becoming active participants to improve society.

Myth: *Social studies has to do with memorizing from a textbook.* Many social studies programs use textbooks, and it is all too common for some teachers to compel students to regurgitate information from those books. A textbook should be used as we use any book. It is a source of information, but similar and different information can be found in other books. A teacher who demands that students memorize a textbook is engaged in indoctrination, not democratic education. In our text we provide numerous strategies to make textbooks sources of investigation and stimulators of provocative thought. The textbook is a means, not an end, a tool to open new avenues of study.

Myth: *Students have to learn theory before they understand practice.* A theory is an opinion, not a fact. Theories arise from studying realities, and students can never grasp a theory without examining its source of reality. The classic example of teaching children "how a bill becomes a law" illustrates the necessity of examining reality in conjunction with theory. The textbook version of neat diagrams and arrows has scant connection with the dynamic process of steering a bill through Congress, a state legislature, or a city council. Interest groups, lobbyists, the legislator's philosophy, or the current state of the economy all influence the process. Theory must be combined with the actual practices or we teach youth an incorrect version of their world.

Myth: *Students don't know anything; they have to be taught information.* Each student represents a piece of the American and human fabric of existence. Many students live in single-parent or blended families, many experience the lay-off of a parent from work, and many walk to school in fear of their very lives. Youth know about drugs, violence, and ethnic hatred. They also know about examples of friendships bridging ethnic boundaries and people caring and loving one another. Students are a rich source of information about the real world of our society, and their knowledge should be incorporated within a social studies program.

Myth: *You can't teach thinking skills.* All humans from birth are thinking creatures. Educators who complain that students "don't know how to think" really mean "students aren't thinking the way I want them to think." Readers of this book thought differently in their younger years, but they engaged in critical thinking. The task of teachers is to assist youth to become reflective thinkers about their own thought process and that of other people. People can improve their capacity to be analytical in problem solving and can learn to understand (although not necessarily agree with) how other people resolve complex issues.

Myth: *Social studies teachers want to impose their values upon children.* There is little question that many teachers impose their values upon children. The "hidden curriculum" of schools is value-laden in its demand for obedience to rules, following school procedures, and punishing those who disobey. Social studies is the place in the curriculum for students to learn about the hidden curriculum, to learn about how values are inherent in educational organizations, and to become familiar with their own value orientations. Schools, by definition, arise from a values base. It is in social studies that students should learn about human values and begin the process of defining their own value belief system.

Challenges and Responsibilities

Teaching social studies from an active stance places new challenges and responsibilities upon teachers. A teacher who moves away from making a textbook the sum total of social studies and seeks to engage students in being active participants in creating schools that are healthy, vibrant centers of learning runs the risk of becoming "controversial." Unfortunately, in too many schools those who "play by the book" easily receive tenure since no parent becomes upset at what they teach. A teacher who asks students to reexamine values or become sensitive about the rights of all humans may anger some members of the community.

The authors of this book have been subject to "black lists" because they challenged members of the community who wanted schools to reflect a narrow range of values. Book censorship exists in many communities, and teachers are discharged because of their concern for equity in the educational process. We would not be truthful unless we brought to the reader's attention that teachers who seek an American society in which diversity is respected and individuality encouraged may run the risk of becoming the targets of angry members of the community.

There are parents, teachers, administrators, and school board members who want schools to indoctrinate youth with their mores and values. It is easy for an author to urge young teachers to take a stand against bigotry or narrowness, but from personal experience we know how lonely it is to give higher priority to the needs of your students than those of powerful community interest groups. We can only urge that you become active members of professional organizations such as the National Council for Social Studies and work to improve the quality of social studies.

Thousands of educators are working to create an American society in which gender issues, mutliculturalism, and global concerns are addressed in elementary and middle school classrooms. They need your cooperation to make social studies the vibrant core of a curriculum that will move America in positive directions towards a 21st century in which all humans can fulfill their inherent capacities. The challenge is awesome, but the rewards are in seeing that each and every one of your students has equity in opportunity and the right to a life of dignity.

Part 1

Social Studies and the Global Community: Directions and Issues

Chapter 1

Social Studies and the Changing Society

Social Studies and the Changing Society

A New Rationale for Social Studies

Social studies is not just the study of cultures or the story of humanity's past, but it is also a vehicle to move people toward a promising future. Many dream of a future world in which the dignity of each individual is respected and all can fulfill their human potentialities. The social studies involve the knowledge, attitudes, and skills which enable children to develop into wise, responsible, and effective citizen-ambassadors.

The globalization of everyday life, in effect, makes each individual a citizen-ambassador. Our decisions and actions in what we purchase, how we vote, or where we spend leisure time impacts the lives of people throughout the world. This generation of teachers is educating the future leaders of the world. One task of teachers is to provide an environment in which students not only enjoy their youth but also learn about the wider world in which one day they will become active participants.

Social conflict is pervasive in the world as nations emerge from the post-Cold War era and enter a period in which the divisive forces of tribalism and nationalism set former neighbors against one another. Elementary and middle school social studies cannot shield children from conflict. Instead, teachers need to help children understand the nature of conflict and learn conflict resolution techniques. When children discover how to resolve problems through tools such as negotiation, compromise, mediation, and arbitration, social studies becomes a relevant and practical source of knowledge.

Social studies has a unique place among academic disciplines. It encompasses every aspect of human life. For example, elementary and middle school social studies incorporates literature, poetry, science, math, music, and art to provide children a holistic view of people, places, and situations. A storybook can become for children a doorway to the past, a graph can clarify facts and figures, and music and art can allow children to enter the spirit and emotions of faraway peoples. Social studies is the story of human existence in all its manifold ramifications.

> Teach history in context so that people and events are seen in relation to consequential social and economic trends and political developments. A richly drawn portrait of a given time and place must also include a sense of the life of the times: the ideas that influenced people's behavior; their religious, philosophical, and political traditions; their literature, art and architecture; the state of their knowledge and technology; their myths and folktales; their laws and government. (Ravitch & Finn, 1987)

The social studies are the study of political, economic, cultural and environmental aspects of societies in the past, present, and future. It has several purposes for young children:

The social studies equip them with the knowledge and understanding of the past necessary for coping with the present and planning for the future, enable them to understand and participate effectively in their world, and explain their relationship to other people and to social, economic, and political institutions.(Ravitch & Finn, 1987)

Social studies differs from history and the social sciences in fundamental ways. The social studies are the social sciences simplified for pedagogical purposes. In history and social sciences the addition of new knowledge to the field is of major importance. Scholars seek to add to the sum total of human knowledge, but the social studies teacher deals with a restricted content and often lacks time or expertise to engage in research. Social studies is more concerned with synthesizing and applying knowledge from history and the social sciences. "It could be said that history and the social sciences are producers of knowledge, while social studies is largely a consumer" (Forino, Elementary School Journal, vol. 67).

The elementary and middle school teacher realizes that knowledge, by itself, does not ensure students will be reflective thinkers and active participants in a democratic society. The task of teachers is to assist students in using knowledge to make rational decisions. Social studies, math, science, or literature lessons can each serve a role in helping students to use knowledge for the betterment of themselves and their world.

Social studies provides students with critical thinking skills for productive problem solving and decision making. An effective social studies program enables students to be reflective, to analyze their values, and to make thoughtful judgments. Elementary and middle school social studies is as much concerned with critical thinking in the home, the playground, the school, the local community as it is with national or global issues. For many children their "real world" is that of school. The ideals of a democratic society, and critical thinking have to be practised in the daily life of the classroom.

School is a laboratory in which students learn to participate in a democratic manner in resolving problems. A successful social studies program is more than a series of random activities or experiences. There is need for system and organization to the process by which students gain understanding and are able to use concepts from history and the social sciences.

Children's attitudes and values are forming, and they need to become acquainted with a variety of ideas and opinions from many diverse sources. "They need to encounter and reencounter, in a variety of contexts, the knowledge, concepts, skills, and attitudes that form the foundation for participation in a democratic society" (NCSS, 1990).

In elementary and middle school, children begin to explore the concepts of time, space, and distance. These ideas are best presented in social studies to enhance their understanding of where they live in relationship to the world. Geography is an exciting and personally relevant topic which involves the story of how each child's ancestors arrived in America. It is as much a human as physical story which explores the study of physical, political, cultural, and economic relationships among people.

▲ The task of teachers is to assist students in using knowledge to make rational decisions. *Courtesy Webster University.*

Americans come from many backgrounds, but share common traditions and values. Social studies in elementary and middle school offers students understandings of their own and other cultures and helps to integrate those values and traditions that perpetuate the democratic spirit of our nation. Americans need knowledge to examine contemporary issues and problems successfully .

Although children have difficulty grasping the concept of time, they can gain an understanding of their historical heritage through techniques such as biographies, historical narratives, and historical fiction. The National Association for the Education of Young Children (1986, p. 34) reports that 8-year-olds are able to learn about people who live elsewhere in the world and that by age 9 they have well-established racial and ethnic prejudices. "Ten-year-olds are interested in the world, and anxious to investigate and learn about current world affairs. These children need exciting experiences in social studies if they are to internalize democratic ideals."

The heritage of Americans encompasses a multitude of conflicting interpretations of the past. Historians and social scientists continue to debate whether there is one or diverse heritages. The elementary school is the first place where children encounter this clash of ideas. We do a disservice to children by depriving them of knowledge from which they can make informed decisions. They require information and skills to analyze this data in order to learn how citizens reach conclusions.

To understand themselves, children have to learn how their own and other ethnic groups are woven into the rich fabric of American society and how each group contributed to the formation of our national heritage. The study of multiculturalism goes beyond the accumulation of names, dates, and facts. Multiethnicity is central to our continued existence as a democratic society, and children must learn and respect ways diverse peoples can live harmoniously. The social studies class has a primary responsibility to build a sense of community and commitment to cooperation.

▲ School is a laboratory in which students learn to participate in a democratic manner in resolving problems. *Courtesy Saint Louis (Missouri) Public Schools.*

Education within a pluralistic society should affirm and help students understand their home and community cultures. However, it should also help free them from their cultural boundaries. To create and maintain a civic community that works for the common good, education in a democratic society should help students acquire the knowledge, attitudes, and skills they will need to participate in civic action to make society more equitable and just. (Boules, 1986, p. 32)

The modern social studies teacher has to be cognizant of the vast array of information impacting the minds of children. Television enables even primary-age children to become aware of complex issues such as those linked to the Gulf War of 1991. Elementary school students read and see stories about drugs, pollution, and AIDS. By age 7, children have formulated fairly accurate conceptions of work, wants, and scarcity in their daily encounters with the economic system (Armento, 1986).

There is much that we know about how to teach social studies, and much that we are still attempting to understand. One apparent conclusion is the vital importance of the elementary years in laying the foundation of the active and informed citizen. The NCSS Task Force on Early Childhood/Elementary Social Studies bluntly states "that teachers who miss these crucial opportunities to build interest, to introduce concepts from history and the social sciences, and to develop social perspectives and civic understanding may make it more difficult for citizens of the 21st century to cope with their future" (National Council for the Social Studies Task Force).

The social studies curriculum is never fixed in time. Among elementary and middle school curricula it is the most complex, the most constantly altered by changing circumstances and events, and the most in need of critical analysis. Traditionally, the elementary and middle school social studies curriculum has been dominated by history and geography, but preparation for the 21st century is more complex. New manifestations of social studies are being created as you read these words. Thirty years ago social studies did not deal with topics such as women's studies, Native American cultures or African-American ethnicity. Social studies are a continually evolving field of inquiry.

▲ Geography involves the story of how each child's ancestors arrived in America. *Courtesy Kirkwood (Missouri) School District.*

Historian Charles Beard stated that in the 1930s social studies represented the "seamless web" of knowledge. The challenge for elementary and middle school teachers in the 1990s is to draw upon a vast array of resources to help students grasp human interaction and interdependence that characterize the closing years of the 20th century. This requires integrating academic disciplines in order to present the varied and complex story of human experience.

The novice teacher discovers there is much to teach and too little time. The elementary and middle school teacher has to focus precisely upon key concepts and teach them in depth. Not every theme included in a required curriculum or textbook is of equal importance. Selectivity always involves the risk of overemphasizing, trivializing, or underplaying material. You, the future teacher, are a curriculum designer and decision maker. You choose which issues to emphasize, the methods of instruction, and the approaches to integrate those concepts in a comprehensive perspective.

Mistakos' (1981) model of three social studies traditions shows how various assumptions about the meaning of social studies lead to different approaches and emphases. These traditions each imply a different approach to organizing curriculum materials. For example, if a teacher organized a lesson on the Revolutionary War using Social Studies Taught as Citizenship Transmission, the emphasis would be upon glorification of American heroes. If the focus was Social Studies Taught as Social Science, the emphasis might be upon the concept of "revolution" and its ramifications for contemporary times. A "Social Studies Taught as Reflective Inquiry" approach might ask students to view the Revolutionary War through the lens of an English or American patriot, and compare and contrast their views in hope that students would be better able to employ these insights in their own school conflict situations.

A teacher who is cognizant of the differing purposes of social studies is able to expand the range of curriculum materials and teaching strategies. Young people have differing needs, and an enriched social studies program is more apt to meet those intellectual and emotional needs.

Scope and Sequence

The term *scope* refers to the range of substantive content, values, skills, and learner experiences to be included in a social studies program. It also involves identifying appropriate life-related issues in order to give students opportunities to apply knowledge, values, and skills. Scope may focus on a narrow aspect of the curriculum, (e.g., map reading skills) or it may also be defined comprehensively to delineate the outer boundaries of subject matter, skills, and learner experiences.

Teachers and curriculum planners decide not only what to include in the social studies program, but the order in which the components appear, i.e., their *sequence*. Topics that are spatially or psychologically close to learners have traditionally appeared in the early grades. The "expanding environment" principle has been used in planning social studies sequences for the elementary school since the 1930s.

Recently this principle has been criticized. The National Council for the Social Studies Task Force on Scope and Sequence (1989, p. 378) did not recommend "that a social studies sequence rely solely on the expanding environment principle." It appears that the media, especially television, plays such a major role in children's experiences that curriculum planning based on the "expanding environment principle" cannot fully account for the rapid and unpredictable media events. Television exposes them to more knowledge about a catastrophe in Bangladesh or warfare in Europe than typical 6-year-olds know about their own local communities.

▲ Multiethnicity is central to our continued existence as a democratic society. *Courtesy Saint Louis (Missouri) Public Schools.*

Table 1-1: The Three Social Studies Traditions

SOCIAL STUDIES TAUGHT AS:		
TRANSMISSION	**SOCIAL SCIENCE**	**REFLECTIVE INQUIRY**
PURPOSE To inculcate appropriate values as a framework for making decisions.	To apply social science concepts, skills, and processes in decision making.	To use inquiry as both the source of knowledge and for problem solving and decision making.
METHOD Textbook recitation, lecture, question-answer sessions, structured problem solving exercises, and others.	Data-gathering and knowledge verification method appropriate to each social science.	Processes involving identifying problems, challenging conflicting views, and structured decision making.
CONTENT Material illustrating values, beliefs and attitudes selected by an authority interpreted by the teacher.	Material involving the structure, concepts, problems, and processes of the various social sciences.	Material for student-selected problems that emerge from the analysis of each student's values, needs and interests.

SOURCE: Charles Mistakos, "The Nature and Purposes of Social Studies," in *Education in the 80's*, ed. Jack Allen, (Washington: National Education Association, 1981), p. 16.

The Task Force stated that "the purpose of extending content outward, away from a self centric focus is to illustrate how people and places interact; how people of different areas depend upon one another; how people are part of interlocking networks that sustain the life of modern societies, and how people and places everywhere fit into a global human community" (NCSS, 1989). An American child is part of the same human experience as children everywhere, and the task of educators is to help them build those linkages.

Some educators organize curriculum around the principle of progressing from the simple to the complex. However, topics are intrinsically neither simple nor complex. For example, graduate students and second graders both study "the family," though at different levels of analysis. Scope and sequence charts depicting subject matter arranged sequentially according to presumed difficulty may create erroneous impressions about the complexity of content.

There are several ways to sequence social studies materials:

1. From simple to complex.
2. In chronological order.
3. In reverse chronological order. Elementary teachers frequently begin with current events and work backwards.
4. From geographically near to geographically far.
5. From far to near. Study other nations, then study the United States and the local neighborhood.
6. From concrete to abstract. Study neighborhood environmental issues, and then national or global.
7. From general to the particular. Examine the idea of poverty, and then deal with specific examples.
8. From particular to the general. Examine local issues of pollution, and then explore the general concept of pollution. (Oliva, 1988)

The Open Education movement of the 1960s and 1970s emphasized that children should decide the order of sequencing. Advocates believed children were able to order their own learning patterns and would select what was needed to be learned. They wanted teachers to be sensitive to the needs of children and use the child's decisions about learning as the starting point for scope and sequence.

▲ Young people have differing needs which can be met through an enriched social studies curriculum. *Courtesy Webster University.*

Psychologists such as Jean Piaget or Arnold Gesell have identified stages of children's growth and development. Their supporters argue that curriculum scope and sequence should be attuned to the corresponding stage of the child's developmental process. This idea is very common in school district curriculum guides.

A continuing source of conflict in scope and sequence revolves around the issue of whether subject matter content or the child's maturation stage should determine what is learned at each grade level. The first assumes adults know which material children can master at each grade level, while the latter emphasizes relating content to the actual children in your classroom. This will probably continue to be an ongoing debate.

The issue of complexity is less important than the way subject matter is taught. A motivated teacher can inspire students to study material they ordinarily would have difficulty understanding. A teacher's excitement is frequently contagious and encourages children to become interested in the lesson. Young children learn best when presented concrete experiences and manipulable materials. They are interested when they see relevance to their own lives in what is being learned.

The National Council for the Social Studies Task Force on Scope and Sequence recommends the following scope and sequence:

Kindergarten: Awareness of Self in Social Setting.

Grade 1: The Individual in Primary Social Groups: Understanding School and Family Life.

Grade 2: Meeting Basic Needs in Nearby Social Groups: The Neighborhood.

Grade 3: Sharing Earth Space with Others: The Community.

Grade 4: Human Life in Varied Environments: The Region

Grade 5: People of the Americas: The United States and Its Close Neighbors.

Grade 6: People and Cultures: Representative World Regions

Grade 7: A Changing World of Many Nations: A Global View

Grade 8: Building a Strong and Free Nation: The United States

Grade 9: Systems that Make a Democratic Society Work: Law, Justice and Economics

Grade 10: Origin of World Cultures: A World History

Grade 11: The Maturing of America: United States History

Grade 12: One year course or courses; selection from the following:

- Issues and Problems of Modern Society
- Introduction to the Social Sciences
- The Arts in Human Societies
- International Area Studies
- Social Science Elective Courses (NCSS, 1989)

Ralph Tyler (1965) defined the scope of the curriculum as the breadth of the curriculum — its content, topics, learning experiences, and organizing threads. There are several factors for teachers to consider in deciding which content fits one of the previously stated general headings. Content has to be relevant to the lives of children. The novelist Herman Wouk in *City Boy* depicts a group of boys sitting on the stoops opposite Public School 50 arguing about baseball averages. They hear the bell sounding time for school, and one boy exclaims, "Now we have to study that dumb old math."

Teachers have to balance student life experiences with the demands of the school curriculum. Society insists that certain information be conveyed to youth, and a skill in teaching is weaving back and forth between the formal curriculum and the world of children. A great teacher makes seemingly dull curriculum come alive in the minds of children.

A key ingredient in a successful scope and sequence is enabling students to visualize and understand the connections between various disciplines taught in the school curriculum. An elementary or middle school teacher, unlike those teaching at the secondary levels, has the unique opportunity to create lesson plans which integrate knowledge. For example, how can reading Snow White be related to a social studies lesson on law?

▲ The social studies curriculum enables American children to understand that they are participants in a global human community. *Courtesy Null Elementary, Saint Charles (Missouri) Public Schools.*

Jerome Bruner (1968) helped popularize the idea of a spiral curriculum. He suggested introducing the basics of academic disciplines in the early grades, and then repeating them with increasing levels of complexity and sophistication throughout a student's career in education. Social studies scope and sequence in this model concerns itself with locating where in the K-12 curriculum to teach a concept, and then where and how it would be taught at increasing levels of complexity. For example, the concept of "interpretation" in second grade could be introduced by discussing Cinderella's version of the ball and a version told by a stepsister. A twelfth grader might deal with the same concept by reading contrasting views of historians about a topic in history.

John I. Goodlad (1963, p. 28) defines scope as "the actual focal points for learning through which the school's objectives are to be attained." He regards expressions such as "activities" or "learning experiences" as too narrow to convey the breadth and scope of what a teacher potentially can include in a single lesson. He prefers to use the term "organizing centers" which can range from a poem, a trip to study soil erosion, a guest speaker, a unit of work or a book.

The novice teacher who is introduced to a school district's curriculum guide can be intimidated by the volume of information it contains. Many teachers find it convenient to use the textbook as a guide for what is to be covered rather than as one of many sources of information. They may allow textbook "conclusions" to replace alternative ideas and views. A strict adherence to curriculum expectations fosters minimal, rather than maximum, student performance. A guide describes the general contours of the trip, but the teacher is responsible for its daily activities.

There is also an *implicit* curriculum in a social studies classroom. Behavior, attitudes, and values in the classroom can frequently assume greater importance than what is being taught. Courtesy and respect for another's opinions are essential in a democratic classroom, but they are means rather than ends in themselves. The integrity and individuality of each child must be respected, and that can only come about when everyone in the class behaves in a democratic fashion. Teachers must be cognizant that adherence to school rules is best internalized when children play an active role in organizing and implementing the democratic processes of the classroom.

▲ A teacher's excitement is contagious. *Courtesy Kirkwood (Missouri) School District.*

Social studies can model for students the democratic process of our nation. Students have a right to be different, and all students have a right to safety and respect for their dignity as humans. Social studies is the proper place to have class meetings, discuss behavior issues, and work toward establishing class procedures which are consistent with our democratic values as a nation.

A related issue facing social studies education is what we avoid teaching. Do we teach the story of the United States as one in which things went smoothly under the guidance of mistake-free leadership? Do we avoid controversial issues? Elementary school teachers cannot include everything, but a decision to leave out material should be a conscious one that is based upon a rationale.

The complexity of social studies need not overwhelm the novice teacher. There are materials that guide, people who are supportive, and one's own personal reservoir of resources to serve as a base, all of which will expand with experience. Social studies is ever-changing, it is exciting material, and it deals directly with life issues facing children. The challenge is great, the reward even greater.

Trends in Modern Society

The future is emerging now since it emanates from decisions and events in the present. We can never precisely define what will happen at a future time, but we can become students of current trends since they ultimately impact the future. "As a society, we have been moving from the old to the new. And we are still in motion. Caught between eras, we experience turbulence. Yet, amid the painful and sometimes uncertain present, the restructuring of America proceeds unrelentingly" (Naisbitt, 1982, p. 1).

Young children live in the present both in mind and body. Yet, in their actions, they also shape trends impacting American society. Elementary and middle school teachers can assist them to draw upon their own knowledge to better understand the dynamic nature of the ever-changing world.

Alvin Toffler (1980) argues that we are in the midst of a new paradigm of change that is analogous in scope and impact to the Industrial Revolution. Elements of these changes are apparent in our everyday lives, but we are so caught in the immediacy of the moment and rapidity of the changes that it becomes difficult to stand apart and witness the dawn of a new civilization.

> This new civilization brings with it new family styles; changed ways of working, loving and living; a new economy; new political conflicts; and beyond this an altered consciousness as well. . . . Millions are already attuning their lives to the rhythms of tomorrow. Others, terrified of the future, are engaged in a desperate, futile flight into the past and are trying to restore the dying world that gave them birth (p. 9).

Teachers can help students become successful citizens in the future by enabling them to grapple with issues of the present. This means teachers have to become familiar with the dynamics of change, particularly with its impact upon the field of social studies. Table 1-2 shows several key trends that are rippling through American society.

▲ A great teacher makes curriculum come alive in the minds of children. Photo by Claudia Burris. *Courtesy Webster University.*

Accelerated Change and an Uncertain Future

American school children are the first generation to confront an unknown economic and social future. Years ago, individuals obtained jobs on farms or in factories, and offices, and it was common for many to remain employed in a single position for their entire lives. Changing technology or global competition forces many to change or lose jobs, and they discover that knowledge learned in school may not be applicable in their quest for new positions.

It is estimated that 25% of jobs that will exist in the year 2005 have yet to be invented. Just twenty five years ago many present day occupations did not exist. For example, jobs in video rental stores, building and working with personal computers or VCRs, positions in satellite and cable television, have only come about in the past two decades. Children throughout the world who live in a modern technological society must be prepared to deal with economic uncertainty of the 21st century.

American corporations are restructuring themselves to meet global competition. Millions of middle managers are being fired and the survivors compelled to do extra work without financial

Table 1-2: Implications of Societal Trends

SOCIETAL TREND	IMPLICATIONS FOR SOCIETY	IMPLICATIONS FOR CLASSROOMS
Accelerated Change and an Uncertain Future.	• Downsizing of corporate America. • Family turmoil. • Occupations of the future are not yet definbed. • Individuals will change careers several times in their working lives.	• Curricula will be transformed. • Skills for dealing with change, ambiguity, and flexibility will be emphasized.
Changing Demographics.	• Aging population. • Increase in children in poverty.	• Aging school faculty and administration. • School must work with children in poverty and drug-addicted.
Telecommunications and Information Technology in a Global Village.	• Immediacy of information. • Information overload.	Schools linked to global network. More information.
Pluralistic, Multiethnic and Multicultural Environment.	• Potentially more conflict, and tensions. • Pressures to include ignored groups increase.	• Challenges to academic disciplines. • Cultural histories to be included in new curricula.
Cultural Revolution.	Increased adult/youth conflict.	Youth challenges authority.
Role Differentiation.	People continually switch roles.	Teacher/students interact on many role levels.
Families Come In Many Forms.	Increase in divorce and single parenting.	Harder to involve parents with school in traditional ways.
Expanding Individual Rights.	Greater conflict and more resort to courts to resolve.	Students aware of rights and more often challenge authority figures in schools.
Decline in the Quality of the Environment, Urban Life, and Health.	• Lower quality of life. • Fewer new cures for diseases, increased medical costs.	• Increased concern about the use, disposal and recycling of teaching materials. • Medical spending may preempt educational spending. • Increased absenteeism in schools.
A Global Economy.	Employment impacted by world events.	Global decisions impact school finances, curriculum, etc.

compensation. In 1991, 20% of the workforce was unemployed at one point or another. Other industrial nations are facing similar projections.

Corporate restructuring directly affects children. Their parents live in fear of being replaced, dealing with a lay off, or may witness the end of a career. It means putting a house up for sale or moving in hope of finding new jobs. Corporate restructuring will continue throughout the nineties leaving in its wake demoralized families and frightened children.

Throughout the 20th century, humans have experienced more and swifter change than at any other time in previous history. There are still people alive who witnessed the introduction of the automobile and the radio. The baby boom generation, which is now pushing their forties, has gone from black and white TV screens to a proliferation of media which has altered the nature of home entertainment. The 55-plus generation recalls outdoor toilets, trolleys, and 5-cent movies while today's youth can't even purchase a stick of gum with a nickel.

Acceleration in change affects every facet of our lives. Human knowledge is doubling every ten years. The United Nations has gone from fifty countries at its birth to over 175 today with more awaiting entry. The skills and information of today may not necessarily be effective tools for people living in the coming decades.

Toffler argues that the human mind cannot assimilate all the changes impacting society at any one period of time. The elementary school teacher cannot hope to keep up with the knowledge explosion. A teacher whose goal is imparting data will be overwhelmed by information. Content is a tool to help educate children in successfully confronting and guiding change in productive ways.

The curriculum for the school of the future has yet to be invented in any nation. This does not imply we must abandon all that was taught in the past because our human heritage is vitally important to the emotional and intellectual health of society. The only certainty we have about the future is that it is uncertain. One of our tasks as educators is to invent a curriculum that enables people to live successfully amidst uncertainty.

▲ The skills and information of today may not be effective tools in the next decade. *Courtesy Null Elementary, Saint Charles (Missouri) Public Schools.*

Changing Demographics

The parents of elementary and middle school children are the post-baby-boom generation. Parents and their children are the largest age cohort in the U.S. population, and they are making America a maturing society. In 1900, the average age of Americans was 17, today it is 32, and in Japan it is approaching 35.

There are too many people in this cohort for the existing top level positions of a post modern economy. They are encountering a slower movement to the top of the career ladder, and a relative decline in income. Some economists predict that those entering the workforce in the 1970s and 1980s may be the first generation of Americans to earn less than their parents. Similar patterns are reported in Europe and Japan.

The 55-plus generation is also rapidly increasing in numbers. This group constitutes a powerful voting bloc which can determine school finances in many districts. An exciting possibility for elementary social studies is to form a bond between today's youth and the generation of their grandparents. This linkage can be educationally powerful as well as help establish among the elderly a vested interest in supporting quality education for youth.

Among the young, there has been a 25% increase nationwide of children living in poverty during the last decade. There is also a corresponding increase in drug-addicted infants (such as "crack" babies). Schools will need to be prepared to work with this increase in the number of children with problems.

Schools also reflect changing demographics. Teachers and administrators, even school buildings, are getting older on average. A large number of educators are expected to retire in this decade, and there may be need for extensive rebuilding of the physical infrastructure of schools. These changes might create new opportunities for extensive curriculum experimentation as a new group assumes leadership in education.

Telecommunications and Information Technology in a Global Village

Time magazine's "Man of the Year" in 1991 was Ted Turner, who developed Cable News Network (CNN). A generation ago Marshall McLuhan (1964) proclaimed the advent of a "global village" in which communication media would transcend national boundaries and link people together in an information network. Turner's CNN was hailed as a major source of information for leaders as well as the average person. It has changed the nature of world diplomacy by compelling national leaders to confront publicly the media's impact on their decisions.

▲ An exciting possibility is to form a bond between today's children and the generation of their grandparents. *Courtesy Saint Louis (Missouri) Public Schools.*

The Information Age is here, and the pace and volume of available information continues to increase dramatically. A stock market rally in London, a summit in Moscow, a violent election campaign in Colombia, or a rock concert in Central Park can be seen live practically anywhere on Earth. School children viewing these events at home take the reality and availability of global information for granted. Students can now obtain information not found in their social studies textbooks from sources simultaneously viewed by children all over the globe.

Changes in technology will accelerate the ability of children to become visually connected. "What we are seeing is not just the globalization of television but also, through television, the globalization of the globe" (McLuhan, 1964, p. 314).

The prevalence of these technologies presents new teaching and learning opportunities and mandates. Schools must assume a role in educating children to manage the constant flow of information. Data overload can lead some people to become lethargic while others may feel confused or inadequate. The ability to organize information and make it serve a useful function in one's professional and personal lives is among the new basic skills necessary for survival in the Information Age.

The availability of these technologies means that school can function effectively without being limited to the four walls of the classroom. Live or archived information and data are available via the cable television or satellite receiver in the building. Teachers and students can access educational materials and library reference materials without leaving the classroom through use of videotape, videodisc, and CD-ROM technologies. This has implications for delivering or receiving instruction on a worldwide basis. The transfer of knowledge and data via telecommunications has the potential to remove barriers of physical distances and travel times across the city or across continents.

Pluralistic, Multiethnic, and Multicultural Environment

The U.S. population mix including white Americans, African Americans, Hispanics, Asians and Native Americans is changing rapidly, and non-whites will constitute an increasing segment of

▲ The social studies curriculum must reflect the cultural heritages of diverse peoples.
Courtesy Saint Louis (Missouri) Public Schools.

the future population. Our social environment, both nationally and internationally, can be expected to be more diverse and more pluralistic. Individual and cultural differences can create more conflict within communities or schools and also lead to increased pressure for inclusion within the curriculum of groups previously ignored or slighted.

There are new challenges within schools to the traditions of Western civilization serving as the basis of the academic disciplines. The Eurocentric social studies curriculum is being transformed to reflect growing diversity in America. The curriculum of schools must become a curriculum of inclusion to reflect the cultural heritages of diverse peoples.

There is controversy regarding how to change the curriculum to reflect the changing ethnic composition of America. There are nearly as many Moslems in America as Jews, and Asians who come from many countries are the fastest growing group in the United States. Teaching about ethnicity in elementary social studies is an exciting challenge. It does not mean abandoning cultural traditions or values but recasting them to reflect who Americans are today.

Similar ethnic issues are arising in other parts of the globe. France has over five million Moslem citizens, Germany has millions of people from Turkey and other southern European nations, Asians and blacks now constitute over 10% of the British population, and each day's newspaper reports strife and ethnic conflict throughout the world.

The elementary and middle school social studies classroom will be at the center of change in the coming decade. In this setting, children will read about, see on television, and meet people from all parts of the world, and they will learn to handle conflict and develop respect for the integrity of each individual. The Los Angeles school system reports the presence of over 100 ethnic groups in its elementary school population. Elementary and middle school children now belong to a world community.

In effect, all, except Native Americans, are descendents of relatively recent immigrants. One out of three Americans in 1914 was an immigrant or the child of one. The United States has been striving for 200 years to create an environment in which diverse peoples can fulfill their individual heritages and function in cooperative ways with other Americans.

Cultural Revolution

Twenty-five years ago young people were enthralled by the Beatles or hummed the latest Bob Dylan song. Woodstock, long hair, and "doing your own thing" characterized the 1960s. Each era in human history had its share of fads, but today's adults were exposed to dramatic changes in dress, sound, and sight far surpassing any previous generation. They were bombarded by over 80,000 commercials prior to high school graduation, and their children are experts about advertising.

The family or neighborhood once shaped cultural tastes. Today, cultural messages come electronically from every part of the world. A visiting British rock group can turn youngsters on to a new fad. A motion picture made in France can create a new look in clothes. A videotape from Germany can expose children to sexual imagery that would embarrass an adult.

Technology has freed youth from adult control over its cultural interests. Children in different societies share similar tastes in music, dress, and behavior. They increasingly expect that schools demonstrate standards of excellent performance equal to those of the commercial world.

The media will continue to direct the flow of youth culture. The elementary and middle school classroom must learn to utilize technology more effectively. Teachers cannot take the place of rock stars, but they can assist young people to examine the values underlying their culture and their heroes.

Role Differentiation

Adults in American society perform several roles: personal, family, occupational, and societal. Each role requires differing skills, and each carries a cluster of stress factors. The parent brings to each conference with a teacher multiple roles and stresses.

The complexity of modern society pulls individuals simultaneously in several directions. The quest for personal satisfaction clashes with the desire for family. Their roles as mother or father carry stresses just as their occupational roles demand time and attention away from the family. A crisis in the Middle East can send father or mother on a dangerous mission abroad.

Christopher Lasch (1978) believes we have become a "narcissistic society" in which personal fulfillment takes precedence over all other obligations. People want careers, children, and a happy home life irrespective of the financial and emotional costs. Elementary school teachers should be cognizant that these demands impose time constraints upon parents. It may require inventing new opportunities for parent involvement in schools and rethinking the schedule for parent conferences.

Families Come In Many Forms

Census figures in 1990 show that the number of households in which a married couple lived with young children was 26% of the total in 1990, down from 40% in 1970. Average family size dropped from 3.58 in 1970 to 3.17 in 1990. It is estimated that half the children entering kindergarten this year will spend some time in either a single-parent or blended family prior to graduation from high school. The traditional "Leave It to Beaver" family portrayed in some textbooks — Mommy at home while Daddy works — is rapidly disappearing. It is estimated that fewer than 15% of American families fit this traditional model. "In a real sense we are beginning a post-ideological discussion of the family" (Klineberg, 1991, p. 15).

In her book on the American family, *Embattled Paradise,* Arlene Skolnick (1991) argues that our stereotypical thinking about family stems from the 1950s which she considers a unique interlude of domestic stability in a century of steady evolution of sexual mores and family structures. And, once the recent changes in the family are viewed as part of a historical continuum, the changing status of women emerges as the major ongoing dynamic from the end of the Victorian era until now.

Dual-career families and single parenting are rapidly becoming the norm. Mom and dad mesh busy work schedules to accommodate the child's needs. Social studies classrooms have to reflect changing gender roles; perhaps mom is asked to discuss future careers while dad gives a cooking demonstration. "Room mothers" may be replaced by "room grandparents."

Single parenting impacts millions of children. Latchkey children are home alone without adult supervision during homework time. Family life must become an important topic in the elementary social studies curriculum. Your classroom may be the only place children can articulate their fears, anxieties, hopes, or concerns about living in a blended family with step-brothers, -sisters, and a stepmother. Social studies offers an opportunity to learn about gay parent situations or the extended family structure common to many ethnic groups. Schools today face greater challenges than ever before in aiding children to function successfully within changing home environments.

Expanding Individual Rights:

The past forty years have witnessed momentous expansion in the definition of individual rights. In *Brown vs. Board of Education (1954)* the United States Supreme Court declared segregated schools to be unconstitutional and ushered in decades of struggle to define the meaning of discrimination and eliminate prejudice in our society.

The definition of rights has benefited youth. PL 94-142 (Education For All Handicapped Children Act, 1975) provided handicapped children equal entry into schools, including architectural adjustments to school buildings. Children have the right of free speech — within limits — in schools, and arbitrary actions by teachers or administrators can be subject to review by outside authorities. These changes require teachers to keep more detailed records and be sensitive to the legal right of children to be treated as unique individuals.

▲ It has been estimated that half the children who entered kindergarten in 1992 will spend time in a single-parent or blended family before they graduate from high school. *Courtesy Saint Louis (Missouri) Public Schools.*

The expansion of rights has benefited minorities, women, gays, and the aged. It has brought the courts into schools leading to enforcement of desegregation, revision of the curriculum, and to the seizure of school districts by officers of the court as in Boston. Educators are in the forefront of America's struggle to create a just and equitable society.

Decline in the Quality of the Environment, Urban Life and Health

The historic American belief in unlimited resources is being replaced with recognition that planet Earth has limited resources that must be safeguarded. Humans have depleted the earth's nonrenewable natural resources in an ongoing quest for personal consumption and living for the present. In addition, we have disturbed some critical biochemical balances such as the ozone layer and carbon dioxide in the atmosphere. Air and water quality is threatened; numerous species of flora and fauna are becoming extinct as rainforests are leveled to satisfy nearsighted human interests.

But even with heroic efforts now, the continuing deterioration of air, atmosphere, and water quality has already taken its toll, and has set in motion health consequences for years to come. This will impact quality of life in general, and increase medical costs. Teachers may notice increased absenteeism due to health issues.

Limited resources means less funding for education. The post-Sputnik thrust of the 1960s to expend monetary resources to improve American education will probably not be replicated in the 1990s. Reform of education will occur with limited resources to support the rhetoric for change. Teachers will be called upon to utilize their ingenuity to scrounge materials or accomplish goals within scanty budgets.

Children are surprisingly sensitive to environmental issues and have a growing awareness about the need to conserve our limited resources. Social studies can draw upon this interest to directly involve students in local efforts at environmental education.

A Global Economy

The United States is involved in an export/import trade worth over $800 billion. We are part of a global economy in which decisions made in Japan or Berlin can impact the lives of children in your schools. American firms seek overseas locations to produce materials cheaper or gain entry to markets such as the European Economic Community.

Foreign organizations are either purchasing American corporations or establishing their own facilities within the United States. America has to borrow billions of dollars each year from foreign investors to cover its annual budget deficit. Many American business leaders head multinational corporations that happen to be headquartered in this nation.

The global economy is more complex than American firms building factories abroad or foreign corporations investing in the United States. It is also an awareness of the interconnectedness and interdependence of nations. We cannot ignore the Berlin wall coming down, the crisis in the Gulf or conflicts in South Africa. The world is becoming smaller and each event directly affects children in your classroom.

It may appear overwhelming, but the elementary and middle school teacher's classroom is part of a world network. Changes at every level of the system impact all classrooms, and schools have to prepare students to function successfully in this new world order.

There is no cookbook which offers easy recipes for solutions to the problems of a changing world. The challenge is to create within each classroom a laboratory in which students experiment with problem-solving techniques and decision-making strategies. Social studies offers children an awareness that they need not be passive receivers of change; they can become participants in directing changes toward a new American society.

The New Basic Skills

Children who entered fourth grade in 1991 will be the first Americans to graduate from high school in the 21st century. If they attain normal life expectancy, these children will die around 2060, and some will be alive for the American tricentenary in 2076. Their mid life crisis will occur around 2020, and their own children will live to witness the birth of the 22nd century.

Fifty years ago schools prepared students to live in an industrial world centered around the assembly line that demanded obedience and conformity to superiors. A strong back, the willingness to work, and a high school diploma were once all that were needed to make a start in America. "They are no longer. A well-developed mind, a passion to learn, and the ability to put knowledge to work are the new keys to the future of our young people, the success of our business, and the economic well-being of the nation" (Secretary of Labor's Commission, 1991, p. 1).

SCANS (Secretary of Labor's Commission on Achieving Necessary Skills) spent over a year examining the changing patterns of work in America. The traditional basic skills are still important — the ability to read, write, and do arithmetic—but the disappearance of high paying unskilled jobs and their replacement with work requiring "smarter" workers requires a new set of basic skills. The emergence of what Peter Drucker calls "knowledge workers" means employees of the future must be able to be creative and responsible problem solvers who put knowledge to work.

The days of standardized rote performance on the assembly lines are disappearing. A modern economy requires a relentless commitment to excellence, product quality, and customer satisfaction. Decisions must be made closer to the frontline of an organization and draw upon the abilities of workers to think creatively and assume responsibility for solving problems.

A new set of "basic skills" is emerging to supplement those taught in schools. These new skills not only pertain to the workplace but are equally important to success in home and interpersonal relations. We are a more complex society and people need more complex skills to function at high levels of effectiveness.

Group Process Skills

Business people report that on a typical day, about 40% of their time is spent at meetings. Effective participation in group sessions will be essential in most careers of the future. An important new basic skill will be utilizing group process skills to make meetings a productive use of time. The individual who knows how to maximize satisfaction of both individual and group goals will be a highly valued team member in the workplace. David Johnson and Frank Johnson have identified the components of this skill:

▲ Creative problem solving is a basic skill for success in the 21st century. *Courtesy Kirkwood (Missouri) School District.*

1. Ability to clarify goals in terms of the best match between the goals of individuals and the goals of the group.

2. Communicating ideas and feelings accurately and clearly.

3. Sharing participation and leadership among group members.

4. Sharing power and influence throughout the group. These dimensions should be based on expertise, ability, and access to information, and not on authority or position.

5. Making productive use of conflict. Minority opinions should be respected and incorporated into the decision making process.

6. Fostering group cohesion and trust among all members.

7. Creating an environment which encourages the fullest use of problem solving abilities.

8. Creating an environment which encourages interpersonal communication. (Johnson & Johnson, 1975)

Preparation for group effectiveness can begin in school. The classroom of the future can emphasize students working in teams, becoming skilled at accomplishing team tasks, and being empathetic group participants. A focus on this skill will shift education away from teacher-centered and teacher-controlled classrooms to those in which teachers coach students to function successfully in achieving team goals.

Success Through Failure

A major function of schooling is selection and sorting of students. Grades are a major mechanism to accomplish the assignment of future social roles and status to students. An "F" grade brands the individual as inadequate and a failure. We need to reexamine our view of failure.

Failure is a normal occurrence in an organization or institution. It is through failure that scientists learn how to create new drugs or products. A major league baseball player "fails" seven out of ten times at bat. We acclaimed Michael Jordan as a superstar even though he "failed" on forty percent of his shots. A teacher would flunk him, yet he was paid millions.

Failure is a learning experience that hones necessary skills and attitudes to be successful in the workplace or in one's personal life. Elementary and middle school children will witness the extinction of many current jobs, and it is highly likely that a majority of them will have three or four different occupations during the course of their worklife.

Students have to learn how to work through failure. We need to rethink the meaning and purpose of failure. Students should be encouraged to try new approaches and rewarded with high grades if the attempt was interesting or innovative. Schools must educate a generation in which failure is respected as part of the process of innovation. For many people, failure may be a prelude to launching a new career or reworking a marriage. Perhaps some students will receive "A" grades if their failure displays creative thinking.

Risk-Taking

The culture of schools emphasizes the need to "play it safe." Many students learn to meet teacher expectations by doing the required work and nothing beyond that point. Is there an intellectual and emotional price young people pay for striving to be obedient students? Creative thinkers are not necessarily "A" students as witness the lives of Thomas Edison, Henry Ford, Franklin D. Roosevelt, and Abraham Lincoln. Few schools encourage students to go beyond the limits established by curriculum guides.

Americans begin over 400,000 new enterprises each year. The vast majority of these go under within a year, but it is not uncommon for these risk-takers to begin afresh with a new idea. A majority of new jobs created during the past decade emanated from the fast-food industry and human service occupations. Our future as a society lies in the hands of enterprising women and men who are willing to risk uncertainty in order to succeed.

Schools can become a birthplace of risk taking. Educators must become willing to encourage students to practice risk taking. They need assignments which go beyond recalling textbook material, and they should be encouraged to gamble on new approaches to classroom work. Students need new rewards for academic risk taking.

Lifelong Learning

Traditionally, society has assumed that individuals can learn all they need to know in school. The ability to read, write, and do arithmetic is only part of preparation for life. Children will live amidst continual flux. They will be educated for a particular job, work in that occupation, witness its demise, obtain new education for the next career step, and so on.

Schools are merely the first rung on the ladder of lifelong learning. Students have to learn how to learn. This will require schools to de-emphasize worksheets and textbooks that foster the belief that once the page or chapter is completed, students *know* the material. It is more important for students to learn how to obtain information they need than to learn assigned material.

The library has to become the center of learning. It is in the library that students gain skills in exploring answers to their own unanswered questions. Their quest for information will require working in pairs or small groups because they must understand the importance of using a network approach to gather data for problem solving.

Respecting the Diversity of Humanity

America is undergoing dramatic demographic changes. California in this decade will become the first state in which white Americans are a minority of the population. Hispanics, Asians, and Afro-Americans will constitute a growing percent of the nation. A significant proportion of business enterprises will be owned by people from other countries.

Elementary and middle school children will be required to interact with people of many cultures and behaviors in a manner that respects the integrity and right of people to be different. Empathy, respect for individuality, enjoying other customs and values will be among the qualities needed in American society. Prejudice, as we know it, cannot be allowed in the future.

Schools have to teach and practice effective human relations skills at an early age. This means school staffing at all levels has to reflect diversity, and curriculum materials have to incorporate a wider range of information than currently in practice. The task is complex. It is not sufficient to discuss "Asians" or "Africans" or "Moslems"; it is necessary to acquaint students with the extraordinary diversity of these peoples' cultures. Teachers must continually educate themselves and develop human resources to provide students with exposure to human diversity.

Creativity

Too often schools have regarded creativity as the province of "gifted" students. Students who earn good grades are not necessarily gifted or creative. In fact, many students who are successful in traditional schools may lack creativity. They frequently are those able to work within the limitations of school structures who are hesitant to go beyond existing boundaries.

Creativity involves the ability to see new patterns within existing information. The individual who took a round object and turned it into a Hula-Hoop was employing creative thinking skills. The individual who developed velcour was a creative thinker. Creative thinking is found within people of all cultures, and is not restricted to those with good grades.

All students need education in creative thinking. We need this type of attitude among secretaries and mechanics as well as among scientists. Every student should be educated to think in a creative manner. We need schools fostering gifted thinking rather than classes in which a select few are exposed to interesting materials. Creative problem solving is a basic skill for success in the emerging world of the 21st century.

The new basic skills can and must be taught in schools. Traditional basic skills will always be important, but they, in themselves, will not prepare students for success in the world that is a-borning. We need a wider range of basic skills if we are to educate youth to assume leadership of an America that is part of a global society.

• •

SUMMARY

This chapter has reviewed the major purposes and goals of social studies including current recommendations on scope and sequence. It has identified several significant societal trends impacting the teaching of social studies, and has reviewed the emerging new basic skills required of educated people in the coming century.

REVIEW QUESTIONS

1. Which societal or international trends would you add to those listed by the authors?

2. Which of the trends discussed in this chapter most personally impacts you?

3. Which aspect of the rationale presented in this chapter do you most support? Which aspect of the rationale do you least support as a goal for social studies?

4. What would you add to the rationale for social studies in elementary school?

5. Which of the basic skills suggested in this chapter would be easiest to present in elementary school? Which, if any, would be difficult?

6. Are there other basic skills that should be taught in elementary school?

7. Do you agree or disagree that the "expanding environment" approach in elementary social studies is no longer valid?

8. What other concepts do you think should be included in elementary social studies?

9. What event in world affairs during your lifetime has most emotionally impacted you? Which aspects of that experience would you like dealt with in an elementary social studies classroom?

10. Give an example of the "implicit" curriculum you experienced during your elementary school experience?

ACTIVITIES

1. Interview parents of elementary school age children, and ask them what they consider to be skills necessary for success in the workplace and in family living.

2. Read several magazines from business, education, politics, entertainment, and family life. Identify societal themes repeated in these publications and how these themes impact educating young people. For example, a business magazine that has several articles concerning layoffs of professional people is indicating that people will be switching careers during their worklife.

3. Visit an elementary school social studies class. Compare what is being taught with ideas raised by this chapter's rationale.

4. Telephone, write, or visit your favorite elementary school teacher. Ask that teacher: Should social studies be taught in elementary school? Why? What changes would the teacher advocate in the social studies curriculum?

5. Interview an individual who has made a career switch. Ask which skills were required in order to make that career change.

READING

What We Know About Teaching Elementary Social Studies
by David A. Welton
Associate Professor of Education, Texas Tech University, Lubbock

Despite all of the things we don't know about teaching social studies, things that Vincent Rogers and others have so ably pointed out, there are occasional bright spots in the shadows. True, not all of what we know is necessarily new, nor is it based entirely on research. Indeed, much of our knowledge is in the form of idiosyncratic and apparently disjointed collections of beliefs that have been gleaned from experience, primarily the experience of teaching children and young adolescents. Although such experiences sometimes reemphasize what we should know but don't, the purpose of this article is to highlight some, but certainly not all, of the things we know, or think we know, about teaching elementary social studies.

1. One of the things we know—and sometimes wish we didn't—is that social studies usually ranks as the subject children like least (or hate most). To make matters worse, they do not see it as useful. Students dislike other subjects too, of course; yet despite an active dislike for grammar, for example, most students still regard it as useful. If nothing else, studying grammar is a necessary evil. Social studies, on the other hand, is apt to be regarded as an unnecessary evil—as something students could just as readily do without.

2. We know that from a student's point of view, social studies is typically seen as a subject one knows, not something one does. Social studies is much like literature in this respect. After studying the Civil War or reading *The Red Badge of Courage*, for example, students know they will be expected to have certain information in their possession. Exactly what might be expected of them will vary from teacher to teacher (which reflects something else we know—that our approach to social studies is seldom consistent), but students will most certainly be expected to know something. Whether they will ever apply their newly acquired knowledge in real-life situations is usually another matter entirely.

Despite some similarities, social studies and literature differ in at least one important respect. *The Red Badge of Courage*—indeed, all literature—has a story line, a plot. Even though students may never apply what they read to their daily lives, the mere existence of a plot can make the process of studying literature bearable, even interesting. In social studies, the apparent absence of readily visible plots poses an obvious problem with which teachers have had to cope for years. When the subject matter lacks inherent interest, as social studies often does, teachers must step in to add the interest element and make it relevant. And that, as many of us are exceedingly well aware, is no easy feat.

No matter how interesting teachers try to make it, we know that social studies is seldom seen as a subject one does. It is not like arithmetic or grammar, for example, which are clearly subjects one knows *and* does. Opportunities to apply one's knowledge of arithmetic and grammar abound. When students actually "do" social studies, however, it is usually in the form of completing an assignment—answering the questions at the end of the chapter, for example. The chances are slim that students will be called upon to apply what they have learned from those assignments to out-of-school situations. When was the last time someone asked you how many states border on Tennessee, for example? (The answer is: 8.) It is not too surprising, then, that mathematics and grammar are regarded as practical, and social studies is not.

3. We know that teachers have traditionally relied on two techniques for enhancing the perceived utility or "practicalness" of social studies. The first technique is reflected in the claim (to students) that "You're going to need *this* some day," while the other is reflected in the more encompassing "teaching children to think" approach to social studies.

"You're going to need this" is not necessarily an invalid claim; somewhere in the future, students may actually be called upon to demonstrate whatever *this* refers to. In other instances, it may be a lame excuse that teachers use when they do not understand why they are doing whatever they are doing; or it may simply be a way of saying "This stuff is going to be on the test" (and after which students promptly forget most of what they have stored in their short-term memories). Whatever the circumstances, we know that over the long run the "You're going to need to know this" claim is seldom more than marginally effective. Among younger children, it is not entirely a matter of validity or credibility, although both can play a role. Rather, children's responses may reflect their perception of time, as well as their conception of "the future."

4. The future-oriented applicability of elementary social studies may be meaningless to children who hold a quite different view of the future. We know, for example, that childhood is a pe-

riod when time creeps. It is a period when children measure their age in half-years, when being seven-and-a-half is considered "much older" than plain ol' seven. We need only to look at how quickly our own birthdays seem to come around as we get older, or to recall those interminable childhood waits from one Christmas to the next, to see additional examples of this. The child's real future, the future that he or she understands and deals with, may be two days, two weeks, or possibly two months hence. Thus, from a child's perspective, a future need that is two years away may be so distant in time that it is beyond comprehension. Likewise, telling children that something happened two hundred or two thousand years ago may be equally meaningless. As Vincent Rogers suggested, if we had an elementary social studies curriculum that really reflected the way children view time and space, it might look quite different from what we have today.

5. We know that although the "expanding environments" approach to elementary social studies has been updated, the basic framework has remained essentially unchanged since its creation in the early decades of this century. Students begin by studying more immediate environments—the family, the school, the neighborhood, etc.—and then move in logical fashion to successively more distant environments—the state, and then the nation. By the end of grade six, students in a traditional program will have completed a survey of the entire world. This approach to social studies curriculum is a masterful example of adult logic. Whether it actually reflects the way in which students look at their world—the world in which they really function—is a matter not often addressed.

5.1 We know that the expanding environments approach to elementary social studies was created at a time when many students left school at the end of grade six (or seven, or eight). At that time, it was reasonable to provide a survey of the earth's environments prior to the end of the student's public school career. Today, of course, most students no longer leave school (physically, at least) as early as they once did, and thus the time available for instruction has almost doubled. Nevertheless, many elementary teachers still find themselves engaged in hurried surveys of the earth as if the students' departure were still imminent, which it obviously is not.

If the "it's our last shot at the student" rationale for elementary social studies is no longer appropriate, why then do we continue doing what we do? Are the forces of tradition, parental expectations, and the availability of teaching materials so strong that we are unable to counter them? Possibly. What we have done, it appears, is sustain a sixty-year-old curriculum by slightly altering the rationale for teaching it. Instead of the "last shot" principle, it appears that we have shifted to a "getting-them-ready-for," foundations-type rationale. In addition to whatever else it may do, the apparent purpose of elementary social studies is to lay the foundation for further study in high school and college. Questioning that rationale, and what we do under it, is tantamount to desecrating motherhood and apple pie. Yet to hear some high school teachers tell it, there is considerable doubt about the effectiveness of elementary social studies programs. On the other hand, since college instructors voice similar concerns about the effectiveness of secondary social studies programs, there is apparently a problem at that level too.

A second strategy for enhancing the practicality of social studies (that was noted earlier) is reflected in the "teaching children to think" or process approach to instruction. This approach, not incidentally, is evident in several subject areas, most notably science. By using social studies (or science) content as a vehicle for teaching information-handling processes—thinking skills that students can use in their everyday lives—the instructional outcomes should be at least as useful as what one learns in arithmetic or grammar. The rationale itself is sound and generally acceptable to most individuals, but we also know that several problems can arise when it is translated into action.

6. We know that one of the problems that students and teachers encounter in implementing a process approach involves the need, and sometimes the inability, to manage multiple objectives. The idea that content can serve as vehicle for teaching transferable thinking skills runs counter

to an academic tradition in which the content itself—knowledge learning—has been the primary, if not the sole, objective. Inasmuch as the sage of process-oriented instruction has been well documented elsewhere (see John Haas, *The Era of the New Social Studies,* Social Science Education Consortium/ERIC ChESS Clearinghouse, 1977), suffice it to say that it has sometimes seemed as if thinking was supposed to replace content as the sole focus of instruction. Information-processing (thinking) obviously cannot take place in a void; one must have something to think about—namely, some kind of content. That social studies lessons can have a dual emphasis, both process objectives *and* content objectives, seems to have gotten lost in the shuffle.

7. There seems to be a growing reluctance to acknowledge and accept the fact that social studies can be something one knows and does. Unfortunately, this reluctance is further reflected in many of the most recent elementary text materials. Publishers have staged a hasty retreat from the process-oriented materials that were available during the 1960s and 1970s. As one publisher's representative put it, *"Process, inquiry,* and *creativity* have become 'dirty words,' and we dare not use them in our materials." For tangible evidence of the back-to-the-basics movement, one need look no further than the most recently published social studies textbooks.

8. The final aspect of what we know about teaching elementary social studies is possibly the most obvious and certainly the most important; namely, that what students take away from a learning episode is determined largely by experience, *their* experience. It really does not matter what form that experience takes; it can consist of *prior* experience (from the student's past), *actual* or participatory experiences that occur in classrooms or elsewhere, or *vicarious* experience, those intensely personal, fantasy-like phenomena that we all create and react to as if they were real. Whatever its form, experience provides the concepts—the mental "hooks," if you will—that enable students to bring meaning to the events and phenomena they study.

8.1 At the risk of overburdening an already obvious point, we know that relevance is determined in part by how closely new information or experience relates to the student's prior experience (and current interests). To state it a bit differently, we know that meaning—personal meaning— is inherent in subject matter only to the extent that students have sufficient prior experience that they can relate to it. This helps to explain why children, when asked to tell something about George Washington, for example, invariably mention "wooden false teeth." Yet if asked to cite the major points from "Washington's Farewell Address," they typically draw a blank.

Why do children remember the seemingly trivial details, like Washington's teeth, and forget or ignore the so-called "important stuff"? It is not because the "important stuff" is not being taught any more, as some would claim. On the contrary, many teachers labor diligently trying to teach the significant aspects of Washington's presidency, only to find that two weeks later their students remember little more than the seemingly inconsequential aspects of study. Consider that most children lack an experiential basis for bringing meaning to something such as "avoiding foreign alliances." They may memorize the phrase for a time, it is true, but unless they have an experiential basis that enables them to deal with "alliances" in a personally meaningful way, it is likely to go the way of the many other things they have supposedly learned. Washington's false teeth, on the other hand, is something children can relate to (1) because of their own experience with dentists or teeth-related problems, and (2) because it is unique. Washington's now-infamous teeth set him apart from the run-of-the-mill colonist (or at least what children know about colonists), and the combination of these two factors enables children to bring meaning to what might otherwise be considered trivia.

8.2 We know that when students' prior experiences provide an inadequate basis for bringing meaning to new data, we have two alternatives to turn to: (1) actual (or simulated) participatory experience, and (2) vicarious experience.

Participatory experiences are so commonplace that they hardly deserve further mention. Some of the better examples include: field trips, mock elections, and hands-on activities such as butter-making or quilting. Time-consuming as such activities are, there is little question that visiting a meat-packing plant or making butter during an in-class activity can provide students with an experiential basis for interpreting such phenomena. However, we also know that unless participatory activities are authentic, or as authentic as it is possible to make them, they can quickly degenerate into mere activity. Despite their current popularity, food-related experiences are particularly susceptible in this respect. Activities that involve eating canned spaghetti on the pretext that children will better understand the Italian culture, or eating raw fish so as to "better appreciate" the Eskimos (or Scandinavians), for example, are so absurd that they border on malpractice. They are "real experiences" to be sure, but what students learn from them— that they hate (or like) canned spaghetti, and that the Eskimos are stupid because they do not cook their fish before they eat them— can be a far cry from what was intended.

When providing actual experience is neither feasible nor possible, the third option, vicarious experience, becomes more viable. By appealing to the child's imagination, and by building mental images so vivid that they cannot be ignored, we can sometimes create experiences that students relate to vicariously—as if they were really happening and the child were actually participating in them. The key to doing that, in a word, is details.

8.3 The role that factual details play in social studies is one of the most widely misunderstood aspects of instruction. In the creation of vicarious experience, details provide the data that enable children to build vivid mental images of what took place. Consider the following statement as an example: "In 218 B.C., Hannibal left Cartegena with an army of over 100,000 soldiers, crossed the Alps, and then met the Roman legions in what is now Italy." Though accurate, the statement is also lifeless, devoid of anything that might capture the imagination. It takes details, such as the fact that Hannibal's 37 elephants had been trained to terrorize enemy soldiers (they practiced by trampling on captured enemy prisoners), and that the elephants had to be lured onto sod-covered rafts before they could cross the Rhone River, to create a sufficiently vivid visual image that students can relate to it. Individually and in the sweep of human history, each detail is insignificant; collectively, details play a significant role in the creation of vicarious experience. (This also implies that a "bare bones" approach to history does not cut it; there is not enough information for students to relate to).

8.4 Unfortunately, we also know that some individuals use the number of details that students remember as a measure of the quality of learning. To do so elevates details to a role that far exceeds their function. Asking students to remember how many elephants were in Hannibal's herd, for example, is like giving star billing to a wardrobe mistress: both are vital to their respective productions, but the attention they receive is out of proportion to the role they play. For lack of a perspective (or possibly something to test students on), teachers often view factual details as important information, the "stuff" that students are supposed to remember.

Details are as essential to the overall fabric of social studies as are the major organizing concepts. In the oft-used metaphor of a loom, the details are represented by the woof, the shorter yarns that run crosswise. The organizing concepts and generalizations of social studies are represented by the longer vertical yarns, the warp, which thread their way throughout the fabric. Unless the warp and woof are meshed properly, the fabric will fall apart. As far as some students are concerned, elementary social studies has already worn dangerously thin. In light of this and despite everything we do not know, it appears that we might be wise to reconsider what we already know about teaching social studies.

(Courtesy © *National Council for the Social Studies*. Used with permission.)

What We Don't Know About the Teaching of Social Studies

Vincent Rogers
Professor of Education, University of Connecticut, Storrs

Despite my attempt to review pertinent literature, sample the views and opinions of experts in the field, and survey current school practice, writing this article remains a personal, idiosyncratic task. The questions I have selected inevitably reflect my own biases, values, interests, and prejudices. This, of course, would be true of anyone who wrote this piece.

It is also possible that this listing will reflect my personal ignorance rather than gaps in the field of social studies in education. That, however, is a chance I must take.

1. First, an observation I consider unavoidable in a discussion such as this. It is not so much an unanswered question in the sense that we lack the appropriate data to deal with it. Rather, it is a dilemma that has disturbed me ever since I have been involved in social studies education. In essence, it concerns the continuing (one might say growing) dichotomy between democratic values and school practice.

We are a society that purports to place great value on individual freedom, equality before the law, individual dignity and importance, and personal opportunity to develop as fully as talents, abilities, and interests will permit. In addition, we value the abstract (yet still meaningful) concepts of liberty, justice, freedom, and democracy. Yet we continue to suffer from a form of schizophrenia when day-to-day life in schools and in classrooms is observed. It is as if, concerning the education of our children, we are quite content to live in a fantasy world. The ideals and values outlined above are of course important, and we must tell each other this from time to time. On the other hand, these ideals need not clutter up the daily practice of schooling. We prefer to believe that such ideals and values will somehow develop despite the way schools are operated. We say we believe that all people are created equal and are entitled to life, liberty, and happiness; but we have no intention of applying that concept to education. We talk about the importance of things of the mind while emphasizing the rewards of more material things. We declare the importance of justice in public and private life, but we practice injustice in our schools in a variety of ways.

The current conservative movement in American education clearly stands for more than literacy and mathematics skills. A desire for obedience, conformity, rigidity, and control seems to lie at the heart of the movement. These goals run a collision course with the most important values suggested by our traditions. Yet they are sought by educators and laypersons alike who seem either to see no ideological conflict in such practices or assume that there is no relationship between what happens in schools now and the sort of human being one becomes following 12 years of schooling.

2. We know a great deal about the development of "negative types of human beings," to use Pitirim Sorokin's phrase. The criminal has been researched far more than the saint. The result is that our social science knows little about positive persons, their conduct, and their relationships. We know a great deal about aggressive, antisocial behavior and very little about how qualities such as empathy, sensitivity, sympathy, and altruism can be nurtured. There is a discouraging lack of evidence that might link technological progress, increased literacy rates, and more efficient means of communication with an increase in sensitivity and concern. Yet, as population increases, as society becomes more complex, as we develop more and more deadly ways of dealing with human conflict, the need for the fostering of such qualities is obviously increased. As teachers, we know virtually nothing beyond commonsense notions about how schooling might support and develop such qualities in children and youth.

3. Despite the considerable professional literature devoted to the subject, we know little about the development, effects, or efficiency of what I shall call genuine student inquiry. A careful ex-

amination of the materials and methods that comprise social studies curriculum projects and packages reveals that the kinds of questions raised, the problems studied, the discoveries or generalizations arrived at, are rarely the children's. We try valiantly; we smile, entreat, and cajole. Some of the students are caught up in it some of the time—perhaps an unusually challenging topic catches their fancy, or perhaps an unusually dynamic teacher draws them out through the force of his or her personality. More often than not, however, we end up with something Vincent Glennon has described as "sneaky-telling." We know where we're going; we know what the questions should be, what the "big ideas" are, and what conclusions one should come away with if one follows the teacher's manual.

Genuine inquiry can be defined as "finding out," to borrow Charles Rathbone's phrase. It need not be goal oriented, and one does not necessarily know in advance what one is seeking. It is an impulse to search—not necessarily to search for. There are a host of questions related to this concept for which we have virtually no answers. What effects does inquiry have on students's attitudes toward the social studies as a school subject? Do such activities transfer to other areas"? Are they appropriate for gifted and other exceptional children?

4. If the homily "we learn best when we care most" is true, we know very little indeed about the effects of human feelings and emotions on cognitive learning in the social studies. A truly integrated human being integrates the intellectual world with the world of feelings and emotions. He sees the relationship between what is known or understood and what is felt or expressed. Since content with emotional impact is often perceived by teachers as dangerous, threatening, or perhaps embarrassing, the emotional aspects are often glossed over so that "safer" material can be discussed. Is it possible to create classroom conditions that encourage emotional expression so that curricular issues may take on personal significance? It may be that social studies programs that deal honestly and completely with all the human emotions may in the long run bring about a better understanding of ourselves and of others. At this moment, we simply do not know whether this is true.

5. We know little about the effects of certain aspects of the school environment on the social and political attitudes of children and youth. How does one begin to think about oneself and about others when physically disabled children become a part of the school milieu, when a new program for gifted children is begun, when the reward and punishment systems are changed, when new dress codes are established? How do disabled and gifted children think of themselves and of others when such programs are begun? What are the effects of academic standards {e.g., competency tests) for promotion and high school graduation on student self-concept and attitude towards others? Such programs may or may not contribute to the development of feelings of powerlessness, alienation, superiority, inferiority, class, race, or ethnic bias. The point is that, at present, we simply do not know.

6. Jean Piaget and his colleagues have developed a body of research on children's thinking that is attracting increased attention among early childhood educators in all parts of the world. His warnings about meaningless verbalization, superficial 'knowing," and the difficulty of abstract thinking on the part of young children are well known. What this suggests for the social studies curriculum is considerably less clear. We have little notion of what a social studies curriculum for 5-, 6-, or 7-year-olds would look like if it were faithful to Piaget's developmental concepts, and even less information about the possible effectiveness of such approaches if and when they are fully developed and tested.

7. The primary teaching tool of the vast majority of elementary and secondary school social studies teachers is the commercially produced textbook. While numerous studies have examined the content and structure of such books (e.g., studies of the treatment of women and Blacks, Jews, and other minority groups; studies of the treatment of places such as Africa, China, or the

Middle East; studies of such things as concept load or readability), little if anything is known about the ways textbooks and their accompanying workbooks affect children's perceptions of the nature of social science concepts and methodology. What do children learn about the social science by being taught almost exclusively from books—that knowledge is inevitably contained between the covers of a book? That social science data are for the experts alone? That there is a right answer for most questions? That "people' lived in the past (and in the present) minus the joy, sorrow, agony, elation, misery, warmth, love, disappointment, blood, sweat, tears, and stink of real human beings? What messages do the books as books convey:? We really don't know.

These seven questions lie at the heart of social studies education' major concerns as I perceive them. While the list could easily be extended and revised. I doubt very much whether any of the seven could be excluded.

(Courtesy © *National Council for the Social Studies.* Used with permission.)

QUESTIONS ON READINGS

1. David Welton says that from a student's point of view, "Social studies is typically seen as a subject one knows, not something one does." Based on your experiences as a student, is this an accurate statement?

2. Welton critiques the "expanding environment" approach and claims it is a "masterful example of adult logic." What does he mean by this comment?

3. Reflect on your own studies of American history. To what extent do you remember facts, and to what extent do you recall meanings?

4. Vincent Rogers notes that "We know a great deal about aggressive, anti-social behavior and very little about how qualities such as empathy, sensitivity, sympathy, and altruism can be nurtured." What implications does this have for the teaching of social studies in elementary school?

5. Rogers says that "We know very little about the effects of the school environment on the social and political attitudes of children and youth." Which effects do you believe emanate from the school environment?

6. Rogers raises a question: "Is it possible to create classroom conditions that encourage emotional expression so that curricular issues may take on personal significance?" How would you respond to his question?

REFERENCES

Armento, B. J. (1986). Research on teaching social studies. In M. C. Wittrock (Ed.), *Handbook of research on teaching* (3rd ed.). New York: Macmillan.

Banks, J. A. (1991). Multicultural education: For freedom's sake. *Educational Leadership, 49,* (4), 32–36.

Bruner, J. (1966). *Towards a theory of instruction.* New York: Norton.

Forino, A. J. (1966). Why Social Studies. *Elementary School Journal, 66,* (5), 229–233.

Goodlad, J. I. (1963). *Planning and organizing for teaching.* Washington, DC: National Education Association.

Johnson, D., & Johnson, F. (1975). *Joining together: Group therapy and group skills.* Englewood Cliffs, NJ: Prentice Hall.

Klineberg, S. (1991, December 29). *The New York Times,* p. 15.

Lasch, C. (1978). *The culture of narcissism.* New York: Norton.

McLuhan, M. (1964). *Understanding media.* New York: McGraw Hill.

Mistakos, C. (1981). The nature and purposes of social studies. In J. Allen (Ed.), *Education in the '80s* (pp. 13–21). Washington, DC: National Education Association.

Naisbitt, J. (1982). *Megatrends.* New York: Warner.

National Association for the Education of Young Children. (1986). S. Bredekamp (ed). Position statement on developing appropriate practice in early childhood programs serving children from birth to 8. *Young Children, 41,* (6), 3–19.

National Council for the Social Studies Task Force on Early Childhood/Elementary Social Studies. (1989). *53,* (1), 14–21. Washington, DC: National Council for the Social Studies.

National Council for the Social Studies Task Force on Scope and Sequence. (1989). *Social Education, 53,* (1), 14–21.

Oliva, P. (1988). *Developing curriculum.* Boston: Scott Foresman.

Ravitch, D., & Finn, C. (1987). A report on the first National Assessment of History and Literature. In Ravitch & Finn (Ed.), *What do our 17-year-olds know?* (p. 205). New York: Harper & Row.

Secretary of Labor's Commission on Achieving Necessary Skills. (1991) p.1.

Skolnick, A. (1991). *Embattled paradise.* New York: Basic Books.

Toffler, A. (1980). *The third wave.* New York: Bantam.

Tyler, R. (1965). *Perspectives of curriculum evaluation.* Chicago: Rand McNally.

SUGGESTED READING

Drucker, P. (1969). *The age of discontinuity.* New York: Harper & Row.

Goodlad, J. (1983). *A place called school: Prospects for the future.* New York: McGraw-Hill.

Kumar, K. (1988). *The rise of modern society.* New York: Basil Blackwell.

Lasch, C. (1984). *The minimal self.* New York: Norton.

McHale, J. (1969). *The future of the future.* New York: Braziller.

McLuhan, M. (1964). *Understanding media.* New York: McGraw Hill.

Naisbitt, J. (1982). *Megatrends.* New York: Warner.

Ravitch, D., & Finn, C. (1987). A report on the first National Assessment of History and Literature. *What do our 17-year-olds know?* (p. 205). New York: Harper & Row.

Secretary of Labor's Commission on Achieving Necessary Skills. (1991).

Shane, H. (Ed.). (1981). *Educating for a new world millennium.* Bloomington, IN: Phi Delta Kappan Foundation.

Toffler, A. (1970). *Future Shock.* New York: Random House.

Chapter 2

Ethics and Values in Social Studies

Ethics and Values in Social Studies

Schools, inescapably, transmit values. The word "value" derives from the Old French, *valoir*, to be of worth. Values are attitudes or attributes we esteem and seek to develop in children. By simply requiring that children attend school or raise their hands before speaking, we are taking a value stand. The issue is not should we teach values, but which values are to predominate in schools. Teachers have to be aware of implicit as well as explicit values presented in the classroom.

On the first day of school when classroom procedures are discussed, a teacher is exposing children to a particular value system. In general, the historical relationship between teacher and student has been based on authority and control. Value-free classrooms do not exist. Teachers must be sensitive to issues arising from imposing values upon children even when they believe it is merely being done in the "best interests" of the child.

The influence of teachers in value development is extremely important in the elementary and middle school years. Teachers have to understand clearly their own value systems and to consider if they are providing a consistent and self-reflective model. Raths (1966) suggests teachers should continually ask questions to clarify their value stance. Among the questions he includes are:

1. Is that very important to me?
2. How did I feel when that happened?
3. What other alternatives did I consider?
4. Would I freely choose this alternative?
5. What do I mean by. . . ?
6. What assumption did I make?
7. Was this consistent with what I did?
8. Do I do this often?
9. What can I do about this idea?
10. Would I do it again the same way?
11. How do I know it's right?
12. Why did I do it that way? (Raths, pp. 56–62)

Children come to school with a set of values reflecting their family, neighborhood, or society. They are not "empty vessels" but are filled to the brim with the values of their parents and community. Children frequently encounter conflict between values espoused by teachers or schools and those established within their own homes. For example, some families enjoy loud conversations with arms waving in excitement, but such behavior would be punished in school. It is critically important for teachers to recognize that behavior is not intrinsically "good" or "bad" but culturally determined.

Teachers must be sensitive to the reality of their own value systems and how they affect the daily operation of the classroom. Educators frequently assume that the rules and regulations of the school are inherently valid for all people. The classroom has to be a safe and courteous environment for all students and respect alternative systems of beliefs.

Raths and his associates (1966) believe values education should enable children to use the processes of "(a) choosing freely, (b) choosing from alternatives, (c) choosing thoughtfully, (d) prizing and cherishing, (e) affirming, (f) acting upon choices, and (g) examining patterns of living" (p. 82).

Is the child to be considered an individual with distinct human feelings and values, or is the child to be molded according to the values of the school and society? We can easily discuss such questions on a philosophical level, but in actual practice the complexity of the classroom interferes with the goals of education. The control functions of schools impact instruction. The dynamic of interaction with 20 children, paperwork, required curricula, interruptions and lack of supplies frequently compel teachers to limit the individuality of the child.

Children display individuality from birth. These traits clash with parental demands, but most children assert their "I" qualities. School is the first societal institution encountered by children that demands strict conformity to adult values. The school may profess its desire to respect the child as an individual, but its organization and procedures stem from adult interpretations and goals concerning what constitutes proper behavior for children.

A teacher continually walks the thin line separating the child's right to be a unique person and society's need to impose a common core of values. Punctuality, completing homework, standing quietly in line, or bringing sharpened pencils are values. A question teachers should ask is which of the values insisted upon within school further learning? Which individual values can a child retain and which must be modified to meet school demands?

▲ Children come to school with a set of values reflecting their family, neighborhood, or society. *Courtesy Saint Louis (Missouri) Public Schools.*

The Democratic Classroom

The school may be viewed as a laboratory in which competing members of society debate the nature of democracy in America. We expect the school to be a microcosm of the democratic process. Democracy for students and teachers, however, is often a case of how well they conform to dominant political forces.

The elementary or middle school teacher has the challenge to create an environment fostering the democratic ethos. Children seek both an exciting, relevant curriculum, and respect for their dignity as individuals. Teachers who are able to meet these needs establish the foundation for a democratic and successful classroom.

Schools transmit cultural heritages which generally depict an idealized version of society. There is a strong pull upon the elementary and middle school teacher to present young children the textbook version of democracy in America rather than the real one that exists in the corridors of power. The school has a responsibility to forge new paths whose avenues are broad enough to accommodate people of diverse backgrounds and aspirations, and whose goals may differ regarding the nature of democracy in America.

This voyage begins in elementary and middle school classrooms that reflect democratic principles of behavior. Teacher and students should share in the responsibility of establishing a social contract that delineates the rules and regulations that will govern how all interact with one another. A teacher who sends home to parents a list of "do's" and "don'ts" deprives children the sense of responsibility and ownership which comes from being part of the creation of a classroom government.

The democratic society, as well as classroom, is predicated upon trust. Most Americans are trustworthy people who pay their taxes and obey the law. No system of democracy is perfect, but as Winston Churchill once said, "Many forms of government have been tried, and will be tried in this world of sin and woe. No one pretends that democracy is perfect or all-wise. Indeed, it has been said that democracy is the worst form of government except all those other forms that have been tried from time to time" (House of Commons, 11 November 1947). Children in a democratic classroom will make mistakes, and can learn from them. They will never learn how to practice democracy unless given flexibility to err and to get another chance at success.

▲ Schools should be a microcosm of the democratic process. *Courtesy Pattonville (Missouri) School District.*

▲ Schools tend to present an idealized version of democracy in America.
Courtesy Null Elementary, Saint Charles (Missouri) Public Schools.

Noted social studies educator Fred Newman (1977) has identified eight approaches to educating students to be responsible citizens in a democracy. These are:

1. Academic Disciplines: This approach teaches facts, concepts, and generalizations about America's past and present. The assumption is that students who gain this knowledge will be educated citizens who can make informed decisions.

2. Law-Related Education: Traditionally we have taught students about the structure and processes of government and our fundamental rights. More recently, law related programs have emphasized case studies and role playing dealing with contemporary issues.

3. Social Problems: This approach focuses upon relevant social issues to students — crime, drugs, pollution, energy, etc. The assumption is that students who become familiar with these issues from an academic perspective will more likely act as informed citizens when confronting these problems.

4. Critical Thinking: This approach provides practice in critical thinking. It often is taught as part of a particular method of how one analyzes problems or issues in order to make decisions.

5. Values Clarification: This approach seeks to aid students to understand their own values and how values impact on the thought processes of people. It is assumed this knowledge will aid students to be sensitive about handling value laden problems.

6. Moral Development: This approach derives extensively from the work of Lawrence Kohlberg who believed moral reasoning goes through stages of development. Students are taught how to recognize their stage of reasoning and guided to function at higher stages of moral thought.

7. Community Involvement: This approach plunges students into real community issues that exist outside the classroom. The assumption is that students will be more interested in dealing with topics related to their own communities.

8. Institutional School Reform: This approach deals with the autocratic structure of schools and classrooms. It seeks to unite teachers and students in fostering democracy as part of their every day life in school.

An elementary and middle school teacher might incorporate all these approaches in order to foster a democratic mind-set within students. Students need knowledge about our democratic heritage, its defects, and ways people are seeking to improve our society. They need experiences in confronting problems and learning how to handle conflict in constructive ways. They also need to explore the world that lies outside the classroom boundary because they are citizens of that society.

Educational institutions exist in a politicized world, but their business is not politics, per se. The elementary and middle school teacher is not charged with governing or holding elections to decide procedures or training students to believe a particular set of values. The task is more complex. The student needs knowledge, but also opportunity to discover new directions in thinking. No teacher has all the information sought by young people, but every teacher has to be willing to allow youth to stumble, fall down, pick themselves up, and pursue their quest for knowledge.

Democracy is not something to be imposed in a classroom. It is an attitude, a way of life, and a rigorous way of thinking. It must be lived and practiced every day by teachers and students. A student teacher once asked "How are expectations for students in your classroom different in May from September?" The same can be asked about democracy in a teacher's room. If education in democracy is successful, then the May classroom will display more sophisticated versions of democratic processes:

1. Students will bear a greater responsibility for initiating what is to be learned.
2. Students will be responsible for ensuring that the dignity and rights of all students are respected.
3. Group processes will be effective sources of student cooperative learning.

Franklin D. Roosevelt said, "I would rather be a builder than a destroyer." The democratic classroom is an edifice that teachers can construct with diligent care for the rights and dignity of students. We sometimes forget the wisdom of youth, but we can never forget our responsibility to model in the classroom the democracy we seek for our society as a whole. Elementary and middle school teachers can add one building block that eventually will lead to the transformation of our nation.

Indoctrination or Choice?

Values education is a two-faceted component of the curriculum. The curriculum contains inherent values that are rarely taught as a distinct subject, and there are values presented as "lessons." For example, when a student must request permission from the teacher to sharpen a pencil, the value of respecting authority is transmitted. A teacher who reduces grades because of late completion of assignments may communicate that punctuality is more highly valued than the quality of work. There are values educators inculcate without conscious thought, and there are values we clearly desire to be accepted by students.

Teacher behavior impacts the behavior, attitudes, and beliefs of students. This hidden or implicit curriculum may be defined as school practices and values that shape the behavior and attitudes of teachers and students. This curriculum raises key questions:

▲ Group processes are effective sources of student cooperative learning. *Courtesy Webster University.*

1. Do you insist students show respect for one another but fail to treat students with respect?
2. What do your words say about the importance of learning?
3. How do your behavior and words convey your feelings about the principal, other teachers, the school, and the community?
4. How do the structure, system of rules, and physical appearance of your classroom influence student attitudes about themselves and the importance of learning?
5. Do you talk about the importance of writing and spelling, but hand out materials that are poorly written and that contain misspelled words?
6. Do you stress the importance of reading and writing, but never allow students to encounter your reading and writing? (Ellis, 1988, p. 235)

A fundamental question facing educators is whether the purpose of schooling is to aid students to "simply discover what beliefs, attitudes, and values people actually hold, or do we not also have an obligation to make inquiries about the beliefs, attitudes, and values they ought to hold?" (Frankel, 1964, p. 22)

This raises further issues:

1. Should we stress the contradictions between principles humans profess, and the principles evident in their conduct?

2. How far do we really want to go in studying beliefs, attitudes, and values in the context of alternatives?

3. Should we present diluted views of difficult social problems, or should we be open and frank in our teaching?

4. Is it appropriate to induce belief on the students' part in the strength and rightness of the society to which they belong?

There are educators who seek to impose a common core of values by compelling teachers to strictly adhere to a standardized curriculum.

A discipline should impose a pattern of behavior on its disciples. The discipline of the social studies should impose itself, then, on the teachers of social studies, directing what they teach and how they teach it; on the pupils in their behavior of learning, making it more purposeful and orderly; and on pupils and teachers alike in their civic behavior. (McCutchen, 1963, p. 65)

Social studies is not a "discipline" with a distinctive body of knowledge, but, rather, a federation of subjects each with its own discipline. It is presumptuous to believe that some person or some group knows which "patterns of behavior" should be imposed through a school curriculum.

Ideally, moral antagonists would respect one another's position and avoid making the classroom their battleground. Unfortunately, "true believers" seek to impose their version of truth upon the school. Charges of "secular humanism" or "pornography" or "racism" are frequently cast against those who appear to be against one or another form of "truth." Moral judgments arise from someone's frame of reference or belief that one set of values is inherently superior to other value systems.

▲ Learning activities should encourage students to inquire, to do their own thinking, and to create their own way to handle problems. *Courtesy Webster University.*

"In order to develop autonomy of thought, students need opportunities to organize their own conceptual systems and to develop their skills for independent processing of information" (Taba, 1971, p. 40). The scope and organization of learning activities should encourage learners to inquire, to do their own thinking, and to create their own way of handling problems. They may need assistance in moral reasoning or rethinking if their moral views damage the rights of other people. A task of schooling is providing information concerning moral principles, to help students learn analytical thinking skills, and to provide opportunities for students to act upon their ethical beliefs.

In a society as diverse as the United States, conflicting values coexist simultaneously. Some people believe it is important to "look out for number one" while others place group concerns ahead of the individual. Two people may claim to share a similar value but differ fundamentally in the implementation of that value. One teacher might lower grades because papers are not neat while another deems content the only criterion for determining grades.

The role of values education can be confusing to the novice teacher. It can become an intellectual exercise in which students learn "about" values but are not required to demonstrate understanding. It is one thing for students to state the importance of treating strangers with respect; it is another if these students mistreat other class members. There is a difference between knowing proper behavior and acting properly. There are value issues discussed in class which may not arise until 20 years later in the life of a student.

An individual might sincerely believe it is wrong to use vulgarity when angry, but each time she becomes angry, vulgar language emanates from her mouth. A person can state the importance of aiding poor people but ignore opportunities to provide economic or moral support to those without financial resources.

Moral behavior entails more than subscribing to a set of values. Morality is not simply something to be believed; it is also something to be practiced. Students must learn that good intentions are merely a step toward the ultimate goal of moral action.

A student can't be expected to make valid moral choices if under duress. A morally mature individual is autonomous, rational, empathetic, and personally responsible for actions. This suggests the need for a classroom environment which fosters autonomous behavior. It also requires opportunities for students to make mistakes without fear of punishment or having grades utilized to guide them to the "correct" answer. Teachers and students can establish autonomy oriented limits. Together they can arrive at consensus regarding boundaries, and establish the limits permissible for each student to exercise autonomy.

The sociologist Emile Durkheim explained the ramifications of school discipline:

> Some see it as a simple way of guaranteeing superficial peace and order in the class. Under such conditions, one can quite reasonably come to view these imperative requirements as barbarous, or a tyranny of complicated values. In reality, however, school discipline is not a simple device for securing peace in the classroom, it is the morality of the classroom as a small society. (Quoted in Power, Higgins, & Kohlberg, 1989, p. 23).

Elementary and middle school children spend half of their waking hours each school day in class. Many children spend more time with their teachers than with their parents. The school is

▲ Classroom environments should foster autonomous behavior. *Courtesy Kirkwood (Missouri) School District.*

the society of the child. Many value conflicts arise for children from school situations. They frequently struggle with values stemming from the "hidden curriculum" of the school which demands specific behaviors under threat of punishment. "Neatness" may be very difficult if a child lives under extreme conditions of poverty or in an abusive home.

A charge often directed at educators is their failure to prepare children for the "real world," but the classroom and school actually constitute the real world of the child. Schools reflect societal values, and this is manifested in ways we educate children regarding values. Teachers have an exciting opportunity to transform the classroom into a microcosm of society in which children confront similar value dilemmas as those being dealt with by adults.

The United States of America is predicated upon fundamental rights guaranteed to all citizens. There is little debate that these rights have frequently in the past and present been denied to some Americans. The democratic classroom remains the best opportunity for teachers to offer "choice" rather than "indoctrination" as the prevailing way of life for children in schools.

> A values emphasis within the social education program should seek to educate (rather than indoctrinate) students (a) about values that exist in the world today that influence, in a major way, human behavior and group choices; (b) about their own values and about the methods humans employ to seek valued goals; and (c) about the reasons, knowledge, and skills necessary for dealing effectively with serious social/civic issues. (Armento, 1981, pp. 117–118)

John Dewey urged that youth should become involved in the task of transforming society in order to create a nation that actualized its guiding principles as embodied in the Constitution. A teacher who involves children in determining classroom procedures and gives children choice in determining rewards and punishments is preparing them for the "real world." Hopefully, their experiences in class will enable children to become caring and concerned citizens who seek a world predicated upon principles of equality and justice. If this proves so, the schools will have become the conscience of society, and within the schools, the social studies program will have become the conscience of the school. Will the social studies teacher accept this responsibility? (Doblein, Fischer, Ludwig, & Koblinger, 1985)

Jack Fraenkel suggests there are several skills which students must possess in order to improve their ability to handle issues relating to values. He believes serious and sustained knowledge concerning values will not come about unless students have key abilities and strategies to examine values. In the process Fraenkel offers, students are able to:

- formulate some idea of what a value is;
- know the difference between a factual-type question, an inferential type question and a question of value;
- make reasonable inferences about a person's values;
- compare and contrast values;
- participate in value discussions;
- evaluate value-claims;
- evaluate evidence offered to support a value position;
- understand why people value different things;
- realize that values conflict;
- explore and evaluate alternatives and consequences in value conflicts. (Adapted from Frankel. NCSS, 1985)

Values Education Strategies

Values education has been integral to the process by which adults influence student attitudes and behaviors. The decade of the sixties was a turbulent era which stimulated extensive thinking regarding moral education. Many educators felt it imperative to move away from authoritarian moral codes which imposed upon children adult moral values, and ignored personal choice.

> When children do not learn to be responsible for each other, to care for each other and to help each other, not only for the sake of others but for their own sake, love becomes a weak and limited object. Teachers and children...must learn to care enough to help one another with the many social and educational problems of school. (Glasser, 1969, p. 14)

Among the most prominent theorists dealing with moral reasoning is Lawrence Kohlberg. Kohlberg built upon the pioneering efforts of Piaget to construct a system which characterized a child's moral progress. His research led Kohlberg to the view that a child's moral development fell into six stages which frequently are grouped into three moral levels.

Level 1. PRE-CONVENTIONAL:
Stage 1. The child's orientation is concerned with punishment and obedience. Rules are obeyed to avoid punishment.
Stage 2. The child conforms in order to obtain rewards. Orientation is to self pleasure.
Level 2. CONVENTIONAL:
Stage 3. The focus is upon behaving as a good little girl/boy in order to maintain good relations. Orientation is avoiding disapproval.
Stage 4. Laws are to be obeyed except in extreme situations when they conflict with other societal obligations. Orientation is to meet your obligations.
Level 3. POST-CONVENTIONAL:
Stage 5. Feeling of contractual commitment. The need to uphold certain laws for the survival of society.
Stage 6. Belief in universal moral principles and personal sense of commitment to them.

Kohlberg's work provides a foundation upon which educators can examine the complex issues of values. Several advocates of Kohlberg's ideas are attempting to create schools based upon the premise that children should daily be involved in struggling with moral dilemmas. For example, students might have the following dilemma posed as a basis for class discussion:

- John is 13 years old. His family is poor, and there is no milk in the house. His mother gives him $2 to go to the corner grocery store and buy milk. While at the store, John notices that the clerk has gone to the back of the store. John realizes he could leave the store without paying for the milk. Should John take the milk without paying for it? Explain your reasons.
- (further information is supplied) John's father is out of work and there is no other money in the house. Should John steal the milk? Why or why not?
- Does your answer change if told there is a baby in the house who needs milk?

Values Clarification

Sidney Simon, noted leader in the values clarification movement, contends that emphasis should be placed upon "the process of valuing" rather than upon inculcating any particular set of values.

He argues that no one person or group has the "right" set of values to provide children, and that adults often act hypocritical in saying one thing but doing something quite different in practice. Teachers who utilize the ideas of Simon employ a variety of activities to stimulate value discussions. For example:

- Children are asked to list thirteen (a baker's dozen) favorite items around the house which require the use of electricity. Students are requested to cross out the three items they could do without in case of a power outage, and then list the three that mean the most to them.
- Students are asked to send a telegram beginning with "I urge you to . . ." to family members, classmates, friends, etc.
- Students are asked to complete the following in ten separate sentences, "I am . . ." (The object is to discover the roles or attitudes children ascribe to themselves)

In one values clarification activity called "Personal Coat of Arms," students are asked to draw a coat of arms, divide it into six sections and enter in the following information:

1. Draw two pictures. One depicts something you enjoy doing, and one portrays something you would like to do.
2. Draw a picture which shows something you value highly.
3. Draw a picture describing something your family highly values.
4. Draw two pictures about what you most like about yourself. (Simon, 1966)

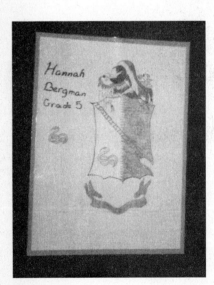

▲ Creating a personal coat of arms is an effective values clarification activity. *Courtesy Perry County (Missouri) School District No. 42.*

Although Simon argues that his approach is value-free, values are evident in his writings. A question he frequently asks is, "How can we get people to see that getting a high paying job is not the final reward of a college degree?" Or, "How can we get men and women to take on some larger share of their personal responsibility for the rampant racism in our nation?" These are values many Americans share with Sidney Simon; but they are "values." It is impossible to avoid advocating values in even the best of value exercises.

Some critics of values clarification believe it is not sufficient to "clarify one's values." They claim this approach ignores the issue of whether or not values should be directly taught children. For example, should a teacher avoid teaching against racism because this is imposing a set of values upon children? Other critics raise the issue of what happens when societal values may be deemed unfair by one part of the community while others seek change. Southern whites imposed segregated schools upon their communities prior to the *Brown vs. Board of Education* decision in 1954. Which values should have been taught children—segregation is wrong, or segregation is a way of life? Should the values presented in school reflect society as it is or as it ought to be? Who decides how it ought to be?

The role of teachers in values clarification is complex. Some argue for a "neutral free" approach in which teachers avoid expressing their values or ideas regarding controversial topics. Merrill Harmin argues that teachers should take a stand. For example, during the Watergate scandal teachers had to deal with a situation in which the President of the United States lied. One approach might have been: "I don't think it is right for a President to lie. Are there situations in which a President should lie? Why or why not?"

Elementary and middle school teachers have a particularly burdensome task since young children frequently believe teachers embody the "truth." The elementary school child is influenced by a teacher's opinion and values. Trust is a heavy responsibility and a test of one's ability to respect the integrity and individuality of human beings.

Conflict between differing values is a normal aspect of our everyday life. It causes teachers to clash with students, parents, administrators, other teachers or spouses. The goal of educators is not to eliminate conflict over values, but to assist students in understanding and accepting differences without the need to resort to violence.

There is a tendency to deny that value conflicts exist within our society. We prefer believing that all Americans accept the same values, and problems arise due to poor communication. We downplay the importance of class conflict and believe all problems can be negotiated without resort to violence. American political parties cross all economic and social groups unlike political parties in Europe which often represent a particular "class" or interest group.

Teachers can assist students in examining value conflicts. First, students have to understand why two values might be in conflict. Second, they need background information regarding ways others have dealt with the value conflict. Third, they need to understand the underlying causes of the value conflict and explore alternative ways people's values may conflict without resorting to anger or violence.

Teachers can pose questions which require children to raise issues of values in their lives. The purpose of these questions is to stimulate thought upon the part of students regarding the nature of values in their lives. Several excellent value provoking questions are:

- What was a recent decision you made in which you had to select from among several choices?

- Give an example in which you made a choice and the consequences were not what you expected?

- What is something about your home and family that you are proud of?

- Tell us something you have done that you are proud of?

- Tell us about a time when other kids wanted to do something and you didn't go along because you thought it was wrong?

Value discussions are extremely important in focusing students upon the nature of values and how they impact their lives. Students also need strategies that enable them to examine value issues in a more systematic manner. The following model is designed to provide students a tool for exploring value conflicts.

▲ The goal of educators is to assist children in understanding and accepting differences without the need to resort to violence.
Courtesy Saint Louis (Missouri) Public Schools.

- TITLE: What value is the source of conflict?

- FACTS: What information do we have about this value conflict?

- TREATMENT: How have people dealt with this value conflict in the past?

- CAUSES: What are the causes of the value conflict?

- ALTERNATIVES: How could this value conflict be handled differently so that all parties are treated with respect for their individual integrity?

The following illustration shows how the model can be applied to a familiar story.

A Case Study between the Three Pigs and the Wolf

- TITLE: A value conflict between the Wolf and three Pigs over private property.
- FACTS: 1. Each of the three pigs built a house. 2. The wolf sought to enter the houses in search of food. 3. The wolf first requested entrance and when it was denied resorted to wind power. 4. The pigs attempted to protect their property.
- TREATMENT: 1. Talk about the problem. 2. Use of wind power. 3. Physical violence against the pigs by the wolf. 4. Murder of pigs by the wolf. 5. Physical violence by a pig against the wolf.
- CAUSES: 1. Hunger pangs inside the wolf. 2. Belief by the pigs that since they had built their houses everything in their houses belonged to them. 3. Wolf had been educated to believe that if a wolf is hungry, the wolf has a right to use violence, including murder, in order to obtain food. 4. Pigs had been educated to believe that a wolf could physically harm them.
- ALTERNATIVES: 1. Wolf offers to do some work for the pigs in exchange for food. 2. Pigs ask a third party — the horse — to be present in order to ensure that no violence takes place. The pigs and wolf meet to discuss how to live in peace. 3. Pigs and wolf agree to have their children play together in order to learn how (a) wolves develop a tremendous desire from childhood to use force in order to obtain food, and (b) pigs are taught the importance of hard work and maintaining their property.

Teachers cannot ignore their own values, and the reality that those values intrude within the classroom, but they can create an environment in which students feel free to explore their own and the values of different peoples. The question of "values" was a highly visible issue during the U.S. election of 1992, and it will continue to be raised by interest groups seeking to exert control over the school curriculum. Elementary and middle school teachers have to be sensitive to the emotions which surround issues of values, but they also have a professional obligation to protect the right of children to be reflective citizens, and participants in furthering the democratic nature of our society.

Religion in the Social Studies Curriculum

Defining the place of religion in the social studies curriculum is often hampered by erroneous information. Despite common beliefs among educators, the Supreme Court did not ban the teaching of religion in schools. In the landmark case of *Abington School District v. Schempp*, the court held that studying religions in school is both legal and desirable. Justice William Brennan noted, "It would be impossible to teach meaningfully many subjects in the social sciences or the humanities without some mention of religion."

Religion has been a driving force in shaping human history. The Bible was central to Abraham Lincoln's education, and today millions of Americans are influenced by the Koran, the Torah, the sayings of Buddha, or Native American religious values. It is difficult to imagine how one could obtain an accurate understanding of America's past without some knowledge of religion.

America's colonial experience stemmed from religious conflict in England. The Pilgrims came seeking religious freedom for themselves, not for others. Opponents of the Puritans such as Roger Williams had to flee. Catholics and Jews fought to obtain legal rights throughout the colonial period, and it was not until after adoption of the Constitution that both groups began to be granted the right to vote. It took decades before Jews could vote in all states.

Children should know that Thomas Jefferson was most proud of his accomplishments in fighting to make religious freedom a right. They should be aware of the struggle by Catholics in the 19th century to overcome bigotry and to prevent schools from propagating anti-Catholic bias. The stories of the Amish, Mormons, and Christian Scientists illustrate the struggle for religious freedom.

The absence of religion from the curriculum ignores the impact of Christian and Jewish theology upon the quest for social justice by the American labor movement at the turn of the 20th century. Churches played a significant role in helping to improve working conditions and ending child labor. The women's rights movement and the antislavery crusade were also religious and moral in nature.

In contemporary times it is difficult to understand events in eastern Europe or the former Soviet Union without discussing religion. The Solidarity movement in Poland was strongly influenced by the Catholic church. Children cannot intelligently discuss the Middle East without some grasp of the religious nature of the conflict. Current tensions in Ireland stem from religious fears between Catholics and Protestants.

We justifiably expect home and church to instill religious values and practices. However, it is unusual for children to learn a great deal about religions other than their own except in school. The Supreme Court has held that a proper function of schools is to teach about religions, their beliefs, their values, and their practices. However, it is not constitutional for public schools to preach or insist upon a particular religion's set of beliefs.

Religions are centered in values. Most religions emphasize honesty, truth, respect for fellow humans, and the need for an individual to pursue ethical standards of behavior. There are significant differences among religions, but also a base of commonality which can help bind students together in an ethical community.

The National Council for the Social Studies in 1985 adopted a position statement and guidelines for teaching about religion. Among its key points were:

- Study about religions should emphasize the necessity and importance of tolerance, respect, and mutual understanding in a nation and world of diversity.
- Study of religions should be objective.
- Study about religions should stress the influence of religions on history, culture, the arts, and contemporary issues.
- Study about religions should be descriptive, nonconfessional, and conducted in an environment free of advocacy. (NCSS, 1985)

Knowledge about religions is a characteristic of the educated person. It is also essential in understanding many of the world's conflicts that regrettably have a religious base. Knowledge about religions can help promote understanding and alleviate prejudice in a world grown increasingly more diverse. The failure to teach about religion gives students the erroneous impression that religions are not important. If schools are to provide students with a comprehensive education, religion must be part of the curriculum.

The Chador

On Monday morning, three teenage girls who have been raised in the Muslim faith entered Jefferson Middle School wearing chadors. The chador is worn by women in many Moslem nations. It is a headscarf covering the hair, ears, and neck of a woman leaving only a wearer's eyes and a small part of the face visible. Fatimah and Samira, age 13, and Lleila, age 14, told the principal that they wished to wear the chador in accordance with their religious faith. The Koran's teaching on the subject is contained in two chapters entitled "Light" and "The Confederate Tribes." Verse 31 of "Light" says:

> Enjoin believing women to turn their eyes away from temptation and to preserve chastity; to cover their adornments (except such as are normally displayed); to draw their veils over their bosoms and not to reveal their finery except to their husbands, their fathers, their husbands' fathers, their stepsons, their brothers, their brothers' sons, their sisters' sons, their women servants and their slave girls; male attendants lacking in natural vigor, and children who have no carnal knowledge of women. And let them not stamp their feet in walking so as to reveal their hidden trinkets.

Verse 59 of the chapter "The Confederate Tribes" says:

> Prophet, enjoin your wives, your daughters and the wives of true believers to draw their veils close round them. That is more proper, so that they may be recognized and not molested.

The principal, Mr. Harris, pointed out to the girls that although an African-American himself, he had taken a strong stand against an attempt by a group of black students to wear hats to school. He pointed out that if the girls could wear a chador, it would open wide the door to students wearing whatever they desired. Mr. Harris said that public schools in America were secular institutions in which religion could not impose its practices. He had already banned Christmas decorations and trees to protect the sensibilities of Jewish and Moslem students. He gave the girls the choice of removing their chadors or going home. They agreed, under protest, to take off their chadors.

The next day Mr. Harris and the superintendent of schools, Ellen Moskowitz, were visited by a delegation of Moslem clergy and parents together with Rabbi Philip Goldberg. The Moslem parents and clergy insisted that the girls be allowed to dress in accordance with their religious beliefs. They were upset that Mr. Harris was compelling the girls to violate their religion. Rabbi Goldberg supported the Moslem parents and argued that Moslem children should be allowed to follow their religious beliefs just as a Jewish student should be allowed to wear a yarmulke. He believed these practices were an excellent opening to expand the educational horizons of all students. (Stopsky, 1989)

Questions:

1. Which are the strongest arguments favoring the position of the Moslem girls?
2. Which are the strongest arguments favoring the position of the principal?
3. Is the position supporting the wearing of a chador in accordance with or in violation of the First Amendment to the Constitution?

Moral Education in a Global Context

Societies tend to adopt an ethnocentric attitude toward value education. We assume our values, attitudes, and beliefs are held by other people in the world. As Americans, we believe in the idea of a democratic society, and it is difficult for us to accept that people might think otherwise. We tend to forget that ours has been a long journey which is yet to be completed.

Interdependence within the world makes it imperative for Americans to understand that other people can have different value beliefs. Japanese society emphasizes group cohesion and loyalty to the group. It is the norm in Japan for an individual to remain with the company or organization which first hired the person. "Looking out for number one" is considered a violation of the need for group solidarity. People do not ordinarily jump organizations to take higher paying jobs.

Many strict Moslem societies such as Saudi Arabia do not believe females should have the freedoms accorded American women. The Gulf War created tensions in Saudi Arabia when its citizens observed American women acting on an equal basis with men. There are people in Saudi Arabia who seek to create a more open situation for women, but others believe women are "free" because they are treated with respect and have control over the home.

The Inca empire, prior to its conquest by the Spanish, was totalitarian and hierarchical in structure. However, the Inca rulers ensured that all citizens had food, clothing, and shelter. People lived in extended family communities, there was no need for money, and they were protected by a powerful army. Inca values ran counter to those of modern-day America. How does a teacher present this society which was not democratic in nature?

Obviously, Inca children did not go through Kohlberg's stages of moral development. This suggests that our endeavor to establish a system depicting the evolution of moral reasoning has a cultural bias. A challenge to educators is to respect differing values in other societies while at the same time enabling children to create a personal system of values centered in democratic ideals.

It is difficult for both teacher and students to understand and respect values which differ from those of mainstream America. Our assumptions are viewed as "normal," and they are continually reinforced through the media and day-by-day interactions with other Americans. Educators need a process which enables students to study other values in order to understand them even though we may continue to disagree.

Following is a process that seeks to provide students an approach to understanding a value that goes counter to a popular idea regarding love and marriage. Americans are raised to believe that a boy and girl who love one another should be able to marry one another.

▲ Children must recognize that people of other cultures can adhere to values other than our own without being condemned. *Courtesy Kirkwood (Missouri) School District.*

> **Example:**
>
> Value Statement: American Orthodox Jews believe Jews should marry only other Jews.
> > Knowledge:
> > - There are fifteen million Jews in the world and five million of those live in America.
> > - American Jews have a low birthrate.
> > - Over 50% of marriages in America by Jews are with Christians.
> > - Less than 40% of children born to Jewish/Christian marriage are raised as Jews.
>
> Analysis: If present Jewish birthrates and marriages with Christians continue, the American Jewish population will dramatically decline over the coming hundred years.
>
> Frame of Reference: What are the concerns of Orthodox American Jews regarding the future of their religion?
>
> Empathy: How can I understand the emotional and religious desire of Orthodox Jews to oppose marriage with non-Jews?
>
> Rethinking: I still believe people should be able to marry one another regardless of their religion, color of skin, or economic situation. I can understand, however, how a particular religious group might seek to protect its survival by avoiding marriage with people outside its ethnic group.

Democratic values regarding equity, choice, and individuality are integral to American society. Schools stress these values as essential to the survival of our nation. It is also necessary to recognize that people in other cultures can adhere to other values than our own without being condemned or denigrated.

An important consideration for teachers is empowering students to take a stand concerning hatred and bigotry in the world, while at the same time being sensitive to the right of people to be different. King Gedminas of Lithuania opposed Christianity in the 14th century but told a delegation of Pope John XXII: "We allow Christians to honor their God according to their own traditions, the Russians according to their customs, the Poles according to theirs, and we, Lithuanians, honor God according to our rituals, and yet, we all have one God" (Oslo Conference on Hatred, 1991).

Nobel Prize winner Elie Wiesel stated in his 1986 acceptance speech that "I swore never to be silent whenever and wherever human beings endure suffering and humiliation." Children can be cruel to one another and often endure cruelty from adults. Hopefully, in classrooms, they can enjoy an environment in which individuals feel free to oppose all forms of hatred, and to escape being its target. The 1991 Oslo Conference on Hatred in its final statement urged that all institutions help lead humanity away from destructive hate:

> Parents, teach your children that to hate is to mutilate their own future. Teachers, tell your pupils that hatred is the negation of every triumph that culture and civilization may achieve. Politicians, tell your constituencies that hatred is, at all levels, your principal enemy, and theirs. Tell all those who listen to you that hatred breeds hatred and can breed nothing else.

SUMMARY

This chapter has discussed issues facing educators when teaching about values. It reviewed issues pertaining to values education and noted the place of religion in the topic of school values.

QUESTIONS

1. Which, if any, of your family values conflicted with those propagated in elementary and secondary school?

2. Did you encounter teachers in elementary or secondary school who consciously sought to persuade students to accept their values? If so, how did students react?

3. The authors state, "The school is the society of the child." Do you agree or disagree with the statement? Give an example to support your position.

4. How would you handle a parent complaint that your selection of educational materials reflected your values?

5. Can you cite an example of a child or yourself as a child acting in accordance with Kohlblerg's stages?

6. Which, if any, values would you consciously impart to students?

7. How would you react to a parent's request to ban holiday activities or songs because they advocate a religious belief?

8. Are there any values that you believe all humans seek?

9. Do you agree with Sidney Simon that teachers can or should teach "value-free"? If so, how would you accomplish this goal?

10. What is your reaction to the NCSS guidelines on teaching about religion?

ACTIVITIES

1. Interview elementary school teachers concerning value conflicts they have encountered with parents and their method of handling those situations.

2. Organize an analysis of the value beliefs of members of an education class.

3. Organize an analysis of the value beliefs of faculty members of the Education Department at your school. Compare and contrast their values and those of students.

4. Identify a fairy tale. Develop a value clarification activity based upon the story.

5. Interview religious leaders of two or more religions concerning their ideas about teaching religion in schools.

6. Analyze a story book used in elementary school for examples of gender bias, values, and racism.

7. Interview elementary school children regarding which values are most important to them.

Moral Advocacy and Social Education

by James S. Leming

Can there be anything wrong in teaching children that they ought to obey the law, be honest in their personal dealings, be respectful of others and their property, shun violence, or value human life? Certainly, we will not have a viable society unless the vast majority of citizens share allegiance to these norms. Surprisingly, however, contemporary approaches to moral education such as values clarification and the moral reasoning approach of Lawrence Kohlberg hold that teachers should not attempt to foster specific moral norms. Both of these approaches are nondirective and content free. They emphasize only open-ended, decision-making rules. They implicitly communicate to students that morality is fundamentally a matter of individual choice. Students learn that moral rules have their origin and derive their legitimacy solely from the act of decision-making. To be morally educated means to be skillful at adhering to procedural decision-making criteria. In this brief essay I would like to argue that social studies teachers should defend the basic moral norms which underpin the society in which all of us live so as to get students to share allegiance to these norms. This position I will call "moral advocacy," for it suggests that teachers ought to advocate, in a well reasoned manner, specific moral norms.

Contemporary approaches to moral education, I believe, represent an overly restrictive and limited view regarding the concepts of morality, moralization, and moral education. These approaches pay little heed to the social basis of morality. The moral norms of a society do not just happen. They are not created anew each generation, nor are they imposed by forces outside of a society's control. They have evolved in response to the social needs of that society. They regulate human behavior, stabilize the society, and, as a result, enhance individual welfare. To the extent that moral norms are unclear to the members of a society or to the extent that individuals are incompletely socialized into allegiance to these norms, a society faces potential instability.

Current approaches to moral education are premised on a view of the development of moral character which most research on moralization does not support. Reasoning does not appear to be a major determinant of socially responsible behavior. For example, in the area of prosocial behavior (behavior intended to aid or benefit another person or group), studies suggest that determinants of this behavior are such variables as: exposure to potent models of the desired behavior, having the consequences of actions for self and others explained, nurturance, and assignments of responsibility.[1] If children are presented with examples of prosocial behavior, if significant others approve of such behavior, and/or if children are provided with an opportunity to practice such behavior and are rewarded for it, evidence suggests they will acquire it as a norm. There is little evidence that we consciously choose our moral character. Thus, perhaps, it is not surprising that moral/values education programs have yet to demonstrate any significant impact on socially responsible behavior.[2]

There are many reasons which explain why teachers have avoided moral advocacy. One argument holds that since we are a culturally diverse society, the only way to respect the cultural heritage of all is for the teacher to accord all moral points of view equal weight. The argument is not persuasive because, in spite of the apparent moral diversity in our society, there exists a shared body of belief within communities regarding root values which can provide a common basis for moral education.

A second reason why teachers often avoid moral advocacy is because they are fearful of antagonizing elements within the community. This often occurs, however, as the result of advocacy of positions which are misunderstood and/or not endorsed by the community. Although this may be a very real problem for many teachers, it is not an inevitable by-product of moral advocacy.

A third reason why teachers, and social studies teachers in particular, have avoided moral advocacy centers around the view of the ideal citizen as an informed and independent decision-maker. There is a common misconception that moral advocacy would result in students slavishly and unreflectively accepting the view that answers to all moral questions lie in authority figures. Moral advocacy as a position about teaching does not demand that students believe as the teacher believes on moral questions. Alternative moral points of view may be considered and questioned, just as the teacher's perspective may be. Unlike current approaches to moral education, however, the teacher as moral advocate act as a strong and reasoned proponent for a specific socially agreed-upon moral point of view. Moral advocacy does not entail indoctrination, for it does not rule out serious consideration of alternative points of view, nor is it based solely on the authority of the teacher. Good reasons are to be stressed constantly as essential for a warranted moral position.

Before moral advocacy can be successfully implemented, however, there are three major considerations which must be addressed. Let me comment on each.

• *First,* there must be significant community input and school/community agreement concerning the moral norms which are to be the focus of instruction. Community/school task groups must be set up with a responsibility of specifying the focus and limits of the moral instruction which is to take place. Both agreement and disagreement are likely. The resulting program may reflect reasoned compromise between divergent positions or possibly a decision not to pursue moral education with regard to specific issues. Regardless of the outcome of such school/community deliberations, alternatives such as not involving the community, implementing programs clandestinely, or hiding moral education under more appealing labels (e.g., citizenship education) do not establish a firm foundation for a long-term successful program. Also, without broad-based school/community dialogue the potential exists for small vocal minorities to exert undue influence regarding single issues.

The widely held commitment to pluralism in the United States entails local community control of schools. There are, however, limits on communities regarding the nature of the moral norms to be fostered and on the rights of majority versus minority positions within the community. These limits are to be found in the root values embedded within the Constitution and specifically, in the Bill of Rights. For example, public schools do not have the right, regardless of the extent of community agreement, to advocate racism or to attempt to instill a sectarian religious perspective. Such activities would, on the one hand, sanction racist behavior, which is illegal and immoral, and on the other hand, involve the schools in activities which are clearly unconstitutional (the propagation of specific religious dogma in public schools). Ideally, teachers will play a significant role in the formulation of the goals of the moral education program through their participation in the school/community dialogue.

Teachers do not have the right to subvert the legitimate moral norms held by the community. Teachers, as employees of the community, are contractually obligated to carry out their duties consistent with legal school board policy. If the community decides that it wishes to have a specific moral standard taught as an explicit component of the school curriculum, it is reasonable to expect teachers as public employees to support this request. Communities, on the other hand, do not have the right to limit teachers's First Amendment right of freedom of speech. In cases where this potential issue becomes a public concern, it will, as it has in the past, be taken to the courts for resolution. In cases where teachers cannot in good faith carry out the dictates of the community, the teacher should work to change community opinion or search out a school district more compatible with his/her beliefs.

•*Second,* there needs to be an additional emphasis involved in the selection and training of prospective teachers. Characteristics associated with a capacity for effective modeling behavior should be given attention by those involved in teacher-training programs. A model's potency has been found to be related to the model's perceived competence, status, and control over resources, degree of prior nurturance, similarity with subjects's background, exhibition of simple rather than complex behaviors, and the rewards accruing to the model as a result of the demonstrated behavior. Although it is unreasonable to expect all teachers to provide exemplary role models for children, these characteristics of effective modeling suggest considerations for enhancing the salience and potency of teachers as moral advocates.

•*Third,* the methodology and content of instruction will need to be reconsidered. As suggested above, through their social behavior in the schools, teachers have the potential to serve as significant models of socially desirable behavior. Teachers can also present, for class consideration, realistic and timely examples of moral behavior which exemplify community standards. An increased sensitivity to the central role of morality in social life can be developed by having students study contemporary and historical examples of the relationship between the social cohesion provided by morality and personal and social well-being.

In our society, one of the central tasks of adolescence is identity formation. Involved in this redefinition of self is a re-examination of one's moral code. This stage of human development suggests that moral instruction in schools should be organized on the principle of a gradient of rationality. That is, in the earliest school years, children's moral options and choices will be necessarily limited by the teacher. Even then, however, we must begin to train children to apply, and expect the application of reason to understand moral questions. As the child progresses through school, the complexity and ambiguity of moral life will become apparent to children and will necessarily receive increased attention in the classroom. However—and this is where moral advocacy differs markedly from contemporary approaches to moral education—the teacher even at the latter stages of public school remains a consistent, strong, and reasoned proponent of specific moral norms. If the teacher carries out his/her advocacy in a considered manner, it should not stifle student thought, but, rather, represent a reasonable position presented by a significant other in a persuasive manner. Much outstanding work has been done by social studies educators and advocates of moral education regarding approaches for fostering thinking about moral questions. This work will continue to play a central role in moral education, especially with regard to the education of older students and in dealing with areas where societal consensus is low.

The evidence regarding schools' and teachers' ability to inculcate specific moral norms in children has not been encouraging. Hartshorne and May's classic study on the effectiveness of the Character Education Movement of the 1920s found that traditional approaches at inculcation were not effective in producing significant changes in student behavior. This general finding has remained unchallenged over the past half-century. Many factors both within schools and in society at large combine to limit the potential impact of any approach to moral education. Some of the more significant factors are: teachers have comprised notoriously poor and inconsistent models for children; major discrepancies exist between what is taught in school and other salient dimensions of the child's environment; teachers have lacked the ability to present moral arguments which are appealing and/or make sense to children; teacher presentations have been overly strident and perceived as old-fashioned; the nature of the schooling experience has led to an increasing devaluation of school and its teachers; and, media, mass culture, and peer group norms have emphasized the trendy and unusual, rather than the stable moral matrix which holds society together.

These factors, although making the task of moral education exceedingly difficult, also suggest considerations which moral advocacy must address if it hopes to be successful. The following are three of the areas involved in the practice of moral advocacy which will require close attention if past weaknesses are to be avoided. *First,* teachers can become more effective as moral educators not only by increasing their capacity for effective modeling, but also by developing a greater sensitivity to the need for consistency between their behavior and the norms they are attempting to foster. *Secondly,* teachers need to develop the ability to communicate with youth in a manner that is both appealing and understandable. Especially useful in this respect are findings from developmental psychology regarding the relationship between stage of moral reasoning and the comprehension of what is communicated. Studies using Kohlberg's stages of moral reasoning have found that children seldom comprehend messages more than one stage above their own. They understand but reject messages below their own level. It has also been found that children judge moral communications that are at the next highest stage as preferable. These findings suggest areas where teachers, by paying attention to their own students' level of reasoning, can maximize the potential for "making sense" when talking to children about moral concerns. A *third* area requiring close attention by teachers is the importance of developing in youth conceptual frameworks which will allow them to understand, without lapsing into shallow cynicism, the booming, buzzing confusion which constitutes moral life in contemporary society. Such a framework would emphasize the web of moral rules which make social life possible. Teachers should play a significant role in developing student understanding of such a framework and in encouraging children to use that framework in interpreting their social world.

If recent Gallup polls are an accurate indication of the public mood, there exists widespread support for moral education in the United States today.[3] It is likely that this support involves not only a desire that schools instruct children in how to think more systematically and clearly about moral questions, but also a desire that schools share with the family in the moral training of youth and foster an allegiance to the moral norms of the community which will manifest itself in the childrens' social behavior. If the schools' only focus is on getting children to think about and develop positions on moral questions, the public will likely be disappointed; for there is little evidence that such training in reasoning has any significant impact on social behavior. To date, contemporary approaches to moral education have focused largely on reasoning and personal choice without attention to the motivational foundation of social behavior. There is a need to broaden the conception of moral education.

Attempting to instill an allegiance to specific normative behaviors in children does not necessarily entail any squashing of the human spirit. Nor does it involve the legitimization of unjust or repressive social structures, the slavish acceptance of arbitrary moral standards, or the inevitable atrophy of the power of reason. Moral advocacy is little more than the attempt to ensure that our children play by the moral rules. For it is by living within and abiding by the moral framework of society that the vast majority of men and women is enabled to achieve happiness and self-realization while at the same time protecting the rights of others to do likewise.[4]

Notes

[1] Paul Mussen and Nancy Eisenberg-Berg, *Roots of Caring, Sharing, and Helping: The Development of Prosocial Behavior in Children,* San Francisco: W. H. Freeman and Co., 1977; Ervin Staub, *Positive Social Behavior and Morality: Social and Personal Influences,* New York: Academic Press, 1978.

[2] James S. Leming, "Curricular Effectiveness in Moral Values Education: A Review of Research," *Journal of Moral Education,* 1981 in press; Alan L. Lockwood, "The Effects of Values Clarification and Moral Development Curricula on School-Age Subjects: A Critical Review of Recent Research," *Review of Educational Research*, Vol. 48, Summer 1978, pp. 325–364.

[3] George H. Gallup, "The 12th Annual Gallup Poll of the Public's Attitudes Toward the Public Schools," *Phi Delta Kappan,* Vol. 62, Spring 1980, pp. 33–48.

[4] For a more detailed treatment of the issues raised in this brief essay, the reader is referred to James S. Leming, "On the Limits of Rational Moral Education: Psychological and Sociological Perspectives," *Resources in Education,* October 1980, ED 187 623.

QUESTIONS ON READINGS

1. What are the author's three major considerations concerning moral advocacy?

2. The author states that teachers "do not have the right to subvert the legitimate moral norms held by the community." Do you agree or disagree with his viewpoint?

3. Do you believe schools can significantly alter the moral values children bring from their homes and community?

4. What role should teachers play in moral advocacy?

LESSON PLAN

Ms. Carla Wallace   First Grade

Objective: Learning about the life of the Sioux Indians.

Rationale: It is important for students to understand the diversity of life-styles and customs among Native Americans.

Activities:

1. Teacher introduces topic using KWL (Know, Want to Know, and Learned). Students indicate what they know, and what they would like to know. When lessons are complete, they fill in what they have learned.

2. Teacher asks students to group themselves based on where they live. Teacher indicates on map of U.S. groups of Native American nations prior to arrival of Europeans.
   - Teacher hands out pictures of different types of houses used by Native Americans. Each group selects one type of house to draw and construct.

3. Teacher indiciates that many Sioux lived in tepees. Students build their own tepees. Teacher reads *Dancing Tepees* which is a collection of poetry.
   - Students use shape of their tepee to make a "shape poem."

4. Teacher demonstrates different ways used by Sioux to communicate—smoke signals, picture writing, sign language, calendar stick and winter count.
   - Class divided into four interest centers. With aid of parent volunteers, each group uses one of the Sioux communication methods to convey a message.

5. Students are divided into groups and asked: "Assume there were no stores. How would you make clothes from something in nature?" Each group is to come up with a solution.
   - Teacher shows examples of Sioux clothing and how they were made.

6. Children sit around a pretend campfire. Teacher reads stories from *Sioux Stories*.
   - Students divided into groups. Each child is to tell other members of their group a family story of their own.
   - Teacher reads the book, *Knots on a Counting Rope*, by Bill Martin. Each child is given a piece of yarn. Children are told that each time they tell a story a knot is to be tied in their piece of yarn.

7. Teacher tells about chores and schooling for Sioux boys and girls. They are shown pictures of Sioux games. Among them are: foot races; moccasin game, in which an object is hidden in one of three moccasins and other person has to guess in which one; and spinning tops, which were made of bone, antlers, or wood. Children play games.

8. Teacher shows film about a buffalo hunt. Students are asked to brainstorm how Sioux killed buffalo before arrival of horses.
   - Teacher reads book, *Gift of the Sacred Dog,* by Paul Goble.
   - Teacher lists buffalo parts. Students in groups are to guess how each part was used by Sioux.
   - Students in groups plan a menu that might have been eaten by a Sioux family.
   - Teacher reads book, *Popcorn,* by Tomie DePaola.

9. Teacher reads book, *I'm in Charge of Celebration,* by Byrd Baylor.
   - Teacher tells about Sioux dances and rituals. Children do several Sioux dances. Students plan a Sioux celebration.

10. Teacher introduces guest speaker who is of Sioux Indian ancestry.

Bibliography:

Banks, Lynne, *Indians in the Cupboard.*
Baylor, Byrd, *I'm in Charge of the Celebration.*
Goble, Paul, *Gift of the Sacred Dog.*
Miles, Miska, *Annie & the Old One.*
Naylor, Maria, *Authentic Indian Designs.*
Native American Youth, *Dancing Tepees.*

REFERENCES

Abington School District v. Schempp, (1963).

Armento, B. J. (1981). A matter of values. In J. Allen (Ed.), *Education in the '80s* (pp. 113–118). Washington, DC: National Education Association.

Dobkin, W., Fischer, J., Ludwig, B., & Koblinger, R. (Eds.). (1985). *A handbook for the teaching of social studies.* Boston: Allyn & Bacon.

Ellis, A., Mackey, J., & Glen, A. (1988). *The school curriculum.* Boston: Allyn & Bacon.

Frankel, C. (1964). Needed research on social attitudes, beliefs, and values in teaching social studies. *NCSS Bulletin, 1,* p. 8.

Glasser, W. (1969). *Schools without failure.* New York: Harper & Row.

McCutchen, S. (1963, February). A discipline for the social studies. *Social Education,* pp. 61–65.

National Council for the Social Studies. (1985).

Newman, F. (1977). Building rationales for citizenship education. *NCSS Bulletin, 52,* 4–8.

Oslo Conference on Hatred. (1991).

Power, F. C., Higgins, A., & Kohlberg, L. (1989). "Lawrence Kohlberg's approach to moral education." New York: Columbia University Press.

Raths, L., Harmin, M., & Simon, S. (1966). *Values and teaching.* Columbus, OH: Charles E. Merrill.

Simon, S. B. (1978). *Values Clarification: A Handbook of Practical Strategies for Teachers and Students.* New York: Hart Publishing Company.

Solé, R. (1989, October 29). French Education in Turmoil over Chador Issue. *Manchester Guardian Weekly,* pp. 15–16.

Taba, H. (1971). *A teacher's handbook to elementary social studies.* Menlo Park, CA: Addison Wesley.

Ubbelohde, C., Frankel, J. (eds). (1976). *Values of the American heritage: challenges, case studies, and teaching strategies.* Washington, DC: National Council for the Social Studies.

SUGGESTED READING

Bridges, D., & Scrimshaw, P. (Eds.). (1975). *Values and authority in schools.* London: Hodder & Stoughton.

Frankel, C. (1965). *The case for modern man.* Boston: Beacon.

Glasser, W. (1969). *Schools without failure.* New York: Harper & Row.

Kohlberg, L. (1981). *The philosophy of moral development.* San Francisco: Harper & Row.

Pawetczynska, A. (1979). *Values and violence in Auschwitz.* Berkeley: University of California Press.

Raths, L., Harmin, M., & Simon, S. (1966). *Values and teaching.* Columbus, OH: Charles E. Merrill.

Schnall, M. (1981). *Limits: A search for new values.* New York: Clarkson Potter.

Scriven, M. (1966). *Primary philosophy.* New York: McGraw-Hill.

Simon, S. (1972). *Values clarification: A handbook of practical strategies for teachers and students.* New York: Hart.

Chapter 3

The Global Curriculum

The Global Curriculum

Today's society functions on a global scale. Global interactions occur daily in our economic, political, cultural, technological, and cultural lives. Satellites, electronic communications, and ordinary TV sets mean we see events anywhere in the world and even in space live or within minutes of their occurring.

The transformation of political systems throughout the world impacts our budgetary process and may determine if funds are available for students to attend college. A decline in Tokyo's stock market is echoed in London and New York's stock exchanges. Even individual human activities have global implications. For example, chloroflorocarbons in aerosol sprays have increased everyone's vulnerabity to skin cancer.

The global reality of the American society can be dramatized by arbirtarily choosing just one item of clothing a student is wearing at this moment. This item is likely to have been subject to several of the following: A foreign nation might have been the source of the raw materials for this item, or the source of the machinery used to manufacture the item. A foreign nation may be where the item was manufactured. Even if the item were manufactured domestically, the garment worker in the plant, the truck driver who shipped the item, the warehouse worker, or the sales clerk may have been a recent immigrant. Or, any of the companies in this chain, from the manufacturer to the department store may be owned by a foreign nation or may be one that operates worldwide, and has foreign nationals on its board of directors.

▲ Social studies teaching is dramatically affected by the globalization process. *Courtesy Null Elementary, Saint Charles (Missouri) Public Schools.*

Social studies teaching is dramatically affected by the globalization process. The social studies teacher today is faced with information in recently purchased textbooks, maps, and globes that is outdated because of rapid global changes. For example, changes in the 1991–1992 school year, such as the dissolution of the U.S.S.R. and unrest in Yugoslavia, dated even the newest maps and textbooks. Schools and teachers are challenged to find ways of teaching social studies that will be stimulating, relevant, and meaningful to students in a world undergoing dramatic change.

This chapter aims to (1) explain what the global curriculum is and why it is important in our schools; (2) discuss ways to globalize teaching; and (3) cite examples of efforts to globalize the elementary social studies curriculum.

The Global Curriculum: What Is It and Why Do It?

The term "global education" is often used to describe the various efforts underway to incorporate within the curriculum a more complex undestanding of the human community. It may carry various meanings such as the following:

1. Broadening the study of world history to incorpoate societies lying outside the traditional Eurocentric focus. This might include the story of Japan, the geography of India, the impact of Arab thinkers upon western thought, or the history of Africa.

2. Studying the customs and lifestyles of particular regions, nations, and cultures.

3. Learning to communicate in foreign languages.

4. Studying world problems such as environmental issues, population problems, promoting human rights, and the importance of peace education.

5. Studying domestic multicultural issues as they pertain to an international focus. For example, learning about racism and prejudice in other parts of the world or the international dimensions of hunger and homelessness.

6. Learning conflict management skills to better undestand ways of peacefully resolving differences with people both on the national and international scene.

▲ The global curriculum includes an introduction to foreign languages. *Courtesy University City (Missouri) Public Schools.*

These approaches fall under the theme of global education. They present the view that differences as well as similarities exist among peoples around the world, and that many mainstream American experiences and values are not shared universally. Some approaches stress understanding the differences and similarities between peoples. Other approaches aim for empathy and appreciation of differences; and still others promote the development of specific skills to think and work with people of diverse backgrounds.

Willard Kniep suggests that global education contains four elements of study: (a) human values; (b) global systems; (c) global problems and issues, and (d) the study of interdependence between peoples. In the 20th century, for the first time, the world's people have begun to establish universal standards for human relations. Global education aids students to recognize diversity of value systems but also to perceive those qualities people share in common. People today are linked to fellow humans to an extent unprecedented in human history. We cannot escape being part of several global systems simultaneously impacting our economic, social and political lives (Kneip, 1986).

Global issues and problems are transnational in scope. The origins and consequences of problems transcend the boundary of any single nation. They can only be dealt with through multilateral actions because any single problem is probably connected to several others. The restructuring of the former Soviet Union requires economic assistance from other nations, conflict resolution activities to prevent war between the splintering pieces, aid from scholars abroad in order to revamp education and cultural structures, and assistance in establishing democratic foundations for society. Each of these problems impacts other nations and none can be solved alone by the Russian peoples.

The complexity of the modern world even overwhelms experts who have spent years studying these issues. Some elementary and secondary teachers hesitate to involve students in

▲ The global curriculum broadens social studies to consider societies outside the traditional Eurocentric focus.
Courtesy Kirkwood (Missouri) School District.

materials they might deem beyond the grasp of the young mind. The media, however, expose elementary and middle school students to sights, sounds, and information about current affairs.

Teachers and students must embark on a joint expedition to examine and learn about the world outside the classroom. Young students frequently display enthusiasm and interest in studying material and topics pertaining to faraway places. This spirit can be channeled into productive study of topics related to world issues. Teachers can foster skills in finding causality in events, bridging disparate concepts, understanding multiple perspectives and employing conflict resolution methods to resolve problems.

In fact the global curriculum is an interdisciplinary endeavor, as Hanvey suggests in his list of five dimensions of the global curriculum:

1. Perspective consciousness: This refers to the recognition of and appreciation for images of the world which differ from one's own.
2. State of the planet awareness: This means that one understands and is concerned about current global issues and events.
3. Cross-cultural awareness: This refers to the general understanding of characteristics that define cultures in the world, and the ability to grasp similarities and differences among the cultures.
4. Systemic awareness: This refers to the familiarity with the patterns of interaction and interdependence in international systems (economic, political, environmental, etc.).

▲ Young people are frequently enthusiastic about studying faraway places. *Courtesy University City (Missouri) Public Schools.*

5. Options for participation: This refers to selecting strategies for playing an active role in local, national or international arenas for working on global issues.(Harvey, 1979)

These dimensions of the global curriculum focus upon the sensitivities students develop rather than the content knowledge per se. This suggests that teachers can develop these perspectives while working with a variety of topics, and particularly when teaching units that are organized in an interdisciplinary manner.

That the global curriculum emphasizes processes rather than content knowledge is echoed by Cleveland (1986), who states that the global curriculum should aim to develop in students:

1. *A feel for basic human needs*: When students can understand their own human needs, they will understand the needs and aspirations of people everywhere. This is the basis for empathy.

2. *A feel for global changes:* In order to manage the major changes in shifting world power balances, the explosion of information and revolutionary technologies, students must be able "to think more freshly, farther ahead, and more widely . . . than ever before."

3. *A feel for "national security":* Although national security has previously meant military defense, the term takes on broader meaning in the global community, because security of the planet from nuclear destruction or environmental abuses coincides with the security concerns of individual nations.

4. *A feel for the way world economy works:* The new dynamics of world economy are based on "human capital," such as education, resourcefulness, and strategic decision making rather than on natural resources, money or the size of the labor force per se.

5. *A feel for cooperation and consent building:* Using rigid or autocratic ways to relate in the world community does not advance the interests of any nation. Fluency with cooperative methods will be required for working on local, national as well as international projects.

6. *A feel for cultural diversity and political pluralism:* The diversity of values, cultures and personalities in a pluralistic society and world requires that all citizens are free of intolerance for this diversity.

7. *A feel for the nature of leadership:* In a global community in which there is no single super-power or a state of nobody-in-charge, individual citizens are increasingly responsible for determining both their individual and collective fate.

In this scheme, each of the aims are defined as "a feel for" rather than more common cognitive formulations of curricular goals. This emphasis on the "feeling for" suggests that the learning processes and the approaches to studying the material may be more important than the specific knowledge or skill per se. Cleveland's approach emphasizes that traditional approaches to mastering information are unmanageable in an era of rapidly expanding knowledge.

The Association for Supervision and Curriculum Development has sought to clarify the definition of a global curriculum. Their definition contains four parts:

1. The study of problems and issues that cross and transcend national and political boundaries;

2. The understanding of the interconnectedness of systems, ecological, cultural, economic, political, and technical;

3. Perspective taking, which is the ability to view things through the perceptions and values of others; and

4. The realization of the commonality of human needs and wants even when individuals and groups differ on surface appearances and expressions.(Tye, 1991)

This is a multidisciplinary definition which, like Cleveland's, recognizes the importance of values and differing viewpoints. It reinforces the concerns of an increasing number of social studies educators that content and process are inextricably linked. The global curriculum can be defined as follows: *The global curriculum includes the conscious knowledge of and involvement in issues, ideas, and activities which relate to humans or other living beings or the planet itself, across political, social and geographic boundaries. It includes the appreciation for the interconnectedness of self with others and the world.*

The components of this definition can be further clarified in order to delineate the basis of a broad global perspective and identify topics to be covered:

▲ When students understand their own human needs, they begin to understand the needs and aspirations of people everywhere. *Courtesy Webster University.*

- *the conscious knowledge of* means that students become aware of their own learning. They must not only know the material, but be cognizant of the fact that they know it. Educators call this self-awareness "metacognition." Teachers can have students practice this skill from the earliest grades.

- *involvement in* means students are engaged in the material they are studying, and actually participating or acting (i.e., doing something) with regard to the topic itself. An example of this is students practicing and advocating paper recycling at home and at school.

- *issues, ideas, and activities which relate to humans or other living beings or the planet itself* The global curriculum is concerned about the various systems in the human and social world, such as the economic, political, psychological, or historical material, which are the usual concerns of the social sciences. This includes the communication systems and technologies that provide the vehicle for global networking. The global curriculum also includes the natural world, as plants and animals are part of the total environmental system of humans. Physical and chemical processes are also the concern of the global curriculum since they too are part of the environment in which human function. The sciences and social sciences are united in the global curriculum.

- *across political, social and geographic boundaries* A global curriculum emphasizes that social studies can no longer confine itself within the narrow constraints of the local community. A study of family life can be expanded to include family life of granparents who emigrated from abroad or how children live in different countries. This global perspective does not preclude teaching about the local environment, but places it within a broader international perspective. The democratic system of the United States can be contrasted with other forms of democracy in Canada, France, Germany as well as autocratic systems in the world.

- *appreciation for the interconnectedness of self with others and the world* A key component in the global curriculum is to stress the individual's relationship to the concepts being studied. It is not sufficient to taste a dessert from Vietnam, or to see the Halloween traditions of Mexico. Students must see how their own diets and holiday practices influence and are influenced by practices and activities in other nations. In the traditional curriculum, students are taught that dictators are evil. In the global curriculum, students learn the processes by which dictators seize power, and make connections between this information and situations in their own society in which people abuse power. Going further, students might be able to better grasp the mentality of a dictator when they discover how their own angry, violent or hostile feelings are universal attributes. The global curriculum seeks to empower students with new skills of understanding in order to bring about a more democratic world.

Social Studies Throughout the World

In addition to teaching students about the world around them, global education strives to familiarize them with how social studies is taught in other nations. Each society presents its ideas about world issues through the perspective of its individual bias, values, and attitudes. Learning about the education of children in other societies enables American children to better grasp disparate viewpoints.

> The transnational character of social studies is little understood or appreciated in the United States. Although American social studies educators are among the leaders in promoting international studies and global education, although they attempt to reduce ethnocentrism and national chauvinism among their students, and even though they read about international affairs and travel widely, they are generally uninformed about their own profession as it is practised in other nations. (Mehlinger, 1979, p. 1)

The term "social studies" is a peculiar American invention. Most children in the world study content areas such as geography, history, political science, and economics. Terminology may appear an unimportant issue, but it reflects how other societies define their attitudes and values. An American teacher who establishes a relationship with teachers in other nations must be cognizant that even such a basic concept as the term "social studies" should be clarified in the early stages of communication. A global perspective requires being sensitive to other ways of thinking.

It is common for people to assume that other humans think, act, and feel in like manner. Two decades ago, anthropologist Edward Hall (1973) argued that culture is a hidden dimension. He explained that culture penetrates our perceptual system, thus masking the basic aspects of our existence which are immediately obvious to an outsider. People tend to think about the learning environment with which they are most familiar, and this is true about people throughout the world.

It is important for children to know that teachers and students in other societies have different ways of behaving. In traditional Asian cultures, students would not openly disagree with a teacher because they believe wisdom comes with age. The sharing of emotions is common in American schools, but not part of the culture of a Korean or Chinese classroom. A value emphasized in American education may not be recognized in a different culture.

Rituals and patterns of classroom interaction also vary from culture to culture. In Jamaica, primary school students flap or snap their fingers to signal they know the answer. In Trinidad, students place their index and middle fingers on their foreheads with the inside facing out to ask permission to be excused. The classroom in an Israeli kibbutz is noisy and interaction is spontaneous, but a Chinese classroom is very quiet.

Global education prepares students to respect diversity of behaviors manifested by people in everyday life. In Italian classrooms, teachers and students touch each other frequently, and children greet a teacher with a kiss on both cheeks. On the other hand, Japanese children show emotional restraint in the classroom. Global education enables children to understand that communication with its verbal and nonverbal messages, systematic patterns, and socialized rituals reflects cultural norms and traditions.

The study of social studies has to be viewed within the contextual framework of how other peoples examine their past and present. The People's Republic of China is based upon Marxist principles so the study of ancient Chinese history emphasizes that early humans lived in communes, and Marxist ideology permeates every aspect of the curriculum. Japan ignores the brutal behavior displayed by its soldiers when invading China in the 1930s just as American textbooks avoid discussing cavalry attacks upon Native American villages in the 19th century.

Global education strives to make teachers more sensitive even in expressions used within the classroom while discussing other societies. For example, some textbooks still refer to "Moorish Spain" when discussing the era of Moslem control of the Iberian peninsula. The word "Moor" has no meaning to people in Islamic nations who employ expressions such as Arabs or Muslims. The year "1994" refers to the Christian era, but Jews, Muslims and Buddhists use different calendars to reckon their origin and the present time.

As teachers become inceasingly more involved in global education, new opportunities emerge to provide a transnational dimension to classroom activities. There are classroom instructional materials prepared in foreign nations which can be adapted for use in American schools. The Schools Council History 13–16 Project in England has created curriculum packets on the topic of "What is History?" and a paperback entitled, *The American West: 1840–1895,* which enables American students to obtain an interesting perspective on their own history as viewed through a different lens (Mehlinger, 1979).

The International Society for Educational Information has developed a vast array of curriculum materials in English that depict life in Japan. *The Life of an Elementary School Pupil in*

▲ Diversity of values, cultures, and personalities in a pluralistic society requires that all citizens are free of intolerance.
Courtesy Saint Louis (Missouri) Public Schools.

Japan is a fascinating account of going to elementary school as told through the perspective of a Japanese child. For example, the following excerpt discusses school rules:

> Among the rules made by pupils, there are ones about what each committee should do. For instance, we have a committee to arrange games and where to play them during recess. The rules made by the committee are announced in each homeroom by the committee chairman or a committee member. Pupils usually keep this kind of rule better than the rules made by teachers.

The more American children learn about the lives of children in other parts of the world and what they study in social studies or history, the more our students can fully grasp the dilemmas caused by change both abroad and in our own past. Nigeria uses social studies education to break down religious and regional differences in order to develop the concept that everyone is a "Nigerian." This process is analogous to what the United States did during periods of high immigration. Germany has drawn upon social studies education in order to dilute the negative ramifications of nationalism and to deal with the horrors of World War II. This is analogous to our endeavors to create a multicultural curriculum that examines negative as well as positive actions toward minorities in America's past.

Global education enables American teachers and students not only to learn and understand about other peoples, but to find new ways to improve our own society. Educational reform is an important issue throughout the world, and we can learn how other societies approach the issue of changing their schools. For example, a cake and chocolate factory in Hargate, England, invited a group of high school teachers to spend several days learning about modern management techniques. They returned to their schools and with the aid of factory managers involved pupils in a project to create a new chocolate product. The emphasis was transnational so the chocolates were designed as a gift to a French school that had hosted an exchange visit. English students had to write covering letters to the French children who would eat the chocolate. It is through learning from examples such as this endeavor at global education that American teachers can broaden their own approaches and make students sensitive to innovative ideas throughout the world (Hirsch, 1992).

In the past few decades American educators have witnessed a globalization of the social studies curriculum. American education cannot be provincial and only concerned with national or local concerns. Social studies, regardless of how it is defined in other societies, remains the place in the American curriculum in which students gain a global perspective. Our efforts to implement a global orientation are matched by the endeavors of other nations to link their students with the wider world. "The point here is to suggest that while other nations may have much to learn from the United States about social studies, the United States may have much to gain from other nations. The exchange will enrich the social studies, an emerging transnational profession" (Tucker, 1979, p. 100).

▲ National security includes non-military concerns such as the environment. *Courtesy Saint Louis (Missouri) Public Schools.*

Case Study of African Education

The country of Dako is located in Africa. It has a population of 22 million people who are divided in six major linguistic groups. Dako was a colony of France for approximately 100 years, and French was the official language during that time period. It was common for outstanding Dako students to be sent to France for higher education.

There are two major cities which contain about five million people, and the remainder of the population lives in rural communities. There are 90,000 people of French ancestry who live mainly in major cities and dominate banking, industry and large farming. Rural Dako raises cocoa, cotton, and engages in subsistence farming. Dako exports about $200 million worth of oil. The average income is about $350 per year.

The government of Dako has mandated compulsory education for children ages 6 to 13. At present, about 65% of children are attending school.

About 20% of children go on to secondary school and about 5% attend college. A Minister of Education directs all schools and makes curriculum decisions. Teachers are hired by the Ministry of Education which also assigns administrators to schools.

The Minister of Education has convened a conference to discuss the future of education in Dako. Your task is to develop a plan of action. In developing the plan, consider the following issues and questions:

1. What should be the goals of education in Dako?
2. Given limited amounts of money, how should money most effectively be allocated? For example, should more money go to higher education or to elementary schools?
3. How should education in Dako be the same or different as education in the United States?

Environmental Education: Global Interdependence

The environmental situation has compelled humanity to face the obvious: physical, economic, and emotional needs are not separable, and only through global cooperation can planet Earth be a healthy place for all. Out of an awareness of problems such as pollution or rising gas prices comes an understanding of our interdependence with others in modern problem solving. Our personal needs are no longer personal, they are interactive.

An effective environmental education program enables children to recognize how their habits, directly or indirectly, affect the ability of other humans to meet their basic needs. Children can profit enormously from early exposure to good energy values. They can learn, for example, that it is possible to be comfortable indoors at a lower temperature, or by dressing warmer they can reduce energy utilization in the school building. Students can carry these attitudes back home and support parental endeavors to reduce energy use.

There are several concepts which serve as guidelines for environmental education in social studies:

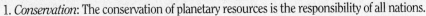

1. *Conservation*: The conservation of planetary resources is the responsibility of all nations.
2. *Energy Interdependence*: All nations depend upon one another for energy and the actions of one impact others.
3. *Energy Resources and Distribution*: Students have to be aware of availability of energy resources and how they are distributed in the world.
4. *Overconsumption:* The United States is the largest user of energy resources in the world, but other nations increasingly are using more and more energy.
5. *Energy Alternatives:* There are many alternative forms of energy, and informed societies employ several of them in order to avoid overdependence upon any one.

The world is threatened by a wide range of threats to ecological stability, and since stability and biological survival are closely linked, an essential task of modern education is preparing students to cope with these issues. The magnitude of threats to the biosphere are great enough to warrant extensive environmental education efforts in schools.

> And yet this education will have failed in its most important role if it treats the environment as an alien place where problems occur due to "human impact. . .," and which, may or may not encumber humankind with inconvenient "limits." The paradox is that to get to the root of our environmental problems, we must learn to see that the environment is not a separate subject at all. (Johnson, 1983, p. 41)

It is possible, based on news reports, to regard environmental issues as raised by overly sentimental people who are concerned by an owl or a fish. Each year a multitude of species disappear from the Earth, and the cumulative effects of these extinctions pose a grave danger to the long-term survival of millions of our fellow species on this planet. Tropical forests are being cut down at the rate of approximately 42,000 acres per year, and if that situation continues, the major portion of tropical forests will have disappeared by the end of the coming century.

▲ Students must be engaged in the material they are studying, and actually participate or do something with regard to the topic. *Courtesy University City (Missouri) Public Schools.*

The growing loss of topsoil, the spread of deserts in places like North Africa, and the growing pollution of the ocean are related to actions by humans. Environmental education has the task of making students aware that long-term survival depends upon short-term actions. This does not mean frightening students with tales of horror and devastation. The educational system should produce students who understand that the global environment is the way our world works, and humans play a vital role in the formation of an environment which is in harmony with all living species.

An effective environmental education has to be multidisciplinary in organization. It requires integrating science, social studies, mathematics, art, and literature in order to broaden the ability of students to see the interrelationships in life on this planet. Environmental problems can be resolved if humans assume responsibility for their actions toward the physical environment and animal species of the planet. Students can learn that the ecological system is a social arrangement and results from natural and human causes which interact with one another.

Teaching Social Studies from a Global Perspective

How does an elementary or middle school social studies teacher implement lessons reflecting a global perspective? This is a special challenge since textbooks and other teaching materials

▲ The global curriculum includes the study of the natural world.
Courtesy Lynn Rubright, Webster University.

reflecting this perspective are only gradually emerging. One approach for doing this is to turn the definition of the global curriculum into a checklist for determining how fully lessons conform to the characteristics of the global curriculum. Such a checklist might include the following:

- Does the lesson enable students to be involved in issues?
- Does the lesson include ideas that cross political, social, and geographic boundaries?
- Does the lesson link human concerns with processes in the living world, physical or chemical processes, or the planet itself?
- Does the lesson demonstrate how individuals are interconnected with other peoples in the world?

Below are examples of elementary school social studies lessons which attempt to incorporate a global pespective.

A Global Perspective in Current Events (grades 4 and above)

In a class of 20 to 30 pupils, the teacher obtains five copies each of four daily newspapers (with the same publication date) from different cities. The teacher divides the class into five groups, 4 to 6 students per group, and distributes one copy of each newspaper and a large posterboard (tag board) to each group. Students scan the papers and clip articles that are "global" in nature. They evaluate and compare the articles on whether the perspectives are local, national, or global. They make a "front page collage" of articles representing the global perspective on the posterboard. They may include news articles, editorials, features, cartoons, advertisements, and artwork that the group determines to be global in nature. Upon completion of this task, each group presents their posters to the class and explains their rationale for selection and placement of the clippings. The teacher guides the discussion toward clarifying students' concepts of what constitutes the global perspective, how the various newspapers compared in their viewpoints and coverage, and how the groups compared in their selections.

Ethnic Origins (grades 1 and above)

Students can understand and appreciate the variety of ethnic backgrounds when they are given opportunities to interview and bring in parents and other people in the community to discuss their ethnic origins. The application of this approach in Orange County was successful in classrooms as young as first graders.

The most significant value of these "ethnic origins" lessons often emerges from the students' work after the actual contact with the interviewee or classroom visitor. The value placed on ethnic origins permits students to reflect about and explore their own individual ethnic backgrounds, even when their ethnic backgrounds differ from that of the interviewee or speaker. In discovering commonalities, students learn to empathize with their classmates and with families in the community. This becomes a foundation for increased understanding and appreciation of the wide diversity of people, ideas, and values in the multicultural and global society.

The Global Marketplace (grade 3 and above)

The most revolutionary change in America's economic life in this century has been the phenomenal growth in trade with all parts of the globe. The United States now exports about $400 billion worth of goods and imports about $450 billion worth of products. People in all walks of life, such as grocers, department store employees, automobile dealers, factory workers, and farmers, are dependent upon international interactions for their economic survival. To illustrate the global interdependence of the economy, student groups visit and interview the shipping/receiving managers for several different kinds of local retail outlets, such as grocers, automobile dealer-

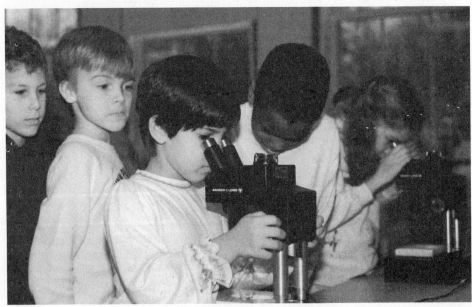

▲ The sciences and social sciences are united in the global curriculum.
Courtesy University City (Missouri) Public Schools.

ships, discount department stores, and restaurants. Students try to identify the sources and means of transportation by which goods arrive at these outlets. They trace the routes of various goods from the retailer back to the warehouses back to the wholesalers back to ports of entries back to the agricultural or manufacturing sources. With their results, the student groups construct color-coded route maps that show the distances and transportation methods involved in transporting the goods. In class discussions and written worksheets, the teacher helps students compare the various route maps and analyze the interdependencies in the network.

A Multidisciplinary Lesson on Water Usage (grades 3 and above)

This lesson involves concepts in science, social studies, writing, and mathematics. It uses a personal survey to raise students' awareness of their own invisible uses of water, and how it compares with water usage in developing nations.

It is estimated that each American is responsible for using an average of 300–500 liters (78–130 gallons) of water per day. Students keep an individual log of their water usage for several days as a way of comparing their individual water useage with this statistic. In their logs, they list every situation in which they use water, from the bathroom and kitchen at home, to the soft drink from the vending machine, to the watering dish for a pet gerbil. The logs also include estimates of the volume of water consumed in each situation listed. Students consult reference materials or do ad hoc experiments and arithmetic calculations to find that volume.

When the students report their average daily use of water, they discover that no one comes close to the 300–500 liters per day cited. A stimulating discussion follows in which students speculate about the discrepancy. The teacher reveals that industrial and commercial use of water is included in the 300–500 liter per person average. Students object to this, as they do not feel it is appropriate to include industrial and commercial water use when estimating children's water use. The teacher explains further. Even though each individual, adult or child, may not directly experience the industrial and commercial water useage, each adult and child is included in the calculation because each benefits directly from the services and products that result from these commercial and industrial processes. For example, the convenience of electricity may not be available to us if water were not used in regulating the temperature in the generating plants. Or the automobile, bus, or bicycle the student used in getting to school would not exist if large amounts of water were not available for processing and shaping the steel, assembling the vehicle, and painting it.

▲ The global curriculum enables students to assume responsibility for their actions toward plant and animal species of the planet. *Courtesy Saint Louis (Missouri) Public Schools.*

Students reflect on this argument. They express their feelings about it, and speculate on how their lives would differ if the nation's per person water usage were reduced to levels comparable to that of developing nations. Each student then composes an essay describing this image.

A global education approach promotes active involvement on the part of students with current issues and problems. Many will argue that schools should not promote social activism and that it is inappropriate to ask children to take sides in debates that are often politically charged. The counterpoint is that children (and adults) must learn that they are responsible for the consequences of their actions, particularly how their actions affect other people, their environment, and ultimately their own futures. Probably the single most effective approach is for teachers to reflect upon how they themselves are involved in the issues and topics they teach, and what kind of example they themselves set for their students.

All academic disciplines have a role to play in furthering global education. The study of literature, music, and the arts have a great deal to contribute to the understanding of human values, the experience of people around the globe in coping with persistent problems and issues of our time and to the development of a historical perspective. While the social studies may have a special role to play in the development of a global perspective, school programs will be truly global when the distinctive content of a global education is reflected across the curriculum.

SUMMARY

This chapter has presented a definition of global education and discussed issues pertaining to the implementation of a global perspective in the classroom. It reviewed the status of social studies education in the world, and discussed the topic of environmental education in the social studies curriculum.

QUESTIONS

1. Examine the clothes you are wearing today. How do they reflect the emergence of a global economy?

2. How do a global curriculum and an international curriculum differ?

3. How is multicultural curriculum related to global curriculum?

4. To what extent is global curriculum present in today's schools? Give two examples to support your answer.

5. Do you agree or disagree with Cleveland's emphasis upon "a feel for" rather than a statement of cognitive goals as a way of defining educational goals?

6. Cite an example of how your own cultural bias would influence the manner in which you teach social studies?

7. What knowledge do you possess about the education of children in other nations? How did you obtain this knowledge?

8. How might learning activities cited in this chapter cause teachers to encounter complaints from some parents?

9. What do you envision as the greatest difficulty in implementing a global curriculum?

10. The authors list five key points about global education. Can you cite any additional points?

ACTIVITIES

1. Contact a foreign embassy and find out how to develop a pen pal relationship with schools in that nation.

2. Make a list of nations that did not exist 5 or 10 years ago. Examine social studies textbooks for information about these nations.

3. Find books in the library written by foreign authors that deal with issues in American life or history. How accurate do you find their analysis?

4. Using a cable or satellite television program guide, identify all the programs in one week devoted to global issues. View at least 5 of these programs. Report on the global issues addressed by each program. Discuss (a) the completeness of coverage in the program; (b) the position advocated by the author, producer or the person/organization featured in the program; (c) the actions teachers and/or pupils can take regarding the global issue highlighted.

5. Identify a problem facing another nation. List all ways in which their problem impacts American society.

Position Statement on Global Education

Prepared at the request of the International Activities Committee by:

John Chapman (Chairperson)
Michigan Department of Education
East Lansing, Michigan

M. Eugene Gilliom
The Ohio State University
Columbus, Ohio

James M. Becker
Mid-America Program
Indiana University
Bloomington, Indiana

Jan Tucker
Florida International University
Miami, Florida

Technological advances, increased trade, tourism and cultural exchanges, environmental concerns, competition for markets and scarce resources, and the continuing arms race are drawing nations and peoples into increasingly complex relationships. Increased human interactions across national and continental boundaries increase the potential for both cooperation and conflict. The day-to-day lives of average citizens, as well as the destinies of nations, are being influenced by our growing international, cross-cultural links.

The phenomenon of globalization is evident in a variety of ways, including: (1) the evolution of global systems of communication and transportation; (2) the incorporation of local, regional, and national economies into a world-wide global economy; (3) increased interaction between societies, resulting in a global culture which exists along with an array of distinctive local, national, and regional cultures; (4) the emergence of a world-wide international system which is eroding the traditional boundaries between domestic and international politics; (5) the increasing impact of human activity upon the planet's ecosystem and the increasing constraints on human activity imposed by the limits of the system; and (6) an expanding global consciousness which enhances awareness of our identities as members of the human species, as inhabitants of the planet Earth, and as participants in a global system.[1]

Human life has been globalized to the point where we must alter the ways we have commonly viewed ourselves and others. The view of the world as a collection of countries pursuing separate destinies is no longer accurate. Rather, globalization has progressed to the point where each of us is constantly touched by interactions within the global system.

The growing interrelatedness of life on our planet has increased the need for citizens to possess the knowledge and sensitivity required to comprehend the global dimensions of political, economic, and cultural phenomena. Although highly trained specialists in foreign languages and in international affairs play a vital role in our nation's transnational interactions, it is imperative in a democracy that public understanding of global events and processes be widely shared. Our nation's security, prosperity, and way of life are dependent in large part on citizens developing the capacity to comprehend transnational, cross-cultural interactions and to participate constructively in decisions influencing foreign policy.

The Meaning of Global Education

Global education refers to efforts to cultivate in young people a perspective of the world which emphasizes the interconnections among cultures, species, and the planet. The purpose of global education is to develop in youth the knowledge, skills, and attitudes needed to live effectively in a

---

[1]The analysis in this section is taken largely from *Schooling and Citizenship in a Global Age* by Lee Anderson.

world possessing limited natural resources and characterized by ethnic diversity, cultural plural-ism, and increasing interdependence. The need to improve the international orientation of chil-dren and youth is widely recognized. Nonetheless, concerted efforts to upgrade and expand the global dimensions of elementary and secondary curricula are not widespread. Furthermore, only a small percentage of those students who attend college have transnational, cross-cultural experi-ences or enroll in courses in international studies. Thus, for most citizens, the elementary and secondary schools are important agencies in our society for nurturing constructive attitudes to-ward global matters and for providing basic knowledge about international events and processes. It is clear that the foundation for our understanding of world events, the impact of international issues on our daily lives, and the interrelatedness of peoples and of cultures must be built at the elementary and secondary levels.

The national Council for the Social Studies recognizes the urgent need to improve and to ex-pand the global dimensions of the social studies curriculum. The recommendations offered here follow from the *NCSS Curriculum Guidelines,* which state that "the basic goal of social studies education is to prepare young people to be human, rational, participating citizens in a world that is becoming increasingly interdependent." The framework of the *Guidelines* presents four goal ar-eas for the social studies: knowledge, abilities, valuing, and social participation. Global education should be interpreted and implemented within this frameowrk. A global perspective should per-meate the total spectrum of social studies goals, offerings, materials, and instructional strategies. Global education needs to be viewed as part of the foundation of social studies education and as being more fundamentally important than a mere addition to the curriculum.

The subject matter and values of global education should not be limited to social studies. How-ever, due to the type of academic and professional training that they have received and the nature of the subject matter of social studies, social studies teachers are in a key position to play a leading role in bringing a global perspective to the school curriculum at the building and district levels.

The two major thrusts of these guidelines are that social studies should assume a major role in providing students with opportunities (1) to learn to perceive and understand the world as a glo-bal system, and (2) to see themselves as participants in that system, recognizing the benefits, costs, rights, and responsibilities inherent in such participation.

Recommendations

The social studies should emphasize:

- **that the human experience is an increasingly globalized phenomenon in which people are constantly being influenced by transnational, cross-cultural, multi-cultural, multi-ethnic interactions**

  Viewing human experience only in relation to a North American or a European frame of refer-ence has been a long-standing bias in education in the United States. Today, the social studies should include a world-centered treatment of humankind. For example, the teaching of history can be improved by the use of a global approach to the study of our past and by the addition to the curriculum of more content focused on developing nations and domestic minorities.

- **the variety of actors on the world stage**

  The dramatic increase in transnational interactions in recent years has produced growing num-bers of individuals, groups, and agencies with international contacts and influence. The character and influence of multinational corporations, church groups, scientific and cultural organizations, United Nations agencies, and local, state, and federal agencies deserve fuller treatment in the so-cial studies curriculum.

- **that humankind is an integral part of the world environment**

The human-natural environment should be seen as a single system. This requires an emphasis on: (1) the ultimate dependence of human-kind upon natural resources; (2) the fact that natural resources are limited; (3) the nature of the planet's ecosystem; and (4) the impact of ecological laws on human culture.

- **the linkages between present social, political, and ecological realities and alternative futures**

Students should perceive the close relationships between past, present, and future. The use of "historical flashbacks," for example, can add to students' understanding of the relation of past to present. Greater emphasis is needed on studies designed to improve students' ability to see present choices as links to possible alternative futures.

- **citizen participation in world affairs**

World affairs have often been treated as a spectator sport in which only the "expert" can participate. The increasing globalization of the human condition has created additional opportunities and responsibilities for the individuals and groups to take personal, social, and political action in the international arena. The curriculum should demonstrate that individuals and groups can influence and can be influenced by world events. Furthermore, the social studies curriculum should help to develop the understandings, skills, and attitudes needed to respond effectively and responsibly to world events.

The Realities of Educational Change

Sound educational responses to the challenges of interdependence, cultural diversity, and competition for scarce natural resources require careful attention to the realities of educational change. Efforts to improve global education in the schools are complex human organizations subject to many demands and pressures. Individuals and groups involved in our educational system include: parents, students, teachers, administrators, local curriculum committees, professional educational associations, accrediting agencies, textbook publishers, state departments of education, and special interest groups.

In light of these realities, improvements in global education, like general educational reform efforts, require: (1) that a thorough assessment be made of existing opportunities to encourage global education and that obstacles to those efforts be identified and confronted; (2) that specific practical steps be taken to strengthen ongoing programs in global education; (3) that successful experimental efforts in global education be expanded; and (4) that new initiatives in global education be stimulated.

To become a more effective agent of citizen education in a global age, the schools in general and the social studies in particular need to continue to expand efforts to globalize the curriculum. The National Council for the Social Studies urges such action and offers a variety of materials and services to help the social studies educators get on with this important task.

(Courtesy © *National Council for the Social Studies*. Used With Permission.)

QUESTIONS ON READINGS

1. What are the three most significant issues facing people on planet Earth?

2. What should be the goals of global education in elementary and middle school grades?

3. What problems would schools encounter if they implemented a global education curriculum?

LESSON PLANS

Fred Stopsky   Grades 4–6
Objective: To replicate the process by which a new nation is created.

Rationale: Students can best understand the intricacies of nation formation by recreating the procedures neccessary in order to be regarded as a nation by the world.

Activities:

Students will be assigned to work on the following topics either on an individual basis or as part of a collaborative group.

1. Identify a name for the new nation.
2. Create a flag for the new nation.
3. Write a national anthem for the nation.
4. Develop and print currency.
5. Establish a system of government.
6. Decide on a language for the new nation.
7. Create an economic system for the nation.
8. Apply for membership in the United Nations.
9. Design government buildings to house officials in the nation.
10. Apply for international airplane and flying routes.
11. Create a customs service, and decide how people can enter or leave the country.
12. Organize a national police force for the country or create local police forces.
13. Create a judiciary system.
14. Design and print passports.
15. Hire ambassadors, and design embassies.
16. Establish road regulations.
17. Establish an army, navy, air force, coast guard, etc. Design uniforms.
18. Identify a national animal and national flower.
19. Decide how TV and radio stations will operate.
20. Apply for international television and air rights.
21. Decide which information should be obtained in your census.
22. Decide on how far into the sea your nation's boundaries will extend.
23. Decide which sports will be emphasized in your nation and which you intend to enter in the next Olympic Games.
24. Apply for membership in the European Economic Community, the North American Free Trade Association, etc.

25. Identify the basic human rights which all people in your nation will be granted.

26. Decide if you will have open borders enabling anyone to enter and live in your country.

27. Establish a school system for your country.

Several of these activities require students to contact government agencies. For example, they will have to research which international body deals with allocating radio or TV bands. After students have gathered the information, it can be organized in the form of a book, a collage, a videotape, radio program, or art exhibit.

Ms. Karen Kenney (Third Grade)
Objective: Students will understand the importance of the rain forest to world development.

Rationale: Students should understand how the rain forest impacts their lives. As a result of this lesson, students will be able to identify rain forests in the world, as well as animals and products found in them.

Activities:

1. Teacher will read *The Kapok Tree* by Lynne Cherry, which deals with cutting trees in rain forests. Students will be asked: "Where does the story take place?" "Why did the wood chopper leave the rain forest?" After discussion about the story students will see "You Can't Grow Home Again," a production of Children's Television Workshop which presents an overview of rain forests in the world.

2. Students in groups will set up a mini-earth experiment using a desk lamp, plastic two liter bottle, cup with water, and a globe. In the experiement students:
   - Place water in the bottle and put on lid. Then shine light from the lamp on the center of the bottle. Teacher asks what the climate would be like inside the bottle, how ould it be like for an animal, does anything escape from the bottle, etc.

3. Teacher will develop a web on the blackboard based on student comments about rain forests. Students will be given pictures of different scenes from forests. They are to decide which animals live in which forests. Which forests would fall into the category of a rain forest?

4. Students will plant a mini-rain forest using a clean, dry glass jar with lid, sterilized potting soil, gravel, bits of charcoal, water spritzer, and plants like boxwood, winter-green, ferns, philodendron, spider plants, mosses, etc.

5. Through use of poetry and pictures students will learn about animals in the rain forest.

6. Teacher will present a "Rain Forest Rap" about characteristics of rain forests. Students will list animals mentioned in rap. Students in groups will develop their own version of a rain forest rap.

7. Students will utilize the school library to identify foods commonly found in rain forests. They will develop a menu for a meal using foods from the rain forests.

8. Students will refer to magazines and newspapers in order to identify plants and animals commonly found in rain forests.

9. Teacher will make a web based on student responses why it is important to save the rain forests. Students will then make posters for display in the school on the topic, "Why Save the Rain Forests?"

10. If school administration grants permission, students will collect money to purchase rain forest land.

Bibliography:

Amadio, N. (1988). *Alice in Rain Forest Land,* Watermark Press, Australia.

Baker, J., (1987). *Where the Forest Meets the Sea,* Greenwillow Books, New York.

Banks, M. (1989). *Conserving the Rain Forests,* Steck-Vaughn, Texas.

Cherry, L. (1990). *The Great Kapok Tree,* Gulliver Books, San Diego.

Dorros, A., (1990). *Rain Forest Secrets,* Scholastic, N.Y.

Forsyth, A., (1988). *Journey Through a Tropical Jungle,* Simon & Schuster, N.Y.

Landau, E., (1990). *Tropical Rain Forests,* Franklin Watts, N.Y.

Mitchell, A., (1989). *Wildlife of the Rain Forest,* Mallard Press, N.Y.

Owen, J. (1984). *Mysteries & Marvels of Insect Life,* Osborne Publishing Ltd, London.

Ross, W. (1977). *The Rain Forest: What Lives There,* Coward, McCann and Geoghegan, Inc., N.Y.

Wood, J., (1987). *Nature Hide & Seek Jungles,* Alfred Knopf, N.Y.

World Wildlife Fund (1988) VCR of *Rain Forest Rap.*

REFERENCES

Cleveland, H. (1986). The world we're preparing our schoolchildren for. *Social Education, 50* (60), 416–423.

Hall, E. T. (1973). *The silent language.* Garden City, NY: Anchor.

Hanvey, R. (1979). *An attainable global perspective.* Denver: Center for Teaching International Relations.

Hirsch, D. (1992, May 27). Multinational partnerships. *Education Week,* 20, p. 20.

International Society for Educational Information Inc. *The life of an elementary school pupil in Japan.* Tokyo.

Johnson, P. (1983, April). Connecting patterns through environmental education. *Education Leadership, 40,* (7) pp. 40–44.

Kneip, W. (1986, October). Defining a global education by its content. *Social Education, 50,* (6) pp. 437–446.

Mehlinger, H. (1979). Social studies education: A transnational profession. In Mehlinger, H., Tucker, J. *Teaching social studies in other nations* (pp. 1–14). Washington, DC: National Council on the Social Studies.

Mehlinger, H. (1979). Social Studies education: A transnational profession. *The American West: 1840–1895.* Washington, DC: National Council on the Social Studies.

Tucker, J. L. (1979). Social studies in the United States: Global challenges. In Mehlinger, H.; Tucker, J. *Teaching social studies in other nations* (pp. 91–102). Washington, DC: National Council on the Social Studies, Bulletin 60.

Tye, K. (1990). *Global education: From thought to action.* Alexandria, VA: ASCD.

Suggested Reading

Barnaby, F. (Ed.). (1988). *The Gaia peace atlas.* New York: Doubleday.

Cleveland, H. (1986). The world we're preparing our schoolchildren for. *Social Education, 50,* 416–423.

Didsburg, H. (Ed.). (1984). *Creating a global agenda.* Bethesda, MD: World Future Society.

Ferencz, B. B., & Keyes, K. (1988). *Planethood.* Coos Bay, OR: Vision Books.

Lean, G., Henrichsen, D., & Markham, A. (1990). *Atlas of the environment.* New York: Prentice Hall.

Mehlinger, H. (1981). *UNESCO handbook for the teaching of social studies.* Garden City, NJ: Anchor.

Perelman, L. (1976). *The global mind.* New York: Mason Charter.

Tucker, J., & Mehlinger, H. (1979). *Social studies in other nations.* Washington, DC: NCSS.

Whitaker, B. (Ed.). (1984). *Minorities: A question of human rights.* New York: Pergamon.

Part 2
Teaching and Learning

Chapter 4

Curriculum
Decision Making

Curriculum Decision Making

The word "curriculum" comes from Latin and means to "run the course or race." A race can be a grueling affair which exhausts the runner, or it can be an energizing and transforming event. John Dewey described curriculum as the lifeblood of teachers while experience is the curriculum of students. Traditionally, curriculum has been defined as a process of pedagogy. "It codifies the basic meaning of the educational process in question, the selection and organization of what is taught, and the methods of instruction" (Lundgren, 1985, p. 21).

Curriculum issues are as old as education. People have been arguing throughout history about what youth should be taught. Plato (1941) commented in *The Republic*, that young men of Athens should study geometry because it "makes all the difference in preparing the mind for any kind of study" (p. 244). Aristotle (1946) was uncertain if education should focus on studies "which are useful in life, or those which make for goodness, or those which advance the bounds of knowledge" (p. 334).

The Chinese education system that prepared youth to pass state examinations was the envy of French intellectuals in the 1700s because it produced people of exceptional ability. Jewish education in the Middle Ages concentrated upon issues of ethical behavior and knowledge of the Torah. Today, supporters of an Afrocentric approach in curriculum note that ancient Egyptian education excelled in math, science, and architecture. Aztec youth were taught history, art, music, and astrology, and many North American Indian societies focused upon a curriculum combining practical knowledge with folklore and religion.

Early colonial Americans were clear about their educational goals—classical education and religion. This approach lasted into the 19th century when critics challenged the presence of classical languages in the curriculum. Post-Civil War America felt pressure to alter the school curriculum in response to industrialization and increasing immigration.

Charles W. Eliot, president of Harvard, chaired the 1893 *Committee of Ten Report,* which urged that academics be emphasized in elementary and secondary education. The Committee supported the introduction of modern languages on an equal basis to classical, but strongly backed the idea that all students should receive an academic foundation in order to succeed in life.

These recommendations were attacked by 20th century reformers who thought modern developments required a shift in education away from the traditional. The "social efficiency" advocates led by Franklin Bobbitt, W. W. Charters, and David Snedden wanted school curriculum to relate directly to the daily needs of people. They discounted the relevance of classical literature, foreign languages, physics, and higher mathematics to life in the industrial world. They wanted schools to prepare youth for work, citizenship, and leisure activities. The *Cardinal Principles Report of 1918* identified seven areas for emphasis in the curriculum: health, command of fundamental processes, good family life, vocation, citizenship, ethical behavior, and good use of leisure time.

The social efficiency supporters emphasized practicality. Bobbitt wanted a "scientifically" structured curriculum that produced measurable results. Social efficiency gained support among business leaders because it promoted well-behaved, knowledgeable, and orderly workers. This would ensure stability and halt inroads by radical elements.

A second curriculum reform movement emphasized the child at the center of learning. Educators like John Dewey, Carleton Washburne, and, in England, A. J. O'Neill, claimed children passed through stages of development, each having distinctive characteristics that should form the core of curriculum. Adolph Ferriere (1933) defined the "Activity School" as "the school of spontaneity, the school which furthers creative expression in the child" (p. 55).

Advocates of child-centered approaches believed young children were interested in myths and legends like their ancestors. They passed through a savage stage and an agricultural stage that necessitated appropriate curriculum materials. A goal of these reformers was to first identify the stages and then create curriculum to match these stages. Washburne argued that children should progress at their own rate while Dewey sought through the "Project Method" to have students work cooperatively.

Colonel Francis Parker in the latter 1800s attempted to rid schools of monotonous drill and replace it with more emphasis upon play and activity. Children were taught the "word" method in reading instead of phonics. G. Stanley Hall, at the turn of the 20th century, rejected a strict academic curriculum since he thought children lacked reasoning power. The birth of the "Project Method" in the 1920s placed the child in a central position to create curriculum. The formal content was de-emphasized in place of children working in groups on topics related to their needs and interests.

A modern manifestation of this thrust was the "open school" movement of the 1960s and 1970s. The child was placed at the center of the curriculum, and teachers employed play and

▲ Child-centered approaches emphasize the need for children to be engaged with manipulable materials.
Courtesy University City (Missouri) Public Schools.

group activities to further learning. Sylvia Ashton-Warner, John Holt, Herbert Kohl, and others rejected regimentation and rote memorization, which they claimed dehumanized children, and impaired learning:

> We like to say that we send children to school to teach them to think. What we do, all too often, is to teach them to think badly, to give up a natural and powerful way of thinking in favor of a method that does not work well for them and that we rarely use ourselves. What are the results?... Most of them get humiliated, frightened, and discouraged. (Holt, 1967, p. vii)

Open education writers argued that children from birth to five were natural and creative thinkers. They wanted curriculum to evolve from the innate creative capacities of children which they believed existed on an equal basis with youth from all socioeconomic and ethnic backgrounds. They sought an open approach that drew upon the interests of children in order to best teach the formal curriculum.

This child-centered approach emphasized the need for children to be engaged with manipulative materials, and that making, doing, and building were often preferable to passive listening or rote learning. Children learned about colonial America by cooking foods or making objects from that period using the tools of the time. Critics charge this approach leads to a dilettantism, and that manipulatable materials in themselves are no guarantee of meaningful learning.

> The real dichotomy is not between passivity and activity in learning. Rather, a much more important dichotomy would be between aimless or superficial activity versus directed or complete activity.... Similarly, activities which provide children with a full and complete knowledge of a skill are probably more beneficial than those which give the child a mere passing acquaintance with the craft. (Elkind, 1981, p. 436)

A third thrust in curriculum reform has urged that children be provided opportunities to engage in social reform. The Great Depression provided progressive educators an opening to introduce into the curriculum the idea of social reconstruction of society. They wanted children to become involved in dealing with issues of social concern. This movement was resisted by school officials who were not anxious to oppose powerful forces in their local community who disliked politicized students. Its legacy, however, can be seen in modern day student programs about peace, the environment or poverty.

Curriculum must continually respond to competing interests. It is simplistic to speak of a clash between "traditionalists" and "reformers." Those supporting the thesis that social studies should emphasize the interests of children, or those seeking to perpetuate our societal heritage or those seeking to reform society have bases of support in all communities. There are numerous sub groupings in each of these positions. Social studies has to address a variety of needs rather than stake out a narrow ideological position which satisfies a particular group. The United States is a diverse society, and social studies should reflect the varied interests and needs of the population.

▲ Making, doing, and building are often preferable to passive listening or rote learning. *Courtesy Perry County (Missouri) School District No. 42.*

Social studies seeks to aid children develop their minds. "One thing is essential to becoming a human being, and that is learning to use the mind. A human being acts in a human way if he thinks" (Hutchins, 1968). Our diversity, however, places a particular responsibility upon social studies to utilize a curriculum that does not stop at thinking, but also educates the whole human being.

The three curriculum thrusts each contains an aspect that when unified bring together the cognitive and affective domains in a powerful relationship stimulating youth to become sensitive, intelligent, and concerned people. Schools prepare children for life in the workplace, and it is only appropriate that curriculum aids children to be happy and effective in their chosen occupation. A school which ignores the interests of children in formulating curriculum will fail just as a business which ignores its customers will go bankrupt. Schools are in the forefront of our society's struggle to create equity and justice, and children have to play a role in that quest.

An effective curriculum offers children entrance to the wisdom of human heritage. It must of necessity view what is to be taught through the mind's eye of children, and place the child's interests and needs before arbitrary standardized norms. Curriculum always entails teaching a content, but the content only has meaning as children are attracted to and able to learn it.

Arguments concerning curriculum frequently revolve around *how* rather than *what* is to be taught. It is common for educators to focus on scope or sequence issues rather than reexamining the nature of what is being taught children. For years, elementary school educators have assumed social studies should begin with the family or neighborhood and expand outward. It is only recently that questions have been raised about the need for a different focus in social studies in the primary grades. Content and methodology are best viewed as an integral whole.

▲ Social studies seeks to aid students develop their minds. *Courtesy Webster University.*

It is important to differentiate between information and knowledge. "Information provided by a teacher or textbook is generally, and wrongfully, perceived as knowledge." Knowledge is something "created through a process of personal involvement" between students and information. Unless students engage themselves directly and with purpose, information conveyed in the text or by the teacher will remain data to be learned rather than knowledge to be used (Bragaw, 1988).

We are a few short years from the birth of the 21st century, but curriculum still remains a prisoner of many 19th century practices. A visitor from the 1890s would not be surprised at the organization of our social studies curriculum. Several inventions during that century continue to dominate the organization of curriculum and the instructional tools used in teaching.

Pestalozzi was a remarkably inventive Swiss educator in the latter part of the 18th century whose work with poor children compelled him to develop new forms of technology and teaching strategies. He is responsible for the slate, which later gave rise to the blackboard, and he helped to develop the idea of a textbook as an instructional device. Pestalozzi profoundly influenced 19th century educators, such as Herbart in Germany. Herbart formalized the concept of organized, planned classroom instruction, and is responsible for the origin of modern teacher education programs. He created formal lesson plans which continue to guide teaching. Two distinctively American developments, grades and grade levels, originated in the latter part of the 19th century.

The post-Civil War generation witnessed dramatic population growth, which necessitated consolidation of smaller into larger school districts. Mass education meant bigger schools, and an increasing uniformity of the curriculum. Teaching became a profession, and curriculum became the instrument of the state to propagate national beliefs.

Despite 20th century technological inventions such as the phonograph, movie projector, slide projector, radio, television, computer, and video recorder, curricula still bear a close resemblance to those used over a hundred years ago. Educators still organize learning employing the principles and organizational model of schools that prepared children for the early stages of the industrial revolution.

Americans have been struggling for 200 years to identify a public school curriculum that respects the integrity of children, the diversity of our nation, and still transmits the core heritage and knowledge of our society. That curriculum has yet to be invented. The challenge for teachers in the 21st century is to forge a curriculum that enables youth to become creative, knowledge-able, productive, and self-actualized humans.

Organizing Curriculum

Curriculum is a process that selects and organizes what is taught and the method of instruction. A lesson or unit plan is a teacher's strategy to facilitate this learning. An effective curriculum creates within children the desire to learn because what is taught is both interesting and meaningful. Elliot Eisner (1982) warns that the "use of a tight, prescriptive curriculum structure, sequential skill development, and frequent testing and reward are classic examples of form becoming content" (p. 12). Curriculum is the vehicle used for the journey, not the journey itself.

▲ Diversity places a particular responsibility upon social studies to utilize a curriculum that educates the whole human being. *Courtesy Webster University.*

The presentation of content to students is organized in daily lesson plans. The preparation of lesson plans always involves "what," "why" and "how" questions. What do I want to teach, why should students learn this material, and how will I teach it? The best curriculum is one that leads children to think, "Oh, this is easy to learn." Teachers can recall their days as students when their grasp of the material being studied culminated in "Aha! Eureka! I understand that." The information contained in a lesson plan will only be effective if it is "translated into the learner's way of attempting to solve a problem" (Bruner, 1966, p. 53).

One of the most popular curriculum models stems from the work of Ralph Tyler (1949). He suggested that curriculum planners obtain data for their objectives from three sources: the learners, contemporary life outside the school, and subject matter. He believed this information should be filtered through the educational and social philosophy of the school and the psychology of learning. Tyler urges teachers to provide learning experiences that (a) develop thinking skills; (b) help students acquire information; (c) encourage the development of social attitudes; and (d) stimulate student interests.

Teachers tread a thin line between imparting information and enabling students to be in charge of learning. Teaching material is a provisional state whose object is to make the learner a self-sufficient problem solver. If students are dependent on teachers for the "answer," the purpose of education is not achieved.

In selecting a particular curriculum content, teachers should consider: (a) the backgrounds and experiences of students, including how they learn; (b) the knowledge being studied in the grade level or subject area; (c) conditions and expectations in American society; and (d) the interests and needs of children. Ronald Brandt (quoted in Bragaw, 1988) argues for a "utilitarian" approach in deciding curriculum content that is concerned with "how will it be used." Teachers want a strong content to undergird their lesson plans, but they can never lose sight that curriculum has to be viewed as relevant by students and centered in the reality of American society.

A common mistake in preparing curriculum is to focus on why students will have a difficult time learning the material. Who can forget the professor stating on the the first day of class, "This is a tough class and many of you will fail." This attitude generates negative reactions among students causing many to conclude that failure awaits regardless of their efforts. Students want to learn and want to feel themselves to be competent people. The organization of any piece of curriculum should begin with a positive belief that students can learn the material in the lesson.

Teachers have to be clear what they expect to teach and what students are to learn. There are distinctions between levels of goals. The Tri-County Goal Development Project distinguishes between types of goals and who sets them as shown in Table 4-1. Goals should be explicitly stated and consistent with the curriculum material. Teachers should avoid education jargon and write in a simple, direct style. Examples of goals at each level of planning are included in Table 4-1.

Writing lesson plans or curriculum units requires knowledge of the content to be covered, an understanding of the children who will learn the material, common sense, and interesting teaching strategies. Ineffective teachers focus upon what is to be taught from their curriculum guide while effective teachers concentrate on how curriculum addresses the learning needs of children. There are several considerations that can guide teachers in the preparation of curriculum:

▲ Schools prepare young people for life in the workplace. *Courtesy Saint Louis (Missouri) Public Schools.*

Consideration 1:   Which concepts are to be taught?
Consideration 2:   How do these ideas pertain to the lives of children?
Consideration 3:   What are the behavioral objectives?
Consideration 4:   Which instructional strategies will be used in attaining the behavioral goals?
Consideration 5:   What do students already know about what is to be taught?
Consideration 6:   What is the content of the curriculum?
Consideration 7:   How will content be organized and sequenced?
Consideration 8:   Which methodologies will be employed to further learning?
Consideration 9:   What materials or equipment is needed to teach this curriculum?
Consideration 10: How will the learning be evaluated?

Consideration 1 : Which concepts are to be taught?

A concept is a general idea or understanding, especially if derived from a specific influence or occurrence. A teacher must always be aware of the concepts being presented in the lesson plan.

Table 4-1: Classification of Curricular Goals

TYPES OF GOALS	GOALS ARE SET BY:	EXAMPLES (4)
SYSTEM LEVEL GOALS	School district.	The student knows and is able to apply basic scientific and technological processes.
PROGRAM LEVEL GOALS	Curriculum personnel.	The student is able to use the conventional language, instruments, and operations of social studies.
COURSE LEVEL GOALS	Group of teachers.	The student is able to employ the techniques, strategies, and methodologies of social scientists and historians in learning social studies.
INSTRUCTIONAL LEVEL GOALS	An individual teacher.	The student is able to correctly classify elected officials according to their level of government.

Adapted from Tyler, 1983, p. 41.

Frequently, attitudinal concepts intermix with content. For example, in teaching the concept "westward movement," a secondary goal might be cooperative learning. Content and attitudes go hand-in-hand. A teacher, unlike a production line worker, is engaged in a multitude of interactions at every given moment. Few, if any, activities such as a lesson plan can be set aside as a discrete action.

Consideration 2: How do these ideas pertain to the lives of children?

How do these ideas pertain to the lives of children? Children want to know why they have to learn curriculum. What does the War of 1812 have to do with their lives? For example, learning the content of the War of 1812 will not excite many students, but if it is presented from the perspective of how conflict can lead people to fight, it takes on meaning to children who daily live with conflict. Why study about city government? City governments establish laws such as where and when skateboards can be used which directly impacts leisure time for children.

▲ An effective curriculum offers children entrance to the wisdom of human heritage.
Courtesy Perry County (Missouri) School District No. 42.

Consideration 3: What are the behavioral objectives?

Curriculum goals should be stated as behavioral objectives to clarify which observable behaviors children will display as a result of learning. For example, "As a result of studying pre-Civil War slavery, students will be able to state three ways slaves fought back." The purpose of behavioral objectives is to make certain both teacher and student know why the curriculum is being studied. It enables teachers to be accountable for their actions, but more importantly provides clear feedback about what is being learned.

▲ Curriculum entails teaching content, but content only has meaning as children are attracted to and able to learn it. *Courtesy Lynn Rubright, Webster University.*

Consideration 4: Which instructional strategies will be used in attaining the behavioral goals?

What instructional strategies will be employed? A curriculum can include many forms. It can be written, visual, a game simulation, a series of cartoons or pictures, or a movie. The curriculum designer has to decide which form most effectively communicates the concept. For example, if the goal is to teach about hair styles of the 1950s, it would be appropriate to utilize visual materials since the written is less effective in conveying information about hair styles.

▲ After the Civil War, mass education meant bigger schools and increasing uniformity of the curriculum. *Courtesy Saint Louis (Missouri) Public Schools.*

Consideration 5: What do students already know about what is to be taught?

What do students already know about what is to be taught? We previously stated Dewey's view that life experience is the curriculum of students. A conceptual approach to curriculum enables teachers to draw upon those experiences. Children encounter hate, love, conflict, change, and friendship as part of normal life. They argue on the playground, they form and break friendships. When teaching the concept of "taxation" as related to causes of the American Revolution, it is easy to draw upon children's knowledge of taxation. Each time they purchase a Big Mac or candy bar they pay a tax. Many children know they have to add the tax cost onto the purchase of a new Nintendo game. The most common error in developing lesson plans is to ignore the vast amount of knowledge possessed by students.

Consideration 6: What is the content of the curriculum?

What is the scope of the curriculum? All curriculum has content. If "Depression" is the concept to be taught, one has to consider which aspects of the Depression will constitute the curriculum. Will the music, personal recollections, poetry, literature, movies, sports, foods, or fashions constitute the content? A content drawn from diverse sources expands opportunities to incorporate all students in learning.

Consideration 7: How will content be organized and sequenced?

How will the content be organized and sequenced? A curriculum needs a scope and sequence which describes the order in which material is presented to students. An effective curriculum proceeds at an appropriate rate. It has an rhythm or flow which moves students through a variety of experiences. There is conscious thought regarding the order of how material is presented. Students enjoy doing a variety of things in school and nothing is more boring than repeating the same sequence.

▲ The chalkboard, a 19th century invention, continues to dominate the organization of curriculum and instruction. *Courtesy Webster University.*

Consideration 8: Which methodologies will be employed to further learning?

Which methodologies will be employed to further learning? A variety of teaching strategies should be employed in teaching. The curriculum can include reading a short story or poem, small group work or individual activities. The flow of the content is complemented by student movement from one activity to another.

Consideration 9: What materials or equipment is needed to teach this curriculum?

What materials and equipment are needed for the curriculum? Preplanning enables teachers to be prepared with all necessary equipment and materials. Students are more likely to be actively engaged in learning if everything is ready to go and checked out. Audio-visual equipment and copy machines in schools may break down leaving the unprepared teacher frustrated and angry. Experienced teachers have alternative plans in case the equipment is not functioning.

Consideration 10: How will the learning be evaluated?

How will the learning be evaluated? A good curriculum experience can appear unsuccessful if the evaluation does not relate to learning objectives. If a teacher's goal is to encourage cooperative learning, pencil and paper tests may not enable that goal to be evaluated. Elementary school teachers can employ art activities, role-playing or story telling to determine if the material has been learned. College students are all too familiar with the professor whose final exam has little relation to what was taught. Evaluation can take many forms but must be consistent with goals.

Madeline Hunter's Model Curriculum

School districts throughout the United States have been encouraging teachers to employ organized methods of curriculum development. Among the most popular of these methodologies is the work of Madeline Hunter. Hunter's approach to instruction is based on the premise that "the teacher is a decision maker," and those decisions should be based "on sound theory rather than on folklore and fantasy" (Hunter, 1985, p. 57).

Her work arises from several assumptions regarding curriculum organization:

1. Teaching and learning are inextricably woven together.
2. Teaching is a process of professional decision making.
3. Appropriate decisions can help most students learn.
4. We can control the teaching decision, but we cannot exert similar control over learning.
5. The professional skills of teaching can be learned.
6. Knowledge that has been validated by research is available to help improve teaching.

Hunter's approach to lesson planning is used by thousands of teachers. In some school districts teachers are evaluated based upon their ability to effectively implement a Hunter lesson plan. It is likely a novice teacher will be required by the school district to become familiar with the steps of a Hunter lesson plan:

▲ Knowledge is constructed through a process of personal involvement between students and information. *Courtesy Saint Louis (Missouri) Public Schools.*

1. *Objective/Rationale:* The teacher informs students what they will be able to do by the end of the instructional period, and why this lesson is important. The objectives should be specific and focus on observable learner behavior.
2. *Anticipatory Set*: The anticipatory set focuses the learner's attention, reviews or relates previous learning, and/or develops readiness and standards for the instruction to follow. It should be brief to allow time for the lesson's activities.
3. *Instructional Input*: The teacher determines what information is needed by the student in order to accomplish the present objective. The teacher also selects teaching strategies—films, lecture, games, etc.

4. *Modeling*: Modeling provides students with an example of what the finished product looks like. The learner's initial exposure to the new information has to be accurate. The teacher should present the models and control their content.

5. *Check for Understanding*: The teacher observes how the students handle the material and employs questioning techniques to ensure they are on the right track. The data received enables teachers to revise instruction.

6. *Guided Practice*: The student's first attempts with the new material should be guided by the teacher to ensure success. The quicker tasks are performed by students, the sooner teachers can offer corrective feedback.

7. *Independent Practice*: The students develop fluency by practicing independently once they can demonstrate performance without errors. This work should be consistent with stated objectives of the lesson.

8. *Closure*: In this aspect of the Hunter Model, the teacher links lesson activities to the original goals in order to reinforce within the minds of children that they have accomplished the purpose of the learning experience.

9. *Evaluation*: The evaluation component of the Hunter Model entails assessment strategies utilized by the teacher in order to determine how well children have learned.

A MADELINE HUNTER MODEL LESSON PLAN

Subject: Pearl Harbor

Rationale: Students will be able to list two reactions among Americans to the Pearl Harbor attack in order to understand the initial reactions of people to war.

Anticipatory Set:	Teacher asks students to write down how they would feel if someone they did not know pushed and punched them in the lunch line. How would they feel if someone they know acted this way?
Instructional Input:	Group students according to (a) those who would fight back, and (b) those who would take other courses of action. Each group collates all their reasons to support their response. Teacher reviews actions leading up to the Japanese attack on Pearl Harbor and reads several eye witness accounts.
Modeling:	Teacher draws two columns on the board and asks each group to supply information for their column. Teacher shows film clips showing how Americans felt after the attack on Pearl Harbor.
Check Understanding:	Teacher elicits student comments comparing their ideas with those shown in the film clips or from the readings.
Guided Practice:	In groups, students read additional eye witness accounts and excerpts from President Roosevelt's speech to Congress. Each group will present its ideas regarding how American leaders reacted compared to how the class reacted to being pushed or shoved in line.
Independent Practice:	Students compile a list of alternative courses of action available to America after the attack and why the leaders decided on war as their response.
Closure:	Teacher will read selections from Japanese participants in the attack regarding how they felt in 1941 and how they feel today about the attack.
Evaluation:	Each student will write a poem, draw a picture, or write a few paragraphs describing how Americans felt about the attack on Pearl Harbor.

Some school districts have developed lesson plans centered around the work of Benjamin Bloom. Following is an example of a lesson plan following this model:

Table 4-2: Lesson on July 4th

CATEGORY	EXAMPLES OF QUESTIONS AND ACTIVITIES
Knowledge:	1. What are different ways people celebrate this holiday?
Comprehension:	1. What do you most enjoy about July 4th? 2. What do the stars on the flag represent?
Application:	1. If you could create a new holiday, what would be its purpose? 2. What type of celebrations would take place on your holiday?
Analysis:	1. If you were a visitor from England, how might you feel about the July 4th celebration? 2. Would all Americans feel the same way about the importance of July 4th?
Synthesis:	1. Create a July 4th greeting card that would make you laugh. 2. Create a July 4th card that would make you feel sad.
Evaluation:	1. What would be the best way to celebrate July 4th? Why? 2. Should everyone be given the day off on July 4th or should some people have to work?

The Hunter model can be a valuable tool for teachers, but it has also been abused by teachers who follow it in a rigid way, and by administrators who use it to evaluate teachers. "Any observer who uses a checklist to make sure a teacher is using all seven elements does not understand the model" (Hunter, 1985, p. 57). She suggests that teachers use those elements of her model which are appropriate to the day's lesson.

A novice teacher is bombarded with a plethora of ideas concerning how best to write lesson plans. State, district, and school curriculum leaders will provide materials and directions about what and how to teach in social studies. "The process of curriculum improvement is more important than the product . . . An emphasis on process recognizes that curriculum improvement should be a continuous effort, rather than a job terminating in a finished product" (Meussig, 1978, p. 3).

The classroom teacher is the "alpha and omega of curriculum improvement" according to Meussig (1978). A good social studies program needs materials and a philosophical base, but without a teacher's commitment, it becomes a dead letter. Teachers have to be skillful adapters of existing materials and shape them to fit the particular requirements of their own students. No cookbook exists to delineate the specific method of effectively teaching social studies. A successful social studies program develops when teachers keep an open mind, ask questions, are willing to experiment, and share in a cooperative manner with their peers.

Democratic Empowerment of Students: Lesson Planning

The lesson plans presented above emanate from teacher interests or the formal curriculum taught in the school. A child's initial contact with formal education is the elementary school. Prior to entering kindergarten, children have been learning how to walk, talk, play, manipulate adults, form friendships, and have gained knowledge about the outside world. Elementary school teachers can initiate children into a learning environment in which child and adult function as a team to identify what is to be learned and share in the exploration how to obtain this knowledge.

A curriculum strategy that offers students choices in learning does not mean all lesson plans should be designed in this manner. Student involvement in determining some portions of the curriculum, encourages within the class, a spirit of democratic cooperation. It enables children and teacher to form a personal relationship requiring teachers to seek understanding of what the child is experiencing and the child to assume responsibility to implement what the teacher is experiencing.

A democracy-centered lesson plan can originate from conscious planning or it can arise from a spontaneous comment by a student. Following are some examples of these two approaches.

1. A child says, "The pond near our house has yukky water." This comment can initiate a class project to explore why the water looks so bad.

2. A student states that her father is in the fire department. Another says her mother is an accountant. Teacher asks the class, in groups, to organize how the class can learn from these two parents. They are responsible for deciding (a) the topic; (b) questions; (c) how the presentation will be made to the class.

3. A child says, "Timmy and Mike were fighting on the playground." Teacher asks students, in groups, to discuss why children fight on the playground and how best can these fights be handled.

4. Teacher asks students to list what they like best or their hobbies. Child has option of working alone or with someone who has a similar interest or hobby to organize a learning experience for either (a) the class; (b) a group of children in the class; (c) or one other student.

5. Teacher asks the class: "What would you like me to learn that you know about? For example, I don't know very much about how to play Nintendo. I would like you to identify something I should learn, and I want you to help me learn. I want you to be my teacher."

Young children are excited about learning. A classroom which combines formal curriculum with student initiated learning experiences builds upon the strength of elementary age children—their intense desire to understand and participate in the world. The democratic empowerment of children sharpens their critical thinking abilities, and develops their abilities to understand the nature and purpose of schooling.

Identifying the Conceptual Focus

A concept is a general idea or understanding, especially one derived from specific instances or occurrences. A conceptual approach to curriculum aids teachers by focusing attention upon major ideas being studied. It avoids the possiblity that the main goal of curriculum becomes imparting data without any clear connection to significant ideas. Teachers have to be clear about the major concepts they wish students to learn.

Conceptual statements express a complete idea. For example, the concept of "slavery" can be made into a conceptual statement that enables teachers to focus the direction of curriculum planning.

Level 1: (very abstract) Slavery existed in the United States prior to the Civil War.

Level 2: (somewhat narrower) Abolitionists wanted to end slavery.

Level 3: (still narrower) Black Abolitionists played a prominent role in ending slavery.

Level 4: (narrower) Female Black Abolitionists were key players in the anti-slavery movement.

Level 5: (very narrow) Southern born female Black Abolitionists influenced the Abolitionist movement's program to end slavery.

And so we could go on, refining and narrowing further and further. The Level 1 statement is so broad it is difficult knowing where or how to begin the unit. The Level 5 statement has specificity that might lead to a too narrow approach. Listing several levels of the original concept enables the curriculum designer to decide which is the level that best fits what is to be taught. A rule of thumb is that a unit based around a concept lasts no longer than ten class sessions. Obviously, teachers can design units that have a shorter duration. The conceptual approach provides a road map regarding what to teach.

Practice Exercise

The same conceptual statements can guide learning at any grade level. They can be either too broad or just about right for a curriculum unit. Circle your choice for each item.

Table 4-3: Conceptual Statement/Breadth

CONCEPTUAL STATEMENT	BREADTH (Circle One)	
1. The history of fashion.	Appropriate	Too Broad
2. Transportation in post Civil War America.	Appropriate	Too Broad
3. Colonial American Foods.	Appropriate	Too Broad
4. Educational innovations.	Appropriate	Too Broad
5. People of Africa.	Appropriate	Too Broad
6. American Indian ideas regarding government.	Appropriate	Too Broad
7. Renaissance art.	Appropriate	Too Broad
8. Female writers of the 1960s.	Appropriate	Too Broad
9. French sixteenth century explorers in North America.	Appropriate	Too Broad
10. Arab nautical inventions.	Appropriate	Too Broad

Key

It is important to know that deciding on the best focus for a concept is a judgment call. Here is one interpretation of the statements above:

1. A bit too broad. It could entail fashion in any century or any country.

2. Appropriate. One could get more specific by suggesting the history of the railroad.

3. Appropriate.

4. Much too broad. An example of a specific direction to this topic would be: "The impact of technology on education innovation."

5. Too broad. Africa is a large continent with many diverse people.

6. Appropriate. It would be too specific to focus upon "Iroquois ideas on government."

7. Too broad. Renaissance art was found in many nations and lasted for a considerable period of time.

8. Appropriate. It deals with many female writers, but the time period provides a concise way to handle the subject.

9. Appropriate.

10. Appropriate. A well-focused idea for a unit.

Once teachers have identified the concept and found the appropriate level, it is possible for them to express ideas in a conceptual statement. A conceptual statement summarizes the rationale regarding why the concept is being taught.

CONCEPT: Freedom

FOCUS: Dissent in American democracy.

CONCEPTUAL STATEMENT: American democracy has utilized various compromises in permitting and restricting dissent.

Practice Assignment

Try writing your own concept, focus, and conceptual statement for a lesson. Review your work with your classmates and your instructor.

CONCEPT: _____

FOCUS: _____

_____

CONCEPTUAL STATEMENT: _____

_____

_____

Sub-Concepts

After a concept has been identified and phrased as a conceptual statement, the next task is to identify the sub-concepts which support the major idea. It is common that several ideas will cluster around a major concept. For example, in teaching multiplication, students first have to learn how to add and subtract.

Let us assume a teacher wishes to teach the concept of "friendship." The following sub-concepts might be included in the unit plan.

- Sharing
- Empathy
- Understanding
- Loyalty
- Forgiveness

Each of these sub-concepts could in itself be a concept, but in this instance they are linked to the major idea of friendship. The curriculum unit on friendship would probably include activities designed around each of the sub-concepts because they interconnect with the major concept. Notice that each of the sub-concepts could be subdivided more narrowly.

There is no specific formula for writing curriculum. It depends to a great extent upon the teacher's awareness, experience and instincts about children and the subject matter. Practice does make perfect if teachers are willing to learn from endeavors and revise the material. A curriculum writer has to listen to the comments of students and to their silences.

Practice Assignment

Expand your conceptual analysis to include sub-concepts. Discuss your ideas with your peers.

CONCEPT: _____

FOCUS: _____

_____

CONCEPTUAL STATEMENT: _____

_____

_____

SUB-CONCEPTS: _____

_____

_____

▲ Despite 20th century technological inventions, curricula still bear a close resemblance to those used over a hundred years ago. *Courtesy University City (Missouri) Public Schools.*

Robert Mager's *Preparing Instructional Objectives* (*1962*) is helpful in writing clean, concrete lesson objectives. Mager emphasizes that teachers must address the following three questions in order to state objectives in clear and meaningful ways: (a) What should the learner be able to do? (b) Under what conditions will the learner be able to do it? and (c) How well must it be done?

Mager believes that an objective always says what a learner is able to do in an observable manner. It also describes the important conditions under which the performance is to occur, and, if possible, describes the criterion of acceptable performance. He cautions against the use of "unclear verbs" such as: enjoy, value, know, appreciate, understand, realize, or become aware of. Mager urges using clear verbs such as list, classify, write, measure, select, define, compare/contrast, or construct. Following are examples of clearly written objectives based on Mager's ideas:

1. Students will list three causes of the Civil War and write a three-paragraph essay explaining why they were causes.
2. Students will compare and contrast the versions stated by the wolf and the three pigs regarding the source of their conflict.

▲ Curriculum planners obtain data for objectives from learners, contemporary life outside the school, and subject matter. *Courtesy Saint Louis (Missouri) Public Schools.*

Behavioral objectives help in clarifying the purpose of a lesson, but they cannot describe all goals. Some valuable lessons are designed to make children laugh or have fun, and that is difficult to measure in behavioral terms.

Lesson Plan

Webster's New World Dictionary (1975) defines a lesson as "something that needs to be learned." Teaching is an art form, and the lesson plan is its working sketch. An artist is concerned that the final product contains a unity of purpose. Teachers and students should be clear at the conclusion of a lesson as to the unifying themes of what was taught.

A lesson plan is a short-term designed activity or part of a sequence constituting a unit. It may not be "new" material, but it is something teachers wish to do in an organized fashion. Many lesson plans exist only for the day, others are linked to broader goals that may last several days, weeks, or months.

A lesson plan begins with a body of subject matter that raises a fundamental question: What does this all mean? Teachers whose only response is that the curriculum guide says they should teach the material ensure that students will fail to grasp relevant meaning and will sense that the teacher is adrift. Once teachers are clear about content and theme, they must establish objectives. Cognitive objectives relate to information and affective objectives pertain to attitudes and values.

A lesson plan involves two components—what the teacher will do and what students will do. These are interactive because any action by teachers requires some reaction by students. A lesson plan should always describe the manner in which this interaction occurs. Lesson plans are more effective if teachers plan the variety of activities in which students engage during the time period.

Lesson plans are guides or maps that present a clear vision of what will happen that day. Unfortunately, lesson plans are frequently written to please a school administrator or to fit into some schoolwide system. The more complex the lesson plan, the less frequently it will be of service. A lesson plan should be easy to write and clear enough for a substitute teacher to carry out its aims that day. Lesson plans are concise statements of what happens in a specific time period.

Following is a sample lesson plan for one class period.

CONCEPT: School as a geographic unit.

FOCUS: Classroom maps acquaint students with idea that maps are a way of describing places.

CONCEPTUAL STATEMENT: Students should be taught to draw a map of their classroom to personalize maps in their mind.

Teacher	Student
1. Tell students: "Close your eyes and imagine you are going home. See all the places in your mind that you see on that trip home." (Allow at least 1 minute for visualization.) Ask students to draw pictures of two interesting places they imagined during the visualization.	1. Students close eyes and visualize trip. Then they draw the pictures.
2. Provide Poloraid cameras or camcorders. Form student groups and direct them to take pictures of their area and direct them to take pictures of classroom.	2. Groups decide which pictures of their area to take.
3. Bring out a large posterboard. Show how to mount the pictures so all can see.	3. Groups paste pictures on posterboard.
4. Direct students to draw a map based upon their picture map.	4. Each group makes a map.
5. Mount all maps on the wall. Take out city map and show location of places students drew. Explain similarity between their classroom maps and the city map.	5. Each group mounts its map. Listen.

This lesson plan is designed as an early introduction to mapmaking. It will be followed in subsequent lessons with other mapreading, mapmaking and map-interpretation activities.

Thoughts About Writing Lesson Plans

1. Consider how much time is to be allocated to the lesson.
2. What percent of the time will teacher talk, and how much time will students work in small groups or individually?
3. What will students like best about this lesson?
4. What will students like least about this lesson?
5. How clear is the central idea to be conveyed in the lesson?
6. What would you best enjoy teaching in this lesson?
7. How can students take responsibility to decide what they will learn in this lesson?
8. Is there a variety of activities and materials in the lesson?
9. Is there an interesting "hook" to open the lesson that immediately captures their attention and interest?
10. What type of activity best follows this lesson?
11. Which, if any, homework activity should follow?
12. A personal way to evaluate the lesson is to ask: "If I were a student in this class, would this be an interesting lesson?

A Curriculum Unit

A curriculum unit is an organization of learning centered around a major concept, issue, problem or theme that extends over a period of time. As a rule of thumb, units comprise activities for five to ten days. Elementary school teachers frequently spread some units over the course of the school year. For example, a unit on weather might entail activities each month coinciding with the weather in that period of the year.

The format of the unit is similar to that of a lesson plan. It describes the interactive process between students and the teacher. There is no need to specify in a unit that the activity will take exactly one day or that it will last a certain number of minutes. It is preferable to describe the flow of action without becoming locked into time constraints. This enables an elementary school teacher to devote more than an hour to the unit if that day students are excited and engaged with the material.

Following is a sample unit.

CONCEPT: Listening

FOCUS: Improvement of listening skills enhances student self concept.

SUB-CONCEPTS:

1. The importance of listening and being listened to.

2. How we hear other people.

3. What we hear.

4. Cooperative learning.

RATIONALE: Listening is a basic communication skill. It is a learned skill which must be developed. Students who practice active listening enhance the self-concept of other people and have their ideas listened to in a more positive manner.

We listen for many reasons: as part of being creative, for enjoyment, to sort out facts, to gain information, and to make decisions. Listening is also an aesthetic experience which enables us to hear the sounds of nature and become more intimate with the natural world.

This unit is designed to improve the quality of a child's listening and to improve sensitivity to others, and the world we are in contact with during daily life.

LESSON 1

Sub-Concept: How we hear.

Behavioral objective: Student will be able to construct a model of an ear.

Activities:

Teacher	Student
1. Brings in a model of an ear. Explain its features. Encourage students to explore it.	1. Students listen to teacher, ask questions, see, touch, and play with model. Then they draw a picture of the ear.
2. Demonstrate how to create a "listening ear." A student who puts on the listening ear will listen carefully to others.	2. In groups, students take turns so each can have a "listening ear."

LESSON 2

(This lesson takes several days.)
Sub-Concept: What we hear.

Behavioral Objective: Students will be able to identify, and recreate sounds and voices.

Activities:

Teacher	Student
1. Asks students the following questions: What sounds do your pets make? What sounds do you hear in the kitchen? Make the sound. What sounds do you hear in the living room? Make the sounds. What sounds do you hear in a music store? What is the nicest sound you hear? What is the scariest sound you hear? Select students who ask the class about a sound.	1. Students listen, and respond to sounds.
2. Say: "We are now going on a listening walk outside. Select a partner, and when we return share with the class sounds you heard."	2. Students walk, talk, and listen. Students share sounds with class.
3. Say: "Draw a picture you think goes along with your sounds." Put drawings together as collage.	3. Students draw.
4. Say: "Tonight, I would like you to listen to sounds. Share them at our next listening time together."	4. Students listen for night sounds.
5. "I would like to form groups of four. Share your sounds with people in your group. Each group will be asked to share with the class the scariest, nicest, and most interesting sounds.	5. Students work in group. Then share sounds with class.
6. Say: "I want each person to put on your special listening ear. Close your eyes. I will make sounds and your job is to identify the sound." Use egg beater, sand blocks, whistle, bell, rattle, xylophone, nutcracker, etc.	6. Students put on listening ears and close eyes. Raise hand and tell the sound.
7. Say: "I would like you to listen to this tape with a partner. Guess the noise. After you tell which sound it is, then you make the sound." Play tape which includes: snapping fingers, whispering, yawning, crumpling paper, washing hands, sawing wood, vacuum, hammer banging, sharpening a pencil, clapping, coughing, writing with chalk.	7. Students listen to tape and raise hands. Then make the sound.
8. Whose voice is it? Tell students to close their eyes. Tap a child on the shoulder. Have the child speak. The class has to guess who is speaking. Tape voices of people in the school. Have students pair off and team to guess the speaker.	8. Hide eyes. Listen with listening ear. In pairs, students guess the speaker.
9. Play music selections with various tempos to which students can clap the rhythms. Include medium, then fast, then slow tempos in order to test their listening. Change loudness also so students respond to rhythmic clues rather than to the tunes themselves.	9. Remain with partner and listen to music. Clap.
10. Have students form a rhythm band by using musical instruments (or other materials that could be used as musical instruments).	10. In groups of 8, students create music.

LESSON 3

Sub-Concept: Hearing other people.
Behavioral Objective: Students will listen to a story and be able to retell it to another student using their own words. Students will ask questions to elicit specific information about the story.

Activities:

Teacher	Student
1. Teacher reads *The Three Little Pigs,* then reads *Little Red Riding Hood.* Direct students to form pairs. One student asks questions about *Three Pigs* and other replies. Reverse roles for *Red Riding Hood.*	1. Listen to stories; ask and answer questions in pairs.
2. Direct students to draw pictures to go with each story, and place five key words from each story on picture.	2. Team draws picture and places key words.
3. Teacher directs students in "Simon Says."	3. Students take turns playing game.
4. Direct "Up or Down" game. Teacher says: "Horses' ears up; Horses' ears down. Cats' ears up; cats' ears down.	4. Students wear listening ears. The ears are put up or down in response to teacher directions.
5. Direct "Chin, Chin, Chin" game. Teacher points to chin and says, "Chin, chin, chin." Then points to another feature, but continues to say, "chin, chin."	5. Students point to what teacher says, not where the teacher points.
6. Describe "Mixed-Up Story:" "I'm going to tell you a story, but you have to listen because every once in a while I'm going to ask someone to do something. Once there was a boy (Tony, touch your nose), and his mother asked him (Gary, stand up) to get a loaf of bread from the store (Gloria scratch your ear). She gave him a dollar and (Ellen, touch your toe), he walked to the store, but on the way (Mike, clap your hands) to the store he met a friend. They played (Elizabeth, wiggle your nose) ball, and during the game he (Mandy, meow like a cat) lost the money. (Sam, wiggle your ears). His mother was unhappy (Jason, shut your eyes) when he came home.	6. Students listen. Student who is asked to do something carries out request. Students form groups of four. Each person tells a Mixed-Up story having things others must do.

LESSON 4

Sub-Concept: The importance of listening and being listened to.

Behavioral Objective: Students will demonstrate to their peers ability to listen by doing what is asked.

Activities:

Teacher	Student
1. Say: "I would like each person to tell others in your group the nicest things about you as a person. Their job is to give examples of how you demonstrate the trait here in school or in your neighborhood.	1. In groups of 6, each student tells nice thing about self. Others give examples of the trait.
2. Say: "Each person in the group should tell other people three things they would like done for them during the next week. For example, you might ask each person to say hello to you everyday when you enter the class. Be sure you say *exactly* what you want."	2. Students make requests and discuss how to carry them out.
3. Say: "I would like you to take 10 minutes thinking about one thing each person in your group has said that was interesting. Write it down. Then share your ideas with that person."	3. Students think and write. Student share.
4. Say: "I would like each group to come up with one thing they would like me to do in the coming week. Be sure to explain clearly what you want me to do. At the end of the week, please give me a grade based on how well I did what you asked. I'll talk with each group and tell you whether or not your directions were clear."	4. Students talk and come up with an idea to give teacher.
5. EVALUATION: Say: "I would like each person to share with someone else an example of how you know they listened to what you were saying. For example, you might say—when you repeated back my story I knew you were listening."	5. Students share.
6. Say: "Share a story with someone and ask them to practice listening with their listening ear."	6. Students share.
7. Say: "Draw a picture showing someone listening to you. Put the words on the picture that tell how you feel when people listen to you." Observe students.	7. Students draw and write.

Reflections on Units

1. Does your unit open with an interesting activity?
2. Does the unit have a flow of activities in which both teacher and students are actively involved in the material?
3. What percent of your questions are: recall or open-ended?
4. Do you have a variety of activities: talking, writing, drawing?
5. Do you have some "fun" activities along the way?

6. What do you believe is the high point of the unit?

7. What is the low point of the unit?

8. What will students find easiest to learn?

9. What will they find hardest to learn?

10. Is your evaluation consistent with your objectives? Does it evaluate what you set out to teach?

Discussions about curriculum reform frequently are stifled by pressures from interests outside and inside school districts. Several factors hinder creating an environment which would facilitate critical analysis of how curriculum can best prepare youth for the coming century. These include:

1. State mandates emphasizing basic skills restrict teacher freedom to experiment or empower students to help shape curriculum decisions.

2. Standardized tests required by district or state education departments narrow the focus of instruction to material covered by the tests.

3. School district curriculum guides are usually created by a committee. They limit individual teachers in deciding upon texts or what to teach.

4. Teacher evaluation models which define "effective teaching' in a narrow prescribed process hamper teacher spontaneity.

5. The absence of time or money limits teachers' availability to work on curriculum change.

6. The professional preparation of teachers and administrators "typically involves limited exposure to critical issues in curriculum theory, social foundations, and organizational/school change. Instead of providing experiences in critical inquiry, such programs emphasize the mastery of technique over analysis" (Bruner, 1966).

7. The influence of national models by individuals such as Madeline Hunter are sometimes uncritically accepted by the central office of a school district as a means to standardize curriculum. This restricts freedom of teachers and students to experiment with curriculum.

8. State adoption of texts places a financial constraint upon school districts since they lack money to turn down free texts from the state.

9. Teacher organizations sometimes fail to assume leadership in curriculum reform. Individual teachers lack backing from their professional leaders to experiment.

10. Isolation of teachers makes it difficult to work on a daily basis with peers. They are unable to cooperatively plan curriculum, nor can they receive ongoing feedback from peers about curriculum experiments in their own classrooms.

The result of routinized mandated education is to trivialize the curriculum. "Trivialization, in the context of the curriculum, refers to instances in which the curriculum is conceived or enacted in a way that oversimplifies, renders it less stimulating or demanding, requires little judgment and expertise by the teacher, or obscures the real ideologies that are embedded in it." (Bruner, 1966) There is strong pressure upon teachers to focus upon procedures or meeting mandated goals rather than assuming responsibility or being given the power to shape curriculum to meet the needs of the children in their classrooms.

Trivialization leads to fragmentation of knowledge. The demands for accountability encourage teaching children information or skills that can be demonstrated on a standardized test. Knowledge is transformed into pieces that fit into fill-ins or multiple choice exams. Controversial or ambiguous materials that require time and active student involvement are de-emphasized since they get in the way of preparing students for the test.

Teachers, as well as students, are victimized, by trivial curriculum. Fortunately, many teachers rise above these pressures and create exciting classrooms in which students engage actively in learning significant materials. Our society needs a new curriculum geared to the demands of the new century, and this challenge to innovate remains the task of those in the teaching profession.

· ·

SUMMARY

This chapter has reviewed historic trends leading to the emergence of modern curriculum ideas. It provides several models of organizing lesson plans and presents a process of how to write a curriculum unit.

QUESTIONS

1. Cite examples from your experiences in social studies classrooms in which teachers represented one of the three curriculum movements discussed in the chapter.

2. Which of the three curriculum movements fits most closely with your philosophy of teaching social studies?

3. Recall the last time you said, "Aha, Eureka! I understand that." Analyze the process of how you came to the "Eureka" moment.

4. If you have ever been in a classroom in which a teacher said, "This is a difficult class," discuss how you felt emotionally and intellectually when told that.

5. Identify two classes you currently are taking and analyze if the course goals are stated in behavioral terms.

6. What do you find most helpful about the Madeline Hunter model of lesson planning?

7. What do you find most helpful about the Bloom Taxonomy model of lesson planning?

8. What would be most exciting about creating lesson plan models that empower students to take the initiative?

9. What do you find most helpful about the model of lesson planning described by the authors of this book?

10. Can you cite examples from your life as a student in which teachers "trivialized" the social studies curriculum?

ACTIVITIES

1. Select an item in your possession and teach about it to another student. For example, what and how would you teach about your watch?

2. Identify something to teach, and write a lesson plan for it using the four models presented in this chapter.

3. Obtain a lesson plan from a teacher and analyze it according to the ideas presented in this chapter.

4. Observe a teacher teaching, and analyze the lesson plan based on the models presented in this chapter.

5. Use your university library to obtain a copy of a lesson plan written 20 or 30 years ago. Analyze the lesson plan based on ideas presented in this chapter.

Middle Grades Social Studies: A Modest Proposal
by Michael G. Allen

Early adolescence has been described as a "metamorphic development, having extraordinary consequences for the individual and widespread implications for social studies educators" (Brown 1982, 30). Within a relatively short time, growth breakthroughs that establish the foundation of late adolescence and adulthood are structured.

In preparation for this special middle school segment in *Social Education,* the writer sought middle grades schools where social studies instruction has involved middle school students in the serious pursuit of education. This included an extensive Dialog search, discussions with middle grades colleagues throughout the nation, and a review of pertinent literature. The search proved fruitless. In fact, findings paralleled those of recent National Science Foundation (NSF) studies on the state of social studies education. It therefore seemed appropriate to redirect efforts by offering a series of recommendations for improving middle grades social studies.

As with other components of an exemplary middle grades school, the social studies program should reflect conscious commitment to "three educational goals seen as dominating the curriculum of the middle school"—personal development, skills of communication and learning, and major knowledge areas (Alexander and George 1981, 56). Though a plethora of scope and sequence arrangements for middle grades social studies exists, there are strong similarities in offerings nationwide ("In Search of a Scope and Sequence," 1984; Project Span 1982).

The following several findings from studies sponsored by the National Science Foundation (Wiley 1977) and reported by Shaver, Davis, and Helburn (1979) are offered in support of recommendations for improving middle grades social studies:

1. Teachers are the key to what social studies will be for early adolescents.
2. The dominant instructional tool continues to be the conventional textbook.
3. The curriculum is mostly history and government with geography included at the elementary and middle/junior high school levels. There is little interdisciplinary teaching and little attention to societal issues.
4. The dominant mode of instruction continues to be large group, teacher-controlled recitation and lecture, based primarily on the textbook.
5. The "knowing" expected of students is largely information-oriented. Students often have to reproduce the content and language of the book. Experience-based curricula are rare as is inquiry.
6. Teachers rely on external motivation. Students are not expected to learn because of their interest but because doing one's lessons is the thing done for grades.
7. Students generally find social studies content and modes of instruction uninteresting.
8. Affective objectives are rarely an explicit part of the curriculum. Implicitly, content and classroom considerations are typically used to teach student to accept authority and the have them learn "important truths" about history and government.

Based on these conclusions, the following recommendations are offered in support of restructuring middle level social studies education (Allen and McEwin 1983).

Recommendations

1. Middle grades social studies textbooks should be carefully selected and used as a major resource in addition to a wide variety of supplemental resources. Steps should be taken to point out the textbook's limitations as well as its benefits.

While the standard social studies textbook is an appropriate resource for instruction, problems arise when it is utilized by educators as the principal source of truth. When viewed as authoritative and unquestionable, the kind of interactive instruction that is most effective with early adolescents is negated. Exclusive use of textbooks in unimaginative ways discourages students from thinking about important issues. Overuse or misuse retards reflective thinking.

The textbook should be used to allow early adolescents to learn in other ways than by memorization of facts presented by whoever authored the text. Limiting knowledge in this manner often results in passive, uninvolved citizens.

2. Middle grades social studies should emphasize history, government, and geography with numerous opportunities for integration of other social science disciplines, humanities, and students' personal life experiences. Interdisciplinary units should be utilized.

An interdisciplinary approach leads to deeper understanding of important concepts, generalizations, skills, and values. While history, government, and geography are vitally important, they should be studied in connection with other social sciences, the humanities, and students' personal life experiences (Miller and Young 1979). Since middle grades students are generally on the threshold of intellectual development, interrelationships among the social sciences may be understood for the first time.

3. A wide variety of teaching methods and materials should be employed in middle level social studies including experience-based curricula like community study and social action projects.

Social studies are unsurpassed in potential when experience-based learning is employed (Schug and Beery 1984). Appropriate techniques, activities, and materials for these youth include simulation games, audiovisual materials, bulletin boards, independent and group projects, guest speakers, open discussions, values clarification activities, learning activity packets, exchange programs, pen pals, festivals of various countries or communities, community study and involvement (Allen 1980; Kohler 1981; Kowalski and Fallon 1986; Lipka, Beene, and O'Connel 1985), oral history projects, social action projects, and acquisition of skills.

4. Middle grades social studies educators should recognize the uniqueness of this age group.

Too often, this age group is viewed as *junior high school* students or even young adults. Until this widespread perspective is abandoned and replaced by understanding of the developmental realities of early adolescence, little improvement in early adolescent education will be realized. . . .

5. Affective education is a crucial responsibility of middle level educators and should be an important component of the middle grades social studies program.

Early adolescence is an opportune time for challenging students with value-laden issues without inculcating a predetermined set of values. Values are being formed and solidified during early adolescence and should be addressed rather than avoided (Raths, Harmin, and Simon 1978). Exposure to value conflicts through literature, film, community involvement, and other activities provides excellent opportunities for understanding developing emotions and belief systems. Open-ended discussions can help students determine direction in life while leading to increased self-understanding of their role in life and society.

6. Middle grades social studies teachers should make their classrooms a forum for democratic action and address controversial issues that have meaning to early adolescents.

There seems to be little concern among social studies teachers or the general public for dealing with controversial issues in social studies. This is an increasing need as the nation moves toward more conservative views and teaching positions become less secure.

Early adolescents ask tough questions as they search for understanding and meaning in life. Such questions must be addressed since "becoming a democratic citizen requires more than an abstract understanding of democratic principles and practices. Behaving democratically is a way of life. It is not enough that schools preach democracy; they must practice it also and be able to instruct through modeling" (Hepurn 1983, x).

7. Skill development should be a systematic and continuing component of middle grades social studies programs.

Too frequently class time is considered too valuable to be devoted to more time-consuming activities that build skills important for survival in a democratic environment and increasingly interdependent world—for example, skills related to acquiring information, organizing and using information, and interpersonal relationships and social participation ("In Search of a Scope and Sequence," 1984, 260–61).

8. Social studies educators should recognize their responsibility to contribute significantly to the personal development of early adolescents.

Social studies properly emphasize citizenship as it relates to government affairs, history, and the social sciences (Barr, Barth, and Shermis 1977). By relating social studies to the needs and interests of early adolescent learners, both the goals of personal development and specialized social studies knowledge and skills may be realized.

9. Aspects of the middle school concept should be studied by social studies educators regardless of their current school organization plan, to determine whether components of the concept may be beneficial to their teaching.

Reorganization of middle grades education has resulted in increased attention to middle level social studies. Though a national study (Brooks and Edwards 1978) revealed that only limited instructional changes have occurred in most middle grades schools advocates of the middle school concept have encouraged various instructional and organizational changes—for example, interdisciplinary units, personal development, team teaching (Johnston and Markle 1986). Such efforts must continue if the middle school movement is to impact successfully on curriculum as well as organizational aspects of education for early adolescents.

10. Middle grades social studies educators should become apprised of the early adolescent period by reading, attending conferences, and participating in other experiences that will increase understanding of this unique developmental period.

Lack of knowledge about teaching early adolescents is not unique to social studies educators. Historically, they have been prepared to teach at the elementary or senior high school level with little mention of the intermediate grades (Alensander and McEwin 1982; NMSA 1986). Therefore, it is rare to find social studies educators who have been trained to teach at the middle grades level.

Since the majority of teachers, administrators, supervisors, and other educational personnel involved with middle level social studies have had little or no special preparation, they should make special effort to acquaint themselves with this age group. Administrators can play an important role in improving middle grades social studies by making information available on early adolescents.

Reflections for the Future

In 1916, John Dewey warned educators and others of the standing danger that "the material of formal instruction will be merely the subject matter of the schools, isolated from the subject matter of life experience." This is no less true today. In fact, as knowledge continues to multiply at an exponential rate and daily life becomes increasingly complicated by dwindling nonrenewable resources, population pressures, and fragmenting social-cultural connections, the need to root social studies in direct, firsthand experience is critical.

Democratic citizenship is based principally in the knowledge gained, skills practiced, values formed, and classroom-community interactions experienced in and through social studies education. Without such experiences, early adolescents will be ill-prepared for citizenship. Social studies educators face a profound responsibility for preparing early adolescents for their future—and ours—by enhancing their ability to engage in active citizenship (Parker and Jarolimek 1984).

Middle level educators enjoy unsurpassed opportunities for effecting such needed changes. No more important task exists than preparing positive and purposeful individuals and implanting a legacy of reflection coupled with the skills and desire to nourish personal powers. Early adolescents deserve no less.

References

Alexander, William, and Paul George. *The Exemplary Middle School.* New York: Holt, Rinehart and Winston, 1981.

Alexander, William, and C. Kenneth McEwin. "Toward Middle Level Teacher Education." *Middle School Journal* 13, no. 3 (August 1982): 3–5.

Allen, Michael G. "Social Studies as Social Action." *Middle School Journal* 11, no. 4 (November 1980): 13–14.

Allen, Michael G., and C. Kenneth McEwin. *Middle Level Social Studies: From Theory to Practice.* Columbus: National Middle School Association, 1983.

Barr, Robert, James Barth, and S. Samuel Shermis. *Defining the Social Studies.* Bulletin 51. Washington: National Council for the Social Studies, 1977.

Brooks, K., and F. Edwards. *The Middle School in Transition: A Research Report on the Status of the Middle School Movement.* Lexington: Center for Professional Development, University of Kentucky, 1978.

Brown, James A. "Developmental Transition in the Middle School: Designing Strategies for Social Studies." In *Developmental Perspectives on the Social Studies,* edited by Linda Rosenzweig. Bulletin 66. Washington: National Council for the Social Studies, 1982.

The Current State of Social Studies: A Report of Project Span. Boulder: Social Science Education Consortium, 1982.

Hepburn, Mary, ed. "The NCSS Position Statement on Democratization of Schools." In *Democratic Education in Schools and Classrooms,* Bulletin 70. Washington: National Council for the Social Studies, 1983.

"In Search of a Scope and Sequence for Social Studies." Report of the National Council for the Social Studies on Scope and Sequence. *Social Education* 48, no. 4 (April 1984): 259–61.

Johnston, J. Howard, and Glen C. Markle. *What Research Says to the Middle Level Practitioner.* Columbus: National Middle School Association, 1986.

Kohler, Mary Conway. "Developing Responsible Youth through Youth Participation." *Phi Delta Kappan* 62, no. 6 (February 1981): 426–28.

Kowalski, Theodore J., and John A. Fallon. *Community Education: Process and Programs.* Bloomington: Phi Delta Kappa Educational Foundation. Number 243, 1986.

Lipka, Richard P., James A. Beane, and Bruce E. O'Connel. *Community Service Projects: Citizenship in Action.* Bloomington: Phi Delta Kappa Educational Foundation. Number 231, 1985.

McEwin, C. Kenneth. "A Report on Middle Grades Schools in North Carolina: A Study of Current Practices." Boone: North Carolina League of Middle/Junior High Schools. ERIC Number 199, 206. 1981.

Miller, James, and Jan Young. "The Social Studies as Personal Development." *The North Carolina Journal for the Social Studies* 26, no. 1 (Fall 1979):1–7.

Parker, Walter, and John Jarolimek. *Citizenship and the Critical Role of the Social Studies.* Bulletin 72. Washington: National Council for the Social Studies, 1984.

NMSA. "Professional Certification and Preparation for the Middle Level: A Position Paper." Columbus: National Middle School Association (NMSA), 1986.

Raths, Louis, Merrill Harmin, and Sidney Simon. *Values and Teaching,* 2d ed. Columbus: Charles E. Merrill 1978.

Schug, Mark C., and R. Beery, eds. *Community Study: Applications and Opportunities.* Bulletin 73. Washington: National Council for the Social Studies, 1984.

Shaver, James, O.L. Davis, and Suzanne Helburne. "The Status of Social Studies Education: Impressions from Three NSF Studies." *Social Education* 43, no. 2 (February 1979): 150–153.

Wiley, Kenneth B. *The Status of Pre-College Science, Mathematics, and Social Science Education.* National Science Foundation. Social Science Education Consortium. U.S. Government Printing Office. #038-000-00363-1. 1977.

The author thanks C. Kenneth McEwin and the National Middle School Association for permission to draw extensively from "Conclusions and Recommendations" in *Middle Level Social Studies: From Theory to Practice* by Michael G. Allen and C. Kenneth McEwin (Columbus: National Middle School Association, 1983), 42–51.

Michael G. Allen is Director of Continuing Education and Graduate Studies at Castleton State College, Castleton, Vermont.

(Courtesy © *National Council for the Social Studies.* Used with Permission.)

QUESTIONS ON READINGS

1. Which recommendations for improvement of middle schools do you believe are most significant?

2. In which ways should middle school curriculum differ from the elementary school curriculum?

3. What do you believe should be included in middle school curriculum that is not listed in this article?

REFERENCES

Aristotle. 1961. *The Politics of Aristotle,* (ed) Ernest Baker. London: Clarendon.

Bloom, B., Krathwahl, David, and Masia, Bertram (1956). *Tatonomy of Educational Objectives: Cognitive Domain.* New York: Longman.

Bragaw, A. (1988). *Content if the curriculum.* Washington, DC: ASCD.

Bruner, J. (1966). *Towards a theory of instruction.* New York: Norton.

Eisner, E. (1982). *Cognition and curriculum.* New York: Longman.

Elkind, D. (1981) Child development and the social science curriculum of the elementary school. *Social Education, 45,* (6), pp. 435–37.

Ferriere, A. (1933). *The activity school.* New York: John Day.

Guralnik, D. (Ed). *Webster's New World Dictionary.* New York: Collins World.

Holt, J. (1967). *How children learn.* New York: Pitman.

Hunter, M. (1985). What's wrong with Madeline Hunter? *Educational Leadership,* 42 (5), pp. 57–60.

Hutchins, R. (1968). *The learning society.* New York: Praeger.

Lundgren, U. (1985). *Current thought on curriculum.* Washington, DC: ASCD.

Meussig, R. (1978). "Social studies curriculum development." Washington, DC: National Council on the Social Studies, Bulletin 55, p. 4.

Plato (1941). *The Republic* (Frances MacDonald, Trans.). Clarendon Press.

Tyler, R. (1983). *Fundamental curriculum decisions.* Washington, DC: ASCD.

SUGGESTED READING

Bank, A. (1981) *A practical guide to program planning.* New York: Teachers College Press.

Bobbitt, F. (1924). *How to make a curriculum.* New York: Houghton Mifflin.

Eisner, E. (1974). *Conflicting conceptions of curriculum.* New York: McCutchen.

English, F. (Ed.). (1983). *Fundamental curriculum decisions.* Washington, DC: ASCD.

Katz, M. (1968). *The irony of early school reform.* Boston: Beacon.

Killpatrick, W. (1936). *Remaking the curriculum.* New York: Newson.

Taba, H. (1971). *A teacher's handbook to elementary social studies: An inductive approach: Reading.* Menlo Park, CA: Addison-Wesley.

Chapter 5

Partners in Learning

Partners in Learning

Social studies offers the primary opportunity in the elementary curriculum for development of group processes and building positive self-esteem. Self-concept emerges through a continuous series of interactions between children and adults in the family, community and school. The classroom abounds with expressions of emotion between teachers and students and between students and their peers. The effective use of group processes and individual learning opportunities enhances the opportunity for social studies activities to foster positive self-esteem.

Each member of the class is a unique individual, but all students share common experiences in schools. Although definitions of success may differ, each wants to earn praise from teachers and peers, and each wishes to be included in the learning process. The classroom group is a social body, and this dynamic offers possibilities in teaching social studies. Many children view class social interactions as more important than the curriculum that is taught. They are interested in behavior and wish to better understand group processes.

▲ Social studies offers the primary emphasis in the elementary curriculum for development of self-esteem. *Courtesy Webster University.*

Imagine a class in which students worked individually, proceeding at individual rates until the material was completed through means of an assessment process. Imagine a class in which students worked in groups, sharing ideas, assisting one another in tasks and homework assignments, and openly discussing their ideas and concerns. Both of these classrooms are found in American public schools. The purpose of this chapter is to describe why both approaches can be used effectively.

Collaborative Learning

In recent years, the idea of collaborative learning has become a popular model for subdividing the class into groups. Collaborative learning activities range from assisting with one another's writing assignments to undertaking a group research project in the library. As students interact with one another, informal factors are also at play. Sometimes, youngsters with poor self-images feel unproductive in an activity requiring sharing and aiding others. The greater their sense of threat, the more they can disrupt the collaborative enterprise of the group.

It is important to create a positive social climate in the subgroup if all members are to feel themselves worthy as individuals. "The warm support, encouragement, and respect which students express for one another can facilitate the development of high self-esteem and a fuller realization of intellectual abilities" (Schmuck & Schmuck, 1971, p. 17). An effective collaborative learning experience will foster positive feelings about self and peers.

Teachers must remember that peer support and intellectual development are important rationales for collaborative learning. Teachers want students in the group to learn the assigned material, to write reports or to engage in group projects. However, teachers should be sensitive to the intra-group process, and ways to assist students in developing positive feelings for their peers.

For us, a positive classroom climate is one in which the students share high amounts of potential influence — both with one another and with the teacher; where high levels of attraction exist for the group as a whole and between classmates; where norms are supportive for getting academic work done, as well as for maximizing individual differences; where communication is open and featured by dialogue; and where the processes of working and developing together as a group are considered relevant in themselves for study. (Schmuck & Schmuck, 1971, p. 18)

▲ The school abounds with expressions of emotion. *Courtesy Pattonville (Missouri) School District.*

Cooperative learning had its origins in group investigative activities fostered by the ideas of John Dewey and in more recent times through the writings of Herbert Thelen (1962). Thelen suggests that the role of teachers is to provide a problem situation that can serve as an inquiry by students as a group. Their task is to identify a group problem and work toward a solution. The task of inquiry is obtaining knowledge, which according to Thelen is using information from the past and applying it to present situations. This will only occur if the group functions as an efficient entity. A group must be large enough to provide diversity but small enough for all to participate.

Organizing for Cooperative Learning

A group of students constitutes a microcosm of the world. Each child brings to the group a personality and past experiences. A group can assume its own personality, which can prove to be productive or counterproductive to the task assigned by teachers. In organizing a group, teachers might consider:

1. Should the group represent a diversity of abilities and personalities?
2. Should students be grouped on the basis of academic ability?
3. Is the assigned task one requiring its components to be subdivided among members of the group?
4. Does the group task entail recall of information already taught?
5. Does the group task entail conveying information to the teacher?
6. Does the group task require verbal interaction among its members?
7. Does the group have flexibility in carrying out the task? Can it go in a new direction?
8. Is leadership of the group clear to all?
9. Is there a group process to organize information?
10. Is the group to provide midpoint feedback to the teacher?

11. Is the group clear from its inception about the assigned task and the manner in which the final product will be presented?

In the traditional classroom, students sit in rows facing a teacher who is conveying information. A classroom designed around group work alters this dynamic. It changes the role of teacher from being at the center of the learning process to becoming a member of the learning team. A cooperative learning organization creates new roles for teachers:

1. *Facilitator*: The teacher's function is to assist students in functioning as a learning team. This requires educating them to operate as a cohesive group, to overcome interpersonal problems, and to develop a sense of loyalty to other members.

2. *Curriculum Developer*: Curriculum materials which are designed for use in traditional classroom situations may not be appropriate for group learning. Teachers have to adapt or create curriculum materials which can be used effectively within a cooperative learning environment.

3. *Resource Expert*: A group continually draws upon the teacher for new sources of information. A teacher has to identify possible resource people and materials which will aid the group in carrying out its tasks.

▲ Effective use of group processes fosters positive self-esteem. *Courtesy Webster University.*

There are many reasons why students might be formed into groups within a class. Teachers must develop a clear rationale why a particular form of grouping is to be utilized. Among the ways group settings can be used are:

1. *Information Exchange*: Students can share information they have studied or researched with other students within a group setting. This format can even be used with homework assignments. Students often gain information by listening to the ideas of their peers.

2. *Review*: A group format aids students prior to a test by providing opportunities for review of material. Listening and asking questions of peers about material to be tested can prove invaluable in memory retention.

3. *Problem Solving*: There are many occasions in which teachers pose a problem to the group and ask for a group solution. For example, ask a group to problem-solve other ways in which Jack could have resolved his conflict with the giant in "Jack and the Beanstalk."

4. *Tutorial*: Students helping students learn is among the most powerful means of conveying information. A group can review each member's homework assignment and suggest corrections or additions. A poem or short story can be presented to a group and comments requested for improvement.

5. *Planning:* A group can be assigned the task of engaging in a planning exercise. For example, a group might plan activities for a Halloween party or a trip to the zoo.

6. *Conflict Resolution:* A conflict between students can be fed back to their group with a request that the group work out alternative ways to resolve the problem between its members.

7. *Evaluation:* The group can be assigned the task of evaluating the work of its members and suggesting grades.

The idea of students working in cooperative ways with one another is an attractive concept to most teachers. It is consistent with beliefs that schools can help educate youth in the democratic processes of our society. At the same time, it imposes upon teachers the need for educating students to function in new roles. Many children arrive at school without extensive experience in functioning as group members. In working with small groups, teachers must remember several factors:

- Instructions to the group should be precise and clear.
- The final outcome of the group activity should be understood before the group begins its work.
- The task assigned should be within the intellectual and emotional capacities of the group.

NAME _____ DATE _____

DISCUSSION TOPIC _____

1. The hardest thing for me to do in this group discussion was _____

_____

_____

2. I find it hard to listen to people who _____

_____

_____

3. The thing I like most about this discussion was_____

_____

4. The discussion helped me to understand_____

_____

Students have to be made aware of their responsibilities as group members. It is important to review procedures for effective participation as a member of a group. In some cases, teachers provide children a "Group Badge" to wear that describes how they will function during this portion of the class period. For example, the badge might contain the following information:

1. I will be an active listener when others speak.
2. I will complete my part of group tasks.
3. I will admit mistakes and accept suggestions from other members of the group.
4. I will ask questions if something is unclear.
5. I will ask for help when necessary.
6. I will help other group members.
7. I will join with others in having fun, but know when to stop.
8. I will try my best to come up with new ideas.

Students in upper elementary and middle school are accustomed to receiving letter or numerical grades for work. They are less clear about grading policies for participation in group work. A self-evaluation process enables them to become sensitive to new demands imposed upon students when they function interactively with their peers. Following is a sample form for self-evaluation of student performance in a group.

Self-Evaluation					
Each week you will be asked to evaluate how well you aided your group to carry out its tasks. Your honesty in completing this task helps not only yourself, but other members of the group.					
	Never		Sometimes	Always	
1. I ask questions that are helpful to others.	1	2	3	4	5
2. I offer aid to other members of the group.	1	2	3	4	5
3. I remain on the assigned task.	1	2	3	4	5
4. I suggest interesting ways to complete our task.	1	2	3	4	5
5. I accept criticism in a positive manner.	1	2	3	4	5
6. I am proud of how I work in the group.	1	2	3	4	5

The creation of cooperative learning experiences within the class covers a wide range of activities. The following continuum depicts the focus of control when organizing students into groups.

```
◄───────────────────────────────────────►
Student              Shared                 Teacher
control              control                control
                     (group)
```

There should be times within the day when students work individually, when they work in a small group setting, and when the teacher is directly in control of the entire class. A balance between these organizational models enables both students and teacher to accomplish their goals in a sharing manner. Each format is conducive to particular learning activities, although in some situations all formats can be utilized.

Development of group skills can be started in the primary grades by involving groups of children in specific tasks— watering plants, caring for the class library, helping distribute supplies, composing a group poem or story, or putting on a puppet show. Prior to a presentation by a guest speaker, small groups can identify one question they would like to pose in the questioning segment of the talk.

Class Meetings are employed by many teachers to foster group participation in planning class activities. The entire class can be involved in identifying interesting speakers or planning class procedures. A subgroup structure makes class meetings even more effective because it enables more children to be involved in discussion. It aids the shy student to express ideas and make suggestions. In some classes, students are offered the right to call for a class meeting when they believe the need exists.

A classroom in which group activities are central to the education mission places demands upon teachers. The advantage of a teacher-centered classroom is that control is clearly vested in the hands of the teacher, and the potential for unplanned occurrences is reduced. It is educationally exciting to share power for learning with students because it opens new potential in curricu-

▲ Each child is a unique individual, but all students share common experiences in school. *Courtesy Null Elementary, Saint Charles (Missouri) Public Schools.*

lum planning. The teacher has to be flexible in response to student ideas, and although this may not always fit into school- or state-mandated educational goals, it can be accomplished.

Educators must recognize that while child-centered education is critically important in fostering the democratic spirit, it does not mean allowing children freedom to be egotistically bent on fulfillment of their personal desires. Teacher-controlled or student-centered classrooms are vulnerable to the danger of satisfying the personal factor rather than stimulating educational inquiry:

> When the emphasis falls upon having experiences that are educationally worthwhile, the center of gravity shifts from the personal factor, and is found within the developing experience in which pupils and teachers alike participate. The teacher, because of greater maturity and wider knowledge, is the natural leader in the shared activity, and is naturally accepted as such. The fundamental thing is to find the types of experience that are worth having, not merely for the moment, but because of what they lead to—the questions they raise, the problems they create, the demands for new information they suggest, the activities they invoke, the larger and expanding fields into which they continuously open. (Dewey, 1930)

The time is gone when we can draw a clear line between teachers and students. We can no longer treat children as though they belong to another species, for when we do treat them in such manner, they behave in ways we find discouraging. We must recognize that a continuum exists between teacher and student and both have responsibilities to ensure that productive learning occurs in the classroom. Cooperative learning is an important factor in affording students opportunities to assume leadership in learning.

▲ Every student wants to experience success. *Courtesy Saint Louis (Missouri) Public Schools.*

Other nations are also emphasizing the importance of groups as part of the educational process. Children in Japanese schools become part of a subgroup as early as the first grade and remain with the group for at least two years. They assist one another with schoolwork and engage in group learning projects. Each day a group has responsibility for obtaining food from the cafeteria for classmates while other groups are engaged in cleaning the school or performing other school-related tasks. The Japanese culture regards effective participation in a group as vitally important for their economic and national success.

Russian schools have long been noted for their endeavors to constitute the group as a primary learning body. Each class is divided into groups and its members are responsible for aiding one another in homework assignments. When children are absent, other members of the group have a responsibility to ensure that homework assignments are delivered to their homes and assistance is provided for anything that is not understood.

American schools do not operate in isolation from other nations. The efforts of schools throughout the world to employ effective strategies of group work can be studied and adapted to the American experience. Pen pal relations with foreign schools can be a jumping-off place for learning how another nation deals with this important issue.

Cooperative Learning Lesson Plans

New curriculum and teaching strategies are required in order to develop educational materials that are conducive to group work. For example, the story of "The Little House," by Virginia Lee Burton, depicts the desire of a house in the country to see the bright lights of the city only to become disillusioned, and then desire a return to country living. A cooperative learning response to the story requires extensive planning on the part of a teacher.

Cooperative Learning Lesson Plan for "The Little House"

1. *Architectural Groups*: Each group is to identify a form of housing in cities, suburban areas and rural communities. In your presentation to the class, show drawings of the housing you have researched.

2. *House Groups*. Group "A" presents the advantages of living in a country house, Group "B" the advantages of living in a city house, and Group "C" the advantages of living in a suburban house. Each group in its report is to put on a dramatic presentation with art work explaining its advantages.

3. *Transportation Groups*. Each group is to investigate a main source of transportation at a particular time in American history.

4. *Recreation Groups*: Each group is to identify forms of play of children in cities, suburban areas and farm situations. In your final report, demonstrate a form of play particular to your area.

5. *Dress Groups*: Each group is to identify how people dressed in cities and rural areas at different points of American history. The group is to create a costume to show the class.

6. *Role Play:* The class is divided into role play groups. One group role plays the feelings and emotions of a rural house, another the feelings and emotions of a city house.

7. *Stories about houses*: Each group is to read at least one story about living in a house. These stories are to be drawn from other societies or cultures. In your presentation to the class, tell about the housing situation and how it compares with that depicted in "The Little House" story.

8. *Writing Groups*: Groups can be assigned the task of writing a new version of the story or composing poems to go along with the existing story.

The extensive possibilities created by moving from a "read and discuss" approach to cooperative learning compels teachers to be much more active in organizing learning materials. Each group activity listed above requires identifying resources for use by the group, working with each group on its project, and helping them to plan their class presentations. This format means teachers move continually around the room, working with a particular group for a few minutes and then going to another part of the class to furnish different assistance to a group.

There are several factors to consider prior to plunging into extensive use of a cooperative learning format.

- A novice teacher should initially feel confident that the class accepts her authority. This also means the teacher should know the students as individuals as well as how they function in class situations. Group dynamics often require structuring the group to include diverse students, and this knowledge is not immediately known to the teacher.

- Begin group work slowly. Each phase should be carefully discussed with the entire class so they understand the process, and can provide their own input.

- A natural tendency of students in a group is to take on too much. The scope of a project or research should be narrowed in order to ensure that it can be successfully completed. It is preferable to narrow a focus rather than extend it. A collage which students think can be done in an hour might take a week.

- Elementary and middle school children are engaged in learning how to research and gather materials. In the beginning stage of group work, make available a considerable amount of resource materials. Later, as students become more skilled in using the library they can assume greater responsibility for gathering data.

- Meet with group members on a regular basis to monitor their progress and address their concerns or questions.

- Develop a feedback form which enables the group to provide an ongoing summary of their progress.

- Be sensitive to problems imposed upon a group when one or two members become disruptive. It is difficult for children to control these individuals, and your assistance will be necessary.

- Encourage students with a special interest to advertise for fellow members of the group. For example, if a student was interested in games played by children in colonial America they could create an advertisement to lure other interested students, e.g. "Wanted: Students Interested in Studying Play in Early America. See Kim for further information."

▲ A group research project in the library is an effective collaborative learning activity. *Photo by Claudia Burris. Courtesy Webster University.*

Child-Centered Classrooms

The struggle to create child-centered classrooms has preoccupied many educators throughout much of this century. Inherent in child-focused education is the view that the child contains within the self capacities to learn, to be caring and to function with mature attitudes and values. This approach to education suggests the need for students to assume a coequal leadership role with teachers in the learning process.

Advocates of child-centered classrooms seek to create a class environment in which children are freer, happier, and less pressured in the learning process. They seek a balance in which the needs of society and schools coexist peacefully with those of children. Child-centered educators recognize that children often learn in different ways than adults; they think holistically rather than fragmenting knowledge into segments and pieces. There is a naturalness to a young child's thought and learning that stands at variance from the traditional school model, which is organized sequentially and in a linear mode.

The essence of a child-centered education is the belief in the child's innate capacity to want to learn. Frequently, this natural desire to learn is stifled at great consequences for the intellectual and emotional development of children. Albert Einstein has stated the problem eloquently:

One had to cram all this stuff into one's mind, whether one liked it or not. This coercion had such a deterring effect that, after I had passed the final examination, I found the consideration of my scientific problems distasteful to me for an entire year. . . It is in fact nothing short of a miracle that the modern methods of instruction have not yet entirely strangled the holy curiosity of inquiry; for this delicate little plant, aside from stimulation, stands mainly in need of freedom; without this it goes to wrack and ruin without fail. It is a very grave mistake to think that the enjoyment of seeing and searching can be promoted by means of coercion and a sense of duty. (Goodman, 1967, p. 6)

Children do not differentiate between social studies or language arts, or between science and math. A group of children at play on the beach may create new games, discuss problems and find solutions or design fabulous castles, and dance and sing. In school, each of these activities would be allocated a period of time and given a designation—social studies, language arts, etc.

Child-centered classrooms are concerned with creativity and self discipline. President John F. Kennedy was fond of recalling the Chinese proverb which states that if you give me a fish I will eat today, but if you teach me to fish, I will eat forever. A child-centered classroom accepts that children have the capacity to make decisions, to organize their play and to devote considerable amounts of time to those activities which capture their interests.

Children can accept inefficiency, confusion, and noise more readily than can adults. They frequently gather vague and seemingly irrelevant pieces of information and put them together in a logical manner. Herbert Kohl has argued that in a child-centered classroom, teachers live in "suspended expectation." It may take a few days or weeks for the child to finally piece together the understanding a teacher seeks to enable or a question of yesterday may finally be understandable tomorrow.

The teacher's role is critical in a child-centered classroom. The ability to live in suspended expectation can test the will of even an experienced teacher. Charles Rathbone (1971) argues that a child centered classroom

▲ The role of teachers is to offer a problem situation that can initiate inquiry by students as a group. *Courtesy Kirkwood (Missouri) School District.*

de-emphasizes the view of the teacher as instructor, possessor of special knowledge, transmitter of answers, filter or mediator between materials and learner, determiner of curriculum, orchestrator of large groups of children, evaluator, standard setter; it empha-sizes, on the other hand, teacher as trained observer, diagnostician of individual needs, presenter of environments, consultant, collaborator, flexible resource, psychological supporter, general facilitator of the learning requirements of an independent agent. (p. 106)

There is a tendency in discussing child-centered classrooms to overlook the complexities imposed upon schools when societal knowledge is imparted to youth. The adult mind is so familiar with logically ordered knowledge that it does not recognize the amount of separating and reformulating that direct experience undergoes to become a branch of learning. An academic discipline is the product of the science of the ages, not of the experience of a child. It is a map pointing in various directions, not an end in itself. The child's present experience is not final, but transitional. It is a step along the path toward being able to enter into an academic discipline in a more mature manner.

The tools of inquiry are important for children if they are to participate in gaining access to the human heritage. The traits of self-reliance and the scientific method of examining informa-tion are invaluable to children as they grapple with personal or societal concerns. The experience of children is rich and varied in relationship to other children; however, children have limited contact with the broad spectrum of human experience.

A teacher in a child-centered classroom recognizes that school represents the larger world in a smaller and more compact model. Children need opportunities to express their ideas and, while respecting the role of teachers, be able to confront conflict in an organized and systematic manner. It is a long, lonely fight for children to escape from believing that one must always do exactly what adults demand. At the same time, it is an equally difficult task to recognize that adults can teach one how to become a fisherperson for life.

Characteristics of a Child-Centered Classroom

1. Children engage in alternative styles of learning. A variety of learning modes are employed in the quest for knowledge.

2. Group, sub-group and individualized organizational designs are utilized in accordance with material being studied

3. The class is a humane environment in which the rights and needs of each child is respected.

4. Self-initiated learning opportunities are available when students identify new paths for exploration.

5. Learning takes place in many environments other than the classroom. Museums, the outdoors, or community facilities are utilized when appropriate.

6. The teacher is a guide as well as possessor of knowledge.

7. Freedom has limits and responsibilities for students and teachers. A child-centered class maintains a delicate balance between school demands and the integrity of each child to be a unique individual.

8. The teacher is both a provider of information and a participant/learner. There are times when teachers join with students on an equal basis in seeking to understand new knowledge.

9. The teacher is an active listener who enters dynamically into the world of others, and seeks to understand issues from the child's perspective.

10. There is humor and joy in the act of learning. Education is a serious matter, but one must never lose sight of the absurdities of life in our quest to understand the human condition.

▲ Each child brings to the group a personality and past experiences. *Courtesy Webster University.*

Organizational Settings for Child-Centered Education

There have been many efforts to restructure schools and classrooms in order to facilitate a more child-centered environment. The Open Classroom experiment of the 1960s and 1970s led to extensive physical changes. Walls were torn down in many schools and children were provided with greater flexibility to move around and interact with one another. The "open walls" approach upset many teachers, who objected to the high noise level and the free manner in which students moved around the room.

The English "informal" or "integrated day" format attracted considerable interest among American teachers at the height of the Open Education movement. In this model, teachers created interest areas such as science or social studies centers. The interest area was stocked with

▲ In the traditional classroom, students sit in rows facing a teacher who conveys information. *Courtesy Saint Louis (Missouri) Public Schools.*

materials for students to work in pairs, alone, or in small groups. Students moved from one interest area to another while the teacher worked with small groups of students or one-on-one with a child.

The integrated day approach sought to capture student-initiated interests as a springboard for multidisciplinary activities. If a child indicated an interest in airplanes, the teacher would attempt to identify other children with a similar interest. This small group might construct, draw or read about airplanes while other groups of students studied something completely different.

There are still many schools in existence which arose during the Open Education movement in an attempt to move children out of school buildings. These "schools without walls" are usually designed for adolescent children and provide opportunities to work with artists, intern in business enterprises, or work with a mentor on a specific project.

▲ Group work changes the role of teacher from being at the center of the learning process to becoming a member of the learning team. *Courtesy Kirkwood (Missouri) School District.*

These endeavors seek to place the interests and needs of children as central to the mission of education. The desires and concerns of children are viewed as the beginning point of learning and emphasis is placed upon making classrooms freer, happier, and less pressured environments. Advocates of a child-centered classroom believe education should flow from the child outward to society rather than society imposing its will upon youth. There have been several experiments in this century which attempted to create child-centered schools. A.S. Neil's Summerhill gave children extensive freedom to decide what and how they should learn. However, most child-centered education has impacted schools in bits and pieces due to the efforts of individual teachers who are committed to respect the integrity of children.

Textbooks as Partners in Learning

Textbooks originated in the 19th century when libraries were few and far between. It was an education breakthrough when textbooks appeared with concise but comprehensive information that was not available in local communities. The McGuffy Reader and Webster's *Blue Backed Speller* became common tools of education for generations of children. By the 20th century, it had become accepted practice to provide free textbooks to children regardless of their parents' income.

Many states have adoption policies under which committees determine which books will be purchased by state education authorities for local school districts. In recent decades, "readability formulas" tightly control how textbooks are written, causing critics to complain about vapid writing that is choppy and monotonous.

Social studies textbooks frequently arouse concerns from special interest groups. Each demands coverage or attention to its concerns. Textbooks must please the hawkeyes of differing persuasions, which often leads to "mentioning" topics in order to assure coverage. A word, a phrase, or a heading is often cited as proof that the topic has been "covered."

▲ There should be times within the day when students work individually. *Courtesy Null Elementary, Saint Charles (Missouri) Public Schools.*

There is little evidence that adopting a social studies textbook series K-8 ensures continuity or transition from one grade level to another. Frequently, social studies series are collections of loosely related volumes; there is no certainty that a fifth grade textbook will complement its fourth or sixth grade companion text.

One of the most disturbing aspects of social studies textbooks is the apparent superficiality of treatment accorded critical thinking, citizenship, map, and research skills. In practice, the skills that receive the heaviest emphasis are likely the ones that could be most easily tested. The rigid standards imposed by state adoption committees force many publishers to offer scanty or disconnected coverage about important topics.

In sum, social studies textbooks are of poor instructional quality because of a combination of factors: preoccupation with superficial yet broad content coverage, lack of care in content choice and presentation, absence of "point of view" and the use of readability formulas that result in "inconsiderate" content presentation involving short sentences, simple vocabulary and the exclusion of connectors and referents that help make text easier for youngsters to comprehend. (Woodward, Elliott, & Nagel, 1986, p. 52)

Although significant problems exist with social studies textbooks, they remain for elementary and middle school teachers a centerpiece of their social studies program. Textbooks will be part of the curriculum for the foreseeable future, and teachers have to make them a partner, not an enemy, in the instructional process. A key factor in making effective use of textbooks is to regard them as an interactive medium in which students dialogue both with the text and other resource materials. In this way, students learn that textbooks contain information that is in transition and frequently will be rewritten to reflect new information.

Textbook information was gathered by authors who researched an extensive array of books and other resource materials in the process of collecting data. They read books, articles, and primary source documents and then selected bits and pieces of their research for inclusion in the text. A different set of authors might have selected different materials. Learning about the process of how a textbook is created enables students to comprehend the process of information selection.

The increased concern about the need to include multicultural and gender materials in textbooks affords interesting opportunities for students to better understand textbooks. College libraries and some school districts have copies of textbooks published 10 or 20 years ago. These books reflect the concerns of a different era.

An activity for students in fourth grade and above would be to select chapters from current textbooks and those written 20 years ago. Compare and contrast how minorities are presented in the textbooks, and select chapters from the textbooks to analyze how girls and women are portrayed.

▲ The development of group skills can be started in the primary grades by performing a puppet show. *Courtesy Lynn Rubright, Webster University.*

Rapidly changing world events make it difficult for textbook publishers to keep abreast of what is happening in history and geography. Countries are emerging while others disappear. The ozone layer problem was not a significant factor in textbooks of 10 years ago, but today it appears prominently in environmental education. Students in third grade and above can select an issue discussed in their textbook and contrast how that topic is presented by current media sources.

Textbooks have the advantage of providing each member of the class the same core of basic information about a topic. This common base of knowledge can become a springboard for further learning activities. Students in the fifth or sixth grade can select a topic from the textbook and then subdivide into cooperative learning groups. Each group is assigned the task of gathering additional information. For example, assume the War of 1812 is the topic. Assign one group the task of researching how the War of 1812 is viewed by the Canadians. Assign a second group the job of researching how military troops were transported during the war; and assign a third group to examine weapons used by the fighting forces. A group can also be formed to research the role of minorities in the war.

Bilingualism is frequently discussed as a source of "problems." The presence of students in class who can read and write in a foreign language opens new opportunities for more effective use of textbooks. A Spanish speaking student in grades 4–6 can be asked to work with the class in contacting schools in Spain, Mexico or Venezuela in order to obtain information from them on how the United States is depicted in their textbooks, or to secure a Mexican view of the Mexican War. These activities ensure that bilingualism plays a vital learning role in the classroom.

Many school districts destroy old textbooks after several years of use. It is beneficial to save these old texts. After a few years, your classroom resources will have grown to the point where students can examine their current textbook in a more critical manner because of the readily available presence of other sources in the room.

Educators must be concerned about what knowledge all students need in order to succeed in their personal and occupational lives. The textbook contains a valuable source of information, much of which can assist students in developing a foundation of knowledge. A task of elementary and middle school social studies is educating students to be critical readers and thinkers. Learning information in textbooks together with becoming skilled at analytical investigation of the textual material is invaluable training in the process of critical thinking.

Textbooks raise questions about what, if anything, should constitute core knowledge and its relationship to critical thinking. A challenge facing teachers is making the textbook a tool enabling students to go beyond rote memorization, and to become instead, advocates of the democratic process and concerned citizens who wish to overcome all forms of inequity in American society.

> The struggle to integrate process and knowledge in a way that respects the diversity of our society and counters the inequities that are perpetuated through schooling is perhaps the central unaddressed question in current debates about educational reform. What we might come up with is a continually emerging and self-renewing curriculum with a changing constellation of central knowledge and a critique informed by student voices and the voices of their communities—that is, with a curriculum that is part of the struggle to make a democracy out of the United States. (Kohl, 1992, p. 461)

Individualized Learning

In addition to concern about students functioning effectively within group settings, teachers also seek to meet individual needs. There is a difference between individualization and one-to-one instruction. Individualization refers to the manner in which teachers plan, collect and organize educational materials to meet the needs of one child while one-to-one instruction refers to the process by which instruction is delivered. The organization of learning materials or creation of an Individualized Learning Program (IEP) is quite different from meeting with a child face-to-face to review material.

Individualization of instruction enables teachers to meet the needs of an increasingly diverse student body. In theory, designing educational materials tailored to meet the needs of a single child is a valid approach to respecting the uniqueness of children. However, individualized instruction is difficult to implement. Among the factors that enter into individualization are:

1. Time constraints imposed on the teacher by the need to develop specific education packets for an individual child. Few novice teachers have this time or ready access to materials.

2. Providing sufficient time for discussion and review with children of their work. As the teacher reviews an individual child's work, the remainder of the class has to be engaged in learning activities.

3. The continuous and careful assessment of a child's performance can become time consuming. It often requires creating new evaluation procedures.

4. Students engaged in an individualized program complete their work at different times. Teachers have to have available additional purposeful work for those individuals. In addition, students who take a long time to complete their individual work also require assistance.

Teachers who seek to develop individualized education programs should proceed in a step-by-step process. The novice cannot plunge immediately into an individualized form of instruction. It might be beneficial to have available individualized instructional packets which are used by a few students. As knowledge is gained during the school year about individual needs, these packets can be expanded to meet the diverse concerns of children. It is also possible to pair two students with similar needs to facilitate sharing and cooperative learning.

Checklist for New Teachers

1. Are you able to correctly pronounce the name of each student?
2. Are you familiar with school procedures such as fire drills?
3. Are you aware of any physical handicaps faced by a student?
4. Are you familiar with library procedures and resources?
5. Are you familiar with procedures for use of media equipment?
6. Will students be involved in the process of establishing class procedures?
7. Are there sufficient books and materials available for students?
8. What emotional feeling do you wish conveyed by the physical arrangement of your classroom?
9. How will you assess student work?
10. Will a substitute teacher be able to follow your lesson plan when you are absent?

Teacher as a Partner in Learning

An enthusiastic class attitude is the best guarantee of success in learning. Experienced teachers frequently comment that each class has its own unique flavor or feeling. A positive class attitude will be of enormous assistance in meeting the individual needs of children. It has often been said that nothing succeeds better than success. A motivated class is the best guarantee that cooperative learning and individualization will be successful in implementation.

Suggestions for Motivation

1. Ensure that students see relevance of what is being studied to issues of their own lives.
2. Draw analogies between the material and events of today.
3. Open yourself to the group. Let them know of your concerns or doubts or hopes. Students are more relaxed when the teacher is viewed as a normal person.
4. Avoid all forms of sarcasm and personal negativism.
5. Be an empathetic person.
6. Display enthusiasm for what is being studied. If a teacher isn't interested, it is doubtful that students will be interested.
7. Observe each child's thoughts and behaviors for signs of motivation or confusion.
8. Trust each child and respect his or her individual needs.

9. Freely admit mistakes.

10. Be an active listener.

A teacher plays many roles in a classroom and the successful performance of them generates high motivation among students. Among the roles of an elementary or middle school teacher are:

1. *Guide:* The teacher is analogous to a scout who points the way into the unknown.

2. *Learner:* The teacher is an active learner who is continually bringing personal discoveries into the classroom.

3. *Model:* The teacher models how to think and work in a class situation.

4. *Storyteller:* Children love stories, and teachers are the source of many interesting stories about life and people.

5. *Scene Designer:* The teacher organizes the class environment to foster a positive learning climate.

6. *Actor:* Teachers and students are performers, and the classroom is a stage upon which they act.

7. *Friend:* Students desperately need good friends in an era in which parents work or struggle under great difficulties. A teacher plays a vital role by being available as a friend.

8. *Authority:* A teacher is an authority figure. An authority is one who possesses knowledge that can be shared.

9. *Community organizer:* Students need to belong to a community, and a primary task of teachers is to create a sense of community within the classroom.

10. *Inspirer:* All humans need inspiration that the world can be a better place, and children, above all, have this need.

11. *Routinizer:* Children find security in routine and the teacher's task is to ensure that routine is a means, not an end in itself.

12. *Evaluator:* Evaluation is a process by which people gain confidence in their unique capacities to learn. A teacher has to develop understanding of why and how evaluation provides emotional and intellectual strength to the child.

The essence of a democratic classroom is mutual respect between teacher and students. Teachers must put to the test the theory that the natural impulses of children are creative, and that given interesting curriculum materials and an environment which fosters a spirit that respects the integrity of people, children will develop powers and abilities hitherto undreamed of.

● ●

SUMMARY

This chapter has reviewed the rationale for collaborative learning and explained strategies for implementing classrooms in which teachers and students work in a team arrangement. It has also reviewed issues relating to use of textbooks in teaching social studies.

QUESTIONS

1. What did you most enjoy about group work activities when in elementary school? What did you least like?

2. Which type of educational tasks are best performed in a group setting?

3. The authors list seven tasks that groups ordinarily perform. Can you list additional ideas for group work?

4. How does a teacher's role alter when students work in groups?

5. What are the advantages in organizing students into groups from the first day of class? What are disadvantages?

6. What are the advantages and disadvantages of giving all members of a group the same grade?

7. Do you agree with the view of child-centered educators that children are innately interested in learning?

8. What do you like best about having textbooks assigned in a class? What do you like least?

9. How can society balance the need to represent the educational goals of ethnic and interest groups with the need for textbooks to be intellectually valid?

10. The authors list 12 teacher roles. Which of these most comfortably fits your personality? Which fit least?

ACTIVITIES

1. Take a lesson plan designed to be presented by a teacher to the entire class and turn it into a group-based learning experience.

2. Develop a lesson plan in which students work as team members in situations outside the school setting.

3. Interview teachers about their group-centered lesson activities.

4. Develop a lesson plan using a textbook as its base.

5. Compare and contrast three elementary social studies texts regarding how minorities and women are depicted.

READING

Conventionally Theirs: An Overview of the Origins, Content, and Significance of the Convention on the Rights of the Child

by Nigel Cantwell

Within just two years of its adoption by the United Nations General Assembly on 20 November 1989, the Convention on the Rights of the Child has already fulfilled its promise of becoming one of the most widely ratified human rights treaties in existence.

Little more than a decade ago, "children's rights" was generally considered a term to be avoided at all costs when taking up problems related to child development, welfare, and protection. Qualified variously as a "concept in search of a definition" and as an indication of an undesirably politicized approach, it met with open hostility or barely disguised anxiety among a wide range of professionals more or less closely involved in work for children. Even now, many remain unconvinced. Indeed, judging from the all-too-frequent expressions of skepticism, and even opposition, to the CRC, one might well believe that the term came from nowhere, suddenly landing upon an unsuspecting world.

Yet, far from constituting a sudden revolution, the provisions of the CRC are essentially the logical outcome of a continuous process of experience gathering and reflection over several decades. It is therefore worthwhile to examine closely the origins, content, and intention of this treaty, in order, among other things, to dispel some of the misconceptions surrounding it and to ensure that its potential as a tool for work on behalf of children is fully realized.

The Right to Special Rights

The evolution of special rights for children took place alongside that of human rights generally, and followed a fairly typical course for the development of international standards: the formulation of basic ideas promulgated in the form of a declaration, the gradual introduction of some of those ideas into binding and nonbinding international texts of wider scope, and the bringing together and updating of the resulting body of pertinent standards in a full-fledged convention.

The idea that children everywhere should have special rights was first formulated on paper in 1923. In that year, the council of the Save the Children International Union adopted a five-point Declaration of the Rights of the Child, setting out basic child welfare and protection principles, which became known as the Declaration of Geneva. The following year, the Assembly of the League of Nations passed a resolution endorsing this declaration and invited its members to follow its principles. In 1948, the newly constituted United Nations adopted a slightly expanded version containing seven principles. The United Nations General Assembly, on 20 November 1959, promulgated a ten-point declaration, which served as the springboard for the CRC and is still valid today.

Some countries had been hoping that the 1959 text could be adopted at that time in the form of a binding treaty and not as simply a list of nonbinding basic principles. It was to take another twenty years, however, before the international community was prepared to consider setting out the rights of children in the framework of a convention. The government of Poland, one of the convention's proponents in 1959, launched the initiative on the eve of the International Year of the Child (1979). In presenting its proposal to the 1978 session of the UN Commission on Human Rights, Poland sought to ensure the adoption of the convention during 1979 so that it would stand as a lasting symbol of the International Year of the Child.

This explains, in part at least, why the first text proposed was modeled closely on the 1959 declaration. It tends to take several years to formulate to the satisfaction of all states the text of binding treaties (and even nonbinding instruments). By putting forward a draft based on principles already unanimously agreed upon, Poland believed that agreement and adoption might be secured unusually quickly. This was not to be, however. Instead, the original draft was deemed inappropriate as the basis for an international treaty and the Commission on Human Rights decided to establish a working group to review and revise the text. This working group (composed of delegates from the commission's member states and observers from other governments and recognized organizations) then proceeded to meet for one week annually until 1987, moving into top gear in 1988 with two fortnight-long sessions in what proved to be a successful attempt to complete the draft in time for its adoption in the symbolic year of 1989 (the thirtieth anniversary of the declaration and the tenth anniversary of the International Year of the Child).

Special Human Rights

Although evolutionary (rather than revolutionary) in nature, one feature of the CRC marks a dramatic change in the way we view special rights for children. Here, for the first time, children's rights are set formally and irrevocably in the context of human rights. This was clear from the start because the Commission on Human Rights, and not any other UN body, oversaw the formulation of the convention (which, of course, now forms part of the body of international human rights law).

This fact has several implications. First, it does away once and for all with the idea that children's rights are to be set against adults rights; it clearly demonstrates, on the contrary, that children need special attention within the framework of human rights, just like certain other population groups. Second, it shows that human rights methodology is as pertinent to the promotion and protection of children's rights as it is to those of others and, in so doing, it takes children's issues out of the realm of the well-intentioned but ill-judged sentimentalism and sensationalism to which they have been so regrettably prone. Third, it increases substantially the potential range of organizations involved in child-related questions. Finally, it means that all kinds of rights are covered: not just those related to welfare and protection, but also civil rights providing for children to become the subjects, rather than the objects, of their rights. In other words, children are to exercise those rights in accordance with their maturity, to be heard in matters affecting their lives, and to participate in society as a whole.

Bear in mind that this convention—like every other binding treaty—is a listing of states' obligations both to undertake and, in certain instances, to refrain from given actions. These obligations may be direct—providing education facilities and ensuring proper administration of juvenile justice, for example—or indirect, enabling parents, the extended family, or guardians to carry out their primary roles and responsibilities as caretakers and protectors. Neither the existence nor the content of the CRC denies or reduces the importance of the family—quite the contrary. Furthermore, the CRC is not concerned with regulating intrafamilial relationships, nor is it a checklist of demands and claims, however legitimate, by children vis-à-vis adults. In other words, it is in no way a children's liberation charter. In the last resort, it is a catalogue of situations and guidelines that governments may accept, in theory at least, as falling within the scope of their individual and collective responsibilities.

In this and other respects, it is also important to view the CRC as a whole. To single out a specific provision and try to gauge its meaning (or, even worse, to consider a sentence or phrase in isolation) is highly misleading. Taken alone, for example, Article 15, paragraph 1—"States Parties recognize the rights of the child to freedom of association and to freedom of peaceful assembly"—is, arguably, potentially dangerous for children and promotes an extraordinarily laissez-faire attitude. Reading the paragraph in conjunction with a variety of other provisions, however, would dispel such fears. For example, the second paragraph of the article sets certain limits on these rights; Article 3 stipulates that the "best interests of the child" are to be a primary consideration in decisions affecting him or her; Article 5 recognizes the need for parental guidance "consistent with the evolving capacities of the child" in the exercise of rights; preambular paragraphs underline the importance of family; and, finally, the legislator's intention (often apparent in the records of the drafting process) in this case was primarily to prohibit arbitrary interference on the part of the state or its agents.

All Rights for Children

The CRC is comprehensive in the kinds of rights it covers. Traditionally, these would be classified as civil and political on the one hand, and economic, social, and cultural on the other. Although Article 4 explicitly mentions "economic, social and cultural rights," this is an exception to the philosophy underlying the convention whereby these traditional distinctions have been avoided. The text reflects the fortunate tendency to look on all rights as indivisible and mutually reinforcing in responding to human needs.

The CRC brings together all these rights in three main ways:

1. It reaffirms, with regard to children, rights already afforded to human beings in general by virtue of existing human rights instruments. Indeed, almost eight such international texts, both binding and nonbinding, have been identified as containing standards and rights that either ex-

plicitly or implicitly concern children. Some of these rights, such as protection from torture, are noncontroversial in terms of their applicability to children. During the drafting process it became obvious, however, that those who formulated basic treaties such as the International Covenants—and, in many cases, those governments that adopted and ratified them—must have been thinking mainly of "human beings" in the very limited sense of "adults." Thus, when it came to reaffirming in the CRC such rights as freedom of expression, freedom of assembly, freedom of religion, and the right to social security—all basic and established human rights—heated debate occurred on whether, and under what conditions, children could and should benefit from such rights. Consequently, reaffirmation was by no means a sterile, superfluous exercise. It was, rather, the result of a deliberate and necessary decision to ensure that the convention constitute a clear statement that could leave no doubt as to the rights to which children are entitled.

2. It upgrades certain basic human rights in order to take into account the special needs and vulnerability of children. For example, standards of acceptable conditions of employment must be much tighter for children and young people than for adults.

3. It establishes standards in facets of life that are pertinent specifically, or *more* specifically, to children. Safeguarding children's interests in adoption proceedings, separation from parents, access to primary education, prevention of and protection from intrafamilial abuse and neglect, and opportunities for play are among the child-specific issues addressed by the convention.

New Rights for Children

Overall, the Convention on the Rights of the Child undoubtedly is a progressive document that contains three kinds of innovations in particular: introducing "participation rights" for children, considering questions never previously addressed in an international instrument, and including principles and standards that have so far figured only in nonbinding texts such as declarations and "minimum rules."

A look at the 1959 Declaration of the Rights of the Child shows that it contains principles concerning provision and protection, but no sign whatsoever of the third *P*—participation. In that declaration, children were not recognized as having the right to do or to say anything—they were simply to be provided with certain things or services (e.g., name and nationality, health care, and education) and to be protected from certain acts (e.g., abuse and exploitation). It is therefore significant that the international community has accepted participation rights as an integral part of this convention. In this connection, it is also worth pointing out a similarly important novelty regarding access to information: Article 42 explicitly obligates the state for the first time to ensure that children, and not just adults, are informed about their rights.

The CRC also breaks new ground in addressing a topic never previously considered in an international instrument: the rehabilitation of children who have suffered various forms of cruelty and exploitation, including the victims of armed conflict. Under the terms of Article 39, governments must undertake to promote these children's physical and psychological recovery and their social reintegration. This is a remarkable step forward, as is another of the convention's innovations: the obligation of governments to take measures to abolish traditional practices harmful to children's health.

The third kind of progressive innovation concerns more specifically the articles on adoption (Article 21) and the administration of justice (Article 40). These issues are the subject of two nonbinding instruments adopted by the UN General Assembly toward the end of the period in which the CRC was drafted: a 1986 Declaration of Social and Legal Principles governing national and international adoption and foster care, and the 1985 Standard Minimum Rules for the Administration of Juvenile Justice, also known as the Beijing Rules. Both—especially the former—were the subject of lengthy drafting processes and considerable negotiation. Just two or three years after their approval, their essential elements were incorporated in the binding text of the convention—a significant step forward.

These innovations not only are important in terms of international human rights law but are equally remarkable in that they both indicate and foster a new attitude toward children. Using the convention as an educational tool in the classroom can be fundamental in securing optimal implementation of the rights it contains.

Nothing Is Perfect

Although progressive, not every aspect of the CRC meets its expectations or hopes. The low standards set in the now infamous Article 38 on protection of children in armed conflict and, particularly, their participation in hostilities, are still contested by all nongovernmental organizations and a good number of governments. They are outraged that it proved impossible to prevent a provision that allows children to engage in combat situations as of their fifteenth birthday. Their efforts to secure consensus on a higher standard before the text was adopted by the UN General Assembly were unsuccessful.

Similarly disappointing was that no acceptable formulation could be found for a provision protecting children from medical experimentation; consequently, the convention contains no mention of these practices that remain an all-too-frequent reality.

Many nongovernmental organizations are also critical of the rights on choice of religion afforded by the CRC's provisions compared to the International Covenant on Civil and Political Rights (the latter's higher standard can be invoked if necessary, however, since it is theoretically applicable to all, regardless of age). Several individual nongovernmental organizations are dissatisfied with the way certain of their specific concerns are addressed (or *not* addressed)—e.g., the absence of any reference to preschool education.

Surely no nongovernmental organization or government would venture to say that it is completely happy with the text of the CRC. This is hardly surprising considering that the convention is an international treaty that must take into account a wide range of beliefs, values, and ideologies and that cannot reflect or promote the standpoint of any individual group. The continued existence of criticism, therefore, should not detract from the indisputable fact that the CRC recognizes substantially more and better rights for children than those they have been granted to date.

Into Force and into Practice?

The CRC came into force on 2 September 1990, thirty days after the twentieth state had ratified it and well under a year after its adoption. Never before had a UN human rights treaty so rapidly received the support it needed to become law. The two most recent conventions (the Convention on the Elimination of All Forms of Discrimination against Women, and the Convention against Torture) took, for example, two and two and one-half years respectively to be ratified by the requisite twenty states. Moreover, most countries from the developing regions of the world have ratified the Convention on the Rights of the Child. This, incidentally, tends to put into perspective the criticism sometimes voiced during the drafting process that third world concerns were not sufficiently taken into account by a working group dominated by the "North."

In 1991, the States Parties (those that have ratified the treaty) elected a committee of ten "independent experts" whose main task will be to review states' compliance with their obligations under the convention on the basis of reports they provide and other information supplied by reliable sources.

This monitoring function is balanced by a clear desire to ground the CRC's implementation in a nonconfrontational frameowrk of constructive dialogue and international cooperation. This approach—set out in the implementation provisions—responds to two realities: first, that monitoring is of limited use on its own because sanctions cannot be applied; and second, that most countries would have virtually no chance of complying with the convention's provisions unless provided with appropriate technical and other assistance. The resulting mechanism is, therefore, yet again an innovative step in the right direction, enabling and encouraging a wide range of countries to envisage ratification and, as a result, fostering the goals of the convention.

It would be misleading not to mention that the nongovernmental organizations will also be active in pointing out violations, problems, and needs, and proposing solutions. Although the formal contributions of international nongovernmental organizations to the monitoring process will be largely determined by the Rules of Procedure that the Committee on the Rights of the Child is developing, they will constantly be seeking ways to maximize respect for the CRC's provisions. In so doing, they will place special emphasis on developing their networking and cooperation with national and local nongovernmental organizations.

The Convention on the Rights of the Child is unquestionably worth fighting for, and the fight must take place first and foremost at the national level where the degree of mobilization will largely determine the treaty's real effectiveness. In the face of a dwindling minority of recalcitrant governments that stubbornly swim against the tide of signature and ratification, the initial task is clear: create widespread awareness of internationally recognized human rights of children and arouse massive public support for ratification. Even before that is achieved, work can—indeed must—begin at the national level on monitoring compliance with the convention, since its provisions can already be considered an integral part of international human rights law. The instrument exists; the challenge now is to become skillful in using it.

Nigel Cantwell is Director of Programmes for Defence for Children International, an international nongovernmental organization founded in Geneva in 1979, whose action is directed toward promoting and protecting the rights of children throughout the world. DCI has sections in nearly forty countries and members in thirty more. It served as secretariat to the NGO Ad Hoc Group on the drafting of the Convention on the Rights of the Child, and is now coordinator of that group in its reconvened form. DCI is in consultative status with the Economic and Social Council of the United Nation,s UNICEF, and the Council of Europe.

Defence for Children International, PO Box 88, 1211 Geneva 20, Switzerland;
(41 22) 734 0558, (41 22) 740 1145 (fax).

(Courtesy © *National Council for the Social Studies.* Used with permission.)

QUESTIONS ON READING

1. What rights are possessed by all American children?

2. Which additional rights do you believe should be accorded American children?

3. Which segments of the American population would most oppose extension of rights to children?

REFERENCES

Dewey, J. (1930, July 9). How much freedom in the new schools? *The New Republic, 63,* (814) pp. 28–32.

Kohl, H. (1992, April 6). Rotten to the core. *The Nation, 254,* (13) pp. 457–460.

Rathbone, C. (1971). *Open education.* New York: Citation Press.

Schmuck, R., & Schmuck, P. (1971). *Group processes in the classroom.* Dubuque, IA: William Brown.

Thelen, H. (1962). *Education and the human quest.* New York: Harper & Row.

Woodward, A., Elliott, D., & Nagel, K. (1986, January). Beyond textbooks in elementary social studies. *Social Education, 42,* (5) pp. 57–60.

SUGGESTED READING

Cattegno, C. (1971). *What we owe children.* New York: Dutton.

de Lima, A. (1926). *Our enemy the child.* New York: New Republic.

Hertzberg, A., & Stone, E. (1971). *Schools are for children.* New York: Schocken.

Holt, J. (1969). *How children learn.* New York: Pitman.

Issacs, S. (1971). *The children we teach.* New York: Schocken.

Kohl, H. (1969). *The open classroom.* New York: New York Review.

Rathbone, C. (1971). *Open education.* Columbus, OH: Charles Merrill.

Weinstein, G., & Fantini, M. (Eds.). (1970). *Toward humanistic education: A curriculum of affect.* New York: Praeger.

Chapter 6

Critical Thinking in the Social Studies

Critical Thinking in the Social Studies

Humans are born with the potential to engage in critical thinking. Sigel (1984) defines critical thinking as an "active process involving a number of denotable mental operations such as induction, deduction, reasoning, sequencing, classification, and the definition of relationships" (p. 19). Children reason, question, and solve problems in the course of normal growth and development. The task of elementary school teachers is to nurture this spirit of inquiry and natural curiosity and direct it into more sophisticated means of problem solving.

Schools often give students the impression that problems lend themselves to right and wrong answers. In the real world, ambiguity is much more common. The best minds in our society are uncertain how to halt drugs or eliminate crime. Critical thinking skills are best developed when students work in an environment that is open to a multitude of possible ways to solve problems and relates both to the concerns of adults and the individual interests of children.

There is a tendency in school programs that teach critical thinking to direct students in a step-by-step process toward a specific outcome. Complex issues of everyday life are seldom solved in such a fashion. Economists have widely different views regarding effective ways to end a

▲ The task of elementary teachers is to nurture children's spirit of inquiry and natural curiosity. *Courtesy Saint Louis (Missouri) Public Schools.*

recession, and educators continue to debate how to help schools succeed in teaching children to be critical thinkers.

> Trying to break thinking skills into discrete units may be helpful for diagnostic purposes, but it does not seem to be the right way to move in the teaching of such skills. We believe that teaching people to think is like teaching someone to swing a golf club. It is more important to get the feel of the whole action. If you start by working on just one small piece of the swing, you'll surely make a mess out of it. (Sandler & Whimbey, 1985, p. 200)

Our daily lives confront people with ill-structured problems. Who to marry, how to invest one's money, and which graduate program will ensure a good job are questions that do not lend themselves to a step-by-step process. Children are confused about how to reconcile pleasing friends, teachers, and parents when these groups disagree about proper behavior. Educators are uncertain whether reading scores, how many books children read or the pleasure of reading is the best indicator of reading effectiveness. Robert J. Sternberg (1987), an expert on critical thinking, suggests:

> The courses we have taken (and the ones we now teach) on critical thinking might also lead us to believe that life's problems will be well-structured. But, few of life's problems are so neatly structured, and it is the solving of ill structured rather than well-structured problems that will prepare us for the challenges we most often face. (p. 196)

The importance of critical thinking is often presented as a given in education. However, there is little certainty among educators about the meaning of critical thinking and how it can be taught to students. Sternberg's (1987) research into the nature of critical thinking programs has identified several ways in which educators operate on assumptions concerning critical thinking that might be erroneous:

1. The teacher is the teacher and the student is the learner. Adults, as well as youth, need help in developing effective critical thinking methods. Teachers, as well as students, need further education in critical thinking.
2. Critical thinking is the students' job and only the students' job. Teachers often seek packaged programs in critical thinking that lift the burden off their shoulders to engage in critical thinking. It is more beneficial to students for teachers to demonstrate how they engage in critical thinking than to follow a prescribed formula of logical thought.
3. The most important thing is to decide on the correct program. First decide upon goals for critical thinking, and then decide which programs best aid in achieving your ends.
4. What really counts is the right answer. A frequent danger in critical thinking programs is a prior assumption that students should eventually agree on predetermined "right" outcomes.
5. Class discussion is primarily a means to an end. Teachers want students to discuss topics, but the presence of discussion in itself is not evidence of critical thinking. There must be substance as well as discussion.
6. The job of a course in critical thinking is to teach critical thinking. Teachers cannot "teach" another to think in a critical manner. They can provide the environment and

means, but the ultimate responsibility rests with the student's critical thinking capabilities. (p. 196)

Programs to teach critical thinking often come in commercially produced packages. Students are provided all the relevant information and a process to work their way through the issue to reach a logical solution. That is an interesting and perhaps a worthwhile exercise. In real life, however, we make decisions without all the relevant data. Deciding what to produce or which stock to buy requires logical thinking, but the final decision is never based on possession of all pertinent information necessary to make an informed conclusion.

The fact that over 40% of marriages end in divorce suggests that the "best laid plans" don't always achieve desired ends. We must be on guard as educators to avoid leading students to the erroneous conclusion that if they follow a particular program of thinking they can achieve the best end goal. Life is too uncertain.

During the development of the Mercury space program, a young engineer, Jack Heberlig, was charged with developing the astronaut's living area. He used a pig to test his ideas, but the pig died. Heberlig was in a quandry since no one at NASA had an explanation for the death. He finally asked a farmer who told him that pigs always died if they were kept on their backs for any length of time. Heberlig learned that ordinary citizens can also solve complex problems.

Obviously, students are always thinking, but perhaps not in ways desired by teachers. A good beginning point for teachers is to model critical thinking. Students usually regard their teachers as fountains of knowledge. They rarely witness teachers grappling with the uncertainties that go hand-in-hand with problem solving. Students should observe teachers involved in the process of solving problem including the false starts and dead ends.

None of us can teach students how to think, because from the moment of birth each individual is a thinking human. We can, however, create environments and experiences that foster critical thought on the part of students. Students reconstruct what happens in classrooms and refashion those events through the filter of internal systems of thought. The social studies lesson enables students to test their capacity for critical thinking with the guidance of supportive teachers.

▲ Students are always thinking, but perhaps not in ways desired by teachers. *Courtesy Null Elementary, Saint Charles (Missouri) Public Schools.*

An important strategy to encourage critical thinking is the teacher's use of precise language in asking questions or providing information. An imprecise statement or question does not lend itself to furthering the development of critical thinking skills. For example, "What do you think about the American Revolution?" is less precise than, "How did the American Revolution change government in our nation?" Following are some examples of precise and imprecise language:

"What happened in the War of 1812?" — "Which battles were turning points in the War of 1812?"

"What did you like about Red Riding Hood?" — "How did Red Riding Hood try to help her grandmother?"

"Why are there so many fights on the playground?" — "How does playing games in a short period of time cause fights?"

The language used by teachers frames the presentation of the content being studied. It identifies student activities, and describes the norms of acceptable or unacceptable behavior. The use of imprecise language impedes learning how to deal with problems in an analytical framework.

Critical thinking may not lend itself to precise grading. Teachers should remember that what is important is the reasoning process followed by students to solve problems, not necessarily the solution. Teachers should emphasize their interest in risk taking approaches that stimulate creative thinking.

Educators want students to learn to think critically. Sternberg does not believe critical thinking can be taught as a set program. On the other hand, practitioners such as Barry Beyer (1983) argue for purposeful, planned programs carried out over an extended period of time. He urges that critical thinking instruction should introduce "students to a skill and then provide guided practice and reinforcement in using the skill in a variety of settings with a variety of media" (p. 46).

▲ Teachers can create environments and experiences that foster critical thought on the part of students. *Courtesy University City (Missouri) Public Schools.*

Critical thinking is a way of life which makes students aware of the range of possible ways to confront problems. Critical thinking programs have to be long range in nature. Students do not learn thinking skills simply by employing them in an unguided manner, nor can skills be learned in one or two experiences. They have to be frequent and include feedback.

Critical thinking is not merely the province of schools. People continually sift through information in daily life and critically analyze situations. A daily drive in a car is an ongoing series of critical decisions as the driver anticipates the behavior of other cars and makes adjustments in order to avoid accidents. Clarke (1990) suggests that in any experience, people engage in several forms of thinking because our minds require organization and management of our encounters with situations. His categories of thinking include:

1. *Scanning and focusing*: People purposely search for meaningful information in their surrounding world. Driving a car requires continual scanning to identify potential problems or erratic driving upon the part of other drivers.

2. *Creating categories and classes*: Our mind clusters data rather than deal with each piece of information as a discrete piece of data. This can lead to stereotyping people because they have some of the characteristics associated with a particular category in our minds.

3. *Inducing propositions from facts:* People select a fact and place it into a larger framework of thinking. For example, you see a child run into the street after a ball, and immediately adjust your driving to take into consideration the consequences of continuing to drive your car in a straight line. Schools often overwhelm students with facts without linking them to broader propositions.

4. *Activating conceptual knowledge*: Most school information is based upon deductive reasoning. Students need experiences with inductive thought that moves them toward conceptual thinking.

5. *Predicting and planning*: The elementary school child is in the process of becoming a future thinker. They need experiences engaging in predicting and planning for future events and situations.

6. *Developing procedures*: Students need to learn a variety of problem-solving strategies to deal with their varied problems.

Students need to become aware of their own mental processes in order to become more adept at problem-solving. Left to their own devices, children may not seek to sharpen or refine their critical thinking capacities. When encountering problems or issues, it is easy to allow emotions, prejudices, or preconceived ways of thinking to assume control over the mind. It is the task of critical thinking programs to provide students more systematic ways of dealing with human complexity.

An important first step in fostering critical thinking is to improve students' abilities to ask questions and engage in classroom discussions that lead to more sophisticated reasoning skills. A good questioner is a good listener. A good questioner can move a discussion in the direction of critical thinking by stimulating new ways of perceiving information. Problem solvers begin by asking questions, not offering solutions. The development of refining questioning abilities within students is a key aspect of developing an effective critical thinking program.

It is equally important for teachers to be aware of ways in which the questions they pose guide thinking processes in the classroom. The way a teacher structures a question can influence the nature of thinking required to respond. A teacher who employs only one form of questioning limits the breadth of potential responses within a classroom. It is the purpose of this

▲ An important strategy to encourage critical thinking is the teacher's use of precise language in asking questions. *Courtesy University City (Missouri) Public Schools.*

▲ Critical thinking makes students aware of the range of possible ways to confront problems. *Courtesy Saint Louis (Missouri) Public Schools.*

chapter to offer a variety of strategies and techniques that extend the range of questions asked in classrooms.

The Art of Questioning

It is the questions teachers pose, not the answers they give, which live in the memory of students. A good question arouses curiosity, motivates learners to branch off in multiple directions, and challenges the mind to refashion the known in new ways. The manner and sequence in which teachers ask questions and handle student responses influences the quality of classroom discussion.

A question is an integral component in processing information. It initiates lines of associations moving in several directions which can produce helpful data. Good questions elicit from children higher levels of critical thinking by engaging them in the task of finding answers and seeking new roads for further investigation. An outstanding teacher knows the fine art of questioning which is the spur to imagination, the stimulus to thought, and the incentive to action.

Good questions aid students to become active listeners. A careful listener is attentive to learning and able to respect the integrity of all class members. A teacher who continually asks for simple recall questions of what has been taught deadens curiosity and produces conformity. Diversity is the lifeblood of creative thought, and it is essential in the questioning process.

Parents are amused or bewildered by the "why" questions of children. "Why is the sky blue?" or "Why is there only one moon?" Children bring to the elementary school classroom the capacity for imaginative questioning. This talent must be nourished and encouraged by teachers.

There are many reasons why teachers ask questions in class. These reasons simultaneously serve several purposes.

▲ An important first step in fostering critical thinking is to improve students' abilities to ask questions and engage in discussions. *Courtesy Saint Louis (Missouri) Public Schools.*

1. To encourage a particular student's participation in class work.
2. To find out what students know.
3. To get discussions going in a new direction.
4. To attract a student's attention.
5. To review what previously has been taught.
6. To serve as a springboard for the teacher to discuss a topic.
7. To stimulate creative thinking.
8. To pose a problem for class discussion.
9. To enable a student to shine before her peers.
10. To determine how a student or the class thinks aloud. (Hyman, 1962, pp. 2–4)

Forty years ago a committee of educators led by Benjamin Bloom created a widely used taxonomy of educational objectives. Questions, as well as behavioral objectives, can be classified

▲ **The questions teachers pose live in the memory of students.** *Courtesy Kirkwood (Missouri) School District.*

under this system. Studies based on Bloom's taxonomy indicate there is a strong relationship between the time it took for children to respond to questions and the taxonomic level. The higher the level of questions, the longer it took for students to answer.

It is not clear whether there is a hierarchical ordering of cognitive objectives or only a simple categorizing of cognitive processes with no rank ordering at all. Hence expressions such as "higher order" or "lower order" may be misleading. It is more significant for teachers to ask appropriate questions that elicit a variety of responses. Recall of information is as necessary as the ability to hypothesize or think in analytic terms.

Bloom's Taxonomy of the Cognitive Domain

Evaluation
Synthesis
Analysis
Application
Comprehension
Knowledge

Applying Bloom's Taxonomy to Social Studies

Cognitive Level	Sample Question
Evaluation:	* If you were in charge of energy policies, how would you allocate monies?
Synthesis:	* In which state's economy does oil make the greatest impact?
Analysis:	* Why do all oil companies seek to maximize their oil production?
Application:	* How does oil production affect the price you pay for the clothing you are wearing now?
Comprehension:	* What is the function of an oil rig?
Knowledge:	* How many states produce oil?

(Bloom, 1956)

Bloom's Taxonomy demonstrates that using different words in a question will elicit different responses. For example, "Would you like pizza for lunch?" can be changed to "What would be your dream topping on the pizza we are having today for lunch?" The former question calls for a one-word response, the latter entails more elaborate analysis by the student.

A properly worded sequence of questions stimulates interaction and active listening. Effective questions energize the natural curiosity of children and, in turn, make teachers and students better listeners. Outstanding teachers learn from children. Students learn from their peers as well as the teacher. But little is to be learned if the classroom consists only of memory work.

Following is an example of a sequence of questions on the topic of the American Revolution which makes an analogy between England as the mother country having a conflict with the American colonists, and student conflicts with parents.

1. Give me an example of what you and parents argue about.

    The question directs students to the idea of a family quarrel. This enables all to participate.

2. How many students have argued with parents about buying things? Give examples of how you argue with parents about homework, clothes, or staying up late at night.

    These questions direct students to think in terms of categories. This can lead toward the idea of multiple causation.

3. Assume you were King George III. What is one reason you would suggest to the colonists why rebellion would hurt their interests?

    This question requires some knowledge of the American Revolution. It is open ended so students can engage in hypothesis thinking.

4. Assume you were a colonist; give one reason you could provide King George why revolution is needed.

    This question is open-ended. To answer students must apply their knowledge in a creative way.

5. Assume you were a colonist; what is one argument you could advance to fellow colonists why revolution is wrong?

    This question compels students to understand there was diversity among Americans about the need to rebel.

6. How are the arguments advanced by King George and the colonists similar or different from the manner in which you argue with parents?

    This question enables students to establish connections between their lives and the American Revolution. It encourages all students to enter the class discussion.

Effective questioning requires extensive planning by teachers. A teacher must consider the knowledge base of students and utilize their life experiences to aid in the learning process. This moves the teacher away from the role of imparter of information to that of listener and coach.

At first, children may seem to prefer the safety of lessons which only require a "yes" or "no" answer to the challenge of engaging in speculative thinking which frequently results in multiple answers or none at all. Teachers must be sensitive that some students are hesitant to participate in open-ended thinking. This requires building trust levels and providing a classroom environment which encourages intellectual risk taking.

▲ A good question arouses curiosity. *Courtesy Webster Univeristy.*

A key factor in being an effective questioner is careful phrasing and planning what to ask. A skilled teacher follows several procedures in formulating questions to ensure appropriate wording:

1. Make questions clear and definite. An ambiguously worded question often leads to silence. For example: "Compare how the American navy fought in the Pacific and in Europe during World War II," is ambiguous while "How did naval support for fighting on islands in the Pacific compare with naval support for the army in Europe?" is more definite.

2. Make questions succinct. For example: "How did the burning of Washington D.C. in 1812 by the British affect the design or structure of the White House?" is clearer than "What happened after the British burned the White House in the War of 1812 and got the American people mad at them?"

3. Use vivid language. "Why did Teddy Roosevelt refer to Woodrow Wilson as having the "backbone of a chocolate eclair'?"

4. Adapt language to fit the audience. "Give me a reason why the North and South fought the Civil War," is more easily understood by elementary school children than, "What are the fundamental factors leading to conflict between the North and South?"

5. Avoid multiple questions. For example, "Abraham Lincoln changed his mind about slavery. How did he change, and why did people in the South become angry toward him?"

6. Avoid guessing questions. "What am I trying to get you to tell me about Thomas Jefferson?"

7. Avoid leading questions. "Do you really believe what you just said?"

8. Avoid fill in questions. "World War I began in. . . ."

9. Avoid annoying questions such as, "What else?" This can be rephrased as, "You just gave me one reason why women are more active in politics; please give me another reason."

▲ Good questions aid students to become active listeners. *Courtesy Null Elementary, Saint Charles (Missouri) Public Schools.*

It is not only the words we use, but our tone of voice, our body language, and our wait-time which determines if students will respond in creative ways to questions. Research indicates that many teachers only wait one second before repeating the question or calling on someone else to respond. An effective teacher waits approximately three to five seconds before taking other action. For example, if a student doesn't respond quickly, say, "Take a few seconds and think about what I asked." This encourages class participation and particularly helps the shy child.

Questioning Tips:

1. Make questions clear so that each child understands its meaning.
2. Avoid questions that trivialize the subject. For example, "How many people were present during the signing of the Constitution?"

3. See the question from the mind's eye of the child. For example, if the American Revolution is being discussed, consider the students' perspective; "What do children in my class know about a conflict between a mother country and its children?"

4. Clarify questions if you sense confusion in the class.

5. The greater the range of your knowledge of subject matter, the broader the range and depth of your questions.

6. Give students quality time to respond.

7. Link questions to the life experiences of children. For example, if studying the Pilgrims, consider their prior knowledge: "What do children in my class know about moving from a home to a new area?" This might lead to: "Could those of you in the class who moved from a different part of the country share with us how you felt being a stranger in a new neighborhood?"

▲ An effective teacher waits three to five seconds for a student to respond to an oral question. *Courtesy University City (Missouri) Public Schools.*

8. Encourage students to ask for additional information if it will assist in responding to your questions.

9. Let students know if there is more than one possible answer to the question.

10. Create a classroom environment in which a "failed answer" becomes a jumping-off place for new thinking. For example, "John just said that rap music was common during the Depression. Let's find out when and why rap music came about."

11. Hold the interest of the class by calling on a student *after* asking the question, not before.

12. Distribute questions among both volunteers and nonvolunteers. A nonvolunteer should not be made to feel harassed, and you can ask if they need further clarification of the question.

13. Encourage students who respond to questions, to direct their answer to the entire class rather than to the teacher.

14. Move your body toward the inattentive student, and if they are unable to answer, ask in a quiet tone if they need further help.

15. Audio or video tape your classroom, and analyze teacher-to-student and student-to-teacher questions.

16. Set aside a class period in which you do not ask a single recall question.

17. Analyze the questions in your textbooks. Alter several of the recall questions and turn them into questions which will stimulate discussion.

18. Analyze questions posed in a presidential press conference.

19. Maintain a file of interesting student questions.

20. Create an examination which does not have any recall questions.

Recall, Analytical, and Divergent Questions

Effective questioning techniques can transform the dynamics of classrooms. Each question asked by teachers affords new opportunities for students to engage in critical thought processes.

Fortunately, children are natural questioners, but this wondrous human instinct needs encouragement and support.

Numerous studies reveal that 90% of questions asked in school require students to recall information previously learned. Memory questions are important because teachers must know what students retain, and students need a data base in order to engage in higher levels of thinking. However, reliance solely upon recall of data will not enable students to engage in critical thinking.

Teachers must reconsider the type of questions being asked to bring diversity into the educative process. Let us illustrate this point by using a piece of history and demonstrating how utilization of a variety of questions makes for exciting learning.

"In August, 1492, Christopher Columbus sailed across the Atlantic Ocean in three ships. He reached the shores of the Western Hemisphere in October, 1492."

1. In what year did Columbus sail?

2. How many ships did he use

3. When did he reach the shores of the Western Hemisphere?

4. What was the name of the ocean he crossed?

These questions request specific information which the teacher or textbook has presented. There is only one answer for each question which precludes creative thought or discussion. The student either knows or doesn't know the answer.

The same information can be turned into an analytic thought question which requires comparing and contrasting information.

"Compare the explorations of Columbus with those of Lewis and Clark. What were the similarities and differences between both journeys?"

The same type of analytical questions can be asked younger children with a slight modification of wordage.

"Compare the voyage of Christopher Columbus to America with an example of when you moved from your old to a new neighborhood. How did Columbus and you encounter the same or different problems?"

The analytic form of questioning requires students to compare knowledge learned on two different occasions. The student is being asked to juxtapose two pieces of information which can create interesting images and extend the range of her levels of thinking.

"Compare Goldilocks taking things from the Three Bears with an example from your life in which you took something without asking permission."

Children enjoy analytic questions because there are many possible "right" or "wrong" answers. The teacher is more interested in the thinking process displayed by students than in their ability to state a predetermined set of answers. This provides students greater freedom to stretch their minds and examine new perspectives.

There are several expressions which lend themselves to analytical questions: "why," "explain," "give us the reason," "tell why you reached that conclusion," "what is the meaning," "tell us why you agree or disagree," "how do the things compare and contrast," or "what is the difference."

Another level of questioning lends itself to higher forms of critical thinking—divergent or hypothesis questions.

"Assume you were going on the first space ship to Mars; what would be your greatest concerns?"

After students discuss this question, the following question can be posed: How do your concerns compare to those of Columbus?

Hypothesis questioning opens an infinite variety of possibilities for students to consider. For example, the teacher might pursue the line of questions regarding voyages in this way: Assume you were on the Mayflower bound for America; what would you like to take along knowing that once you arrive it will be necessary to survive?

After students give their responses, they can do library research to gather information regarding what actually was taken on the Mayflower. Once the information is collected it can be utilized to compare and contrast what Columbus took or what astronauts take on a spaceship.

Divergent thinking frequently can be posed in a personalized question format: "Imagine you were a woman farming in North Dakota in the nineteenth century; how would concerns for your children be similar or different from those of an urban mother today?" Or "Your neighbors say that since they don't have children, they should not pay school taxes. How would you respond to that statement?"

Questioning techniques change the dynamics of a classroom. The teacher assumes the role of guide to critical thinking or becomes a stimulator of ideas. Students interact with one another and there are fewer teacher-to-student exchanges. The classroom becomes a laboratory of ideas in which both teacher and students explore the known in new ways and venture into the unknown as a collaborative team.

New Questions for Old Materials

The following pages contain materials that have been taught or can be taught as traditional recall of information. Ways to pose new questions that can stimulate students to engage in critical thinking processes are illustrated. The suggestions are merely examples, and we hope readers can uncover even more interesting ways to make these materials thought provoking.

Gettysburg Address

Fourscore and seven years ago our forefathers brought forth on this continent a new nation, conceived in liberty, and dedicated to the proposition that all men are created equal. Now we are engaged in a great civil war, testing whether that nation, or any nation so conceived and so dedicated, can long endure. We are met on a great battlefield of that war. We have come to dedicate a portion of that field, as a final resting-place for those who gave their lives that this nation might live. But, in a larger sense, we cannot dedicate—we cannot consecrate—we cannot hallow—this ground. The brave men, living and dead, who struggled here, have consecrated it, far above our poor power to add or detract. The world will little note, nor long remember, what we say here, but it can never forget what they did here. It is for us the living rather, to be dedicated here to the unfinished work which they who fought here have thus far so nobly advanced. It is rather for us to be here dedicated to the great task remaining before us, that from these honored dead we take increased devotion to that cause for which they gave the last full measure of devotion; that we here highly resolve that these dead shall not have died in vain; that this nation, under God, shall have a new birth of freedom; and that government of the people, by the people, for the people, shall not perish from the earth.

1. What can you tell about the nature, form, values, and beliefs of the society in which the author of this document lived by just relying upon information in this paragraph? For each statement you make, give the specific reference in the paragraph which led you to make your comment.
2. What can you tell about the author of this document by just relying on information in this paragraph? What do you know about the author's personality or values?

General Braddock's Defeat

James Grahame, *The History of the United States of North America* (1846, pp. 244–245).

Filled with that pride which goes before destruction, Braddock commenced his march from Will's Creek, on the 10th of June at the head of about two thousand two hundred men . . . After a laborious progress, which was still unnecessarily retarded, and yet unaccompanied by the precaution of reconnoitring the woods, Braddock arrived at the Monongahela on the eighth of July.

Francis Parkman, *Montcalm and Wolfe* (1899, pp. 212–213).

It was the tenth of June before the army was well on its march. Three hundred axemen led the way, to cut and clear the road: and the long train of packhorses, wagons, and cannon toiled on behind, over the stumps, roots, and stones of the narrow track, the regulars and provincials marching in the forest close on either side. Squads of men were thrown out on the flanks, and scouts ranged the woods to guard against surprise: for with all his scorn of the Indians and Canadians, Braddock did not neglect reasonable precautions. Thus, foot by foot, they advanced into the waste of lonely mountains that divided the streams flowing to the Atlantic from those flowing to the Gulf of Mexico—a realm of forests ancient as the world. The road was but twelve feet wide, and the line of march often extended four miles. It was like a thin, long parti-colored snake, red, blue, and brown, trailing slowly through the depths of leaves, creeping around inaccessible heights, crawling over ridges, moving always in dampness and shadow, by rivulets, and waterfalls, crags and chasms, gorges and shaggy steps.

1. On which points do both authors agree?
2. List those points on which the authors disagree?
3. How does the style of writing influence what and how you learn?

Japanese Haiku Poems

The Beginning

Spring starts:
new year; old rice
five quarts.

You Unknown Flower

To bird and butterfly
unknown, a flower blooms:
the autumn sky.

Autumn Leave

To Lord Taba's hall
    five or six horsemen hurry hard—
        a storm-wind of fall.

On the Road to Nara

Oh, these spring days!
    A nameless little mountain;
        Wrapped in morning hazel.

1. What can you tell about geographical characteristics of the society which produced these poems?
2. By reading these poems, what can you tell about people, products, animals, etc. in this society?
3. By reading these poems, what can you tell about the governmental structure of this society?
4. How are the authors' way of perceiving or describing the world similar or different from that of an American?

(Henderson, 1958)

Student-Initiated Questioning

A recurring theme in developing critical thinking is empowering students to initiate topics to be studied. As long as adults ask questions or suggest issues, students are passive recipients rather than active investigators. In a successful critical thinking program, students formulate what is to be examined, and influence how the process unfolds.

▲ Student-initiated questioning develops a sense of mastery and shifts leadership to students. *Courtesy Webster University.*

Student-initiated questioning develops a sense of mastery and shifts leadership to students. Students may not be accustomed to sharing responsibility with teachers in determining which questions willl focus classroom discussion. A teacher's role changes in student-initiated questioning. Teachers become a source of information, a guide to resources, and a colleague in the joint quest for knowledge.

A student-initiated questioning program best proceeds in small steps allowing students to gain confidence in their capacities to raise questions and guide discussion. The questions posed in May should be of higher quality and involve a greater number of participants than in September. Following are examples of techniques to move students toward greater control of the questioning process.

Party Games can be used to introduce students to questioning techniques.

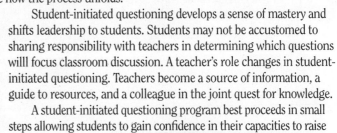

A is dead, there is broken glass and water on the floor, the room has bars on the window, and the door is locked from the inside. Your task is to find out what happened. You may ask any question that has a yes or no answer on my part. If you ask the right questions you will be able to reconstruct the story (the actual story is about a cat who crawled through the bars, overturned a fishbowl, and killed the fish).

Twenty Questions is another technique that both adults and children enjoy. Students could be paired and asked to develop a topic for a session on Twenty Questions. The Twenty Question topic can be related to current events or something being studied in social studies.

It is important when using these techniques to provide ample time for students to debrief the process. They have to become conscious of how questions must be organized in order to be used effectively. The danger is that the "game" becomes the object rather than analytical thinking.

There are many ways to incorporate questions in existing curriculum in order to foster questioning skills. For example:

- Which questions could Little Red Riding Hood have asked to determine if the wolf was or was not her grandmother?
- Which questions could Dorothy have asked the Wizard of Oz to determine if he could help her return home?
- Which questions should the seven Dwarfs have asked Snow White to determine if she should live with them?
- Students could create a questionnaire for parents or grandparents in order to learn about the past—what was school like when they were children?
- A class meeting can be held prior to a visit by a guest speaker in order to put together questions which assist in learning.
- A weekly class meeting in which students develop questions to pose the teacher to learn more about what will be studied in the future and why.
- Students put together questions to ask people around the school—the custodian, a secretary the principal, etc . . . The object is to learn about their work.
- Students can create mini questionnaires to send in the mail to people. The object is to learn specific things rather than engage in general questioning.
- Students can create a questionnaire that might be put together by a Martian sociologist who wants to learn about the Earth and its people.
- Students can create a questionnaire to send children in another country to learn about their lives.

The Cherry Tree Story

One day in the garden where he often amused himself hacking his mother's pea sticks he unluckily tried the edge of his hatchet on the body of a beautiful young English cherry-tree which he barked so terribly that I don't believe the tree ever got the better of it. The next morning the old gentleman, finding out what had befallen his tree, which by the way was a great favorite, came into the house; and with much warmth asked for the mischievous author, declaring at the same time that he would not have taken five guineas for his tree. Nobody would tell him anything about it. Presently George and his hatchet made their appearance. "George," said to his father, "do you know who killed that beautiful little cherry tree yonder in the garden?" This was a tough question; and George staggered under it for a moment, but quickly recovered himself, and looking at his father with the sweet face of youth brightened with the inexpressible charm of all conquering truth, he bravely cried out: "I can't tell a lie, pa; you know I can't tell a lie. I did cut it with my hatchet." (Weems, 1909)

- Assume you were a detective who has been called in to determine if the Cherry Tree story is historically accurate. Your task is to organize a set of questions to pose an historian in order to determine the historical accuracy of the story.

For example:

1. Where is the first written record of the story?
2. Who wrote the first account of the story?
3. What is the date of the story's first appearance in print?

Good questions can be found in every aspect of life. A photograph, picture or cartoon in a magazine can be used to pose questions. Following is an example of a simple cartoon. Students can be asked: "What question is one alien posing to the other? "After students provide some questions, they can be asked to make up answers to the questions.

▲ A cartoon or picture can be used as a basis for questioning: "What question is one alien posing to the other?"

The use of effective questions expands the possibility for analytical and divergent thinking in the classroom. Teachers and children are happier when students engage vigorously in discussions. Young children want to share their ideas, but need questions that stimulate their natural inquisitiveness and wonder.

Organizing the Questioning Process

Outstanding teachers reflect before asking questions in order to be clear about the focus of class discussion. After 10 or 20 years of practice, these individuals appear to have an instinctive grasp of questioning. A novice teacher, however, has to begin in a well-organized and conscious manner. The story "Goldilocks and the Three Bears" will be used to demonstrate a method of questioning that encourages analytic and divergent thinking.

TOPIC: Goldilocks and the Three Bears

KEY ISSUES:

1. Family life of the three bears.

2. Breaking and entering without permission.

3. Animal rights.

4. Private property.

5. Punishment for wrong doing.

ISSUE: Breaking and entering without permission.
RECALL QUESTIONS:

1. Who owned the house that Goldilocks entered?

2. Why did the occupants of the house leave?

3. Why did Goldilocks enter the house?

4. What did Goldilocks find in the house?

5. What happened after the Bears returned?

ANALYTIC QUESTIONS:

1. Have you ever taken something from a brother, sister, or friend without asking permission? Why did you do this?

2. How do you feel when someone takes something from you without permission? How would the reaction of the Bears be the same or different from your feeling?

3. What would be the strongest argument Goldilocks could state to defend her behavior? Her weakest argument?

DIVERGENT QUESTIONS:

1. What would have been the reaction of Goldilocks if the Bears had come to her house and taken things without permission?

2. Imagine that you were walking by the house of your friend and saw a fire in the window. Would it be OK to enter the house without permission to warn the people?

3. Imagine that the Three Bears took Goldilocks to court and asked that she be punished. How would the jury and judge rule?

● ●

CASE STUDY

TOPIC: Snow White and the Seven Dwarfs

KEY ISSUES:

1. _____

_____

2. _____

_____

3. _____

_____

4. _____

_____

5. _____

_____

ISSUE: _____

_____

RECALL QUESTIONS:

1. _____

_____

2. _____

_____

3. _____

_____

4. _____

_____

ANALYTIC QUESTIONS:

1. _____

_____

2. _____

_____

3. _____

_____

DIVERGENT QUESTIONS:

1. _____

_____

2. _____

_____

3. _____

_____

SUMMARY

This chapter has focused upon the relationship between questioning and critical thinking. It presented several strategies for using new forms of questioning in order to elicit higher levels of thinking.

QUESTIONS

1. What do you prefer most about being asked recall questions? What do you like least about such questions?

2. As a student or teacher, which type of questions do you most frequently ask in class? Which type of questions do you avoid asking?

3. What is most interesting about applying Bloom's Taxonomy to the questioning process?

4. Do you agree or disagree with the authors that children prefer the safety of "yes" or "no" responses? Why are such answers safe?

5. What would be your greatest challenge in posing analytic or divergent questions?

6. How did the authors' suggestions for teaching the Gettysburg Address alter your view of the document?

7. What is most intriguing about using new questions for old materials as suggested in this chapter? What would you find difficult about using this method?

8. What would be your greatest concern about encouraging student-initiated questions? What do you like most about this process?

9. What process do you follow in organizing questioning? Do you have prepared questions or do you make them up as you go along?

10. What are the most interesting insights into questioning that you learned in this chapter?

ACTIVITIES

1. Write down every question a teacher asks in one of your classes and categorize them.

2. Create a mini-lesson using only analytic or divergent questions.

3. Have yourself taped while teaching children. Analyze the questions you posed students.

4. Spend one hour on a playground. Write down every question posed by children. Categorize the questions.

5. Analyze questions in a textbook. What percent are analytic, and what percent are divergent questions?

6. Select a fairy tale, and create new questions for it.

7. Tape a portion of a presidential press conference. Analyze the questions posed by reporters.

8. Obtain test questions from teachers at elementary, secondary, and college levels. Analyze and categorize the questions.

READING

A New Framework for Developing Classroom Questions
by Roberta M. Woolever

An accepted goal for social studies education is to teach thinking skills (National Council for the Social Studies 1984). The most widely used method to achieve this goal has been teacher-developed questions designed to stimulate students to use different mental processes, such as the six levels of cognitive outcomes in Bloom's taxonomy (Beyer 1984).

As noted by Beyer, the use of a variety of questions by the teacher does not in itself teach students how to think, but it can provide them with opportunities to practice thinking skills and opportunities for the teacher to evaluate their skill development. This article acknowledges the limited—but still useful—role of classroom questions in developing students' thinking abilities.

Evidence to date generally supports the use of higher cognitive questions by teachers as a means to stimulate higher-level thinking and increase student achievement (Gall 1984). Left to their own devices, however, teachers typically ask only low-level, fact-recall questions (Davis and Tinsley 1967; Gall 1970; Gallagher 1965; Hare and Pulliam 1980).

It has proven difficult to change teacher questioning behavior; studies of the *immediate* effects of *prolonged* training in questioning strategies—based on Bloom's taxonomy or Guilford's structure of intellect—have documented only limited changes in teachers' classroom behavior (Winnie 1979).

A New Approach to Developing Classroom Questions

Given the role of teacher questions in promoting student thinking and achievement and the minimal effect over the last two decades of teacher training based on Bloom's taxonomy or Guilford's model, alternative models should be explored.

One such option is the framework of children's language use developed by Joan Tough (1976, 1977a, 1977b, 1982). Working in England, Tough did a longitudinal observational study of children, aged 3 to 7½ years, in classroom settings, in which she recorded their spontaneous use of language. Tough's naturalistic observations of children's verbal behavior resulted in a framework of seven categories based on the *function* for which language was used. Tough's categories have subsequently been validated by Staab (1984) for analyzing the spontaneous language use of children in the United States.

While thought and speech are not the same, noted Russian psychologist L. S. Vygotsky (1962) concluded that the development of language in children cannot be separated from their intellectual development and that verbal intercourse with adults is a powerful factor in their cognitive development. Thus, insofar as teachers ask questions that require students to use language for a variety of functions, they also stimulate students to use a variety of mental processes.

Application of Tough's framework when developing classroom questions also has merit as a means for promoting educational equity. When Tough (1977a, 1982) studied children from two divergent socioeconomic groups, she found group differences reflected in the proportions of the various language categories used. Children from the low socioeconomic group used language less frequently to predict and consider alternative possibilities, to project into the lives of others, and for imaginative play. With effective training, teachers could use questions to elicit a full range of thinking and language use by all pupils, regardless of background.

The remainder of this article describes Tough's framework of children's language use and suggests how it can be used as the basis for developing a classroom questioning strategy.

Tough's Framework

Tough's framework is not a taxonomy. Each of the seven categories represents a different function or purpose for which children spontaneously use language; the categories are not ordered into a hierarchy from simple to complex, with each more complex behavior dependent on the ability to perform the lower-order behaviors. The categories are not mutually exclusive; it is not possible that the same utterance may, in a different situation, serve a different function. Tough's (1976, 1977a) categories are described and illustrated below.

1. For *self-maintaining,* children use language to protect or assert their own interests. Language may be used to state needs or wants, to justify behavior, or to criticize or threaten others. For example:

"I get to have the first turn on the computer today."

"If you don't stop bothering me, I'll tell the teacher."

2. For *directing,* children use language to monitor their own actions, to give instructions to themselves or others, or to plan collaborative action. With younger children, the directing function may frequently take the form of a monologue and appear not to be dependent upon the presence of a listener.

"As soon as I finish my math worksheet, I need to hurry to the social studies center."

"You check the encyclopedia under 'George Washington' and I'll check under 'U.S. Presidents'."

3. For *reporting,* language is used to label components or details of a picture, scene, situation, or incident; to refer to a sequence of events; to make comparisons; to recognize related aspects; to make an analysis of several aspects; to recognize the central meaning; and to reflect on the meaning of one's own experiences or feelings. In essence, the student reports what she or he has read, heard, seen, experienced, or felt.

"The area of California is approximately the same as that of Japan."

"The book I read was about the difficulties of growing up as a member of a minority group."

"I felt sorry for the Native Americans who were killed or driven off their land by the European settlers."

4. For *logical reasoning,* children use language to explain a process, recognize causal and dependent relationships, identify problems and alternative solutions, justify judgments and actions, draw conclusions from general principles, and form concepts and generalizations. In logical reasoning the child goes beyond the facts—beyond who, where, when, what next, or how much—and explains why, how, or what makes me think so. The child may also deduce conclusions from general rules (as in recognizing examples and nonexamples of concepts) or induce the general rule from the particular (as in Taba strategy for "discovery" of concepts).

"If you find a dollar bill on the playground, then you can decide to keep it, try to find the owner, turn it in to your teacher, or just leave it on the ground."

"I think that the use of seat belts by car drivers and passengers should be required by law because it will save lives but not cost much money."

"Based on the five cultures we studied, we can conclude that all people are faced with the problem of unlimited wants and limited resources."

5. For *predicting*, language is used to anticipate or forecast events, details of events, or a sequence of events; to anticipate problems and possible solutions; to anticipate alternative courses of action; and to predict the possible consequences of events or actions. The essence of predicting is to anticipate the unknown. While predictions ideally involve the use of logical reasoning to arrive at an informed forecast of what might come to be, this category may also include wild guesses.

"I think that we are soon going to face the problem of a shortage of good farmland."

"I think that the salt and flour map that we are making will fall apart if we don't add more water to our mixture."

6. For *projecting*, language is used to say what one believes other people or things (nonhumans or inanimate objects) feel, think, or would like to have or do. Projecting may also be used by children to speculate on what they would feel, think, or like to have or do in a hypothetical situation. The essence of projecting is to empathize, to put oneself in another person's place. Projection—like prediction—m ay be the product of rash, rather than reflective, judgments.

"I think that she must have felt very sad and lonely when no one talked to her on the first day of school."

"I think that a sled dog must be very happy at the end of the day to get some food and rest."

"If I were an ocean, I would want to be the Pacific so that I would be warm and have tropical islands and colorful fishes."

7. In *imagining*, language is used to make up or act out an imaginary story or situation. In the context of an imaginary situation, children may use language for each of the other six functional categories. Examples of this category should be self-evident; they might spontaneously occur in a dramatic play or block center or in creative writing.

Using Tough's Framework to Develop a Questioning Strategy

Teachers can learn to use Tough's framework to develop a questioning strategy to stimulate students to engage in a variety of cognitive processes and to use language for a diversity of purposes. The first step is to understand Tough's categories and the ability to use the framework to correctly classify sample questions. The next step is to gain skill in developing questions that can be expected to elicit language use in each category. The final step is to implement a classroom questioning strategy that includes an optimal proportion of each of the categories in the framework.

A description of the seven categories has already been presented. In our experience, teachers need use only four of the seven categories—reporting, logical reasoning, predicting, and projecting—to develop a variety of questions for use in teaching reading or the content areas (see Harms, Woolever, and Brice 1986). The other three functional categories (self-maintaining, directing, and imagining) are of little use in developing classroom questions to follow up on material taught by strategies such as lecture, textbook, newspaper article, direct observation, role play, or simulation activity.

First, check your knowledge of Tough's framework by classifying the questions in Figure 1. While the questions in Figure 1 were selected as reasonably clear-cut examples, it is by no means necessary that a teacher be able to classify questions (or student responses) with 100 percent accuracy in order to benefit from training in Tough's framework. The goal is to ask a *diversity* of questions to stimulate thinking and language use for a variety of purposes; it is generally not important that a particular question, asked at a given moment, be of a particular type.

Without specific training, teachers can be expected to ask primarily reporting questions. In one study of 58 elementary student teachers who had not yet been trained in Tough's framework, the average proportion of each type of question asked to total questions asked during a 20- to 30-minute discussion lesson, was as follows (Harms, Woolever, and Brice 1987):

85.7%—Reporting
9.8%—Logical reasoning
3.2%—Predicting
1.4%—Projecting

Such a restriction to the almost exclusive use of reporting questions by teachers places concomitant restriction on the range of children's thinking and language use in school.

The second step in training to ask a diversity of questions is to practice developing questions based on a hypothetical or anticipated

---

Figure 1
Classifying Teachers' Questions

Classify each of the following questions as to the expected category of Tough's framework of an appropriate student response.

___ 1. What was this newspaper article about?

___ 2. How do you think the sheep felt when it was being sheared by the cowboy?

___ 3. What do you think our governor will do next?

___ 4. What makes you think that the story takes place in Africa?

___ 5. If you were an anthropologiest, where in the world would you most like to go to do fieldwork?

___ 6. What might be some negative consequences of the president's choice to fill the vacancy on the Supreme Court?

___ 7. (Follow-up to question 6) Why?

Answer Key for Figure 1

1. Reporting (the central meaning)
2. Projecting (into the feelings of a nonhuman)
3. Predicting (an event)
4. Logical reasoning (to draw conclusions)
5. Projecting (into one's own desires in a situation never experienced)
6. Predicting (to anticipate problems)
7. Logical reasoning (to justify opinion)

learning experience in which students take in new information. This could include, but not be limited to, taking a field trip, reading or listening to a story or newspaper article, looking at a picture, observing or participating in an experiment, listening to a lecture, reading a textbook, or viewing a film.

To maximize the likelihood of asking a diversity of questions, the teacher should, after selecting the material to be taught and considering the needs and abilities of the students, establish a target *proportion* of questions from each of the four categories. For example, one teacher might establish as a goal to ask 65 percent reporting questions, 15 percent logical reasoning, 10 percent predicting, and 10 percent projecting, while a teacher working with a different group of students might decide to ask 30 percent reporting questions, 30 percent logical reasoning, 20 percent predicting, and 20 percent projecting.

At this time, there is no empirical evidence to help one select the *optimal* proportion of each type of question. In each of the examples above, the teacher would ask a diversity of questions that is not characteristic of an untrained teacher.

Finally, the teacher must be committed to routinely asking questions in all categories. Knowledge of Tough's framework and skill in classifying and developing questions are of little use if teachers do not change their classroom questioning behavior. As reported by Harms, Woolever, and Brice (1987), preservice teachers can be taught the framework—including practice in classifying examples of children's statements, classifying examples of teachers' questions, and developing appropriate questions in each category from a picture or text selection—in just two hours.

Six weeks after a two-hour training session, elementary student teachers (who were not informed that they were being observed for questioning strategies) asked significantly fewer reporting questions and significantly more logical reasoning and predicting questions when compared to a group of untrained student teachers. The proportion of projecting questions was also greater for the trained student teachers, but the difference was not significant.

Summary and Conclusions

We need not make an either/or choice. Teacher knowledge of Tough's framework, Bloom's taxonomy, and Guilford's model may be the ideal. But given the limited impact of teacher training in Bloom's taxonomy and Guilford's model over the last 20 years, it seems worthwhile to explore the relative effect of training in Tough's framework. Tough's framework is based on children's spontaneous use of language and groups utterances into seven functional categories. Only four categories need be used as the basis for a comprehensive questioning strategy.

References

Beyer, B. 1984. "Improving Thinking Skills—Defining the Problem." *Phi Delta Kappan* 65: 486–90.

Davis, O. L., Jr., and D. Tinsley. 1967. "Cognitive Objectives Revealed by Classroom Questions Asked by Social Studies Student Teachers." *Peabody Journal of Education*. 45: 21–26.

Gall, M. 1970. "The Use of Questions in Teaching." *Review of Educational Research* 40: 707–21.

———— 1984. "Synthesis of Research on Teachers' Questioning." *Educational Leadership* 42: 40–47.

Gallagher, J. 1965. "Expressive Thought by Gifted Children in the Classroom." *Elementary English* 42: 559–68.

Hare, V. C., and C. A. Pulliam. 1980. "Teacher Questioning: A Verification and Extension." *Journal of Reading Behavior* 12: 69–72.

Harms, T., R. Woolever, and R. Brice. 1986. "A Questioning Strategies Training Sequence Based on Language Use Categories." Unpublished manuscript. School of Education. University of North Carolina at Chapel Hill (27514).

National Council for the Social Studies. 1984. "In Search of a Scope and Sequence for Social Studies." *Social Education* 48: 249–62.

Staab, C. 1984. "Yes, Tough's Categories Do Work." *Educational Review* 36: 17–25.

Tough, J. 1976. *Listening to Children Talking: A Guide to the Appraisal of Children's Use of Language.* London: Ward Lock Educational, Ltd.

———. 1977a. *The Development of Meaning: A Study of Children's Use of Language.* New York: John Wesley & Sons.

———. 1977b. *Talking and Learning: A Guide to Fostering Communication Skills in Nursery and Infant Schools.* London: Ward Lock Educational, Ltd.

———. 1982. "Language, Poverty, and Disadvantage in School." In *The Language of Children Reared in Poverty,* ed. L. Feagans and D. Ferran. New York: Academic Press.

Vygotsky, L. 1962. *Thought and Language.* Cambridge: MIT Press.

Winne, P. 1979. "Experiments Relating Teachers' Use of Higher Cognitive Questions to Student Achievement." *Review of Educational Research* 49: 13–50.

Roberta M. Woolever is an associate professor in the Division of Teaching and Learning of the School of Education at the University of North Carolina at Chapel Hill.

QUESTIONS ON READING

1. What are the seven categories of children's language according to Tough?

2. After listing questions asked by a teacher in college, secondary or elementary school, fit them into Tough's classification system.

3. What is the greatest difficulty using Tough's classification system to organize the questioning process?

LESSON PLAN

Ms. Vicki Kahlert

Objective: Developing problem solving skills in children.

Rationale: Students need specific strategies and techniques to deal with solving problems.

Activities:

1. Teacher arranges to have argument with another teacher. Students overhear the argument.
   - Teacher asks students: "What were the main things I argued about with Ms. Jones? Were we able to solve our problems? Did we listen to one another's ideas?"
   - Teacher asks each student to give an example of an argument they had with someone else that was not resolved. Class takes one example and brain storms several ways the problem could have been solved.

2. Teacher presents a problem solving method to students:
   1. Stop and think (take a deep breath).
   2. Identify the key issue in the problem.
   3. What do I see? What are the facts?
   4. Alternatives: What are several ways to solve this problem?
   5. What are the consequences?

3. Teacher shows several episodes of a TV show and halts the video before resolution of the problem. Students brainstorm ways to resolve the problem. Then watch how the TV program handled the conflict.

4. Teacher shows videos of cartoon shows with problems. Again students brainstorm ideas and compare.
   - Teacher hands out "Robbie Raccoon" letters from the Weekly Reader. These letters are from real problem situations faced by students in school. Students in group are each given a situation and asked to come up with a solution. The group is to follow the methodology presented by the teacher.

5. Read the story *Snow White* and discuss what things could really have happened in the story (facts) and what was probably fantasy. Teacher leads a discussion about fact and fantasy in our life and how they get mixed up in an argument.
   - Teacher asks students to list things that could not happen—a pumpkin turning into a coach or a mirror speaking.
   - Students divided into pairs. One pair makes up a list of statements containing facts and fantasy. The other pair have to decide which is which.
   - Each student makes a list of facts about self and fantasies. The list is presented to a classmate who has to decide which is which.

6. Teacher presents four person group with a situation drawn from the *Weekly Reader.* Each group is to present their situation to the class, but with two endings. One ending results in the problem still going on and one ending resolves it.

7. Students role play fairy tales like *Jack and the Beanstalk,* and the class discusses several ways in which problems could have been resolved.

8. Teacher shows class situations from the *Peanuts* comic strip. Each group gets a comic strip sequence and has to role play another way to resolve the situation.

9. Students in groups identify a conflict situation they have faced. The situation is to be role played and the class has the task of identifying a positive resolution of the conflict.

Bibliography:

Adrent, Ruth, (1992) *Trust Building With Children Who Hurt: A One-to-One Support Program for Children Ages 5–14.* New York: The Center for Applied Research in Education.

Freed, Alvyn, (1974) *TA for Kids . . . and Grown-Ups Too!* California: Price/Stern/Sloan Publishers.

Goldstein, Arnold, (1988) *The Prepare Curriculum.* Illinois: Research Press.

Vernon, Ann, (1989) *Thinking, Feeling, Behaving: An Emotional Education Curriculum, Grades 1–6,* Illinois, Research Press.

REFERENCES

Beyer, B. (1983, November). Educational Leadership, *41*(3), pp. 44–49.

Bloom, B. (1956). *Taxonomy of educational objectives.* New York: Longman, Green.

Clarke, J. H. (1990). *Patterns of thinking.* Boston: Allyn & Bacon.

Everwine, P. (1970). *In the house of light: Thirty Aztec poems translated by Peter Everwine.* Iowa City, IA: Stone Wall Press.

Fuson, R. (1987). *The log of Christopher Columbus.* Camden, NJ: International Marine Publishing.

Henderson, H. (1958). *An introduction to haiku.* New York: Doubleday.

Hyman, R. (1962). *Strategic questioning.* New York: Prentice Hall.

Parkman, F. (1899). *Montcalm and Wolfe.* Boston: Little Brown.

Sandler, W., & Whimbey, A. (1985, November). A holistic approach to improving thinking skills. *Phi Delta Kappan, 63*(3) pp. 199–203.

Sigel, I. (1984, November). A constructionist perspective for teaching thinking. *Educational Leadership, 42*(3) pp. 18–22.

Sternberg, R. (1987, February). "Teaching critical thinking: Eight Easy Ways to Fail Before You Begin." *Phi Delta Kappan, 68*(6) pp. 456–59.

Sternberg, R. (1985, November). *Phi Delta Kappan, 67*(3) pp. 194–98.

Weems, M. L. (1809). *The Life of George Washington.* Philadelphia: Mathew Carey.

SUGGESTED READING

Clarke, J. (1990). *Patterns of thinking,* Boston: Allyn & Bacon.

Collins, C. and Mangieri, J. *Teaching thinking.* Hillsdale, NJ: Lawrence Erlbaum.

Heiman, M. (Ed.). (1987). *Thinking skills instruction: Concepts and techniques.* Washington, DC: NEA.

Hyman, R. *Strategic questioning.* Englewood Cliffs, NJ: Prentice Hall.

Sanders, M. (1966). *Classroom questions: What kinds?* New York: Harper & Row.

Sund, R. *Creative questioning.* Columbus, OH: Charles Merrill.

Sternberg, R. (1977). *Intelligence, information processing and analogical reasoning.* New York: Halstead.

Wasserman, S. *Teaching for thinking.* New York: Teachers College Press.

Chapter 7

Creative Thinking in Social Studies

Creative Thinking in the Social Studies

This chapter offers a rationale for the importance of creative thinking skills in the elementary social studies curriculum and provides strategies to implement this form of thought process in the daily life of the classroom. All children are capable of creative thinking; the challenge is to translate this abstract theory into the specificity of a lesson plan. An event such as the American Revolution can be taught as recall of information, or it can become the vehicle for creative thinking.

An important component of creative thinking is mental flexibility. A rigid approach to any form of problem delimits the opportunities to uncover alternative ways of exploration. Creative problem-solving entails mental "play" in order to free the mind from mental constructs of preconceived ways of examining situations. In this chapter the influence of a humorous perspective will be emphasized as another strategy to direct students into creative thinking processes.

Creative Problem Solving

Creative thinking is the ability to identify new patterns within existing information. Creative thinkers break out of stereotypical patterns and generate new ways of looking at experience. The capacity to diverge from normal thought patterns is found in people from all walks of life. A mechanic, a baker, a scientist, an athlete, or a teacher can each become the catalyst for formulating new ways of performing the tasks required by their occupations.

Creative problem solving abilities are not restricted to children with high IQs, but are present in many students. Ever since Aristotle, logic has been regarded as the best way to solve problems. However, creative problem solvers use a host of approaches, some logical, and others that turn logic upside down. The individual who took a rock, termed it a "pet rock" and sold it for several dollars was a creative thinker. Everyone has come across inventions that seem simple. These are the ideas which elicit the comment: "Why didn't I think of that before?"

Edward de Bono, who coined the term "lateral thinking," points out the fallacy of logical thought processes in dealing with crime. Logic argues for higher police budgets in order to reduce crime rates. De Bono (1968) believes this logical solution leads to the reverse of its goal. Increasing police budgets causes more crime! The presence of more police enables more criminals to be caught, more people to report criminals, more trials, the need for more jails, and

▲ All children are capable of creative thinking. *Courtesy University City (Missouri) Public Schools.*

more taxes to pay for increased expenses. He argues for a "reverse" solution which focuses upon decriminalizing certain categories of crime such as gambling or increasing the speed limit.

There is an old folktale about a merchant who was deeply in debt to a money-lender. The merchant had a beautiful daughter who the moneylender wanted to marry. The moneylender suggested a bargain. He would place a black pebble and a white pebble into a bag. If the girl selected the black pebble she would marry him and her father's debt would be canceled. If she chose the white pebble, her father's debt would be canceled, but she would not have to marry the moneylender. If she refused to pick a pebble, her father would be jailed.

The girl and her father agreed to the bargain. The girl noticed that the money-lender picked two black pebbles from the pebble-strewn path, and placed them in the bag. He then asked the girl to select a pebble. What were the girl's alternatives?

1. She could refuse to select a pebble. In that case, her father went to jail.
2. She could open the bag and expose the money-lender as a cheat. Her father would still go to jail.
3. She could take a black pebble and marry the money-lender.

In this case, the girl found a creative solution. She placed her hand in the bag, fumbled with the pebble and dropped it among the pebbles on the path. She then said: "Look inside the bag. I obviously selected the opposite of whichever pebble is left."

Creative "thinking" encompasses a wide variety of human thought processes. Sometimes, it refers to genuine creations; at other times it is nothing more than combining things in new ways. Creative problem solving in schools most often relates to helping young people view existing problems through the perspective of a new lens.

The task of creative thinking is educating children to approach problem solving with a different attitude and mind set. Teachers will be successful in fostering creative thinking to the extent they are willing to allow a temporary ban on logical thought, and allow time for creative play with ideas. For example, in studying about frontier life, students can speculate about the West's future if there had been no demand for buffalo fur among the settlers or Europeans.

A great many new ideas come about when new information gathered by observation compels a reappraisal of old patterns of thought. Although new information can lead to new ideas, solutions to problems can also come about without years of hard work or any new information at all.

Albert Einstein did no experiments, and gathered no new information before he created the theory of relativity. He looked at the existing information which everyone else was content to fit into the Newtonian structure, and put it together in a different way. The airplane was developed by two bicycle mechanics. There is a capacity for generating new ideas that is better developed in some people than in others. This ability is not related to sheer intelligence but emerges from people who have a particular habit of mind, and an interesting way of thinking.

Depression era children in New York created footballs by rolling up discarded newspapers. The famous Notre Dame football coach, Knute Rockne, was relaxing at a vaudeville show when he got the idea of training his backs to move in a cadence just like the dancers on stage. The "T"

▲ Creative thinking is the ability to identify new patterns within existing information. *Courtesy University City (Missouri) Public Schools.*

▲ Creative thinking sometimes refers to genuine creations.
Courtesy Saint Louis (Missouri) Public Schools.

▲ Teachers must allow time for creative play. *Courtesy Saint Louis (Missouri) Public Schools.*

formation was created by moving the quarterback a few steps forward behind the center. It took basketball 40 years before someone got the idea of shooting with one hand, and another person built on that development to create the jump shot.

In years past, Eskimos depended upon seal meat, blubber, and skin for survival. Seals keep breathing holes open in the ice, and although they can remain underwater for long periods of time they eventually have to come to the surface to make use of these holes. Eskimos waited by the hole with spear in hand, but seals had excellent hearing. The seals remained underwater when they heard the sound of hunters approaching.

This used to be a life and death problem for Eskimos. They solved the dilemma by restructuring the environment. Two men walked to the breathing hole, keeping in step. One man stopped and the other went on. The seal heard the man who departed and assumed the coast was clear. The seal surfaced only to find death at the hands of a creative problem solver.

Fostering creativity in children requires teachers to adopt a different frame of reference within the classroom. Children will not openly express their creative capacities unless the environment encourages them to express ideas freely. Creative thinkers make many mistakes before finally reaching their goals. Failure is a necessary component in moving toward the new. Children need opportunities to fail in productive ways if creativity is to emerge.

Our preoccupation with practicality hinders the nurturing of creativity. The creative process requires time, and it does not readily lend itself to worksheets and sequential testing. President Franklin Roosevelt could not order scientists to deliver an atomic bomb by a certain date. Creative thought is akin to gardening. One must nurture the buds, feed them with healthy nutrients, and await the blossoming which comes in the spring. Teachers who pose problems requiring creative thought must have patience and trust in the innate imaginative capacities of children.

Following are examples of strategies that encourage creative thinking. Our task is to encourage the creative thought process that best suits each child.

▲ An open class environment encourages students to express ideas freely. *Courtesy Saint Louis (Missouri) Public Schools.*

Brainstorming

Brainstorming is a commonly accepted practice to generate ideas when confronted with problems. It encourages a small group of people to manufacture many ideas within a relatively short period of time. Alex Osborn (1948) suggests four basic rules students should follow when engaged in a brainstorming exercise:

1. Defer judgment. No idea is initially criticized since it deters students from making suggestions. The analytic component of brainstorming comes at a later stage.
2. The session should be conducted in a free wheeling environment. Humor and laughter encourage speculation and adventurous leaps into the unknown.
3. Students should tag on to one another's ideas. They should be encouraged to piggy back on someone else's suggestion in order to move the process ahead.

4. An important objective of brainstorming is quantity. The qualitative aspect comes after the group has generated a host of ideas. A list of many ideas increases the probability that an interesting solution will be discovered.

Brainstorming can be continually employed to assist in dealing with classroom issues. Students can brainstorm questions to pose a visitor or provide teachers new ways to get homework assignments completed. A teacher who enables students to brainstorm solutions is fostering a democratic environment within the classroom as well as gaining access to new ways of handling old problems.

Cross Matrix Problem Solving

Children have many desires and often assume all their wishes can be fulfilled. The concept of "consequences" or "limited resources" has yet to take root in their consciousness. It is difficult for children to recognize that each choice impacts all other choices. Sometimes, one choice can trigger a series of beneficial or negative consequences. For example, the decision by an elderly couple to retire to Florida could result in a disaster if they moved to an area at risk from hurricanes. Or the choice of a child who saves her allowance money to buy a computer game only to discover that she then lacks money for a weekend movie.

▲ Preoccupation with practicality hinders the nurturing of creativity. *Courtesy University City (Missouri) Public Schools.*

The cross matrix problem-solving method enables students to recognize how choices impact our range of alternatives. It is a process in which students learn how decision "A" alters the manner in which other goals can or cannot be attained. For example, in writing behavioral objectives we frequently lose sight of how objectives interact with one another. Assume our topic is improvement of education. Following are several goals:

1. Raise test scores of all students.
2. Improve self esteem of all students.
3. Increase school year to 220 days.
4. Improve school/parent relations.
5. Increase number of teachers obtaining advanced degrees.

Each of the above are excellent goals, which all schools might seek to accomplish, but they also contain contradictory aspirations. If the school goal is to raise test scores, reality suggests that "X" percent of the students will fail to attain this goal, which will result in lowering student self esteem. If the school year is increased to 220 days, it will negatively impact "X" percent of parents who will need to alter their child-care requirements or perhaps encounter difficulties scheduling vacations. Teaching school in the summer can create problems for teachers seeking advanced degrees. College schedules may not coincide with their summer instructional times. Listing goals without exploring how goals interact with one another may foster unrealistic attitudes.

Following is a model by which students can learn how to solve problems using the cross matrix approach. The topic is energy. Ordinarily, students will suggest various ways to handle problems arising out of the topic of energy conservation. However, without a model such as the cross matrix, they will not have information regarding the interrelationships between their suggestions. For example, as the model below indicates, greater use of electric cars increases the need for electricity and this will increase demands for expansion of solar or nuclear energy.

Table 7-1: The Cross Matrix Approach Helps Students Solve Problems in New Ways.

	ELECTRIC POWERED CARS 1	RAISE PRICE OF OIL 2	SOLAR ENERGY 3	HOUSE INSULATION 4
1. Use electric powered cars		reduce need for oil.	increase need for solar energy.	less critical
2. Raise price of oil.	greater need		greater need	greater need
3. Use solar energy.	greater need for electricty	less need		less need
4. More house insulation.	less need	less need	less need	

The cross matrix process enables students to understand how goals interact with one another. The repeated use of this process gradually makes students understand that each time a desired goal is sought, it will affect the manner in which their other goals can be achieved.

Creative problem solving entails both the art and science of thinking. It is a combination of knowledge and intuition. Brainstorming, idea trees, morphological forced connections, synectics or the cross matrix process extend the human mind beyond the boundaries which ordinarily restrict our ability to step outside the norm. The nine dot exercise illustrates this concept. Without lifting your pencil from the paper, draw exactly four straight, connected lines that will go through all nine dots, but through each dot only once.

This problem can only be solved by going outside of the boundaries. Children, prior to school, live in a world that is infinite in all directions. A program of creative thinking seeks to capture that innate spirit, and nurture its further growth. Creative problem solving in elementary and middle schools enables children to generate ideas that are new to them, although not necessarily new to humanity. The creative process is a tool for children to become more effective in their everyday lives.

The more experiences children have with creative problem solving, the greater is their capacity to draw upon a more extensive range of ideas when seeking solutions. Louis Pasteur once said that inspiration is the impact of a newly observed fact upon a mind that has previously been fully prepared by prior absorption of knowledge. A mind rich with ideas, strategies, techniques, and comfortable with tresspassing restrictive boundaries is fertile ground for creative thinking.

Morphological Forced Connections

Brainstorming can play a vital role in the creative process. It can be utilized to better prepare students to function as inventive thinkers. Students assume that the ability to invent requires extensive education and specialized training. Authors Koberg and Bagnall in *The Universal Traveler* (1976) describe a process that enables students to become instant inventors. Inventions are merely new ways to combine old bits and pieces. An inventor is the one who uncovers new patterns and translates that information into something different. Students are inherently conservative when confronted with new solutions. They need a process that is nonthreatening, to enable them to explore new directions.

The morphological forced connections process is a variation of brainstorming that guides students through the process of inventing in a nonthreatening environment. It involves several steps:

1. List the attributes of the situation.
2. Below each attribute place as many alternatives as possible.
3. When completed, make many random runs through the alternates picking a different item from each column, and assembling the combinations into entirely new forms of your original subject.
4. Draw a picture of the new design.

Task: *To invent a new type of pen.*

Attributes of a Pen:

Cylindrical	Plastic	Separate Cap	Steel Cartridge, etc. . . .

Alternates:

Faceted	Metal	Attached Cap	No Cartridge
Square	Glass	*No Cap*	Permanent
Beaded	*Wood*	Retracts	*Paper Cartridge*
Sculptured	Paper	Cleaning Cap	Cartridge Made of Ink

▲ **Invention: A cube pen, one corner writes, leaving six faces for ads, calendars, photos, etc. . . .**

This activity is best done in groups in order to encourage playing with ideas. It enables the student who has artistic ability to play an active role in the creative process or the shy child to feel more comfortable expressing ideas. For example, assume you are studying the covered wagon and its impact on westward movement. The morphological forced connection enables the entire class to participate in the creation of a new covered wagon model. In the process of inventing the new model, students are compelled to learn about the existing ones. Thus, the creative process reinforces learning about the past as students explore the future.

Synectics

William J. Gordon (1973), developer of synectics, describes it as a process of joining together different and apparently irrelevant elements or ideas. The French mathematician Henri Poincare emphasized that to invent one had to step outside the problem. Gordon believes one way to step outside is to view the problem from the context of analogies.

The Schick injector razor was invented by an army officer who saw an analogy between loading a repeating rifle and loading a razor. Charles Duryea, an engineer, could not solve the problem of how to develop an efficient system for introducing fuel into the engine of an automobile until one day in 1891 he observed his wife at her dressing table spraying herself with her perfume atomizer. George Westinghouse was baffled by the problem of how to improve train brakes until he read an article about a rock drill being operated by an air hose 3,000 feet from the compressor. The article led him to invent the air brake.

William Gordon's synectics process is designed to make problem solving available to everyone. It draws extensively upon making analogies between the problem at hand and the natural world. For example, Gordon was asked by a manufacturer of potato chips to discover ways to package them in a tighter fashion without causing breakage. His team drew an analogy between wet and dry leaves. Dry leaves are very brittle, but once wet, they do not easily crumble. Therefore, they hit upon the idea of wetting potato chips, placing them in cans, and allowing the chips to dry out.

Gordon developed a short process of synectics. For example, he believes the following took place in the mind of Louis Pasteur, inventor of vaccination:

Step 1: — Paradox Established theory says that infection comes from within but no soldier becomes infected until wounded.	Step 2 — Analogue Fermentation of grapes.
Step 4 — Equivalent Skin must be cut to allow infection to begin.	Step 3 — Unique Activity Grapes must be crushed to allow fermentation to begin.

His epoch-making theory that derived from his equivalent was that germs were carried by air (Gordon & Poze, 1980, p. 55).

Using Synectics to Invent a Poem

Synectics draws heavily upon imagery much like poetry. Poetry entails combining words to create images and feelings. Synectics offers an opportunity to involve all students in an unusual form of creative problem solving—inventing a poem.

The synectics process involves four stages in the "invention" of a poem. In step 1, students are provided practice in the use of metaphors, which play a critical role in poetry. Metaphors engage the imagination and encourage children to think in visual terms. In Step 2, children are asked to think and act like an inanimate object in order to alter the boundaries of logical thinking.

Step 1 Practice in Metaphor Usage

1. How could cavepeople have invented the concept of clothes from looking at bears? _____
_____

2. Which bird would have inspired prehistoric people to carry things in a container? _____
_____

3. What in the natural world would have led prehistoric people to invent:
   a. The zipper: _____
   _____

   b. The safety pin: _____
   _____

   c. The pencil: _____
   _____

4. What things would have given ancient people their first notion of the wheel? _____
_____

5. A woodpecker is like what object found in a house? _____
_____

6. A doorbuzzer is like which animal? _____
_____

7. Summer is like a bridge because _____
_____

8. A water hose reminds you of which animal? _____
_____

Step 2   Personalization
The Teabag Lesson
You are now officially a TEABAG!
How does your body feel when you are plunged into a cup of hot water? Act and feel like a teabag:
_____
_____
_____

Describe the changes in your body as you sit in the cup for a few minutes. _____
_____
_____

As you sit in the cup, what do you think will happen to you? _____
_____
_____

You have been taken out of the cup. What changes take place in your teabag body after you are out of the cup?

_____

_____

_____

What plant is like you, the teabag?

_____

_____

What animal is like you, the teabag?

_____

_____

_____

Step 3   Practice in guided imagery.

The Blue Balloon

Picture in your mind a blue balloon. Breath air into it until it is blown up. Put a string on it. Throw the balloon in the air. Catch it. Have it bounce up and down the wall. Make the balloon come right to your face. Change the balloon to orange. Blow the orange balloon up until it is twice as big. Prick the balloon and watch the air go out. Feel the air blow against your face. Turn the air into a stream of water and feel it wet your face. Turn the balloon back to its original blue.

The Apple

Visualize an apple inside your head. Go over the apple carefully. Notice its color and texture. Cut a piece out of the apple. Smell the piece. Take a bite and feel the apple inside your mouth. What does the rest of th apple look like without the piece? Watch the rest of the apple slowly turn brown. Have your hands feel the apple's skin. Put the piece you ate back inside the apple. Smell the apple.

Step 4   Creating the Analogy

Students are asked to do the following: "When I mention the next word, write down the name of the first animal that enters your mind. The word is FOG." After students write down the name of the animal they are asked to write ten descriptive sentences about the animal. The sentences are to describe the animal, how the animal moves and thinks, its fears, hopes and anxieties, etc.. Students are urged to use as many adjectives as possible. For example, assume you wrote "cat" as your name.

1. My skin is black, silvery and sleek.
2. I love to purr when I am happy.
3. I move tenderly and with caution.
4. I fear dark wet nights when dogs wander the streets.
5. I am proud, demand attention, and refuse to serve anyone.
6. I creep over damp ground smelling the earth's aroma.
7. I love to sit on the window sill watching morning be born.
8. My claws rip the green carpet when I feel anger.
9. I love to sit in the warm, snuggly human's lap.
10. My green eyes glow when I become angry.

Step 5   The Invention of a poem.

Students are then asked to select four descriptive sentences, and turn the subject from cat to fog. The sentences are placed under one another in the following fashion:

Fog
Black, silvery, and sleek
I move tenderly and with caution
Creeping over damp ground,
smelling earth's aroma.

I am proud
demand attention
and serve no one

My green eyes glow at night
Purring with happiness
Then, snuggling warmly
I watch morning be born.

Students can also be asked to place the three most descriptive words they wrote under one another in a variation of a Japanese Haiku poem.

Glow
Silver
Anger

The creative act is not restricted to a small group of "gifted" students. Each child is unique and views the world through an individual lens which can be used to unleash the power of creativity. In this section we propose that most children are capable of insightful thinking if only provided the tools and opportunity to take advantage of their innate imagination. Harry Truman never went to college and failed in most of his business ventures. However, he had perserverence, a willingness to work hard, and an ability to continue learning on his own. Eventually, these qualities led him to the presidency. There are many children with the same capacities, and they should be encouraged to take advantage of them.

Memory as a Creative Problem-Solving Skill

Memory is among the most important human faculties, but it is rarely taught in schools. Without memory there would be no learning from experience, no language development, and no intellectual reasoning. Problem solving depends upon our ability to recall information and use that information in old as well as new ways.

There are varieties of memory experiences which play a role in problem solving:

1. *Episodic Memory.* The memory of past episodes and events in one's life such as going to a fair.
2. *Factual Memory.* The memory of facts, such as George Washington was president or two plus two equals four.

3. *Semantic Memory.* The memory for meaning. We recall that "rough" describes a tactile experience or that tigers growl.

4. *Sensory Memory.* People have visual memory and recall faces. They also can remember the sound of music or the smell of a perfume.

5. *Skill Memory.* People recall skills such as how to dress, drive a car, play basketball or use a fork.

6. *Instinctive Memory.* The newborn baby "remembers" how to suck at its mother's breast, and to breathe, sleep and digest food. (Russell, 1979, pp. 82–83)

The decision of what to memorize continually assaults our mind. Our senses are bombarded with stimuli from a bus trip to school, a walk in the park or what is taught in the class. Of the potential millions of possibilities of memory events, only a small percent become incorporated into our long term memory. Following is a diagram illustrating the process:

Practice

	Sensory	Short Term		Long Term
Stimulus - - - -	Register - - -	Memory - - - - - - - - - - - - -		Memory

Millions of Americans recall one event on a November day in 1963—the assassination of John F. Kennedy. The stimuli impacted their sensory register and became part of short-term memory. During the following years they discussed and recalled the event until it became part of long-term memory. This November, they most probably will recall the event from their long-term memory and make it part of the Short Term Memory.

People recall what registers. For example, recall everything you know about a "penny" without looking at one. You most probably easily recalled its color and size because that is how we identify a penny. Our long term memory is like a giant library. Imagine entering a library that contains millions of volumes, but lacks a card catalog. The purpose of training students to improve memory is to provide them with a card catalog system that makes retrieval of information much easier. The following story illustrates how to make stimuli strongly impact the memory system.

> ## The Planet Exercise
> Shut your eyes and in your mind go to a park or forest. It is a beautiful spring day. Sunlight glittering through the leaves and a warm breeze on your face. Your feet crunch on branches. You come to a brook, lie down on the grass, and go to sleep. You awake feeling fresh and happy. You walk until a lush green meadow appears. There is a silver mercury object in the center. You discover it is an old *Mercury* car. As you stand admiring the Mercury car, a noise on your right makes you turn. It is the Goddess *Venus*! She walks toward you with her golden hair swaying in the sun. Venus reaches the Mercury car, smiles, and slips into the driver's seat. Suddenly, there is a noise on your left. It is a beautiful woman—*Eartha* Kitt, the singer. She comes to the Mercury car, smiles at you and gets in the back seat. Eartha reaches into a bag and pulls out a five pound *Mars* bar. She takes a bite of its rich carmel and eats the Mars bar. The sound of pounding makes you turn. It is the giant *Jupiter*. He jumps on top of the Mercury car. Venus turns on the ignition key and the car moves. You can see the back license plate— SUN. It stands for *Saturn, Uranus, Neptune.* Now the sound of barking. It is *Pluto*. Pluto is chasing the Mercury car with its license plate—SUN. Saturn, Uranus Neptune, and Pluto barking.

People use imagery in memory quite naturally. It would be easy for you at this moment to shut your eyes and return to your childhood home, wander through the kitchen and once again "see" your bedroom. A picture is truly worth a thousand words in memory association. The power of associative memory enables students to remember and also to create.

Imagery plays a vital role in social studies. For example, if students are studying the Depression era, implanting images in their minds will assist in memory retention. "Shut your eyes and see a young boy and his father walking in a park. Each carries a shovel. On the back of the boy's T-shirt are three letters—CCC. On the father's shirt one can see WPA. The boy works at planting trees while the father is busy making a road." This image conveys that the CCC involved boys planting trees while older men built highways in the WPA.

The "Planet Exercise" can be replicated in virtually any social studies lesson. In the following story, several key battles in the Pacific region of World War II are taught through use of imagery. "Shut your eyes and imagine that you are sailing on an ocean. Cool breezes caress your face as you sit on the desk gazing outward. Your ship comes to a *harbor* and you decide to join some people who are seeking *pearl*s. *Midway* through the swimming, you look back to the ship and hear a woman singing, "*Tara wa* boom de ay, tara wa boom de ay." She calls out to you, "Did you hear, *Phil* has some *pains*, but he will be *OK in a wa*le. He asked you to *Guard* the *canal*'s entrance so no one will take the blue fish he wants to use as a *new guinea* specimen." (Battles: Pearl Harbor, Midway, Tarawa, Philippines, Guadacanal, and New Guinea).

Memory education is an opportunity to both impart knowledge and teach creative thinking techniques. A considerable amount of time in the elementary and Middle School classroom is devoted to imparting information, but rarely are students furnished skills in retention of what is being taught. The effective use of memory strategies improves how much material is remembered. For example, the following list of words can easily be taught by turning them into a fun story:

Car, sunglasses, orange, pencil, mint, paper, tree, clock, radio, airplane, fire.

You are seated in a *car*. As you look through the front window you realize it is shaped in the form of *sunglasses*. At the end of the hood is a giant *orange*. Sticking into the orange is a purple *pencil*. A sticky *mint* is on top of the pencil in place of the eraser. The wind blows a piece of *paper* which sticks to the mint. When you think of paper it brings to mind a *tree*. On a branch of the tree is hanging a red *clock*. On another branch is a black *radio*. On top of the tree is a tiny *airplane*. You open the door of the tiny airplane and out comes *fire*.

Creative storytelling to recall information offers students an opportunity to become active participants in learning. Memory techniques require the individual to become engaged in the process of retention. Memory education excites students because it is both fun, and empowering. Once students understand they *can* remember what is taught in class, their self-concept is enhanced.

For example, assume the objective was teaching the following facts about the Civil War period. Lincoln was President of the North, Jefferson Davis of the South; Robert E. Lee and Stonewall Jackson were outstanding Southern generals, and Ulysses Grant and William Tecumseh Sherman were Northern generals. The North lost the Battle of Bull Run but won at Vicksburg and Gettysburg. The Civil War began in 1861 and ended in 1865 at Appomattox.

Story: Abe Lincoln and Jeff Davis were presiding at a dinner given on a steamboat captained by Robert E. Lee. Their waiter, Stonewall Jackson, who served people seated in the southern half of the dining room, got into a fight with two other waiters, Ulysses Grant and William Sherman, who served the northern part of the room. "You won this first fight," said Grant. "Since it took place under the picture of the bulls running, we'll call it Bull Run. But, Sherman and I will beat you when you come to our part of the room. See the pictures of Vicksburg and Gettysburg? Just wait till we beat you there." Jackson was sent to room 1861 to cool down and Grant and Sherman to room 1865, which is known as the Appomattox area.

To create a mental image is to "imagine," and the power of imagination is almost limitless. The ability to put common images together in the mind to create vivid new images is an exercise in problem solving. It is essential to the process of memory, and it is necessary for students to learn these techniques, not merely to improve recall of what has been learned, but also to improve organizational skills.

Imagery is valuable in memory because it strengthens associations and linkages. It makes the mind interact with material being learned and makes the learner a participant. In the animal kingdom and among humans, memory evolved to record the routes and location of food, shelter, mates, and foes. Children retain the imagery capacity, and this talent can be channelled into productive ways of learning and problem solving.

Memory Tips

1. The acronym technique entails forming a word that incorporates information to be memorized. For example, TISQ: Tea Act, Intolerable Acts, Stamp Act, and Quartering of soldiers. These are events from the Revolutionary War period.

2. Encourage students to translate information being studied into a song:

Red River Valley (tune)

There's a battle at Midway we'll remember,
Where we sank a lot of Japanese ships,
It came after the attack on Pearl Harbor,
Which got us into the great World War II.

3. Assist student to create "memory tapes." Information is put on an audio tape followed by classical music, more information, and additional music. These tapes can be played at bedtime.

4. Encourage students to form name associations for historical figures: Dwight Eisenhower's name is linked to an eye pushing a lawn mower.

5. Have students draw an object map of their room at home. The location of items related to school should be placed in specific places on the map.

6. An important memory technique is to place information being studied on key places along a street that is familiar. For example, the planet information could be memorized in the following manner: A *Mercury* car is placed on top of the Harris roof; a golden flashing *Venus* is placed on the mail box of the Barton residence; a large blue *Earth* is on the front door of the Lewis family; a red *Mars* is attached to the lamp post in front of Mandy's house; *Jupiter* is attached to the basket of the Klein family driveway, the word *SUN* flashes on the garage door of the Stopsky family, and *Pluto* is barking on the front lawn of Morgan's garden.

▲ Humor encourages speculation and adventurous leaps into the unknown. *Courtesy Webster University.*

Humor in Education

Schools should be an interesting and exciting place because children learn best in a happy environment. Creative elementary and middle school school teachers employ various forms of humor in order to make a subject matter come alive in the minds of children. A dictionary defines humor as "the ability to perceive, appreciate, or express what is funny, amusing, or ludicrous." Humor is a state of mind or disposition to see unexpected or new patterns within existing situations.

Teachers know that happy children are less prone to become discipline problems. They are more receptive to new ideas and more willing to engage in sustained work. Harvey Mindess (1971) has identified six attributes of people who have a humorous frame of mind: flexibility, spontaneity, unconventionality, shrewdness, playfulness, and humility. These characteristics are frequently found in outstanding teachers and are among the characteristics we seek to instill within children.

Humor is an underexplored subject in education. Few recognize that just as people go through stages of personality development, they also go through stages of humor (Tamashiro, 1979). The newborn baby laughs if the body is tickled or when objects, especially large toys, are brought into direct bodily contact. These forms of interaction address the child's concern to identify the boundary where the body ends and the outside world begins.

At the next stage, the terrible 2s, children assert an emerging sense of self, largely by using the word "no." This is the impulsive stage because the child seems to be governed by impulses and places the self at the center of life. The child is concerned about motor control and mastery of body functions. Noises of the body—hiccups, burps, and passing gas—often draw laughter.

At this stage, children laugh at bodily and facial contortions, physical clowning, and most slapstick humor. Accidents resulting from clumsiness or other gross physical misfortunes also elicit laughter. Children's beginning mastery of language enables them to enjoy nonsense words or verses. Simple teasing chants such as "Tommy is a cry baby, Tommy is a cry baby," illustrate the combination of beginning language competence and aggressive impulsivity.

Children about the age of four are capable of delay when it is to their immediate advantage. The child's sense of self-definition shifts from impulses to concrete self-interests and wants. The child discovers the boundary between self and others in the form of psychological territory and begins protecting it. This is the self-protective stage. The notion of blame is understood, but the blame is externalized.

▲ Creative problem solving enables children to generate ideas that are new to them, although not necessarily new to humanity. *Courtesy Saint Louis (Missouri) Public Schools.*

Children at this stage are capable of forethought and delay of gratification. These cognitive activities enable the child to play and set up a practical joke. Insults and "put-downs" are common because the child is more adept at using language.

> Adam and Eve and Pinch-Me went to sea in a raft. Adam and Eve fell in the water. Who was left? If the unsuspecting child says, "Pinch-Me," she receives a sharp pinch.

The next stage of humor development occurs when children enter school. They identify with a social group and learn that conformity to rules liberates them from the unpredictable social world. This is the conformist stage since social acceptability is important. Children enjoy conventional humor—cliched, unoriginal jokes. These include most riddles, moron jokes, concrete puns, and knock-knock jokes.

> What has four legs and can't walk? Answer: A table.
> Why does the fireman wear red suspenders? Answer: To hold his pants up.
> How did the boy get out of the Holy Church? Answer: He crawled through one of the holes.

Ridicule of "undesirables" and racial and ethnic humor are also prevalent at the conformist stage because they highlight the desirability of being in the "right" group. Teachers should be sensitive to the prevalence of this attitude and anticipate cruel jokes directed toward minorities or outcasts.

The next stage is called "conscientious" and most often occurs in later adolescence. Conscience, values, and sense of personal satisfaction govern thoughts and actions more than social desirability. At this stage children are able to consider the positive and negative consequences of their actions. Many children at this stage enjoy original, noncliched and good natured humor.

> A leopard went to an eye doctor and complained that whenever he looked at his wife, he saw spots in front of his eyes. The doctor said: "Well, what do you expect, you're a leopard!" The leopard replied: "Yes, but my wife is a zebra."

An awareness of the stages of children's humor development enables teachers to anticipate how their class will react to fun activities. A class in which the sound of laughter is heard is frequently a class in which learning occurs. Sam Levinson, a former social studies teacher, who became a famous humorist in the 1950s and 1960s often told the story of the best teacher he ever had in school. She knew Sam was the class clown who continually disrupted his classmates. This wise teacher gave Sam one minute each day to tell jokes in a rapid fire manner while she took attendance. Each day she began her lesson teaching happy children, and Sam kept his part of the bargain by being an attentive student.

Humor in Social Studies

Social studies is the story of people in all their manifold ways of behavior. Educators often forget that life is not merely a linear ride toward some predestined future. It also involves false starts, chance, and hunches as part of the voyage. The creative factor may later appear to be the result of logical processes or planning.

During the early days of the New Deal, when America was in the grip of a severe depression that left one-third of the workforce without jobs, an assistant to Franklin Roosevelt was reviewing with the president details about establishment of the Works Project Administration (WPA). As the assistant was leaving, he turned and asked: "Mr. President, what about artists, musicians, and writers? Should they be included in the WPA?" President Roosevelt thought for a moment and replied, "Oh sure, throw them in, they also need jobs." Thus was born, in a moment, a creative endeavor to foster arts and humanities in America.

A humorous minded individual is a creative thinker who observes the obvious and discovers unexpected twists and turns. The creative thinker uncovers new patterns within existing information. Humor entails the same process. All jokes jar our sense of reality by revealing new patterns.

> "Doctor, doctor, my husband is crazy. He thinks he is a horse. He sleeps in a stable, eats hay and barley and walks around on all fours. Can you cure him?" The doctor pondered for a

▲ Creative processes help students understand the past to prepare for the future.
Courtesy Perry County (Missouri) School District.

moment and replied: "I think I can cure him, but it will be expensive." "Oh, money is no object," said the woman. "He has already won four races."

Children can be educated to employ a humorous perspective in order to enhance their critical thinking capacities. Humor, more than any other facility, enables children to get past the obvious and more readily grasp the subtle and hidden factors of life. Children enjoy playing with words and ideas because it provides them powerful tools to employ in the complelxity of an adult controlled world. Following are a variety of activities that draw upon a humorous perspective in creative thinking.

Limericks: Children enjoy the sounds of music, and limericks have a musical beat which transforms words into action. A social studies limerick enables children to express themselves in creative ways. A limerick can only be written if the child has some knowledge concerning the topic. Information can more readily be retained if it is linked to rhythm and imagery. For example:

> There once was a girl named Snow White,
> Who an evil queen banished from sight,
> In the forest so wet,
> Seven dwarfs she met,
> Till Prince Charming made everything right.

> R is the great Jackie Robinson,
> Who could play baseball better than anyone,
> A man so patient and fine,
> Broke the old nasty color line,
> Now the Major League's are open to everyone.

▲ Schools should be interesting and exciting places because children learn best in a happy environment. *Courtesy Saint Louis (Missouri) Public Schools.*

Puns: The magic of language is integral to social studies and to humor. Children love to play with language and rearrange words to create new images. Puns are a form of word play that can be used to assist children in remembering their social studies lessons. For example:

> Abraham Lincoln was uncertain of the location of the best Italian restaurant in Washington. He told his wife: "I seem to have lost my Spaghettsburg Address."

> Brutus to Caeser: "How many hamburgers did you consume at lunch today?" Caeser: "Et tu, Brutus."

> A wise old crow perched himself firmly on a telephone wire. He wanted to make a long distance caw.

The young child being introduced to writing benefits by exposure to fun ways of expressing ideas. Puns form visual images in the minds of children which are so critical to recall. For example, "As General Lee said to the blue-coated waiter, thanks for the bottle of Bull Rum." (Battle of Bull Run in the Civil War). Students can even create a Pun Dictionary to aid in their memorization of information or manipulation of words and ideas.

Pun Dictionary:

Aardvark: Heavy labor. "It's aardvark, but it pays well."

Beatnik: Santa Claus on the day after Christmas.

Dewey: In 1948, the voters thought he didn't get up in due time.

Gerrymander: The lines roam and meander all over the state.

Hoover: During the 1928 election, one of the presidential candidates promised to clean up with a new vacuum cleaner.

Nixon: "I told you, nix on those tapes."

Biograffiti

Dr. Jekyll isn't himself today.

Humpty Dumpty was a fall guy.

Thomas Jefferson liked to declare himself.

Benjamin Franklin was a real hot wire.

Running up and down Bunker Hill made Molly dip into the pitcher for a drink of water.

"I have a dream" was a King-sized image sitting atop a mountain.

Visual Writing: The old adage "A picture is worth a thousand words" applies dramatically to children in elementary and middle school. Children love art and drawing as a way to express feelings and ideas. Social studies can utilize this interest to motivate children to learn in new ways. There is a growing body of knowledge regarding learning styles that indicates that many children are visual learners who need picture images in order to understand the material (Gardner, 1983). Following are several examples of ways to combine art and social studies in a dramatic way to stimulate student interest.

▲ Humorists, like Will Rogers, are creative thinkers who observe the obvious and discover unexpected twists and turns.

▲ Children love art and drawing to express feelings and ideas. *Courtesy Null Elementary, Saint Charles (Missouri) Public Schools.*

▲ Edison

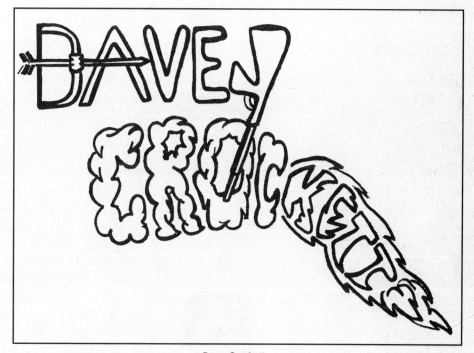

▲ Davey Crockett

▲ George Bush

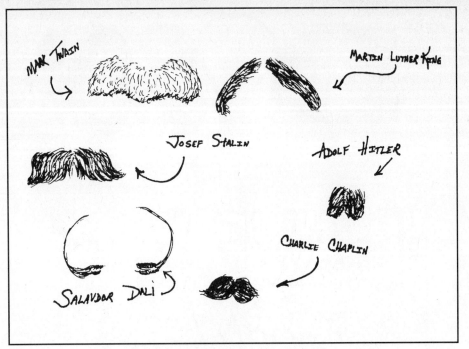

▲ Moustaches. *Drawings by Kate Barton Stopsky.*

Rebus: A rebus is an expression presented in a visual form. Each word is represented by visual images and the images are linked together. Following is an example:

▲ Rebus

Why Do We Say That? The study of expressions enables children to uncover the fascinating and creative ways in which language works its way through history. Students can learn about the past by uncovering the mystery as to why we use current expressions.

Mind Your P's and Q's: People who mind their P's and Q's are careful about their behavior. The expression arose in nineteenth century England when sailors ran up tabs in waterfront bars. The sailors and worker would buy pints and quarts of ale which the salon keeper would abbreviate on a slate with a "P" and a "Q." If the keeper didn't keep the record straight, he could lose money. Later, children were told to mind their "P's" and "Q's" to ensure proper behavior.

Predictions Gone Astray: People in the past continually made predictions about the future world. They were correct sometimes but often erroneous. It helps students to understand the present if they can understand how people in the past viewed their own futures. Following are some past predictions that went astray:

"Everything that will be invented has been invented."
—Charles Duell, 1899, Director of U.S. Patent Office
"Who the heck wants to hear actors talk?"
—Harry Warner, 1927, President of Warner Brothers
"There is no likelihood man can ever tap the power of the atom."
—Robert Millikan, 1923 winner of Nobel Prize in physics

Newspapers: Newspapers of the past and present are rich sources of information about the daily lives of people. They provide information not merely about the political world, but also regarding everyday events. For example, following is a menu reported in *Le Figaro* on December 4, 1870 of a dinner given in Paris for distinguished guests. Paris was under siege and there was a shortage of food.

Consomme of horse with birdseed
Skewered dog liver, maitre d'Hotel
Shoulder of dog, tomato sauce
Stewed cat with mushrooms
Ragout of rats, Robert.
Dog leg flanked with ratlets
Elephant's ear au jus.

Letters to the editor: History is ordinarily presented from the perspective of what happened to famous people. We rarely devote sufficient time to learn what life was like for an average person. Ann Landers and "Dear Abby" are familiar columns to readers, but few people know that similar columns appeared in newspapers over 80 years ago. Following is a letter which appeared in the *Jewish Daily Forward* in 1905:

Esteemed Editor:
We were sitting in the shop when the boss came over to one of us and said, "You ruined the work, you'll have to pay for it." The worker answered that it wasn't his fault, that he had given out the work in perfect condition. The boss got mad and began to shout, "I pay your wages and you answer back, you dog! I should have thrown you out of the shop a long time ago!"
The worker trembled, his face got whiter. When the boss noticed how his face paled, he gestured and spat and walked away. The worker said no more. Tired and overcome with shame, he turned back to his work and later he exclaimed, "For six years I've been working here like a slave, and he tells me, 'You dog, I'll throw you out!' I wanted to pick up an iron and smash his head in, but I saw before me my wife and five children who want to eat."

Obviously, the offended man felt he had done wrong in not standing up for his honor as a worker and as a human being. In the shops, the machines hummed, the irons thumped, and we could see tears running down his cheeks.

Did this unfortunate man act correctly in remaining silent under the insults of his boss? Is the fact that he has a wife and children the reason for his slavery and refusal to defend himself?

Editor Responds: The worker cannot help himself alone. To defend their honor as men, the workers must be well organized. There is no limit to what must be done for a piece of bread. One must bite his lips till they bleed, and keep silent when he is alone. But, he must not remain alone. He must not remain silent. He must unite with his fellow workers and fight.

SUMMARY

This chapter has presented a rationale for creative thinking, and demonstrated how problem solving techniques, memory approaches, and humor can be utilized in educating students to function in creative ways.

Below is a list of twenty creative ideas that could be used to humorize social studies lessons.

1. Have a day in which the class is governed by unusual "laws" created by the students.
2. Have students invent a school in which humor is the main curriculum.
3. Invite a local political cartoonist to discuss humor.
4. Have students study the history of humor in America.
5. Have students invent something that could have altered history, for example, tea made from cotton. This would have eliminated a major cause of the Revolutionary War.
6. Take a little known president such as Franklin Pierce and create activities to go along with his birthday celebration.
7. Have students develop "what if" stories. What if the South had won the Civil War?
8. Have students collect outdated laws that are still on the books. For example, "In Garfield County, Montana, it is illegal to draw cartoons or funny faces on window shades." Students could hypothesize the origin of such laws.
9. Have students collect jokes from parents and grandparents and analyze similarities and differences.
10. Present history from the bottom up, for example, Paul Revere's ride as told by his horse.
11. Obtain a recording of an old radio comedy. Analyze its humor.
12. Have students invent a business for the year 2030.
13. Put together a dictionary of school slang.
14. Have students create a false document, for example, a Puritan description of a baseball game. The task of students is to identify every error in the document.
15. Have students create bumper sticker slogans related to what is being studied in social studies.
16. Have students design "Wanted Posters" for people such as Hitler, Billy the Kid, etc.
17. Students are to assume they are Martian scientists. The only knowledge they possess about Earth has been obtained by watching television. Students are to give a "Martian Interpretation" about life on Earth.
18. Have students create a future sport.
19. Have students create menus for different societies or periods in history. Younger children can put together a feast for animals in the forest.
20. Have students create "Recruiting Posters" for events in the past. For example, "Sail With Magellan and See the World."

QUESTIONS

1. What place, if any, do you believe humor has in social studies curriculum?

2. Where do you personally fit in the stages of humor?

3. Which comedy shows or comedians would most interest: (a) primary age children; (b) upper elementary age children; (c) the middle school child.

4. What would be your greatest anxiety about emphasizing humorous activities for students?

5. Which of the materials in this chapter would you find easy to teach? Which might prove difficult?

6. What did you find most enjoyable about social studies when you were in elementary school?

7. Do you agree or disagree with the authors that humor can be used to teach creative thinking?

8. What are your favorite memory strategies?

9. In which ways do you employ creative thinking in your voting behavior?

10. Which comedian do you enjoy the most? Why?

ACTIVITIES

1. Collect jokes from young children and organize them into categories.

2. Read an autobiography or biography about a humorist in order to explore the theory of humor.

3. Do a report on the history of comic strips and how they reflect changes in American society.

4. Follow comic strips for a few weeks and make a list of all political and social issues dealt with in the comic strips.

5. Compare three comedians representing different gender and ethnic backgrounds and examine their ideas concerning humor.

READING

Don't Stamp On Me: Postage Stamps As a Teaching Device
by David Curtis Skaggs
Professor of History Bowling Green State University
and
Larry Dean Wills
Associate Professor of Education Bowling Green State University

Often the most common of objects provide some of the most useful classroom educational inovations. Postage stamps allow opportunities for developing not only a wide-ranging interest in themes, but also skills in such areas as collecting, language arts, data gathering, and critical analysis. While such skills may be acquired with stamps pertaining to countries throughout the world and a variety of time periods and topics, we have chosen the American Revolutionary era to illustrate this teaching technique.

The most obvious skill acquisition derived from using stamps involves data gathering. Not only do official Postal Service publications[1] provide information in this regard, but also more de-

---

[1] See the easily acquired (at every post office) *United States Stamps and Stories* (published annually) and the more detailed *United States Postage Stamps* (Washington: Government Printing Office, 1972, plus supplements). The latter book provides important technical information about each stamp of particular interest to those involved in stamp collecting.

tailed material and additional library skills may be developed by sending students to standard reference works like the *Dictionary of American Biography, Who Was Who, Dictionary of American History, Notable American Women*, and other such sources. Most students easily recognize such standard postage stamp figures as George Washington, Benjamin Franklin, and Thomas Jefferson; but who, for instance, were Peter Francisco, Sybil Ludington, Salem Poor, and Haym Salomon, who were honored in the 1975 "Contributors to the Cause" series? Such research should open inquiry into the roles of enlisted men, women, blacks, and Jews in revolutionary America. Moreover, work in these reference books should open up all sorts of avenues for additional study.

To illustrate stamps being used as a springboard for data gathering, consider the "Drummer" stamp from the 1973 "Rise of the Spirit of Independence" series.

First, what is happening in the picture? What does the drummer do and why? (When students understand that, like a bell, the drum was a means of communicating in an era before telephones and sirens, you may wish to send some students to gather information on particular drum beats.) The stamp also shows a woman handing a weapon and another object to a man. What kind of weapons were used in the revolution? (This could prompt a long discussion about rifles and muskets and why the latter were mostly used.) What other object is the woman handling the man? Is it a powder horn or a pouch for gunpowder and shot? Why does he carry his gunpowder and not have it in a shell like we do today? (The technology of firearms might excite the interest of students turned off from the traditional approaches to the study of history.) The stamp shows men riding and running away from the drummer. Are they afraid? Or are they seeking fellow soldiers who may not hear the drum?

Where does the scene take place? This is most difficult, and obviously the Postal Service desired a universal depiction, but two indications might place this in the Middle Colonies. Both the buildings in the right foreground and background appear constructed of brick. This was much more normal in the Middle and Southern colonies than in New England, where wood was the most common construction medium. The stepped gable on the building behind the dummer indicates a northern European influence, especially Dutch, more likely to be found in New York or Pennsylvania. (All this might prompt some students to study colonial architecture.)

One skill frequently ignored in the social studies classroom is viewing. Though much of what we know is based on what we perceive, the ability to get as much as possible out of a stamp, picture, or any experience for that matter, can be developed. Stamps serve as a useful tool for this purpose.

For example, having viewed a particular stamp, ask each student to list what each sees happening. Next, ask the students to share with the class what they have observed, writing student responses on the chalkboard. Ask your students to compare their responses with oothers in the class, using such questions as (a) Why did I not see what others did? (b) Was I mistaken in what I did see? (c) Did I see anything that nobody else saw?

Once the facts shown in the stamp are discussed, the teacher may turn to hypotheses on what people are doing. For what purpose is the drummer calling the men to arms? Is it for practice? Are they expecting a British or Indian attack? How would they form for maneuvers? Once such issues are raised, and based upon what students know and what they think they know about the stamp, what unanswered questions emerge? Where might they go to answer their questions?

Let us use the "Sybil Ludington" commemorative for the progression from facts to hypotheses to generalizations.

Again the factual questions emerge. What happens in this picture? A woman (we assume a girl, from the caption "youthful heroine") is riding a horse side-saddle past colonial-style homes. The bicentennial logo after her name hints at the Revolutionary era. What possible thing is this girl doing? Is she riding fast or slowly? Why? Her mouth is open; is she shouting something? We can hypothesize that women did play important roles in the securing of national independence. What could a girl do to merit a postage stamp? Is she a female counterpart to Paul Revere? How does her exploit compare with his? After you have asked these questions, you may begin to make generalizations about the role of women in the Revolution. The skillful teacher will send such inquiring minds to available resources.[2]

Students without interests in the common historical topics of politics and military action may find a variety of other areas of interest. Artists and their work may intrigue numerous students. Probably few artists have had more of their work used as postal illustrations than did Charles Willson Peale. On what stamps do we find his paintings utilized? A good beginning would be the January, 1977, issue of Peale's painting of Washington at Princeton. Why is he called "the artist of the Revolution"? A higher level of study involves the artistic genre represented by particular painters. Why, for instance, are the artistic styles of John Trumbull, shown in the "Declaration of Independence," and of Archibald Willard, in "Spirit of '76," both of which appeared in 1976 strips of stamps, described as being "Romantic?"

Similar interests may be developed in period costumes. What kind of clothing and accessories did men and women of various social classes wear in the eighteenth century? How was this clothing made? For instance, what were the differences in military uniforms shown in the 1975 continental uniform series? Another discussion could involve the costumes of women or the artisans of the 1977 "Skilled Hands for Independence" block.

Somewhat sophisticated skills may be shown in a critical analysis of Henry Sandham's depiction of the initial combat on Lexington Green.

Does the artist imply the British were the aggressors in this engagement? If so, why does the American artist want to show the British started the war? Two avenues of investigation might ensue from a discussion of this particular commemorative. First, who fired the first shot?[3] Second, what is the role of propaganda and mythology in the national self-image?

The physical property of stamps may prompt some students to become involved in or to share their previous passion for collecting stamps. Here the teacher may find an opportunity to teach collecting skills such as the care and organization of a collection, how to be thorough, and trading with other collectors. Other skills, stemming from the costs of collecting, involve economic questions. Why are some stamps more valuable than others? The law of supply and demand can easily be taught when one views the typical price list for stamps.[4]

Stamps may also serve as an aspiration for essays, poems, or even plays on a theme depicted. Here the instructor may allow students to select a stamp of individual interest and write about it. Rather than requiring one form of communication over another, give the students the freedom to express themselves in their own idiom. It might be in the form of a collage, a tape recording of the student's impression of the stamp, or any number of literary or artistic self-expressions.

A variety of language arts skills may be developed in conjunction with stamp units. What is meant by such words as "tread" in "Don't Tread on Me" or "liberty" in "Give me liberty or give me death"? These slogans appeared in the "Historic Flags" series of 1968 and the "American Credo" series of 1960. Also of interest should be the definition of such words as "declaration" and "independence" as depicted in the special four-stamp strip of 1976. The "Sic Semper Tyrannis" motto of Virginia, displayed on its flag, should give pause to those interested in classical languages, the place of classical studies in colonial education, and the rationale for John Wilkes Booth shouting it when he leaped to the stage of Ford's Theater after shooting Abraham Lincoln. On a more sophisticated level, one might use the *Oxford English Dictionary* to trace the etymology of the word "liberty" from a meaning including a personal or group privilege to one denoting an equality of citizens' rights.

---

[2]Lonnelle Aikman. "Patriots in Petticoats," *National Geographic*, 148 (October 1975), 475–495, provides numerous examples.

[3]Peter S. Bennett, *What Happened on Lexington Green?* (Menlo Park, California: Addison-Wesley Publishing Co., 1970), provides resource materials for an inquiry lesson using this incident.

[4]For the most comprehensive information and prices of American stamps, see the first volume of the latest edition of the *Scott Postage Stamp Catalogue*.

Language arts skills may be expanded to examinations where a stamp may be used to require students to write about an illustration in order to apply a concept learned earlier. Or one may provide a group of stamps and ask students to rearrange them to construct a logical sequence of events concluding with a written generalization based upon the series. Chronology is unimportant in such exercises. What is critical is the development of logical analysis. Thus stamps may be used to apply facts and hypotheses in the development of generalizations.

One of the most important of all skills is that of critical analysis. Here the teacher should be concerned not only with factual knowledge, but rather with the whys and why nots of history and of our image of the past. For instance, who is *not* depicted among the individuals of the age is often more interesting than who has been pictured. No stamp honors Horatio Gates, victor at Saratoga; Richard Montgomery, hero of Montreal and Quebec; Daniel Morgan, who fought from Canada to the Carolinas; nor are there any for the presidents of the Continental Congress, like John Hancock or John Laurens; and none depicts the Southern partisan leaders, like Francis Marion, Thomas Sumter, or Andrew Pickens. What does this say about the Post Office's image of the war effort?[5]

Of the revolutionary women, only Sybil Ludington actually was involved in the war effort. The first woman on a stamp, Martha Washington, has as her sole claim to fame being her husband's helpmate. Betsy Ross' title as designer of the continental flag is somewhat tenuous. That leaves only Mary Hays, known as "Molly Pitcher," who is anonymously honored with an overprint of the George Washington regular issue to commemorate the sesquicentennial of the Battle of Monmouth, in which she participated. One could question the omission of Mercy Otis Warren, Abigail Adams, and Eliza Lucas Pinckney from stamps honoring distinguished persons of the revolutionary age.[6]

Similar criticisms might be leveled at the battles commemorated in postage stamp illustrations. The relatively small engagements from Lexington to the lifting of the seige of Boston have merited seven commemorative issues and, aside from Princeton and Yorktown, no battle south of New York was honored during the sesquicentennial or during the bicentennial. One wonders why such victories as those at Trenton, New Jersey, Great Bridge, Virginia, Fort Moultrie, Cowpens, and Kings Mountain, South Carolina, and Moore's Creek, North Carolina have not been commemorated. Certain stalemates, such as those at Germantown, Pennsylvania, Monmouth, New Jersey, Guilford Courthouse, North Carolina, and Quebec, deserve to be remembered. When one considers that more and bloodier fighting occurred in the Middle Atlantic and Southern states, the distortion of historic truth represented in previous postal issues becomes increasingly obvious. Will the presence of a Southerner in the White House mean greater representation for this region in fugure postal issues? Only time will tell.

Do your students have particular persons or events they feel are deserving of such an honor? A good class project might involve the gathering of data to support such a claim and the forwarding of the conclusions to the Philatelic Affairs Division, U.S. Postal Service, Washington, D.C. 20260, and to members of Congress. Another exercise would be for students to design their own stamps depicting events or persons they feel deserve recognition. Such an exercise would involve not only the fact-finding activities which may be of interest to some students, but also utilize the artistic talents of others.

---

[5] For a more detailed analysis of the postal image of the Revolution and a complete list of all stamps relating to the period, see David Curtis Skaggs, "The Revolution through Postage Stamps: Icons of America's Birth," in Ray B. Browne and Marshall Fishwick, eds., *Icons of america* (Bowling Green, Ohio: Bowling Green Popular Press, 1977).
[6] See Richard C. Brown, 'Postage Stamps and American Women: Stamping Out Discrimination in the Mails," *Social Education*, 38 (January 1974), 20–23, for the postal image of women from Martha Washington to the present.

Another critical insight into the postal image of the Revolution would be our drift away from the "great hero" stereotype. From 1847 until 1975 our regular issue stamps invariably depicted Washington, Franklin, and Jefferson. The newly-issued "Americana" series is entirely devoted to symbols—drum, liberty bell, printing press, Old North Church, eagle and shield, and the 13-star flag with Independence Hall. Does this new issue represent a modern age without heroes whose most prominent figures are transitory celebrities whose fuzzy images cross our television screens and disappear with the flick of a switch?

Or, on the other hand, does the recent commemorative stamp drift from the traditional heroes to ones depicting the efforts of ordinary citizens mark a greater awareness of the common man and woman? Such bicentennial era series as the "Colonial Craftsmen," "Colonial Communications," "Contributors to the Cause," "Revolutionary Uniforms," and "Spirit of '76" certainly demonstrate this possibility.

The 1977 commemorative issues demonstrate this dualism of heroes and ordinary citizens. Washington and Lafayette are again honored, as is General Nicholas Herkimer of Oriskany fame. The July 4th block of four civilian artisans contributing to the war effort marks a continuation of the imagery of the common people's role in securing America's independence. Which of these images would your students prefer?

Some hints for classroom usage of stamps seem appropriate. The small size and delicate condition of stamps provide obstacles to their use that must be overcome. One way would be to have students with a photographic bent make slide transparencies for classroom use. Another might involve placing the stamps in inexpensive, clear plastic mounts which may be passed around the class. Obviously, one must acquire several copies of each issue, but this can be turned into class projects provoking student interest. (For those teachers utilizing learning centers, independent study activities can be constructed which involve one or two students viewing selected stamps.)

One may wish to purchase the Postal Service's Bicentennial Mint Set and Album ($7.50) containing 30 stamps printed from 1971 through 1976. Another "Stories of the American Revolution" album ($3.00) contains 23 United States and foreign cancelled stamps depicting our struggle for independence. These may serve as teacher's guides for a philatelic unit. "The Post Rider" is an interesting filmstrip with cassette tape which integrates one of the stamps from the 1974 "Spirit of Independence" series into an effective grade school teaching unit.

However they are used, postage stamps provide a springboard to wider learning. Of course, they may illustrate other times and nations; but effectively employed, stamps represent a too-little-used tool for encouraging student activity and inquiry.

(Courtesy © *National Council for the Social Studies*. Used with permission.)

QUESTIONS ON READING

1. How do postage stamps reflect the interests and emotions of society?

2. How does the author use postage stamps to demonstrate analytical and divergent thinking?

3. Which recent stamps reflect events or people in American history?

LESSON PLANS

Peggy Crump   Grades 4–6
Objective: To develop creative thinking skills through use of comic strips.
Rationale: Remedial reading students are frequently drawn to comic strips in newspapers. Comics offer fresh opportunities to draw upon student motivation in order to develop critical thinking.

Activities:

1. Open-ended discussion about why students enjoy comics. Pass out newspapers and use comics for discussion.

2. Display a comic strip that has been cut up and its order jumbled. Discuss why it doesn't make sense. Students are paired, cut up comic strips, scramble them, and place in an envelope. Each team exchanges its cut-up comic with another team. They race against one another as to which team can put the comic back into its correct sequence of action.

3. Teacher opens discussion about conclusion and predictions. Teacher reads a comic strip and halts before the end. Each team is to predict the ending. Later, each team is to write and draw the ending they would prefer.

4. Teacher discusses the idea of a "summary." Students pair off and read a comic strip. They are to agree upon a summary of what they read and present it to the class.
   • Students find a comic strip about a dog and one about a cat. They are to compare and contrast the story line of each strip.

5. Teacher displays a comic strip on an overhead with a word whited out. Students are to infer what is the missing word and state why they came to that conclusion.
   • Students take a favorite comic strip and white out some words. They are to write new dialogue.

6. Students are placed in groups and asked to dramatize a comic strip. Their presentation is to be videotaped for discussion. Class is to predict which comic strip is being acted out.

7. Students are introduced to different types of humor such as irony, satire, and puns. They are to work in groups and identify examples of each from comic strips given by the teacher.

8. Teacher leads discussion about "setting" of the comic strip and how characters "fit" the setting. Students in teams create new "balloon" statements for characters that don't fit the setting or the personality.

9. Class is divided into four groups and each group given a funny incident. The group is to create a comic strip to fit the incident.
   • Each group is given a situation in which characters from two different comics meet. For example, Snoopy meets Garfield. The group task is to write a comic strip about the meeting.

10. Extension Activities:
   • Make a crossword puzzle using words or characters from this unit plan.
   • Image you are interviewing a comic strip character. Which questions would you pose?
   • Imagine aliens got copies of our comic strips. What ideas would they have about planet Earth?
   • Interview people about their favorite comics. Chart and graph results of interviews.

Bibliography:

Adams, A.H. and Woods, E.E. (1976) Study guide to Reading the Newspaper, Perry-Neal Publishers.

Diamond, Sandy, (1988) Newspapers in Education Lesson Ideas, St. Louis Post-Dispatch.

Robinson, J. (1974) The Comics: An Illustrated History of Comic Strip Art, N.Y., Putnam.

Lori Gunn   4th Grade

Objective: To improve spelling using memory techniques.

Rationale: Children need better techniques in order to improve their retention of words. Memory techniques will assist them in knowing spelling words.

Activities:

1. Teacher explains that spelling words will be learned a new way—through use of special memory powers that each person has within their own mind.
   - Teacher reads list of 25 words. If child misspells word, a big "X" is placed over the incorrect letter. Then, the correct letter is written with a colored marker and made very big. For example, "abot" would be written, "aboXt" and then "aboUt."

2. Teacher explains that spelling words will be made into pictures. Or, the letters of the word are to represent its meaning—JOY. Students work in groups on spelling picture project. Student work is hung in the hallway.

3. Students shut eyes and recall pictures of words written the previous day. Each student in a group lists words recalled and group compiles a correct list of spelling list.
   - Each group makes a word puzzle using at least six words from their list.
   - Groups exchange their word puzzles with others.

4. Teacher uses words from list in sentences and students write the word.

5. Teacher reads a new list of words. If students mispell words, they are to cut the letters of the mispelled words from a newspaper and paste the word together correctly.
   - Students work in groups to paste correctly spelled words.

6. Teacher tells students their task is to take a long word in the spelling list and find short words in it. Those short words are to be used in a sentence. For example, "handker-chief" becomes, "I will hand the chief his kerchief."
   - Students in groups work on the project. Groups share their completed project.

7. Teacher tells students that today, instead of making short phrases from their words, they are to make longer sentences. Students work in groups on the project. Teacher encourages students to come up with silly or weird sentences.
   - Teacher reads words from list in a sentence and students write them correctly.

8. Teacher hands out new list of words. Students are told that each group will be given some of the words. The group's task is to act out the spelling of the word using their bodies, for example, "tiger." Students are to make their bodies look like that of a tiger, or they are to make their bodies look like the shape of a letter in the word and spell out the word using their bodies.
   - Teacher goes around the room snapping Polaroids of the word shapes. These are displayed on the bulletin board.
   - Each group acts out its words for the class.

9. Students are asked to place their words into categories. Each group is to make up its own system of categories. The categories are shared with the class.

10. Each group is asked to make up a short story using all the words from their spelling list. The stories are shared with the class.

11. Teacher gives test to determine how many words are correctly recalled.

REFERENCES

de Bono, E. (1968). *New think*. New York: Basic Books.

Gardner, H. (1983). *Frames of Mind: The Theory of Multiple Intelligence*. New York: Basic Books.

Gordon, W. J. J., & Poze, T. (1980). *The basic course in synectics*. Cambridge: Porpoise Books.

Gordon, W. J. J. (1973). *Synthetics*. New York: Macmillan.

Kornberg, D., & Bagnall, J. (1976). *The Universal Traveler*. Los Altos, CA: William Kaufmann.

Mindess, H. (1971, August). "The Sense of Humor." *Saturday Review*.

Osborn, A. (1948). *Your creative power: How to use your imagination*. New York: Charles Schribner's Sons.

Russell, P. (1979). *The brain book*. New York: Hawthorn.

Tamashiron R. (1979, November). "Children's Humor: A Developmental View." *The Elementary Journal, 80*, (2).

SUGGESTED READING

Cerf, B. (1947). *Try and stop me*. Garden City, NJ: Garden City Publishing.

deBono, E. (1969). *New Think*. New York: Basic Books.

Gordon, W. J. J. (1973). *Synectics*. New York: Macmillan.

Kornberg, D., & Bagnall, J. (1976). *The Universal Traveler*. Los Altos, CA: William Kaufmann.

Lorayne, H., & Lucas, J. (1974). *The memory book*. New York: Ballantine.

McGhee, P., & Chapman, A. (Eds.) (1980). *Children's humor*. New York: Wiley.

Osborn, A. (1948). *Your creative power*. New York: Charles Scribner's Sons.

Stopsky, F. (1992). *Humor in the classroom*. Lowell, MA: Discovery Enterprises.

AN AFTERTHOUGHT

Are You Ready to Become a Teacher?

1. Do you murmur "no cuts" when a shopper squeezes ahead of you in line?
2. Do you move your dinner partner's plate away from the edge of the table?
3. Do you ask if anyone needs to go to the bathroom when you enter the theater?
4. Do you hand a tissue to anyone who sneezes?
5. Do you ask guests if they remembered their scarves and mittens as they leave your home?
6. Do you refer to it as "snack time" instead of "happy hour?"
7. Do you say, "I like the way you did that" to compliment the mechanic who repairs your car?
8. Do you say, "Are you sure you did your best?" to the mechanic who fails to repair your car?
9. Do you sing the Alphabet song to yourself as you look up a number in the telephone book?
10. Do you say everything twice? Do you repeat yourself?
11. Do you hold your spouse's fingers over the coins as you hand them to him?
12. Do you ask a quiet person at a party if he/she has something to share with the group?

   • If you answered "yes" to more than three of these items, you are hooked on teaching.
   • If you answered "yes" to more than half of these questions, you will probably spend your life in teaching.

Chapter 8

Integrating Technology into Social Studies

Integrating Technology into Social Studies

In the summer of 1938, the American essayist E.B. White first saw the flickering image on a small television screen. That fall he wrote in *Harper's Magazine* that television would be the test of the modern world. He thought television would be either an "unbearable disturbance" in our daily lives or a "saving radiance" in the sky. Television was the first of a series of new technologies which dramatically altered American life in post World War II America. The focus of this chapter is on how the elementary social studies teacher can effectively utilize technology in the classroom.

The 20th century is rife with examples of technologies that promised to "revolutionize" education. In nearly a century preceding the coming of personal computers, teachers have seen radio, 16mm film, filmstrips, overhead transparencies, and various forms of telelvision heralded as answers to education's problems. As early as 1922, Thomas Edison (quoted in Wise, 1939) believed that the "motion picture would revolutionize our educational system, and that in a few years it would supplant largely, if not entirely, the use of textbooks." Film was regarded as a visual and concrete experience that would increase student motivation and learning efficiency, but various factors like cost, availability of film copies, access to projectors, and teacher hesitation to use technology prevented Edison's prediction from achieving actuality.

The Industrial Revolution gave us machinery to substitute for physical labor. The information revolution is giving us machinery and tools to extend our mental labor; they will not replace that mental labor. The computer does not replace mental energy; it requires additional mental energy. Training the mind to use information technology is far different from training the body to use machines correctly. It means a new burden on the schools if students are to learn how to think in different ways.

New Technologies

The computer is the dominant linchpin among technologies that have emerged in the past decade. The desktop computer affords interesting avenues to develop flexible programs and provides an interactive process between student and technology. Teachers and students can actively interact, manipulate, or even produce media rather than merely watching or listening as passive observors.

Learning activities with the new technologies range from structured drill tutorials to open-ended tools such as writing, graphic design, or group brainstorming; from viewing a tour of a zoo to student groups producing a video animation sequence illustrating the water cycle. The computer is a multifaceted invention, a tool for making, exploring, and thinking in various domains. With pre-computer media, the extent of teacher or student manipulation was when to show the film or how much to view. The computer enables teachers and students to manipulate the sequence of what is viewed, which pictures will be juxtaposed and compared, or superimposed and highlighted.

The computer offers opportunities to go beyond manipulation and engage in creative activities. Students and teachers can create, add, or edit text material (as in a word processor), voice or music enhancements, and include drawings, maps or charts, snapshots and homemade video clips. In essence, new technologies move consumers from being passive recipients to managers, creators, authors, and producers of information.

The presence of new technologies raises social and economic questions for educators. The definition of literacy" as the ability to read, comprehend, judge and produce written material is a definition from the era of the printing press. Most schools lack resources to invest heavily in new technologies, but some wealthy districts can, and this means their students will have a head start in computer age literacy. This will further increase the equity gap between rich and poor children in American society.

The emerging Information Age is computer and video based, which means that students who become proficient with these new technologies while in public school will have enhanced opportunities in higher education or the work world. Their ability to manipulate new technologies is a valuable tool that will be in demand from employers.

Elementary and middle school teachers have an important role to play in developing technological skills among all students regardless of economic or ethnic background. Youth must be educated to think and act critically and effectively in the techno-logical environment. Some educators believe that expanding access to technology may eventually foster greater equity for all students to develop their intellectual skills.

The mere introduction of technology will not in itself resolve problems of unequal educational opportunities or motivate

▲ New information technologies have become increasingly visible in elementary classrooms. *Courtesy Webster University.*

children to learn. A teacher with autocratic tendencies is likely to use the computer to further regiment and dehumanize learning, whereas a teacher who practices the values of democracy will be more likely to utilize the computer to foster equity. Change will only occur when teachers seek to join technology with the principles of a child-centered democratic classroom.

If the information technologies are to be truly integrated into elementary and middle school settings, teachers must learn how to work with technologies to promote desired atittudes, foster knowledge and create a class environment which generates self discipline. New technology is rich in its breadth of exciting educational programs. The word processor can be used to write reports and stories or become part of a multimedia presentation on local recycling activities. A generation raised on video games is more inclined to work with technology that requires a hands-on approach.

Access to technology continues to be limited. For example, even though the number of computers in schools worldwide increases as computer technology improves rapidly and its costs decrease, the ratio of computers to students in the U.S. in 1989 was still 1 computer for every 30 students. In the early 1990s, schools in the U.S. still vary greatly in how classrooms are outfitted with computers. There may be no computers, one or a few in a classroom, and in a few situations a coordinated network of computers in a classroom. Frequently the learning center, lab, or library houses a roomful of computers where computer-based activities for a whole class can be scheduled.

Instructional Computing

The most common use of instructional computers in elementary and middle school grades is drill and practice of math, word processing, keyboarding, and English.

Activity

In groups of 3 to 4 persons, review 3 instructional software packages including the program disc and manual. Report on each of the packages by answering the following questions.

1. Give the program title and description.
2. State which grades and subject areas the program is appropriate for.
3. List the content objectives of the software.
4. Can the objectives be achieved effectively without using this software? Describe how.
5. Identify other (*collateral*) objectives (i.e. implicit or hidden curriculum) that are being achieved when students use this software.

Computer Simulations

A "simulation" in the classroom is any activity or tool that imitates a process or situation. As such, many teachers already do simulations without computers in the form of role-playing, personifications, and mock trials, or in using models like a globe or solar system. Computer simulations, however, affords the opportunity for students to role-play more complex situations and concepts. Students can interact with the simulation and control variables separately, thereby learning concepts or skills in a self-directed manner.

▲ Teachers and students can produce media rather than merely watching. *Courtesy Saint Louis (Missouri) Public Schools.*

Computer simulations can be used in both the cognitive and affective domains to achieve lesson objectives:

1. The personal engagement of students increases motivation about the lesson to be studied.
2. They can get students to think analytically and critically about the subject.
3. The use of simulations encourages students to employ constructive social skills in their interactions with one another.

Teachers should follow several guidelines in doing computer simulations with students.

1. It is important to provide worksheets and conduct class discussion that directs students to think and reflect about the activity in relation to concepts in the lesson because some students perceive simulations as "games."
2. Teacher should plan to help students make the link between the strategy they used in the simulation activity and the lesson concept.
3. Teachers should review the lesson materials thoroughly before the lesson. Simulations cannot stand alone.

4. It is important that simulation lessons do not contain too many factors and variables because students get distracted, and may venture onto paths far removed from the central goals of the lesson.

Activity

Preview a simulation such as *Odell Lake, Oh, Deer!, Oregon Trail, The Marketplace* (MECC), *Decisions, Decisions* (Tom Snyder Productions), *Where in the World Is Carmen Sandiego?* (Brøderbund Corporation), or *Whatsit Corporation* (Sunburst). Address the following questions in reporting about your preview:

1. List the advantages of using this simulation pacakage.
2. List the disadvantages.
3. List the key concepts that are meant to be taught by the simulation program.
4. Describe three ways these concepts can be taught without using the simulation package.
5. Compare the overall value of the simulation package with the approaches in #4.

The Computer As A Tool

In addition to teaching or illustrating material, students and teachers can use computers for their intellectual or artistic exploration and expression. The computer becomes a tool in writing, planning, model building, graphic design, or music composition. These applications are considered tools in that they automate some of the computational (e.g., creating a graph), mechanical (e.g., automatic formatting or outlining), and cognitive (checking spelling or grammar) burdens involved in the associated tasks. Tools include empty "shells" like word processors, databases, and spreadsheets, as well as those filled with a particular content, such as prepared databases.

▲ Educators find the computer to be a multifaceted tool for making, exploring, and thinking. *Courtesy Null Elementary, Saint Charles (Missouri) Public Schools.*

The open-endedness of computer tools makes them highly flexible, enabling students and teachers to gain access to a wider choice of strategies and materials. Computer tools allow students to engineer their own cognitive realities, hence stimulating the development of high-level cognitive skills. These applications enable students to qualitatively enhance their academic performance without relying on different software packages for each topic of study. The same tool, for example, a database program, can be used whether students are tallying voting patterns in the county or cataloging various nations' environmental efforts following an Earth Summit. Computer tools enable students to be more autonomous, and to assume greater personal responsibility for learning. The use of computers moves the class and teacher away from didactic processes of learning and toward collaborative endeavors.

Of course, using computer tools does not by itself result in these gains, or other improvements like better writing (as a result of using a word processor). These changes seem to occur only when the teacher systematically plans for and guides students toward the particular objective such as clearer writing, responsibility for learning, or other higher-level cognitive skills. The word processor, for example, improves writing only when it is integrated fully into a coherent writing curriculum.

Expert Systems

"Expert systems" are computer programs that model the reasoning of experts on a particular topic. They store and catalog information, as do computer data bases, but can also guide the inquiry. For example, a student might consult an expert system to help her decide which high school to consider attending. The student would respond to questions like, "Do you prefer a public school as opposed to a private or parochial school?" or "Do you prefer a specialty magnet school?" The system determines which questions to ask and makes a recommendation based on the students' answers and the characteristics of the schools. The student can also find out how the system arrived at its conclusion by retracing the reasoning path used by the expert system.

In one system called *Knowledge Works,* the teacher or student enters the possible outcomes on a selected topic (e.g., the list of high schools), composes the questions that refer to the relevant characteristics, and fills out a table of "yes" or "no" responses for how each outcome relates to each question. Once the information has been entered, the system can show how the knowledge base is organized either in table form or in a tree-diagram. The system also handles the logic during a consultation session, including (1) determining which questions to ask and in what order, (2) systematically eliminating outcomes based on the individual's sequence of answers, and (3) tracing the reasoning used to reach its conclu-

sions. *Knowledge Works* is practical for teachers as well as pupils as young as 7 years old.

In the classroom, expert systems have been used as:

1. *Instructional Aids:* Teachers build an expert system to introduce or reinforce concepts. For example a teacher might use an expert system about U.S. presidents as way of getting students to become familiar with the biography and beliefs of these presidents.

2. *Medium for Student Research and Reports:* Students themselves research a topic and use that knowledge to design and build a system. These student-built

expert systems often accompany students' written reports, cooperative research group activity, or book reports. Student systems are shared by having other students "consult" the student-built expert system.

3. *Tool for Studying Knowledge Organization:* Expert systems are often used to teach thinking skills or processes themselves. For example, teachers use expert systems to work with classification skills, seriation, and scientific method. Young children take a list of items they know well, such as brands of athletic shoes or favorite ice cream flavors, and create criteria for classifying, identifying, or choosing these items, and then evaluate the classification system they use to construct their system.

▲ Before computer-based media, decision making was limited to when to show the film or filmstrip or how much of it to view. *Courtesy Perry County (Missouri) School District No. 42.*

Some teachers show students how to use the expert system and gain a level of comfort with the medium before applying the understanding to the teaching of their subject. Others do not feel the preliminary work is necessary. These teachers incorporate students' understanding of the technology with content objectives. Following are three synopses of lessons teachers created involving expert systems.

- "Differentiating Personal Characteristics," grade 2, teacher: Jan Engdahl
  This lesson introduces students to classification of observable personal characteristics, and the graphic representation of this classification using a tree diagram. It involved the whole class creating a human tree diagram. Students practice the brainstorming technique. Students stand in a straight line, shoulder to shoulder. Students took one step forward when a characteristic the teacher named was true about themselves. In this way, students were divided by their personal

characteristics, such as gender, hair color, hair length and texture. An expert system was created. Students answered the questions, thus comparing the expert system's results with the physical characteristics observed in the earlier activity. Students examined the resulting tree diagram and discussed what it represents.

- "Native American Tribes," grade 3, teacher: Joyce Belrose

  Students spent several days reading about Native Americans. They then decided what categories they would like to research. Categories included environment, homes, food, dress, jobs, and traditions. They entered the information into a database and used it to select common characteristics. Groups of students, using the database as a resource, devised an expert system with which could isolate individual tribes. After entering their designs into Knowledge Works, each student group explained their tree diagram classification of the tribe characteristics to the class.

- "Classifying Books Using Tree Diagrams," grade 3, teacher: Paula Hertel

  Students were asked how they might categorize books about Native Americans. They devised eight questions, such as "Do you want a fictional book about American Indians?" "Should the book have illustrations?" and "Do you want a book that takes place in a desert?" The questions and the students' responses were entered into the expert system, which displayed a tree diagram. Students explained to the class how individual books could be recommended by following the path on the tree diagram.

4. *Telecommunications*. Telecommunications is the transmission of audio, video or data information via telephone, radio, television, teletype, satellite, facsimile (fax), modem, and other electronic media. Often, telecommunications is used to refer only to computer-to-computer communication. "Local" communications refers to computers linked together by cable in pairs or in groups called "networks." On the other hand, "remote" communications refers to computers linked by telephone. A modem, enables a computer to interact with another computer via telephone lines. Classrooms across the hall, across town, or anywhere in the world can interact with each other by utilizing a modem for remote communications. These communications are typically coordinated through a network service or bulletin board system (BBS), allowing interaction with a wide audience.

In the classroom, telecommunications examples today consist of text-based interactions over modems and phone lines. These are typically student exchanges of personal information, "pen-pal" interactions, and cooperative data exchanges on shared comparative projects on topics like acid rain, recycling methods, or family traditions. Although telecommunications activities do not typically include face-to-face interactions, students are motivated to search for ways to compensate for this limitation (Sproull & Kiesler, 1986).

The following are telecommunications activities for either a local or remote system in the classroom.

1. *Introductions by Electronic Mail.* Have students compose a brief description about their hobbies and interests and post it as a bulletin on a bulletin board service, or on the local network. This language arts activity can be reviewed by the teacher prior to posting and disseminating it among other children in the school.

2. *Fractured Facts.* A "Fractured Facts" board includes "informational bulletins" (such as those describing a famous person, historical event, science facts, etc.). There are factual errors contained in the bulletins. The student assignment is to sign-on, read the bulletin(s) and reply with the corrections. Later the original sender may give feedback to the replies indicating how many "fractured facts" were identified.

3. *The Chain Story.* One person starts the bulletin board (or electronic conference) with the beginning of a story. The next student signs on, reads the story beginning and then adds a bulletin which is a continuation of the story. As other students sign on, they read the continuing story bulletins and add a bulletin.

4. *Studying Characters' Feelings.* The students read or listen to a novel or short story. The teacher or a student group selects key characters to be "players" on the bulletin board. The teacher signs on each character on the board, as though the character is a person on the board. An alternative is to have the teacher assign students to particular characters. Students sign on the board and read the bulletins posted by the "characters". They react to the characters' comments on the bulletin board through the "reply" option.

5. *Father Lost-Time.* On one conference board, "Father Time" has lost his calendar. He posts bulletins which describe important historical events during a period in history (relevant to the curriculum). He points out that he cannot place the correct dates for these events. Students sign on and read the bulletins. They reply to Father Time or to the Bulletin Board with the dates for the events. Later the teacher can check to see whether the students' reply dates were correct.

6. *Letters to the Editor:* A current events topic is presented at the beginning of a bulletin board or electronic conference. Students give their reaction, opinions or comments about the topic in the form of a "letter to the editor." Students may also reply to those who wrote previous letters. Later the teacher can conduct class discussions based on the various opinions expressed by students.

Videodisc Applications in Social Studies

Videodiscs are laser-based media capable of storing visual and audio information, including photographs, diagrams, maps, animation, film clips, music, and oral explanations. They are "as easy to play as phonograph records, and because nothing touches the playing surface except a beam of light, they should last indefinitely" (Van Horn, 1987). The material on the disc can be accessed directly using a remote control, a computer connected to the player, or a bar code wand and printed bar codes that the teacher or student prepared beforehand. Since the material on the disc is more quickly accessed than videotape, videodiscs are extremely flexible as an instructional aid.

▲ Teachers' roles in relation to new technologies change from consumers of information to managers, creators, authors, and producers. *Courtesy Webster University.*

Examples of classroom applications of the technologies described here are ones that have been applied in regular classroom settings where student or teacher access has been limited.

- "Carnivores and Herbivores," grade 4, teacher: Chris Ravens, Webster Groves (Missouri) School District

  In this social studies/science and technology lesson, the students had been studying food chains and could define carnivore, herbivore, and omnivore. They were introduced to the videodiscs, *Encyclopedia of Animals,* Vol. 1–2, which contains motion-video segments of animals and a world map showing where each animal lived. The disc also contained still pictures of animals comparing their size to humans. Students located and played videodisc segments. Students recorded observations made from the discs in their science journals. Observations included information on eating habits, predators, habitat, regions where they lived, and other interesting facts. Their individual reports involved classification of the animals according to one of these characteristics.

- "Attributes and Tree Diagrams," grade 3, teacher: Colleen Brugnara
  Videodisc and expert system technologies were combined in this lesson designed to reinforce the following concepts and thinking skills: (1) all matter has attributes; (2) a hierarchical classification system, as illustrated by a tree diagram, makes decision making efficient, (3) skills including inference and the process of elimination can be used to solve problems. Students reviewed properties of matter in science. They then made and explained the placement of blocks in a Venn diagram. Students were shown eight objects on the videodisc "Visual Almanac." On worksheets, they answered questions that required them to follow paths of inference on a tree diagram. Students could then confirm their answers with the bar code and videodisc. They could also consult an expert system for validation.

▲ Some educators suggest that computers in classrooms meant greater equity for all students. *Courtesy Kirkwood (Missouri) School District.*

Television and Videotape

Television has been viewed as a potential educational tool ever since its widespread acceptance in the 1950s. With at least one television set in practically all homes in the U.S.A., television has become the most dominant form of mass communication. Television is among the most powerful tools in social studies education. It provides instantaneous access to the world and dramatic real-life stories about people and places. It offers a vast weekly array of informational films, thought provoking dramas and an opportunity to see world leaders in action.

Quality television programs can transport students around the world, present fascinating graphics and tell interesting stories. The sight of a volcano whose erruption has covered an area cannot be replicated by a geography book's explanation of volcanoes. Television offers immediacy and unlike print, favors movement over stillness, simplification over complexity, personality over conceptualization and the present over both past and future.

Public television offers many quality programs and in some areas, full course and diploma programs are delivered via television today. Programs on virtually every level and topic taught in school have been created by local or state schools districts, by public television and independent producers. They are accessible via broadcast, cable or satellite television systems, close-circuit and microwave transmissions. Many programs are also available on videotape or videodisc.

Live instructional television includes courses by satellite or cable which is a practical solution when instructors are not available or affordable for in-person instruction. Today, these courses are primarily designed for high-school, undergraduate, graduate and adult enrichment audiences, so they may not have particular applicability in elementary or middle school grades. A privately funded project called Channel One delivers daily live 15-minute news broadcasts via satellite to participating schools across the U.S.A. The cable network, C-SPAN, which airs

Congressional activities, government and other public affairs programs, provides teachers' guides to use both live and taped material in the classroom.

Pragmatic and pedagogical obstacles have resulted in the limited use of live television for classroom instruction. These obstacles include unavailablity or problems operating the equipment, teachers' lack of time or access to preview material, scheduling difficulties, poor quality or less than relevant programs. However, with the emergence of "archived television," e.g. the videotape and videodisc media, educators are more able to utilize instructional media within classrooms. It is relatively easy for teachers to preview videotapes or videodiscs within their own homes and decide which pieces of the tape or disc to use in lesson plans. The widespread availability of videocassette recorders (VCR) makes it possible for teachers and students to record programs (broadcast, cable, or satellite) for later preview, or showing. In addition, broadcast services are increasing by making tapes of aired programs available to schools for instructional uses. Video collections such as those of the Public Affairs Video Archives at Purdue University and PBS Video make previously aired programs readily accessible.

Is instruction using television and videotape effective? This question has been debated in educational research for decades, with no definitive conclusion about exactly how effective the media per se is. There is much evidence that learning from television can occur, from the preschool ages on (Chu & Schramm, 1979). In particular, television is effective in traditional content-based instructional goals (Schramm, 1977). However, when television is judged alongside *well-designed* instructional units without television, the results are varied. In general, television is not any more or any less effective than other well-planned means of instruction (Clark & Salomon, 1986). As with other media, the effectiveness of television instruction depends on how the teacher helps pupils integrate the media experience with the objectives of the lesson.

▲ The computer offers opportunities to develop powerful intellectual skills. *Courtesy Saint Louis (Missouri) Public Schools.*

The increasing availablity of camcorders add yet another dimension to this technology. Camcorders allow students and teachers to become producers of video, not just consumer-viewers. The opportunity to make video is a key element in completing the "video literacy" metaphor. Just as one cannot be considered literate until one can intelligently read and write; video literacy consists of both intelligent viewing and making of video. Although still novel, classrooms are increasing devoting time to create news programs, and use personally produced video in reporting on their library or field research. Student produced work is being viewed on community cable systems, or exchanged with other schools, as a way of sharing knowledge. The camcorder can be incorporated into multimedia lessons as discussed below.

Activity

Choose a grade level. Then consider the following statement: "It is possible to achieve all the social studies content objectives in that grade level through television and video programs." Obtain recent issues of *TV Guide,* satellite and cable television program guides, and catalogs from educational video services. Make a list of all the programs aired or on tape that may be used to achieve the content objectives for your grade level. Summarize your results.

Television programs can be used to stimulate critical thinking. Many sitcoms depict problems or conflicts. Teachers video tape these programs and present them to the class. In one activity, the teacher halts the program prior to its ending and asks students to hypothesize what will next occur. In some cases, students are asked to rewrite the entire script or change personalities of the cast in order to create new dynamics in the story. Some classes have a video exchange program with schools in other nations; interesting video tapes are exchanged which depict one another's society. Hopefully, in the coming decade, videoconferences or the videophone will become less expensive and children around the world will be able to see and speak with one another.

Television is established as a fact of life, an integral part of virtually every American's life, and a major source of information about what happens in the local community, throughout the country and around the globe. The medium helps shape our understanding of ourselves, our society, and our place in the world. Television has also helped create the "information age." It is a tool for managing the demands of an information-driven society because it serves to integrate rather than segment information.

There are several unfortunate consequences of student interaction with television. They come away with the idea that even the most complex problem can be solved in thirty minutes, with time out for commercials. They learn that emotion is frequently equated by volume of voice and vigor of gestures. Students are often passive receptors of information, sitting in front of the tube without careful thought, and become accustomed to the idea that violence is the best way to solve problems.

Television must become a tool that educators use to their advantage in teaching social studies. We are only beginning to learn efffective ways to integrate television within the curriculum. It is not a substitute for teachers, but another means teachers can use to attract and sustain student interest.

Films

Films have been used in conjunction with social studies instruction for over sixty years. They are frequently employed to illustrate material being covered in reading and discussions or to supplement material already studied. Students learn about the westward movement and then view a film in order to reinforce what was taught. Many teachers also use films as a "change of pace" in order to entertain or catch a few minutes of rest in the hectic day of teaching.

These are valid uses, but films can also be used to stimulate high levels of critical thinking. There are many films which raise critical issues or present problems for analysis as well as films which depict historical events. Hollywood films tend to skirt historical accuracy and this failure can be turned to advantage by the enterprising teacher. For example, in the summer of 1992, a film depicting the life of Christopher Columbus was widely shown. One of the textbook authors and a class of undergraduates discovered, after research, at least 20 factual errors in the film as well as insensitive presentations of Native Americans.

The typical elementary or middle school school child watches hundreds of films and TV programs, goes to the movies and rents videotapes. They are experts regarding what constitutes a poorly produced film, but their interest in the medium can be used to foster critical thinking.

One strategy is to link students with the film to be shown. For example, prior to showing Rudyard Kipling's *Rikki-Rikki-Tavi*, students are divided into groups and each group is asked to view the film through the mind's eye of their character. The story is about a mongoose in India who is taken in by a boy and his family. In the story, Rikki saves the boy and his parents from snakes. However, from the viewpoint of the snakes, Rikki is an intruder who murders them, kidnaps, holds one baby egg hostage, and finally kills all their baby eggs. The birds in the story view Rikki as a hero who saves them from attacks by the snakes. In one teacher's class, the students held a mock trial in which Rikki was charged with tresspassing as well as assault and battery.

Another strategy is to halt the film at key points in order to elicit discussion or have students hypothesize what will occur. The film *Joseph Schultz* tells the story of a German soldier who refused to participate in the execution of civilians and was then placed against the wall to be shot. The film can be stopped at the point where Joseph Schultz initially refuses to fire on the civilians. Students frequently respond to the question of his alternatives by saying Schultz should shoot over their heads or kill the officer and his fellow soldiers. A few moments later students are asked what alternatives were open to the officer and other men in the firing squad. At each place the film is halted, students become active participants in discussion and the film takes on new meaning.

Almost all films are designed to influence our attitudes and thoughts, particularly those made for commercial purposes. Teachers use films as an effective way to teach children about propaganda techniques such as the way children are manipulated to purchase games, toys, and clothes. Commercials and programs can be taped for discussion and analysis of how opinions are controlled through use of camerawork, editing, and direction.

The growing availability of camcorders will make it possible for students to create their own films. A student "documentary" of pollution or local traffic congestion can be a spur for the class to become change agents seeking to improve the quality of life within the community. This experience can benefit children who have difficulty expressing themselves in writing and to students who have ideas which take them beyond the library. Films can be a doorway toward expanding possibilities for media use in the classroom.

Chalkboard

The chalkboard was among the first pieces of technology to dramatically alter education within classrooms. Its introduction and widespread use in the 19th century enabled teachers to present information visually and allowed students with limited amounts of money to share their ideas in a written form with classmates. For many teachers, the chalkboard is the most-used piece of technology in their daily teaching.

Writing on chalkboards enables children to see as well as hear words being spoken. There are several factors to consider when using chalkboards:

- Write in large letters and legibly.
- Transform a collection of words into a chart to aid children understand the concept of categories.
- Arrows or pictures dramatically enhance the visual imagery being presented.
- Ask students to draw their responses if they are struggling with speech or writing.
- Continue speaking even as you write or draw on the chalkboard in order to maintain student involvement.

Multimedia

Change to multimedia can be defined as an instructional delivery or presentation that involves a variety of media technologies. These technologies may include: text, graphics, photographs, motion video or animation, music or speech. Likewise, the "media technologies" refers to any combination of video technologies (videotape, videodisc, CD-ROM, live television), computer technologies, and audio (live or recorded music or speech). Multimedia also implies interactivity, the ability of the teacher or student to control the order and the timing of material to be viewed or heard. This interactivity may be preprogrammed, so a particular sequence is shown to a class, for example; or it may be spontaneous, so the sequence can be modified during a session.

Multimedia has the potential for being more effective than the individual technologies or media, because the teacher can choose the most effective elements of several technologies and link them. It makes possible the juxtaposition of ideas and concepts from separate media, which were previously perceived as unrelated. The links themselves make possible the communication of new ideas and concepts.

Using multimedia usually involves creating new information: whether it is adding an oral commentary, labeling a chart in the presentation, or shooting new video. However, even when the material is only assembled, rather than created, the process is a thought-stimulating, creative, and integrating. Students have the opportunity to document their learning through another media.

The use of multimedia with young children poses several issues pertaining both to availability of materials, time considerations, and teacher knowledge. The more media technology employed, the increased probability something will go wrong. Few teachers have the time, background or motivation to invest considerable energy in complex technological endeavors. The novice teacher should take one step at a time in the implementation of multimedia presentations.

Technology has been at the foundation of human economic progress in the past few centuries. It has enabled humans to make significant advancements in health care, diet, living conditions, and life style. There are critics who worry that reliance upon the technological "fix" also poses problems. Technology will not in itself lead children to learning or higher standards of education. Technology is a tool, not a cure.

Teachers cannot ignore children's powerful attraction to technology. Their reliance upon such things as video games for entertainment has made electronics as integral to their lives as the farm was to the childhoods of children two hundred years ago. Teachers have to invent new ways to integrate technology into the curriculum without diluting traditional academic materials such as books and writing. The challenge is dramatic, but the possibilities are awesome.

· ·

SUMMARY

This chapter has reviewed the role technologies play in the social studies curriculum. It discussed the use of computers, TV, and radio in social studies education.

QUESTIONS

1. What is your greatest source of information concerning national and international issues?

2. Which forms of technology do you most frequently employ in your daily life?

3. What is your greatest anxiety about using technology as part of your teaching plans?

4. What is your greatest strength in utilizing technology?

5. Assume every American child was provided a personal computer. How would that impact learning?

6. How has technology impacted your learning in college?

7. Cite an example in which the media significantly impacted your values and shaped your atittudes.

8. What is the difference between your utilization of technology and that of today's school children?

9. Which do you prefer—a teacher who makes extensive use of chalkboards or one who ignores them in teaching?

10. What type of information do you obtain from the radio?

ACTIVITIES

1. Interview parents about their attitudes toward the relationship between media and their children.

2. Interview elementary school children about what they like best about using technology.

3. Critique an existing piece of computer software that is currently being used in schools.

4. Interview elementary school teachers regarding their views about using technology in the classroom.

5. Interview curriculum coordinators and computer advocates in elementary school. Obtain their ideas regarding the use of technology and compare those findings with ideas provided by teachers.

READING

Computers for Intellectual Regeneration

Editor's Note: *The following article is the result of an interview conducted by Diane Kendall and Howard Budin with Robert Taylor, an Associate Professor of Computing and Education at Teachers College, Columbia University.*

Q. *What do you see as some of the exciting things happening in computing and education today?*

A. The most exciting thing that's happening because of computer use in schools and universities today is the intellectual regeneration occurring among the people using computers. People who had stagnated and gotten bored are alive again. Their students sense it and appreciate the more energetic ethos that it creates.

The dominant type of computing going on in education apart from the old types (programming, computer science and statistical analysis) is probably word processing. All kinds of people have discovered how useful computers can be in all kinds of writing, and they're relishing their value. But other "newer" types of computing are also gaining prominence along with word processing: data base building and use, graphical representation of all kinds, telecommunicating (including bulletin board use), and so on.

What people are finding through these new applications is renewed interest in understanding and improving what they do educationally. And through all these uses, people are getting a new appreciation of the truly endless, ongoing character of education: constant change is the norm for hardware and software, and to use either regularly requires learning to live with change. Finally, student computer use frequently demonstrates that student attention and interest can be intensely focused on intellectual activity for long periods of time, certainly far longer than the traditional length of a school or university class period.

With the huge increase in the last five years in the number of people using computers in education, we are seeing the effects of hardware developments that put much more computing power into a much smaller space, at a much lower cost. Such developments have spread computing use from a relatively small group of people who had to be specially trained, to a very large group who need very little special training. Part of the stimulation is volume alone; we now see a lot of people who use computers and are excited about them who had no connection whatsoever with them a few years ago. The implications for school activities are significant.

One is that widely accessible, powerful computing motivates people to think about things in a new way, to think about new possibilities with respect to whatever subject they're using computers for. Computing also requires people to learn to live with change.

It forces them to develop a strong sense of the need to be more flexible instead of having a number of small fragments of activities as we do in a typical university or school day, where we have 2 hours for this course or 40 minutes for that subject. We see people working on the computer for 4, 5, 6, 7 or 8 hours at a time or working over a period of weeks on some project. This pattern has important implications for the way our overall school system is structured and for ourselves as faculty members and teachers, and for the way our students work on the assignments we suggest.

Computing is likely to help us change the role of teachers and professors from people who are authorities primarily because of the information they possess to people who are revered and respected primarily because of their coordination and judgment about information that everybody has equal access to, and that neither they nor anyone else can entirely master because there's just too much of it. In this sense, we'll see movement away from the traditional assumption that a relatively small, commonly agreed upon body of knowledge comprises the information that any educated person must know to an assumption that the educated person is one who has a way of operating or thinking that enables her or him to come to terms with much larger bodies of information, including information yet to be developed.

Q. *Could you expand a little on how the role of teachers is going to change because of new computer technology that may be entering their schools and classrooms?*

A. As I said, I think that the current view of the teacher in our school system (and probably the professor in our universities as well) is more often than not based upon a belief that the teacher has a significant body of information at his or her command, that that information is part of a particular sacrosanct pile whose internalization is considered by everybody to be the essence of getting educated, and that the teacher commands appropriate techniques for dealing with that information. Moreover, it is because the student commands neither so well that the teacher enjoys control over her or his students.

I like to think that the teacher will become more often a sort of coach, because a coach is a model everyone can understand. Suppose you are a vocal coach. You won't really put on a good operetta or musical if you insist on being the best singer in your group. If you insist on being better than any of the students you're going to have in your production, it probably won't be a very good production.

The successful coach, whether in athletics or music, is someone who emphasizes judgment, skill and the ability to urge people on or, alternately, to restrain them within the skills and knowledge that they possess. We can look at another model and see that computing might push us in that direction because it constantly brings home to us how little we know and how little we can hope to master all the increasingly large body of information available on a particular topic. The principal role of the teacher may move from being master of the classroom to coach of information navigators, teaching students how to navigate all this information and form judgments based on it.

Q. *What resources do you think technology is providing now or is likely to provide to students of social studies for learning about the world that were not previously available?*

A. I think that's an extension of what I was just saying—computing tends to bring home to us more and more the fact that there's far more information than we can easily internalize. When there were few books on Plato's *Republic*, we could all read them and memorize what they said and discuss these ad nauseum; what we're seeing now is mass multiplication of information about our world physically, socially, politically and so on. What the computer makes possible is access to this information in ways that we did not have before.

One example would be the use of electronic connections to access and navigate information. With more information than people can put into a particular personal computer, we can have a repository of information set up so that many people can talk to it and ask questions through electronic connections. There might be a whole library on the computer that people could access from all sorts of perspectives.

Examples of this on a small scale are beginning to go forward now, which will have a large impact on classrooms. Instead of having a small library with a couple of hundred volumes, through electronic connection students would have access to vast quantities of information—maybe from all over the country, maybe all over the world—that they previously would have had to go to all those places to see. So, electronic connections or networks are another form of access to information that is going to impact and affect the social studies and social science classroom.

Another form of computer information manipulation and use that is going to be important to social studies is what we call simulation, or an imitation of some aspect of life. We build models all the time of what life is like, and every theory of history is really a model. Sometimes it is contradicted by another theory, but we use models to talk about things intellectually. In terms of simulation, what the computer makes possible is something that seems more real than a mere discussion, since the computer can be programmed so that it appears to make some things happen as they "really" do. You can have simulations of war, business activities, explorations, discoveries, landing on the moon, and of course you can have all sorts of social simulations.

Such simulations can give students a perspective different from the one they get from reading a book or searching a network for information. Others may bring into interactive time/space a sort of re-creation of time past. People can play these simulations in the classroom, they can play at night, they can play together, and they can even play alone, with just the computer, but through them all they can realize some new perspective on information that's been around for a long time but has not been so dynamically presentable before.

Another aspect that the computer emphasizes and, like simulation, provides a whole new perspective into certain parts of the social studies information bank is graphics. Our whole educational system has become increasingly oriented around text as we've mastered our means of putting information into alphabetical form and printing it over the last couple of thousand years, especially since the invention of movable type. But we have always had the tendency to represent things graphically, also. In social studies the most common example may be a map, but in other cases pictures, graphs or diagrams help to convey information or understanding of it that text alone is not very good at.

With computers and the advent of tools like the Koala pad, the Macintosh computer, and "draw" and "paint" software, it's possible for people with minimal artistic skill and minimal skill in representing objects graphically to borrow these skills from other people via the software and hardware. Thus the graphically unskilled can represent all sorts of things graphically, in a form that's recognizable and aesthetically acceptable.

Where information might better be represented graphically, there is no longer the barrier there once was to so represent it. Earlier, it might have been very expensive to produce even a few images, so although the historian or geographer might say, "Gee, this is the best way to show people what I mean here," he or she often was restricted by the cost from producing it in a graphic form. The teacher might have said, "I'd like to give a test showing this diagram, but it's much easier or faster or cheaper to produce a test with words only, so that's what I'll do." Now, with the computer it's just as feasible to present information graphically as textually, so the teacher will be free to use the more effective of the two and blend the two into any combination. This will surely improve learning within many topical areas of social studies.

What the computer makes possible, if we put the video on a videodisc or similar device, is direct, instant access to any segment or frame of the video regardless of its order within the particular video product. It's an instantaneous forward or rewind with complete precision over where you stop. You don't even realize that you're moving from the end to the beginning, you're just suddenly there. You're free to create any navigation sequence and to leap back and forth as you wish. You can create software that lets the viewer navigate by names and concepts he or she chooses without any idea where any picture or segment is physically. For example, you can put the costumes of Central Europe during the 17th century on videodisc and allow students interested in this period to zoom back and forth, looking at them from different perspectives: Bavaria in 1640, what women wore on their feet during this whole period, and so on. They can pick and choose still or animated material and even sounds. And a very impressive component of videodisc is volume. You can store an awful lot of individual pictures on one disc. The important thing is that the computer makes it possible to have that direct access to video images.

Finally, a last example, related to videodisc, is CD-ROM. There we have a technology which makes it possible to store large, multivolume texts like an encyclopedia in a single disc, only a few inches in diameter and no thicker than a credit card. Through software, you can access any information in the encyclopedia by citing the appropriate key words. If you couple that with graphic image possibilities and with telecommunications or network possibilities, you've just introduced into the classroom so much more information and so many more ways to conceive of it and understand it that it has to have a massive effect on the way students conceive of history, geography and social interaction.

Q. *How do you think the use of computers in the classroom is going to change students' views of the world?*

A. Well, I don't know; I suppose a better way to phrase that would be how might it, because we don't really know. Certainly the role of the teacher is crucial. Hardware and software packages in isolation, no matter how expert the design, are not going to accomplish X or Y. They may provide a lot me information in the abstract sense, but without a teacher to provide some guidance and to help the various youngsters interact with that information, it's questionable what such packages will provide. But with teachers who are interested in helping young people prepare to live in a much more interconnected world, the possibilities with computers are wonderful.

Instead of having just a book on the Americas, which has only brief information on some specific place like Colombia or Nicaragua or Panama, on the computer the student can have a brief framework on the Americas, and then go to any of these rich, full bodies of information that exist on videodisc or CD-ROM or in some network to a much higher proportion of all the information that exists on that place. The student can literally find out as much as he or she would like to find out about a given place.

I think we desperately need to have this sort of support available, because, as a country with an administrative whose policies, right or wrong, encourage military activity in Central America, one of the difficulties with the citizenry supporting or rejecting those policies is that they don't know much about Central America. If you ask the average person basic questions like, "What countries border Nicaragua?" or "What export crops may be interdicted by the Contra movement?" or "How long did the United States intervene in Nicaraguan affairs prior to the ouster of Somoza?" they don't know the answer. No wonder when someone in Washington says something about Central America, most of our citizens don't have any idea whether it's even reasonable.

If children learned in school how to use electronically accessible banks of information, when an issue came up and somebody said, "Such and such is the case with respect to Honduras," people would know how to find out how likely it might be that this was really the case. Just in terms of a useful increase of access and perspectives on information, the computer might prove very helpful.

One would hope that if we have the much broader access to information that computers can provide, and people learn how to use this information as they're going through school, they'll be in a better position to judge policies and actions that are increasingly going to be a part of everybody's life, as long as this nation remains a democracy.

Dianne Kendall teaches the Computers in the Social Studies Course at Teachers College. Kendall previously taught junior and senior high school social studies and she has been an editor of Intercom.

Howard Budin is an instructor in the Computing and Education program at Teachers College. With Kendall, he co-authored *Using Computers in the Social Studies.* Budin taught elementary school for many years and has consulted extensively with school districts on teaching training for computer use.

(Courtesy © *National Council for the Social Studies.* Used with permission.)

QUESTIONS ON READING

1. What does Taylor consider to be the major benefits of utilizing computers in education?

2. How will computers alter children's sense of the world?

3. How will computers alter the nature of what is taught in social studies?

4. Will computers change the role of teachers? If so, how?

Sample Lesson: "The INs and OUTs"

Title: The INs and OUTs (Author: R. Tamashiro, Webster University)

Target Pupils: Grade 4–8

Objectives/Rationale: Students will be able to:

1. Describe their own thinking strategies used in solving a classification problem.
2. Define thinking processes, dialectical reasoning, observation, inference, and divergent thinking.
3. Exercise dialectical reasoning by discussing and evaluating strategies with peers.
4. Evaluate efficiency of thinking skills strategies.

Note: This lesson is designed as a follow-up lesson to thinking skills already studied. Prior lessons defined and elaborated on the skills identified.

Preparation:

Equipment: Overhead projector; videodisc player with large monitor; videodisc remote control and/or bar code readers for player.

Materials: National Gallery of Art videodisc; student worksheets for "INs and OUTs," and "Debriefing THE INs AND OUTs." Optional: overhead transparencies of each worksheet.

Resources: Optional *Bar 'n Coder* software if students or teacher will create new barcodes.

Set Up: Set up videodisc player and monitor, test barcodes and check frame numbers of selected items. Duplicate student worksheets, prepare overhead transparencies.

Activity Sequence:

1. ANTICIPATORY SET: Engage students with the following questions listed below. Students take turns answering the questions orally. Several students respond to show variety of answers:

    a. In this school, there are some IN groups and some OUT groups? How many of you have ever been in an OUT group when you really wanted to be in the IN group?

    b. What are some of the IN groups in this school?

2. INSTRUCTIONAL INPUT: Introduce lesson purpose: "Today we will study about IN groups and OUT groups using pictures. You will get to practice some of the thinking skills you learned this week such as observation, inference, divergent thinking, and classification. We'll be using pictures from a videodisc to do this."

3. MODELING: Distribute worksheets A ("INs and OUTs") and B ("INs and OUTs Dialogue Worksheet"). Explain to students that they will be seeing pictures corresponding to frame numbers on Worksheet A. They must give each picture a title; and attempt to identify the "rule" for all the INs. Show first frame. Say: "This picture is IN."

4. GUIDED/INDEPENDENT PRACTICE: Proceed through pictures sequentially. "IN" PICTURES are: 1, 4, 5, 10–12, 14, 16–18. "OUT PICTURES are: 2, 3, 6–9, 13, 15, 19, 20. Have students enter checkpoints on Worksheet B after every 5 pictures. Review previous pictures as necessary. Students may take turns sending the bar codes to access the picture as directed by teacher. Students write answers in worksheet B as directed by teacher.

5. CHECK UNDERSTANDING: Teacher distributes worksheet C. Ask students to respond to question 1.

6. Form groups of 3–4 students. Allow 20 minutes. Students answer remaining questions.

7. CLOSURE: Assemble class. Ask a reporter to share group discussions. Review definitions. Orally, students provide definitions.

Evaluation: Collect student worksheets to check ability to identify steps and strategies, identify abilities to do metacognition.

WORKSHEET A: The INs and OUTs

No.	Frame	Picture Title	INs	OUTs
1	2018			
2	1978			
3	1980			
4	2006			
5	1200			
6	1240			
7	1258			
8	1474			
9	1522			
10	1154			
11	1174			
12	1216			
13	1224			
14	3308			
15	3296			
16	2468			
17	2762			
18	3339			
19	1790			
20	1158			

Rule: _____

Worksheet B: INs and OUTs Dialogue Worksheet

Your Name: _____

Checkpoint #1:

(a) What do you think is the rule to be IN?

_____

_____

(b) How sure do you feel about 'b'? *(Check ☑ one)*

☐ Very sure   ☐ Somewhat sure   ☐ Unsure

Checkpoint #2:

(a) What do you think is the rule to be IN? [Check here ☐ if your rule is the same as #1.]

_____

_____

(b) How sure do you feel about 'b'? *(Check ☑ one)*

☐ Very sure   ☐ Somewhat sure   ☐ Unsure

Checkpoint #3:

(a) What do you think is the rule to be IN? [Check here ☐ if your rule is the same as #2.]

_____

_____

(b) How sure do you feel about 'b'? *(Check ☑ one)*

☐ Very sure   ☐ Somewhat sure   ☐ Unsure

Checkpoint #4:

(a) What do you think is the rule to be IN? [Check here ☐ if your rule is the same as #3.]

_____

_____

(b) How sure do you feel about 'b'? *(Check ☑ one)*

☐ Very sure   ☐ Somewhat sure   ☐ Unsure

Worksheet C: Debriefing "The INs and OUTs"

INSTRUCTIONS: Answer the questions below.

1. List the thinking steps (or strategy) you used in trying to solve the INs and OUTs activity.

    Step 1: _____

    Step 2: _____

    Step 3: _____

    Step 4: _____

    Step 5: _____

2. In your groups, review the list you made in #1 above among members of your group.
    (a) Who has the LONGEST list of steps: _____
    (b) Who has the SHORTEST list of steps: _____

3. Compare Worksheet 3b among group members. Is it possible to tell that one person had a more *efficient* solution than others?
    (Check ☑ *one)* ☐ Yes ☐ No. Explain your answer by describing what you mean by *efficient*.

    _____

    _____

4. Compare your lists and make ONE list which your group feels is an effective strategy for solving the INs and OUTs actively.

    Step 1: _____

    Step 2: _____

    Step 3: _____

    Step 4: _____

    Step 5: _____

5. The strategy you described above might be useful in other situations in or outside school. List three situations in which these strategies might be helpful.

    a. _____

    b. _____

    c. _____

REFERENCES

Chu, G. C., & Schramm, W. (1979). *Learning from television: What the research says.* Washington, DC: National Association of Educational Broadcasters.

Clark, R. E., & Salomon, G. (1986). Media in teaching. In M. Wittrock (Ed.), *Handbook of research on teaching* (3rd ed.) (pp. 464–478). New York: Macmillan.

Schramm, W. (1977). *Big media, little media: Tools and technologies for instruction.* Beverly Hills, CA: Sage.

Sproull, L., & Kiesler, S. (1986). Reducing context cues: Electronic mail in organizational communication. *Management Science, 32,* 1492–1512.

Van Horn, R. (1987). Laser videodiscs in education: Endless possibilities. *Phi Delta Kappan, 68,* 696–700.

Wise, H. A. (1939). *Motion pictures as an aid in teaching American history.* New Haven, CT: Yale University Press.

SUGGESTED READING

Chu, G. C. (1979). *Learning from television.* Washington, DC: NEAB.

Diaute, C. (1985). *Writing and computers.* Reading, MA: Addison Wesley.

Office of Technology Assessment. (1988). *Power on: New tools for teaching and learning.* Washington, DC: USGPO.

Pea, R. & Sheingold, K. (1987). *Mirrors of minds: Patterns of experience in educational computing.* Norwood, Ablex.

Schramm, W. (1977). *Big media, little media.* Beverly Hills, CA: Sage.

Chapter 9

Communication in Social Studies

Communication in Social Studies

Social studies, at the most fundamental level, is the examination of social relationships, and communication is the very essence of human interaction. Language links everything that is taught and learned in schools. For this reason, reading, writing, speaking, viewing, and listening are vital skills that help children make sense of their world.

The social studies offer excellent opportunities to develop students' communication skills. In this chapter, we will focus on reading, writing, visual, and oral communication as both process and content in the social studies.

Reading

Textbooks remain the foundation of most social studies programs. In addition, children spend time in the library doing research or reading books outside class. The development of good reading skills among students is a vital responsibility of the social studies curriculum. It is important for children to recognize bias in text writing, grasp the main points being presented, and understand how best to retain information they have read.

▲ Textbooks remain the foundation of most social studies programs. *Courtesy Null Elementary, Saint Charles (Missouri) Public Schools.*

Outlines

Reading skills begin with ensuring that students know how to make effective use of textbooks. Teachers should review the table of contents with students prior to reading assignments in order to give them an overview of the entire book. A table of contents is a road map that students should consult in the course of reading the text. Some strategies to make effective use of a table of contents are:

1. Review all the main headings in order to outline the textbook's scope and sequence.
2. Explain the purpose of main headings and subheadings to students.
3. Indicate where maps, charts, and graphs are found and how they present information.
4. Prior to the first reading assignment carefully review the scope of the chapter and the meaning of each subheading.

Note Taking

Teachers must recognize that children need assistance in every aspect of the reading process, including how to outline and take notes on what they read. Prior to reading a chapter, review the

▲ Children need assistance learning how to outline and take notes.
Courtesy University City (Missouri) Public Schools.

contents of the chapter, how it is sequenced, and the type of information to be found in it. Students should be given practice in outlining the chapter and how to take notes. Consider the following example:

The New Deal

A. Economic Issues

    1. Unemployment

    2. Lack of money to begin new businesses

    3. Bank failures

    4. Factory closings

    5. Lack of access to world markets

B. Political Issues

    1. Overwhelming Democratic Party majority in Congress

    2. Need for immediate action

    3. Presence of Communist and Nazi party groups

C. Social Issues

    1. Fear and anxiety

    2. Middle class people suddenly poor

    3. Anger and violence on horizon

This process offers a way to teach students how to take notes when reading a chapter. As an incentive, they may be told these notes can be used on exams. The important factor is enabling students to recognize that outlining and note taking provide easy access to material that has been read and may clarify the seeming complexity of the ideas. Some teachers provide detailed outlines of the first few chapters to be read and gradually reduce the detail of these outlines until they believe students are prepared to handle the task independently. This step-by-step process enables all students to gain confidence in their ability to put into writing the information they have read.

A common student concern is not knowing *what* is important and what should become part of their notes. The availability of teacher notes on several chapters provides an effective frame of reference for students, and they should be encouraged to consult the teacher material until they are confident of how to take notes. In taking notes, students should be encouraged to:

1. Write in large letters.
2. Underline key points with a magic marker.
3. Draw arrows from one point to a connecting point.
4. Make a rough sketch to visualize a key point. For example, sketch a mountain and a woman carrying a pitcher of water in order to remember Molly Pitcher on Bunker Hill.
5. Ask oneself if a friend would understand what has been written in the notes.
6. After completing note taking for a chapter, draw a diagram linking key points to one another.

Visualization in Reading

Memory experts emphasize the importance of visualization in reading. Students should be encouraged to halt after reading a passage to form a mental image of it. For example, in reading about the westward movement they can form a picture of a covered wagon and people crossing the plains. Or, if reading about the 1920s they can visualize people dancing the Charleston. Visual imagery assists students to recall information they have read.

Another effective memory technique is to pause at particular places in a chapter and hypothesize what will happen later in the book. For example, after reading about Lincoln's election, students might visualize soldiers fighting, men on horseback waving swords, ships attacking other ships, and soldiers getting off trains. The teacher can ask them to predict what will occur in the following chapters. These reading strategies enable students to link what is read in one chapter to what will happen in the next chapter.

It is all too common for students to be overwhelmed by the social studies textbook and miss its central points. Social studies textbooks contain fascinating stories of real people. Visualizing stories breathes life and reality to reading. Reading with visualization makes the presence of a "forest" clearer to students as well as enables them to identify the 'trees' within it.

Comprehension Skills

The young reader in elementary and middle schools is introduced to the method of analytical reading. It is preferable to realize that students need assistance in basic reading skills. Mastery of reading skills ensures an improved understanding of text material.

A. Vocabulary skills.
   1. Children frequently encounter unfamiliar words in the text. They should be encouraged to use these words in complete sentences. For example: "The pioneers built *sodhouses* on the open plains which lacked trees."
   2. Students should be encouraged to refer to dictionaries for word meanings.
   3. Teachers should set aside a day in which the entire class uses words from a reading selection in the normal course of daily activities. For example: "My mom and I agreed on a *Bill of Rights* to govern my freedom to make choices about going to the mall."

4. Teachers should use words encountered in social studies for vocabulary and spelling activities and tests.

B. Comprehension Skills

1. Identification of a main idea and the supporting details. For example: "The Progressive Era witnessed the growth of government intervention in economic life. Laws were passed to regulate child labor, to end monopolies, and to establish safe and healthy working conditions. Many manufacturers resisted efforts to protect the welfare of workers."

2. Cause and effect: Students learn the relationship between a central factor and its impact upon consequences. "Passage of the Social Security Act in the 1930's ensured that the elderly would have financial support after retirement."

3. Categories: It is important for students to cluster information into groups. For example: Brown v. Board of Education, Civil Rights Act, Birmingham bus boycott, and Martin Luther King Jr.'s Washington D.C. march all fit into the category of efforts to reduce discrimination against African-Americans.

4. Comparison: Students identify similarities and differences in a reading selection. For example: "In the Civil War, the Confederacy won the initial battles around Washington, D.C. while Union troops were victorious in the west. Both sides in the early stages of the conflict relied upon volunteers."

C. Critical Analysis

1. A critical reader must distinguish between fact and opinion in a reading selection. For example: "Andrew Carnegie was a brilliant industrialist who treated workers unfairly." The words "brilliant" and "unfairly" are opinion statements.

2. Social studies textbooks contain numerous statements reflecting author bias. It is impossible to write a textbook without making biased statements. For example: "The failure of Prohibition demonstrated that supporters of the temperance movement were out-of-touch with the American people." The author indicates that the temperance movement was wrong to advocate the Prohibition Amendment.

3. A textbook usually has many assumptions that the uncritical reader accepts without question. For example: "The colonists opposed the British King." Many colonists were loyalists who supported the King and left America after Britain lost the Revolutionary War.

Students With Reading Problems

It is normal in any class to encounter students who have difficulty reading the material in a social studies text. After checking records to ensure that the student has a history of reading difficulties, teachers rely upon several strategies to assist these children:

1. Read the material to the student. This should be done quietly without attracting much notice from classmates.

2. Ask another student to read the material as part of a buddy system. If at all possible, find a strategy that allows the children receiving help to give help to the readers. For example, perhaps they can play with them on the playground or help in some sport or art activity.

3. Record the material and establish a "listening center" which is open to anyone who would like to hear the text material. Or, ask a volunteer to do the reading.

4. Secure the help of a teacher aide or parent who wants to assist in the classroom.

5. Seek aid from an older student interested in tutoring younger children.

6. If possible, rewrite material at an easier level. This is time-consuming and should be regarded as a long term project.

It is important that children who receive assistance in reading be afforded opportunities to enhance their self concept. A child who feels positive about the self and has success in several areas is more prone to accept reading help without developing a sense of inferiority.

Literature-Based Approaches

Social studies textbooks have been criticized as being disconnected and sterile, with trivial content and passionless rhetoric. They have been accused of omitting or only superficially addressing issues of real interest to young people (Sewall, 1988). Students' lack of interest in textbooks is evidenced by the fact that youngsters "rarely curl up in bed at night with a good textbook (Tyson & Woodward, 1989)."

Researchers and creative teachers have begun to advocate that we rely less on textbooks and use literature (trade books or real books) as the basis of the social studies curriculum. Trade books offer important advantages over textbooks. Authors of trade books feel less commercial pressure to appeal to a wide audience. This results in less censorship and oversimplification than we often find in textbooks.

Real books approach subjects from diverse perspectives and offer a breadth and depth of information that can genuinely interest readers. They are the work of imaginative, creative authors who write in order to communicate new understandings of specific social phenomena to readers. Literature offers students opportunities to discover or construct answers to their own authentic questions rather than identifying sentences from textbooks to complete end-of-chapter exercises. Reading trade books helps children become independent, critical, and creative thinkers and problem solvers. Involving students in the process of selecting books builds enthusiasm for literature and interest in social issues.

▲ Creative teachers use literature as the basis of the social studies curriculum. *Courtesy University City (Missouri) Public Schools.*

> Real books . . . are written by authors who know how to unlock the world with words and to open our eyes and our hearts. Each real book has its own voice—a singular, clear voice—and each speaks words that move us toward increased consciousness (Peterson & Eeds, 1990, p. 10).

Trade books of many genres are appropriate for use in social studies learning. These include biography, autobiography, nonfiction narrative and expository writing as well as fiction. Using literature as the basis of social studies instruction is best accomplished through thematic units, which may be interdisciplinary. Developing a thematic unit includes several procedures:

1. Select a theme. This may be the teacher's choice, or students might be involved in collaborative decision-making.

2. Scavenge for related, inviting books. Encourage children and parents to help.

3. Set objectives. These may be related to both social studies (e.g., map skills) and reading (e.g., making inferences).

4. Assess students' prior knowledge. This includes determining what they know, what misinformation they have, and what they want to learn.

5. Develop a reponsive plan that draws on students' interests and natural curiosity.

6. Include read-aloud activities. It is important for adults to model expressive oral reading.

7. Assist students in planning and completing related activities such as storytelling, oral reports, map making, art projects, performances, and creative writing.

8. Encourage students to engage in problem-solving by formulating questions, developing hypotheses, and doing research to find answers.

Writing

Many social studies teachers require students to write, but it has more often been used as an evaluation tool than a means to help children learn. Writing both facilitates learning and creates products that help us assess students' knowledge and understanding of social studies.

▲ Students learn as they write. *Courtesy Webster University.*

Writing is an important means of learning. Students learn as they write. They discover or construct ideas about the focal subject that they did not previously know or understand clearly. Any writing is contingent on something to write about: without a subject there is no way to begin. The various subject areas that comprise the field of social studies offer rich possibilities for learning by writing. Any teacher who assigns writing and grades it is teaching writing.

Writing is thinking. As we write we sort relevant from irrelevant information, prioritize ideas, draw inferences, build relationships, and logically develop arguments. Simply by writing—that is, by composing information—the writer becomes aware of connections and thereby knows more. As the writer composes, new knowledge emerges. Writing also expresses the emotions, intuitions, and creativity of the writer. When students write about social studies, they think about social, historical and political concerns. They develop new insights and enhance their cognitive skills.

Writing instruction facilitates students' mastery of content, develops appreciation and understanding of that content, and enhances thinking skills and processes. No matter what the subject, no matter how much one already knows about it, simply writing about that subject creates new awareness of how the fragments of information about that subject relate to each other. This awareness is new knowledge. It also helps develop communication skills necessary for young people to succeed in social interactions within and beyond the school.

The nature of writing makes learning inevitable. Writing is not grammar, not punctuation, not spelling. Writing is composing, and composing is a sustained activity of discovery and stating relationships among bits of information. These relationships evolve as one writes by means of continually grouping pieces of information into clusters, and regrouping them with more information into new clusters. The writer's learning depends not on some static value of information but on the way the writer relates the information fragments to one another.

Expository Writing

Expository writing in the soical studies usually is in the form of student reports. Expository writing offers at least three benefits:

1. Students develop thinking and writing skills.
2. Students learn the content of their reports.
3. Students apply reference and research skills. (Welton, 1989)

Social studies teachers often settle for what David Welton (1989) calls "pseudowriting." Pseudowriting is a process in which students simply locate and copy or paraphrase information. It is a mechanical routine which does not require thinking, organization, analysis and synthesis of ideas. Pseudowriting is common when students copy sentences verbatim from the textbook to answer end-of-chapter questions. Pseudowriting also occurs when young people simply plagiarize information from encyclopedias. Real writing requires students to organize and express ideas in their own words. Teachers should never settle for less.

There are several strategies to help students do real expository writing:

1. Introduce young people to the librarian and the library. Be sure they understand how to use the card catalog, encyclopedias, and nonfiction works in appropriate ways.
2. Show students copies of well-written reports by other students.
3. Using an overhead projector, review why a particular report demonstrates quality writing.
4. Use peer editing and review.
5. Regularly assess students' progress and offer ongoing feedback based on specific comments concerning organization, writing style, and content.

Freewriting

Many social studies teachers complain that their students do not write well. Students do not write well because they do not write often. Studies show that young people are seldom expected to write more than a paragraph (Olson, 1984).

The most effective way to help students become better writers is to offer more opportunities for them to write. Having students maintain a freewriting journal is a relatively easy way to increase young people's writing opportunities.

Freewriting has been defined as "simply writing without stopping to direct or redirect the flow of words" (Tamura & Harstad, 1987, p. 256). It provides an excellent start of the day or lesson routine because it helps establish a purposeful, thoughtful classroom climate.

Ask students to provide spiral notebooks or folders as their journals. Begin the day or lesson by writing a topic on the board, reading aloud to students or watching a brief clip from a film or video. Writing prompts might focus attention on current events, historical themes, community concerns, cultural events, or anything that would trigger students' curiosity and imaginations. They may choose to write about the given topic or select another, but all must write during the established time, usually five minutes or less. Tell students in advance that the freewriting journals are private and personal and will not be read.

Make certain pupils also understand that their journals will not be graded on the basis of content or writing mechanics. Evaluate their work only on quantity. This frees the student from trying to conform to the teacher's expectations and encourages young people to risk consideration of new ideas and experimentation with different ways of writing. This evaluation plan encourages the development of trusting relationships between teacher and students. In addition, it offers pupils many opportunities to write without overwhelming the teacher with mountains of grading.

Creative Writing

Social studies topics offer opportunities for young people to extend their learning through creative writing. Developing a newspaper to reflect another era or location enables students to vicariously experience other times and places. Writing letters or journal entries from the perspectives of people in other historical periods or contemporary cultures challenges students to examine the world from new viewpoints. Young people may also be encouraged to write poems or short stories as social studies activities. For example, in studying Moslem and Jewish life in medieval Spain, students will encounter poetry of that era that might stimulate creative thinking. A popular form of poetry at that time was "puzzle poems" such as:

Jehuda Halevi

What is it that is blind, but has one eye,
which men cannot live without,
because it devotes all its life to clothing others
but itself is always naked and bare?

Answer: eldeen (needle)

▲ Writing and presenting eulogies enables students to vicariously experience other times and places. *Courtesy Robert Tabscott, Elijah Lovejoy Society.*

The creative thinking of the past has relevance to the present. Students should learn about the human heritage in order to assist them to become creative thinkers. The exposure of students to interesting and provocative writing is a stimulant to their own creative writing.

Oral Communication

Oral communication involves both sending and receiving information. In other words, both speaking and listening are vital skills which should be developed through the social studies. Large and small group discussions as well as role playing are excellent means to enhance students' speaking and listening skills. Because these teaching/learning strategies are considered in other chapters, we will focus attention in this section on other methods to develop students' oral communication skills—storytelling, drama, and music.

Storytelling

Story is at the center of language, culture and learning. For generations, childen have begged, "Tell me a story." Storytelling breathes life into characters and events. In contrast to film or television, storytelling depends on the imaginations of listeners.

Storytelling is a responsive art. The story may change each time it is told based on the involvement of the listeners, the situation, and the mood and purposes of the teller. It is a fun and effective teaching method because it draws children into the tale. Storytelling is especially useful in helping children understand and appreciate the values of their own and other cultures.

Classroom storytelling is usually based on classical litera-ture, personal stories and folktales. Folktales are a part of the oral tradition of every culture and are the mainstay of the repertoire of stories used in the social studies. Four characteristics of folktales make them inviting and exciting to children:

▲ Role-plays are excellent means to enhance students' communication skills. *Courtesy Perry County (Missouri) School District No. 42.*

1. The magic in the tale lies in people and creatures being shown as they really are, not as results of wishes and dreams. In fact, wishes are usually shown to be foolish, as in the Grimm Brothers' *The Fisherman and His Wife*, in which the wife's discontent causes her to lose all she gained by wishing.

2. Natural wit, intelligence, and goodness generally outsmart evil, as in Molly Bang's (1987) *Wiley and the Hairy Man*, in which the brave Wiley outwits the wicked Hairy Man.

3. The magical heart is limited. It cannot change a heart or the state of the world, but only outward conditions. Cinderella's clothes and conditions are changed, not her personality or character.

4. Evil does not win, but receives its due or is recognized as evil. Sometimes this includes a harsh treatment of evil, such as in the German *Cinderella*, as retold by the Grimms (Bosma, 1992).

▲ Puppet plays develop children's listening skills. *Courtesy Saint Louis (Missouri) Public Schools.*

▲ Storytelling is an effective teaching method because it draws children into the tale. *Courtesy Lynn Rubright, Webster University.*

Storytelling involves careful planning, but it is not based on a memorized script. The storyteller and listeners are immersed in the tale; they live the story together. When planning to tell a story, consider the following questions:

1. What is the purpose of telling the story?
2. Which aspects of the story are essential and which can be omitted?
3. What is the plot of the story?
4. What is the best sequence of events?
5. What is the setting of the story including time, and the physical, geographical, and cultural surroundings?
6. What information about the appearance and personalities of the characters should be shared?
7. Who are the listeners?
8. How should I involve the listeners in the telling of the story?
9. What costumes or props are needed to tell the story?
10. Which facial expressions, pacings, gestures, tones of voice, and volume levels will be most effective?

Teachers should not be the only storytellers in the social studies classroom. Many parents and people from the local community have wonderful stories to share with youth. After students have had opportunities to listen to adult storytellers, they should be encouraged to tell personal stories or accounts of books they have read in a storytelling manner.

▲ Music activities are important teaching/learning strategies in the social studies. *Courtesy Saint Louis (Missouri) Public Schools.*

Music

Music activities are important teaching/learning strategies. Through the universal language of music, young people understand and appreciate the perspectives, experiences, and cultures of others, past and present. For this reason, music should be incorporated into almost every social studies unit.

Singing is a universal activity of children. Through songs students vicariously experience the emotions of others: the pride of the patriot, the expectancy of the pioneer or the suffering of a slave. Songs can serve as launchpads for lessons about historical periods (e.g., "Yankee Doodle," "Swing Low, Sweet Chariot,") and communities around the world ("Kookaburra," "Don Gato," "Hato Popo").

Rhythmic activities are an important means of self-expression. Musical games and dances offer children opportunities to be released from the conformity of rows of desks and to develop physical coordination, poise, cooperation and teamwork. Musical games and dances are expressions of various cultures and periods of history that can help children understand the life experiences of peoples in other times and places.

Popular songs are a revealing index to life in a society. They depict the habits, the slang, the intimate character of every generation, and they tell as much to future students of a civilization as any history, biography, or newspaper of the time. Historically, folksongs were not only a major form of entertainment but a means by which people spread information from one place to another.

Popular songs and folksongs, unlike history textbooks, do not deal mainly with the leaders or famous generals, but focus on ordinary men and women. They depict their pains and joys; their hopes and despairs. For example, in the midst of the Depression of the 1930s, Woody Guthrie

▲ Through the universal language of music, young people appreciate the perspectives, experiences, and cultures of others. *Courtesy Francis Howell (Missouri) School District.*

▲ Rhythmic activities develop physical coordination, poise, cooperation, and teamwork. *Courtesy Francis Howell (Missouri) School District.*

▲ Listening to the music of various ethnic groups enhances cultural understanding.
Courtesy Saint Charles (Missouri) Public Schools.

wandered the roads of America singing about ordinary people and sharing their emotions:

Rambling through your village,
Rambling through your town,
I never meets a friend I know,
As I go rambling round.

My mother dreamed that I would be,
A man of great reknown,
But, I am just a refugee,
As I go rambling round.

▲ Dances are expressions of various cultures and periods of history that help children understand the life experiences of peoples in other times and places.

Folksongs of the past and popular songs of the present are motivating devices enabling children to grasp the emotions of another time and place. People have always sung songs about their concerns and these are valuable additons to the field of social studies. They can be used in several ways:

1. Have students collect songs from grandparents which describe another era. Hold a "Grandparents Jamboree" in which their songs are sung and discussed with children.

2. Have students identify songs that depict bias or prejudice as a part of a lesson on prejudice. For example, the nineteenth century song "No Irish Need Apply" describes how the Irish were treated, while Simon and Garfunkel's "The Sound of Silence" notes anti-Semitism in American society.

3. Hold a "Global Jamboree" in which songs from people throughout the world are sung.

4. Have students listen to radio stations whose songs are aimed at specific ethnic groups. These songs can be recorded and played in class.

5. Organize a unit that only uses music in order to depict an historical period.

6. Develop a unit that uses songs to examine how outlaws are viewed in American history.

7. Develop a unit that uses songs to examine the lives of women throughout history.

Art

Throughout human history, art has played an important function in communicating cultural, philosophical, and emotional feelings. Not only do the arts convey in part what it means to be human, the arts also give coherence, depth, and resonance to other academic subjects. An important task in elementary and middle school social studies is educating youth to know, love, and respond to the products of the human spirit.

The great works of art constitute an incomparable record of our past and the evolution of humanity. The wonderful ancient cave paintings found in France and Spain give us a glimpse of the Paleolithic world. The cathedrals of Notre Dame and Canterbury represent the endeavors of medieval people to express their relationship to God. Students should know about these works because they offer a unique doorway into the past.

Great works of art are part of our common culture in that they are among the finest expressions of the values we cherish. In the lines of the Pantheon, we learn about the Greeks and their desire for order and harmony in the universe. Picasso and Van Gogh teach us about the end of an agricultural era and the birth of modern technological times. Great art communicates values of freedom and individual expression.

Great art is part of our common culture as Americans and citizens of the world. Art engages the human mind; it conveys order and structure, freedom and experimentation, beauty and triumph of the human spirit. Art is among the most important social studies tools to make the human experience come alive in the minds of children. Art education in elementary and middle school strives to: (1) heighten student awareness of self and sensitivity to the environment, (2) enable students to express their ideas visually, (3) foster the creative spirit, (4) provide knowledge of our cultural heritage, and (5) educate youth to make qualitative visual judgments.

▲ Art communicates values of freedom and human expression. *Courtesy Null Elementary, Saint Charles (Missouri) Public Schools.*

▲ Art is a way for children to express themselves in nonverbal ways. *Courtesy Webster University.*

There are several strategies teachers can employ to incorporate art into the social studies curriculum:

1. Offer students opportunities to create self-portraits in conjunction with writing assignments.

2. Involve parents and grandparents in developing a "school museum of art" exhibit depicting a period in history, past or present.

3. Work with local art museums to plan student visits or link to art outreach programs.

4. Invite members of ethnic groups to present an art exhibit portraying the artistic endeavors of people from many cultures.

5. Help students develop an art history mural for display that incorporates examples of art across the world. These can be pictures, drawings made by students, or portraits loaned by parents.

6. Use commerical product logos as exercises in critical thinking. One group of students draws logos and another group identifies the products represented by the logos.

7. Collaborate with an art teacher to study a particular period of history in a multidisciplinary unit. Students should connect the art of a period to events of that time in history.

Art and social studies are mutually supportive in that both deal with manifestations of the human creative spirit. Art is an opportunity for childen to express themselves in nonverbal ways. Art is found in all cultures, and the art of each society has a contribution to make in human history.

Photographs and Pictures

Pictures, drawings, and photographs in social studies are potentially useful teaching aids. Photographers have been depicting human life for over a hundred years. The pictures of Matthew Brady still remain among the most vivid examples of life during the Civil War and provide an important insight into conditions faced by the soldiers. A picture of a starving child or houses destroyed by a hurricane impact people more vividly than any textual material. Pictures and photographs can be used to stimulate critical thinking as well as interest in the subject matter.

Teachers have to bear in mind that pictures or photographs do not necessarily speak for themselves. Much of the information has to be deliberately and patiently extracted, and this requires educating children to see in new ways. Visual education is vital in a world which relies increasingly upon visual means to communicate ideas. For example, after showing students a picture of a frontier American town in the 1870s, one might ask:

1. Why are there no sidewalks?

2. What does the wooden construction of houses suggest about permanency?

3. How does the dress of people fit the time and environment in which they live?

A sequence of pictures enables the teacher to direct student thinking along a systematic path. For example, showing students several pictures of people in work situations can generate discussion regarding the nature of work in contemporary life. Students could categorize the pictures into occupations: (a) requiring physical labor, (b) work in offices, (c) providing service. This could lead to a student project using pictures in newspapers and magazines in order to create a photo collage of work in America.

Textbook pictures and photographs can be used to help students identify biases and values. Pictures are no less value-laden than words. The idea that pictures convey a point of view can be demonstrated in social studies. The famous picture of the Boston Massacre can be cited as part of a lesson asking students to draw pictures of the event from a British perspective.

Students can be asked to skim through an American history textbook and analyze the type of pictures used to portray famous Americans. They will probably discover that pictures, paintings, and photographs tend to emphasize the dignity of individuals and their positions in life. The political cartoons that are often reproduced in textbooks are also useful for analyzing political biases. It can lead to a student project of drawing political cartoons about a past or present situation.

The manner in which a society portrays itself is a value statement. Students live in a visually oriented world that requires visual literacy if students are to be critical analyzers. Photograph and picture analysis can assist in educating youth to be critical thinkers.

▲ Drama enables students to see the world from new perspectives. *Courtesy Francis Howell (Missouri) School District.*

Drama

Drama is one of the most expressive and flexible of communication arts. It includes such genres as mime, puppetry, chamber (readers') theater, theatrical improvisation (including role-playing), as well as the traditional staged or publicly read play.

Drama is especially valuable as a means of instruction because it enables students to both visualize and vicariously participate in significant historical events or the lived experiences of others. It also enhances self esteem, encourages teamwork and cooperation, and improves verbal and nonverbal communication skills. Students learn both facts and concepts while simultaneously exploring individual creativity.

▲ Drama enhances self-esteem, encourages teamwork and cooperation, and improves verbal and nonverbal communication skills. *Courtesy Francis Howell (Missouri) School District.*

▲ In chamber theater, actors do not memorize roles, but interact much as they would in a traditional play. *Courtesy University City (Missouri) Public Schools.*

▲ **Fieldtrips bring children to the magic of live theater.**
Courtesy Webster University.

For example, when studying the American Revolution, students might pantomine Paul Revere's ride while listening to Longfellow's poem or the "William Tell Overture." During a lesson on conflict resolution, students could write and perform a puppet play showing both appropriate and inappropriate ways of dealing with conflict.

Chamber (or readers') theater is the public performance of a play in which actors do not memorize their roles. Actors carry scripts, but interact much as they would in a traditional stage production. The emphasis is on suggestion rather than illusion. A chamber theater performance of excerpts from *Huckleberry Finn* would offer students an historical perspective of racial interactions.

Career exploration might be addressed through a simple game of charades which is a form of theatrical improvisation. While studying issues leading up to the Civil War, students could improvise their own version of the Lincoln-Douglas debates. Role-playing has proven to be an effective tool in helping students view the world through the eyes of others.

▲ **Students perform "Bambi" as part of their own ecological study.**
Courtesy Francis Howell (Missouri) School District.

Students might learn social responsibility and compassion from a field trip to a professional stage production of *A Christmas Carol.* Watching a video of *The Sound of Music* would help students begin to understand the impact of World War II on children and families. Students might perform their own stage version of *Bambi* as part of an ecological study.

Social studies teachers can effectively use drama with or without costumes, scenery, elaborate equipment, or extensive preparation and rehearsal. Scripts may be commercial publications, teacher generated, the result of student projects, or extemporaneously improvised. The social studies classroom is a stage upon which students can learn about others and themselves.

Communication is a means by which students express their ideas, feelings, and beliefs. An exciting communication program affords opportunities for students to gain valuabe insights regarding the nature of how people have interacted in the past and how they communicate with one another in the present to prepare for improved understanding in the future.

SUMMARY

This chapter has explored a variety of communication strategies and ideas pertaining to social studies. It has presented specific examples of using drama, photography, art, storytelling, music, and literature to convey ideas. It has also examined ways to improve students' reading and writing skills.

QUESTIONS

1. How do you utilize a book's table of contents or index in reading?

2. How effective do you find notes taken in class in making lecture presentations understandable? How effective are your textbook notes?

3. In which ways, if any, does visualization aid in your comprehension of a book?

4. Which books have most personally impacted you? How many of these books were read as part of school assignments?

5. What type of writing do you most enjoy? Which do you most dislike?

6. The authors mention "pseudowriting." To what extent, if any, does being a student encourage pseudowriting?

7. Which stories from parents or relatives have impacted your way of thinking?

8. Analyze the process by which you learn a song.

9. To what extent do pictures in newspapers and magazines shape your perception of events?

10. Which play, if any, has most impacted you on a personal or historical level?

ACTIVITIES

1. Collect popular, country, rap, and rock songs. Analyze the themes found in each of these genres.

2. Rewrite a section of a textbook into language you believe students would find enjoyable.

3. Compare and contrast the writing styles found in textbooks with those found in magazines or newspapers.

4. Visit an art musem. Identify how art works could be used in conjunction with social studies.

5. Describe how a play could be used in conjunction with teaching social studies.

READING

Oral History in Elementary Classrooms
by George L. Mehaffy

*George L. Mehaffy is Director, School of Education at
Eastern New Mexico State University, Portales, New Mexico.*

For adults, abstract ideas can be interesting, even fun. Having traveled or seen films and pictures, we can envision places and events far removed from our present. Having had enough history to give us some sense of chronology, we can easily put events into a time context. In other words, we can imbue ideas and events with meaning. But imagine trying to study abstract ideas or distant events without context. The exercise could quickly become meaningless.

How much of elementary social studies teaching comes from our adult, experienced perspective? How often do we teach certain ideas or events far removed from the experiences of children, without attention to the lack of context that experience provides? How often do we ask children to do meaningless seat work, work that we ourselves would be offended to do if asked to perform? How often are students actively engaged in their own learning, as Dewey and a host of others have suggested they should be? In far too many circumstances, we ask children to perform empty exercises, devoid of life or spirit, and then express surprise when students report that social studies has little meaning or impact on their lives.

Oral history holds promise for actively involving students in learning about the world around them. Oral history is often described as recollections and reminiscences of ourselves about our past. It is the systematic collection of a uniquely personal history—the history of common people, not kings or wars, as has been so often the case in the past.

Prior to the invention of the tape recorder, oral history was often collected informally or only by historians. Much oral history is still scholarly, but it has moved beyond the academic world. Families are collecting their histories by interviewing older family members as never before, while small oral history projects have been begun by local community groups across the entire United States. Most importantly, elementary teachers are now employing oral history to inquire about local communities, family backgrounds and neighborhood traditions. In the process, students are beginning to understand that history is not simply the lifeless recounting of distant events memorized for tomorrow's test, but rather an intriguing glimpse into our collective past.

By far the most successful of the student oral history projects is the Foxfire Project in rural Georgia. Started by an English teacher tired of the status quo, Foxfire has evolved into an enterprise that seeks to understand and preserve the unique folkways of that Appalachian region. Over two hundred other Foxfire-like projects are in place in various sections of the United States. Students in these projects have demonstrated beyond doubt that oral history has the capacity to encourage learning by actively involving them in their own history.[1]

Although many student projects are conducted by high school students, oral history projects can be, and have been done, by elementary schoold children. An elementary school project in California, for example, publishes an annual magazine on local folk customs and traditions. In North Carolina, elementary school students publish an illustrated text, portions of which focus on rural life there. A fourth-grade project in Louisiana examined the quickly vanishing culture of the French Acadians.

Some oral history projects are large and well established; others exist precariously from year to year. Beyond these formal projects, countless teachers employ oral history techniques in their classrooms as opportunities arise and as time permits. The point is simple: oral history is being used by elementary teachers with results that have greatly exceeded their expectations.[2]

Values of Oral History

Oral history can be valuable in a number of important ways. It provides a sense of self identity, nurtures a concept of neighborhood, develops research and writing skills, and perhaps most importantly, encourages a sense of curiosity, wonder and excitement about history.

Who Am I?

Children are, by nature, egocentric. They wonder first about themselves and then gradually begin to appreciate others. All of us, as adults, have similar needs. History serves to establish who we are and how we fit into the larger life around us. After talking with parents and grandparents, some teachers have students develop elaborate family trees, while others ask students to collect stories about themselves, typically in projects entitled "What was I like when I was young?" Other students have collected funny family anecdotes or embarrassing family moments. Oral history interviewing techniques have also been used successfully in a bilingual social studies program to encourage greater understanding of different cultural settings,[3] while oral history materials have been used by children studying their community's ethnic heritage.[4]

A Sense of Neighborhood

Oral history can be used to develop a sense of neighborhood, a sense of place. Some oral history projects, for example, have studied jobs, and interviewed neighborhood workers, while others have tried to trace the history of a neighborhood by focusing on commercial development or the history of a building. Early transportation, recreation, housing patterns, or just stories about the way things "used to be"—all can be useful for developing a sense of community. On other occasions, local legends, ghost stories, or major local historical events could be examined. A study of the history of the school or stories about when teachers were young also would be of value in a community study project.[5]

Research and Writing Skills

The oral history projects have reported that students develop greater research and writing skills through their work on the projects. This hardly seems surprising. After all, if students are required to transcribe an interview, or write up the interview in their own words, writing skills are developed. In addition, the need to pose questions helps develop better questioning skills. Developing background information on a subject requires that students examine other forms of historical documentation. Furthermore, most oral history projects involve some form of product, even if it is a simple, mimeographed paper at the conclusion of an oral history unit. Developing a project encourages artistic talents, and begins an exploration of various print media.

Sense of History

Perhaps most importantly, oral history can "turn kids on" to history as the most fascinating school subject one can study. No longer a dead subject filled with empty dates and useless names, history can become the examination of everything around us, and the question "How did it get that way?" After all, individuals are what they are as a product of their own personal history, and the history of those around them. Furthermore, oral history allows students to become active learners, not passive recipients of facts and figures. Suddenly students can become inquirers, listeners, and writers; publishers and producers; observers and researchers.

Suggestions for Beginning an Elementary Oral History Project

An oral history project need not be a major undertaking. Too many textbooks imply that enormous resources and planning are required for successful oral history projects. Although that may be true for scholarly projects, for teachers, however, oral history can be as elaborate or simple as time and resources permit. Oral history techniques can be used next week to study milk production; the same techniques also can be used to develop a four-year, comprehensive study of the neighborhood. In other words, oral history techniques can be applied to ideas large or small.

Teachers should begin in small and simple ways: elementary students have some natural limitations that may preclude some sophisticated projects. The first task is to identify a "do-able" project. Students participate in selecting what should be studied, how will they go about it, what kind of final product they want, and determining how long it should take? These critical elements must be considered at the beginning of a project.

Involving students in the decision-making process is also essential in order for them to feel they have ownership in the project. Student involvement in selecting a topic helps insure that it is of interest to them, not just interesting to the teacher. In Austin, Texas, for example, students chose to study the development of the city's leash law, a topic in which they were emotionally involved. The resulting study was more meaningful to students precisely because they had such high interest in the subject. (It was not a topic the teacher would have chosen, yet students probably gained greater understanding of the political process from their study than they would have from the more typical study of "How a Bill Becomes Law.")

Once the project is selected and the topic is clearly defined, students need to become literate about the subject area. Some reading, some discussion by the teacher, perhaps some guest speakers, can all be devices for helping students understand more about the topic. Elementary students must also develop logical questions to ask, and the teacher must provide guidance. To interview, students need some good open-ended questions that encourage the interviewee to talk at length. Questions that can be answered yes or no, or that tend to discourage talk, should be avoided. On the other hand, students should not simply read a list of questions mechanically. The delicate balance lies in having enough questions that students feel comfortable in the interview process, yet not rely solely on those questions.

Once the topic, background information, and sample questions are identified, students should begin learning about interviewing. They might begin by interviewing their teacher, or they could interview each other. Preliminary interviews could be conducted in front of the entire class, with the teacher providing feedback about good and bad techniques. Once basic interviewing skills have been developed, interviewees could be brought into the classroom. Several schools do this in programs entitled "Living History." Bringing the informant into the classroom eliminates having children to go out into the community, which invariably requires parental participation (though in some projects parents have been willing sponsors). Children can then be assigned interviews with family members, school personnel, or other children, depending on the project.

Just as students need practice developing interviewing skills, they also need practice with the mechanics of an interview. Cassette tape recorders have become simple to operate, yet to record clear conversations without background noise requires some practice. Many projects ask two students to conduct an interview together; while one student asks most of the questions, the other operates the tape recorder and provides general moral support. Some teachers ask students to take photographs of the interview, and the second student can often be responsible for that.

Academic oral history projects usually transcribe the tape-recorded interviews, an unbelievably time-consuming and complex project. Most elementary projects, by contrast, do not transcribe tape recordings. Sometimes excerpts from an interview are transcribed, or a story is written from the interview. When transcription is required in some upper level classes, the students themselves do it. In other situations, parents can help.

The products spawned by oral history projects can be as varied as the projects themselves. Some students have produced picture books of local history with small sections of writing. Others have simply had a party at the conclusion of a unit and invited all the interviewees to attend. Others have given the collected materials to a local history society or library, or deposited the material in the school library for use by other classes. Other projects have produced elaborate finished products including printed books or pamphlets with photographs and illustrations. Still others use collected peripheral materials such as old letters and photographs to create displays in the school library or local museum.

Most teachers who have incorporated oral history techniques into their classroom teaching emphasize the importance of having some kind of product, some culminating activity. The product, and the pride in having produced something tangible, sets this form of school activity apart from so many others. Indeed, the fact that students are doing something real, substantive and related to their own lives, may be the secret of the success of this particular form of classroom activity.

Conclusion

Oral history represents a threat to some teachers. The journey into this new approach is unfamiliar, and the road may reach unforeseen destinations. The journey may involve new relationships with students, noise, or disturbing questions. Getting started may also require an investment in learning about oral history and its many applications to classrooms. Yet for those teachers willing to make the investment, the rewards can be worth the risk. Students will look at the world around them in new ways, asking questions about themselves and others that they never thought to ask before. They will learn that history invokes the most profound questions about being human. They will develop new insights into older people around them, and, in the process, perhaps understand what John Dos Passos meant when he said that "a sense of continuity with generations gone before can stretch like a lifeline across the scary present." They will grow socially as they try to talk with adults. They will begin to understand that grammar is not a cruel joke imposed on children by adults, but a means to enhanced understanding, particularly in translating spoken language to written language. They will take pride in the things they have accomplished. But most of all, they will be a joy to teach, for the spirit that animated them when they first came to school—the inquisitiveness and pleasure of learning for learning's sake—will once more be present.

(Courtesy © *National Council for the Social Studies*. Used with permission.)

Notes

[1] There have been a number of dexcriptions of the Foxfire Project and the many projects it has spawned around the country. For example, see: Wigginton, Eliot. *Moments: The Foxfire Experience.* Kennebunk, Maine: Ideas, Inc., 1975. Sitton, Thad. "The Descendants of Foxfire" *The Oral History Review* 1978:20–35.

[2] For a somewhat outdated list of elementary projects and some not-so-outdated tips on how to conduct elementary school projects, see: Reynolds, Sherrod. "Golden Hindsight, Homespun, Lagniappe, et al." *Teacher* 96 (March 1979) 68–71.

[3] See:
Olson, Mary; Hatcher, Barbara. "Cultural Journalism: A Bridge to the Past" *Language Arts* 59 (January 1982) 46–50. Martinez, Paul E. "Integrating Oral History into the Bilingual Social Studies: An Instructional Technique that Is Successful" Detroit: Paper presented at annual Bilingual Bicultural Education Conference, 1982. (ERIC Document Reproduction Service No. ED 220 238).

[4] There are a number of these project descriptions in the literature. An example would be: D'Amico, Joseph J.; Newcombe, Ellen. "History, Heritage, and Hearsay: A Children's Guide to Ethnic South and Southwest Philadelphia". Philadelphia: Research for Better Schools, Inc., 1982. (ERIC Document Reproduction Service No. ED 209 140).

[5] The field of community history offers countless topics for study by elementary school students. A number of excellent descriptions of how to conduct community history studies exist. Among the best: Weitzman, David. *My Backyard History Book.* Boston: Little, Brown and Company, 1975. Metcalf, Fay D. & Downey, Matthew T. *Using Local History in the Classroom.* Nashville: American Association for State and Local History, 1982.

QUESTIONS ON READING

1. What are several benefits students can derive from utilizing oral history in social studies?

2. How does oral history improve reading and writing skills?

3. Which difficulties might teachers encounter using oral history?

LESSON PLAN

Pickett Pat Lema, Curriculum Coordinator,
Pattonville School District

Objective: Students will analyze fictional or nonfictional characters and identify inferred qualities.

Activities:

Before reading a well-known story, provide students with a matrix that identifies the major characters from the story. Identify a selection of qualities, relationships, and interests. As students read, have them make notes regarding how story characters fit or don't fit the listed qualities. After the story is finished, have students compare their analysis with other students. Each group can present its agreements and disagreements to the class.

	Wolf	1st Pig	2nd Pig	3rd Pig
Qualities				
lazy				
playful				
mean				
serious				
Relationships				
friend				
enemy				
leader				
Interests				
having fun				
hard work				
eating				

Broadening Applications:

Repeat the model using a brief biographic sketch of an important historical figure such as Lincoln, Columbus, Eleanor Roosevelt, Booker T. Washington, etc. You may add categories such as "physical characteristics" or "personal experiences" in your left column. Students can present their ideas in written form such as in a "postcard" to another student.

After several group experiences in class, students should be encouraged to employ this model in their own personal reading. They can be given freedom to create their own matrix categories. Observations, pencil/paper products, or personal interactions with students will provide the evaluation of objective mastery.

Further Applications:

For those interested in connecting reading and writing within social studies from an "author's perspective" this activity lends itself to the eventual writing of a biographic or character sketch. The steps of the process should include:

I   Gather Details
    A.   Physical Characteristics
    B.   Personal Characteristics

II   Connecting
    A.   Other's reactions (in text)
    B.   Main Impressions.

III Getting It Down
    A. Expand on main impressions
    B. Bring character to life; describe a typical day; use dialogue.

IV Correcting
    A. Share aloud with others and revise
    B. Edit

V Publishing
    A. Class book, read aloud, exchange and draw caricatures, etc.

Sources and References:

Johnson, D.D. & Pearson, P.D., (1984) *Teaching Reading Vocabulary,* New York: Holt Rinehart & Winston.

Marzano, R.J., Paynter, D.E., Kendall, J.S., Pickering, D., & Marzano, L. (1991) *Literacy Plus: An Integrated Approach to Teaching Reading, Writing, Vocabulary and Reasoning,* Columbus: Zaner-Bloser, Inc.

Sebranek, P., Meyer, V., & Kemper, D. *Writing Source 2000* Wisconsin: Write Source Educational Publishing House.

Marna Romeo   Primary Grades
Objective: Learning about African-American culture through literature.

Rationale: Students can learn about ethnic cultures through literature and gain greater understanding of similarities and differences among ethnic heritages.

Activities:

1. Teacher reads story, "The Village of Round and Square Houses," by Ann Grifalconi, which depicts a village in Cameroons where the men live in square and the women in round houses. The houses sit on the side of a volcano.

   • Children build a tiny volcano. Teacher asks what type of house they would build if they lived on the side of a volcano.

2. Teacher asks what students would do if they saw a purple, four-legged chicken or a woman who could take off her head? Teacher reads traditional Creole Folktale, "The Talking Eggs," which is about two sisters. One sister is sweet and hardworking and the other is nasty and lazy.

   • During the story, teacher stops and asks students what they would have done in the situation.

   • After story is read and discussed, children in groups decide if they want to write a new ending.

3. Students receive copies of song, "Follow the Drinking Gourd." Learn words and sing the song. Teacher tells about origin of the song.

4. Students listen to recording of "Why Mosquitoes Buzz in People's Ears," and then read "Anasi the Spider."

   • Teacher passes out a reproduction of a kente cloth, which is worn by the tribal story teller. Teacher says "The Black Snowman" is a modern fiction story based on the African tradition of the kente cloth. It is about two brothers who discover the pride of the kente cloth and get new pride in their own African-American culture.

- Students listen to and read parts of the story. Teacher gives each student a piece of kente cloth which will help in writing and reading.
5. Teacher introduces book, "Tell Me a Story, Mama," by Angela Johnson, which is about a young girl who asks her mother to tell her stories and soon knows all of them.
   - Teacher asks if anyone in class knows stories told by parents. Asks them to share the story.
   - Teacher asks students to illustrate one family story they remember. Students share stories.
6. Teacher asks children to tell about their first trip away from home. Teacher shows cover of book, "Rhema's Journey," which is the story of a nine-year-old girl who lives in the mountains of Tanzania and accompanies her father on a trip to Arusha City, where he works as a guide at the Ngorongoro Crater animal preserve.
   - Teacher distributes glossary of some Swahili words. Children recite the words. The book has many photographs, and teacher shows them as she reads the story. Children follow on a map of Africa. Teacher asks questions such as: "How are your chores the same or different from those of Rhema? What does she study in school? Would you rather use a toothbrush or a miswaki?"

Tina Christen
Objective: Strategies to increase comprehension across the curriculum.

Rationale: Students need techniques and strategies in order to improve their understanding of what is being learned.

Activities:

1. Teacher says, "A butterfly flew across the meadow." Teacher asks students to imagine the statement in their minds by turning it into a picture. Teacher reads the poem, "The Butterfly," by A. Delancy.
   Students draw pictures of images that came into their minds when they heard the poem. Students in groups share their illustrations.
2. Each student selects a story that has been read. Students are given story maps to depict their story. Each student will be giving a TV presentation of the story, including ads that depict a key scene in the story.
3. Teacher writes a word problem on the board which has a missing last sentence. Students in groups develop ideas as to what the problem wants them to do.
   - Students in groups develop word problems with a missing sentence. These are shared with other groups that have to identify the missing sentence.
4. Distribute copies of a local newspaper, and ask students to list all the theaters that are showing their favorite movie.
   - Students are divided into groups. Each group is given a chapter from the social studies text and asked to create a way to identify all the key issues mentioned in the chapter. Strategies are shared with other groups.
5. Teacher provides students information about a topic in social studies. In groups, students are to predict what will happen, for example, the outbreak of World War I. They are to predict what will happen in the war. The reasons for the predictions are to be explained.
6. Students in groups read newspaper. They are to write a summary of an article, but it should contain several mistakes. The task of the class is to identify the mistakes.

Sharon Whittington   Primary Grades
Objective: To learn about farm life through means of storytelling.

Rationale: Students learn more effectively when knowledge is related to stories.

Activities:

1. Students are asked what kinds of animals live on farms. The teacher introduces the story, *The Barnyard Boaster*. Story is told and acted out by the teacher.
   - Students role-play animals in the story.
   - Students give names of other animals that live on a farm and sing "Old MacDonald."
   - Teacher talks about farm tasks. Students pantomine the farm tasks.
   - Students create a mural about farm life.
2. Students role play the story, *The Barnyard Boaster*. Teacher introduces information about what farm animals eat.
   - Students cut out pictures of farm animals and draw pictures of what the animals eat.
3. Students go on field trip to local farm and identify animals read about in the story.
   - Students discuss what games children play on farms. Go on a field trip to a farm and have a hay ride.
4. Students observe pigs on a farm. Do an origami project on designing a fence and pen.
5. Teacher introduces the story, *Charlotte's Web*. After reading the story, students put on their own play to reenact the story using puppets they have made.
6. Students read the *Three Pigs* story.
   - Students in groups take turns retelling the story.
7. Teacher brings in pictures about farms in Japan, Ghana, Vietnam, and Peru.
   - Students identify similarities and differences between farms they have been studying and the pictures of farms in other nations.
   - Students draw pictures of animals found on the other farms, such as a llama.
8. Students go to the library and look for books about farms in other nations. They also look for books that tell stories about life on farms in other nations.
9. Children draw pictures of farms from other nations including animals.

REFERENCES

Bang, M. (illustrator)(1987 reprinted from 1976) *Wiley and the Hairy Man: Adapted from an American Folktale.* New York: MacMillan's Children's Book Group.

Bosma, B. (1992). *Fairy Tales, fables, legends, and myths* (2nd ed.). New York: Teachers College Press.

Olson, L. (1984, September 5). Let Them Write: The Call for More Time on Task. *Education Week,* p. L12, L13, L54.

Peterson, R., & Eeds, M. (1990). *Grand Conversations.* Richmond Hills: Scholastic.

Sewall, G. F. (1988). American history textbooks: Where do we go from here? *Phi Delta Kappan, 69,* 552–558.

Tamura, E. H., & Harstad, J. R. (1987, April). Freewriting in the social studies classroom. *Social Education, 51,* (4), pp. 256–59.

Tyson, H., & Woodward, E. A. (1989). Why students aren't learning very much from textbooks. *Education Leadership, 47,* 14–17.

Welton, D. A. (1989, October). Expository writing, pseudowriting, and social studies. *Social Education,* 444–448.

Suggested Reading

Bosma, B. (1992). *Fairy tales, fables, legends, and myths* (2nd ed.). New York: Teachers College Press.

Elbow, P. (1973). *Writing without teachers*. London: Oxford University Press.

Fader, D. (1986). *The new hooked on books*. New York: Berkeley.

Goodman, K., Meredith, R., Smith, E. B. (1987).

van Nostrand, A. D. (1977, May). The inference construct: A model of the writing process. *ADE Bulletin, (57)*.

Chapter 10

Assessment of
Student Learning

Assessment of Student Learning

"There can be no teaching without learning." Israel Scheffler offered this simple but profound observation of teaching in 1960. Common sense tells us that learning can be either a solitary or shared activity. Students may learn alone or in groups, with or without a teacher. Teaching, by its very nature, however, must be an interactive process. Teachers can carefully write objectives, plan lessons, stand before the class and talk, but unless students are learning, the teacher is not teaching.

Successful teachers are reflective practitioners; they continuously question themselves. "Do my students understand this material?" "Have they discovered its relevance to their own lives?" "Are they ready to move on to a new topic?" The information-gathering and decision-making process necessary to answer these questions is called *assessment of student learning*.

The purpose of this chapter is to examine assessment practices that enhance student learning. Let's consider the following classroom situations as we begin.

Mike Smith's second graders were working in small groups. They were finishing a unit on pollution. Mike had handed each group pieces of red and green poster board. The red were titled "Causes of Pollution," and the green were labeled "Ways I Can Help." The groups had markers, scissors, glue, and old magazines. Mike clearly explained the directions, and the children got started making posters.

▲ Teachers can stand before the class and talk, but unless students are learning, the teacher is not teaching.
Courtesy Webster University.

As he circulated among the groups, Mike noticed the students were able to generate several ideas for the posters on "Causes of Pollution," but had real difficulty getting started on the second poster. His questions and prompts didn't seem to help.

Later he commented to a group of teachers at lunch, "My kids know a lot about pollution, but they don't see any connections with themselves. They don't understand that they are part of the problem. They can be part of the answer."

Maria Gonzales' third graders were studying the three branches of government. She gave her students short true-false and matching quizzes twice weekly so they and she could see how much they were learning. The final unit test would also include short essay questions. Maria's students had been successful on the earlier quizzes, but she didn't know how well they would respond to essay questions.

So, Maria asked her students to write a paragraph explaining the "balance of power" among the three branches of the federal government. As she scored their paragraphs, Maria was disappointed. "The kids don't understand this as well as I thought," she reflected. "They

▲ Teaching must be an interactive process. *Courtesy Webster University.*

can choose the right answer if I give it to them, but they can't express these ideas in their own words. We need more practice."

The fourth graders in Susan Yoshida's class were passing their social studies homework in to her. They were studying the geography of their own state. Using commercial road maps Susan had obtained, each student had planned a family camping trip to a state park. They marked the route, described the relative location, measured the distance, estimated the travel time, and described family activities at the campsite.

Susan smiled in response to the enthusiastic chatter as the children passed their folders to the front of the rows. "We're going hiking at Thousand Hills." "My dad said mine was so good that we're really gonna go fishin' at Finger Lakes." "We're goin' to Indian Trails and look for arrowheads." Susan was anxious to see their projects, but she was already confident the students had been successful.

"You should be so proud!" she said. "Your camping trips sound exciting. I'm sure you're ready for the next project. Let's get started."

▲ Effective teachers continually assess student learning.
Courtesy Saint Louis (Missouri) Public Schools.

Some teachers equate assessment with tests. Effective teachers, like those described on the previous page, however, continuously assess student learning. As indicated in these vignettes, assessment includes informal observations of students in the classroom and analyses of students' classwork and homework. Teacher-made and commercially produced tests offer more formal means of assessment. It is important to use both informal and formal processes to determine how well students learn and how effectively teachers have taught.

Children's facial expressions and body language are important indicators of boredom or curiosity, pleasure or frustration, confidence or failure. The oral questions and answers of students reveal their level of engagement with and mastery of material, as well as their ability to formulate and articulate ideas. For these reasons, insightful teachers carefully observe students during instruction, group activities, and independent work.

Authentic assessment in the social studies involves more than paper-and-pencil tests, quizzes, and drills. It requires genuine representations, simulations, or replications of the kinds of challenges faced by citizens or professionals who do something with their knowledge. Authentic assessment in the social studies may be more difficult than in spelling, mathematics, or science because social learning involves understanding self and others, exploring diverse perceptions, analyzing competing points of view, and confronting uncertainty. The depth, richness, and complexity of the social studies must be reflected in our approaches to the assessment of student learning.

What We Teach

"Teach what you test, and test what you teach." This common sense advice reminds us of the close connection between curriculum and lesson planning and assessment. The decision about how to assess learning is part of the planning process that occurs before instruction begins. While

▲ Children's facial expressions and body language are indicators of boredom or curiosity, pleasure or frustration, confidence or failure. *Courtesy Saint Louis (Missouri) Public Schools.*

teachers must be open to emergent and serendipitous learning opportunities, it is important to have clear objectives in mind before presenting lessons. It is unlikely an archer will hit the bull's eye if he doesn't know what the target is.

One useful way to analyze instructional objectives is to think of learning in terms of three broad categories or domains: (1) the cognitive domain, (2) the affective domain, and (3) the psychomotor domain. In basic terms, the cognitive domain involves academic or intellectual kinds of learning. The affective domain is concerned with learning related to values, beliefs, and attitudes. The psychomotor domain involves learning related to the sensorimotor system and large and fine muscle control.

The Cognitive Domain

The cognitive domain, as stated above, is concerned with academic or intellectual learning. Much of what we know about this learning stems from the work of Benjamin Bloom and his associates (1956). They developed a hierarchical classification system for levels of cognitive learning. Commonly referred to as Bloom's taxonomy, their work identifies six levels of thinking from simple to most sophisticated. The levels are arranged in a hierarchy, meaning that each level is dependent on and assimilates lower levels. Ordered from simple to most complex, the six levels of Bloom's taxonomy are:

> Knowledge
> Comprehension
> Application
> Analysis
> Synthesis
> Evaluation

As teachers establish learning objectives, choose instructional strategies, and assess student learning, it is valuable to consider Bloom's taxonomy. This analysis helps teachers emphasize higher level cognitive processes rather than narrowly focusing on simple recall.

Knowledge is the lowest level of Bloom's taxonomy. It involves the ability to remember information in the same way it was presented. At this level, students are not required to do anything to manipulate or interpret learned material. They simply recognize, recall, and reproduce given information.

- Who wrote the Declaration of Independence?
- What are the names of the two houses of Congress?
- Where was the treaty signed that ended World War II?
- When did Missouri become a state?

Comprehension, a more complex cognitive ability than knowledge, involves processing information so that the meaning is clear. Comprehension is the lowest level of understanding. According to Bloom, comprehension can be separated into three subcategories: translation, interpretation, and extrapolation. Students demonstrate understanding when they translate ideas into a different form (e.g., verbally describing data from maps, charts, graphs, or written text), interpret information (e.g., explain why something occurs), or extrapolate it (e.g., project a trend beyond information given).

- What is the main idea of this paragraph?
- How is the geography of the United States and Canada alike? How is it different?
- Describe the events that led the United States to enter World War II.

Application, the third level of Bloom's taxonomy, requires students to apply previously learned information in a new situation. They must actually do something with what they have learned. The process of application usually involves two phases. First, a principle, generalization, abstraction, or formula is learned. Second, students encounter a new challenge or situation and are expected to apply what they already know. The second phase is more difficult.

- Explain how one of the inventors we've studied is like a friend of yours.
- If you lived at the time of the War Between the States, would you have supported the Union or the Confederacy? Why?
- Using your map, determine the latitude of Moscow.
- Which of the people named on the front page of today's newspaper would you least like being and why?

Analysis involves students' abilities to take apart a complex phenomenon to show how and why it works. It might involve examination of some communication process (e.g., a speech, essay, story, play, poem, work of art, or musical composition) and an explanation of how the components fit together and contribute to the effect of the work. Or, it might include attempting to understand an existing situation by carefully looking at the influences that created it.

- Let's write down the major events since the War in the Gulf. Then, let's discuss how these are interrelated and why we are where we are today.
- How might this situation have been handled differently?
- What point was Dr. Martin Luther King, Jr. trying to make in his speech?
- What evidence can you find to support the view that job opportunities for women are/ are not the same as for men?

Synthesis is different from other levels in important ways. It involves creativity and is oriented toward producing a tangible product. Synthesis requires students to take separate pieces of information and combine them to create knowledge that is new (at least to the student). Pieces, parts, or elements are arranged to create a new pattern or structure.

- How would St. Louis be different today if early settlers were from Japan?
- If Ross Perot had won the 1992 presidential election, how would the United States be different today?
- How could we change recess rules and activities to avoid playground arguments?
- What are some ways we could use to get our families and friends involved in recycling?

Evaluation is the highest level of Bloom's taxonomy. It involves making judgments about the worth or merit of an object or idea. Evaluation requires a two-step process. First, criteria must be established as the basis of judgment. Second, the criteria are applied to the phenomena to be evaluated. It is important to note that sharing unsupported personal opinion is *not* evaluation.

- Do you think executing convicted murderers encourages or discourages violence in our society? Why?
- Was W. E. B. DuBois a great American leader? After providing your own definition of "greatness," respond to the question.
- How well did the United States use its resources in the Vietnam War?

The Affective Domain

The cognitive domain is concerned with improving the brain, while the affective domain focuses on developing the heart. Goals for student learning that relate to motivation, cooperation, initiative, and persistence as well as behaviors related to attitudes and values belong in the affective domain. It deals with students' likes, dislikes, needs, interests, feelings, and emotions rather than knowledge or skills. The scope of affective goals may be as narrow as attitudes toward specific homework and class projects or as broad as core values such as honesty, appreciation of differences, and respect for the rights of others.

In considering the affective domain, it is important to distinguish between the implicit and explicit curricula. Explicit goals are consciously and deliberately chosen by teachers to guide instruction. A first-grade teacher who encounters a problem with missing lunch money or pencils and responds with a lesson on honesty or respecting others' property is teaching to an explicit goal.

The implicit, or hidden, curriculum refers to the affective learning that occurs naturally through the teacher's interactions with students. The teacher's personal attitudes and values are presented through his actions, words, tone of voice, and nonverbal communication. The topics and student behaviors the teacher emphasizes, downplays, or ignores send powerful messages that are part of the hidden curriculum.

The implicit curriculum is also reflected in commercially produced and teacher-prepared instructional materials. For example, the old Dick and Jane reading books (from which one of the authors learned to read in the 1950s) featured only white, middle-class children in nuclear families. The exclusion of the experiences of people of color, the working class, or members of nontraditional families suggested their unimportance or unworthiness. In addition, Dick was portrayed as brave and adventurous while Jane was gentle and careful. When Puff the cat ran up the tree, Jane cried, but Dick climbed the tree and rescued the cat. Representing males as strong, active, and decisive and females as weak, emotional, and dependent reinforced gender stereotypes. In the preparation, selection, and use of curriculum materials, it is important for teachers to be sensitive to ways the hidden curriculum influences students' learning within the affective domain.

To assist teachers in planning instruction, Benjamin Bloom and his associates have also developed a taxonomy of the affective domain (Krathwahl, Bloom & Masia, 1964). In this taxonomy, interests, attitudes, values, and appreciations are compared to a continuum that ranges from the lowest level of awareness to the highest level of internalization in which an individual is characterized by specific values and attitudes. Each level, from lowest to highest, represents a tendency toward character formation. A brief description of the taxonomy of the affective domain is presented here.

Receiving or attending is the lowest level of the affective domain. Clearly, the student must pay attention as the first critical step to learning. Because of previous experience, each learner begins a new situation with a point of view or mind-set that enables or hinders learning. Within this level, a range of behaviors is possible. Students may only passively attend to the material presented, and it is the teacher's responsibility to capture their attention. Or students may willingly focus attention during the learning process.

- Do students listen carefully when others speak?
- Do they recognize there may be more than one acceptable point of view?
- Are they willing to listen to a variety of musical styles?
- Are they conscious of ethnic differences?

Responding, the second level of the affective domain, requires that students go beyond a simple willingness to attend to the learning opportunity. The students must show interest, choose to become involved or engaged in learning, and receive satisfaction or pleasure from the experience.

- Are my students willing to participate in the activity?
- Do they voluntarily look for books or other sources of information on this topic?

- Do they voluntarily choose to engage in this activity outside school?
- Do students seem to enjoy the activity?

Valuing represents the third level of the affective domain. At this level, the students internalize and consistently demonstrate certain values or ideals. The learners not only accept a value, but commit to it. They are willing to take a stand, put themselves on the line, and articulate or defend their position. Students exhibit loyalty and confidence and attempt to persuade others to accept their positions.

- Do students actively listen and participate in discussion of this topic?
- Do they take an active interest in drawing others into the discussion?
- Do they deliberately consider a variety of perspectives on issues in order to form opinions?
- Do learners exhibit loyalty to groups in which they participate?
- Are they willing to take a stand on issues of human rights?

At level four, *organization*, the student prioritizes values into a system which guides decision making. At this stage, the learner conceptualizes the value, relates it to other values, resolves value conflicts, and establishes an integrated framework.

- Do students compare their own ethical standards to the actions of historical and contemporary women and men?
- Are they forming judgments about the future directions of American society?
- Have they developed strategies for dealing with aggression in culturally appropriate ways?

Characterization by a value or a value complex is the highest level of the affective domain. At this point, the individual has organized her or his beliefs into a personal philosophy or worldview. This personal philosophy persistently and consistently guides behavior so that others describe and characterize the person by these central values. These fundamental beliefs are generalized in a way which enables the individual to reduce and order the complexities of life and act consistently and effectively.

▲ Learners need to be active. *Courtesy Saint Louis (Missouri) Public Schools.*

- Do students reconsider opinions and alter behavior when presented with new evidence?
- Do they make decisions based on situations, issues, goals, and consequences rather than dogmatic, inflexible rules or emotion and wishful thinking?

Values have been an important emphasis in American education since colonial days. The hornbook, *Blue-backed Speller*, and McGuffy readers stressed values derived from Protestant theology and capitalism including hard work, thrift, temperance, self-control, humility, and charity.

Explicit emphasis on affective goals has continued in the 20th century. An important facet of education in the 1920s and 1930s was the focus on the "whole child." World War II and the postwar conflict involving communism impacted education in the 1940s and 1950s. In the 1960s and 1970s, the emphasis was on humanistic and confluent education. The 1980s and 1990s have been dominated by a call for the return to traditional values. All these eras shared at least one common theme—there is more to education than mastery of objectives in the cognitive domain.

Yet, cognitive objectives continue to receive the overwhelming commitment of time and resources in American classrooms. Joseph E. Bogen (1975), a pioneer in split-brain research, drew attention to the excessive dominance of cognitive objectives and suggested methods to bring balance to the curriculum (1975). Carl Sagan (1977) agrees. He contends that the most valuable contributions to law, philosophy, the arts, science, and technology are the products of combined cognitive and affective processes. Leonard Kaplan (1978) claims that affect actually increases intellectual power.

The philosopher, Alfred North Whitehead, believed that affect is pervasive in all content areas. All learning, he argued, is shot through and through with emotion. Attitudes, beliefs, values, and appreciations are vital to an understanding of the social studies. Stripped of emotional content and value, the social studies are little more than lists of dates and facts for students to memorize and packaged rhetoric to be regurgitated.

Psychomotor Domain

The psychomotor domain classifies human movements on a continuum ranging from simple to complex. Basic human movements (running, jumping, climbing, lifting, carrying, hanging, and throwing) do not require teaching. According to Anita Harrow (1972), these movements represent the need of learners to be active. Harrow includes all observable voluntary human motion in the taxonomy. A shortened version of her taxonomy of the psychomotor domain is presented below.

1. Reflex Movements
    a. Segmental Reflexes
    b. Intersegmental Reflexes
    c. Suprasegmental Reflexes
2. Basic-Fundamental Movements
    a. Locomotor Movements
    b. Nonlocomotor Movements
    c. Manipulative Movements
3. Perceptual Abilities
    a. Kinesthetic Discrimination
    b. Visual Discrimination
    c. Auditory Discrimination
    d. Tactile Discrimination
    e. Coordinated Abilities
4. Physical Abilities
    a. Endurance
    b. Strength
    c. Flexibility
    d. Agility
5. Skilled Movements
    a. Simple Adaptive Skill
    b. Compound Adaptive Skill
    c. Complex Adaptive Skill

6. Nondiscursive Communication
   a. Expressive Movement
   b. Interpretive Movement

   At first, the taxonomy of the psychomotor domain was seen as useful only to physical education teachers. The psychomotor domain, however, cuts across all disciplines. Learners process information in three basic ways—by seeing, by hearing, and by doing.

   Many students need physical activity to learn. In the social studies, objectives in the psychomotor domain may include handwriting, artwork, constructing maps or other projects, dance, singing, playing instruments, pantomime, gestures, and other forms of nonverbal communication.

   Learners are physical, mental, emotional, and valuing beings. The cognitive, affective, and psychomotor domains are artificial constructs that provide teachers with valuable heuristics, ways to consider independently human qualities that emerge in concert. The cognitive, affective, and physical are intricately interrelated. Successful teachers emphasize learning and assessment in all three domains.

Assessing What We Teach

Three general principles are important to consider when planning to assess student learning:

1. What we are assessing must be clearly related to what we are trying to teach.
2. Assessment should occur frequently so external factors do not cause us to make judgments about students that do not accurately reflect their true learning.
3. Because teachers have a clear understanding of the learning we expect from our students, we should create our own assessment tools.

▲ Learners process information by seeing, hearing, and doing.
Courtesy University City (Missouri) Public Schools.

Let's consider each principle individually. The first principle suggests that assessment must be clearly tied to instruction. Evaluating students on assignments or tests that are not related to what has been studied in class sets youngsters up for failure. To avoid this, teachers must plan assessment at the same time we set learning goals and construct unit and lesson plans. For example, a lesson devoted to living habitats of Native Americans prior to European colonization should not have questions on an assessment device which deals with songs and dances.

The second principle suggests that we assess youngsters' progress at frequent intervals. This offers several advantages. Students may become nervous when they are evaluated. They feel less intimidated when learning is assessed more frequently. Frequent assessment also helps us diagnose problems students may be having so that we can review, revise, and expand our teaching. Frequent assessment may also offer us a more accurate picture of student learning. If Justin did not feel well when completing an assignment, his teacher might incorrectly conclude he did not understand the material. If Jared made several "lucky guesses" on a particular test, we might decide he knows more than he really does. Frequent assessment balances unusually high or low scores. In addition, when teachers assess learning often, they can adjust materials and teaching approaches if it appears the lesson is not achieving its goals.

The third principle suggests that we, as teachers, should be actively involved in choosing and developing the assessment tools (e.g., tests, quizzes, individual and group projects, class and homework assignments) we use in our classrooms. It is highly unlikely that assignments or tests developed by commercial publishers and testing services or even school district curriculum committees will be perfectly congruent with the specific learning expectations each of us has established for our own students. The most appropriate, pertinent, and relevant evaluation tools are created by teachers who are intimately involved with the children whose learning is to be assessed—not district administrators, government bureaucrats, or commercial testing experts who have never met your students.

We do not suggest that standardized tests are unimportant. They are valuable to help schools and districts understand how groups of students compare with national averages or criteria. Such tests, however, may assess student learning in areas that are not closely related to the actual experiences of children in an individual classroom. Overemphasis on standardized tests often results in a narrowing of the curriculum to focus on only the lowest levels of the cognitive domain, perhaps because they are easily evaluated on multiple-choice tests. Too often educators have attempted to adjust curricula to match the requirements of standardized tests. Here the tail wags the dog. Instead, we should be choosing assessment processes that are consistent with the things we are trying to teach.

Assessment Options

When planning to assess student learning, many teachers immediately think of formal tests. While paper-and-pencil tests are important, there are numerous possibilities to consider before evaluating student learning. Depending on what we are teaching, we might want students to demonstrate learning by making a peanut butter and jelly sandwich, drawing a map of their own neighborhood, creating a puppet play, performing ethnic songs and dances, or developing a portfolio.

Student Portfolios

The development of portfolios by students offers an exciting approach to authentic assessment. Each student should purposefully select artifacts that document personal learning. Appropriate evidence to collect in a portfolio might include:

1. Student writings.
2. Rough drafts and finished products.
3. Group assignments and team projects.
4. Student reflections, such as journal entries.
5. Collections of data entries, such as research logs.
6. Creative expressions/e.g. art, photographs, audio and video recordings.
7. Teacher comments and assessments.
8. Questions.
9. A sample that reflects the student's approach to problem-solving.
10. An example that shows how the student went about learning something new.
11. Any work of which the student is particularly proud.
12. An example of a project that was a comical disaster.
13. A sample of a work in process that the student wants to continue.

Adapted from D. Adams and M. Hamon. (1992, February). Portfolio assessment and social studies: Collecting, selecting, and reflecting on what is significant. *Social Education, 56,* pp. 103–5.

Our assessment program sends powerful messages to students about the real purpose of their learning experiences. For example, in a unit on American history, Frank Williams told his sixth graders the primary purpose was to analyze major historic trends. His tests, however, consisted only of completion (fill-in-the-blank) items that required memorization of isolated information from their textbook. Frank's students quickly learned that the real purpose and the best way to succeed was to memorize discrete historical facts. For this reason, it is vital for us as teachers to establish and maintain consistency in what is taught and how it is assessed. Let's consider some assessment options.

Rating Scales

Rating scales are particularly effective when assessing youngsters as they perform authentic tasks such as developing portfolios, participating in discussions, presenting speeches, or constructing projects. Rating scales can be used to evaluate objectives in all three learning domains—cognitive, affective, and psychomotor. Teachers might use rating scales to communicate evaluation information to students or design an instrument so that students can offer feedback to each other. A rating scale for a small group discussion might be established like this:

Outstanding	5	Always
Above Average	4	Frequently
Average	3	Occasionally
Below Average	2	Seldom
Unsatisfactory	1	Never

- During discussion, does the student actively participate to help move the group toward its goal?
- Is the information s/he presents factually accurate?
- Does s/he show respect for the contributions of other group members?
- Are the student's points communicated clearly?
- Are his/her comments related to the topic?

▲ Rating scales are effective when assessing authentic tasks such as presenting speeches. *Courtesy Saint Louis (Missouri) Public Schools.*

Evaluative Checklists

Checklists, like rating scales, are appropriate to evaluate students' physical performances. They may be used to assess objectives in all three domains of learning. Checklists, however, are limited to a yes or no answer that indicates the presence or absence of a behavior. For example, if a teacher were interested in monitoring the progress of student groups in planning puppet plays about occupations, the checklist on the following page might be used.

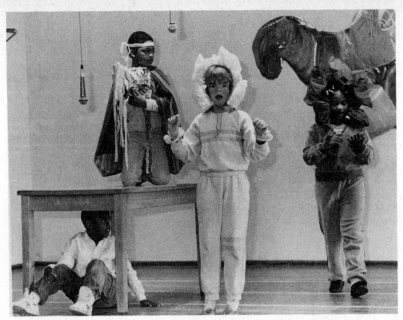

▲ Checklists may be used to evaluate students' physical performances.
Courtesy Saint Louis (Missouri) Public Schools.

Students' Names: _____
_____
_____

	Yes	No
Occupations selected and approved		
Rough outline of script turned in		
Final script turned in		
Puppets made or selected		
Play performed for class		

Essays

Essays are powerful evaluation tools. They are capable of assessing student learning in both the affective and cognitive domains. Essays can be used to assess learning at every level of the cognitive domain (knowledge, comprehension, application, analysis, synthesis, and evaluation). However, essays are not often used at the lower levels (knowledge and comprehension) because they require a great deal of time to correct.

It is important to write directions carefully to guide students as they write essays. Consider the following sets of instructions for sixth graders who were studying current events.

A. Write a paper in which you discuss the 1992 United States presidential election.

B. Write an essay about two pages in length. Compare and contrast the 1992 United States presidential candidates. Explain the strengths and weaknesses of each candidate, who you would have voted for and why.

Students responding to the first set of instructions are likely to ramble. The second set of directions is more likely to enable students to succeed.

We should consider these helpful hints when preparing and scoring essays:

1. Determine in advance whether to grade based only on content or to include writing mechanics in the score.
2. Write a sample essay to help determine what content should be included.
3. Devise strategies to keep from identifying the writer of an essay until after it is scored in order to avoid favoritism.
4. Read all essays written in response to a specific question before scoring other items.
5. Read essays more than once.
6. Adjust scoring in comparison with other essays in order to maintain consistency.

Completion

Completion or fill-in-the-blank items are most useful to assess student thinking at the lower cognitive levels of knowledge and comprehension. Because completion questions must be carefully constructed so that only one answer is logically correct, they discourage divergent and creative thinking.

Compare the following items:

A. The man elected president of the United States in 1992 was

_____ .

B. The name of the president of the United States who was elected in 1992 is _____ .

Most students would probably answer "Bill Clinton" to both questions. But some students might correctly answer the first question "Democratic," "Liberal," or "from Arkansas." Each completion item should have only one blank which ought to be near the end of the sentence.

▲ Essays are powerful evaluation tools. *Courtesy Webster University.*

Matching

Matching items are most useful to assess student learning at the cognitive levels of knowledge and comprehension. They are easy for teachers to construct and grade. Like completion items, matching assignments discourage creative or independent thinking.

All matching items should focus on the same topic, which is clearly identified. The list on the right (from which students select answers to place in the blanks on the left) should contain about 25% more items than the list on the left. This discourages guessing and makes it possible for a student to answer one incorrectly without automatically missing two items.

Midwestern State Capitals Matching Exercise

Directions: Find the capital in the column on the right that matches each state in the left-hand column. Place the letter identifying each capital in the blank space by its state.

_____ 1. Missouri	a.	Topeka
_____ 2. Illinois	b.	Lincoln
_____ 3. Iowa	c.	Cleveland
_____ 4. Kansas	d.	Lansing
_____ 5. Nebraska	e.	Columbus
_____ 6. Indiana	f.	Jefferson City
_____ 7. Ohio	g.	Kansas City
_____ 8 Michigan	h.	Madison
_____ 9. Wisconsin	i.	Springfield
_____ 10.Minnesota	j.	St. Paul
	k.	Des Moines
	l.	Indianapolis

Multiple Choice

Multiple-choice items are probably the most widely used type of assessment. They are easy for teachers to construct and score and can be used to assess objectives at the cognitive levels of knowledge, comprehension, application, and analysis. A multiple-choice item consists of two parts, a stem and alternative choices. Among the alternatives, one is correct, and the others are distractors.

The principal river of the United States is the
a. Colorado.
b. Mississippi.
c. Arkansas.
d. Ohio.

The first European who circumnavigated the globe was
a. Columbus.
b. Cortez
c. Magellan.
d. DeSoto.

The Women's Suffrage movement was closely related to the
a. Temperance movement.
b. organization of labor unions.
c. Civil Rights movement.
d. entry of women into the workforce during World War II.

Multiple-choice items have been criticized because they limit students' opportunities to think critically, creatively, and independently. Grant Wiggins (Nickel, 1992), a leader in authentic assessment, contends that multiple-choice items do not challenge students to perform with knowledge or produce documents, artifacts, or performances. They just point at answers.

Multiple-choice items, however, can be rearranged in order to stimulate creative thinking. Consider the following multiple choice questions,

Which of the following is not an important New Deal Law?
a. CCC
b. WPA
c. Social Security Act
d. Civil Rights Act

▲ Teachers understand important things about students' learning when they observe them construct a museum exhibit. *Courtesy Perry County (Missouri) School District.*

In this example, students recall information without any indication that they understand the actual functioning of the laws. Consider this alternative:

Which of the following is not an important New Deal law?
a. CCC—I am a teenager seeking work rebuilding forests;
b. WPA—I am an adult who seeks work;
c. Social Security Act—I am retired and need income.
d. Civil Rights Act—I am an African-American who wants the right to vote.

True/False

True/false items are most often used to assess knowledge level thinking. Although they can be quickly prepared and scored, they have several disadvantages. First, they encourage students to guess. Even if they don't understand the material, students have a 50:50 chance of correctly responding. Second, it is difficult, especially in the social studies, to prepare statements that are absolutely "true" or absolutely "false." Much of the content of the social studies tends toward gray rather than black or white.

Assessment Tips

1. Ask students to furnish questions for the examination.

2. Allow students to refer to notes or textbook during the test.

3. Vary the day of the week and time of day for tests.

4. Allow students to take home essay questions.

5. Be aware of students with reading problems who require additional time to complete written tests.

6. Meet with students on a one-to-one basis, and conduct the test by means of verbal interaction.

7. If you are requiring an essay, teach students how to write an essay. Prior to an exam, review the process of essay writing. For example:

Essay Question: Causes of the American Revolution

  A. Political
1. Taxation: Discuss the Stamp Act.
2. Representative Government: Discuss how colonists wanted to elect governors.
3. Property Rights: Discuss why colonists were upset when British troops were quartered in their homes.

  B. Economic
1. Colonists wanted to trade anywhere in the world.
2. Colonists wanted an end to governmental monopolies.

8. Teach students how to use memory techniques in order to improve memory retention.

9. Give students some flexibility regarding ways they are evaluated. For example, allow a student to have an art or math question integrated with social studies.

10. Include one humorous question on each exam as a tension release. For example: "All but one of the following is an important female political leader: (a) Eleanor Roosevelt; (b) Susan B. Anthony; (c) Madonna; (d) Senator Nancy Kassenbaum."

11. Assess performance in the affective domain. For example, "I will give an 'A' this week to anyone who has demonstrated a willingness to help at least one other person with homework."

12. Each month ask students to create an exam to test teacher knowledge about what is being studied or current events.

Charles Colton, a 19th century British writer, once said: "Examinations are formidable to the best prepared for the greatest fool may ask more than the wisest man can answer." Examinations, tests, and grades still bring shivers, shudders, and fear to students. Successful teachers, however, never use assessment as a means to control, punish, or embarrass youngsters. Instead, they use creative assessment strategies to produce information that is useful to both teachers and students. We understand important things about students' learning when we observe them constructing a museum exhibit, doing an oral family history, or participating in a mock trial in an historical time

▲ Authentic assessment gauges students' learning through substantive activities such as mock debates or trials.
Courtesy Pattonville (Missouri) School District.

and place. Master teachers know that the challenge of authentic assessment is not to measure students' abilities to answer questions on paper-and-pencil tests, but to gauge youngsters' abilities to apply what they are learning to confront the challenges of the 21st century.

SUMMARY

Assessment is among the most sensitive interactions between students and teachers. Students frequently evaluate teachers on the basis of tests rather than the content of a course. Children face enormous pressures from parents, teachers, and peers to excel on tests. National leaders and the media cite test scores as an indication of success or failure in American schools. Assessment can become a tool or an end in itself. The goal of education is the improvement of learning and helping youth to better understand themselves, their society and the human heritage. Teachers who employ assessment for these purposes are acting in a professional manner.

Assessment impacts the novice teacher in direct ways. School districts assess teachers and influence both what is taught and how teachers teach. The challenge to teachers is creating assessment techniques that respect the integrity of what is being taught while affording children opportunities to attain the full extent of their innate capacities.

QUESTIONS

1. What was the most common form of assessment you encountered in elementary school? At the secondary level?

2. What has been the most interesting form of testing you were given as a student?

3. Cite an example in which you were evaluated based on the affective domain, for example, grade reduction due to lateness.

4. To what extent should factors from the affective domain influence grading in elementary and middle school?

5. Should students be evaluated in the area of psychomotor abilities?

6. Which do you prefer: frequent assessment or long period assessment?

7. Cite an example in which you were tested on items not heavily emphasized in a course. Discuss your feelings.

8. What do you like best or least about essay questions?

9. What do you like best or least about completion and multiple choice tests?

10. How does testing impact your motivation to learn?

ACTIVITIES

1. Collect assessment tools from elementary and middle schools. Categorize and analyze the data.

2. Develop an assessment device that reflects ideas discussed in this chapter.

3. Interview elementary and middle school teachers regarding assessment. Present your analysis of their ideas.

4. Interview elementary and middle school children about testing. Present your analysis of their ideas.

5. Rewrite a standardized test in order to make it a more effective assessment tool.

READING

Testing and Evaluation of Social Studies Students

In the last decade of the twentieth century, contemporary American education is gradually turning from centrally-mandated educational reforms toward improvement efforts based in the schools themselves. Across the nation, citizens and educators are restructuring schools in line with the 1986 recommendations of the Carnegie Task Force on Teaching as a Profession. Although restructured schools may differ greatly from one another, their common denominator is shared decision making and local leadership at the school level rather than a uniform curriculum or accountability defined only by scores on standardized achievement tests. The National Governors Association supports this new wave of educational reform and the reform has received the endorsement of both of the nation's major teacher unions.

The image of the restructured classroom is one in which students participate in higher-order thinking and in which learning activities and curriculum materials engage and challenge them. Student-to-student interaction and cooperation are hallmarks of such classrooms. Restructured schools call for decentralized decision making, differentiating instructional roles according to teaching skills and expertise, and assessment and accountability based on learning outcomes valued by individual schools.

Paralleling this new wave of restructuring are efforts to transform student assessment from an overreliance on machine-scored standardized tests to approaches that balance such measures with alternatives such as performance assessments or authentic assessments. The design of such assessments reflects actual learning tasks such as speaking effectively or taking a reasoned stance on a controversial social issue. They focus on the processes students use, not merely the answers they choose.

In this environment of shared instructional leadership and authentic assessment, the social studies teaching profession can enhance learning in history and the social sciences and develop the skills necessary for participatory citizenship. The purpose of this position statement is to demonstrate how testing and evaluating social studies students can contribute to those ends.

Testing in Social Studies

Evaluation refers to the collection and analysis of assessment information, often in the form of test results, to assist in judging student progress in learning. Social studies educators at all levels recognize a need to evaluate their programs, with testing geared toward measuring and assessing objectives as one of its major components. Social studies teachers test students to gauge how well their students are accomplishing stated learning objectives in order to make informed decisions for improving the effectiveness of their programs.

A comprehensive evaluation plan for social studies includes appropriate use of both teacher-made achievement tests and standardized achievement tests. These two types of tests serve complementary, sometimes overlapping purposes. Tests in social studies serve a number of purposes. Social studies teachers use tests:

- to determine the learning needs of students
- to provide learners with information and assistance on their progress toward social studies objectives
- to provide information for assigning grades and for making decisions about promoting students to the next grade level
- to compare the social studies achievement of their students with those of a broad population of students

For assessing individual students' accomplishments in terms of stated social studies objectives, teachers develop tests tailored specifically to the objectives related to the learning experiences in their classrooms. In constructing these tests, teachers may make judicious use of test items developed by the publishers of their social studies textbooks. These tests may be either norm-referenced, to compare students' retention of a body of social studies knowledge and skills, or criterion-referenced, to determine the extent to which each learner has mastered each of a number of specific social studies performance objectives.

Teachers may use published standardized tests to supplement the information derived from locally-developed teacher-made tests. Standardized tests may provide data on how well students in a particular school or school system perform on social studies objectives in comparison to learners in many other schools across their state or nation. In addition, test publishers may provide norms that permit comparison of local students with a wide sample of peers in their particular cultural or ethnic group. Although most standardized tests are norm-referenced, many allow teachers to interpret test results on a variety of social studies skills.

To meet the requirement of content validity, the objectives of published tests adopted for local use must closely match those of the local studies curriculum. Social studies teachers need to participate actively in content validation as part of the test selection process. By helping to select standardized tests for use in their schools, teachers may discover some important objectives they address inadequately in their classrooms and thereby make adjustments in their curriculums. They may also identify highly valued social studies objectives not represented in any of the published tests and recommend limits for interpreting the results of standardized testing.

As the social studies curriculum requires close interaction with a variety of information media, social studies tests, whether locally-constructed or nationally-marketed, should include items that require students to use and interpret various sources. Tasks in social studies tests should use materials such as maps, photographs, tables, charts, graphs, editorial cartoons, newspaper clippings, artifacts, documents, film or video clips, and audio recordings.

The overriding purpose of testing in social studies classrooms is to improve learning. To accomplish this goal, social studies teachers must be proficient in interpreting and reporting test results, including those from standardized tests. Standardized test data collected in social studies classrooms must be available to the teacher for study. The teacher can then examine the picture they present of each learner and weigh those descriptions against the evidence that has accumulated from teacher-made tests and other measures over weeks and months of social studies learning experiences. Teachers can then make judgments about the appropriateness and effectiveness of their social studies curriculum. To accomplish this, teachers will require some in-service education since the measurement background of teachers varies widely and tests and reporting formats change from time to time and differ from one publisher to another.

Evaluation Beyond Testing

Social studies education, as envisioned by NCSS in numerous publications, involves the acquisition of essential knowledge of history and the social sciences. It entails the development of the skills and attitudes required for competent, participatory citizenship in our democratic society and in the global community. Social studies programs designed to educate for effective democratic citizenship emphasize gathering information from a variety of disciplines and experiences along with thinking, decision making, communication, social interaction, and civic participation.

Evaluation of student progress in a sound social studies curriculum requires more than the typical objective-type paper-and-pencil test. To gauge effectively the efforts of students and teachers in social studies programs, evaluators must augment traditional tests with performance evaluations, portfolios of student papers and projects, and essays focused on higher levels of thinking. The development of a comprehensive, systematic, and valid evaluation for a social studies program requires the creative cooperation of social studies professionals with educational measurement specialists. Ideally, evaluation design is integral to the curriculum development process and proceeds simultaneously with it.

Fairness in Testing and Evaluation

Social studies educators in our pluralistic society must see that their teaching and curriculum materials are fair to all people, regardless of their ethnic backgrounds, beliefs, genders, or handicaps. It follows that they must also assure that all assessment materials, whether produced by publishers or by teachers, are blind to learner characteristics, such as culture and gender.

In recent years test publishers have conducted staff development programs aimed at sensitizing test writers to prejudice, stereotyping, and denigration of particular groups. They have employed item writers from minority groups. In addition, they have subjected their test materials to reviews by members of minority groups and others familiar with the needs and learning styles of pupils from various cultural backgrounds. When selecting standardized tests for local use, social studies educators should review the publishers' tests and their statements on fairness and bias to determine the extent to which the authors and editors have succeeded in making the test fair to all learners. When developing local tests and alternative assessment strategies, teachers should apply procedures similar to those used by test publishers to minimize culture or gender bias.

Just as social studies educators see that the content of testing and evaluation materials and strategies are fair to all, they must also exercise vigilance that they make fair comparisons between their students and others and in their decisions about pupils from test results and other assessments. Test publishers provide national norms to compare student achievement. Test users should examine the composition of the group used to establish those norms and juxtapose the socioeconomic, cultural, and gender characteristics of the local school with those of the publisher's norm group. Many publishers offer norms reflecting the typical performance of specific groups, such as African Americans or Hispanics, and may produce local or state norms as additional frames of reference. Social studies educators can and should avoid the mistake of using only one form of measurement in interpreting their students' test results. Social studies educators can and should use *all* the information available about their students' social studies achievement—data gathered from a variety of assessment instrument and techniques—when making decisions about assigning grades, class placement, promotion, or retention.

Recommendations and Guidelines for Evaluating Achievement in Social Studies

Evaluation in social studies should be based on clearly formulated curriculum objectives that social studies professionals have developed and adopted. Teachers use these objectives for evaluating their performance and their students' achievement. Social studies teachers, curriculum developers, supervisors, and methods professors, as well as scholars in history and the social sciences, must influence testing and evaluation programs through the curriculum materials used in classrooms and through consultation on the content and behavioral dimensions of social studies tests and other assessment instruments. Only carefully designed evaluation strategies and tests will enable social studies educators to assess both the academic content and the thinking or performance skills stated in or implied by the objectives.

To improve the assessment and evaluation of student achievement in social studies, the NCSS Advisory Committee on Testing and Evaluation has recommended the following guidelines:

Evaluation instruments should:
- focus on stated curriculum goals and objectives
- be used to improve curriculum and instruction
- measure both content and process
- be chosen for instructional, diagnostic, and prescriptive purposes
- reflect a high degree of fairness to all people and groups

Evaluations of student achievement should:
- be used solely to improve teaching and learning
- involve a variety of instruments and approaches to measure students' knowledge, skills, and attitudes
- be congruent with both the objectives and the classroom experiences of the students examined
- be sequential and cumulative

State and local education agencies should:
- secure appropriate funding to implement and support evaluation programs
- support the education of teachers in selecting, using, and developing assessment instruments

- involve teachers and other social studies professionals in formulating objectives for social studies instruction and evaluation and in the design and selection of social studies evaluation instruments
- measure long-term effects of social studies instruction

In an era of teacher empowerment and school-based curriculum reform, the opportunities for improving teaching and learning in social studies seem boundless. Testing and evaluation of social studies student achievement should support such efforts. Nevertheless, a caution from an earlier period (*NCSS Position Statement on Graduation Competency Testing in the Social Studies,* 1978) bears repeating:

> We hope that preoccupations with testing programs do not deflect social studies educators from the important responsibilities of communicating to parents, legislators, and community members the purposes of social studies instruction and of continuing to provide the highest possible level of social studies instruction.

References

Association for Supervision and Curriculum Development. "Transforming the Test." *Update* 32, no. 7 (1990): 3–6.

Burrill, L. E., and R. Wilson. *Fairness and the Matter of Bias.* Test Service Notebook, no. 36. New York: The Psychological Corporation, 1980.

Carnegie Forum on Education and the Economy. *A Nation Prepared: Teachers for the 21st Century.* Report of the Carnegie Task Force on Teaching as a Profession. Washington, D.C.: Carnegie Forum, 1986.

Fitzpatrick, R., and E. Morrison. "Performance and Product Evaluation." In *Educational Measurement,* edited by R. L. Thorndike. 2d ed. Washington, D.C.: American Council on Education, 1971.

Gronlund, N. E. *Measurement and Evaluation in Teaching.* 5th ed. New York: Macmillan, 1985.

Kurfman, Dana G. "Testing as Context for Social Education." In *Handbook of Research on Social Studies Teaching and Learning,* edited by James P. Shaver. New York: Macmillan, 1991. This chapter is the most recent research statement on testing in social education and contains an extensive bibliography on the subject.

National Council for the Social Studies. *Graduation Competency Testing in the Social Studies.* Position statement prepared by K. A. Fox, P. L. Williams, and L. Winters. Washington, D.C.: National Council for the Social Studies. 1978.

O'Neil, J. "Piecing Together the Restructuring Puzzle." *Educational Leadership* 47 (1990): 4–10.

Thomas, B. *On Their Own: Student Responses to Open-ended Tests in Social Studies.* Boston: Massachusetts Department of Education, 1989.

NCSS Committee Members Contributing to Position Statement

Sheila M. Ager, Princeton, NJ; Janet Alleman, East Lansing, MI; Glen Blankenship, Lawrenceville, GA; Margaret Branson, Bakersfield, CA; Judith Bristol, Houston, TX; Marsha L. Burch, Florence, SC; Regan Carpenter, Edwardsville, IL; Boone Colegrove, Salt Lake City, UT; Patricia J. Dye, Plymouth, MA; Stanley E. Easton, Jacksonville, AL; Richard T. Farrell, College Park, MD; Mary M. Graham, Nashville, TN; Carter B. Hart, Concord, NH; Rachel Hicks, Clinton, MD; Jack N. Hoar, Long Beach, CA; Lewis E. Huffman, Dover, DE; Ray W. Karras, Lexington, MA; James Killoran, Lake Ronkonkoma, NY; S. Rex Morrow, Norfolk, VA; Julie Mortier, Gary, IN; Pat Nickell, Lexington, KY, Board Liaison; Helen W. Richardson, Atlanta, GA; Kathy Skau, Calgary, Alberta, Canada; Dennie L. Smith, Memphis, TN; Warren H. Solomon, Jefferson City, MO; Cheryl Summers, Albuquerque, NM; Terry Trimble, Naples, FL; Roger Wangen, St. Paul, MN; Hines L. Wommack, Americus, GA.

QUESTIONS ON READING

1. What are the main purposes of testing and evaluation in social studies?

2. What is meant by the concept of "evaluation beyond testing?"

3. What should be the goals of assessment in elementary and middle school grades?

LESSON PLANS

David King, Webster Groves School District, Missouri, Grade 5–7

Introduction: The lesson is for the software *Where in the World is Carmen Sandiego?*

Objective: To familiarize students with the mystery exploration game, *Where in the World is Carmen Sandiego?* To apply "look up" skills using encyclopedia, almanac, dictionary, and atlas.

Preparation:

Equipment: Overhead projector and screen; one large monitor and computer system which will run Carmen Sandiego.

Materials: "Where in the World is Carmen Sandiego?" software pack, atlases, almanacs, (*The World Almanac and Book of Facts—1986*) dictionaries, encyclopedias.

Set-Up: Monitor and equipment must be set up where all students can see them. Desks should be arranged into four groups, one for each of the following: Atlases, Almanacs, Dictionaries, and Encyclopedias. The fifth group should be situated around the computer. All students should be familiar with how to locate information in each of the four types of reference materials. Using an index is an important skill. The teacher should be familiar with the software's manual and program.

Activities:

1. Students assigned to groups.

2. After students familiarize themselves with reference materials, explain to fifth group at computer that their tasks are to enter information into the computer, record clues; to read Dossiers to the class; to coordinate the researchers and make all final decisions when game options are presented; and to assist researchers by utilizing their "Official Interpol Map" on pp. 10–11 of the manual.

3. Explain the purpose of the activity to the class (pp. 3 & 6).

4. Boot the software and follow directions to Signing In (p. 4).

5. Read the crime together, and review the uses of the four options on the Main Menu (p. 7). It is best to take time to show how each option works as you explain.

6. Be sure students understand keyboard controls as explained on p. 5 of the Manual.

7. Assist students as they chase the criminal by giving key words and phrases to each research group and guiding the search very closely through the first couple of trials.

8. Once the thief is captured or escapes arrest, have students rotate to another group so they have opportunities to use all reference materials as well as work at the computer.

Teacher Notes:

1. Explain how to use information given in order to guess the criminal's next move. See pp. 8 and 9 of User's Manual.

2. Utilize the See Connections option to limit the cities which need to be researched before making each move.
3. Students should know that a warrant is needed in order to make an arrest.
4. Students should know that they must investigate and obtain as many clues as possible before going to Interpol.
5. During demonstration, show students the various characteristics available in the Interpol Data Base so they will know what to look for while investigating.
6. It is helpful to supply each group with several questions similar to those encountered in the game (p. 8) in order to research during Step 2 of the activity.
7. Projecting an overhead transparency of the "Official Interpol Map" located on p. 10 and 11 of the User's Manual might assist all research groups throughout the lesson.
8. Emphasize the importance of a dictionary as a research tool.

REFERENCES

Bloom, B. (ed), Krathwahl, D., and Bertram, M. (1956). *Taxonomy of educational objectives: Handbook I: The Cognitive Domain.* New York: David McKay Co., Inc.

Bogen, J. (1975). The other side of the brain, VII: Some educational aspects of hemispheric specialization. *UCLA Educator, 17,* 24–32.

Harrow, A. (1972). *A taxonomy of the psychomotor domain: A guide for developing behavioral objectives.* New York: McKay.

Kaplan, L. (1978). *Developing objectives in the affective domain.* Columbus, OH: Collegiate Publishing.

Krathwahl, D., Bloom, B., & Masia, B. (1964). *Taxonomy of educational objectives, Handbook II: Affective domain.* New York: McKay.

Nickel, P. (1992, February). Doing the stuff of social studies: A conversation with Grant Wiggins. *Social Education, 56,* (12), 91–94.

Sagan, C. (1977). *The Dragons of Eden.* New York: Random House.

SUGGESTED READING

Berliner, D. C. (1987). But Do They Understand? *Educator's Handbook.* New York: Longman.

Hathaway, W. E. (1983). *Testing in the Schools. New Directions for Testing and Measurement.* San Francisco: Jossey Bass.

Stiggins, R. J. (1984). *Evaluating Students Through Classroom Observation: Watching*

Students Grow. Washington, DC: National Education Association.

Stiggins, R. J. et al. (1985). *A feeling for the Student: An Analysis of the art of Classroom Assessment.* Regional Education Laboratory. Portland, OR: Northwest.

Part 3

Student as a
Citizen Participant

Chapter 11
Our Historical Heritage

Our Historical Heritage

What is History?

Can we ever know the past? Even more fundamentally, what is in the past that we would like to know? The German historian, Leopold von Ranke, said the task of history was to recreate the past "wie es eigentlich gewesen"—as it really was. Can a society as culturally diverse as the United States come to a consensus about the nature of life that existed on this continent a hundred or two hundred years ago?

History is a process by which a culture seeks to explain its development from its origin to the present. We expect that a person today can enter the mind and spirit of people living thousands of years ago. We assume that past behaviors are understandable or analogous to present situations.

Historians make a daring leap of the imagination in their reconstruction of the past. An infinite number of "facts" exist in the past. The historian selects among facts and weaves a fabric that gives meaning to the present. Historians are artists imposing their mental designs upon the myriad of events constituting the past.

▲ The task of history is to recreate the past as it really was. *Courtesy Perry County (Missouri) School District No. 42.*

Henry Steele Commager (1965, p. 1) has stated that "the past is not dependent on us for its existence but exists in its own right." Theoretically, that might be true, but the moment we read a document from the past our present viewpoints enter the dialogue. Our education, our occupation, our ethnic heritage, and today's events all shape how we will interpret the past. History is usually written by winners for winners.

Imagine being suddenly transported in a time machine to America in 1776. You are at a meeting of American revolutionaries. Your observations of events would be colored by 20th century bias. You would hear the word "freedom" not as it was intended in 1776, but distorted by the intervening years. After the time machine brought you back to the present, the facts recalled would be selective.

History is a moral tale written by people with values who call upon the past to buttress contemporary beliefs. Each generation rewrites the past to fit present circumstances. For example, the rapprochement between the United States and the Soviet Union is already altering history. We may expect more balanced views regarding the origin and development of the Cold War in which mutual misunderstandings and misconceptions play a larger role in the story.

Students often do not recognize that historical evidence relies upon feelings. Marc Bloch (1953) has noted that "historical facts are, in essence, psychological facts." A fact is called into existence by the mind of the historian. Millions of people crossed the Rubicon, but an historian decided its crossing by Julius Ceasar was worthy of note. It is historically valid for women or minorities to raise questions about which facts should constitute history. Historians have neglected the experiences of nondominant groups. The past is not falsified by discussing the lives, activities, customs, sports, foods, or ideas of ordinary people. The lives of Solomon Northrup or Harriet Tubman, who escaped from slavery, help us to understand that condition from a different perspective than a life of John Calhoun would provide. We need a more varied chorus than is presently offered by textbooks.

The task of the historian is to collect, interpret, and explain evidence utilizing methods which are similar to those of a detective. A police officer knows that an eyewitness account has to be treated with care; this principle also applies to historians. We are all historians in everyday life just as we are all detectives; we examine evidence, read documents, analyze people, interpret facts, and reach conclusions. Teachers should insist that those who wish to reinterpret the past are duty bound to adhere to strict standards of historical procedures, such as utilization of primary sources and intensive investigation of all relevant materials.

Children can enjoy history for its mystery and drama. Thomas Macauly commented that history is a trip to foreign places. It transports children to new worlds filled with fabulous customs, new foods, dress, hair styles, and sports. History, more than any other discipline, enables children to understand the variety and diversity of the human condition. It is a tale of wonder opening vistas into an exciting future.

▲ History is the process by which a culture seeks to explain its development from its origin to the present. *Courtesy Francis Howell (Missouri) School District.*

Tools of Historians and Social Scientists

Each occupation compels workers to employ specific tools in order to accomplish their tasks. A secretary relies upon a word processor, a carpenter uses hammer, nails, and a saw, and social scientists have their own set of useful tools. Once children understand the way social scientists and historians function, it is much easier to understand social studies.

Historians and social scientists use similar methodologies in dealing with problems, but there are several differences. Sociologists, economists, and political scientists are more prone to focus on topics that can be dealt with in a methodologically precise manner. They rely more upon mathematical methods of model building. "Opinion surveys, sampling techniques, projective tests, content analysis, scaling, and the like are the new procedures with which the scientists of human behavior have enriched our knowledge of contemporary society and, by extrapolation, our understanding of history itself" (Hughes, 1960).

Both historians and social scientists rely upon several key processes of analyzing issues. They can be taught to students at any age from elementary to graduate school.

Fact and Opinion

A fact is an act or event which has happened. The moment a fact occurs, it takes its place in history. The social scientist no longer deals with the event which has taken place, but with a statement about that event. The facts we know that occurred in the past come to us through the statements of other people. It distorts the past to speak of "true" or "false" facts since all come to us through the biased perspective of the human mind.

Webster's New World Dictionary defines a fact as "a thing that has actually happened or is true." Students have to distinguish between a fact and an opinion. For example, which of the following statements can be objectively determined and which is an opinion?

Snow White was more beautiful than the Queen.

Snow White cooked in a house belonging to seven dwarfs.

The day's events compel teachers to assume the role of judge or become a social scientist in order to resolve conflict. A playground dispute involves separating fact from opinion. Students who understand the difference are more able to intelligently resolve social conflicts in their lives.

An exercise that helps students see the difference between fact and opinion is to create a series of statements mixing facts and opinions:

Roger Clemens is the best pitcher in baseball.

George Bush was elected President in 1988.

Madonna is the most popular female singer.

Bill Cosby appears on television.

Students should be asked to identify fact and opinion statements. They can rewrite a fact statement and make it into an opinion or vice versa. Each week a group of students can create a list of fact or opinion statements as a class exercise.

▲ Cultural performances may help children understand the experiences of women and minotiries who have been neglected by historians. *Courtesy Webster University.*

Interpretation

The observations of social scientists about the past or present vary greatly. Each social scientist's interpretation of events is unique. Marc Bloch (1953) illustrates the complexity of interpretation by citing problems facing an army commander who had to write a report concerning a recent battle. Does he describe what he saw through the smoke-filled sky while peering through binoculars? Should he rely upon the accounts of his subordinates who scurried back and forth from the front lines to headquarters? Or, should he ask the frightened men and women crouching in foxholes what happened? Obviously, each person would tell a different account of the battle.

Children continually encounter the problem of interpretation. A fight on the playground generates many views about what happened. Parents and teachers are familiar with "he said, she said" accounts of a conflict. Many teachers have employed the exercise of whispering a story to a child in the first row, and then having it whispered throughout the class until the last child presents a totally different version from what was originally given.

Children who learn the dynamics of interpretation are better able to understand their own world as well as the past. They can be more effective in resolving conflicts or understanding another child's view of a situation. Following are several activities aimed to improve understanding of interpretation:

- After a baseball game, ask each player to give his/her account of the game. For example, how does the account of the catcher differ from that of the center fielder?
- The delightful African folk story, "Why Mosquitoes Buzz in People's Ears," contains differing versions of an event. Many Dr. Seuss stories reflect the idea of interpretation.

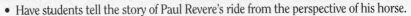

- Have students tell the story of Paul Revere's ride from the perspective of his horse.
- Select two versions of an historical event as reported in two history books.
- Read the children two versions of the same fairy tale.
- Ask another teacher to pretend to be King George III. Students can ask "King George" his version of what caused the American Revolution.
- Ask students to report the landing of Columbus as it might be told by a Native American. "One day strangely dressed people landed. Despite the warm weather they covered themselves with layers of clothing."
- Ask a Spanish-speaking person to translate a Mexican textbook's interpretation of the Texas War of Independence or the Mexican-American War. Contrast that view with ideas presented in an American history textbook.
- Read two poems that have different reactions to a rainy day or a sweltering summer evening.
- Read an excerpt from the autobiography of Frederick Douglass and contrast his view of slavery with that of a southern white.
- Ask children to describe what they like best about their parents and list on the board all the different views.

▲ Children enjoy history for its mystery and drama. *Courtesy Webster University.*

Students can be educated to understand the importance of viewing events from other than their own interpretation. This knowledge will improve classroom behavior and provide students a better grasp of the adult mind. The tool of interpretation is not only important for social scientists, but is vital to the daily life of children.

Causation

It is a major intellectual leap for children to learn that events do not occur magically but have identifiable causes. However, children and adults are often inclined to think that a single cause exists for each event. Richard Hofstadter (1965) in his classic study, *The Paranoid Style in American Politics*, noted that Americans want to believe in conspiracies as the explanation of complex problems. This attitude can be disastrous when unscrupulous people play upon this simple approach to problem solving. For example, Adolf Hitler blamed Jews for Germany's problems after World War I.

The single cause approach seeks to locate the factor which, when removed, would make a decisive difference in a given sequence of events—that is, the factor which, if removed would render the events in question inconceivable. This is a subjective process dependant upon the perspective of the historian or social scientist.

History teaches there are multiple causes behind human events. There was no single cause for the Civil War anymore than there is one cause for unemployment today. Economic, political, cultural, psychological, physical, and religious factors intermix. Social scientists seek to uncover the multiple factors entering into the origin of events. Social studies offers an excellent arena in which students can learn multiple causation's impact upon their interpersonal relations.

Edward Carr (1962) illustrates how to get across the concept of multiple causation by relating a simple story. Mr. and Mrs. Jones go to a party to celebrate her boss's birthday. At the party, a waiter accidentally pushes Mr. Jones, causing him to fall and hurt his back. Mr. and Mrs. Jones decide to leave early. That day Mr. Jones took his car into have the brakes checked, but a power outage caused the garage to close before his car was checked. On the way home, Mrs. Jones fails to see a stop sign because it is obscured by leaves that were not cut that day due to a strike by government employees over vacation pay. The Jones car hits and kills Mr. Smith, who was on his way to purchase some cigarettes because he worked overtime and couldn't get to the store. What is the cause of Mr. Smith's death?

Humans are complex beings whose emotions intrude into everyday actions. There are people who seek to blame problems upon a single cause or a particular ethnic group. Students who learn that multiple causes are to be sought in understanding life will be less prone to accept simplistic explanations of complex issues.

Omission

It is common for people writing about events to omit items that do not fit into their desired outcome. They report one aspect of a story and neglect to report other pieces. This can be inadvertent or deliberate. Imagine a visitor from Great Britain attending his first baseball game. His report of that game would fundamentally differ from a baseball writer's version. Although both "see" the same action, their prior knowledge selects, omits, or adds data.

An historian can also omit material to fit changing events or to rewrite the past. John M'Culloch wrote the first textbook in American history. Following are his two versions of the battle of Long Island during the American Revolution. The original description appeared in the first edition of his textbook, printed in 1795, and another version appeared in the third edition, published in 1807.

▲ The task of the historian is to collect, interpret, and explain evidence using methods similar to those of a detective. *Courtesy Robert Tabscott, Elijah Lovejoy Society.*

The Americans were completely defeated. All who were engaged in the actions of this day did not display courage; nor was it to be expected from such raw troops. Many escaped from the want of discipline; for they broke at the sight of danger, and saved themselves by flight, whereas otherwise they must have been killed or taken.

The Americans suffered great loss in killed and wounded. General Sullivan, Lord Stirling, and eighty officers of inferior rank, were made prisoners, together with one thousand privates. The loss to the British, in killed and wounded, did not exceed four hundred and fifty men.

There are several ways teachers can help students become familiar with this concept. Collect magazines for several weeks and compare their differing versions of the same story. What was ommitted from one account? Why? Children could be asked to report what happened during a dispute on the playground and their versions placed on the blackboard so all could see how each version ommitted some details.

Partiality

The mindset of the person describing an event has to be considered by students. One's use of words conveys how partiality is present. Following is Henry Villard's account (1904) of meeting Abraham Lincoln in 1858 while he was covering the Lincoln-Douglas debates. Note his choice of words:

> I was introduced to Lincoln at Freeport, and met him frequently afterwards in the course of the campaign. I must say frankly that, although I found him most approachable, good-natured, and full of wit and humor, I could not take a personal liking to the man owing to his inborn weakness for which he was then notorious, and so remained during his great public career. He was inordinately fond of jokes, anecdotes, and stories. He loved to hear them, and still more to tell them himself out of the inexhaustible supply provided by his good memory and his fertile fancy. There would have been no harm in this but for the fact that the coarser the joke, the lower the anecdote, and the more risky the story, the more he enjoyed them, especially when they were his own invention. He possessed, more-over, a singular ingenuity in bringing occasions in conversations for indulgences of this kind. (pp. 93–94)

The problem of partiality can even be seen in how a painter depicts an event. Allen Nevins (1938) points out that the painting by Emanuel Leutze of "Washington Crossing the Delaware" is a product of the artist's imagination, not historical reality. Leutze painted 75 years after the event, he used the Rhine River, not the Delaware for the scene, and his model was Worthington Whittredge, an American artist, rather than a picture of George Washington. If Washington had stood up he would have fallen overboard, and the flag is incorrect for the time period. Leutze wanted to portray an heroic Washington and rearranged events to fit his desired objective.

These social science tools can be taught children. It is important for the teacher to introduce these ideas over the course of a year and continually reinforce them with interesting and varied activities. The examples cited in this brief review of social science tools can be supplemented by each teacher's own imagination and ingenuity.

▲ History transports children to new worlds filled with fantastic customs, foods, dress, and hairstyles. *Courtesy Francis Howell (Missouri) School District.*

Our Human Heritage

The Columbus Quincentenary in 1992 raised issues surrounding what should be taught students about the human heritage. Traditionally, Columbus has been depicted as a discoverer who found savage peoples. This approach is not only morally questionable but factually incorrect. It ignores the sophisticated civilizations present in the Western Hemisphere, and the economic, social, and political expertise of the island peoples encountered by Columbus.

Social studies has generally presented the past through a narrow perspective. The majority of historians and social scientists who wrote textbooks in the past were white males trained in a politically centered approach. They relied upon written records, focused upon "great people," and ignored Asian sources, indigenous American materials, and African history. Author Norman Cousins once commented that he was half educated. "I was educated to live in half a world—the white western half" (quoted in Kellum, 1969, p. 45).

Social studies textbooks have traditionally reflected their authors' training in European history. Students have been exposed to a history which presents the past from a "top down" approach rather than one which is balanced by history from the "bottom up". The social sciences have failed to reflect the diversity of human existence and to reflect the past in a manner that is meaningful to students. The tendency of the majority is not to accept what is different or what lies outside of one's own education, and to deny the notion that anything distinct from the dominant society can be of value in its own right.

This attitude is vividly reflected in textbooks which ignore the presence of minorities and women or present them as passive participants in the drama of the past. For example, the following quote from the text, *The Free and the Brave* (McCutcheon, 1967, p. 140) distorts the African American experience in the New World:

"The first Negroes were shipped to America—to Jamestown—in 1619, the year before the Mayflower arrived . . . the first of millions of Africans who were transported toward these shores in the next hundred years."

This statement is factually incorrect. Africans were involved in several Spanish expeditions during the 1500s, including the conquest of the Aztecs and Incas, the exploration of the southern half of the United States, and there is some evidence Africans predated the European presence in the New World. They were seamen, farmers, soldiers, and slaves.

A time traveler from the 25th century who suddenly appeared in our midst would be interested in all aspects of our lives, not merely how we are governed. The traveler would be interested in how we dress, eat, talk, and would want to experience our music, art, and poetry. The time traveler would read our literature, our newspapers and magazines, and sit glued to the TV screen. The traveler would be interested in our hair styles as well as our system of government, military weapons, and sources of cultural conflict. This holistic approach to studying a society is exactly what students are entitled to receive when studying the human heritage.

▲ Children need to experience the myths and stories that have historically bound societies together.
Courtesy Pattonville (Missouri) School District.

A current controversy in the field of social studies concerns the emphasis to be given ethnic minorities and women in social studies. Some critics wish to replace a "Eurocentric" approach with one that places women and minorities at the center. They often urge that children should be taught about the brutalization by dominant whites of minorities, and greater emphasis should be placed upon the contributions of other than European cultures to world civilization. Molefi Kete Asante (1991) argues that African-American children are disadvantaged because the language of the classroom conveys a "white culture."

> Most teachers do not have to think about using the white child's culture to empower the white child. The white child's language is the language of the classroom. Information that is being conveyed is "white" cultural information in most cases; indeed, the curriculum in most schools is a "white self-esteem curriculum." (p. 29)

Asante urges teachers to obtain knowledge concerning minority cultures and to incorporate that information into the curriculum. An Afrocentric program should be infused throughout the school year rather than tagged on as a once-a-month exercise. James Banks (1991), while supporting the legitimization in the curriculum of world cultures, and particularly the debt Western civilization owes Africa, also warns supporters of Afrocentrism:

However, these groups must acknowledge that they do not want to eliminate Aristotle and Shakespeare, or Western civilization from the school curriculum. To reject the West would be to reject important aspects of their own cultural heritages, experiences and identities... African-American culture resulted from a blending of African cultural characteristics with those of African peoples in the United States. (pp. 33–34)

A key issue facing educators is which attitudes and knowledge will enable youth to live successfully in a multicultural world that continues the positive aspects of the American experiment. The sins and blemishes of America are real, but so are its contributions to world democracy—for example, the Bill of Rights and our system of representative government. Is there a common core of values that pertain to all Americans, or should we focus on ethnic and group heritages?

A society as diverse as America needs a common core of values that politically and socially bind people together. Rights such as freedom of speech, press, religion, or due process have a greater chance of being woven into the fabric of our national design if everyone supports their implementation. Throughout human history societies have bound its members together as a group by sharing myths, stories, and values. This does not mean that a simple and unquestioning American patriotism must be accepted by all.

At the same time, we must notice aspects of this heritage which have generally been ignored. The main lineaments of American history can continue, but it will be enriched with material that combats errors, distortions, and imbalances. The Spanish presence prior to the English settlement of the 13 colonies will be told, and more emphasis will be placed upon the impact of slavery on blacks and whites. We can still tell the story of the American Revolution, but also note roles played by Pulaski, von Steuben, or Haym Solomon. Ethnic histories restore the truth of life as it really was.

History books emphasize political history and ignore the lives of ordinary people. They tend to chronicle the lives of the powerful and rich—men who were presidents, generals, and captains of industry. Critics who justifiably condemn this white male approach—our political leaders have been white males—frequently forget that many whites are also left out of the story. Frontier women, Italian and Polish immigrants who fought to improve labor conditions, and Irish immigrant school teachers are also given scant treatment in textbooks on the history of America. Social studies has to weave a more varied design that incorporates the diversity of people who make up the history of human societies.

Children easily identify with people who do ordinary tasks. The overemphasis upon political history has narrowed the range of social studies and helped make this subject one that students often find boring. Teachers must be on guard against substituting for poorly taught Eurocentric social studies a poorly taught curriculum emphasizing minorities or women. Lists of names, dates, and facts do not challenge students. Social studies has to engage students intellectually and emotionally, and lists of female or minority contributions will not make social studies come alive in the minds of children anymore than lists of the accomplishments of white males.

We have shielded students for too long from confronting conflicts. Conflict has been a critical aspect of our heritage since Europeans first stepped on the shores of the Americas. Conflict affects children every day in their interactions with adults and classmates. Our focus upon political leaders has led to ignoring leaders who may have "lost" battles but influenced history in the long run. African-Americans have fought for over 200 years to attain equality; women, Hispanics, and Native Americans have also challenged those in power in order to fight for a just society. We need their stories to inspire children with the knowledge that a loss today does not end the struggle.

▲ The interdependence of people in the world is a necessity for global survival. *Courtesy University City (Missouri) Public Schools.*

Social studies is a human drama reflecting the lives of all people. It must be based upon historically valid information. For example, some critics claim that black-skinned people lived in ancient Egypt and wish to rewrite the curriculum in order to portray Egypt as a black society that gave birth to much of modern knowledge.

John Baines notes that we have mistakenly portrayed Egypt as a white society when, in reality, it comprised people with white, brown, black, and yellow skins. According to Yurco, these terms are a

chimera—cultural baggage from our own society that can only be imposed artificially on ancient Egyptian society. . . . The ancient Egyptians, like their modern descendants, were of varying complexions of color from the light Mediterranean type, to the light brown of Middle Egypt, to the darker brown of Upper Egypt, to the darkest shade around Aswan and the First Cataract region, where even today, the population shifts to Nubian. (quoted in Yurco, 1989, p. 24)

The issue is not whose particular viewpoint about the past should be taught, but "What competencies must students demonstrate in order to deal intelligently with the complexities of history and contemporary society?" (Armour-Thomas & Proefriedt, 1991, p. 30) Multicultural education is not a threat to traditional liberal arts education. It is an exciting extension of that tradition. America has always been a multicultural society composed of diverse peoples who, willingly or not, left different cultures all over the world to come here. Multiculturalism will enable students to live in a healthier society that encourages critical reflection on the values we share in common as well as those which make different groups unique.

Elementary and middle school teachers face increasing pressure to present a particular group's version of America's past. We do an injustice to our historical heritage by falsifying the record. The Founding Fathers were white males but they were also creative thinkers in their abililty to establish a vibrant democratic society. The majority of them could not transcend the limitations of their era in regard to female equality, equal rights for minorities, or real religious freedom. Thomas Jefferson said each generation has to reinvent liberty. Hopefully, our invention will be continued and expanded by women and men, Asians, Hispanics, and African-Americans, rich and poor, farmers and workers, including the children in your class.

E. D. Hirsch (1987, p. 63–70), a noted critic of the child-centered approach to social studies, argues that American schools in the 19th and early 20th centuries created a literate middle class sharing common traditional values by teaching poor children through means of a textbook-centered approach. Children's "literacy is more effectively enhanced when they are successfully taught durable traditional subjects like Ulysses and the Cyclops than when they are taught ephemera like Dick and Jane at the Supermarket." He believes providing all students access to traditional literate culture "gives all students the key to mainstream economic and political life."

Hirsch raises important issues concerning the need to provide a common core of cultural heritage. His emphasis upon textbooks as the conveyor of our past indicates a lack of understanding the reality of classroom education. "Professor Hirsch seems to take the existence of texts themselves as evidence that youngsters actually learned the material in them" (Tchudi, 1987, p. 72–74). All children should share common knowledge about the past, but an important issue is the nature of this past.

Our historical heritage has to be broadened to include people from other than mainstream backgrounds. But, it also has to be meaningful to children. The interdependence of people in the world is a necessity for global survival. Social studies is the proper place in the curriculum for children to learn how they are bound together in a common human heritage. Santayana said if we do not learn from the past, we are doomed to repeat it.

If history teaches anything, it is that values, principles, and morality vary greatly from one time period to another just as they vary within our contemporary society. Justice Oliver Wendell Holmes once said, "I prefer champagne to ditch-water, but I see no reason to suppose the cosmos does." American society is not homogeneous, nor should it be. Social studies can present a portrait of America in which people differed, engaged in conflict, but in the majority of cases utilized the political process or civil disobedience to attain their aims.

It is important for all ethnic groups to be aware of their historical heritage. This knowledge can instill personal pride as well as patriotism. Every ethnic group has played a role in the formation of American society. It is important that history focuses not just on the accomplishments of the great men. It must reflect the everyday lives and experiences of women, men, and children from every social and ethnic group. Social studies has to be presented under a big tent, but it must be meaningful knowledge that impacts the intellectual thought processes of children. John Dewey believed we do not merely have to repeat the past, but we can use our past experiences to construct new and better ones in the future.

Nobel Prize-winner Nelson Mandela (1990) who led the struggle in South Africa to create a free society, has urged that people throughout the world challenge the seeds of hatred wherever they are found and become partisan fighters on the side of peace and democracy:

> We seek to build a society wherein a person's colour will matter no more. A society in which all our people will be united in their diversity. In so doing we are challenging the scourge of racism which is negating the humanity of the whole world. We are opposed to white domination as much as we are opposed to black domination. The solution to our problems does not lie in the enslavement of others; rather it lies in our ability to free all, for in so doing, we shall be freeing ourselves in this regard. Male domination and sex discrimination should not find any place in any truly democratic society.

Social History and Historical Narratives

Students are trained to believe that our cultural heritage deals with important people, governmental actions, and key events. Traditionally, youth learned about their past through the words of elders who passed on not only important stories but also information about foods, health, and ethical behavior.

Elementary school children learn best through stories and involvement in activities that engage the mind and body. They are at an age when listening to a grandparent recount tales of the past is enjoyable. They identify with the past through people.

> Children can learn amazing things if presented in language they fathom and in ways that engage their lively minds and imagination. What they need most is what every generation of young people needs: ways to find meaning in the world and insight into what other people have made of their lives. Over the years gifted teachers have found that children love myths, fables, legends, tall tales, and biographies. Great stories help children understand the world, past and present, and reach beyond the confines of their own immediate experience. (Ravitch, 1986, p. 29)

Millions of children throughout the world have gained understanding of World War II because of a single child—Anne Frank. Her diary is not a political tale but a story of everyday life and the feelings, emotions, and dreams of a young girl. The opening pages of the autobiography of

Frederick Douglass are powerful because they depict what life was like for a slave child in pre-Civil War America. Who can forget the wonderful story of how young Frederick tricked some white boys into teaching him the alphabet.

Historical narratives through both written form and storytelling enable children to identify with people and through the lives of those people learn about our cultural heritage. A dramatic reading of the letters of Abigail Adams to her husband John gives valuable insight into the reaction of women to the Constitution and slavery—"How odd it seemed for us to be fighting for our rights, and still supporting slavery."

The personalization of historical figures brings to life people from the past whose story is merely a name on a page to a generation which has never personally experienced that individual. For example, following is a storytelling account of President Franklin Roosevelt and his wife Eleanor as told by one of the authors:

I was a little boy during the Depression and my parents were rather poor. I remember how poverty often made people tense or nervous, which would lead to arguments and shouting. But, then would come those wonderful nights when President Roosevelt spoke on the radio and for a few hours, at least, everyone would feel reassured and less worried. My parents had total trust that President Roosevelt and his wife, Eleanor, would always take care of poor people. I remember how in 1944 President Roosevelt took a car trip through New York City during the election. They told us he would be in our neighborhood around midmorning, but there were thousands of people lining the street by eight o'clock. We waited in the rain. Hours passed. The rain drenched us, but we waited. Then, about noon, I heard thunder in the distance. But it wasn't thunder, it was the shouts of people. The thunder rolled over the crowd and soon the President's car appeared and we cheered wildly. Then he was gone and all around me people were laughing and crying because they had seen President Roosevelt. A few months later, we were getting ready for dinner when they announced President Roosevelt was dead. My mother began to cry. She asked me what would happen now that President Roosevelt was dead. I tried to explain to my immigrant mother that Truman was now the President. She was confused. She kept on saying that at least Mrs. Roosevelt would be in the White House to look after the poor people. We went into the street and people were crying and finally they got some rabbis and opened the synagogues so people could pray. My mother cried all night because she was scared. A few years later, my high school gave an award to Eleanor Roosevelt and she came to accept it. There were over 2000 kids in the auditorium and when she spoke there was absolute silence. She told us that we must love one another and fight to end injustice and prejudice. When she finished we stood to cheer her and all around me kids were crying. As she walked up the aisle to leave she walked right by me and I touched her sleeve. I was so happy. When she died I cried because I felt that someone in my family had died.

▲ Stories help children understand the world, past and present, and challenge the boundaries of their own immediate experience. *Courtesy Null Elementary, Saint Charles (Missouri) Public Schools.*

Historical narratives and storytelling expands the range of material available to teachers. Diaries, letters, and personal recollections bring to life the world of people other than the great men who led our nation. Grandparents can be invited to class to tell stories about the Depression or World War II. Children can be encouraged to write their own family histories and gain understanding that the feelings and activities of their relatives are also part of the panorama of American society.

In virtually every human society, past and present, the family has been the most fundamental and durable of institutions. A study of family life brings women and children to the center stage along with males. Our neglect of family life leads to misinterpretation of events. Anthropologist Carol Stack (quoted in Downey, 1982, p. 31) found in a study of a poor black community in the 1960s that "families were flexible groups united mainly for mutual aid in the face of scarce resources and recurrent crises. Cooperating kin groups of both relatives and fictive kin—friends who assume the rights and obligations of blood kin—shared the rearing of children and other domestic tasks." This information helps explain that single parent families in the black community are not living in isolation.

▲ Storytelling enables children to identify with people, and through the lives of people learn about their cultural heritage. *Courtesy Francis Howell (Missouri) School District.*

It enables children to realize that social history, which is a focus on the activities and outlook of ordinary people, is as vital to understanding the past or present as is learning about governmental actions. In one Missouri school, two teachers introduced children to games from around the world as part of global education, including playing the ancient Aztec game of Tlachti. Students are interested in how children dressed, played, what they ate or how they dressed in the early history of America.

Few children of Irish-American ancestry realize that the potato was native to the Western hemisphere but eventually found its way to Ireland. The introduction of the potato dramatically altered Irish life, culminating in the potato famine of the 1840s, which compelled millions to migrate to America. The simple potato contains a fascinating story that directly relates to the lives of many American children.

Teachers know that food is an easy way to get the attention of students. It would be interesting to prepare a meal containing only those foods native to this hemisphere topped off with popcorn which was discovered by the Indian population. Preparing the meal, learning about foods, or eating Inca potato soup can introduce children to the past in a fascinating manner that is bound to heighten their interest in social studies.

Social history and historical narratives can be integrated into any curriculum. Teachers can take an adult version of a person's life and transform it into a story for children. Social history enables teachers to engage students with material they find interesting. Social history does not replace, but it can broaden existing social studies.

Perhaps it is impossible to attain Leopold von Ranke's hope that the past could be presented as life really was. The past is continually shifting its focus as we learn more about it or contemporary events compel a new look backward. Construction workers in New York City recently uncovered the oldest known African-American graveyard. The information obtained by examining the graveyard is already altering our view of African-American life in colonial America.

If we can not replicate the past "as it was" we can at least offer students a varied and exciting portrayal of their human heritage. A heritage of inclusion is more intellectually valid than one which arbitrarily excludes or focuses upon a selected few. The ancestors of all children deserve a place in the story of human development and the process by which the United States of America became a democratic nation.

SUMMARY

This chapter has discussed issues related to inclusion or exclusion of people and groups in social studies education. It suggests the need to broaden the base for including diverse people within the social studies curriculum.

QUESTIONS

1. Why should students study social studies?

2. Explain what March Bloch means by "historical facts are, in essence, psychological facts." Give an example to illustrate this point.

3. Which school experiences in social studies did you believe were most valuable to your intellectual or emotional development?

4. Cite an example of how your interpretation of current events or important social issues differs significantly from those of your relatives? What accounts for the differences?

5. The authors state that studying the lives of minorities, women, and ordinary people does not distort but more clearly describes our historical heritage. What are the advantages and disadvantages to this approach?

6. As you prepare to become a teacher, what do you consider the biggest gap in your knowledge of the past?

7. Do you believe students in elementary school should be told critical aspects of the lives of Americans? For example, should they be told Washington and Jefferson owned slaves?

8. Which tools of the social scientist are most important for elementary school children?

9. What did you learn in elementary or secondary school concerning your own ethnic heritage?

10. How would you like students in your classroom to deal with issues raised by the clash between Eurocentric and Afrocentric views of cultural heritages?

ACTIVITIES

1. Conduct an analysis in an education class regarding how many students took course work in African, Asian, Latin American, and women's studies.

2. Interview several relatives or neighbors who are over 50 about a particular period in the history of their lives, for example, life in the 1960s.

3. Study the story of one food such as corn and its impact upon human history.

4. Interview people from an ethnic group other than your own regarding their ideas about what should be taught in social studies.

5. Write the story of your life that you would like to tell your grandchildren. Do it in a storytelling format.

6. Create your own activities to teach concepts of interpretation, partiality, causation or omission.

7. Select a fairy tale and develop a lesson plan that teaches about the tools of the social scientist.

The Report of the New York State Social Studies Review and Development Committee, "One Nation, Many Peoples: A Declaration of Cultural Interdependence," raised many important issues regarding the teaching of America's heritage. The authors of this book have incorproated several of those ideas within the framework of this chapter.

There were dissenting opinions concerning how best to teach America's heritage. Following are three of those reflections on the report.

READING

Additional Comments
by Nathan Glazer

This report is not a document that stands by itself, without interpretation. Different members of the committee, as well as different elements of the public, will read it differently, and selectively. Probably no member of the committee accepts every part and point in the report with equal commitment, and we differ in the way we see dangers in how the report will be read, and how we would like the broad direction it sets for the development of social studies in New York State developed in detail.

The report does reject two extremes in the treatment of ethnic and racial diversity in American social studies: One is the emphasis on forceful Americanization and assimilation that characterized much of American public education during the period of the great European immigration and for some time after. The other one is the parceling out of American history into a different and incompatible story for each group, generally told by a few activists and militants speaking for the group, a vision which seemed to be advocated in an earlier report. The first danger is scarcely a present one: The kind of history which gave an exclusive role as the carrier of American civilization to immigrants from England and their descendants, and the kind of educational practice in which children might be fined for speaking a foreign language, are dead and gone. The second danger is more alive, but the report steers clear of it. It does tell us there are many perspectives from which the story of the American people and the key episodes within that story can be told, and that commonly agreed-on accounts have changed and will change over the years, with both new findings, and, in truth, findings activated by the interests and concerns of new groups in the American population. It accepts the role of the social studies as a socializing and nation-building force, while it applauds an evolving society in which all people of whatever race and ethnic background now find a place. This was not always so, but it is so today.

Within the broad spectrum that remains after the extremes have been rejected, the report points out a very general direction, rather than specifies the details of a syllabus or curriculum. It continues a debate, rather than concludes it.

Even within the bounds of this broad arena of development and debate, there is one major danger I see against which we must be alert, one to which the report offers some support. This is the danger of the hypostatization of race, ethnic group, culture, people. (To hypostatize: "to make into, or regard as, a separate and distinct substance; . . . to assume a reality.") The various ethnic groups, races, sub-cultures, and components of what we like to call with some exaggeration "the peoples of America," are not composed of a "distinct and separate substance." The groups we refer to when we speak of "multiculturalism" are not monolithic and unchanging realities. Each is made up of different classes with different interests, each has been marked by differences created by the time of arrival of different waves under different circumstances, each has undergone various degrees of assimilation, acculturation, intermarriage, and each carries different attitudes to its past: European immigrants overwhelmingly see their assimilation to the United States, under the system of public education they experienced, as a good thing, even if their specific culture and language at the time played no role in the curriculum. Many of us recognize no identity other than American. When we speak of "multiculturalism," we should be aware there are no fully distinct cultures in the United States, aside from American culture. We should not make of something labile, changeable, flexible and variable—the cultures people bring with them to the United States or develop as variants of our common American culture—something hard and definite and unchanging, something that establishes itself as a distinct and permanent element in American society and polity. That is not the way our society works, or should work.

A conception of American multiculturalism that is true to its complex reality does not lend itself easily to teaching to children and adolescents: They want something more definite, the teachers want something more definite and specific to give them, the tests want something more definite on which to test them, and so we fall into teaching a false but easily transmissible picture of American society. And since people are shaped to some extent by their education, we fall into the danger, by presenting a conception of separate and different groups fixed through time as distinct elements in our society, of making our future one which conforms to our teaching, of arresting the processes of change and adaptation that have created a common society, a single nation.

At one time, to teach children about the variability of human culture, we taught them about the Eskimo, adapted to the treeless Arctic, and the pygmy, adapted to the deep tropical jungle. The triumph of these peoples over their environment was truly admirable. But they were also the most isolated and distinct cultures on the face of the earth. Let us not turn our teaching about the peoples of America, who have received every possible cultural influence, and have changed in ways that make then unrecognizable to the relatives who stayed behind, into a story of Eskimos and pygmies. That is not the reality of American society.

The Need to Examine the Origin of Racism and Its Relationship to Skin-Color Devaluation
Submitted by Diane Glover

Winthrop Jordan states in a chapter entitled "First Impressions—Initial English Confrontation with Africans" that England's concept of blackness was loaded with intense meaning. "Long before they found that some men were Black, Englishmen found in the idea of blackness, a way to express some of their most ingrained values. Black was an emotional partisan color, the handmaid and symbol of baseness and evil, a sign of danger and repulsion. White and black connoted purity and filthiness, beauty and ugliness, God and the devil. The Negro was ugly by reason of his color and his "horrid Curles" and "disfigured lips and noses."[1]

Added also were the notions that Africans had a defective religion (heathenism), savage behavior, likened to beasts (particularly the ape) and had libidinous men. The complexion of Africans in the 1550s posed problems about its nature, especially its permanence and utility, its cause and origin, and its significance.[2]

Anderson and Cromwell (1977) reported what White Americans have devalued black skin color. They indicated that blackness has been associated with discouragement, despair, depression, coldness, evilness, nightmares, etc. This negative black concept, they believed, fused with skin color devaluation. Thus the American Black, as well as other Blacks of the African Diaspora, had resigned himself/herself to the fact that he/she was negative, inferior, and less attractive. The study also noted that the social result from accepting negative blackness was devastating. Besides the acceptance of the White ideal and negative blackness, American Blacks have utilized skin color to discriminate among themselves.[3]

Reaves and Friedman (1982) reported that a number of studies in the past demonstrated that standards of physical attractiveness for Blacks were derived from White perceptions of physical beauty.[4]

Williams-Burns's (1980) study also pointed out that an underlying assumption in most investigations appeared to be that low self-esteem was related to skin color.[7]

Fish and Larr (1972) stated that racism has had and continues to have a staggeringly massive and pervasive negative force in the childhood development of Black children; the social layer of identification did not occur as a secondary, superimposed one, but was a major negative influencing factor in their basic identity from the first. Children feel about themselves as they have experienced others feeling toward them. The others include not only members of their family but society and its effect through their parents, who taught them their roles from the beginning.[6]

Several studies have indicated that children become aware of skin color at the age of two and one-half years. Gordon Allport's *Nature of Prejudice* stated that Negro children are by and large "racially aware" earlier than are White children. They tend to be confused, disturbed, and sometimes excited by the problem. Negro children ask more diverse questions about racial differences, fondle the blond hair of a White child, and are often rejective toward Negro dolls.[7]

In 1991, much of what has just been cited still permeates our overall society, and continues to plague communities of the African Diaspora. Skin color devaluation has not disappeared. The topic of racism can no longer be a taboo, if we want an effective multicultural curriculum. The educational community (Giant Step, Head Start, Day Care, community and cultural institutions, colleges and universities, libraries, parents, and public school personnel) need informational and training sessions that address racism and its relationship to skin color devaluation. The educational community needs to know the devastating psychological damage that has been inflicted upon members of the African Diaspora. They need to know society's role in the debasement of physical characteristics of people of African ancestry (their noses, lips, hair, etc.). They need to know the role of European scholarship in promoting psychological and historical inferiority. They need to know or try to understand how racism has impacted on children of African descent and its relationship to self-concept, economic and sociological variables.

In closing, the African Proverb, "An ignorant man/woman is always a slave," best describes how effective this training would be.

Notes

[1] Winthrop Jordan, *The White Man's Burden: Historical Origins of Racism in the United States.* Oxford University Press, 1974, p. 6.

[2] Jordan, pp. 7–16.

[3] C. Anderson and R. Cromwell, " 'Black Is Beautiful' and the Color Preferences of Afro-American Youth," *Journal of Negro Education,* 1977, 46, 76–88.

[4] J. Reaves and P. Friedman, "The Relationship of Physical Attractiveness and Similarity of Preferences to Peer Affiliation among Black Children," *Journal of Negro Education,* 1982, 51, 101–110.

[5] W. Williams-Burns, "Self-Esteem and Skin Color Perception of Advantaged Afro-American Children," *Journal of Negro Education,* 1980, 49, 385–397.

[6] J. Fish and C. Larr, "A Decade of Changes in Drawings by Black Children," *American Journal of Psychiatry,* 1972, 129, 421–426.

[7] Gordon W. Allport, The Nature of Prejudice. Anchor Books, 1958, p. 288.

A Dissenting Comment

Kenneth T. Jackson
Jacques Barzun Professor of History and the Social Sciences
Columbia University

The purpose of this Committee is a good one. Certainly, we should celebrate the cultural diversity which has made the United States almost unique among the world's nations. Certainly, we should acknowledge that heterogeneity has made this land rich and creative. Certainly, we should give our students a varied and challenging multicultural education.

Just as certainly, we should celebrate the common culture that Americans share. Unfortunately, our report seems to disparage "Anglo" conformity. Leaving aside the debatable question of whether or not we in fact have conformity (from Broadway in New York to Broadway in Los Angeles we can easily find more diversity than exists anywhere else on earth) or whether earlier immigrant groups were "required" to "shed their specific cultural differences in order to be considered Americans," I would argue that it is politically and intellectually unwise for us to attack the traditions, customs, and values which attracted immigrants to these shores in the first place. The people of the United States will recognize, even if this committee does not, that every viable nation has to have a common culture to survive in peace. As our own document indicates, one need look no further than Yugoslavia, the Soviet Union, or Canada to see the accuracy of this proposition. We might want to add India after the events of the past two weeks. The dominant American culture might have been German or French or Chinese or Algonquin or African, but for various historical reasons the English language and British political and legal traditions prevailed. Whether or not we would have been better off if Montcalm had defeated Wolfe on the Plains of Abraham is beside the point.

It is poor strategy, poor history, and poor logic for our committee to bemoan the "Anglo" culture that supposedly emerged. After all, does anyone expect that there is more tolerance for multiculturism in Tokyo, Caracas, Istanbul, Copenhagen, Mexico City, or Beijing than there is in New York or Los Angeles? Of course not. In France, for example, the citizenry has even agreed on a common time to vacation, eat, and sleep. There is scarcely a 24-hour restaurant, grocery store, or gasoline station in Paris, and there is even an "academy" to pass judgment on which words are acceptable and which signs can be placed in windows.

A better strategy for this committee would have been to argue in a positive rather than a negative way. Because we are made up of many peoples and cultures, because all these peoples and cultures have contributed to national greatness, and because the United States has typically done a better job of integrating newcomers into its social and political fabric (with racial prejudice being a glaring and persistent exception) than other places, its educational system should reflect that experience. We have been multicultural, we are multicultural, and we hope that we will always be multicultural. Moreover, the enemies of multiculturalism are not teachers, textbooks, or curricular guides, but shopping centers, fast food outlets, and situation comedies, all of which threaten to turn us into an amorphous mass.

The report highlights the notion that all cultures are created equal. This may be true in the abstract, and I have no problem with the philosophical concept. But I cannot endorse a "Declaration of Cultural Interdependence," which is the subtitle of our Committee report. Within any single country, one culture must be accepted as the standard. Unfortunately, our document has virtually nothing to say about the things which hold us together. As Professor Schlesinger notes in his comment, the emphasis is too much on the *pluribus* and not enough on the *unum*.

Finally, I should like to emphasize that history and geography should be the core of the social studies. Three full years—one each of world history, European history, and American history—should be required for high school graduation. Moreover, the State of New York should require social studies teachers to study history and geography themselves. Unfortunately, New York State does not currently require social studies teachers to study any history or any geography at any time.

QUESTIONS ON READING

1. Nathan Glazer says, "A conception of American multiculturalism that is true to its complex reality does not lend itself easily to teaching to children and adolescents." What are the implications of his statement to teaching elementary school children?

2. Glazer says, "When we speak of 'multiculturalism,' we should be aware there are no fully distinct cultures in the United States, aside from American culture." Do you agree or disagree with the statement?

3. Diane Glover says, "The educational community (Giant Step, Head Start, Day Care, community and cultural institutions, colleges and universities, libraries, parents, and public school personnel) need informational and training sessions that address racism and its relationship to skin color devaluation." Do you believe this need exists? If so, should the training be compulsory for teachers?

4. Diane Glover quotes the African proverb: "An ignorant man/woman is always a slave." In which ways are you a "slave" to racist feelings?

5. Kenneth T. Jackson comments: "I would argue that it is politically and intellectually unwise for us to attack the traditions, customs, and values which attracted immigrants to these shores in the first place. The people of the United States will recognize, even if this committee does not, that every viable nation has to have a common culture to suvive in peace." What is your reaction to this statement?

6. Kenneth Jackson argues that "within any single country, one culture must be accepted as the standard." What are the implications of this concept for you as an American? As a teacher of children?

LESSON PLANS

Patricia Miller   Primary grades

Objective: Study characteristics of Japanese culture.

Rationale: The lesson is designed to make young children more aware of some aspects of Japanese culture.

Activities:

1. Children are told they are taking a plane trip to Japan. A map showing the route is given to the students, they are told to fasten their seat belts, and are given Japanese snacks. As they eat their snacks, teacher reads a story about Japan.

2. Teacher takes out a puppet named Susumu who teaches them to say "konnichi wa" (hello) and "sayonara" (goodbye).

3. Susumu invites children to visit his traditional Japanese home. Children remove shoes. Children observe a model of a traditional Japanese home. Susumu explains about eating, sleeping, the flower arrangement, and why shoes are taken off before entering.

4. Susumu asks children to name "traditional" American clothes like a cowboy outfit or old fashioned dresses. Susumu shows children examples of traditional Japanese clothes like a kimono. Children cut out examples of a kimono and color and make designs on it.

5. Susumu introduces a Japanese student from a local university. The student teaches children how to count and several Japanese expressions. The student discusses elementary school in Japan, what they study, and how they play.

6. Susumu shows a video depicting karate. Children are shown the Japanese version of the game Scissors and Rock—Jan Ken Po. Children play it. They then play the Go

game. Several other games, like Hanafuda, are shown. Children divide into groups and take turns playing the various games.

7. Susumu asks children to help in preparing a Japanese meal. The class helps make fried rice, Sunomono, and Almond Cream. Later, the food is eaten.

8. Susumu leads children in singing traditional Japanese songs and a modern hit song.

9. Susumu tells children they are going to celebrate two Japanese holidays—Girl's Day and Boy's Day.
   - Each child brings doll to class. All dolls are placed in the c the room and the class brainstorms ways to sort the dolls—by color, size, etc. Class looks at pictures and hears story about how Girl's Day is celebrated in Japan. Then they listen to stories about Boy's Day. Children make banners telling about Boy's Day and Girl's Day.

10. Susumu greets children and tells about origami. He shows children how to make three animals out of a piece of square paper. Children divide into groups and make animals.

Bibliography:

Branson, Mary K. *A Carousel of Countries,* Bringham, 1986.

Japan Information Center, *What I Want to Know About Japan,* Consulate General of Japan at N.Y., 299 Park Ave., 10171-0025.

Kawai, Toyoaki, *Origami,* Osaka, Japan, Hoikusha's Color Book Series. 1982.

Richie, Donal, *Introducing Japan*, Tokyo: Kondansha Int. Ltd., 1982.

Yoshida, Yasuo, *Japanese for Today,* Tokyo, Gakken Co. Ltd., 1981.

Laura Holt   Upper Elementary
Objective: To acquaint children with traditional West African culture through art objects.

Rationale: Students will learn about West Africa and its people by creating art activities related to this area of the world.

Activities:

1. Teacher greets children dressed in N'Debele clothing and wearing a Poro mask. African music plays softly in the background. Teacher shows maps of modern Africa with particular emphasis upon West Africa. Teacher emphasizes the mask and dress are from traditional African culture and that today there are many modern cities in which people wear western style dress.
   - Teacher hands out objects from St. Louis Art Museum kit on African Art.
   - Teacher leads class discussion on why masks would be worn by people. Asks if they use "a mask" to cover their own face.
   - Students in pairs sketch an idea for a mask. Each team explains to class the purpose of their mask.

2. Teacher creates a drum using a gallon ice cream container. Four tacks are pushed into the bottom, glue is added to wood pieces and a wooden embroidery hoop or rubber band holds down a stretched balloon for the drumhead.
   - Teacher plays a rhythmic beat and while playing explains the use of drums in traditional West African cultures.
   - Teacher shows slides of African drums and talks about uses. Teacher demonstrates how to make a drum. Students design their own drums. As they work, teacher reads "Talking Drums of Africa" by Christine Prince.

3. Teacher carries a traditional Masai shield. To make one, get two 30" long kite sticks, cut a center stick 11" long. Wet sticks and shape into position and glue together. Wrap string back and forth across this frame and tie. Paper mache around the whole surface. Add cardboard handle while wet. When dry, paint surface white and add designs using red, blue, and black paint.
   - Teacher discusses reasons for use of shields and explains that in the Cameroons an irregular shaped shield was made of hippopotamus skin. Asks students for other reasons why shields might be used.
   - Students view slides of actual shields. Students pair off and design their own shields.

4. Teacher explains about the Adinkera Cloth, "The Saying Goodbye Cloth," which is used in celebrating the memory of the dead. Students learn that the designs on the cloth are a message to the dead.
   - Teacher explains how to make an Adinkera cloth. Need: 36" wide white or pastel cloth (sheets or pillow cases will do). Cut cloth into three one-yard strips and then stitch them back together with the satin stitch. Yellow, red, or green thread can be used. Cut small stamps from erasers, styrofoam, cardboard, or linoleum blocks. Ink the stamps and print carefully with newspaper under the cloth for a cushion. Set the ink by soaking the cloth in distilled white vinegar. Iron cloth until dry. A rod can be inserted to make a wall hanging.
   - Teacher reviews how Adinkera cloth evolved in West African culture and the meaning of symbols. Students create their own design messages.

5. Teacher introduces guest speaker from a local university who is from Africa to discuss traditional music. Students listen and ask questions.

Bibliography:

Clifford, Mary Louise & Ross, Edward, *The Creative Africans: Artists and Craftsmen,* N.Y. Noble & Noble, 1971.

D'Amato, Janet and Alex, *African Crafts For You To Make,* N.Y. Julian Messner, 1969.

Glubok, Shirley, *The Art of Africa,* N.Y. Harper & Row. 1965.

Kerina, Jane, *African Crafts,* N.Y. Sayre Publishing, 1970.

Prince, Christine, *Talking Drums of Africa,* N.Y. Charles Scribner's Sons, 1973.

REFERENCES

Armour-Thomas, E., & Proefriedt, W. (1991, December 4). Multicultural Perspectives. *Education Week*, p. 27; 36.

Asante, M. K. (1991, December). Afrocentric curriculum. *Educational Leadership, 49,* (4), p. 28–31.

Banks, J. A. (1991, December). Multicultural education: For freedom's sake. *Educational Leadership*, 33–34.

Bennett, W. J. (1986). *First lessons: A Report on Elementary Education in America.*

Washington, DC: U. S. Department of Education.

Bloch, M. (1953). *The Historian's Craft.* New York: Knopf.

Carr, E. (1961). *What is history?* New York: Knopf.

Commager, H. S. (1965). *The Nature and Study of History.* Columbus, OH: Charles Merrill.

Downey, M. (1982). Teaching American history: New directions. NCSS Bulletin 67.

Hirsch, E. D. (1987, December). Restoring cultural literacy in the early grades. *Educational Leadership, 45,* (4), p. 63–71.

Hughes, H. S. (1960, October). Historian and the Social Scientist. *American Historical Review, 66,* p. 20–46.

Kellum, D. (1969). *The social studies: Myths and realities, a search book.* New York: Sheed and Ward.

Mandela, N. (1990). Olso Conference on Hatred. Unpublished transcript.

McCutcheon, B. (1967). *The free and the brave.* Chicago: Rand McNally.

Nevins, A. (1938). *Gateway to history.* New York: D. Appleton-Century.

Spieske, A. (1938). *The first textbooks in American history.* New York: Teachers College.

Tchudi, S. (1987, December). A reply to Hirsch. *Educational Leadership, 45,* (4), p. 74–75.

Villard, H. (1904). *Memoirs.* Cambridge: Houghton Mifflin.

Yurco, F. (1989, September). Were the ancient Egyptians black or white? *Biblical Archeology Review, 15,* (24), p. 24–29, 58.

Chapter 12

Geography

Geography

The word *geography* means writing about or describing the earth. Geography education involves studying about this planet and how humans interact with it. It provides students a systematic understanding of the world that encompasses the variety of environments and habitats that characterize our earth. Geography begins with "where" questions but also moves into "how" and "why." Students learn not only where they are in relation to places but how events elsewhere impact their lives.

Geographic knowledge is used in making decisions that affect our everday lives. We analyze complex geographic factors such as physical features, climate, topography, or drainage in determining where we choose to live. A beautiful house on a hillside outside Los Angeles may be in a physically attractive environment, but knowledge concerning earthquake potential can alter a decision whether or not to purchase. Geography is as much a part of our lives as any subject taught in school.

The way we live, work, play, or dress is impacted by geographical factors. Many societal problems have a geographic connection. Geographical knowledge determines nuclear plant safety or the disposal of radioactive and toxic wastes and is crucial in making intelligent environmental decisions. A sound grasp of world geography provides students the perspectives, information, concepts, and skills necessary to understand the interrelationships between peoples.

▲ Geography begins with "where" questions. *Courtesy Null Elementary, Saint Charles (Missouri) Public Schools.*

The study of geography enables students to compare and recognize similarities and differences between regions of the world. It permits them to become familiar with physical and human features and patterns. Geographical knowledge enhances our appreciation of cultural and environmental diversity and is a key factor in developing multicultural perspectives in the classroom.

The Joint Committee on Geographic Education of the National Council for Geographic Education has identified five key themes in geographic education:

1. *Location*: Absolute and relative location are two ways of describing the positions of people and places on the earth's surface.

2. *Place:* All places on the earth have distinctive tangible and intangible characteristics that give them meaning and character and distinguish them from other places. Geographers generally describe places by their physical or human characteristics.

3. *Relationships Within Places: Humans and Environments*: All places on the earth have advantages and disadvantages for human settlement. People modify or adapt to natural settings in ways that reveal their cultural values, economic and political circumstances, and technological abilities. Geography focuses on understanding how such human-environment relationships develop and what their consequences are—for people and for the environment. It also shows that our actions produce both intentional and unintentional consequences.

4. *Movement*: *Humans Interacting on the Earth:* People interact with one another and travel from place to place. They communicate with each other or they rely upon products, information, and ideas that come from beyond their immediate environment. In practical ways, geography helps to explain the varied patterns in the movements of people, ideas, and materials.

5. *Regions: How They Form and Change:* The basic unit of geographic study is the region, an area that displays unity in terms of selected criteria. Geographers have developed regions as tools to examine, define, describe, explain, and analyze human and physical environment. Regions provide a context for studying current events, and help us to see the earth as an integrated system of places that we can comprehend as a planetary ecosystem.

Geography enhances skill development of students. According to Walter Kemball (1989), broad categories of geographic skills include the use of maps and globes, charts and graphs, photographs, pictures and images, and scale models. Together with field studies, these skills strengthen student abilities in collecting, classifying, interpreting, analyzing, and reporting.

▲ The way people live, work, play, or dress is impacted by geographical factors. *Courtesy Francis Howell (Missouri) Public Schools.*

▲ Understanding world geography provides students the perspectives, information, concepts, and skills necessary to understand interrelationships between people. *Courtesy University City (Missouri) Public Schools.*

▲ Geographical knowledge enhances appreciation of cultural diversity.
Courtesy Saint Louis (Missouri) Public Schools.

The study of geography has many uses in developing critical thinking capacities. It introduces and develops the concept of scale as a way of distinguishing different levels of generalization, and organizes quantitative and qualitative data into meaningful units such as regions in order to formulate hypotheses. "A geographer is an investigator of some aspect of the earth's surface. He does more than collect factual data. He thinks in geographic relationships" (Mitchell, 1963). Geography suggests to students alternatives for human settlement on earth within the contexts of values and environmental concerns.

Geography uses maps to identify, define and interpret both simple and complex physical and human patterns on the earth's surface at a variety of scales. It draws upon field studies to develop within students increased ability to observe, record, and organize complex phenomena in the natural world. Most importantly, geography deals with human issues and how people interact and interelate with one another.

The Guidelines of the Joint Committee on Geographic Education spelled out specific concepts to be studied in elementary school:

K through 2nd Grade: Self in space, homes and schools in different places, and the neighborhood.

3rd and 4th Grades: Community and sharing space with others, the state, nation, and world.

5th and 6th Grades: The United States, Canada, Mexico, Latin America, Europe, Russia, Middle East, and Africa.

Lucy Sprague Mitchell, a pioneer in geographic education, has identified several stages of the geographical thinking of children.

▲ It is important to use a variety of maps and globes that depict planet Earth. *Courtesy Null Elementary, Saint Charles (Missouri) Public Schools.*

Table 12-1. Stages of Children's Geographical Thinking

STAGES	ORIENTATION	CURRICULUM IMPLICATIONS
Before walking and talking	Attention to qualities of things. Relationship of self to not-self. Spacial relations in things.	Material for sense and motor experiences. Motor exploration.
14 months to 3 years	Interest in body, stepping, and motor experiences. Position of things in room.	Color to designate own possesions. Block play and crayons.
3 years to 4 years	Self still important. Orientation to room and building becomes more elaborate.	Trips in house. Explore living things in immediate environment.
4th and 5th years	Interest in external moving objects like cars, boats, animals, planes. Sense of direction from school to home.	Trips to streets other than own. Trips to zoo and other places. Drawing and building.
5th and 6th years	Street environment and neighborhood. Sense that other places exist.	Chalking maps. Perspective maps. Field trips to see places. Building maps.
7th and 8th years	Beginning to leave here and now. Distant places still have to be connected with here and now.	Practice in scale relief maps. Use of compass. Out-of-door maps. Field trips. Photographs and stories of faraway places. Environmental issues.
9th and 10th years	Interest in distant and past. Ability to think in geographic terms.	Atlases, globes, outdoor maps. Environmental issues. Animal geography.
11th And 12th years	Interest in social thinking. Ability to deal with abstractions.	History and geography integrated. Charts, globes, atlases, all types of maps. Economic geography.

(Adapted from Mitchell, 1963)

Geographic Skills

There are several basic skills young children should acquire in the process of learning about geography. Children in primary level classes should have the following competencies:

- They should be able to classify and categorize objects according to function or size.
- They should understand terms such as east, west, north, or south.
- They should know the difference between right and left.
- They should understand symbols used on maps and be able to construct symbols for maps they create depicting their immediate geographical environment.
- They should be able to identify their city, state, region, or country on a map or on a globe.
- They should know the difference between land areas and bodies of water on a map or globe.
- Students should be able to identify and understand time or temporal concepts such as second, minute, hour, day, week, and month.

Children in the upper elementary grades should develop the following competencies and skills:

- Students should be able to distinguish between "relief," which refers to terrain, and "elevation," which refers to the measurement of altitude.
- Students should be able to interpret and use map legends and to devise their own map symbols in conjunction with drawing or constructing maps.
- Students should be able to use city, state, and national maps to measure distance and ascertain time.
- Students should be able to identify time zones and link them to the idea of longitude.
- Students should be able to understand, make references, and use information ordinarily associated with maps such as density, food production, precipitation, etc.
- Students should be able to understand grid systems and relate them to latitude or longitude.
- Students should be able to locate areas on the map such as the equator, the north and south poles, the Tropics of Capricorn and Cancer, etc.
- Students should be able to identify the planets in our solar system.
- Students should be familiar with issues concerning the presentation of the Earth from a multicultural perspective.
- Students should be able to discuss economic geographical problems confronting developing nations.
- Students should be able to discuss the cause of day and night in relation to the rotation of the earth.

The most common type of map found in classrooms is the Mercator projection. The Mercator projection depicts a flat earth and distorts reality. On the Mercator, lines of constant compass direction are straight lines whereas on the earth they are, with some exceptions, curving lines. It is important to use a variety of maps that more accurately depict planet Earth.

Geography, like history or anthropology or sociology, has its own language. Students have to become familiar with these words and expressions in order to function with geographical materials. Among the most frequently used geographic terms are:

- Altitude: The height above sea level of any area.
- Bay: That portion of a body of water from an ocean or lake which extends into the land.
- Canal: A waterway dug by humans across an area of land for purposes of irrigation or transportation.
- Canyon: A rather deep or narrow valley with steep sides which often has a river or stream at the bottom.
- Cape: A piece of land that extends into a sea or lake.
- Desert: A dry region with limited rainfall and few plants.
- Equator: An imaginary line around the earth halfway between the north pole and the south pole.
- Foothills: A range of low hills usually found near the base of mountains.
- Highlands: Mountainous areas or a high plateau.
- Isthmus: A narrow strip of land connecting two large bodies of water.
- Marsh: Swampy, wet areas of land that are covered at times by water.
- Plain: A region that has level land.
- Plateau: An area of high land that is usually flat.
- Prairie: A region of level land with grass and few or no trees.
- Rain Forest: A region experiencing high levels of rain that contains large numbers of trees.
- Reef: A ridge of rocks close to the surface of an ocean or lake.
- River Basin: Land that is drained by a river and its tributaries.
- Tributary: A stream that flows into a river or large body of water.
- Valley: Low land lying between hills or mountains.

(Adapted from Hunt, 1968)

Home and Neighborhood

Young children who enter school are still becoming oriented to their street and neighborhood. Geography is a tool to help them find out where they are and know how to reach other places. An effective beginning point is to associate their own home to basic geographic concepts. For example:

- Have students make a map of their own home or apartment. They can indicate which rooms are smaller or larger. They can draw pictures of furniture and appliances and make symbols to represent these features.

- In previous chapters, we have described various memory techniques. These strategies can be employed in aiding students to become more familiar with their home and neighborhood. For example, pose the following questions to students regarding their home:

    1. Is the refrigerator handle on the left or right side of the door?
    2. How many chairs are in your kitchen and living room?
    3. If you lay down on the floor, how many of your body lengths would it take to go across your bedroom? How many across the kitchen or living room?
    4. How many windows are in your home?
    5. How many doors are in your home?
    6. How many beds are in your home? Which is the biggest bed? Why?
    7. How many steps does it take to go from your kitchen to where you sleep?
    8. How many steps does it take to go from your house or apartment to a neighbor?

Maps can be confusing to young children. Their home city may appear as a dot or their suburban area may not appear at all on the map. They see in their class a round world portrayed on a flat surface. The following activities may assist students to recognize ways their perspective influences how an object is portrayed. They are to gaze at the following objects as though floating in air and:

1. Draw a picture of a ball, a cat, a can, a tree, an umbrella, a flag, or a shoe.
2. Have students stand on top of the teacher's desk and describe items placed underneath them.
3. Have students present to the class their picture of an item drawn from the view of floating in air. The class is to guess the object being depicted.

The creation of maps in schools frequently focuses upon a child's artistic rendition rather than reflecting accurate information. Initial map activities can help students begin the process of translating information from one form to another; to recognize that many structures are purposely designed, and to understand that maps have to omit some information due to lack of space.

Relief Maps

There are several ways to build relief maps describing the school or its immediate environment. Clay is a costly but effective material to use in map construction. Many teachers prefer papier-mâché maps which are made by tearing newspapers into strips and soaking them in water overnight. Students then mix wheat paste with warm water and make a thin cream. After the water is squeezed out of the newspaper strips, they are dipped into the paste and applied to an outline of the map that is being constructed.

Maps can be built by using sawdust and glue. Mix thinned white glue with dampened fine sawdust until you are able to use it in map making. Another approach is to use salt and flour. Mix four cups of flour, two cups of water and two cups of salt. You can add food coloring and then knead the mixture thoroughly. It may take a few days for the mixture to dry.

Constructing a Globe

Following are instructions for student constructed globes:

1. Inflate a balloon to the desired size—12 to 18 inches is a good diameter. Attach a heavy cord to provide a hanging arrangement to the finished globe.

2. Mix wheat paste to a thick consistency.

3. Cut newspapers into three-inch strips that are tapered to a point at one end. Dip each strip into the paste, and apply it to the globe.

4. After applying two layers of newspaper, hang the globe on a rope or wire which has been stretched across the room.

5. Add three more layers of newspaper. Finish the globe with a layer of white tissue strips.

6. Mark continents and oceans after lines of longitude and latitude have been determined. If a relief map is desired, use a recipe of salt and cornstarch mixture. Before applying this mixture, shellac the globe so moistutre will not cause it to sag.

Neighborhood

The neighborhood is the initial world outside the home for young children. Urban children encounter a variety of apartment buildings and houses, empty lots, and stores. Suburban children tend to initially encounter family homes in their immmediate surroundings, while the neighbors of farm children are not easily accessible. Teachers can introduce the concept of neighborhood on walking trips to streets adjoining the school. On these strolls the teacher can raise several topics:

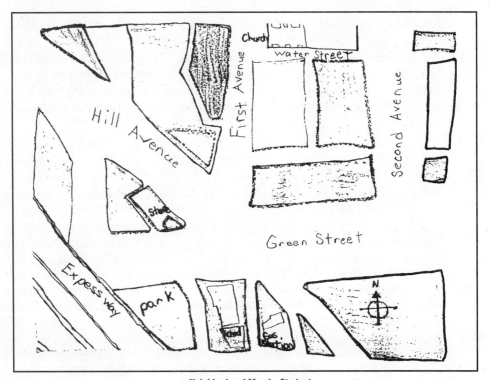

▲ **Neighborhood Map by Student**

- Are house numbers getting larger or smaller?
- What can we learn from reading street names such as Maple, Willow, or Apple streets?
- Why are there stop signs at certain places?
- Are the streets straight or do they wind around?
- Are there traffic lights at certain places?
- Do you find trash cans in front of certain houses or apartment buildings?
- How many streets have a water hydrant?

After the class returns to the school, they can immediately draw a map of their walking tour. They should indicate on the map information they obtained by analyzing geographical features of the neighborhood around the school. Some teachers bring a Polaroid camera on the walk and have students take pictures. These pictures could be transformed into a pictorial map. A follow-up activity could involve having students draw maps of the neighborhood streets around their own house or apartment building. If a group of students are taking a bus to school, they might take pictures of places on the way to school, and these could be incorporated into a collage.

Scale

Time, distance, and space are still abstractions to elementary-age children unless they can graphically encounter these concepts. The maps they construct about places they know and see can be used to teach many geographical concepts. For example, the "grid" which is found on

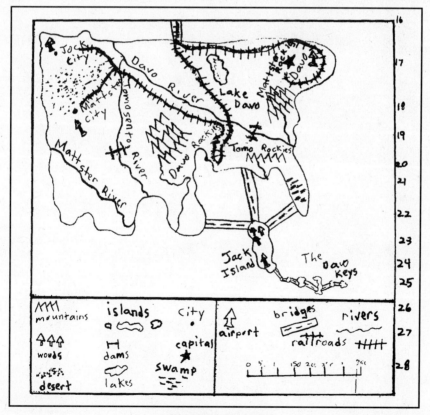

▲ Student Map with Legend

maps can be incorporated into their neighborhood map. After they construct the grid of the neighborhood map, a commercial map of their area could be used to locate their grid in relationship to the local geographic area. In some classrooms, teachers transform the room into a large grid pattern. Students practice moving by the grid system in a variation of Simon Says. For example, "Simon says move two steps north into the next grid box." Students can also create their own maps of fictional areas and utilize a grid to indicate distance and location.

As students enter the upper elementary grades, the concepts of latitude and longitude will be studied. Parallels of latitude are imaginary lines encircling the globe. They measure distances north and south of the equator in degrees ranging from 0 degrees at the equator to 90 degrees at each pole. Meridians of longitude are also imaginary lines encircling the earth and are used to measure distances east and west of the prime meridian, which passes through Greenwich, England. Unlike parallels of latitude they are not parallel lines and do not decrease in size. Each meridian of longitude passes through the north and south poles and has the same circumference. They are measured in relation to the prime meridian and range from 0 degrees longitude at the prime meridain to 180 degreees east longitude and 180 degrees west longitude.

It is difficult to teach the ideas of latitude and longitude on a flat map. It is preferable to use a globe for this instruction. The use of strings, ribbons, pieces of paper or even licorice can illustrate the lines of latitude and longitude on a globe. A large beach ball or volley ball can be used to demonstrate the grid system on a spherical object. There are a variety of physical education activities which lend themselves to reinforcing education about latitude and longitude. For example, students can link themselves together to represent latitude or longitude.

Locating Latitude and Longitude

Following are twelve words. Students are asked to identify which area of the world gave birth to a word and then to locate its latitude and longitude.

Words:
1. yam	2. silk	3. wigwam	4. canyon
5. chili	6. tattoo	7. coffee	8. kimono
9. history	10. dungarees	11. kindergarten	12. khaki

Country	Latitude	Longitude
1.		
2.		
3.		
4.		
5.		
6.		
7.		
8.		
9.		
10.		
11.		
12.		

▲ Student Map

Problem Solving

Maps are puzzles to some children, and this idea can be used to pose "puzzle situations" for investigation by sub groups in the class. For example, in the following problem, a car can not make a right turn. Question: How can the car reach the house of a friend?

The concept of distance can be taught by having students draw a map of the classroom, then a map of the school. Students can pace off distance with their feet or body lengths in order to determine the size of various places in the school. They can be asked to take Polaroid pictures of the school and paste them together to form a map.

On their walking trips, several students can carry a pedometer or they can count how many paces it took to walk one street. This information can be incorporated onto their maps. It is very common for students to ride buses to school. The bus driver can be asked to cooperate by indicating distance traveled along the way to school. For example, students picked up at 110th Street would be told the mileage on the speedometer and then told what it reads when they reach the school.

Action Geographic Projects

Geography offers an unusual opportunity to involve elementary age children in community action projects. E. Dwight Zirschky (1989), an elementary school teacher in Dundee, Oregon, had his students become involved in the controversy regarding the town's refusal to allow a traffic light at the school intersection. The students organized into committees and conducted research

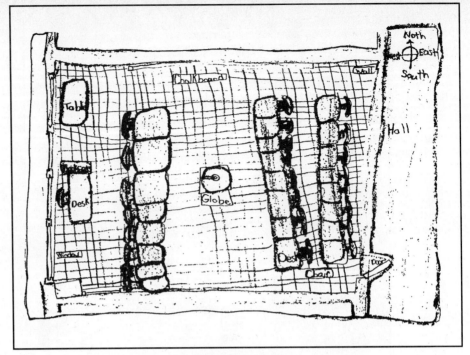

▲ Student Classroom Map

about work, land use, and business activities in the town. They studied traffic patterns and did their own traffic count of cars passing by the school. They studied the relationship of Dundee to the county and state, investigated future buildings to be constructed in the town and studied their town's history. Their project culminated with extensive pictorial displays that were presented to the city council. The school site was granted a traffic light without further discussion.

Elementary school children can study housing available to the aged in their community, the process by which trash is removed and what happens to the trash, how much land is set aside for parks or recreational facilities, or how a school district decides which children ride buses or walk to school. These and other projects enable the class to organize themselves into committees, conduct research and create interesting pictorial displays to culminate their activities. Projects which lend themselves to changing a community boost student self concept and demonstrate that school learning can impact one's immediate environment in positive ways.

Geography Through Picture Books

The five basic geographic terms previously identified—location, place, relationships within places, movement, and regions—can be incorporated into the study of children's literature. One way is to create maps to accompany favorite children's books. For example, *Aladdin and the Wonderful Lamp,* by Carol Carrick is an excellent depiction of this classic tale.

Location:
- Draw a map of Aladdin's town.
- Draw a map of Aladdin going from the town to the valley.

Place:
- Describe the climate changes in the story.
- Draw pictures of flowers or trees in the story.

Relationship Within Places:
- Tell how the weather depicted in the book affects the way people dress.

Movement:
- Describe various types of transportation in the story.
- Create symbols for buildings, roads, the palace, and the cave.

Regions:
- Draw pictures of one type of neighborhood depicted in the story.

Students can accompany the reading of *Tom Sawyer* by creating maps depicting where Tom and Huckleberry Finn traveled. A Dr. Seuss book lends itself to developing a map showing where people move or the action of the story takes place. A geography exercise can emerge from reading nursery tales, short stories, or classic children's literature. For example, draw a map from Snow White's castle to the house of the Seven Dwarfs.

Zoos and Maps

An emphasis of a successful geography program in elementary school is relating maps to the everyday lives of children. Their parents rely upon maps on car trips, while a field trip to the zoo can become a geography lesson by using zoo maps to identify places to visit. On return to school, the students can create their own zoo maps and indicate with symbols the location of the animals or zoo attractions. Students with cameras can help make their zoo maps become even more vivid by placing photos in the appropriate places.

Many zoos have developed educational programs that can be adapted to geographic instruction. Following are two examples from the St. Louis Zoo.

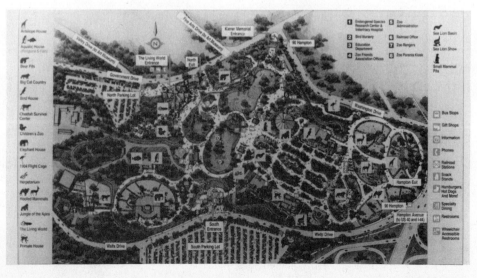

▲ Zoo Map

CONSERVATION CODE

To help save endangered species, zoos and aquariums are working together to breed certain animal species. The name of this project is written in code below. Each symbol has two different meanings. Can you crack the code and discover the name of the project?

A or Z	B or Y	C or X
☞	✕	✳

D or W	E or V	F or U
→	✺	☾

G or T	H or S	I or R
✕	⊃	♣

J or Q	K or P	L or O
☕	☐	⤚

M or N
✳

THE PROJECT'S NAME

_____

_____ _____

TURTLE TREK

Sea turtles hatch from eggs laid in holes on the beach. The baby sea turtles must find their way into the ocean as quickly as possible, without getting eaten on the way. Help the sea turtles make it to the water. Be careful — not all paths lead to safety!

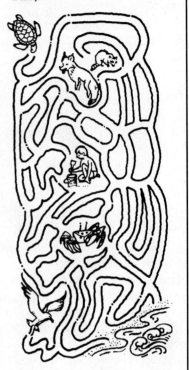

▲ Zoo Project

What If . . . ?

Hypothesis speculation opens opportunities for students to engage in critical thinking. An interesting activity to foster such thought processes in geography is asking students to consider the impact upon society if certain geographical features were altered or did not exist. For example, imagine that the Mississippi River ran east/west rather than north/south. How would that geographical change have affected American history?

A teacher can originate the exercise by posing this question: "What if the earth had no mountains?" This can lead students to discuss how this change in geography would affect their daily lives. After students analyze this geographical change, they can be asked to brainstorm other "What ifs?" For example:

- What if the earth had no rivers?
- What if the earth had no deserts?
- What if the earth had no oceans?

- What if the earth had no winds?
- What if the earth revolved faster around the sun?
- What if the earth revolved slower around the sun?
- What if the earth was triangular shaped?
- What if the earth was flat?

Students can be asked to draw pictures or write about their responses to these questions. Or, a group could be assigned to develop a complete picture of the earth in response to one of these questions. Among the factors to consider might be:

- How would recreation be affected?
- How would clothing be affected?
- How would our cities change?
- How would our housing change?
- How would plant life be affected?
- How would transportation and communication be affected?
- How would wildlife be different?

Students can be encouraged to map a shopping trip. Ask them to draw a map of a toy store indicating where different toys and games are located. On occasion, the store has its own map, which can be brought to school for analysis. Subway systems and bus routes usually have maps indicating places to stop. These maps help students extend their perspective from the local neighborhood to the broader concept of a town or section of a large city.

Sports and Geography

The phenomenal growth of sports in the past decades has brought through television vivid scenes from distant cities and nations. Professional baseball, football, and basketball have evolved from sports confined to cities east of the Misssissippi River to multinational contests spanning the world. Latin-American children have made baseball their number one sport; football is now played in Barcelona, basketball in Rome, and each year American baseball teams tour Japan.

This interest in sports can be tapped to extend interest in geography. Students can research the expansion of professional leagues by creating maps and constructing bar graphs to depict this development. Newspaper accounts of sporting events from different nations can be obtained to give graphic evidence of the transnational influence of sports in the everyday lives of people. If your school is located near a metropolitan area that has professional athletes, foreign born players can be invited to the class for a discussion of sports and play in their home country. If you are not in such a location, a local college might be contacted for information about foreign students on their soccer or other athletic teams.

Suggestions:

1. Have students gather information concerning place of birth of professional hockey players. They can see if areas with the most snow and cold weather produce the greatest number of hockey players.
2. Have students indicate on a map the sites of original professional baseball, basketball, and football teams and current membership in professional leagues.

3. Have students construct a bar graph indicating which states produced the greatest number of professsional baseball, basketball, or football players. Much of this data can be obtained from baseball or football cards.

4. Have students produce a similar bar graph for home states of female tennis players.

5. Have students utilize a map of the world to indicate the main sports of nations.

6. Have students identify a sport team, and construct a map indicating origin of each player. The final map can be sent to the team for possible display.

Map Lesson

Select a day with a full sun. Take the class outdoors to observe and record the position of the sun in the morning, at noon, and just before leaving for home. Point out to students that when they face east, north is on their left, south on their right, and west at their backs. When they face west, north is on their right, south on their left, and east at their backs. In the class-room, continue discussion of cardinal directions by having pupils face east on a sunny morn-ing. As each direction is discovered, label the walls or corners as east, west, north and south.

Map Lesson

One pupil is asked to hold a flashlight to represent the sun; another pupil represents the earth. The "earth" moves slowly around the "sun" enabling students to see that as the earth turns toward the sun, the sun seems to rise, as the earth turns away, the sun seems to set. Students will understand that half of the earth is always toward the sun and half is always in shadow.

Concrete Geography

The names, places, and animals inhabiting the world lend themselves to visual exercises in geogra-phy. The name of an animal can trigger visual images in the mind of a child. For example, a polar bear usually elicits images of cold regions and snow. Concrete geography is a process by which students utilize artistic and photographic imagery to depict geographic areas of the world. Following are several examples of ways children have depicted geogaphic concepts in a visual manner.

▲ Montana, Venice

Concrete geography can help children see the world around them in a more dramatic fashion. It enables children who are visual learners to more readily grasp geographical concepts. The names of countries, mountain ranges, or oceans are abstractions to children, and few are able to relate those words to a specific image. Concrete geography forms associations in the minds of children between a faraway place and an animal they know or a physical feature that is familiar.

Special Feature Maps

A great deal of information can be conveyed about life on this planet through geography lessons. There are a variety of maps, charts and graphs that further student understandings and enable them to obtain a more vivid grasp of material being taught. Physical maps and globes

▲ State Names

▲ Nation Names

employ several colors to indicate water and land areas and to depict land elevation or sea depth. There are also maps that indicate economic activities, population, migration patterns, political voting, military campaigns and a host of other conceptual ideas.

Some map makers have chosen to portray the world from other than the traditional Eurocentric perspective. A map that places the north pole at the center shifts perceptions regarding size and distance of nations or bodies of water from what children normally obtain by viewing a map in which Europe and America are at the center (Forsyth, 1964).

A special purpose map explains an explicit feature, condition or incident. For example, a map can show where and how cotton was produced in pre-Civil War America while another special purpose map can depict slaveholding patterns. The special purpose map enables teachers to focus student attention to a particular aspect of geography (Stopsley, et al., 1975).

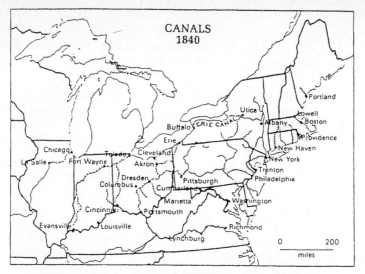

▲ This map illustrates the growth of the nation's transportation systems during the mid 19th century.

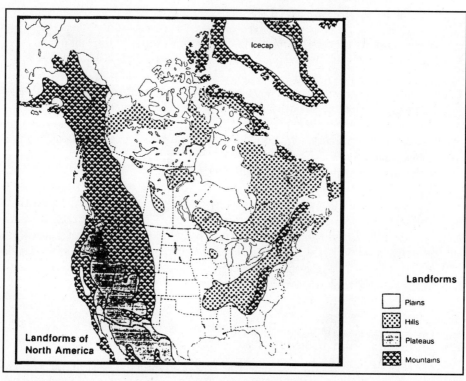

▲ This map illustrates land forms of North America.

> **Building Utopia**
>
> Brasilia, capital of Brazil, was built from scratch in the 1950s in an endeavor to develop resources located in the nation's interior. The planners had free rein to create a modern city free of the traditional grid pattern of cities or individually designed buildings. Their dream was to create a city of the future. Imagine, if you could design a city, how would it be organized? What would be included that presently is absent from cities? What would be excluded?
>
> Motorists travel on highways throughout Brasilia unimpeded by cross traffic or traffic lights. The city is segregated into work areas and residential areas. Apartment buildings are self-sufficient units. Schools and shops are located within the apartment complexes. A service road from the back of buildings leads to the highway. There are no sidewalks and children never have to worry about traffic.
>
> A common complaint of people in Brasilia is their inability to find places to walk. An individual has to cross the large highways to get to a building on the other side. This forces people to use cars to travel about the city. In this planned city, there is no street corner society, no downtown shopping area, no crowds, no window shopping, and no sidewalk interaction. There aren't even street names so one's address might be some letters and numbers—BGS 102-G-321.
>
> The upper class of Brasilia has moved to the suburbs in order to build their own private houses. Brasilia illustrates the need for geography to be linked with sociology, anthropology, and psychology if cities of the future are to be healthy environments for life and work. The historic manner by which cities emerged due to trade patterns may alter in the future. Geography has a role to play in helping prepare for cities of the future.

Changes in the world economy are causing educators to rethink traditional ways of presenting geography. It was common to link possession of natural resources as a key factor in industrialization. However, the emergence of Singapore, Taiwan, and Hong Kong as major centers of production and trade suggests that nations without natural resources can play a vital role in contemporary economics. The world is entering a post-industrial era in which an educated population, an entrepreneurial spirit, and long range planning may be more critical in economic development than natural resources.

It is still typical to find elementary children being taught that people in Mexico wear sombreros or that people in Holland wear wooden shoes. Geography has to address the urban explosion that is congregating millions within densely packed areas. Children should become aware that many African societies are a combination of rural agriculture and urban factories. The growing complexity of geographic education places burdens upon teachers to keep abreast of rapidly changing borders and economic development.

Charts, Graphs, and Tables

Charts, graphs, and tables are highly effective ways of organizing material in visually motivating ways. These tools can be introduced as early as the primary grades. A simple bar graph can represent how many students were born in the community and how many moved to the area from other cities. Graphs and charts lend themselves to cooperative learning activities in which students having diverse talents can each play a role in the final product.

These tools enable students to practice interpreting data, formulating generalizations, and engaging in divergent thinking. For example, a study of the height of American presidents and the height of their opponents will graphically demonstrate to students that the taller they are, the more likely they will be elected. A graph or chart with this information will stimulate students to raise questions and formulate interesting hypotheses.

Richard Schwartz (cited in Forsyth, 1964) has written extensively about ways to incorporate math within global education programs. He selects problems and examples from key global issues of our time. For example:

1. The amount of solid waste (garbage) thrown out by the average person in the U.S. increased from 2.50 pounds in 1960 to 3.43 pounds in 1984. Find the percent increase.

2. If the air quality in a certain area is unfavorable 50% of the time, what is the probability that in one six-day period there will be:
   (a) 4 unfavorable days; (b) 4 or more unfavorable days; (c) no more than 4 unfavorable days?

Students should be continually encouraged to organize ideas using charts, graphs, and tables. Constant practice will strengthen their capacities to employ a variety of critical thinking skills in problem solving. It is important to employ charts and graphs when studying other areas in the curriculum such as science or literature. They provide opportunities for students to organize information in a more illustrative manner (Stopsky, et al., 1975).

▲ Students should be encouraged to organize information using charts, graphs, and tables. *Courtesy Lynn Rubright, Webster University.*

This chapter has stressed the importance of geography in building a global perspective in the curriculum. The development of international understanding requires an empathetic attitude, but unless students have knowledge, attitudes may not achieve the aim of global awareness. Geography is most effectively presented in relationship to other academic disciplines. There needs to be a balance between the physical and human dimensions of geography. Geography does not exist in a vacuum but is linked to cultural, political, and economic considerations.

The future of humanity is closely related to how well people understand the nature of other cultures, values, and geographical factors. Students need to develop a holistic perspective, and geography can play a significant role in helping them internalize such a view. Geography has to play a central role in creating global awareness in education.

Below is a list of suggestions for teaching geography.

1. Have students create a country including its geographical features, economic resources, and climate.

2. Develop a "Capitals Quiz Game." For example:
   • Coiled metal plus a meadow (Springfield, IL)
   • 1920's dance (Charleston, SC)

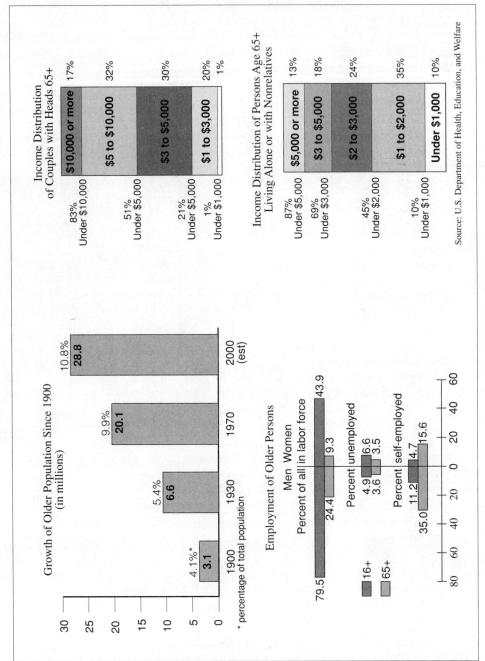

Growth of Older Population Since 1900
(in millions)

4.1%*
3.1
1900

5.4%
6.6
1930

9.9%
20.1
1970

10.8%
28.8
2000
(est)

* percentage of total population

Income Distribution
of Couples with Heads 65+

83%
Under $10,000 $10,000 or more   17%

51%
Under $5,000 $5 to $10,000   32%

21%
Under $5,000 $3 to $5,000   30%

1%
Under $1,000 $1 to $3,000   20%

1%

Employment of Older Persons

Men   Women
Percent of all in labor force

79.5
43.9
9.3
24.4

Percent unemployed

4.9   6.6
3.6   3.5

Percent self-employed

11.2   4.7
35.0   15.6

16+
65+

80 60 40 20 0 20 40 60

Income Distribution of Persons Age 65+
Living Alone or with Nonrelatives

87%
Under $5,000 $5,000 or more   13%

69%
Under $3,000 $3 to $5,000   18%

45%
Under $2,000 $2 to $3,000   24%

10%
Under $1,000 $1 to $2,000   35%

Under $1,000   10%

Source: U.S. Department of Health, Education, and Welfare

▲ Examples of charts and graphs

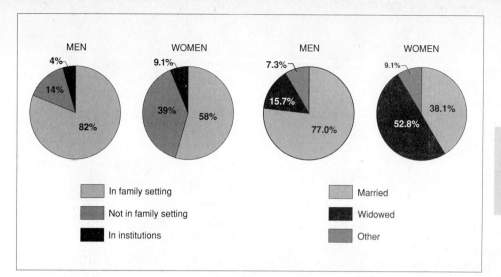

| MEN | WOMEN | MEN | WOMEN |

4% — 14% 82%

9.1% — 39% 58%

7.3% — 15.7% 77.0%

9.1% — 52.8% 38.1%

- In family setting
- Not in family setting
- In institutions

- Married
- Widowed
- Other

▲ **Examples of graphs**

- Summer month plus short vowel (Augusta, GA)
- Wealthy plus a small hill (Richmond, VA)
- Another word for *we* plus a type of metal (Austin, TX)
- Part of foot plus quick look plus short vowel (Topeka, KS)
- Animal's home plus animal hair (Denver, CO)

3. Have students draw a map of the U.S. identifying states by flowers or animals. Do the same for other countries.

4. Create an "orienteering couse" on the playground or in a park. This requires establishing check points which have a word or letter. The students navigate the course with a compass and record each check point.

5. Develop jigsaw puzzles for geographic areas.

6. Lay out a map of the playground but have pieces missing. Divide the class into teams that take turns placing a puzzle piece in the correct area.

7. Have students create maps that might have been drawn by cavepeople.

8. Turn the classroom into a minature town. Each group has a responsibility to create its own area of the town. City Council meetings and town planning can be linked to this activity.

▲ **Studying human and physical dimensions of geography is important in building global awareness.** *Courtesy Webster University.*

▲ The future of humanity is closely related to how well people understand other cultures, values, and geographical factors.
Courtesy Null Elementary, Saint Charles (Missouri) Public Schools.

9. Rearrange the classroom. As students enter have them put on a blindfold. When all are in the room, they are to remove the blindfolds and quickly draw a map of the new room. After completing that task, they are to make maps of the room as it used to be. A follow-up can be discussion comparing the two room designs.

10. Have students pace off the size of the classroom, then the school. They can compare their paces to standard units of length.

11. Scramble word activity: Present scrambled words for geographic areas. For example:
   • Madison is the capital of this state—Coinswins.
   • Mountain range in southern Missouri—Krazo.

12. Students can be asked to identify words inside the names of states or other geographic areas. For example:
   • Washington—wash and ton.
   • Nebraska—ask and a.

13. Have students do an outline map of their own bodies. They can create geographic features for their body.

14. Have one student ask another for directions to go some place in the school. The other student draws a map to indicate the way.

SUMMARY

This chapter has offered a rationale for the teaching of geography in elementary and middle school classrooms. It has reviewed several strategies to implement effective geographic education.

QUESTIONS

1. If you were to purchase a house, which geographic factors would weigh in your decision?

2. How have your ideas about the geography of the world changed in the past four years?

3. When in your life did you first grasp the concept of distance?

4. How does TV reporting help or hinder the way students grasp geographic concepts?

5. Which environmental issues should be most emphasized in elementary social studies?

6. How can motion pictures be utilized in teaching about geography?

7. Which geographic concepts are hardest for suburban, rural, or urban children to grasp?

8. Which do you believe elementary age children know more about—the geography of their city or that of the United States?

9. Which technological developments will have the greatest impact in teaching geography?

ACTIVITIES

1. Make a map of the area around the university based from memory. Then, compare it with reality.

2. Create a geographic problem-solving technique. See chapter for suggestions.

3. Compare maps of the world from 1914, 1939, 1945, and today.

4. Create a geographic lesson based upon a fairy or folk tale.

5. Create a geographic lesson utilizing songs.

READING

Geography—Public Awareness and the Public Arena
by Saul B. Cohen

Throughout the nation, Geography Awareness Week (November 15–21, 1987) was marked by a series of media reports, public hearings, protocol materials, statewide quiz contests, and campus-based activities. At the heart of this important and unprecedented effort that has, to the gratification of geographers, been spearheaded by the National Geographic Society is the concern with geographic ignorance and illiteracy, a spotlight on the sad state of geography in the schools, and a call to arms to teach students geographic facts and concepts. Such concern is congruent with the more widely felt need for schools to return to the basic of civics, history, and geography as part of the social studies curriculum. In the current initiative, teacher training and curriculum development are being promoted as twin strategies for remedying geography's fall from grace in the schools.

We live in a nation in transition that is experiencing profound change and charting a new and unknown economic and geopolitical destiny. It is a transition in which time, space, and technology are intertwined.

Although pleased with the increased attention that geography is receiving, I have a nagging concern that Geography Awareness Week may have overemphasized the obvious—the astonishing lack of knowledge of the face and features of our earth that has been exhibited by American students for close to half a century—while sliding over the root of the problem: the status of geography as a university field. The university is the wellspring for improving geographical education in the schools and for deepening knowledge in the public arena. What is taught to undergraduate and graduate college students, especially those destined for the teaching profession, and the quality of the research enterprise are what gives overall meaning and stature to a field and ultimately to its public acceptance. The university is where theory and methodology are tested and reformulated and where a discipline is reinvigorated by the questions it asks—often as a result of interaction with other disciplines.

Most of the reports that Geography Awareness Week cited in the press referred to the absence of direct locational information—we are in conflict in the Persian Gulf (or is it the Arabian Gulf?)—yet only 60 percent of the public surveyed knew that the Gulf is in the Middle East. So quickly has the memory of Vietnam receded that 95 percent of American college freshman could not locate Vietnam on the map. (I suppose the statistic would be 99 percent for French Indochina.)

These examples do not do justice to the gravity of the problem. In the last analysis, the worth of a discipline is based on how seriously the leadership and lay public weigh its concepts and theories and how useful they find its tools of analysis. Although I am more sanguine about geography's impact in the realm of tools of analysis than in the realm of theory, it is only when the public comes to accept geography as a field that deals with tested "laws and principles" that we will have come of age scientifically.

Whatever definition we use, geography generally focuses on the relationship between human activity and the environment, describing and explaining the significance of location, distance, direction, spread, and spatial succession. It deals with place at varying scales and the interconnectedness of place.

Narrow, Intolerant View

Pervasive ignorance of geographical approaches and concepts is disadvantageous to Americans in their economic, military, and political affairs, and promotes a narrow, intolerant view of the world. The ignorance, however, is far more than simply not knowing where Panama, North Korea, and the Horn of Africa are located.

Thus, the debate over the return of the Panama Canal to Panama was distorted because so many Americans had no idea that changes in the geographical patterns of the world movement of goods had substantially reduced the strategic importance of the "Big Ditch." And the American military was caught unprepared psychologically as well as logistically for the rigors of North Korea's humid continental winter. Moreover, we know that our choice of allies is based on more than political ideology. Both Ethiopia and Somalia have Marxist regimes, and yet our selection of the smaller, weaker, and less strategically positioned Somalia betrayed a disregard of the geographic implications of such a choice.

I have mentioned that both tools of analysis and theory are important to furthering the public interest in geography. The progress that analytic geography has made in the use of geodata handling and automated cartography as well as in the application of remote-sensing materials has revolutionized the study of terrain analysis, deforestation, environmental planning, and urban dynamics. We have to increase public awareness of geography's contribution to those areas of inquiry and to policy application.

Let me illustrate from recent personal experience an educational research project that uses modern analytic tools to promote the public good with respect to the travel and tourist industry, an industry to which geography has much to contribute, as evidenced by the vigor of several undergraduate geography department major programs in Travel and Tourism. A New York City educational project deals with how taxi drivers learn to find their way in the city of New York. All new drivers, and there are 6,500 of them each year, must enroll in a program that includes geography. The geography course is currently taught by excellent instructors, using traditional lectures and map material displays.

Upon evaluating the program, our advisory committee concluded that student taxi-driver learning would be considerably enhanced if a mapping software package were developed to allow for interactive practice in learning about distance, direction, traffic flow patterns, alternative route identification, optimization of travel time, and identification of landmarks.

We have organized a research team at Hunter College that is well on its way to completing the mapping system for the five boroughs of New York (Manhattan at the block scale, and the other four boroughs at neighborhood and main thoroughfare scales). When more effective learning takes place at the two taxi-driver schools, the public will be better served. Moreover, if the learning process is enhanced by modern technology, students are likely to take their classes and themselves more seriously—contributing to one of our committee's fundamental aims, which is to help professionalize the taxi industry.

Although learning the map of New York City is a component of geographical knowledge, it is hardly its essence. Indeed, if place-name identification is viewed as fulfilling the geographic educational need by those who now are leading the back-to-basics movement for social studies—through emphasizing the "facts" of history, geography, and civics, then we will have lost a great opportunity for geographic renewal.

In reducing geographic illiteracy, we must deal with problems of attitude, and not just with the mere memorization of facts or the more important cognitive skills. When a student recently interviewed on a national CBS-TV newscast was asked whether he was bothered by not knowing where the Antilles were located, his response was, "No, as long as I know where I am, what difference does it make?"

Now we could drill into that student's head the location on the map of Cuba, of the Greater Antilles, of the Lesser Antilles, of the entire Caribbean Basin, but if the student does not know the content of the Antilles—their physical settings, their economic resources, and their cultural landscapes, and if the student has no grasp of spatial relations, the patterns of the islands' sociopolitical, cultural, and economic links with the rest of the region and the world, then the student is not thinking geographically. Moreover, if the student has no grasp of how distance-decay theory—the curve of drop-off in political, social, and economic interests—affects the American public's attitudes toward different parts of the world, then understanding will occur in a vacuum.

Correct location of places is the ABC of geography, but not its vocabulary. Just as the alphabet is the means of learning to read, so place content must be intertwined with place identification. Whether learning the geographical alphabet should precede place content; whether the former should flow from the latter is a question that deserves greater attention. Just as reading is the basis for enjoyment and comprehension of literature, so spatial patterns and relations are understandings that flow from the analysis of place content.

Finally, just as literature is the means for reflecting on or understanding fundamental social, psychological, economic, and political processes within a spatial and temporal dimension, so geographical theories are the explanation for certain spatial processes.

There are, therefore, four interrelated components of geographic learning: place identification, place content, spatial patterns and relations, and theory. Clearly the emphasis at the university level must be on the latter two, but we dare not relegate geographic awareness in the schools to the first two.

Person-Environment Relations

I have already given an example of a sophisticated approach to place location through the computer mapping process. Place content includes careful measurement, an ability to select meaningful elements of the physical and cultural landscape to achieve intelligent description, and alertness to the role of boundaries and cores in giving character to place. Place content studies can be important vehicles for understanding person-environment relations.

An immigrant to a new city can, with the use of personal diaries, sketch maps of the perceived environment and the recording of important transactions and interactions, learn the personal meaning of place-content—the geography of fear and the geography of attraction, the geography of the perceived environment and the geography of the ignored environment, the role of anchor points and desire lines in shaping circulation patterns, and the like.

Thus, place content for some who study a foreign region like the Antilles might be an objective set of phenomena, whereas for others studying their own reactions to their local environments, it is a subjective learning process.

Spatial relations can be examined at a variety of scales. The spatial accordion effects of stock market behavior is one illustration. The New York stock market crash of October 19, 1987, had a chain effect upon Tokyo, Hong Kong and Sydney, London, and then back to New York. The general public now knows the meaning of global interdependence in a very concrete time-space sense.

Some spatial patterns are obvious to the observer—that the growth of suburbs hastened the process of central city neighborhood blight, and that the diffusion of population into suburban and exurban areas has been accompanied by industrial and commercial growth.

However, a study like the recent one by geography professors Peter Muller and Truman Hartshorn (*Suburban Business Centers: Employment Implications,* U.S. Department of Commerce, 1987) helps the public to begin to think about suburbs not as amorphous, sprawling areas, but as regions on the verge of being dominated by new cores or nodes—"outer cities" whose central place functions are independent and competitive with the major central city. Whether these new cities started as old, small satellite towns, as in the Northeast, or from scratch, as in much of the South and West, where they emerged first as industrial parks or agglomerations of shopping centers, many outer cities now have full urban forms and functions. Their implications for the central city are obvious. They are interceptors of journeys to work, shopping, business, government, and recreation.

As they in turn age—and some are beginning to show signs of aging—and the pattern of flight and abandonment from them begins, can outer suburbs and even exurbs continue to plan for a two-acre zoning world to maintain their low-rise profiles, or will they become a second tier of outer cities? Whatever the case, it is in these new outer cities that the jobs of the new high-technology era are being generated, and the socio-economic gap between them and most central cities is widening.

Exposition of theory is, perhaps, the most difficult of geographical challenges. The public knows very little geographical theory. More dangerous perhaps than the theory that is unknown is the theory that is out-of-date. The espousal of an American geopolitics by leading State Department officials and military strategists is a case in point.

The geopolitical view of the world, built upon the Heartland Theory, was initially propounded by Sir Halford Mackinder in 1904 and expanded upon in 1919. The theory is simple: that one part of the world, the heart of Eurasia, held the advantage of Central Place. From the continent's interior reaches or pivot area, power can be applied quickly, sequentially, and efficiently against the populous peninsular lands of Western Europe, the Middle East, South Asia, and East Asia.

Given the advantages of land mobility, and the options to strike out in one direction without having to mass forces against other peripheral areas because of the barrier zones of deserts and mountains ringing the Continental Interior, it was assumed that control of the Heartland (Western and Eastern Europe), would give a nation command of Eurasia and thus the world.

The Heartland Theory was embraced by German geopolitik and explains why Germany's opening salvo in World War II was against Poland and why Germany invaded the Soviet Union in 1941 after France had fallen.

Mackinder rejected his own theory in 1944 in favor of a world balanced by four components on the basis of population and national resources.

Moreover, American political geographers wrote extensively in repudiation of the scientific pretensions of German geopolitik. However, the Heartland Theory did not die. It became the basis for a post-World War II interpretation by some American government officials. According to this interpretation, the American-Soviet contest is an enduring historical rivalry that is a dispute over the Eurasian landmass, with parallel drives by the two powers for control of the Eurasian Rimlands shaped by their respective geographical locations. This theory influenced George Kennan's containment strategy, and later became the basis for the Cold War pragmatism that was propounded on geopolitical grounds by Robert Strauz-Hupe, Henry Kissinger, and Zbigniew Brzezinski.

Thus President Reagan, Vice President Bush, Admiral Poindexter, and Lieutenant Colonel North all invoked the Russian drive to warm waters to justify the events that were exposed in Irangate. Keeping the Russians out of the Persian Gulf was also the first rationale for our tanker-reflagging strategy there.

The problem here is with geographical ignorance. European-born political scientists with a map of the world that has changed long since their grade school days have retained a view of the world based on this map that has shaped their thinking as intellectual standard-bearers of a grand strategy.

Illustrative of this kind of thinking, in a recent volume Professor Brzezinski develops his strategic "game plan" for the United States, based upon a statement that then Soviet Foreign Minister Gromyko is reported to have made to a visiting foreign diplomat to the effect that he spends a great deal of time looking at a flat wall map of the world that is centered on Moscow. Brzezinski assumes that Soviet strategy revolves around this exaggerated cartographic projection, rather than an appreciation of the globe. He then rationalizes U.S. policy as a counterpoint to Gromyko's assumed mental map and, in effect, adopts the same distorted wall map in posing an American strategy (*Game Plan,* Boston: Atlantic Monthly Press, 1986).

Changing Mental Maps

As the world changes, so must our mental maps. A valid basis for geopolitical theory today is built upon a world globe that is a seamless web of interconnections. No single place has strategic dominance. Time, technology, resource substitution, and population change have seen to that.

Pipelines and supertankers permit maritime choke points to be bypassed, space-age missiles can breach the barrier zones of interior Eurasia, and regional powers in their home settings challenge superpowers for control over their regions. Think of the map of the world, the globe of true area, shape, and distance—projected on a map to give appropriate weight to area and distance—as a series of nodes of varying sizes and strengths, reaching out to one another through a variety of links and pathways.

In effect, think of the world as a grid system, with patterns of contact that are hierarchically organized and regionally framed—a world in which all 175 nations are political actors, although clearly some have greater vigor than others.

In such a view of the world's map, there is no place for dominance by the center of the "Old World Parallelogram"—the mental map that is held by those who remain bound to the world of the past. Instead of central place theory, we must adapt a theory of systems development, of parts-to-whole relationship in which a complex series of nodes and paths binds our world together in geopolitical regions and overlapping geopolitical realms that are increasingly specialized and integrated. Such a system provides for alternative lines of interaction, and therefore for global policy options.

Calling attention to an ignorance of geography is a necessary but not sufficient condition for improving the American public's state of geographical knowledge. That required long-term commitment by both universities and schools to educating an entire generation, something that cannot be done piecemeal. Research in the university must be linked to 4th grade home geography—or to an elective in a global sequence at grades 10 and 11—or to an introductory college course for prospective teachers.

Although state governments, private organizations, the Congress, and the executive branch of government provided new impetus for geography in the schools, success depends ultimately upon parallel and more fundamental commitment at the university level. The renewal of public interest in geography presents a major challenge for all educational sectors to act cooperatively in restoring this nation to geographical literacy and scientific progress.

This is an opportunity for all of us to work together. The purpose is not to trivialize geography as the memorization of place names, but to understand and promote its role as a mature field of humanistic and scientific study that has an important role to play in helping to educate and enlighten citizens and their leaders in this interdependent world.

Note: This paper was delivered originally at Western Michigan University, Kalamazoo, Michigan, on November 20, 1987, as part of the observance of National Geography Awareness Week.

Saul B. Cohen is cochair of the Governor's School and Business Alliance, President Emeritus of Queens College, and University Professor of Geography at Hunter College and the City University of New York.

(Courtesy © *National Council for the Social Studies.* Used with permission.)

QUESTIONS ON READING

1. How does geographic "illiteracy" impact work life and the American economy?

2. If you were to draw a map of the world, what would you place at its center?

LESSON PLANS

Diane Dressel   First Grade
Objective: The effect of changes in the seasons upon our dress and behavior.

Rationale: The aim of the lesson is to make students more sensitive and observant of how changes in the environment impact human behavior.

Activities:

1. Several days prior to beginning lesson, teacher will display pictures of seasons on bulletin board. Students will discuss pictures and label each one. Teacher will pictorially chart weather and lead discussion about weather and time of the year.

2. Several activities will be done to fit into time of the year. In winter, students will check weather page of newspaper and record sunrise and sunset over a two-month period. In spring, they will record temperature or rainfall.

3. Throughout the year students will study several trees near or on the school grounds to identify changes. Class will visit school library and read books about leaves and how leaves change according to the seasons.

4. In winter, class will draw pictures of trees or collect frozen leaves. They will attempt to plant seeds in winter as well as the spring and compare differences in outcomes.

5. Teacher will read *A Year of Birds* by Ashley Wolff as an introduction to the impact of weather upon animals. Students will discuss their own feelings as the weather and seasons change. Students will draw pictures of animals in relation to the time of the year.

6. Teacher will divide class into groups and ask them to develop lists of activities for each season.
    *   Teacher will display various items such as rakes, seeds, skates, beach ball, etc. Students will walk to music and when music stops, the teacher will name a season. Students then pick up items that fit the season.

7. Students will be asked to draw pictures of themselves according to the season of the year and list activities they would do in the season.

Extension Activities:

1. Students share poems for each season.

2. Students write about their favorite season indicating which of their five senses comes most into play.

3. Class will write and illustrate a "Four Seasons Book" including poems, pictures, and stories.

4. Students will create paper dolls with changing clothes for each of the four seasons.

5. Students collect pictures from magazines and sort them into appropriate columns for the season of the year.

6. Students and teacher construct a time line indicating holidays throughout the year.

7. Students identify a nation in another part of the world such as Africa, Asia, or the southern half of South America. They will study the weather in those nations as compared to weather in their own neighborhood.

Bibliography:

Adams, Richard, *Nature Through the Seasons*.
Allen, Marjorie and Rotner, Shelley, *Changes*.
Bancroft, Henrietta, *Animals in Winter*.
Bennett, David, *Seasons*.
Fisher, Aileen, *I Like Weather*.
Gordon, S., *First Day of Spring*.
Ichikawa, Satomi, *A Child's Book of Seasons* (poetry).
Livingston, Myra, *A Circle of Seasons*.
Parker, Bertha, *Spring is Here*.
Provensen, Alice, *A Book of Seasons*.

Cozetta Vernell   Spec. Ed. K-3

Objective: To increase children's awareness of their senses and bodies.

Rationale: The sense of touch, sight, haring, and smell are windows for children into the world. We learn through our senses.

Activities:

1. Teacher has glasses filled with different types of juices. Each child drinks at least two different types of juice. The child has to use at least two words to describe the difference in taste of the juices.

2. Teacher has an array of objects such as a bar of soap, peanuts, apples, cheese, etc. Students smell the objects.
   - In groups students identify a place they like which has interesting smells—a bakery. They draw pictures and place words that sound like the smell on their pictures.

3. Students are asked to bring in interesting objects that have an interesting touch.
   - Students are paired off. Pair touch several objects and attempt to guess what they are.
   - Students draw pictures of the object that is most interesting and place descriptive words inside the picture.

4. Teacher places an array of objects of differing sizes and colors on the desk.
   - Students in pairs describe an object by its size, color and use. The rest of the class has to guess what is being described.

5. Teacher brings in various musical instruments and things that make sounds.
   - Students in pairs have to guess the sound that is being made. If it is a musical instrument they must guess name of instrument.
   - Several objects are hidden. One group of children makes a sound from the hidden object and the other group has to guess the object.

6. Students put on a play using sight, sound, smell, size and color to demonstrate their learning.

Bibliography:

Brandenberg, Aliki, *My Five Senses,* Harper & Row, N.Y. 1989.

Gibson, Myra Tomback, *What Is Your Favorite Thing to Hear?*
Grosset and Dunlop, N.Y. 1966.

Moncure, Jane, *The Look Book,* Children's Press, Chicago, 1982.

Moncure, Jane, *The Touch Book,* Children's Press, Chicago, 1982.

Moncure, Jane, *What Your Nose Knows,* Children's Press, Chicago, 1982.

Perkinds, Al, *The Ear Book,* Random House, N.Y. 1968.

Smith, Kathie Ellingslea, *Seeing,* Troll Associates, Mahwah, 1988.

Smith, Kathie Ellingslea, *Smelling,* Troll Associates, Mahwah, 1988.

Smith, Kathie Ellingslea, *Tasting,* Troll Associates, Mahwah, 1988.

Smith, Kathie Ellingslea, *Touching,* Troll Associates, Mahwah, 1988.

Jill Bartam   Primary Grades
Objective: The four seasons and ways to preserve the environment.

Rationale: Students need to learn at an early age how nature, humans, and the environment interact with one another.

Activities:

1. Teacher shows several objects such as ice skates, mittens, swim cap, sweater, rake, seed packet, kite, baseball, etc. Children tell how and why items are used.
   - Teacher writes word, "seasons" on board. Students in groups list seasonal words and activities.
   - Students create a mural depicting the current season and its activities.

2. Teacher holds up pictures depicting trees at different times of the year, hills covered with snow and grass. Students in groups categorize the pictures.
   - Each group selects one item, e.g., a tree, and depicts how it looks throughout the year.

3. Teacher tells class the following story: "It was a cold winter day when four children decided to go for a hike in the woods. They brought along a small box of raisins and a thermos of water. They found a cave and explored it. Later, they came out of the cave. It had snowed several inches, and the children were not certain in which direction to head for home. The food and water would not last long. How might these children survive in the woods until help came?"
   - Students in groups come up with a survival plan and share with the class.
   - Teacher asks groups: "Come up with suggestions how people can help animals during the seasons of the year." Students make list of foods they could feed animals in different seasons of the year.

4. Teacher shows photos of people littering a park.
   - In groups students identify how littering will create environmental problems in each season of the year. Students brainstorm ways to deal with the littering problem.

5. Teacher shows pictures of children in other parts of the world doing various seasonal activities.
   - Students in groups are to create a short story about an activity a child in another culture might do in winter or summer or fall or spring. They are to research the culture.

6. Teacher and class examine songs in order to identify information about the seasons of the year. "Mary Had a Little Lamb" or "Twinkle, Twinkle Little Star" will be sung and then closely examined for clues about seasons and environment.
   - Students in groups will write a song telling about ways to protect the environment.
   - Same groups will write a poem to go with a season of the year.

Bibliography:

Allison, Linda, *The Reasons for Seasons,* Yolla Bolly Press, 1973.
Breiter, Herta, *Weather,* MacDonald-Raintree Inc., 1978.
Day, Jennifer, *What is a Tree?,* Golden press, 1975.
Forrai, Maria, *A Look at the Environment,* Lerner Publications, 1976.
Hollander, John, *The Wind and the Rain,* Doubleday & Co., 1961.
James, E.O., *Seasonal Feasts and Festivals,* Barnes & Noble, 1961.
Sechrist, Elizabeth, *One Thousand Poems for Children,* Macrae-Smith, 1946.

REFERENCES

Commager, H.S. (1965). *The Nature and Study of History.* p. 1. Columbus, OH: Merrill.

Forsyth, E. (1964). *Map reading.* Normal, Washington, DC: National Council for Geographic Education.

Hunt, L. (1965). *Map skills project book III.* New York: Scholastic Book Services.

Kemball, W. (1989, December). The objectives of geographic education. *NASSP Bulletin, 16,* p. 15–18.

Mitchell, L. S. (1963). *Young geographers.* New York: Bank Street.

Schwartz, R. *Mathematics and global survival.* Cited in A. Forsyth, Successfully integrating geography: The front door approach and the back door approach. *Social Education* (1992, October), p. 324.

Stopsky, F., Madgic, R. and Teaburg, S. (1975). *The American experience.* Reading, MA: Addison Wesley.

Zirschky, E. D. (1989, July). Traffic light geography. *Journal of Geography,* p. 44–46.

SUGGESTED READING

Bell, N. (1982). *The book of where or how to be naturally geographic.* Boston: Little Brown.

Getis, J., & Getis, A. (1982). *Geography.* Boston: Houghton Mifflin.

Knapp, B., & Codrington, S. (1987). *Themes in geographic development.* Melbourne: Longman Cheshire.

Rowland-Entwistle, T. (1988). *The pop-up atlas of the world: A globe in a book.* New York: Simon & Schuster.

Staff. (1984). *Guidelines for geographic education.* Washington: National Council for Geographic Education.

Stanley, L. (1982). *Where it's at: Geography for the quick.* New York: KAV Books.

Vuicich, G. (1974). *Geography in elementary and secondary education.* Boulder, CO: Social Science Education Consortium.

Chapter 13

The Social Sciences and Student Action Research

Years ago, it was commonly believed that science was a discipline in which people patiently collected facts from nature and objectivley reported them. The conclusions of science were supposed to be nothing more than the summary of facts. Actually, scientists record what they judge to be important and leave out what is not important. One day, another scientist makes a new judgment, and this can create a new theoretical model that changes our view of the universe. The social sciences, like other sciences, deal with approximations made by people who are intimately involved and perceive through their own biases and perceptions of reality.

The social sciences collect facts, but these are selected facts, and the manner in which they are selected depends upon the conceptual organization of the inquiry. Sociologists, anthropologists, psychologists, and political scientists are continually involved in the process of interpreting data through the prism of their discipline, personalities, and mind-sets.

A political scientist examining the Constitutional Convention of 1789 would be interested in the political thought processes of participants. A sociologist would be interested in ways culture or family shaped the thinking of the Founding Fathers, while a psychologist might be interested in how personality influenced ideas of the participants. Social scientists begin the inquiry seeking facts pertinent to their discipline. Different disciplines have different conceptual frames, seek different kinds of data, and formulate their respective bodies of knowledge in widely different forms. It is not uncommon, however, for social scientists to begin from different points but reach similar conclusions.

The differences among the social sciences are fascinating because they introduce students to various phenomena and cast a different focus on similar issues of concern. Modern social scientific inquiry tends to seek patterns—patterns of change or patterns of relationships—as their explanatory principles. A pattern may throw a new and more revealing light on how items were previously understood. The social sciences enable teachers and students to expand their focus from lists and factual data to broader issues of human behavior.

The social sciences contain several conflicting theories about the nature of knowledge or of human behavior. It is sometimes difficult for young children to reach into social science's collection of knowledge and extract information that would be useful in pursuing a current interest. Students come to the task with limited learning competencies making it extremely difficult to intelligently separate bits of data from the structure of the discipline and put that information to productive use. As Joseph Schwab (1969) suggests, "In brief, truth is a complicated matter. The conceptual structure of a discipline determines what we shall seek the truth about and in what terms that truth shall be couched" (p. 12).

The social sciences in elementary school education are not simply a body of information to be mastered. Children live and practice the social sciences in their everyday lives. The child is born into a family, experiences a variety of cultures, and lives the content of sociology, psychology, political science, and economics. The tasks of the social sciences in elementary school are to help children clarify what they experience and translate into action what they seek to attain.

This chapter first provides an overview of the social sciences. Then it presents a methodology that enables students to become observers and practitioners of social change. For young children, understandings from the social sciences that enable meaningful participation in their homes, schools, and neighborhood societies are most productive and meaningful. Practical knowledge is more beneficial to students than content knowledge per se, and this should be the focus of elementary social studies.

Sociology

The relationships of elements in society are the most important understandings for children to gain. Sociology deals with the study of social phenomena ranging from the family, communities, and crime to the way we dress, speak, and enjoy our leisure activities. The sociologist is interested in events as they exemplify social processes resulting from the interaction and association of humans in various situations and under various conditions. The sociologist seeks to uncover patterns underlying human behaviors, and the social arrangements through which values gain their force.

Social patterns are visible because human social behavior is repetitive. The result is stability in social structures and routinization of life. Sociologists are interested in the origin and persistence of social structures. They are also interested in the linkage between social structures and how change occurs within them.

A major research area in sociology is the institution of the family. The rise of dual-career and single-parent families has furthered interest in the impact of modern family patterns upon behavior of children. The psychologist might be more interested in personality formation than the sociologist, who seeks to uncover group processes and interactions within the family.

It has been said that history occupies itself with the differences in similar events, whereas sociology is concerned with similarities in different events. The sociologist is more concerned with the phenomena of revolution than with uncovering the causes of a particular revolution. Sociology helps students perceive the patterns of human behavior and the recurring cycles of events and actions.

▲ Practical knowledge is more beneficial to students than content knowledge. *Courtesy University City (Missouri) Public Schools.*

Sociology focuses on the nature of groups to which individuals belong and the nature of the societies in which they live. The study of local communities, crime, juvenile delinquency, and even schools are major targets of inquiry for sociologists, who seek to uncover patterns of behavior.

These topics deal with the world of the child and provide raw materials from which students can gain greater understanding of how they function within groups and how their local institutions of family, school, and neighborhood impact their everyday lives. The study of sociology enables students to grasp several key ideas:

- Groups are the central organizing body of humans.
- Families differ, but they are a basic institution found in all human societies.
- People in modern societies work, learn, and engage in leisure activities within organizational structures.

Anthropology

In the early years of the 20th century, anthropology was concerned primarily with the study of nonliterate cultures scattered about the world in jungles, deserts, and forests. Anthropologists were interested in how modern humans "got this way," and why one society became a monarchy while another was communal in nature. Since the end of World War II, anthropologists have widened their scope to include industrial societies as well as the nonliterate.

Anthropologists explore the structure and artifacts of society. This requires anthropologists to cross over into different disciplines as they examine culture, literature, technology, societal organization, medicine, and political structure. They seek universals in human behavior and societal structures. According to Clyde Kluckhohn (1949, p. 3), it is the task of anthropologists "to record the variations and the similarities in human physique, in the things people make, in ways of life." He believes only when we understand how humans confront problems in different ways will we understand what humans have in common.

Although most current anthropology literature is written for the professional anthropologist, there is a growing movement to make anthropology more visible to the general public by examining issues and phenomena of mainstream societies and cultures. Anthropology provides a special lens through which we can view our society with a fresh perspective.

Anthropologists increasingly are integrating ideas from psychology, sociology, and archeology to examine contemporary cultures. Modern communication easily transmits cultural mores throughout the world, but anthropologists are interested in how cultural groups maintain their identities in the face of changes in dress, speech, and occupations.

In an age of rapid change it is important to step outside our own culture in order to see ourselves from different perspectives. We are too much caught up in who we are to see how we have come to be or how we can change societal directions. Anthropology can assist students to understand several key concepts about human existence:

▲ It is important to step outside our own culture in order to see ourselves from different perspectives. *Courtesy Webster University.*

- Each society has one or more cultures. In modern times, these cultures increasingly incorporate values and ideas from other cultures.
- Each society deals with basic human needs, but addresses them in different ways.
- To understand American culture, we must trace its antecedents from the past.
- Societies are always in the process of change. It is necessary to study present culture to understand future changes.

Political Science

Political science relates to the study of how government bodies function in the governance of human societies. This entails concern for electoral processes, decision-making processes, the organization of government bodies, and political leadership within a society. A basic function of political science is to examine how societies allocate values, power, and resources. Political science issues within an educational context pertain to policy procedures within schools and legal constraints imposed by outside governmental bodies upon school systems.

Political scientists describe the legal structure of society, analyze how policies are made, trace the historical heritage of political systems, and suggest new ways in which government can improve the quality of life for its citizens. Robert Dahl (1963) defines a political system as "any persistent pattern of human relationships that involves, to a significant extent, power, rule or authority" (p. 6). The school exemplifies issues of power, rule, and authority.

Political science provides a framework for students to understand how their own lives are directed and controlled by governmental procedures. It enables them to see the difference between the form of any governmental entity and its reality. The study of political science provides students several key understandings:

- All groups of humans are governed by formal and informal rules and regulations.
- Each individual is entitled to due process procedures to ensure that everyone has equal opportunity and equal protection under the laws.
- Law allows people to solve conflicts without resort to violence.
- Democracy enables humans to achieve the fullest access to participation in government and involvement in determining future directions of their lives.

Economics

Economics is concerned with the process by which humans create and exchange products, organize the financial interactions of society, and achieve occupational identities. Economics also has to do with the way individuals are allocated to certain roles and status positions in society. It is the social science that most obviously affects the daily lives of children.

A key concept that frequently is stressed in elementary school economics education is that of scarcity. Children believe adults have access to unlimited amounts of money. They are unfamiliar with the idea that allocating financial resources to one item might preclude obtaining another item. Children want money given to the homeless or poor and are not aware of economic considerations affecting problems of homelessness or poverty in our society.

There are several key economic ideas that ordinarily are taught in elementary school:

- Economics deals with issues pertaining to choice. Each choice carries consequences.
- There is an imbalance between wants and resources available to attain goals.
- People work to meet their economic needs and to find personal satisfaction.
- A market economy derives from choices made by consumers regarding allocation and production of resources.
- Service occupations rather than factory work are now the dominant mode of work in American society.

Psychology

Psychology is the social science discipline most concerned with personality development. Its major focus is upon the individual and how a person's attitudes and values develop. Psychology offers new perspectives on the manner in which individual personality affects how people make decisions.

Psychology in the elementary school aids children in dealing with basic questions: "Who am I?" and "How did I become who I am?" Its primary focus for young children is upon the attainment of healthy self-concepts and insights into ways youngsters can be more effective in dealing with conflict in their lives.

There are several key ideas that are usually emphasized in psychology programs for younger children:

- Personal self-actualization.
- Learning about self in order to learn about others.
- Understanding how different personalities view the same things or issues.
- The impact of personality upon ways we employ the five senses.
- The importance of accepting and respecting individual differences.

The social sciences for children relate more with "doing" than obtaining information. Children are, by nature, social beings who seek to understand themselves and the adult world. They need opportunities to utilize the tools of the social sciences in meaningful ways that enlarge their grasp of the social environment that constitutes their daily lives.

It is only recently that teachers are beginning to explore how the methodologies of the social sciences can be transformed into more effective ways of engaging students in civic education. There are excellent curriculum materials that help students obtain a more realistic awareness of contemporary issues and problems. Education also occurs outside schools, and other agencies are also engaged in the educative process. An exciting civic education program combines a variety of strategies including opportunities for students to function as change agents.

Civic education involves making students aware of their own personal connectedness to the larger world around them. A sense of civic awareness requires a capacity to discover what is common amidst all the diversity of interests in a pluralistic society like our own. People who are civic minded seek to connect with others in making society a more humane place. Failing in that, we would be what the Greeks called "idiots." The term was not used to describe people of low intelligence but those who understand only their private worlds.

Action research is one such strategy which uses the tools of the social sciences to more actively involve students in learning about problems of their school and community, and developing ways to move from a knowledge base to an action design. It moves civic education from the realm of discussion and analysis towards some form of action. Action research is designed to make students active participants in creating a democratic environment within their school and community.

Action Research

Within the social sciences, action research transcends the boundaries of individual disciplines. Because it is widely used across the social sciences as a means to discover, construct, and apply knowledge, action research is an effective means for students to understand the content and to experience the process of the social sciences.

The phrase "action research" was coined by Kurt Lewin in the 1950's to describe the research methodology he was developing. Drawing from the work Lewin initiated, Carr and Kemmis (1986) define action research as:

a form of self-reflection enquiry undertaken by participants in social situations in order to improve the rationality and justice of their own practices, their understanding of these practices, and the situations in which the practices are carried out. (p. 162)

Action research, then, has two basic purposes: to *improve* and to *involve*. Improvement focuses on three areas: to improve practice; to improve participant's understanding; and to improve the situation in which the practice occurs. Involvement is equally important as improvement. Action research must be initiated by individuals directly involved in the practice to be considered. Participants must be involved in every aspect of research. As the project continues, the cycle becomes a widening spiral including in the research process more of those affected by the practice.

In order to be viewed as action research a project must meet three requirements. First, the focus of research must be a social practice that can be analyzed both in terms of its effectiveness and according to ethical criteria. In other words, action research attempts to answer two questions: Does the action accomplish the intended purpose? And are the consequences of the action good, worthy, and just? The social practice that is the focus of the project must offer the possibility of improvement.

Second, action research must begin as a cycle of planning, acting, observing, and reflecting. If the process stops there, however, it cannot be regarded as action research. The project must progress from the initial loop to a spiral of cycles that develops into a more participatory and collaborative process of reflection and improved practice.

Third, action research is not the work of objective observers, but of insiders—genuine participants in the practice to be examined. Participants must be involved in the action research cycle, gradually widening participation to include others affected by the practice. Participants maintain collaborative control of both the practice being examined and the action research project.

Action research offers students meaningful involvement in the process of social change. Student action research projects enable youngsters to view themselves not just as products of social, cultural, economic, political, and historical forces, but as active participants who shape these processes. As students collaborate to improve their own actions, understanding, and situations, they create classroom models for rational and democratic societies.

▲ The social sciences help children clarify what they experience and translate into action what they seek to attain. *Courtesy Kirkwood (Missouri) School District.*

Student Action Research

Student action research programs provide students at all grade levels opportunities to translate knowledge into action. Instead of just studying the meaning of sociology, political science, anthropology, or psychology, they can use the skills of these social sciences to improve the quality of life within their environment. Student action research exemplifies what John Dewey urged when he called for schools to be social agents for the reconstruction of society.

Organizing student action research entails several developmental stages to prepare children for new roles as agents of change.

Posing Questions

Children are naturally curious, and they ask many questions such as "Why is the sky blue?" or "Why are some people poor?" out of natural curiosity. These inquisitive questions are the child's entry point into the complex world of adulthood.

Sometimes, through questions children can accidentally stumble into social problems. A group of first graders in Hamburg, Germany were on a field trip to a hospital when one inquired why there was only one person in some rooms, but in other rooms there were many people. The child had innocently raised a fundamental question about health care and its relationship to socioeconomic status. Many student action research projects originate from such unplanned questions.

When teachers ignore or dismiss such complex questions or provide simplistic answers, they discourage students from exploring and investigating topics that genuinely interest them. Student action research encourages teachers and students to seize questions as launch pads for student-initiated projects.

Statement of the Problem or Issue

Once the class is aware of a question and reacts to it, there is need to move toward clarification of the issues at stake. A child who says, "How come I have to stay after school, but Mary gets to go home?," is inquiring into the nature of school detention policies. A teacher can assist the class to identify the problem by posing, "Is the issue, what are school discipline policies and how are they put into practice?"

Identify Sources of Information

After clearly stating the problem, it is necessary for students to begin the process of identifying potential sources of information that will aid in responding to the issues. Books, magazines, personal interviews, newspapers, television programs, graveyard headstones, a pond, a forest, or a city street can all be important sources of data depending on the problem being studied.

Gather Information

A child in an English rural school mentioned in class that, while at a funeral, she noticed that many headstones indicated the persons had died in 1919. A class discussion focused on the topic of whether many people from the village had died in 1919 and what could be the cause. The class charted and graphed data obtained from headstones, interviewed local people, examined local newspaper records, did headstone etchings, and consulted encyclopedias. They learned that an influenza epidemic had been widespread in 1919. While gathering information, students should review all potential sources, because even what may be considered unimportant can eventually play a role in the conclusions.

▲ Graveyard
headstones can
be important
sources of data.
*Courtesy Robert
Tabscott, Elijah
Lovejoy Society.*

Visualize the Information

Elementary age children learn visually. They learn best when a combination of media are used, which include pictures and other graphics. Charts, graphs, pictures and maps are important means of presenting data obtained from research. A group of California children created bar graphs to depict places of origin and dates of death for people in their community from 1848 to 1858. The graphs helped to clarify that most of the original settlers of the community were from eastern states.

▲ Headstone rubbings or etchings offer valuable historic data. *Courtesy Robert Tabscott, Elijah Lovejoy Society.*

Analyze Information

In the analytical phase of investigation, students identify patterns or clusters of data in order to pinpoint key factors. One group of fifth-grade students studied at what time of the day teachers reported the highest incidence of discipline problems. Their bar graphs and interviews pinpointed the time at approximately 10:30 A.M. This information helped focus attention on a key factor in the study.

Formulate Conclusions

Action research directs students toward conclusions in order to move further into the next stage of change. Students who examined the discipline issue concluded that teacher and student fatigue were key factors in morning discipline problems. They observed that many children stayed up late or skipped breakfast, and teachers rose early to attend to their family needs. It appeared that in this school, lunch and recess gave teachers and students an opportunity to deal with fatigue. On many occasions, members of the class may differ regarding conclusions, but this can generate healthy discussion and provide new thought for further research.

▲ A forest may provide needed data for action research. *Courtesy University City (Missouri) Public Schools.*

Action Planning

Student action research is both an academic experience and a mandate for action to improve the quality of life within the school. It should culminate in some form of action planning to carry out the conclusions of the material studied. These plans could range from having health food bars in candy machines to discovering new ways to keep the lunchroom clean. Action plans provide students a sense that they do make a difference in improving the school as a place for healthy living.

Implementation

The implementation phase enables students to learn about and practice the process of moving from a plan to action. This might require interacting with teachers, school administrators, parents, or outside groups in order to translate ideas into action. Implementation provides students access to negotiation skills, compromise, and resolution of conflict processes.

The essential model of action research concerns itself with four key moments. Carr and Kemmis (1986) believe Action Research is a self-reflective spiral consisting of: (a) a plan; (b) an act; (c) observation; and (d) reflection. The ability to be self-reflective is among the most important attributes children can gain from schooling. It enables them to gain a dynamic understanding of the past and present in order to move forward in a constructivist stance. Through self-reflection, student action researchers move from being passive receivers to creators of a more humane and positive environment.

Classroom Action Research Projects

Each classroom is a microcosm of American society. Students reflect diverse ethnic and socioeconomic backgrounds. Their lives and those of parents are case studies dealing with the meaning of work, the nature of family life, health, or how we participate in leisure activities.

Family history offers an interesting opportunity to explore cultural diversity. Each family history is a tale concerning how America came to be and the people who played a role in its creation. Action research projects within the classroom can involve:

▲ Family history offers an interesting opportunity to explore cultural diversity. *Courtesy Webster University.*

- Maping birthplaces of parents or other family members.
- Investigating nations of origin, year of arrival, or initial jobs held by ancestors upon arrival in America.
- Studying leisure activities of people in the past.

Textbooks and reading materials are a rich source of topics for student investigation. They can be studied to obtain a clearer understanding of gender or cultural bias and its impact upon young minds.

- How are young girls depicted in children's stories?
- How are ethnic groups portrayed?
- Which roles do mothers and fathers portray in children's literature?

These questions can initiate a variety of activities, including discussions, charting, graphing, and writing. The class, as part of its implementation phase, might write publishers or authors in hope of changing literature to reflect ethnic and gender diversity. They can also meet with the school district's textbook committee to discuss their concerns regarding textbook adoptions. This might lead to placing students on textbook committees, which would enable them to play a more forceful role in determining the educational process as it affects their daily lives in school.

School Topics for Action Research

The school is an exciting piece of Americana. In some cities such as Los Angeles or New York, ten or more language groups can be found in a single school. The school and its policies and procedures mirror many issues confronting other organizations in our society.

There are many topics that lend themselves to student action research. The students, teachers, administrators, and the organizational structure reflect issues confronting society. For example, the following topics concerning teachers would be informative to students:

- Years of teaching experience.
- College degrees held by teachers.
- State or country of origin of teachers.
- Age of teachers.
- Ethnicity of teachers.
- Gender of teachers

Discipline is frequently the major topic of discussion among educators and parents. It is surprising how few action research projects on discipline have been initiated within schools. We know a great deal about the general topic of discipline, but few individual schools have concrete data about their own situations. A class project could investigate several of the following topics:

- Number of students in detention by the day, week, or month.
- Variety of ways in which students are disciplined.
- Which form of misbehavior leads to which form of discipline?
- Relationship of absenteeism, grades, ethnicity, or gender to discipline.
- Which hour, day, week or month has the lowest or highest incidence of discipline problems?

After completion of these studies, students could share their information with teachers, school administrators, or even the school board. It would provide an opportunity for students to play a vital role in dealing with discipline problems in a school.

Teachers may identify many problems in school, such as excessive paperwork. Instead of complaints, these topics can be turned over to student action research teams for further investigation. How can students play a role in assisting teachers to use time more effectively? Students can gather important data that is probably not readily available to school districts. For example, students in an elementary school collected data on this form:

▲ Locating birthplaces of ancestors is a valuable lesson in diversity.
Courtesy University City (Missouri) Public Schools.

Activity	Minutes
Daily Attendance Forms	
Collection of Money	
Documenting Discipline Problems	
Writing Notes Home to Parents	
Lunchroom Duties	
Supervision of Toilet and Corridors	

The data furnished by this survey provided teachers and administrators new information. It enabled students to discuss with teachers how they could assume responsibility for relieving teachers of tasks that took them away from teaching.

Community

Schools are located within communities. The community can be the area near the school, a town, a suburb, or a section of a city. The specific geographic, environmental, or demographic factors of the community influence the direction of student action research projects.

A small town offers opportunities to study changes in the natural habitat. A suburban area lends itself to investigating facilities available for youth while an urban community might lend itself to a study of pollution or trash collection. Each community offers varying problems or interesting issues to be examined. It is not uncommon for students to have a grasp of the issues facing their local community.

Use the following strategies to identify key issues facing the local community of your school:

- Brainstorm with students about community issues.
- Visit fire departments, police stations, recreation facilities, and business people and have students ask about their greatest concerns.
- Have students survey their parents about local concerns.
- Have students examine local newspapers to identify issues.

A student study of a local community concern can lead to newspaper or television coverage of their results. In many communities, cable television provides community access for programs of local concern. Students can use a camcorder to create programs or program segments to be shown on these community access channels.

The Family as a Focus for Student Action Research

The family is for the child the center of life and the major source of feeling positively or negatively about the self. Today's children live in a variety of family situations. In a recent glance at *TV Guide,* over 20 forms of family were identified that encompassed a wide variety of family types. Ironically, due to mobility or lack of frequent contact with grandparents, many children lack access to traditional sources of family history—their elders.

The study of one's family is an exciting opportunity for children to "enter" the past in a personal way. Every child has a family history even if the child is currently in a single-parent situation or living with a grandparent. Adopted children, however, may lack access to their personal past, but teachers can identify alternatives such as studying foster parents or an adult whose life is of interest to the child. Research into family heritage enables the child to realize that a social studies book is referring to real people like a grandparent or a relative who served in a war being studied. The personalization of the past or present makes social studies more relevant for children.

Student action research into family history is multidisciplinary in nature because the child is engaged in reading, interviewing, examining pictures or drawings, and hearing the music of another era. It is also a bonding process that ties the child to a world that exists only in the minds or behaviors of their elders.

There are several stages in organizing a student action research project about family history. As an anticipatory set, a teacher might share with children something about his or her own family history. Children are vitally interested in the lives of teachers and welcome learning something about this significant figure in their lives. The initial sharing experience enables the class to begin discussing something about their families and what they know or don't know about their family past. Once the groundwork has been laid to create interest in the project, teachers should consider these five stages:

- Each child identifies a family member who will serve as an entry point into the journey of discovering the past. If, for some reason, a child is unable or unwilling to identify a family member, they can be encouraged to study the family history of any adult.
- Children develop tools for the investigation. This may include creating an interview form, identifying questions to pose, or resource material such as newspapers, magazines, albums, etc.
- Children conduct interviews, examine old photograph albums or newspapers, listen to records, view movies or read books discussing the period under study.
- Students analyze the data they have collected in order to reach conclusions or to organize the process of their family history. This involves putting together a way to present their findings.
- Presentation of material to the class is an important phase of the process. Students usually are interested in one another's lives. An exciting presentation can be of vital importance in educating class members about an aspect of the past.

A frequent byproduct of family history in student action research is exposing children to the connection between global issues and their own family members. A grandparent could have served in World War II, or a great-grandparent might have passed through Ellis Island in the heyday of European immigration. A parent could have witnessed a Martin Luther King speech in person or be able to personally remember the assassination of John F. Kennedy.

The intimacy of family experiences stimulates concern among students about gaining further knowledge. A grandmother who can recount working in a World War II factory may be able to open new ideas about issues pertaining to women's rights and changes in family structures. The elders of our society lived at a time when pollution took a different form or juvenile gangs engaged in nondrug-related crime. They can help present-day students understand the process of change and hopefully suggest new ways to improve future directions of society.

Learning about the history of families provides several new ways for children to understand about family life. First, there is new knowledge about the past and the world of their ancestors. Second, there is a more sensitive understanding of their own family situation. Third, there is realization that global issues are, in essence, family and individual issues. Examples can be drawn from family histories which aid students in their endeavors to improve their own, their local community's, and the world's quality of life.

There are many other ways family history can be incorporated within existing curriculum topics. For example:

- Utilize a Cinderella story from their own family history in which an individual overcame poverty or neglect to become successful, and compare that tale with the story of Cinderella.
- Use family history stories about migration in connection with a social studies unit on immigration.
- Recount the story of a relative who was a whaler, trapper, hunter, or lumberman in the context of rising world awareness and concern for endangered species.

- Use pictures from family albums to illustrate a period of the past.
- Gather information about educational experiments in the past and share them with teachers in hope of incorporating some of the ideas within the school.

The linkage of family histories with academic topics and social concerns can be a powerful tool in motivating students to become active participants in learning and social change. It can give new meaning to the idea of multiculturalism by demonstrating that each child represents an ethnic thread in the history of the United States. Student action research into family pasts forms new bonds between class members that transcend academic activities in the classroom.

When children share family stories they discover common themes in their family backgrounds. This leads to improved understanding of one another and fosters feelings of empathy. Some of these connections would not otherwise have come about because of different ethnic backgrounds, cliques or academic standings. Students can not only learn about similarities among themselves, but can gain new understanding about similarities in experiences among people of all societies.

Civic education is among the most important components of the elementary social studies curriculum. It is the place where students are first introduced in a systematic manner to the moral, social, and political dilemmas of their society. Action research can assist teachers in stimulating student motivation to become active participants in furthering the democratic process. It should be used as one of many strategies to bring alive to students the issues our nation has confronted, and continues to face as we seek ways to improve the quality of life for all citizens.

. . . .

SUMMARY

This chapter has reviewed the place of social sciences in social studies and explored ways to employ action research to further civic education among students.

QUESTIONS

1. What would most interest a sociologist, a psychologist, an economist, an anthropologist, and a political scientist about a presidential campaign?

2. The authors state that "children live and practice the social sciences in their everyday lives." Cite examples from your life to illustrate this idea.

3. Make a list of all social groups to which you belong. Compare and contrast your group memberships with other class members. How would a sociologist or economist interpret the data?

4. Which artifacts from our present society would most interest an anthropologist living in the year 3000?

5. How do government decisions and procedures impact your life as a student?

6. Is it possible to be an effective teacher without having a clear grasp of one's own self? Why?

7. Do you believe "action research," which strives to involve students in the improvement of the quality of life, has a place in the elementary school curriculum? Why?

8. What would be your greatest concern if students in your class investigated discipline procedures? What would you find most beneficial?

9. What is similar and different about student library research and student action research projects?

10. What would be your greatest concern if students engaged in an action research project concerning a community issue? What would you find most beneficial?

ACTIVITIES

1. Conduct an action research project related to your college.

2. Invite a government official, a school administrator and a teacher to discuss student action research.

3. Conduct a survey among elementary-age school children concerning which problems or issues most concerned them in their daily life in school.

4. Conduct a survey among parents to ascertain their reactions to student action research.

5. Develop a "Bill of Rights" for students in elementary school that would protect their rights to study social concerns.

READING

Social Reconstructionism for Today's Social Education
by William B. Stanley

William B. Stanley is an Assistant Professor at Louisiana State University at Baton Rouge

The social reconstructionist position emerged in the 1920s and reached its peak of influence during the Depression decade. The reconstructionists were a small faction on the left of the much larger progressive education movement. Eventually their views developed to the point where they were in conflict with the basic tenets of more mainstream progressives such as Dewey, Bode and Kilpatrick. A good sense of the reconstructionist position can be found in the major works of George and Theodore Brameld (Stanley, 1981a).

Although the reconstructionists were few in number, they seem to have aroused the attention and animosity of educators of all political persuasions (Bowers, 1970). for example, many conservatives viewed the reconstructionists as at best naive and at worst a dangerous, un-American influence on our educational system. On the other hand, the American communists rejected reconstructionism and criticized it as another rationalization of capitalism (pp. 22–23). Mainstream progressive educators like Dewey (1933, 1937) also rejected reconstructionism, and it appears to have had little or no influence on recent approaches to social education (Stanley, 1981b).

This background raises a fundamental question, i.e., of what possible value is reconstructionism, a position apparently rejected by most conservative, radical and mainstream social educators for over 50 years? I will try to make the case that reconstructionism, despite its detractors, is directly relevant to today's social educators. In particular, the reconstructionists addressed issues concerning ideology, indoctrination, relativism and social welfare as they relate to the process of social education. In essence, they have raised questions and made proposals of direct relevance to social education theory and practice.

The reconstructionists have made several basic points and recommendations. First, the very nature of education involves some form of imposition. Education cannot (and should not) be neutral. Second, given the inherent bias of education, it will tend to serve the interests of certain groups and not others. Third, our educational system functions mainly to transmit and reproduce the dominant status quo culture and institutional arrangements. Fourth, our dominant culture and institutions are dysfunctional in many respects and do not serve the interests of most of our people. This fact is often masked by an ideology which rationalizes the status quo and makes current conditions appear normal and better than they actually are. Finally, the schools can and should play a role to help ameliorate these conditions by assisting in the reconstruction of our culture and institutions in accordance with democratic values and social and economic justice. This requires that social education be oriented by a just theory of social welfare and that such an orientation be imposed on students. But at no time should teachers inentionally distort or suppress knowledge. Let us consider some of these views in more detail.

Education and Indoctrination

The issue of indoctrination has troubled social educators for some time. In general, the concept "indoctrination" has been viewed negatively. However, the definition of the concept allows for other interpretations. For instance, indoctrination can be defined as instruction "especially in fundamentals or rudiments" or "to imbue with a usually partisan or sectarian opinion, point of view or principle" (*Webster's New Collegiate Dictionary* 1975, p. 586). It is difficult to conceive of any educational program that instructs without promoting some partisan or sectarian views.

A number of approaches have been proposed to help avoid indoctrination or at least mediate its worst effects (Stanley, 1981b, "Indoctrination . . ."). None of these is without serious limitations. Some reject indoctrination as incompatible with a democratic society and believe we can teach without indoctrinating (pp. 201–202). For others, it is acceptable to impose the core values of our democratic culture (e.g., human dignity, basic rights, rational consent, etc.). however, there is general opposition to imposing the way such values should be applied to specific issues, e.g., job opportunities, housing or welfare (pp. 202–204).

For the reconstructionists, indoctrination was a necessary part of the educational process. Counts (1932) maintained

> that all education contains a large element of imposition, that in the very nature of the case this is inevitable, that the existence and evolution of society depend upon it, that it is consequently eminently desirable, and that the frank acceptance of this fact by the educator is a major professional obligation. (p. 12)

Counts believed that it was a myth to assert that we are born free. In fact, we are born helpless and achieve freedom through the medium of the culture. Thus the "individual is at once imposed upon and liberated" (p. 15). The same reasoning holds for our educational system.

In practice students are continually exposed to a contrived and filtered environment in classrooms. Education is compulsory and teachers must select content and instructional methods. There is no rational way to make such choices without holding certain values to establish priorities. Thus education is not a random or neutral process but purposeful and value oriented. The question, therefore, is not will we indoctrinate, but in what way and in accordance with which values and ends. Given its inherent value orientation, education will always tend to serve certain group interests and not others. Thus the reconstructionists would take issue with those social educators who would only impose a problem-solving process (e.g., Engle 1970; Goldmark 1968) or with those who would limit imposition to the core values of our culture (e.g., Oliver and Shaver 1966; Newmann 1975). These approaches to social education are well illustrated by Newmann (1975) who argued that it was never correct to try to convince students to endorse policies that would strengthen core values like rational consent. This is indefensible because it is seldom clear which policies would best serve our ends. We should teach the skills required to make policy decisions (p. 72) but not specific social or political goals, e.g., the eradication of poverty (p. 166).

Conversely, the reconstructionists believed it was necessary, where possible, to specify how core values should apply in specific situations. There were several reasons for doing this.

First, young children at the elementary level are not capable of understanding or applying complex problem-solving methods to analyze social issues. We cannot wait until students are able to reason abstractly before we start the process of social education. Second, cognition is not reducible to a mere set of skills. There is also a nonrational or affective component to the cognitive process. Children must learn to care about certain values or issues if they are to develop an interest in inquiry into social problems. This entails exposing students to social education content and methods designed to have emotional impact and to get students to care. Finally, if the problem-solving methods we are willing to impose are so effective, how is it that they have never produced any solutions worth transmitting to our youth, even on a tentative basis? In a social environment in which other institutions constantly seek to impose specific values and behavior on our young, what must students think of adult social educators who have no proposals to offer on any of today's pressing issues? This last concern is examined in more detail in the last section of this article.

Education and Cultural Reproduction

The reconstructionists argued that our schools function mainly to help reproduce our dominant culture and institutions. This is reflected in the content and values transmitted to students in classrooms and the "hidden curriculum" of schools. The same argument is made by many current "revisionist" educators (e.g., Giroux, 1981, 1983; Giroux and Penna, 1979; Anyon, 1978, 1979, 1980; Cherryholmes, 1981, 1983), and acknowledged as well by a number of "mainstream" social educators (e.g., Morrissett and Hass, 1982; Stake and Easley, 1978; Fielding, 1981; Fetsko, 1979; and Shaver, Davis and Helburn, 1979). The studies and commentary cited above indicate that the major goal of social education appears to be conservative socialization, i.e., the overt and covert indoctrination of students in our society's norms and values. This probably helps to explain the persistent resistance to reform movements in social education.

In many respects it is natural that schools, as agencies of the state, would emphasize the reproduction of the dominant culture. Certainly, one would not normally expect the schools to stand in direct opposition to our main social values and institutions. Furthermore, in a society in which the culture and institutions were progressive and democratic, cultural reproduction would be a healthy emphasis. Indeed, there is no way to maintain *any* society without a certain amount of cultural transmission and reproduction.

But the reconstructionists saw two basic problems with our tendency to overemphasize cultural reproduction. First, every culture and society is supported by an ideology, i.e., "the complex of attitudes, beliefs, ideas, purposes, and customs that express, more or less accurately and more or less systematically, the programs and practices of a culture" (Brameld, 1971, p. 395). Ideologies are a critical part of the knowledge one learns in social education. We must recognize that they are socially constructed and historically conditioned. This creates certain problems, because ideologies "do not always mirror the structures and practices of their cultures with equal accuracy" (p. 395). Furthermore, they often reflect a cultural lag as no culture or society is static, and ideologies often change "more slowly than the cultures they symbolize" (p. 395). Thus they may become outmoded and turn into a device by which a culture and "its institutions are preserved even when their effectiveness has declined" (p. 395).

Often such a lag is unintentional, a result of the difficulty of accurately assessing the need for change combined with the normal resistance to change present in most cultures. But on other occasions the resistance to change reflects the power arrangements in the culture. Certain dominant groups can be well served by status quo values and institutions. Consequently, they will work to preserve and reproduce the extant system. This requires the exercise of power, but it is also facilitated by the maintenance of an ideology that rationalizes the status quo.

In the reconstructionist view, our culture was in a state of crisis (Brameld 1971). This involved an imbalance in a number of the basic aspects of the social structure, as well as value conflicts, contradictions and discontinuities in the culture. This has resulted in confusion, loss of purpose and gradual social disintegration. Among the concrete indications of these developments are social and economic inequality and injustice, crime, drug abuse and moral decline. One major obstacle to overcoming such problems is our cultural tradition (ideology) of progress and optimism, which tends to mask these problems and conceal the abnormalities of our schizophrenic age (pp. 23–24). Thus the ideology of the dominant culture serves to rationalize dysfunctional institutions, and the schools assist in this process, possibly "unaware of the disparity between their ideological descriptions and cultural actualities" (Brameld, 1950, p. 396).

The Role of The School

Given the problems noted above the reconstructionists believed the schools must be involved in the process of transforming the culture and institutions to help ameliorate negative social conditions. However, the schools cannot merely choose to transform or transmit the culture. They must do both and constantly seek the proper balance between the two. Obviously to only reproduce the culture tends to intensify the effects of cultural lag and perpetuate dysfunctional power arrangements. Yet our culture also has many positive aspects, and these must be encouraged and reproduced.

For the schools to be effective in helping to transform our culture and institutions would require a number of conditions. First, we must develop a theory of social welfare to orient the process of social education. As Counts (1932) noted, the chief failure of progressive education was its lack of any theory of social welfare "unless it be that of anarchy or extreme individualism" (p. 7). Brameld (1956, 1971) believed that his reconstructionist ideas contained both the social orientation and epistemology necessary for initiating a new educational program for the constructive transformation of the culture. The reconstructionist position emphasized the core values of democracy and a commitment to change our economic system in ways that would result in more equality and social justice.

Brameld (1938) was influenced by Marxism and believed it to be a valuable methodology for orienting social criticism and social change. But it was not a sufficient method. The Marxist position presented an oversimplified analysis of culture by "reducing it to economic class alignments without sufficient regard for other relationships and structures" (Brameld, 1971, p. 352). It also suffered from a view of historic laws that was overly deterministic. Finally, Brameld rejected the Marxist support for the necessity of a proletarian dictatorship (p. 352). For the reconstructionists, collective ownership of the means of production was not essential, but the private economy must be regulated to help ensure full employment, economic opportunity, and adequate income for a fair standard of living (pp. 437–439). But the ultimate reconstructionist value for orienting educational change was whether or not educational "experience contributed to social-self realization" (p. 450). Social-self realization connotes "the maximum satisfaction of the wants of individuals and groups" (1956, p. 119).

A second condition for cultural transformation is the use of a critical method to penetrate the ideology of the dominant culture so that we may accurately assess the need for change. The reconstructionists emphasized the importance of social criticism to reveal the extent of cultural lag and noted the tendency of social institutions (including education) to be dominated by and function in the interests of certain groups. In addition, they used those elements of Marxism that helped to reveal the role of social class in the process of cultural domination. But a significant problem still remained. An adequate reconstructionist philosophy must provide an epistemological position that reconciled the problems related to indoctrination and relativism. The reconstructionists' attempt to resolve the apparent dilemma posed by choosing either indoctrination or relativism is perhaps their most important contribution to social education.

As noted earlier, there is a great deal of consensus regarding the tendency of mainstream social education to transmit a conservative cultural position and reproduce the status quo. This problem has been compounded by the failure of any social education reform movements to provide an adequate alternative capable of promoting meaningful social change. A major problem in this regard is connected to a flaw in the Deweyan philosophy that oriented most progressive educational reform movements. In social education, this is found in approaches based on using reflective inquiry to analyze social problems (e.g., Hunt and Metcalf 1968; Massialas and Cox 1966).

Dewey (1933) shared many of the reconstructionist concerns regarding the negative aspects of the culture and dominant institutions. However, like other progressives, he would only commit to the instrumental method of intelligence, i.e., reflective inquiry (p. 32). Should this method lead to social improvements (and he assumed it would), so much the better. But he rejected all attempts to impose preconceived conclusions or programs on students. He agreed that much of our current education involved indoctrination, but this did not "prove that the right course is to seize upon the method of indoctrination and reverse its object" (Dewey, 1937, p. 238).

The reflective inquiry process espoused by Dewey was a useful way to analyze the culture. It was open to all forms of knowledge, and no limits were set on the possible outcomes of the inquiry process. However, it also fostered an agnostic attitude toward social issues, i.e., the development of an individual "who sees all sides to every question and never commits himself to any . . . action until the facts are in" (Counts, 1932, pp. 20–21). For Counts, this was a self-defeating approach. Every social problem may have scores of possible solutions and the resolution of such problems requires selecting or rejecting values. This is not possible without a value system and a theory of social welfare. Even so, solutions would always have to be made on the basis of incomplete information.

Brameld (1936), like Counts, agreed that Dewey's progressive ideas had considerable merit but felt they must be extended. He summarized Dewey's approach as "a continuous effort to achieve satisfying adjustments with the world through painstaking analysis of obstacles, the discovery and selection of hypotheses, and the testing of those hypotheses by determining actively whether they solve the problem at hand" (p. 8). The way we view problems will shape the kinds of hypotheses we generate. There is always an interaction between problems, hypotheses and problem solutions. According to Brameld, "the more deep-rooted the social problem . . . , the more thorough-going the suggested solution, and the more vigorous the means of correction" (p. 8). Furthermore, every hypothesis oversimplifies reality and in attempting to avoid all oversimplification, one may fail to choose any hypothesis as a solution and paralyze productive effort. Such a tendency is evidenced by Dewey's followers who

> in their plastic eagerness to learn *all* the facts and to shift their objectives in accordance with their welter of interests . . . are never likely to agree that any hypothesis is sound enough to try. The gravest danger from the "objective" attitude, indeed, is that decisions, if they are reached at all, are reached too late. (p. 11)

Those who fear indoctrination are in fact blocking attempts to establish the truth of theoretical positions, which may be regarded with tentative yet enthusiastic respect. We seem to grant the natural sciences the right to gather evidence to demonstrate the validity of various hypotheses as far as possible, but deny the same right to the social sciences (Brameld, 1936, pp. 15–16). Thus Dewey's instrumentalism as applied to social education is ultimately dysfunctional when

> out of habit of fair consideration of every side of a question, we refuse to conclude that any side is sufficiently good to fight for, or any side sufficiently bad to fight against. Scientific method, despite its glorification of action, becomes an apologist for inaction when it cautiously weighs all possibilities *ad infinitum;* and a devotee of reaction when meanwhile the evils of the status quo threatened to engulf the scientist himself. (Brameld 1936, p. 131)

Brameld (1971) believed that Dewey recognized "the need for positive farsighted conclusions" (p. 162). Dewey's notion that immediate experience is "capable of becoming an intrinsically valued end provides an ontological basis for the view that intelligence mediate in behalf of such experiences" (p. 162). More important, however, is that "the test of truth lies in the consequences of thinking. Thus to argue that ends are not important along with means would be an absurd distortion" (p. 162). But the issue must not be oversimplified to a mere dichotomy between ends and means. Rather the focus should be on the point of stress. "The stress for the progressivist is upon 'how' rather than 'what,' upon process rather than product, upon hypothesis rather than commitment" (p. 163).

Brameld (1947) believed that education must move beyond the "innocuous consideration of all sides of the question" (p. 138). Instead, teachers should strive for group consensus via a process that includes the critical examination of as much evidence as possible in an environment of open communication (pp. 137–138). The tentative conclusions reached by this process would be

> "defensible partialities," i.e., partiality to crystallized ends which fuse at every point with the deepest cravings of the largest possible majority; at the same time ends exposed to the bright light of maximum evidence and public inspection of a free flow of communication (Brameld 1948, pp. 333–334).

It would be better form of pedagogy for teachers to make explicit their "defensible partialities." Students would then have the opportunity to know and examine their teachers' beliefs and the reasoning they used as they went through the process of clarifying and developing their own views on controversial issues (Brameld, 1950, p. 468).

This was the reconstructionist's way of eliminating the central weakness of the progressive approach to problem solving. They granted the importance to the reflective inquiry approach as a mechanism for discovering the truth or solving problems. But one must question "whether the centrality of problem solving as a process does not invite philosophic justification for lack of strong commitment to anything so much as the process itself" (p. 162).

Conclusions

The reconstructionists have raised a number of questions and made specific proposals for improving the process of social education as currently practiced. Many of their ideas anticipated the recent revisionist critiques of social education (see Newmann, 1984, for a brief review of such ideas), a fact often ignored by the revisionists. It is clear that after decades of social education reform we still have not resolved the problems discussed by the reconstructionists. Again, the current growth of revisionist criticism is an indication of the failure of prior reforms.

We could be at the start of a new period of reform. It is not certain how extensive such reform might be, or the direction it will take. But we should consider the history of our field (especially the history of other attempts at reform) as we engage in this process. Too often we have neglected to do this, and it appears to have contributed to the general failure of most past reforms (Nelson, 1980; Hertzberg 1982). The reconstructionists provide us with a rich source of ideas for discussion, and for the creation of new policies and practices in social education.

References

Anyon, Jean. "Elementary Social Studies Textbooks and Legitimating Knowledge." *Theory and Research in Social Education* 6 (September 1978): 40–55.

Anyon, Jean. "Ideology and United States History Textbooks." *Harvard Educational Review* 49 (August 1979): 361–386.

Anyon, Jean. "Social Class and the Hidden Curriculum of Work." *Journal of Education* 162 (Winter 1980): 67–92.

Bowers, C. A. "Social Reconstructionism: Views from the Left and the Right, 1932–1942." *History of Education Quarterly* 10 (Spring 1970).

Brameld, Theodore. "Shifting Winds in Education." *University Review* 5 (Autumn 1936).

Brameld, Theodore. "A Concluding Perspective." *Social Frontier* 4 (May 1938).

Brameld, Theodore. "Workers' Education in America." *Educational Administration and Supervision* 33 (March 1947).

Brameld, Theodore. "The Philosophy of Education as Philosophy of Politics." *School and Society* 63 (November 13, 1948).

Brameld, Theodore. *Ends and Means in Education—A Mid-Century Appraisal.* New York: Harper and Brothers, 1950.

Brameld, Theodore. *Toward a Reconstructed Philosophy of Education.* New York: Holt, Rinehart & Winston, 1956.

Brameld, Theodore. *Patterns of Educational Philosophy—Divergence and Convergence in Culturological Perspective.* New York: Holt, Rinehart & Winston, 1971.

Cherryholmes, Cleo H. "Discourse and Criticism in the Social Studies Classroom." *Theory and Research in Social Studies Education* 9 (Winter 1982): 57–73.

Cherryholmes, Cleo H. "Knowledge, Power and Discourse." *Journal of Education* (Fall 1983): 341–359.

Counts, George S. *Dare the Schools Build a New Social Order.* New York: Arno Press and the New York *Times,* 1969; John Day Company, 1932.

Dewey, John et al. *The Educational Frontier.* New York: Appleton-Century Co., 1933.

Dewey, John. "Education and Social Change," *The Social Frontier* 3 (May 1937).

Engle, Shirley H. "Decision Making: The Heart of Social Studies Instruction." *Social Education* 24 (November 1960): 301–304, 306.

Fetsko, William. "Textbooks and the New Social Studies." *Social Studies* 70 (March/April 1979): 51–55.

Fielding, Roger. "Social Education and Social Change: Constraints of the Hidden Curricula." In Irving Morrissett and Ann M. Williams, eds. *Social/Political Education in Three Countries: Britain, West Germany, and the United States.* Boulder, CO: Social Science Education Consortium and ERIC Clearinghouse for Social Studies/Social Science Education, 1981.

Fraenkel, Jack. *How to Teach About Values: An Analytical Approach.* Englewood Cliffs, NJ: Prentice-Hall, 1977.

Giroux, Henry A. *Ideology, Culture and the Process of Schooling.* Philadelphia: Temple University Press, 1981.

Giroux, Henry A. *Theory and Resistance in Education.* South Hadley, Ma: Bergin and Garvey, 1983.

Giroux, Henry A., and Anthony N. Penna. "Social Education in the Classroom: The Dynamics of the Hidden Curriculum." *Theory and Research in Social Education* 7 (Spring 1979): 21–42.

Hertzberg, Hazel W. *Social Studies Reform: 1880–1980.* Report of Project SPAN. Boulder, CO: Social Science Education Consortium, 1981.

Hunt, Maurice P., and Lawrence E. Metcalf. *Teaching High School Social Studies,* 2nd ed. New York: Harper & Row, 1968.

Massialas, Byron G., and Benjamin Cox. *Inquiry in the Social Studies.* New York: McGraw-Hill, 1966.

Morrissett, Irving, and John D. Haas. "Rationales, Goals, and Objectives in Social Studies." In *The Current State of the Social Studies: A Report of Project SPAN,* edited by Project SPAN Staff and Consultants, Boulder, CO: Social Science Education Consortium, 1982.

Nelson, Jack, L. *Introduction to Value Inquiry: A Student Process Book*. Rochelle Park, NJ: Hayden Press, 1974.

Nelson, Murry R. "Social Studies: Something Old, Something New, and All Borrowed." *Theory and Research in Social Education* 8 (Fall 1980): 51–64.

Newmann, Fred M. *Education for Citizen Action: Challenge for Secondary Curriculum*. Berkeley: McCutchan, 1975.

Newmann, Fred M. "Social Studies in U.S. Schools: Mainstream Practice and Radical Potential." Paper presented at the Annual Meeting of the Social Science Education Consortium, Irsee, Federal Republic of Germany, June, 1984.

Oliver, Donald W., and James P. Shaver. *Teaching Public Issues in the High School*. Logan, UT: Utah State University Press, 1974. (Originally published by Houghton Mifflin, 1966.)

Shaver, James P., O. L. Davis, Jr., and Suzanne W. Helburn. *An Interpretive Report on the Status of Pre-Collegiate Social Studies Education Based on Three NSF-Funded Studies*. Washington, DC: National Science Foundation, 1979.

Stake, Robert E., and Jack A. Easley, Jr. *Case Studies in Science Education*. Washington, DC: National Science Foundation, 1978.

Stanley, William B. "The Radical Reconstructionist Rationale for Social Education." *Theory and Research in Social Education* 8 (Winter 1981): 55–79.

Stanley, William B. "Indoctrination and Social Education: A Critical Analysis." *Social Education* 45, (March 1981): 200, 202–204.

Stanley, William B. "Toward a Reconstruction of Social Education." *Theory and Research in Social Education* 9 (Spring 1981): 67–89.

Webster's New Collegiate Dictionary. Springfield, Ma: G. & C. Merriam Company, 1973.

(Courtesy © *National Council for the Social Studies*. Used with permission.)

QUESTIONS ON READING

1. Restate the main arguments for and against reconstructionism.

2. To what extent should teachers consciously advocate certain values in the classroom?

3. How do student action research projects fit into Reconstructionist theory?

LESSON PLANS

Linda Kertz, Kindergarten Teacher
J.L. Mudd Elementary School
Fort Zumwalt School District,
O'Fallon, Missouri

Objective: Students will identify people and characteristics of nuclear and extended families and understand the nature of their own family.

Activities:

1. Teacher reads *Peter's Chair* by Ezra Keats (Harper & Row) which describes how Peter becomes jealous and runs away when his old furniture is repainted for his new baby sister. Prior to reading, children are asked if they have a baby brother or sister at home. Among questions asked during the story are:
   - How did Peter feel when he saw his furniture painted pink and being used by his baby sister?

- Why did Peter want to run away?
- What would you have done if your furniture was repainted for a baby sister or brother?
- Does anyone besides mother, father, Peter, and his sister live in this family? Are there any uncles, aunts, or grandparents in the family?

2. After reading the story, children draw a picture of their own family and identify its members. The next day they bring pictures of their family to share with friends.

3. Teacher reads *A Chair for My Mother* by Vera Williams (Scholastic) which is the story of how a girl's house burns down and she moves into an apartment with her mother and grandmother. She saves money to buy a chair for her mom.
   - Why did the girl's relatives and friends give things to her family?
   - How is the chair in this story like or different from the chair in Peter's story?
   - Is this an example of a nuclear or extended family?

4. Using butcher paper, graph the number of people in each child's family. Children draw a face for each family member. The class counts the number of family members for each child.

5. Teacher reads *More, More, More Said the Baby* by Vera Williams (Scholastic, 1990) which contains three "love" stories about babies and what their mother, father, or grandmother does to play with them.
   - Why would a baby say "more, more, more"?
   - Who has played with babies? What do you like about playing with babies?
   - How are all babies alike? How are they different?
   - Of the three babies alike? How are they different?
   - Are the three babies in the book, which one would you like to be? Why?
   - If you were a baby again, what are some things you would like someone in your family to do with you?

6. Children take home a sheet which has places for parents to put pictures of the child as a baby. These are shared with classmates.

7. Teacher reads *The Relatives Came* by Cynthia Rylant (Bradbury Press, 1985) which describes how Virginia's relatives came for a summer visit.
   - How would you feel if all your relatives came for a visit?
   - Is this story about a nuclear or extended family?
   - What do you like best to do when relatives visit?

8. Children bring pictures of members of their extended family. Pictures are shared with classmates. Teacher passes out a sheet for a family tree that children are to do at home with parents. Each family tree is posted on the bulletin board.
   - Children are given time to develop their own family books.
   - Each child has a chance to invite a relative to spend a day in class.

Bibliography of Books Dealing with Family:

Ackerman, Karen, *Song and Dance Man,* Scholastic, 1988.
Bauer, Caroline and Feller, *My Mom Travels a Lot,* Viking, 1981.
Hutchins, Pat, *The Very Worst Monster,* Scholastic, 1985.
MacLachlan, Patricia, *Mama One, Mama Two,* Harper & Row, 1982.
Mayer, Mercer, *Me Too,* Western, 1983.
Roy, Ron, *Breakfast With My Father,* Houghton Mifflin, 1980.
Wells, Rosemary, *Noisy Nora,* Scholastic, 1973.

REFERENCES

Carr, W., & Kemmis, S. (1986). *Becoming critical: Education, knowledge, and action research.* London: Falmer Press.

Dahl, R. (1963). *Modern political analysis.* Englewood Cliffs, NJ: Prentice Hall.

Kluckhohn, C. (1949). *Mirror for man.* New York: McGraw-Hill.

Schwab, J. (1969). The concept of structure of a discipline. In M. Feldman and E. Seifman (Eds.), *The social studies: Structure, models, and strategies,* pp. 4–12. Englewood Cliffs, NJ: Prentice Hall.

Shaver, J. P. (Ed.) (1977). *Building rationales for citizenship education.* Washington, DC: National Council on the Social Studies.

SUGGESTED READING

Ambrose, E., & Miel, A. (1958). *Children's social learning.* Washington, DC: ASCD.

Carr, W., & Kemmis, S. (1986). *Becoming critical: Education, knowledge, and action research.* London: Falmer Press.

Shaver, J. P. (Ed.). (1977). *Building rationales for citizenship education.* Washington, DC: National Council on the Social Studies.

Chapter 14

Conflict Resolution
and Law Education

Conflict Resolution and Law Education

Conflict exists in every facet of human existence. From the moment of awakening, individuals are confronted with conflictual choices regarding what to eat, how to dress, or should a cold keep one from going to work. The intensity of conflict is even greater for students since adults largely control the decision making process in their lives.

Conflict resolution seeks to enhance the well-being of all participants in a dispute. Unfortunately, there is a persistent tendency among educators to regard conflict as a negative action rather than as possibly a productive force in human interaction. Lewis Coser (1956) defines social conflict as "a struggle over values and claims to scarce status, power and resources in which the aims of the opponents are to neutralize, injure or eliminate their rivals." (p. 8) However, he also points out that social conflict fulfills a "number of determinate functions in groups and other interpersonal relations; it may, for example, contribute to the maintenance of group boundaries and prevent withdrawal of members from a group."

Conflict is, for the most part, a "rubber concept," being stretched and molded according to circumstances or philosophy. Many teachers and administrators regard the presence of conflict in their school as evidence that the system is not functioning in a healthy manner. Inherent in the perspective that "conflict-free" schools can exist is the belief that people, rather than structural factors, are the reasons for conflict.

▲ Conflict has existed in every facet of human existence. *Courtesy Perryville Newspapers, Inc.*

A goal of conflict resolution is moving individuals away from the view that conflict entails a winner and a loser towards a perspective that it can result in a "win-win" resolution. This approach requires a shift in attitudes. There is greater need to seek "associative" bonds that link people in a cooperative spirit.

The study of conflict resolution raises questions as well as provides some answers. Why do serious situations sometimes result in violence while at other times there is the absence of destructive conflict? Why do some conflicts quickly run a natural course while others remain like festering sores? How does the size of a group influence the intensity or direction of conflict? How does one's identification in a group influence participation or abstention from group conflicts?

Varieties of Conflict

Unless the phenomena denoted by the term "conflict" are limited and differentiated, the concept itself is vague. Social conflict is an interactive relationship between two or more parties. It can not exist without some form of action, be it verbal, nonverbal or physical. Conflict relations involve attempts to gain control of scarce resources or positions or to influence behavior in certain directions. This means there must be "parties" and a particular type of interactive relationship between those parties in order to have conflict.

A *pathway conflict* involves two or more people having similar goals or aspirations but differing about the means to achieve these objectives. Pathway conflicts are commonly found in schools. Teachers, administrators, parents, and students all want an educational environment that fosters learning, but they differ on how best to create such an atmosphere.

Conflicting parties in a pathway conflict should be directed toward their commonalties rather than their differences. If they grasp how they share common values or objectives, it is easier for them to modify positions and resolve the conflict. The vast majority of teachers and students share common desires that every student should have opportunities to perform at high levels. That is the commonalty that can serve to redirect conflict towards a positive outcome.

A more difficult form of disagreement is a *mutually exclusive conflict*. In this conflictual behavior, two or more people differ on goals but are thrust into situations requiring cooperative behavior. A student wants to quit school but must remain due to compulsory education laws. A teacher wants an equal voice in school decision making, but an administrator insists power comes from the top down. Both parties differ on goals and process.

In handling mutually exclusive conflicts, it is necessary to uncover something that constitutes commonality between the warring parties. In the early stages of resolving this form of conflict, there is need to establish a dialogue or to have both parties recognize that they share something between them. This small opening can constitute the basis for moving toward the resolution of conflict.

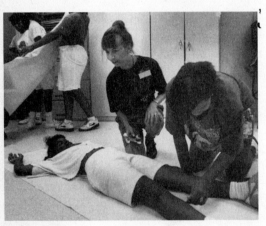

▲ There is a need to seek associative bonds that link people in a cooperative spirit. *Courtesy Webster University.*

A *distributive conflict* involves clashes between people over allocation of limited positions, goods, power, or space. A limited number of "A" grades are available or positions in gifted classes, cheerleading squads or athletic teams. A pie has only so many pieces. More pies can be baked, however. One school in Indiana allowed all interested boys and girls to become members of the cheerleading squad. Their 149 cheerleaders added a new dimension of enthusiasm to athletic events that far surpassed the former ten-member squad. Multiculturalism is an example of expanding the curriculum pie to include a wider variety of people and cultures into topics being studied. The number of pies available is not unlimited, but too frequently we fail to recognize that many more pies can be baked without diluting the quality of the food.

Value conflicts exist in all human groups. A nation as complex and diverse as the United States contains people with widely differing values. Religious, political, dietary, music, or art beliefs can lead to angry conflicts over which values should predominate. Value conflicts have always existed within the United States, and there is little likelihood they will disappear in the future.

Value conflicts demonstrate the importance of conflicting parties accepting the need for differences in life and peaceful resolution of divergent values. We can not always compel the minority to abandon its value structure nor can the majority always be asked to subordinate its basic values. Value conflict resolution requires finding ways to compromise that enable individuals to maintain the integrity of their beliefs while coexisting with differing values.

Role conflicts stem from responsibilities inherent in fulfilling role expectations. A principal is charged with evaluating teachers just as teachers evaluate students. Personality influences how the role is carried out, but role determinants permeate, delimit, and direct role interactions. Novice teachers often fail to recognize that student anger is directed toward the role of teacher more than to personalities.

Intra-group conflict pits members of the same group against one another on issues of status, power, and rewards. A class is a group, and it is only normal that students will have conflictual relationships as they struggle to get the teacher's attention, receive rewards, or seek power. Teachers must be sensitive to the nature of these conflicts and assist students to resolve conflicts in peaceful ways.

Ironically, the closer knit the class is as a unit, the more intense will be any conflict. Positive attitudes between students in a class will not avoid conflict. Only by accepting conflict as a necessary process in relieving tension or bringing hidden feelings into the open will teachers be aiding the process of conflict resolution.

Inter-group conflicts erupt in schools as classes compete with one another over issues as diverse as who is better in athletics to which class had the highest PTO membership. It is important for teachers within a school to model cooperative behavior. Healthy competition can improve class cohesion, but it can be destructive if it comes at the price of fostering negative attitudes in the school.

Lewis Coser (1956) differentiates between conflict as a means, and conflict as an end in itself. Conflicts that arise from

> "frustration of specific demands with the relationship and from estimates of gains of the participants, and which are directed at the presumed frustrating object can be called *realistic conflicts*, insofar as they are means toward a specific result. *Non-realistic conflicts*, on the other hand, although still involving interaction between two or more persons, are not occasioned by the rival ends of the antagonists, but by the need for tension release of at least one of them." (p. 49)

▲ Conflicts may arise over which students get parts in plays. *Courtesy Francis Howell (Missouri) School District.*

▲ A teacher's calm attitude helps reduce conflict in the classroom. *Courtesy Webster University.*

Nonrealistic conflict is less stable, and more difficult to resolve. A student engaged in a violent struggle with an authoritarian father might manifest this anger toward a teacher. This type of conflict will continue to crop up until the student is able to deal with deep seated emotional factors that are at the heart of the matter. This may require the intervention of a school psychologist or some form of counseling.

Realistic conflict lends itself to resolution. Student complaints about homework can be negotiated and resolved. Classroom rules can evolve from the endeavors of the teacher and students to create a sense of mutual ownership. A novice teacher should consider the significance of a conflict situation and avoid escalating a minor issue into a major problem.

Intensity Levels of Conflict

Normal level conflicts are part of everyday life. A slow-moving checkout line, traffic congestion, or failure to collect the trash can cause agitation. Schools are the scene of continual Normal level conflicts ranging from arguments about seating in the cafeteria, who gets a part in the play, the use of the computer, or a failure to do homework assignments.

A sign that one has become experienced in education is the ability to handle these daily hassles without loss of composure. Normal level conflicts are here to stay. A key factor is keeping them to a low level of intensity and avoiding having them blow up out of proportion. A sense of humor and a calm perspective are the best tools to maintain the intensity at a low level of operation.

Pervasive level conflicts are characterized by a tense and emotional atmosphere. Their occurrence can disrupt an entire school and create tensions that affect everyone's behavior. Two children who move from arguing to shouting obscenities are escalating normal level to a more pervasive level of conflict. Fortunately, teachers don't necessarily come across this higher level of conflict every day. If they did, it would indicate a serious breakdown in relations within the class.

▲ The daily newspaper is an important source of information in helping children understand global conflict. *Courtesy Webster University.*

It is necessary when pervasive level conflicts erupt to quickly dampen their intensity. Time out or separation of the students in conflict allows tempers to calm down. Logic and reason do not immediately work well if both parties are still emotionally angry. It is more important to reduce the tension and at a later time work for conflict resolution.

An *overt crisis conflict* occurs when the parties involved become physically or verbally out of control to the point where people can be hurt. These violent forms of conflict are extremely emotionally draining to the point where individuals may be unable to continue functioning in the school setting. Few teachers or students can maintain emotional health if continually subjected to this level of stress intensity.

A major goal of conflict resolution is to prevent disputes from escalating into overt crisis conflicts. If participants are functioning at the overt crisis level they are not readily able to employ conflict resolution strategies. A third party or some form of mediation may be necessary to assist conflicting parties to resolve their problems in an emotionally healthy manner.

The ideas of conflict resolution can be applied to the social studies and language arts curriculum. American history can be viewed from the perspective of conflict analysis. What were the conflicting needs of farmers and cattlemen? Wars can become case studies in conflict resolution. A conflict approach moves away from making value judgments or viewing situations in terms of "good" or "bad" people to an examination of causal factors and a focus on ways to avoid conflict.

Conflict analysis can also be incorporated into stories and varied activities. For example, the story of Cinderella is the tale of conflict between several people over power, status, and beauty. The story begins with Cinderella as a hard-working, beautiful, and decent person who is powerless because she is a stepdaughter. Her stepsisters initially have power and status, but in the end they lose everything to Cinderella, who now has possession of power as well as status and beauty. Following is a model lesson design to employ conflict analysis techniques in studying a story.

The following chart is a model lesson depicting how conflict analysis can be employed in studying a story. Students are to place appropriate comments in each box. For example, they would provide examples of choices made by Cinderella and her stepsisters.

Table 14-1. Conflict, Characters, and Choices

TITLE: *CINDERELLA*			
Characters:	Cinderella	Stepsister 1	Stepsister 2
Choices Made:			
Reasons for Choices:			
Conflicts Arising from Choices:			
Resolving Conflicts:			

Mediation in the School

The rise of programs to assist children in resolving conflict addresses the need for overcoming "emotional illiteracy." The concept of emotional literacy has yet to gain more than a toehold in schools. Children have always needed emotional education to help them deal with the daily conflicts in school settings.

How different a world it might be had we learned the ABCs of dispute resolution at an early age. What if we saw conflict as an inevitable companion to living, a signal that change might be in order, and an opportunity for collaborative problem solving? What if we possessed a repertoire of responses to conflict, and could use them with creativity, care, and confidence? (Davis, 1986, p. 287–98).

Among the most popular approaches to school conflict resolution is training children to be peer mediators. These peer mediators handle fights, deal with interracial incidents, taunts and threats, and the other potentially incendiary incidents of school life. Their tactics include sitting down with those involved and getting them to pledge to listen to the other person without interruptions or insults, and phrasing their own statements in ways that make both parties feel the mediator is impartial. The settlements that emerge are often in the form of signed agreements.

The formal mediation sessions generally take the following format: an opening statement by the mediator, statements by each disputant; additional meetings to elicit information and influence future conduct between the disputants; and usually a final written agreement. There are follow up meetings by a counselor or teacher to ensure that the agreement is working.

Following is a mediation process followed in many schools to educate young children as student mediators:

Purpose of Mediation

Mediators are:

- Not a court
- Not here to judge guilt or innocence, or decide punishments
- Providing an opportunity for parties to talk and try to come to a resolution
- Listeners and helpers

Ground Rules

- Respect each other (no name-calling or put-downs)
- Do not interrupt each other
- Remain seated
- Work towards a solution
- Be as honest as you can
- Keep it confidential (what is said in the room, remains in the room)

Phases of Mediation

Phase 1: Introduction Process

- Everyone is introduced.
- Role of mediators is explained.
- Ground rules are explained.
- Steps of mediation are explained.

Phase 2: Telling What Happened

- Both parties tell their side of the story to mediators.
- Mediator summarizes both sides of the stories.
- Mediator makes certain both sides understand the reasons for conflict.

Phase 3: Understanding the Problem/Identifying Facts and Feelings

- Parties tell their side of story to each other.
- Mediator helps bring out facts and feelings of what is being said.
- Parties change role to get into other person's shoes.
- Mediators summarize facts and feelings of both sides.

Phase 4: Alternative Solutions

- Mediators ask both sides how the problem can be solved.
- Mediators write down all alternative solutions.
- Mediators review all possible solutions and help both parties agree on at least one.

Phase 5: Resolution/Reaching an Agreement

- Final solutions are clearly identified.
- A contract is written up in the words of both parties.
- Everyone signs the contract.

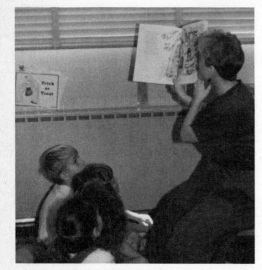

▲ Literature offers opportunities for children to examine conflict and various approaches for resolution. *Courtesy Null Elementary, Saint Charles (Missouri) Public Schools.*

Phase 6: Departure
- Mediators review how the follow-up will proceed.
- Mediators thank everyone for cooperating.

Phase 7: Report
- Mediators file a report with the faculty coordinator.

THE CASE OF THE LUNCH LINE TANGLE

Summary of Conflict: Ms. Smith has broken up a fight in the cafeteria between two sixth grade students, James and Julie. The fight broke out over alleged butting in the lunch line. James and Julie will be punished for breaking the school rule prohibiting fighting. Ms. Smith suggested that James and Julie take this conflict to the student mediators and work out an agreement so it won't happen again. Julie said she would go to mediation if James did, and James said he would try it.

Background information:

Student 1: Julie says a fight broke out in the cafeteria line because James was butting into the line. She said, "James was pushing and butting in line. And when I told him that I was going to tell the teacher, James called me a name." Julie claims that James knocked her down when she started after him. She insists

that James started all of this and that she should not be punished.

Student 2: James admits that he and Julie were pulled apart after rolling on the cafeteria floor while fighting. James claims that his friend had been holding a place in line for him, and when he went to get in line, Julie went off on him. James says Julie had been "bothering him" all morning. James said Julie gives you this mean look. He said, "That girl's crazy. She's always going off on people." James says he only defended himself after Julie jumped on him. James says that Julie said she was going to get her big brother on him after school.

Mediators: The task of mediators is to use the prescribed steps and to help Julie and James reach a satisfactory resolution of their conflict. They are asked to develop a resolution of the conflict by employing the previously described process.

Programs in emotional literacy are part of a larger movement in education to define more broadly the varieties of ways people can be considered intelligent. The work of theoreticians such as Howard Gardner (1983) of Harvard have introduced the concept of multiple intelligences. Among these forms of intelligence is "emotional giftedness" or the ability to manage one's own feelings and help others to function in emotionally healthy ways.

Student peer mediation efforts have begun as early as fourth grade in some schools. Students who participate in the program are selected by their peers based on leadership and ability, both negative and positive. These are students who think well on their feet, are willing to try new things, and are trusted or followed. Special care is taken to select students who represent the gender division and racial/ethnic identity of the school as a whole. Students receive training and work in pairs during lunch and recess to assist their peers in resolving conflicts.

▲ Wars can become case studies in conflict resolution. *Courtesy Francis Howell (Missouri) School District.*

Mediation training shifts the responsibility for solving appropriate school conflicts from adults to students. This frees teachers and administrators to concentrate more on teaching than

▲ Freedom of speech is affected by the rules teachers and students establish in determining how each person in the classroom is allowed to speak.
Courtesy Saint Louis (Missouri) Public Schools.

▲ Multicultural approaches expand the curriculum to include a variety of people and cultures into topics being studied. *Courtesy University City (Missouri) Public Schools.*

upon handling discipline problems. It recognizes that young people are competent to participate in the resolution of their own disputes, and gives students skills such as listening, critical thinking, and problem solving which are basic to all learning.

Many students and teachers who are exposed to mediation find that not only are new skills learned, but old ones are unlearned. They come to have a more complex understanding of the way conflict arises and is maintained. Mediation training helps young people and teachers to deepen their understanding about themselves and others and provides them with lifetime conflict resolution skills. Mediation training, with its emphasis upon listening to others' points of view and the peaceful resolution of differences, assists them in functioning within a multicultural world.

Law-Related Education

Law-related education seeks to improve citizenship education by teaching students about law, the legal process, and the legal system. Law education provides students some necessary tools for understanding our constitutional system of government. It is an educational thrust endeavoring to relate the abstraction of government to the everyday lives of elementary school children.

David Taylor (1977) has identified six components of a law-related curriculum: (1) introducing law; (2) exploring the nature of law; (3) examining legal concepts and issues; (4) understanding the legal process; (5) clarifying values and attitudes about law; and (6) forecasting possible futures based on assumptions about law and law-related issues.

Law-related education is not designed to make students amateur lawyers or prepare them for careers in law. It is more concerned with promoting student understanding of how citizens interact with law. Law-related education helps students to clarify their attitudes and values about laws affecting their lives, and improves their problem-solving abilities.

Many elementary social studies programs teach students an idealized version of government that focuses upon structure rather than actual processes. Law education enables students to balance ideals against the realities of the system and to "critically examine these conflicts from various points of view; to choose an effective course of action, and to clarify one's values and attitudes in relationship to the basic concepts that form the fabric of democracy—liberty, fairness, equality, and the proper balance of power" (Gerlach & Lamprecht, 1975).

Law-related education defines the legal system more broadly than ordinary study of government in elementary school social studies. It examines the roles of police, judges, prosecutors, public defenders, probation officers, and youth service workers. While many civic education programs present government in terms far removed from the consciousness of students, law education seeks to make law relevant to the lives of people in their everyday interactions.

Many law-related education programs take the issues of the street and examine them through case studies and role playing. It sees the Constitution as a living document whose content has been and is still being shaped by legal cases raising significant issues that have troubled Americans for generations. (Henning, 1975, p. 13)

Historically, children in the United States have been denied protection of law. Until the 1970s they were even denied access to due process procedures if they ran afoul of the law. It is only during the past 40 years that the Supreme Court has begun to define the rights of students. Freedom of speech for students was not a legal right until 1969, when in the case of *Tinker v. Des Moines School District* the Supreme Court granted students freedom of expression.

But, in 1988, the Supreme Court ruled in *Hazelwood v. Kuhlmeier* that school officials have broad powers to regulate school newspapers in their effort to maintain a proper educational environment.

Teachers tend to ignore that the first day of school in which class rules are defined by adults establishes legal guidelines for students. Do they have to raise a hand to speak, sharpen a pencil, or go to the toilet? Is lateness or being absent a factor in their grades? Law relates to what children can wear to school, smoking, medication, the privacy of their lockers, the schools they can or can not attend, and P.L. 94-142 details educational programs for handicapped students. These issues interest students and are a natural motivating force to involve them in the study of law.

▲ Students may have conflictual relationships as they struggle to get the teacher's attention or receive awards. *Courtesy University City (Missouri) Public Schools.*

These everyday concerns frequently constitute the raw materials for a successful law-related education program. Teachers miss a wonderful opportunity to introduce the study of government by involving students in formulation of the laws that will govern class behavior. Freedom of speech is affected by the rules students establish in determining how each person in the classroom is allowed to speak. In *Hazelwood v. Kuhlmeier*, the principal censored a student publication; do you as a teacher wish to exercise the right of censorship over what students write or how they express their ideas? Discussing these ideas with your class gives law meaning to students.

Law education is not a substitute for the existing social studies curriculum. It can be woven into many existing pieces that ordinarily are not viewed as pertaining to issues of law or social justice. Many fairy tales involve incidents in which characters violate existing laws in pursuit of their own ends. For example, consider how the following classic tales fit into law education:

Table 14-2. Fairy Tale Legal Issues

FAIRY TALE	LEGAL ISSUES
Cinderella	Child abuse Privacy (can women be forced to try on a shoe?)
Jack and the Beanstalk	Breaking and entering Stealing
Three Little Pigs	Forced entry Destruction of private property
Hansel and Gretel	Kidnapping Attempted murder

Law education adds a new dimension to studying literature and dealing with issues of everyday life. Children are familiar with the mechanisms of law through television and the movies. It is increasingly common for women to be presented as prosecutors or defense attorneys, and the drama of the court, from the frivolity of *Night Court* to questions of life and death, are part of what students watch and consider.

Most law-related education programs use the case study technique. There are a number of procedures that can be used in employing case studies, but the following process is integral to most approaches.

1. Present a short synopsis of the case. This can be recited aloud by the teacher or read by students. For primary age children, a puppet character can recite the case.

2. The teacher reviews the facts of the case with students to ensure that the main points are clear to everyone.

3. Students discuss which laws are involved. They may make reference to cases viewed on TV or in the movies. Older students can be guided through the Bill of Rights in order to identify rights violated in the case study. Primary age children can focus on rules that are broken by the behavior of characters in the case study.

4. After the issues have been reviewed, students can be subdivided into groups. One group may be assigned the role of defense, another the prosecutor while a third may organize themselves into a jury and decide how to reach a judgment.

5. A mock trial can be held or each group may present its arguments to the jury. The jury, after hearing evidence, will render its verdict.

6. The teacher can lead students through a debriefing process to ensure they understand legal issues of the case. In some situations, teachers have invited a lawyer to observe the case and then present an interpretation regarding how effectively the students functioned in their roles. Older students may be provided actual court decisions regarding the issues involved in the case. A local American Bar Association group is an excellent source for additional material about law-related education.

A CASE STUDY

Goldilocks and the Three Bears

1. One day while walking, a young girl named Goldilocks found herself becoming very hungry. She came upon a house in the forest. It belonged to three bears who had gone for a stroll before eating their supper. Goldilocks entered the house while they were gone and ate their supper. She also broke some furniture. Goldilocks was so tired after these activities that she fell asleep in the bed of a bear. When the bears returned from their walk, they found their food eaten, furniture broken, and a stranger asleep in their bed.

2. *Facts*: The house belonged to the three bears. Goldilocks entered without permission. Goldilocks was hungry and tired. Goldilocks ate the food because she was hungry. Goldilocks broke furniture by mistake. Goldilocks fell asleep in a bed. The bears did not know Goldilocks. They found her sleeping in one of their beds.

3. *Issues:* Breaking and entering. Does hunger give people the right to eat the food of strangers? Is breaking furniture by mistake a crime? Are you allowed to sleep in a stranger's house without permission if you are very, very tired?

4. Group One organizes defense arguments for Goldilocks. Group Two organizes arguments for the three bears. Group Three becomes the jury and decides how they will go about deciding the case. If a trial is held, other students can be assigned the roles of judge, bailiff, court recorder, etc.

5. Trial is conducted and the jury explains why it reached a particular decision.

6. Debriefing process.

With primary age children, the Goldilocks trial can be conducted through means of puppet characters. These puppets can be constructed by students who then assume the voices of the characters.

The American Bar Association and other groups working with law-related education have developed extensive literature on the methodology of conducting mock trials. A great deal has also been written on role-playing, which is the essence of mock trials. Following are some guidelines to consider in using mock trials in your classroom:

1. Match the trial to the skills and abilities of your students. Your goal is not to teach students to become amateur lawyers or judges but rather to understand our legal process and to become sensitive about its impact in their everyday lives.

2. Educate students about the general rules of evidence and procedures. Remember, an important goal is helping students understand that there is always more than one side to a story.

3. Cooperative learning is essential to mock trials. Many students can participate in development of ideas even though only one might actually present arguments to the jury.

4. The actual questions can be written or, in some cases, students have the option of creating questions as they proceed.

5. Allow cross-examination.

6. A teacher should not interrupt to point out errors. Wait until debriefing to point out any problems in trial procedures.

7. It is interesting, for educational purposes, to have the jury deliberate before the entire class.

8. It is essential to have a debriefing in order that students learn from the experience. A series of mock trials throughout the school year will develop within students more sophisticated ways to conduct the process.

Law-related education best succeeds if it deals with issues that students find interesting, relevant, and pertinent to issues of their present and future lives. There is a paradoxical aspect of law-related education: it should emotionally engage students while at the same time teach them to control their emotions in dealing with conflict situations. Law education strengthens the analytical and divergent thinking skills of students.

Teachers should be continually seeking ways to integrate legal processes into the curriculum in order to motivate students. Linda Reikes and her associates (1984) developed a curriculum centered on sports and the law in order to stimulate student interest. All games are based upon rules and regulations, and there usually is a figure playing the role of a judge. The draft system in football or baseball raises legal issues while the salary cap in basketball deals with the right of individuals to obtain the highest possible salary.

Law education has a place in the thrust of global studies. Students could compare student rights in different societies. Many Scandinavian societies and France restrict how much home-work can be given young children. A pen pal program with children in other countries could be initiated by exploring how adults treat children. Space offers an exciting new area for law education since we are currently in the process of creating laws to govern human behavior in space. For example, the following case study could assist students in understanding the initiation of the American system of government:

CASE STUDY

Space: The Last Frontier

Situation: A new human colony has been established on the planet of Voronk. Voronk has no known life species. The human group has 25 people including ten children. There are three dogs and four cats. Of the fifteen adults, three are in their sixties while the remainder range in age from 22 to 43.

Task: The class is to create a system of government and create laws to govern human behavior on the planet of Voronk. The colony will be out of contact with Earth for at least twenty years and it has complete freedom to establish any set of rules or government.

Law-related education programs employ a wide range of activities in order to stimulate interest among students. In addition to case studies and mock trials, many visitors are encouraged to participate in the educational process. A police officer can be invited to a class in order to discuss student rights in regard to the police. In one class, episodes of a crime story were shown, and the officer discussed examples in the film in which TV police may have violated constitutional rights.

The American Bar Association has been active in many areas in order to assist law education. They have cooperated in furnishing lawyers to visit classrooms and discuss legal issues. Teachers have created opportunities for students to visit jails, detention centers, courtrooms, and government offices. Older students have been involved in conducting mock legislative hearings, and in some cases, their results have been evaluated by local government officials.

Law-related education lends itself to developing student skills in interviewing, canvassing, polling, investigating local problems, and organizing the process of instituting changes in laws. It is an opportunity for them to engage in action research. Children of all ages can become involved in government and witness the process as well as participate in the creation of more equitable laws.

The Chalk Exercise: Hand a piece of chalk to a student. When the student asks what she is to do with the chalk, ask the students to develop some rules and regulations regarding chalk in the classroom.

Inventing a Sport: Ask students to invent a new sport together with a set of rules and regulations governing the sport.

A New Look at Checkers: Ask students to completely revise the rules regarding how to play checkers.

School Rules: Ask students to identify and list school rules and regulations. They are then to develop a new set of rules for the school.

CASE STUDY

School Rule: Do Not Wear Hats Here

The school policy contains the following rule: "Do Not Wear Hats Here." This rule is posted in highly visible locations throughout the school. The principal has asked a group of students to review the hat rule. On the first day of working on this task, the group encountered the following students:

1. Aaron, an Orthodox Jew, wears the traditional yarmulke.
2. Taffy has a plate in her head since she was involved in an accident. She is embarrassed by it and wears a ski cap to conceal it.
3. Floyd, the team quarterback, has on his entire football uniform including his helmet. The team always dresses this way for a pep rally.
4. Mary was running late this morning. Her hair, still in rollers, is not yet dry. She plans to comb it out later.
5. John Henry is wearing his baseball hat. He says it is a lucky charm that will ensure that his favorite baseball team wins.
6. Hannah, recently arrived from Hungary, always covers her hair with a brightly colored babushka like back in her native land.
7. Alan contracted lice while on vacation. His head has been shaved, smeared with medicated ointment and has been wrapped in a turban-like bandage.
8. James, an African-American student, says he wants to wear a knitted blue cap.
9. Abdullah wears a turban like people do back in his native land of Punjab.
10. Susan takes great pride in her hair ribbons. Today, she is wearing several yellow rosebuds in her hair.

Would your group change the rule: *Do Not Wear Hats Here*. If so, what would be your new rule?

[Developed from an idea from Steve Jenkins of the Conflict Resolution Center in St. Louis.]

Law Education Instructional Strategies

1. Present the 1975 Supreme Court case of *Baker v. Owen,* which allowed school officials to paddle students. Ask students to collect "Letters to the Editor" from their parents addressing this topic and write their own. Put out a school newspaper issue dealing with the topic and conduct a mock trial on it before the student body.

2. Present the following list of laws to students:

   • No person who has not yet attained 16 years of age may appear on the streets of this municipality between the hours of 8:00 P.M. and 6:30 A.M. unless accompanied by a parent or legal guardian.

   • The manufacture or sale or transportation of intoxicating liquors for beverage purposes is prohibited.

   • No person shall conduct himself or herself in a noisy, loud, rude, or disorderly manner with the intent to annoy another person.

Students can be asked to decide why each law was originally enacted and if they are still necessary.

Each of us views the law through a different lens. For some, a law can be an instrument of oppression and for another, a lofty ideal. For better or worse, laws touch all aspects of our lives. The issues of social studies are the issues of law and this area of study can become an important method for making students more aware of the impact of government in their everyday lives.

Role-playing

Programs centered around conflict resolution and law education are most effective if students can separate their personal feelings and examine issues in a more analytical and objective manner. Role-playing is an important tool in enabling students to explore problems and dilemmas from mind-sets other than their own.

Role-playing enables students to respond spontaneously, even emotionally at first, and then gradually, through many enactments, to consider in depth the data needed, the consequences to be faced, the value decisions to be made (Shafted & Shafted, 1982).

Role-playing is a communication process that requires the participant not simply to play another person, but to understand that individual's attributes and feelings. Elementary school children are in the process of becoming less ego-centered and more able to understand others' emotions and viewpoints. Role-playing is an important step in the development of mature attitudes in children:

1. It enables children to put themselves in the shoes of other people and to temporarily suspend their own judgments in order to understand other viewpoints.

2. It fosters empathy by allowing children to feel how other peoples' emotions influence their perception of a situation.

3. It is an important skill that can be of use in many aspects of the lives of students. They can use it when applying for jobs or interacting with people.

4. It simultaneously develops cognitive and affective skills, attitudes and emotions.

Elementary-age children continually interact with people and problem situations such as how to respond to name-calling or being pushed in the line. They need skills to resolve these problems without feeling victimized or becoming an oppressor. Law education and conflict resolution programs are excellent opportunities for children to utilize role-playing as a tool for mature analysis of situations. Shaftel and Shaftel (1982, p. 4) recommend the following steps in role-playing:

1. Identify the problem by confronting childen with the issues or situations to be addressed. An effective strategy is to read a problem story and halt at the dilemma point. This presents a dramatic way to highlight the issues of the role-play.

2. Select the participants or role-players. Some teachers use the opportunity for role-playing to place a child in a situation that differs from their own attitudes or values in order to expand their understanding of human behaviors.

3. Prepare the audience to participate as observors. They should understand the ground rules and their function as observors. The participants in the role-play situation need preparation time.

4. Set the stage, which might include physical rearrangement of the room as well as reminding the audience of how important it is to be supportive to the role-players.

5. Role-play. Some teachers video the role-play in order to use it for further debriefing of what happened.

6. Debrief and evaluate what happened in the role-play.

7. Further role-playing. An incident in the role-play may spark discussion or lead students to examine an idea that arose naturally from the role-playing situation.

8. Sharing experiences and generalizing. It is important to avoid angry statements dircted at any individual and to conduct the discussion in a stress-free environment.

Role-playing is particularly effective in social studies, which is centered around dilemmas posed by human relations issues. Young people need help in acquiring the skills of good judgment, and being able to decide which is the more ethical or humane way of dealing with problem situations. They can learn how to deal with crises of decision making by entering the minds of other people and gaining new understandings of the way others think and act.

Practice in making decisions as part of or apart from a group is an essential feature of role-playing. It is not the student who makes the decision, but the individual into whose mind the child has entered. As each member of the class experiences other roles, he is being sensitized and made more symapthetic to the dilemmas people encounter when confronted with problems.

Simulations

A popular form of role-playing is the use of simulation activities in the classroom. Simlulations are designed to physically, intellectually, or emotionally involve students in examining issues and dilemmas. Simulations can be seen as analogues to the laboratory experiences a student encounters in the physical science courses. Simulation activities are not a substitute for learning material by means of reading or writing. They supplement the existing curriculum through use of strategies that enable students to view situations from a fresh perspective.

Simulations are not only interesting in themselves, but they provoke further student interest in the subject matter. A student who engages in an election simulation may be more prone to follow an election campaign. Simulations may also help students who do not respond well to traditional methods of teaching. They utilize interaction skills and are less threatening to students. Frequently, simulations provide new evidence about student skills, and a quiet child can blossom into a verbally active participant.

A simulation ordinarily poses a problem that students can better understand by participating in some form of reenactment of events. They are required to temporarily suspend individual bias or attitudes in order to examine how others would interpret the situation. Ordinarily, the simulation involves students in physical movement and the use of dramatic techniques. Following are several guidelines for use of simulations in the classroom:

1. Students need sufficient information about the roles they are playing or the situation being explored.
2. The rules of the simulation should be clearly reviewed with all participants and the entire class.
3. Students should be provided sufficient time to prepare for the simulation.
4. Students should be given some leeway in enacting the role, but they should not be allowed to exceed the emotional or intellectual parameters of the role or situation.
5. After completion of the simulation, time should be set aside for debriefing by the entire class. A simulation without follow-up discussion dilutes the educational experience.
6. Students should not be assigned grades on the basis of their role-play or participation in the simulation. Perhaps the role was difficult to reenact or the student decided to experiment with an interesting strategy. Grades inhibit student performance, and lead participants to behave in ways they believe are desired by the teacher.

Simulation: Earth on Trial

Unknown to humanity, representatives of planets from throughout the universe have been observing the earth. It is the responsibility of these representatives to determine if humans are fit to enter the Galaxy Confederation. The Galaxy Confederation is concerned about the behavior of humans and are considering the imposition of a quarantine that would prevent earth people from exploring the universe until they have demonstrated ability to behave in peaceful ways. The task of humans is to convince the Galaxy that Earth is qualified to enter the Confederation.

Following is a description of each Galaxy representative. The representatives of Earth should take into account how each of the Galaxy delegates behaves and thinks.

Tumor: Tumor is from planet Dakeg. On Dakeg, all living forms are linked with one another through telepathic means. They think, act, and feel as part of the whole being of Dakeg. The concept of conflict is unknown to them. All living things on Dakeg exist in a state of harmony with one another.

Zadek: Zadek is from the planet Cruzz. There is only one gender on Cruzz. Zadek has a mate, lives in a shelter, and is an individual. Zadek prides itself on individuality and respect for the individuality of other members of the planet. All life-forms at birth are trained to cooperate and respect other life-forms.

Flom: Flom is from the planet Vetasor. Vetasor went through terrible conflicts thousands of years prior in its history, but all life-forms finally agreed to end warfare because they feared total annihilation of the planet. There are millions of different life-forms on Vetasor and each has the right to exist separately and in peace. All life-forms consume only vegetables for sustance.

Triar: Triar is from the planet Cotr which is highly mechanized and computerized. Androids handle most tasks and recently have been accorded full citizenship rights. All problems or conflicts are handled by central computers which are programmed to resolve problems in peaceful ways.

The task of the simulation is for several class members to enact the role of Galaxy delegates while other students present Earth's case for entry into the Galaxy Confederation.

SUMMARY

This chapter has reviewed the role conflict plays in the daily lives of students and teachers. It discussed ways to employ law education to peacefully resolve conflict situations and to sensitize students regarding ways to deal with conflict in their lives.

QUESTIONS

1. Prior to reading this chapter, would you have viewed conflict as a positive or negative process?

2. Cite examples from your own life of a pathway, a mutually exclusive, a distributive, and a role conflict. Which of these created the most anxiety and stress?

3. Make a list of roles you will play as a teacher in the classroom. Which of the roles will be most difficult?

4. Cite an example from your own life in which a conflict escalated from normal level to pervasive level. What caused the escalation process?

5. What do you consider the most positive aspect of a student mediation program?

6. What would be the most difficult aspect to implement in a student mediation program?

7. The authors state that elementary social studies programs present an "idealized" version of government? Do you agree or disagree with that assessment?

8. Which legal rights are possessed by American children? Which others do you believe they should be accorded?

9. What most interests you regarding law-related education activities?

10. Which critical thinking skills do you believe are best taught through a law-related education program?

ACTIVITIES

1. Have students make a list of all conflicts engaged in during the past few weeks. Categorize these conflicts and analyze the results.

2. Ask students to create a game or activity to use in teaching law-related education.

3. Have students make a list of all roles they perform. Collate their data, and analyze the results.

4. Have students interview teachers and school administrators about roles they perform in their professional lives. Collate the data, and analyze.

5. Have students visit a courtroom to observe law in action.

READING

Teaching About Constitutional Issues and Values
by Dick Merriman

"Americans," Garry Wills wrote in 1978, "like, at intervals, to play this dirty trick on themselves: Pollsters are sent out to canvass men and women on certain doctrines and to shame them when these doctrines are declared—as usually happens—unacceptable. Shortly after, the results are published: Americans have, once again, failed to subscribe to some phrase or other from the Declaration of Independence."[1]

Given our appetite for this sort of self-inflicted embarrassment, it is not surprising that the observance of the bicentennial of the United States Constitution finds pollsters hard at work. They have produced the expected results.

Eighty-two percent of respondents to a recent national survey mistakenly believed that Lincoln's phrase about "government of the people, by the people, for the people," is part of the Constitution. Eighty percent attributed the words in the Declaration of Independence concerning our rights to "life, liberty, and the pursuit of happiness" to the Constitution. Almost half (45 percent) assigned Marx's famous maxim—"From each according to his ability, to each according to his ability, to each according to his need"—to the Constitution.[2]

On some less trivial matters, Americans proved, fortunately, to be more knowledgeable. More than 90 percent of respondents knew that in America anyone accused of committing a serious crime must be provided a lawyer if he or she cannot afford one, and 94 percent knew that police must show a judge that they have "probable cause" to suspect illegal activity before a home may be searched without a resident's permission.

Unfortunately, only 37 percent of respondents knew a basic fact about the Constitution's checks and balances, namely that the president must obtain Senate consent for appointments to the U.S. Supreme Court. A majority of respondents with an opinion on the subject mistakenly believed the president can suspend the Constitution in time of war or national emergency.[3]

The obvious remedy for such gaps in knowledge is for the Senate and C-SPAN to find a way to make Supreme Court confirmation hearings as interesting as the television program "Hill Street Blues." Until that happens, social studies educators need to give special classroom emphasis to those parts of the Constitution that are not regularly interpreted and applied by public defender Davenport and police captain Furillo. I refer to the body of the Constitution that specifies the institutions and processes by which Americans try to achieve self-government through politics.

To focus on the institutions and processes of government and politics may seem at first to involve turning away from alluring discussions about the Bill of Rights—church and state, freedom of the press, pornography and obscenity—in favor of such mundane matters as the separation of powers, federalism, and checks and balances. The Bill of Rights is debatable and thought-provoking. By discussing it, students are challenged to examine their values. Can such things be said about the study of institutions and processes? I think so.

In fact, examining the body of the Constitution is an extremely rich way to stimulate thinking about key political and citizenship values. Some thoughts are presented here on teaching about American civic values through study of our constitutional institutions and processes, and on the place of political theory, history, and debate in such teaching.

Political Theory in Education On the Constitution

Students love a good mystery, and political theory probes some of life's great mysteries. No one is consulted in advance about whether, when, or where he or she wants to be born. We are thrown into the world without our permission. The matter of why life works this way and what this might lead us to conclude about lie's meaning is not a political question. But the very next question—"Now that we are all here, how will we live together?"—is unmistakably social and political.

Nothing about the Constitution can make much sense to students until they understand that it contains and embodies an answer to just these questions of what humans are like and how they can live together and govern themselves. The answer given by the Constitution has obvious roots in the contract theory of such natural rights theorists as the English philosopher John Locke.

Locke asserted in the 17th century that in a presocial and pregovernmental "state of nature" humans had—and knew they had—the rights to life, liberty, and property.[4]

Locke claimed that rational humans would create governments only to facilitate the secure enjoyment of their rights. Locke's bedrock claim was that people and their rights had temporal precedence to the first government and always have moral precedence to any government.

In declaring their independence from England, American colonists claimed similar rights to "life, liberty, and the pursuit of happiness," and invoked contract theory in stating that "to secure these rights, governments are instituted among men, deriving their just powers from the consent of the governed."

The preamble to the Constitution asserts that "the people of the United States" have, for certain purposes and by conscious choice, created the system of government spelled out in the document's subsequent articles. The primal, originating power of our government is in the people, who confer certain powers for certain purposes on their creation, the government.

Who could understand the claims of contract theory as embodied in the preamble and still believe that the president, or for that matter any combination of governmental officials, may suspend the Constitution? Students need to understand that to be an American citizen in the fullest and best sense requires an understanding of the preamble's claim and a readiness to apply it to real life. It should be applied when the police officer knocks on the door and when we find people in the basement of the White House congratulating each other for deceiving us and our representatives in Congress.

There is more to understanding a concept like the sovereignty of the people, however, than acquiring a prickly awareness of what governments may not do. Americans established our national government to *act,* and they must, therefore, be able to communicate to the government their expectations and preferences.

Students will generally assert that Americans accomplish this by relying on government through elected and electorally accountable representatives. But this was not originally the case and, to some extent, still is not. The original Constitution only provided for popular election of members to the House of Representatives. The president and senators were to be chosen in ways that gave state governments a much more substantial role than was given to the people themselves. Even with the progressive democratization of our government and politics, federal judges and Supreme Court justices remain beyond the reach of "We the People" in our role as voters.

An ideal approach to teaching about the civic values that informed the design of the Constitution is to encourage students to identify the different claims about politics and government embodied in it. On one hand, there is the preamble's plain claim that the people themselves created our government. On the other hand is clear evidence of the belief of the Constitution's framers that the purposes for which our government was created could not be attained by letting the people, or a numerical majority of the people as voters, simply have its say and have its way about the content of governmental policy.

While national referenda are common in other countries, our Constitution provides no process by which the people themselves may vote directly on the substance of public policy. We rely on elected representatives to make national policy. Why? How was government by representatives expected to be substantially different from and qualitatively better than popular direct democracy?

Judicial decisions, the framers believed, could not be entrusted to officials chosen by the people. Why? How were the actions of an independent judiciary expected to be different from and better than the decisions of judges who periodically faced the electorate? Under our amended Constitution, the president may serve only two four-year terms, while members of Congress may serve as long as their constituents will retain them in office, and judges enjoy life tenure "during good behavior." Why? What values do we hope to encourage through such an arrangement?

These are not rhetorical questions. They have answers, and students should be encouraged to search for them. In the process of trying to answer such questions, students will come to understand that our political institutions and processes are not so dry; they are, in reality, living expressions of civic values.

History in Education On the Constitution

Even as students are being encouraged to understand the political theory that lives through the Constitution, it is important to guard against the view that the Constitution was the product of philosophical speculation undertaken with Olympian detachment. No view could be less accurate.

The Constitution's designers were history-minded. They read history not just for the sake of knowing what had happened in the past, but in order to learn history's lessons. These lessons shaped the Constitution. The provision of life tenure for federal judges was clearly a product of and a reaction against historical abuses of royal prerogative made possible where English judges served at the King's pleasure.

The separation of powers, and the arming of each branch of government with checks on the others grew from, among other things, one of the key concerns that prompted the American Revolution: the belief that the King's subversion of the balance of the English constitution was about to plunge England, and the British Empire, into tyranny.

The history that the framers themselves had helped make following the Declaration of Independence also influenced their design of the Constitution. The successes and failures of the states' experiments with popular republican government were repeatedly invoked and debated as the framers considered the proper scope of legislative and executive power, the role the people might properly play in their own governance, and the necessary guarantees of individual rights.

The history of government under the Articles of Confederation, and the lessons to be drawn from it, became a major source of contention at the Constitutional Convention. Should a new and more powerful national government be created or should the articles be "tuned up" through amendment?

Attention to history will illuminate the practical constraints that historical circumstances placed on the framers' theorizing. The fact that the colonies, later states, existed before the birth of a national government profoundly influenced the Constitution's design.

While the preamble speaks for "We the People," many provisions of the Constitution (for example, representation in the Senate, the mechanisms of the electoral college) recognize and reinforce the identities and influence of the states. How could it have been otherwise? The framers, however clean their slate when compared with the nations of the Old World, were not in a position to act simply as political *theorists*. Many key provisions of the Constitution cannot be convincingly explained or properly understood except by reference to the numerous instances in which theory was constrained by historical circumstances.

Thinking about political theory and studying history will make it clear to students that the men who designed the Constitution brought great vision to their work of fashioning an effective government in difficult historical circumstances. It will also reveal that some of the framers' contemporaries were not pleased with the convention's handiwork.

Several delegates at the 1787 convention, most notably George Mason, found the Constitution so objectionable that they refused to sign it. Laboring under the disadvantage of a negative label, *"Antifederalists"* (they tried to turn the tables by calling themselves "Anti-rats" and the friends of ratification "Rats"), these opponents mounted a sufficiently serious challenge to ratification that the Federalists finally conceded the necessity of adding a Bill of Rights to the Constitution.[5]

Of course, calls for changing the Constitution did not cease with the adoption of the Bill of Rights. The Constitution's history presents a great spectacle of change. George Washington acknowledged the inevitable need for, and value of, constitutional change. He wrote in a letter to his nephew, Bushrod Washington (November 10, 1787):

> The warmest friends and the best supporters the Constitution has do not contend that it is free from imperfections. . . . I think the People (for it is with them to Judge) can. . . . decide with as much propriety on the alterations and amendments which are necessary [as] ourselves. I do not think we are more inspired, have more wisdom, or possess more virtue than those who will come after us.[6]

In line with Washington's advice, students should be challenged to reflect and deliberate about issues of constitutional change in the past and present. During the bicentennial period, students were invited to "sign on" to the Constitution. A good way to bring the examination of civic values and history into an otherwise ceremonial exercise is to ask students which of our several constitutions they would be happy to sign. Would they sign the Constitution before, or only after, the addition of the Bill of Rights? Before or after the addition of the Reconstruction amendments, provision for popular election of U.S. senators, adoption of women's suffrage, or extension of vote to 18-year-olds?[7] At what point did our institutions of government become sufficiently amendable to electoral influence?

Debating the Constitution's Future

Inviting students to say at what point the Constitution came to reflect their values is also an invitation to some students to conclude that, even with all its amendments, it could still be improved. In reaching such a conclusion, students will find themselves, perhaps surprisingly, in the company of a majority of Americans. The Hearst survey found that a startling 70 percent of respondents favored amending the Constitution to provide limited but renewable terms for Supreme Court justices.[8]

Each decade sees the introduction in Congress of numerous proposals to amend the Constitution to change certain facets of our governmental institutions and political processes. Some of these proposals are hardy perennials, focusing on the manner of selection or terms of office of the president, members of Congress, and the federal judiciary. More recently a good deal of attention has been given to proposals for establishing a presidential line-item veto, a congressional legislative veto, a national initiative and referendum process, and limited campaign spending in federal elections.

Each proposal is eminently debatable, as thousands of adults and students are discovering through their participation in Jefferson Meetings on the Constitution.[9] During Jefferson Meetings, participants confront questions like the following:

- Should the electoral college method of selecting the president be eliminated in favor of direct popular election?

- Would the president be more, or less, effective if given a single six-year term of office? Should the two-term limitation be repealed?

- Would the House of Representatives be more effective if members had longer terms? Should there be a limit on the number of consecutive years a member of Congress may serve?

- Should the current life tenure of federal judges and Supreme court justices "during good behavior" be changed to provide for a fixed term or retirement age? Should the manner of their selection be changed?

- Does the separation of powers, so carefully crafted by the framers, contribute to or hinder effective government? Would line-item and legislative vetoes for the president and Congress respectively enhance the performance of the government without dangerously upsetting the scheme of separated powers?

- Should the processes of initiative and referendum, common in states and localities, be available for making national policy decisions? Would such processes undermine or complement our system of representative government?

- Has the expense of running for national public office invited too many moneybearing special interests into the political process? How can regulation of campaign contributions and spending be reconciled with constitutional guarantees of free speech and association?

- Should a national convention be called, as provided by Article V, for the purpose of proposing amendments to the Constitution? Or should the amending process be confined to consideration of separate amendments proposed by Congress?

In discussing such questions, Americans find themselves in a situation very much like that of Hamilton, Madison, Mason, and other delegates to the 1787 convention. They must ask what values live through the Constitution, whether those values are both agreeable and effectively pursued, and whether proposed amendments would help bring about desirable change.

Some Americans find the electoral college, with is potential to choose as president a candidate who did not win the popular vote, a dangerous anachronism. They complain that the winner-take-all system, which allows a candidate who receives 50 percent + 1 of a state's popular vote to claim all its electoral college votes (except in Maine), is unfair and discourages voting. Others reply that the electoral college reinforces state identities and influence and gives both key states and strategic minorities within key states a voice they would lack in a direct election. They add that, by inflating in the electoral college the popular mandate received by the winning candidate, the electoral college mechanism enables the president to lead an often fractious Congress.

Jefferson Meeting debates about such issues stimulate fresh thinking about civic values because such handy identities as "conservative" and "liberal" offer little guidance. One might say that conservatives would tend to oppose change. But Ronald Reagan repeatedly endorsed an amendment to give the president a line-item veto and favored eliminating—effective after he left office—the two-term limit on presidents.

Taking Responsibility for the Constitution

When Americans discuss issues and values that transcend the constraints of partisanship and self-interest, something refreshing and important happens: They think, really think, about what is good for the whole country. In doing so, Americans cultivate an attribute, republican virtue, that the Constitution's framers exalted above all others.

Parson Weems' moralizing has reduced George Washington's virtue to a trite tale about a small boy's honesty concerning the demise of a certain cherry tree. But to his contemporaries, Washington, who left the contentments of domestic life to lead the nation in war and to launch its new government, was an exemplar of the purest republican virtue; he repeatedly sacrificed his own interests to the pursuit of the public good.[10]

In an odd way, our observance of the Constitution's bicentennial tended to teach just the opposite lesson: that the continuation of our government and our Constitution is inevitable. How many times in the bicentennial season were we told that our Constitution is the oldest constitution continuously in force in the world? How many times lately, by contrast, have we been encouraged to consider how such a happy claim may be reconciled with an event like the American Civil War or the internment during World War II of U.S. citizens of Japanese ancestry?

There is *nothing* inevitable about the Constitution or our continuing enjoyment of the rights it protects. It will live only as long as Americans understand and cherish the values that live through it and only as long as they remain ready to adapt its provisions to meet changing circumstances. It is ours to preserve and ours to lose. This lesson about ownership and the responsibilities that come with it is without doubt the most valuable one we can offer our students. The tools for teaching that lesson—political theory, history, and debate—are, fortunately, familiar and handy.

Notes

[1] Garry Wills, *Inventing America: Jefferson's Declaration of Independence* (Garden City: Doubleday, 1978), xiii.

[2] A Hearst Report, *The American Public's Knowledge of the U.S. Constitution: A National Survey of Public Awareness and Personal Opinion* (New York: The Hearst Corporation, 1987).

[3] Hearst Report.

[4] John Locke, *Two Treatises of Government,* Peter Laslett, ed., (New York: Cambridge University Press, 1960), 309–18.

[5] On the Antifederalists, see Cecilia Kenyon, ed., *The Antifederalists* (Indianapolis: Bobbs-Merrill, 1966).

[6] Quoted in Michael Kammen, ed., *The Origins of the American Constitution: A Documentary History* (New York: Viking Penguin, 1986), 83.

[7] The good idea of asking students which of our Constitution's several versions they would be happy to sign comes from Richard Rabinowitz of the American History Workshop.

[8] Hearst Report.

[9] Jefferson Meetings on the Constitution can be held as community forums or as classroom learning activities. Materials for conducting Jefferson Meetings on the Constitution can be obtained from The Jefferson Foundation, 1529 18th Street N.W., Washington, DC 20036. See also Alice O'Connor, Mary L. Henze, and W. Richard Merriman, Jr., *Rediscovering the Constitution: Reader for Jefferson Meeting Debates* (Washington: congressional Quarterly, Inc., 1987).

[10] On the founders' and framers' fixation on republican virtue, see Bernard Bailyn, *The Ideological Origins of the American Revolution* (Cambridge: Harvard University Press, 1967) and Gordon Wood, *The Creation of the American Republic, 1776–1787* (New York: W. W. Norton, 1969). On the republican virtue of George Washington, see Forrest McDonald, *Novus Ordo Seclorum: The Intellectual Origins of the Constitution* (Lawrence: University of Kansas Press, 1985).

Dick Merriman is Director of The Jefferson Foundation. He earned a Ph.D. degree in political science from Indiana University in 1986.

(Courtesy © *National Council for the Social Studies.* Used with permission.)

QUESTIONS ON READING

1. The author states that the Constitution reflects what people are like and "how they can live together and govern themselves." How do our everyday laws reflect this idea?

2. How did conflict play a role in the creation of the Constitution?

3. Which legal changes would you like to see instituted in the Constitution?

LESSON PLANS

David Sanford   Fifth Grade

Objective: Aiding students to develop positive friendships within the class.

Rationale: Students need to learn ways to build friendships in order to assist in their own self-concept development.

Activities:

1. Open-ended discussion about what students like about friends. Teacher role-plays with a student how to make a friend with a stranger.

   • Students draw pictures of friends. If students say they don't have a friend, ask them to draw a picture of a friend they would like to have.

   • Students write five sentences beginning with: "A friend is . . . " Class statements are placed on large sheet and posted.

2. Students receive sheet headed: "Things My Friend and I Did Last Week." Fill out and share with class.

3. Students receive colored cards. Students with same color become a team. Each student takes a turn interviewing the other about things they like to do, see, eat, etc.

4. Students make a list of what they like about themselves. Each makes an abstract drawing of the self and places their list of words on the page. These are hung in the room. Each student selects one abstract drawing and spends a half hour with that person.

5. Divide class into subgroups of about five. Each group is to create a "perfect friend" using physical features from members of the group. They are to give the friend qualities drawn from those in the group. Their perfect friend is shared with class.

6. Teacher opens class by giving each student a compliment. Class discusses why they liked to be complimented. Students are divided into even-numbered groups. Within the group, students pair off and practice giving one another at least one compliment. Students then pair off with another person in the group and repeat the process.

7. Students brainstorm a list of topics they would like to talk about. Those students who select the same topic for discussion are given time to talk. The members of the discussion group are to eat lunch together and play together for at least one week.

8. Members of the discussion group can compose a letter to their parents asking if they all could do something together on the weekend.

Vivian Boyce   Grades 2–5

Objective: To teach students about the messages a body reveals regarding attitudes and emotions.

Rationale: Body language knowledge is important in aiding children to understand how humans act and feel.

Activities:

1. Pantomine is acting out situations without verbalizing. The teacher holds up words and asks students to make their face coincide with the word, for example, snarl, happy, puzzled.

   • Teacher holds up pictures of people and asks students to guess their emotions.

   • Teacher asks students to role play a traffic cop giving someone a ticket, and a student asking the principal for permission to use the school gym for a party.

2. Students sit in circle. Teacher plays music and children follow what she does. After music stops, a student becomes the leader.

   - After game, students sit in a circle holding a mirror. They practice waving hands and making faces.

   - Students pair off. Each takes a turn doing exactly what the partner does—becomes a mirror of the other.

   - Teacher gives examples for both students to do without speaking—pickup a comb, comb hair, put down comb, put letter in envelope, lick it shut, put a stamp on it. Students do other such exercises such as brushing teeth.

3. Students pretend they have blown up a huge bubble. Child imagines stepping inside bubble. A gust of wind comes up and bubble is floating across the room. Each child is to pretend walking on eggs, cotton, nails, ice, through snow and water.

   - Child moves body as though a robot, a boxer, a skier, a motorcyclist, a ballet dancer, a baseball player, etc.

4. Teacher shows class video of zoo animals. Video is stopped at certain points to note how a lion or gorilla moves.

   - Students pretend they are moving like a cat or a snake or walking like a penguin.

5. Students divided into groups. Their task is to pantomine different parts of the house—toaster, dishwasher, pan, iron, broom, clothes, etc. The pantomines are presented to the class.

   - Each group makes up situations—sibling wants to watch a program on TV or make a phone call. The group presents their pantomine to the class.

6. Teacher plays familiar songs and students in groups take on task of acting out the song.

7. Class puts on pantomine version of *Jack and the Beanstock*. It is presented to other classes.

Bibliography:

Foley, Kathy, et al., *The Good Apple Guide to Creative Drama,* Carthage, Ill., Good Apple Inc., 1981.

Goodridge, Janet, *Creative Drama and Improvised Music for Children,* Boston, Mass. Plays Inc. 1971.

Kay, Drina, *All the Desks a Stage.* Nashville, Tenn. Incentive Pub. 1982.

Keysell, Pat. *Mime Themes and Motifs.* Boston, Mass. Plays Inc. 1980.

Siks, Geraldine, *Drama With Children.* N.Y. Harper & Row, 1977.

Wilson, Robina. *Creative Drama and Musical Activities for Children,* Boston, Mass. Plays Inc. 1979.

REFERENCES

Coser, L. (1956). *The functions of social conflict*. New York: Free Press.

Davis, A.M. (1986, July). Teaching ideas: Dispute resolution at an early age. *Negotiation Journal, 1* (3), p. 287–98.

Gerlach, R. & Lamprecht, L. (1975). *Teaching about the law*. Cincinnati: W. H. Anderson.

Henning, J. (1979). *Mandate for change: The impact of law on educational innovation*. Chicago: American Bar Association Press.

Riekes, L., Appenzeller, H., Engler, T., Mathews, N. and Ross, C. T. (1984). *Sports and law*. St. Paul: West.

Shaftel, F., & Shaftel, G. (1982). *Role playing in the curriculum*. Englewood Cliffs, NJ: Prentice Hall.

Taylor, D. (1977, March). *Law Studies in Schools: A Compendium of Instructional Strategies. Social Education, 41*, (3), p. 170–78.

SUGGESTED READING

Coser, L. (1956). *The functions of social conflict*. New York: Free Press.

Festinger, L. (1964). *Conflict, decision and dissonance*. Stanford: Stanford University Press.

Henning, J. (1979). *Mandate for change: The impact of law on educational innovation*. Chicago: American Bar Association Press.

Himes, J. (1980). *Conflict and conflict management*. Athens: University of Georgia Press.

Jandt, F. E. (Ed.). *Conflict resolution through management*. New York: Harper & Row.

Lamprecht, L., & Gerlach, R. (1975). *Teaching about the law*. Cincinnati: W. H. Anderson.

Riekes, L., Appenzeller, H., Engler, T., Mathews, N., and Ross, C. T. (1984). *Sports and law*. St. Paul: West.

Shaftel, F., and Shaftel, G. (1982). *Role playing in the curriculum*. Englewood Cliffs, NJ: Prentice-Hall.

Stone, J. (1977). *Conflict through consensus*, Baltimore: Johns Hopkins University Press.

Chapter 15

The World and the Classroom Community

The World and the Classroom Community

The classroom is an active participant in the local and world communities. Children continually interact with community resources and facilities, and the sights and sounds of the outside world are always present in their daily lives. It becomes increasingly necessary in contemporary life to integrate the classroom into the dynamic flow of the world that exists not merely in the immediate environment, but in faraway places.

Current events are an important way of helping students become aware of our complex world. Current events lessons enable students to investigate what they hear, see, and read outside school in a more systematic manner of inquiry. Students benefit in several ways from well-organized current events programs:

1. They enable students to study materials or issues not found in textbooks.
2. They make students aware of dramatic and fast changing events in the modern world.
3. They dramatize the multicultural dimensions and interconnectedness of contemporary world events.
4. They provide practice in examining controversial issues in an objective manner.
5. They form linkages between present events and the historical background leading to current situations.
6. They make possible wider application of community resources to the study of national and world problems.
7. They teach students to be selective readers and to examine sources of information in a systematic manner.
8. They enable students to grasp the underlying factors influencing persons and nations and how these may change or remain constant over time.

The disintegration of the Soviet Union, the unification of Germany, and other dramatic events testify to the acceleration of change in the modern world. The map of the world is vastly different from a few years ago. Children and adults increasingly find themselves unable to keep pace with fast breaking events.

The study of current events is popular with children because they link the work within schools with what is happening outside. Television has transformed the way people obtain information.

▲ Current events lessons enable students to investigate what they hear, see, and read at home in a systematic inquiry. *Courtesy Null Elementary, Saint Charles (Missouri) Public Schools.*

Visual images of current events carry greater impact than the printed word, and both adults and children increasingly obtain knowledge from television rather than the newspaper.

The teaching of current events poses several fundamental problems since teachers lack the support of professionally designed instrument such as a textbook. Teachers have to make choices about which events are worthy of study and how to organize the class during the process of the investigation. There are other factors that generate difficulty in teaching current events:

1. *TV Sound-bite:* A typical 30-minute local or national TV newscast devotes approximately 3 minutes to world or national affairs. Lack of time and concern over ratings limits time allocated to serious discussion of major world problems. Viewers obtain limited information concerning issues and problems facing the world.

2. *Background Information:* The fragments of information concerning complex issues generally fail to provide students with historical antecedents of the problem. Few stories on television go beyond a superficial examination concerning past aspects of the event. Students have to evaluate based upon incomplete knowledge regarding how the situation has evolved to its present state.

3. *News Story Drama*: Media dramatizes those aspects of a story that lend themselves to dramatic visual images. The old media adage is that Boy Scouts helping old ladies to cross streets does not "sell" on the six o'clock news. Viewers are frequently overwhelmed by violent and confusing images that lend themselves more to the media's desire for emotional impact than for careful and objective analysis of topics.

4. *Limited Diversity of Views:* Few newspapers or TV programs present more than a limited perspective on contemporary events. The views of people on the extremes of the political spectrum are generally ignored nor are the ideas of politically unpopular people presented in a systematic manner. Mainstream ideas are welcomed because they tend to avoid creating controversy. Corporate sponsors fear.that controversy will prove detrimental to the sale of their products.

5. *Ignorance Influences News:* There are many areas of the world and topics that are not well known to media people. For example, few American newscasters or reporters are familiar with events in Moslem nations, African politics, economic conditions in Latin America or Chinese history. The limited number of experts on topics such as these affects the depth and sophistication of information presented to viewers, listeners or readers.

News is essential to a free society. Despite the proliferation of news media in the past decades, voter participation has declined in the political process. It is important for students to understand the manner in which citizens obtain information and the uses of that knowledge. Following are several activities to stimulate analytical investigation by students into the issue of how does the media impact our knowledge of current events.

Activity

Students conduct a survey of parents and neighbors regarding their sources of knowledge of current events. Participants could be asked to indicate what percent of their knowledge comes from the following sources: radio, magazines, newspapers, television, people. The results can be charted and graphed.

The manner in which current events are made known to the general audience is a key factor in how well students are able to present informative reports to their classmates. Without an historical sense, young children are not able to follow in a meaningful way the changing story of world events. The upper elementary and middle school grades can be more systematic in gathering data and making effective presentations, but they need accurate background information.

In organizing current events, teachers should consider several factors, such as the knowledge base of students, the complexity of the current event, the availability of information, and the manner in which information is to be shared with the class. Current events should be viewed as a year long process in which students continually improve the sophistication of their comprehension of world and national affairs.

▲ Teacher and student can jointly identify issues that the class will investigate. *Courtesy Kirkwood (Missouri) School District.*

Organizing for Current Events

1. *Planning Period*: Teacher and students can jointly identify issues, topics, or problem areas that the class will investigate during the academic year. After compiling these topics, the class can develop a list of resources that will enable students to follow these current event issues. For example, the *Weekly Reader,* newspapers, magazines, pen pal letters from children in other nations, and videotaped TV newscasts are just a few of the many resources students can use in current events reports. Groups can be assigned topics and given access to a variety of resources to assist in their preparation of reports.

2. *Research Period:* During this stage, students actively read, write, and compile information. In the process of gathering data, students decide which are the best ways to present their findings to classmates. Time must be allocated for student research in the library, contacts with outside resources, and planning opportunities with the teacher.

3. *Presentation Period*: Current events requires students to give presentations to the class. Each group may be allocated time during the week for its presentation. This will require time for planning the method of giving the report. In some cases, students may design a collage or show a video or use the chalkboard to give their report. The manner in which the report is given should emerge from a well thought out decision.

4. *Evaluation Period*: Students need feedback from other students and the teacher about the effectiveness of their presentations. This information can come in the form of oral

remarks, written commentary, cumulative checklists, rating scales, drawings, or through visual means. For example, the class might draw pictures depicting events presented by a group, or individual members of the class might add additional information to the report.

Teachers employ many strategies as part of current events lessons. An interesting approach is having weekly role-plays of press conferences in which the teacher, a student, or an outside speaker is questioned by the class regarding a topic. This requires students to study topics discussed at the press conference, or it might involve group-initiated questions for the panelists.

A popular activity is organizing current events scrapbooks that contain stories, pictures, or tapes about pressing problems or issues. From this source, students can produce a monthly class newspaper containing the 10 most interesting current events studied during this time period.

Students can submit photographs or drawings to an editorial board that would select pictures for a collage or to form the basis of a monthly picture magazine of national and world affairs. These can be placed on a current events bulletin board.

▲ **Student research in the library includes opportunities to discuss with teachers the current state of their research efforts.** *Courtesy Webster University.*

The increased presence of VCRs in homes enables students to tape reports of current events. It is now possible for the class to become producers of news programs that could be shown to other classes in the school. They can use camcorders to create their own programs or tape commercial programs and select from among the news items in order to produce a current events program. If a pen pal relationship is established with a school in another nation, videos could be exchanged or news programs developed to share with one another, though you should be sure the video formats you are using are compatible.

In many schools the controversial Channel One developed by Chris Whittle offers free video equipment in exchange for the right to show current events programs accompanied by commercials. It is still too early to gauge the effective of this program upon learning. Some teachers are disturbed by the presence of commercials in the classroom, particularly since students are a captive audience.

In the social studies segment of the elementary school curriculum the focus on current events is accepted without question, but the need to incorporate current events in other disciplines such as language arts, art, music, or mathematics is not so obvious. Yet, current events affect every aspect of the curriculum and can add a new dimension to what is presently being taught. A current events emphasis across the curriculum more readily ensures that students will become aware and understand the wider world beyond the classroom.

Language Arts

Even the best language arts lessons improve when composition, vocabulary, and literature derive at least part of their content from the daily concerns of the modern world. Written and oral communication skills are learned more effectively when students write about and discuss problems that have visual and emotional significance in their lives.

For example, a news account of an eruption of a volcano can spark interest in investigating stories about volcanoes or other natural disasters. The plight of children in Ireland, Lebanon, or the Sudan who are experiencing war and conflict can be correlated to stories or poetry from literature that deal with children living through terror. The classic, "I Never Saw Another Butterfly," which contains poetry of Jewish children in the Holocaust can be linked to poetry or stories from children today who are surviving death and destruction. An effective way of making the present come alive is to involve students in the literature and culture of other societies.

Many children face difficulty dealing with the vocabulary of current events, and language arts experiences in writing and research can be incorporated into social studies lessons. Spelling and vocabulary lessons can be drawn from words encountered by students on TV or in newspapers. Research and writing skills that are vital in developing effective current events presentations can be integrated within the regular language arts program.

Art

The art of other cultures is continually present in daily news reports. Posters, editorial cartoons, or propaganda pieces dealing with a variety of topics such as the environment, pollution, or political parties can be discussed in the art segment of the elementary school curriculum. Students can create visual materials to accompany current events reports.

Foreign Language

A major objective in the study of foreign languages is an improved understanding of the people and cultures of other nations. Even beginning students can use foreign language newspapers or magazines for information about another country. Students can also write to embassies for tourist information about countries in the news. Advanced students can read excerpts from textbooks from other nations in order to obtain a different slant on topics being discussed by the media.

▲ Student presentations about current events may include artwork or other visual media. *Courtesy Kirkwood (Missouri) School District.*

Mathematics

Word problems in mathematics lend themselves to discussion of current topics. Daily newspapers contain charts and graphs as well as economic and financial data about other countries. The decline in the rain forest is a social as well as mathematical issue that students can pursue by using mathematical computations. Levels of income in America or the disparity between economic classes can be approached through mathematics lessons.

Science

Scientific issues increasingly dominate the newspapers as international conferences meet to discuss environmental issues and pollution. Scientific literacy begins by connecting current events to significant scientific developments in the modern world. The disposal of radioactive waste or timber cutting are at base scientific problems that can only be resolved if our population has the knowledge for intelligent analysis.

Music

The invasion of the Beatles in the 1960s marked a change not only in music but in dress and culture. Rappers and rock stars, country western and pop singers all incorporate topics of current concern to our society. The music of other nations also brings out transnational issues that students can more readily grasp through music.

Current events has a role to fulfill in every aspect of the elementary curriculum. This does not mean abandoning texts in use, but utilizing the richness of current events to enhance what is being taught in the prescribed curriculum. The use of current events also requires further thought about the best method to present material of this nature to students.

Although materials designed specifically for children are available, a great amount of the information students obtain regarding world events emanates from sources geared to adults, not children. It is natural that many words or ideas are not easily understood by children. Teachers should consider taping segments of news broadcasts and playing them in class in order to provide guidance to students about vocabulary and the concepts being discussed.

A major problem in current events presentations by students is the manner in which the material is shared with the class. The listener is bombarded with confusing words and information. Many children hesitate asking questions for fear of placing themselves up for ridicule or embarrassing a classmate. It is necessary for teachers to regularly check student comprehension of what is being presented in a current events lesson.

A final problem concerns how current events presentations are evaluated. It may not be possible to use normal grading criteria to evaluate the confusing tangle of contemporary world events. Effort, in many cases, is as vitally important as the actual product of the current events lesson. Many students will require months before they become sufficiently knowledgeable to offer well-constructed ideas about current affairs. Teachers should consider in evaluation the growth and development of student knowledge concerning current events.

▲ An interesting approach to current events is a "press conference" in which a guest is questioned by students. *Courtesy University City (Missouri) Public Schools.*

Students as Participants in the World Community

The inhabitants of planet Earth represent a world community even though world events may belie this concept. Children in a classroom no longer are isolated from events throughout the world. Their dress, music, values, and behavior are all shaped by forces emanating from every part of our planet. It becomes increasingly necessary for the classroom to become a microcosm of the world in order to prepare children to effectively function in a multinational environment.

A choice often confronting teachers is whether the class should reflect the values of the local community, the United States, or the emerging force of the global community as exemplified in the United Nations. Not all areas of the world adhere to democratic principles, and not all regions of America are equally as comfortable with schools modeling democracy. Each teacher has to determine the extent to which democracy can become an operating principle of the classroom.

The idea that classrooms should replicate the democratic process is not new. The great Polish educator Janus Korzcak urged during the pre-World War II era the creation of a children's world parliament in which children from all over the world would elect representatives who would pass laws governing children. He created schools in Poland in which students shared with teachers responsibility for organizing the learning process in schools. John Dewey and other American educators have emphasized the importance of making the classroom not merely a democratic environment but one in which students practice how to be successful in today's world.

Classroom Organization

The collapse of communism as an important ideology attests to the desire of people throughout the world to incorporate the tenets of democracy as part of their everyday lives. The principles of democracy should initially be practiced in the elementary and middle school classroom from the first day of school. Students can negotiate social contracts with the teacher in establishing democratic processes to govern how everyone functions in the daily life of the class.

For example, students can identify the rules that govern proper behavior in the classroom as well as consequences for violations. Each week time can be set aside for students to identify a topic to be studied and their individual responsibilities for learning.

Democracy encounters problems in its implementation. Jury systems sometimes fail to function in a responsible manner, or leaders are tainted by corruption. A democratic classroom will not always function in a smooth manner, but this failure is the essence of how children learn the pitfalls and virtues of democracy. The birth within the past few years of dozens of new democratic nations is creating enormous problems. Ethnic groups in the former Soviet Union and Yugoslavia engage in bloody wars of attrition because of ancient grudges and conflicts. The old Soviet and Yugoslav dictatorial systems forcibly prevented such brutality. Dictatorial regimes prevent people from gaining experience in the peaceful resolution of problems, and the sudden emergence of democracy has ill-prepared the conflicting forces to overcome their problems without resorting to war.

The problems students encounter within a democratic classroom may mirror difficulties occurring in newly established democratic societies. An important instructional strategy is to relate a classroom breakdown in democracy to the breakdowns happening throughout the world. In this way, students learn that democracy is a living force in their daily lives rather than a set of abstract principles learned from books.

For example, the ability to accept people having differing values, religious practices or coming from another heritage is not always present in the classroom or in democratic nations. A clash between students can become not only a lesson in how to resolve conflicts in a peaceful nonviolent manner but also provides a starting point to examine a similar problem occurring elsewhere in the world. Each time a link is made between the operational components of democracy in the classroom with the dynamics of democracy in nations, the student is genuinely experiencing the democratic process.

▲ An effective way to make current events come alive is to introduce students to the children and culture of another land. *Courtesy Webster University.*

Charting Democracy

An effective way to establish correlations between classroom democracy and issues of world democracy is to develop a chart that indicates strengths and weaknesses of the democratic process. This chart would be updated and discussed each time an event happens in the classroom or in the world. It would provide students a visual depiction of how their behavior in the class reflects what is happening elsewhere in the world.

Classroom	World
1. An argument took place today when two students argued over possession of the swings.	1. Country "X" last week took over control of all foreign-owned oil resources.
2. The class was unable to decide who should represent it at a mock U.N. Assembly in the state capitol.	2. The Italian parliament is dead-locked over who should be the prime minister.

A common complaint leveled at schools is that they do not represent the "real world." Teachers know classroom issues are as relevant to real life as what occurs in any corporation or human service enterprise. The process of involving students in exploring how their daily experiences relate to what happens elsewhere is vitally important in aiding them to become knowledgeable citizens.

Mock U.N. Assemblies

One technique favored by teachers is to assign pairs of students to represent a country throughout the course of the year. The team reports on the country's culture, foods, sports, issues, and problems. Periodically, a mock assembly is held in which students represent their country's interests in the resolution of problems. A mock assembly can be more readily done with children from the upper elementary grades.

The authors elsewhere in the text have described techniques of creating simulation activities in which students engage in negotiation and discussion in order to resolve problems. Simulation activities can become part of the ongoing process of involving students in resolving conflict and understanding how people can either peacefully settle differences or resort to violence.

The Media as a Doorway to the World

Many educators regard television with disdain because of its violence, excessive commercials, or because it distracts students from reading. It has been estimated that children who daily watch several hours of television may be exposed to over 20,000 commercials per year. There is little question that television and radio are the child's main entry into the global village. We may bemoan the negative effects of television, but educators must learn how to employ this powerful medium effectively in the instructional process.

Over half of American homes are now linked into cable television, which offers programming ranging from the violent to educationally stimulating programs that appear on such channels as the Discovery Channel or the Arts and Entertainment channel. In a typical week, *TV Guide* lists programs about World War II, the Inca civilization, life in China, or depictions of education in Japan.

The VCR offers teachers opportunities to tape programs that reveal important information about other parts of the world. Programs dealing with the disappearance of the rain forest or the plight of animals in Africa enable children in the class to compare and contrast what is happening in their local community with events in other parts of the world. It is important to allocate time each week for students to review publications such as *TV Guide* to identify programs relevant to the school curriculum.

Radio offers a wide variety of programs that students can connect to topics of broad relevance in their lives. There are many talk shows, special programs on topics being studied in class, and a variety of music stations. These enable students to study music from different cultures or compare their own interests in music with those of other people. Some students may have radios that can receive shortwave broadcasts from other nations. Students could write to these radio programs asking questions or use them to help build connections with children in other nations. Students can also organize a daily newscast for presentation over the PA system to the entire school.

In the coming years it will become increasingly possible for students to view programs from other nations. Students will have satellite dishes at home that enable them to pick up programs from throughout the world. These connections enable students to learn a foreign language, to view children's programs from other societies, and to learn about holidays, foods, customs, and current problems. In the process of linking to worldwide media, the student increasingly becomes an integral member of a world society.

For example, weather reports from the local community can form the basis of a worldwide study of weather. Students can follow patterns of winds, rain, snow, or sunshine as they move across the world by viewing satellite weather reports broadcast from other nations. The media have the potential of making the world come alive in the classroom and concretizing abstract knowledge presented in textbooks.

Students as Participants in the Local Community

World events impinge upon the daily lives of all Americans. Communities do not exist as isolated entities but are inextricably linked to decisions made elsewhere. Current events are not only happening far away but also within the local community. The call-up of the National Guard to handle a conflict abroad or massive layoffs caused by another nation's decision not to purchase airplanes can disrupt the lives of children. The failure of one community to deal with energy or pollution issues creates problems in other regions of the nation or world. Students are participants in the drama of local life and they need opportunities to help make their immediate environment a safe and healthy place to live.

Some schools, particularly at the secondary level, have introduced the concept that students should perform some form of local community service as part of their graduation requirements. This concept can also be applied to students in elementary and middle schools to encourage involvement in local community affairs. There are many tasks elementary-age children can perform, such as being responsible for keeping an area free of debris, collecting food and clothing for poor or homeless families, offering companionship to people in retirement homes, or improving the cleanliness of parks.

Community's Economic Life

Elementary and middle schools are appropriate places for students to investigate the economic dimensions of their local community. An understanding of the economic framework of their community helps students make sense of the flow of events in their daily lives. They also learn an important concept in the democratic process— choice. Economics in American society entails decision making based upon individual preferences.

▲ A culminating experience might involve a schoolwide presentation of the economic life of the community at different stages in time. *Courtesy Francis Howell (Missouri) School District.*

Studying the local community actively involves students with agencies such as commerce, tourism, sanitation, police, firefighters, or the mayor's office. They can collect data pertaining to industries, occupations, housing, recreation, transportation, communication, services, etc. Schools in many communities are an important aspect of the community, providing jobs and pumping money into the local area. Students might be interested in studying the origin of the school system, how it impacts the local economy, or how many people in it not only work but live in the community. A multicultural dimension of such a study is exploring how members of the school system represent the ethnic composition of the community.

A culminating activity to studying local economic history is organizing a schoolwide presentation in which the class could depict the economic life of the community at different stages in time. Charts, collages, pictures, music and written commentaries would explain how people lived and worked from the founding to the present stage of the community.

It might also be possible for students to obtain artifacts from the past—a milk bottle from the 1940s, a picture of a candy store, trolley car, or a horse-driven ice cart, clothes from the 1930s with labels indicating where they were manufactured, something manufactured in another country, or an old black-and-white TV set. These pieces of the past tell an economic story about the community which helps explain the present. They can be reinforced by asking grandparents and parents to give class presentations about economic life in their childhood.

After completing such a project, the class can establish a pen pal relationship with a school in another city, state, or nation to share information about economic conditions in their respective communities. It opens new avenues for investigation as students compare their own community's economic life with that of a rural, urban, or foreign situation. They may discover how children in different parts of the world often wear similar clothes or consume the same products. It is through this process that children become sensitive to the growing globalization of the world economic system and its impact upon the economic life of each local community.

Field Trips

There are many resources and facilities in the local community that relate to current events topics. The beating by Los Angeles police of an African-American raises questions about how local police behave toward minorities. The shutdown of a local factory may be connected to world events, or a visit to a dairy can lead to discussions about diet and health.

Elementary social studies curricula include a number of units entailing trips out into the neighborhood or the local community. Some elementary school teachers take their classes on field trips regularly, overcoming considerable costs in money, time, and aggravation because they recognize the educational benefits that can result from such journeys. A field trip is another opportunity for teachers to link a piece of the local community to current events issues.

The novelty of a trip to a historic site or museum and the experience of seeing and touching serves to fire the curiosity of students who may have read but never seen firsthand these pieces of our heritage. Standing besides a fire truck alters the dimension of size in the mind of a child who has seen its picture. Sitting in a courtroom with an actual jury and judge differs from reading about it.

▲ In a field trip, direct physical experiences rather than words are at the core.

▲ The novelty of a field trip fires the curiosity of students.

A field trip is an experience in which *things* rather than words are at its core. This broadens the opportunity for each student to actively participate in the learning experience. It makes the content equally accessible to every class member since all can physically interact with the event. A field trip also provides children who may be quiet in the classroom a new avenue to discuss their ideas or feelings in a less threatening environment.

The field trip offers teachers a new source of curriculum content that adds to the richness and diversity of the existing course of study. Questions or comments during the field trip can become a springboard for further investigation when the class returns to school. A field trip should be viewed not as something apart but as integral to the school's educational process. It is an opportunity for a new opening, not an end in itself.

Economic constraints make it increasingly difficult for teachers to take field trips. There is also growing concern that an injury to a child exposes teachers and school to legal action. In the winter of 1992, several children were hurt on a field trip to a Chicago airport when a car went out of control. It may be increasingly necessary for teachers to engage students in fund-raising activities in order to have money for field trips. There is also the distinct reality that some school districts will discourage field trips to avoid accidents and law suits.

Museums

Museums are changing. Children are discovering that the once stuffy, sterile, and intimidating halls of museums are now scenes of exciting hands-on activities, stimulating lectures, and engaging media presentations. Dusty displays have been transformed into vivid experiences as curators, teachers, and parents have opened new channels of communication. Museums not only contain our cultural heritage but also are sources of materials that relate to current events topics.

Museums are designing exhibits and activities that appeal both to children's interests and levels of understanding. Perception games, sensory explorations, improvisations, inquiry, and simulations are techniques that museum educators increasingly employ to stimulate children's thinking. Museum tours now emphasize in-depth studies as opposed to surveys that bombard student senses with too many ideas.

Another trend is providing authentic settings for museum collections. By using contextual displays, children gain a greater understanding of relationships between items and events or between an item and its purpose. Some museums have constructed rooms or buildings where children can become immersed in the feelings of other times and places.

A visit to a museum has greater impact if students receive a pre-visit orientation. It helps if the teacher has already been to the museum and knows what students will experience. In some museums, pre-visit kits are available,

FIELD TRIP SUGGESTIONS:

1. Do you have school permission for the field trip?
2. Do you have signed permission forms from parents?
3. Is transportation arranged?
4. Have you visited the site of the field trip and determined how it is to be used for educational purposes?
5. What activities are planned at the site?
6. Is there a person at the site who will conduct educational activities? Have you discussed their presentation with them?
7. Are you familiar with procedures if a child gets hurt?
8. How will you ensure that children don't get separated on the field trip?
9. How long will the field trip last?
10. What activities do you have planned going and coming from the site? If a bus is to be used, will you lead a discussion on the way and on the return?
11. Do you wish students to do something during the field trip, such as take notes?
12. Do you have phone numbers of all students? What will you do if parents fail to pick up their children?

or it may be possible to have a museum staff member visit the class to help prepare them for the field trip to the museum. There are also volunteer docents working on museum staffs who can give presentations in schools. Teachers need to be aware of the unique features and services of a museum prior to planning a field trip.

In an age of economic scarcity and cost-cutting, teachers have to rely upon outreach programs offered by museums. Some museums offer traveling mobile exhibits, lending libraries, and programs of special interest that can be delivered to the school. Lending libraries may provide objects for display in the class. Teachers should develop a human resource catalog of parents or people in the community with special interests who may be of assistance in discussing these objects or providing additional information. A student-parent initiated museum exhibit can result from these resources.

Follow-up activities assure that a museum visit becomes an integral part of the child's learning experience. Documenting a museum experience with tape recordings, slides, photographs or videotapes serves as a catalyst to stimulate children's thinking and imagination. Many of these materials are available in a museum shop or they can be developed by students in the course of the visit.

Videotaping in a museum requires prior approval, but the reward is self-evident. It not only reinforces the actual experience but also enables children in other classes to share in the museum trip. Other follow-up activities to consider are:

1. Recreate the experience in the classroom. Use materials gathered during the trip such as pictures, tape recordings, or items purchased in the gift shop to dramatize the visit. If students saw an exhibit of dinosaurs, they could collect pictures of dinosaurs, show film clips, display artifacts they purchased or construct their own dinosaur. They might even organize a mini-museum that other classes could visit.

▲ Museums are now scenes of exciting hands-on activities and engaging media presentations.

2. Language arts activities can add a creative dimension to the visit. Students can write stories, compose poems, or do art activities to illustrate what they saw or experienced.

3. Students can create their own museum, drawing upon knowledge gained in their trip. If they visited an exhibit on colonial life, the students could create a similar exhibit to depict the World War II or Vietnam eras. It may be possible for students to obtain from family sources artifacts to exhibit in their museum. Obviously, expensive items should not be included in such an exhibit.

4. The class can develop a book depicting their experience at the museum that would be shared with children in lower grades. This makes the students become teachers and improves their observational and organizational skills.

5. In addition to the traditional thank-you letter to museum staff, students can write letters to parents, pen pals, or relatives explaining what they learned at the museum.

6. We have discussed geography in previous chapters. A museum visit is an excellent illustration of how mapping skills can be employed to add a new dimension to the trip. The students can draw a map of the museum or the trip from school to the museum and develop symbols to depict significant points of interest.

Museums are an important source of information for students. Teachers can use these field trip experiences to add zest and enthusiasm for material being studied in the class.

▲ Social studies curricula call for trips out into the local community.
Courtesy Robert Tabscott, Elijah Lovejoy Society.

People in the Community

It has been traditional in the elementary classroom to have guest speakers present information about their occupations, areas of expertise, or interests. Virtually every child in elementary school has heard a talk by a police officer or firefighter. People in the community are valuable resources whose talents should be used to the fullest extent possible.

America, historically, has been a nation encompassing people of diverse ethnic origins. It is currently estimated that within 40 years, a varying range of 30 to 40 percent of students in schools will be of minority backgrounds. The multicultural composition of American society suggests that increasingly within communities valuable resource people are available who can link the child's immediate neighborhood to broader international dimensions.

Guest speakers are available who can bring the outside world into the world of the classroom. Poetry, art, music, foreign language, and cultural differences and similarities can be presented in an exciting manner to students. The use of community people enables children to see their own parents play an active role in the life of the school. Children more readily form connections with a neighbor who discusses an army experience in Germany or their early childhood in Japan or their journey from Mexico to America. These resource people are also much more willing to do follow-up activities with children from their own neighborhood.

It is vital in the use of guest speakers to pay particular attention to pre- and post-activities. Speakers have greater impact if the class has been prepared than if the speaker hits them cold. Following are some suggestions:

1. Carefully select the speaker and review with the guest topics to be covered in the class presentation. Make certain you know the exact nature of what is being discussed.

2. Brainstorm questions to be posed to the speaker and assign teams to raise these questions. Ask students what they would like to know regarding the topic being discussed.

3. In some cases, it might be preferable to have a panel pose the questions.

4. Have students ask their parents for suggestions about questions to ask. This might uncover a parent who has further information about the topic.

5. It helps if the teacher reviews with the speaker the format of the presentation.

6. During the presentation, students can ask the speaker for suggestions about related activities.

7. There should be an activity to follow-up the guest speaker's presentation.

In the coming years there will be greater availability for telephone hookups in classrooms that will allow students to have phone discussions with people who are outside the local community. As classrooms form relationships with schools in other societies, the guest speaker format can be linked to a global interactive process. Students can audio- or videotape their guest speakers and send that to children in another country and receive back tapes of guest speakers from different societies.

The opportunities to link children from throughout the world in a global community exist for the first time in human history. The technology is finally available, barriers are disintegrating as democracy spreads throughout the world, and children share cultural and personal values. The classroom is part of the global community, and the social studies curriculum has to change to reflect this new dimension of human existence.

SUMMARY

This chapter has examined the role of current events in the social studies curriculum. It also examined the use of field trips, museum visits, and guest speakers in expanding student knowledge of the world.

QUESTIONS

1. As an elementary school child, what did you like best about current events lessons? What did you like least?

2. What do you find most difficult today about keeping abreast of current events?

3. Which current events issues in the past few years have most captured your interest? Why?

4. What are your views about the Channel One program that presents current events accompanied by commercials? Should this be allowed in public schools?

5. Which criteria would you use in the evaluation of student current events reports?

6. Describe the various forms of media from which you obtain information about current events.

7. If parents object to speakers appearing in a classroom, should they have the right to remove their child from hearing the presentation? Why?

8. When you were in elementary school, what did you like least or best about presentations made by people from the local community?

9. Based on your school experiences, what is most or least effective about field trips?

10. Describe three exciting ways to get students involved in community affairs.

1. Have students study the news content of newscasts for an extended period of time. Analyze the data in order to identify key issues.

2. Have students list which newspapers and magazines are read on a regular basis. Analyze these periodicals on the basis of political leanings and then interpret the collated data.

3. Have students examine the history and social science courses taken at college.

Which knowledge areas stand out most pointedly?

4. Divide the class into three groups. One group only collects data about world affairs from TV, one from newspapers only, and one from magazines only. Compare and contrast what was learned.

5. Have students react to a current event from a social studies, an art, a music, and a language arts perspective.

READING

Americans Glued to the Tube: Mass Media, Information, and Social Studies

by Mary A. Hepburn

News is essential to a free society. Democracy requires that sources of political information be independent from the government and widely available to the public. Recent events in the People's Republic of China are a grim reminder of that principle. The traditional model of American civic education envisions a citizenry obtaining and digesting information from multiple news sources and using information to take positions on public policy debates.

It would seem that rapid advancements in communications technology would encourage higher levels of public civic interest and involvement. But instead we find that public political interest and voter turnout are the lowest levels in several decades. Is the public failing to obtain the news it needs? Is social studies education failing to develop a critical awareness of the news media? The answer is probably some of both. See what you think as you read about the following public information sources.

Information About our Information Sources

Sources of News. In the past 25 years news delivery has changed dramatically in the United States. National surveys of the 18 and over population (Roper 1985, 1987) show that in 1961 newspapers were the main source of news (57 percent) with television a fairly close second (52 percent), while 34 percent cited radio, and only 9 percent mentioned magazines. (The total is greater than 100 percent because many people used more than one source.) By 1986 television had become the dominant source of news for 66 percent of the people, while only 36 percent cited newspapers, 14 percent cited radio, and only 4 percent cited magazines. Fewer people used more than one source. Most remarkable in the 1986 survey was the finding that 50 percent of American adults were relying *solely* on television for news.

Among college-educated Americans, newspapers persisted as the main source of news until the early 1980s. However, by 1984 they too cited television as their main news source—by ten percentage points more than newspapers—and their reliance on more than one source of news was declining (Roper 1986).

Television Viewing Time. It is not so surprising that television dominates all other mass media as a source of news when one reviews the amount of television viewing time reported in American households. In 1955 the average daily viewing time per television household was 4 hours and 51 minutes. In 1965 it was 5 hours and 29 minutes. By 1975 it was 6 hours and 7 minutes, and in 1986 the average daily viewing time per American television household was 7 hours and 45 minutes (Roper 1986). Keep in mind that today, close to 99 percent of American households have television. It appears that we are fast becoming a nation of "couch potatoes."

Differences by Age Groups. Average viewing time differs by age group. The heaviest viewers are people over 55 and young children 2 to 6 years old. Females in every age group are heavier viewers than are males. Nielson reported that in November, 1986, women over 55 watched an average of 45.3 hours of television per week, while men in this age group watched 38.3 hours per week. Children 2–5 watched 28.2 hours per week and children 6–11 watched an average of 25 hours a week. Young people 15–24 were relatively light viewers, watching television an average of 21.2 hours. Apparently other activities reduce viewing time. It should be remembered that the hours reported do not include time spent viewing movies played on the home VCR or playing video games, so it is likely be that many more hours than reported are spent in front of the video screen.

Use Patterns by Young People. Teenagers are particularly heavy users of radio and television. A survey of 13- to 17-year-olds conducted in the mid-eighties indicated that radio was the most popular (91 percent) of the mass media with television (89 percent) the second most frequently used. By 1989, both radio listening and television viewing were equally high (93 percent). Newspaper reading, however, had declined 7 percent from 68 percent in 1986 to 61 percent in 1989. Notably, newspaper reading was most prevalent in students doing "above-average" school work (Gallup 1989).

Earlier research (see Stanley and Niemi 1988, chapt. 2) provides data on young adult audiences 18–24 and offers some clues about youthful news interests. The study determined that newspaper reading by younger readers was heaviest during prime time (8:00 P.M. to 11:00 P.M.), but only about a third of younger viewers 18–24 watched the news programs that precede or follow prime time shows.

A study of Virginia 8th and 11th grade students in four school districts provides additional insight into television news viewing preferences (Fleming and Weber 1983). They also found that television was student's main source of news. The Virginia students viewed more local news than national news, and the stories that most interested male students were sports items, while human interest stories on local news were the main interest of female students.

A recent report on media use by 21,364 students in the Santa Barbara County School District (1989), entitled *The Wired Bedroom,* revealed that K–12 students had in their bedrooms: radios (79.9 percent), television sets (43.6 percent), stereos (45.7 percent), telephones (38.3 percent), and VCRs (12.9 percent). (Percentages for the 7–12th grade students were higher for every type of equipment.) Reported average weekday television viewing time for the Santa Barbara K–12 students was: 1 to 2 hours for 39 percent, 3 to 5 hours for 24 percent, more than 5 hours for 11 percent, and 1 hour or less for 27 percent, while 54 percent listened to radio every day. Students with better grades in the school district were less likely to have television sets in their bedrooms. The Santa Barbara students appear to be less hooked on television than overall national samples; nevertheless, electronic media are pervasive in their daily lives.

Public Attitudes Toward Information Gained from Mass Media. The American public considers television to be the most credible of the news media. People are more inclined to believe what is seen in active, picture news on television than what is read in print news stories. Asked which source they would believe if given conflicting news reports, 55 percent of adults (18 and over) said they would believe television over other news sources. Less than one-fourth considered newspapers more credible than other news sources, and less than 10 percent said they would believe radio or magazines over other news sources (Roper 1987).

Another eighties study of public attitudes toward news media provides some insight into sources of credibility. Robinson and Kohut (1988) found that people are more likely to believe "well established" news sources rather than lesser known sources regardless of whether they are electronic or print. Such well established sources included the well known network anchors, such as Dan Rather and Peter Jennings, and well known papers such as the *Wall Street Journal*. However, among the top fifteen believable news sources rated by 2,100 people in the national sample, thirteen were television news personalities and network news organizations; only two were print news sources. Hence, the generalization that television news has more clout and credibility with the public is reinforced.

Students in Virginia 8th and 11th grade classes showed the same trust of television: 67 percent believed television to be the most accurate news source, compared to 21 percent for newspapers and 8 percent for news magazines.

Image and Political Judgment. One aspect of this heavy reliance on television for information is the increasing importance of "presentation" or personal style. Image, or how one appears, as opposed to the substance of what one says or does, has increasingly become the concern of public figures on television and media researchers affirm that public opinions on candidates and issues re heavily influenced by image. For example, Graber (1980) analyzed the substance of all types of news coverage for the 1976 presidential campaign and found that three-fourths of the media discussion of presidential qualifications focused on personal style rather than professional qualifications.

A post-election article on the Bush presidential campaign attested to the importance of the campaign manager's skill in carefully controlling the candidate's image on television (Warner and Fineman 1988). The candidate was taught to speak in "sound bites"—very short, cleverly worded statements that are likely to be picked up for broadcast on television news. The candidate was also taught to present the image of strength and assertiveness by careful orchestration of body movements, voice, facial expression, and choice of words. Undoubtedly, clever phrasing and strength of expression have long been used by political leaders addressing the press and public gatherings. But with the dominance of television, the presentation of an appealing (or negative) image is sent rapidly, briefly, and directly into nearly every U.S. home with little or no accompanying background information or clarifying context clues.

Postman (1982, chapt. 7) aptly describes the process of television image television. "Television . . . does not call one's attention to ideas, which are abstract, complex, and sequential, but to personalities, which are concrete, vivid, and holistic. . . . In the television age, political judgment is transformed from an intellectual assessment of propositions to an intuitive and emotional response to the totality of an image."

Implications for Social Studies Education

This is but a small dip into a large cauldron of 1980s data on mass media and public information. But I think it is enough to make the case that the mass media, especially television, have a strong, long reach into the lives and minds of Americans. As the source of news, information, and political imagery, the mass media heavily influence public opinion and citizen decisions and, consequently, public policy. Some consider television to be currently the most powerful citizen educator. As civic educators, how shall we respond?

The temptation is to respond with hopeless negativism. Like Adlai Stevenson we might groan in disgust over television campaigns that merchandise candidates for high office like breakfast cereal. Stevenson viewed the process as the "ultimate indignity for the democratic process." He felt the public would be better served if a political party purchased a half hour of radio and TV silence and asked the audience to "think quietly for themselves." Today, we are aware from so much Nielsen data that the vast majority of the audience would switch channels!

As individuals we may feel unable to do anything about the inexorable drift of media information toward glitzy, brief, often shallow news communication. But as educators we have to recognize that developments in electronic communication will have human effects that require not only a historical record of change over time and continuing observation and analysis by means of the social science disciplines, but they will also require persistent critical study in the social studies curriculum. This means more thorough discussion in textbooks and formal inclusion in the curriculum.

An Analytical Approach. Study of the mass media in the nineties will have to be much more than the historical exposition found in American history textbooks. The means, methods, and effects of mass media as public information sources are the substance of Sociology, political science, economics, and history. But, more importantly, their study is essential to democratic education. Both the subject matter and requisite skills for citizen consciousness call for an analytical approach. For example, students should become aware of the *interactive relationship* between the news media, especially television, and the users. As media users are influenced by broadcast and print, developers of media are influenced by public reactions and expectations of public reactions. The linkage with the public is vast. More than 92 million households have television, more than 62 million newspapers are sold daily, and millions of radios are heard by Americans as they drive, work, exercise, or relax. In social studies we should be teaching about and analyzing these connections and assessing effects of the interaction.

Why do people attribute credibility and accuracy to visual presentations of the news? In social studies classes we must analyze the *power of visuals,* probe the symbols and sources of image formation, and discuss how images can influence attitudes and actions.

Another feature of our news sources that should be examined is the *mix of news and entertainment.* Electronic and print media both convey information on public issues in the overall context of daily entertainment. The subtlety of the mix is greater on television because of its potential for conveying images and evoking instant emotions. One media researcher has observed that "the American polity conducts its business on borrowed time. It is borrowed from a commercial, entertainment-oriented media system" (Neumann 1987). The commercial entertainment mission of the great majority of television broadcast companies means that most programming decisions are not based on public information needs but on the selling of audiences to advertisers for a profit. That profit is based on numbers of viewers determined by Nielsen and Arbitron audience ratings. Students need to be alert to these cross-purposes and the resulting mix of entertainment with news.

Television entertainment in the U.S. is probably the most violent of any industrialized society. Attitudes directly related to citizenship responsibilities are shaped by non-news viewing. Summarizing recent studies collected and reviewed by his research staff, Senator Paul Simon (1989) stresses that the old view of psychologists in the 1950s, that television violence had a cathartic effect on viewers,. is clearly outmoded by newer evidence. There are several types of evidence suggesting that children become less sensitive to the pain and suffering of others; they become more aggressive toward others as a result of excessive violence viewed on television. The violence in television entertainment has increased considerably since the 1950s. Simon notes that by age 16, the average child has viewed 33,000 murders in the 200,000 acts of violence seen on TV. How does this daily dose of vivid entertainment violence affect the attitudes of young people toward the actual destruction, death, starvation, and catastrophe in the news? Do they become immune to concerns about their fellow man? Awareness and discussion of this social phenomenon is social studies.

Critical comparison of the several types of news media is necessary in developing the power of choice. What are the useful attributes of information communication? Which takes the least effort to obtain? Which costs the most? Which gives the most news? (Do students realize that in a 30-minute television news program, only about 14 minutes of actual news is offered? Are they aware that over half of the typical newspaper is advertising?) Which sources give the broadest and deepest coverage of news? Which sources provide news the fastest? Which sources of news present the most vivid and memorable coverage? Do we need more than one source to learn the alternatives regarding a current issue?

Comparative analysis also can be applied to information provided by several examples of the same type of media. Are there differences in the way that different networks and local stations present information about the same issue or event? Does there seem to be a standardization of format in radio news? Do several newspapers carry the same national press release?

Critical review of information specials will offer insights into the selection, organization, and delivery of information by press, television, and radio sources. A prime topic is the political "debate." (I place the word in quotation marks because there is much argument by journalists and social science researchers about whether in the recent presidential campaigns these programs can actually be considered debates.) When presidential debates were initiated in 1960, each candidate responded to set questions; each had the opportunity to rebut statements made by the other candidate; and newsmen were able to ask follow-up questions. Some reviewers consider the "debates" of the 1980s as no more than competing public appearances arranged by campaign managers with a format that discourages discussion of public issues and avoids rebuttal and follow-up question (Kalb 1988).

There is a body of literature, films, and video tapes that can be used to determine the strengths and weaknesses of candidate debates. Do they increase voter information and interest? Do they stimulate political participation? One analysis of the 1980 presidential debates concluded that the networks promoted them as television events. Then, following each debate, news commentators set themselves up as judges of "who won" and assessed presentation and image skills of the candidates as the criteria for victory, thus further obscuring the issues (Berquist and Golden 1981). Students viewing a "debate" on tape could be guided to evaluate systematically its content and contributions to public information.

There are many other possibilities for developing an analytic approach to the use of mass media as sources of information. The point is that if much of what Americans are receiving from these information sources is fleeting, episodic, lacking depth, and quite devoid of an examination of alternatives, then it is necessary to become aware and develop the skills needed to determine which information sources best serve specific needs. Now is the time that news media analyses must become standard in social studies instruction. The CNN classroom news program made its debut in September, and the Whittle Communications news show is expanding is reach into the schools. The need for awareness and reflection on public news access is imminent.

Thirty-four years ago Earl Johnson, a social studies thinker for all seasons, inspired many social science educators with a framework combining substantive knowledge, theory of social studies for a democratic society, and perspectives on the art of teaching (Johnson 1956). He urged that the mass media be a special focus of the curriculum. He could not have known the rapid-fire development of electronic communication that would occur, but he knew the powerful role of information in the democratic society. Wrote Johnson: "The mass media are the means by which true and false leaders seek their following. Hence skills and understanding concerning the nature and role of mass media may, it is hoped, develop a generation of citizens whom the demagogues cannot fool, as well as develop a way of life which will produce fewer demagogues." I think his remarks are appropriate for social studies education in the 1990s. At no time has critical thinking about our sources of information been a more necessary skill for Americans.

Activity 1
Where Do We Get Most of Our News in the United States?

	Magazines	Radio	Newspapers	Television	Other People
1961	9%	34%	57%	52%	5%
1971	5	23	48	60	4
1980	5	18	44	64	4
1984	4	14	40	64	4
1986	4	14	36	66	4

(Source: Roper Reports, 1985 and 1987)

Using the information above, answer the following questions:

1. Describe changes since 1961 in the way Americans get their news. Which main news sources have gained audiences and which have lost them? What reasons would you give for these changes?

2. The percentage totals for each year are larger than 100 percent because people use more than one source for their news. How many sources do you use? Why would it be useful for the public to have more than one source of information?

3. Which newspaper, television station, magazine, radio station, or person do you turn to find out the facts and background about a public issue or a national political event? Make a class list of sources.

4. Which of these sources provide the most information about a news event? Which convey information to people most quickly?

Activity 2
Who Are the Viewers?
Average Hours of TV Viewing per Week by Age Groups

	Age	Hours		Age	Hours
Children	2–5	25.4	Men	12–17	22.4
	6–11	23.2		18–34	25.4
				35–54	27.1
				55+	37.3
Women	12–17	21.2			
	18–34	28.5			
	35–54	32.3			
	55+	41.0			

(Based on Nielsen Audience Demographics Report, November 1988)

From the table above, determine the following:

1. Which age group spends the most average weekly hours watching television? What do you think accounts for this age group's heavy viewing?

2. Which group spends the least amount of time watching television weekly? What explanations would you give?

3. Make a line graph showing the weekly viewing data for men and for women by age groups. How do they compare generally? How does age affect the amount of TV viewing for males? For females?

4. Does this report reflect the amount of time spent watching television by the people of different age groups you know well?

5. How about you? How much time do you watch television each week? Record your TV viewing hours for an entire week. Divide the total by seven to determine your daily average. Compare your average with that of your classmates and with your age group in the 1986 table. How much of your weekly viewing time is spent getting news?

Activity 3
Which News Media do People Believe?

"If you get conflicting or different reports of the same news story from radio, television, magazines, and the newspapers, which of the four versions would you be most inclined to believe?" This question was asked of a national sample of people in the United States aged 18 or older. Their responses are shown on the graph below.

Study the results on the graph and answer the following:

1. Which of the news media is considered to be the most "credible" or believable by American adults? What portion of the public believe this news source? Why do you think so many people believe this news source?

2. What is the second most trusted source of news? Why do you think people do not have greater faith in this news media?

3. Why do you think radio is considered to be the least credible source of news?

4. After answering these questions, what conclusions do you draw about what influences the believability of news sources in the U.S.?

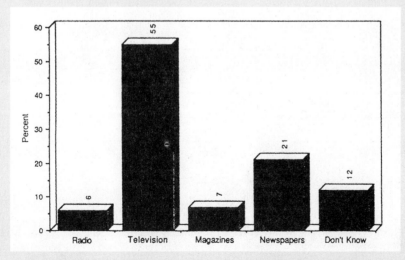

Source: 1987 TIO/Roper Report

Activity 4
Comparing Sources of News About Government, Politics, and Public Issues

According to the 1986 Roper Poll, 66 percent of American relied on television as a major news source while 36 percent relied on newspapers. How much political news can we get and how quickly can we get it from these two main sources of information? In this experiment, you can look and listen to make a comparison.

1. Watch a 30-minute evening TV news broadcast. Use a stopwatch to record the time the newscasters spend on news about public issues, government, and politics. (Exclude weather, sports, chitchat, and other general news.)

   For the same day, measure the column inches of the same kind of political news found in your state or local paper. For comparison purposes, assume that a person can read about 4 column inches of newspaper print in 1 minute. Therefore, count 4 inches of print as 1 minute on the chart below.

2. Compare the quality of coverage of key news items including background information. Rate from 1 (low) to 10 (high) on the chart.

3. Compare the picture coverage. Which source provides the most memorable picture images of the news events? Rate from 1 to 10. Analyze why these images stick in your memory.

4. Compare the timeliness of the news coverage. Rate from 1 to 10. Which source gives the most up-to-the-minute coverage?

Advantages and Disadvantages of
Newspaper and Television as News Sources

	Time and Space? (in minutes)	How Much Coverage?	Picture Coverage?	How Up-to-Date
Newspapers	_____	_____	_____	_____
Television	_____	_____	_____	_____

Make summary statements about the (1) adequacy, (2) speed, (3) depth, and (4) vividness of news coverage from newspapers and television below:

Newspapers: _____

_____

Television: _____

_____

References

Berquist, G. F. and J. L. Golden. "Media Rhetoric, Criticism and the Public Perception for the 1980 Presidential Debates." *The Quarterly Journal of Speech* 67, no. 2 (1981): 125–137.

Fleming, Dan B. and Larry J. Weber. "Getting the News in Virginia." *Social Education* 47 (March 1983): 16–218.

The Gallup Organization. *Gallup Youth Survey*. Princeton, N.J.: The Gallup Organization, 14 June 1989.

Graber, Doris A. *Mass Media and American Politics.* Washington, D. C.: Congressional Quarterly Press, 1980.

Johnson, Earl. *Theory and Practice of the Social Studies.* New York: Macmillan Co., 1956.

Kalb, Marvin. "How the Media Distorted the Race." *Atlanta Journal/Constitution:* 6 November 1988, 1D.

Neumann, W. R. "Knowledge and Opinion in the American Electorate." *Kettering Review* (Winter 1987): 56–64.

Patterson, Thomas E. *The Mass Media Election: How Americans Choose Their President.* New York: Praeger Publishers, 1980.

Postman, Neil. *The Disappearance of Childhood.* New York: Delacorte Press, 1982.

Robinson, Michael J., and Andrews Kohut. "Believability and the Press." *Public Opinion Quarterly* 32 (1988): 174–189.

The Roper Organization. *Public Attitudes Toward Television and Other Media in a Time of Change.* New York: Television Information Office, 1985.

The Roper Organization. *America's Watching: Public Attitudes Toward Television.* New York: Television Information Office, 1987.

The Santa Barbara County Superintendent of Schools. *The Wired Bedroom.* Santa Barbara, Calif.: The Santa Barbara County School District, 1989.

Simon, Paul. "Reducing Violence on Television." *Education Week.* 4 October 1989.

Stanley, W. and R. G. Niemi. *Vital Statistics on American Politics.* Washington, D.C.: Congressional Quarterly, Inc., 1988.

Warner, G. and H. Fineman. "Bush's Media Wizard." *Newsweek,* 26 September 1988, 19–20.

Mary A. Hepburn is Professor and Head of the Citizen Education Program at the University of Georgia in Athens, Georgia 30602.

QUESTIONS ON READING

1. What have been the most significant changes in sources of information for Americans?

2. How does the nature of mass media impede the ability of viewers to obtain information about current events?

3. How can a teacher use the ideas presented in this article in teaching social studies?

LESSON PLANS

Jane Walker   First Grade

Objective: To assist students in gaining an understanding of life in Korea.

Rationale: First grade students need to gain knowledge of how people live in other cultures.

Activities:

1. Teacher has mysterious box and asks students to guess what is in it. After several guesses, a map of the world is shown and Korea is pointed out. A puzzle map of the U.S. is shown and Korea is superimposed on it to equal in size the state of Indiana.

   - Teacher takes out doll named Kei Joon Song who explains the symbols on the Korean flag. Kei says he will be a guide to help the class learn about Korea.

2. Kei tells children they will learn about traditional Korean homes. Kei explains why shoes are removed before entering. He shows Korean pillows and explains the decorative knots. Children make decorative knots. Children play with fans and look at pictures of traditional Korean home, including sleeping mats.

   • Teacher shows pictures of modern Korean cities and buildings.

3. Kei greets children and introduces guest speaker, who is a Korean college student from a local university. Korean student shows children how Koreans write names and gives each child a card with their name written in Korean. Children practice saying their names in Korean. Children are taught how to count to 10 in Korean.

4. Kei greets children and asks them to smell the aroma in the classroom—it is Korean food! Children sample the Korean food. The class cleans up.

5. Kei greets children and tells them they will be playing games today. Children are taught how to play games like Yut, the Five Small Stones game, the Hwato card game and see a video of Korean taekwondo.

   • Teacher shows pictures of Koreans playing baseball and basketball.

6. Kei tells children they have a special treat today since they will be learning about the Korean New Year and traditional ways of celebrating it. Children see traditional Korean costumes. They learn about the celebration for a child's first birthday.

   • Teacher shows pictures of Koreans celebrating New Year's day in the city of Seoul.

7. Kei greets children with Korean music. Teacher shows children a traditional Korean dance in which fans are used. Children do a dance.

8. Children compose a class letter which includes pictures of everyone. The letter is sent to an elementary school in Korea. This begins a pen pal connection with a Korean school.

Bibliography:

Ashby, G. M. (1987) *A Family In South Korea,* Lerner Pub. Minneapolis.

Burns, W. J. & Kim, D. (1987) *A Letter from a Korean Village,* Hanji-munhwa-sa Publishing Company, Seoul.

Chung, O. & Monroe, J. (1988) *Cooking the Korean Way,* Lerner Pub., Minneapolis.

Kubota, M. (1987) South Korea: *Children of the World,* Gareth Stevens Publishing, Milwaukee.

McWhirter, M. E. (1970) *Games Enjoyed by Children Around the World,* American Friends Service Committee Inc., Philadelphia.

Shin, S. (1979) *Children in Korea,* Samhwa Printing Ltd., Seoul.

Tamara, St. (1970) *Asian Crafts,* The Lion Press, N.Y.

Bonnie Shiller   Preschool to Kindergarten

Objective: To make children aware of breads eaten in different parts of the world.

Rationale: One aspect of internationalism is making young children aware that other people eat the same or different foods.

Activities:

1. Record the child's answers to the following questions on a blank 3x5 card.

   "What kind of bread would you like to make?"

   "How would you make it?"

   "What things would you put in the bowl to make it?"

"What do you do next?"
"Where do you cook it?"
"What temperature do you bake it at?"
"How long would it take to bake it?"

Title the recipe with the child's name and the bread they described. Example: "Casey's Croissant."

2. Illustrate the recipe. Include all the recipes described by students into a book and allow one child each day to take it home to share with parents.

3. Read *Bread, Bread, Bread* by Ann Morris, which describes breads eaten around the world. Compare those breads with breads eaten by students. Chart and graph the favorite breads of children in the class.

4. Bring in the following items:

> 3 pita (Mediterranean)
> 3 croissants (France)
> 3 tortillas (Mexico)
> 6 rice cakes (Japan)
> 3 Matzoh (Jewish)
> 3 black bread (Russia)

Each child receives one piece of a bread plus bite sizes of the other breads. They are to sample the breads. Graph the favorite breads of the students.

• You may blindfold each child prior to eating the breads and have them smell them.

5. Make and bake bread like whole wheat, pretzels, quick bread, gingerbread, or pizza.

6. Make bread dough sculptures, necklaces or ornaments.

Bibliography:

Multicultural Cooking with Kids #LC165
Foods From Around the World #LC437
Breads From Around the World #LC913
Asian Cooking Set #LC1315
Hispanic Cooking Set #LC1317
> All available from:
> Lakeshore Learning Materials, P.O. Box 6261, Carson, CA 90749

Carle, E. *Walter the Baker.*
Galdone, P. *The Little Red Hen.*
Hoban, R. *Bread and Jam for Frances.*

Mary Wolf 6th and 7th grades
Objective: Making students aware of the American tradition of immigration.

Rationale: Studying immigration can assist students to gain greater knowledge of their own heritage as well as those of classmates.

Activities:

1. Students in groups discuss "What do I call myself?" How do people account for different ways in which people classify themselves. Students discuss how each person is the result of several ethnic influences.

2. Students engage in a "Family Heritage Research Project" which enables each individual to learn more about family history.

3. Students will examine charts from "Immigrants to the United States by region of origin, 1820–1974."

   • Students in groups use maps to link what they learned in charts to countries of the world impacting American society. Each group is to develop a hypothesis about immigration to the United States.

4. Students observe videotape, *Journey to America* from "The American Experience" series. Among questions posed are: What was the peak year of immigration in 1890–1920 period? Why did industry encourage immigration? What was immigrant attitudes toward police and government? What was a compelling reason to remain in America?

5. Students read Upton Sinclair's, *The Jungle*. In groups, they discuss relationship of immigration to conditions described in the book.

6. The Student Theater Project of the St. Louis Municipal Theater will put on a production dealing with reasons people leave Central America today to live in the United States.

   • Students will be involved in the play by the actors. A discussion will follow the play.

7. Students will examine cartoon depictions of immigrants in the 19th and 20th centuries. In groups they will ientify common themes running through these portrayals of immigrants.

   • Students are to compare and contrast issues raised by the play about Central American immigrants and issues raised by 19th and 20th century cartoonists.

8. Each student will present a family history report on their own ethnic heritage.

   • In groups, students will create a bulletin board using material from their reports on family heritage. Their creations will be displayed.

SUGGESTED READING

Crowder, W. (1973). *Persistent problems approach to elementary social studies.* Ithaca, NY: F. E. Peacock.

Hopkins, M. (1968). *Learning through the environment.* London: Longman.

Kinney, L., and Dresden, K. (Eds.). (1949). *Learning through current materials.* Stanford, CN: Stanford University Press.

Rogers, V. and Roberts, A. (Eds.) (1988). *Teaching Social Studies: Portraits from the Classroom.* Washington: NCSS Bulletin, *82.*

Chapter 16

Social Justice and the Elementary Classroom

Social Justice and the Elementary Classroom

Since the early days of the colonies and the young republic, the architects of American public education have viewed the schools as a potent force to achieve social justice. They recognized that a literate citizenry was an essential aspect of the emerging democracy. The history of American education reflects a continuing trend toward extending educational opportunities to diverse groups.

The school is the arena in which the struggle for justice in American society occurs. Americans believe individuals should have opportunities to succeed and attain full development of their innate capacities. We expect schools to provide an even playing field that offers all children access to economic and social advancement. Yet, schools merely mirror the larger society that is struggling, and often failing, to provide equal opportunity for all citizens.

From the early years of our history, Americans have insisted that schools assume responsibility for political education of the citizenry. Thomas Jefferson articulated in his "Bill for the More General Diffusion of Knowledge," introduced in the Virginia legislature in 1779, the new political function expected of schools:

> Experience has shown that even under the best form of [government], those entrusted with power have, in time and by slow operations, perverted it into tyranny and it is believed that the most effective means of preventing this would be to illuminate as far as practicable, the minds of the people at large.

The earliest laws regarding education in an English-speaking country were established in the Massachusetts colony. The belief that education was necessary for individual and social well-being resulted in legislation in 1642 that required parents and master craftsmen to teach their children and apprentices to read and write. Reading was viewed as essential for youngsters to understand both the laws of the country and the religious principles necessary to obtain salvation. In 1647, the "Old Deluder Satan Act" was passed, which required communities of at least 50 families to hire an elementary teacher and communities of 100 families to hire a Latin grammar (secondary) school teacher. These laws set momentous precedents for government involvement in schools, public funding for education, and the use of schools to achieve social purposes.

In the last half of the 20th century, efforts continue to promote justice by extending and improving educational opportunities. For example, *Brown v. Board of Education* (1954), the landmark Supreme Court decision that struck down the separate but equal doctrine that had justified segregated schools, was intended to address racial inequities. The Elementary and Secondary Education Act of 1965 was part of President Lyndon B. Johnson's "War on Poverty." The goal was to improve the educational opportunities and enhance possibilities of social mobility for children with low socioeconomic status (SES). Title IX of the Education Amendments of 1972 addressed gender discrimination in schools by withholding federal funds for noncompliance. And the Education of All Handicapped Children Act of 1975 (Public Law 94-142) deals with the needs of handicapped children. The law requires that all handicapped children, depending on the severity of the disability, be placed in the "least restrictive" school setting that most nearly approaches the climate of the "regular classroom."

Too often inequities in American society have been regarded only as educational problems, and educational remedies have been expected to solve the complex moral dilemmas that pervade every aspect of American culture. Schools are a powerful force for societal change, but meaningful progress requires the united efforts of government, media, business and industry, and religious and cultural organizations, as well as the commitment of individual Americans. For example, does transporting an African-American child to a predominantly white school offer her a better education if she is faced with the prejudice of teachers, students, or parents when she arrives? Does desegregation offer a genuine promise of social mobility without changes in housing and employment opportunities?

Despite the emphasis in the United States on universal schooling, various social groups have not had equal access to education. This perpetuates injustice because education serves as an important gateway to the social, political, and economic benefits of the mainstream of American society. The educational opportunities offered each student are influenced by socioeconomic status, race and ethnicity, gender, and handicapping conditions. In this chapter, we will consider these key variables in students' backgrounds and examine ways these factors and society's attitudes toward them affect educational opportunities. In addition, we will explore the connections between our individual classrooms and the broader society, reflecting on ways our beliefs and actions as teachers perpetuate or resolve social injustices.

Social Class

Every society has a system that allocates individuals to certain positions of prestige and power. Some individuals have a higher status than others. This system, known as *social stratification*, is a hierarchy by which people are categorized in terms of the degree of superiority or inferiority with which society regards them. Variables can include income, occupation, formal education, and organizational membership.

Social stratification may be based on *ascribed status*, an involuntary or inherited social position based on characteristics beyond the control of the individual. Such characteristics include membership in a racial or ethnic group, gender, and the income and occupation of parents. Social stratification may also be a result of *achieved status*, a voluntary social position that reflects an individual's abilities and accomplishments. *Social mobility*, movement from one social class to another, largely depends on whether social status is ascribed or achieved. *Caste systems*, like those found in Hindu villages of rural India or South Africa's system of apartheid, are based almost completely on ascribed status. They allow little social mobility. In the United States, however, greater emphasis is placed on achieved status, which offers greater social mobility.

The American dream is largely drawn from the conceptualization of status based on merit. In a *meritocracy*, social status results from talent and hard work; people are able to move up or down the "social ladder." If the American meritocracy were fair, we would expect individuals from all social groups to be relatively evenly distributed across social classes. The fact that great differences exist among the status of social groups in the United States suggests that status and the resulting prestige and power continue to be greatly influenced by ascribed rather than achieved characteristics.

Schools are a powerful influence in determining adult status. Everett Reimer (1971) contends that teachers must recognize that decisions they make about students accomplish

> the sorting of the young into the social slots they will occupy in adult life. . . . The major part of job selection is not a matter of personal choice at all, but a matter of survival in the school system. . . . Age at dropout determines whether boys and girls will be paid for their bodies, hands, or brains, and also how much they will be paid. This in turn, largely determines where they can live, with whom they can associate, and the rest of their style of life. (p. 17)

Research indicates that the educational opportunities offered to children of different social classes varies greatly (Kozol, 1991; Anyon, 1980). Most teachers are from the middle class and tend to establish middle-class norms and expectations in their classrooms. Children of the middle and upper classes are more likely to succeed in school because the values presented in their homes and communities are consistent with those taught in the school. In addition, more emphasis is placed on reading, learning, achievement, and planning for the future in middle- and upper-class families.

Teachers tend to favor students who are like them. In fact, it has been suggested that most teachers are involved in a "Pygmalion" project, shaping students in our own image. Teachers generally view students who are attractive, clean, quiet, and respectful as brighter than others. Teachers have difficulty giving low grades to students they like and interact more often with students for whom they have high expectations (Ortiz, 1988). They praise these students more when they are correct and criticize them less when they are wrong(Grant & Rothenberg, 1986). They encourage them to be more independent, self-directed learners and punish them less severely when they violate rules.

In contrast, lower-class students are given less attention and receive fewer hours of real instruction. Teachers interact with these students less often, offer less praise and encouragement and more criticism, and expect them to fail (Volverde, 1987; Borko & Eisenhart, 1986; Fine, 1986). As a result, lower-class students fall farther and farther behind academically, have lower self esteem, and mentally stop attending long before they physically drop out of schools.

One of the authors' sons was in a first-grade class of 20 students. Eighteen were middle-class white children. Two students, Candace and Swahli, were lower-class African-American children who attended the school as participants in a voluntary desegregation plan. The first week of school, their young, white, female teacher divided the class into three reading groups. The top group, the Redbirds, was composed of eight children; all were white. The middle group, the bluebirds, included ten children; again, all were white. The lowest reading group, the Yellowbirds, was composed of Candace and Swahli. In addition, the teacher formed two math groups. Eighteen children were in the top group. I'm sure you can predict which two students were in the bottom group. Joshua, one of the first graders, explained the significance of the groupings: "It's OK bein' a Bluebird, but I'd rather be a Redbird. But I sure don't want ta be a Yellowbird. The Yellowbirds are really the Blackbirds."

It is amazing that a six year old could penetrate the inequity of a classroom system that the teacher failed to understand. The children who enter our classrooms are not equal in terms of talent, ability, motivation, self-esteem, experience, access to resources, or family support. Teachers cannot erase the inequities among students, but we can make decisions based on students' achieved rather than ascribed characteristics. And we can make a commitment to empower every child to achieve. Each of us as teachers must continually examine our own attitudes and behaviors to move our classroom practices closer to the realization of social justice.

Suggestions for Improving Educational Opportunities for Lower-SES Children

- Assess each student's abilities and create individual opportunities to experience success.
- Rethink the curriculum to make it interesting, relevant, and pertinent to lower-SES students.
- Design group activities which engage all learners and offer structure and support for learning.
- Use a variety of teaching/learning strategies and materials to accommodate diverse learning styles.
- Provide opportunities for lower-SES students to know challenging and worthy role models.
- Resist stereotyping, and avoid labeling children as "slow," "bad," or "problems."
- Establish high expectations for students so they live up to–rather than down to–your expectations.
- Help students develop close, affirming relationships with significant adults.
- Enable parents to be involved in their children's education in symbolic and substantive ways.
- Teach and encourage good nutrition and health practices.
- Avoid tracking and ability grouping because they create self-fulfilling prophecies.
- Create a classroom atmosphere of trust and acceptance of differences.
- Continually examine your own values and behaviors to guard against prejudice.
- Advocate with school district, state, and federal officials for lower-SES children to receive adequate educational resources.

▲ Multiethnic education includes an emphasis on overcoming stereotypes, prejudice, and discrimination. *Courtesy Webster University.*

Race and Ethnicity

Race is usually defined by certain physical characteristics. The three major racial classifications are Mongoloids, Negroids, and Caucasians, although there are no pure races due to racial mixing.

The use of race to classify people is arbitrary. It depends on who is doing the classifying and the criteria they use. Many factors (e.g., skin color, facial features, blood type) could be used, but universal definitions do not exist. Many anthropologists agree that there are 3 races, but William Boyd recognizes 5 races, Carleton Coon identifies 9, and Joseph Birdsell identifies 32 (Dobzhansky, 1962). Some anthropologists have even argued there is no such thing as race.

Despite disagreement among scientists, many Americans accept the notion of race and characterize racial groups as having differences in intelligence, motivation, personality, physical abilities, talents, and personal character. This has often resulted in *racism*, the view that one race is naturally superior or inferior. Racism is usually accompanied by *prejudice*, a derogatory view not based on factual evidence, and *discrimination*, unjust treatment of individuals due to race.

Members of a particular ethnic group share a common culture, including patterns of language and behavior, life style, attitudes, and values. James Banks (1988) defines an ethnic group as an "involuntary collectivity of people with a shared feeling of common identity, a sense of peoplehood, and a shared sense of interdependence of fate." (p. 61) Murdock (1967) recognizes 892 ethnic groups in the world. From its conception, the United States has been home to people of diverse backgrounds. Today, America is a microcosm of the zesty diversity of ethnic groups around the globe.

Some ethnic groups can be classified as *minorities*, people who share certain physical and cultural characteristics and are socially disadvantaged. By the year 2000, one third of elementary and secondary students will be minorities. Census projections for the year 2000 predict that minority students will outnumber whites in many states, including Texas and California. In many large urban school districts, minority students are already the majority group. For these reasons, "ethnicity" is becoming a more accurate and useful term than "minority."

The tapestry of American society is woven from the threads of many ethnic groups. Yet the culture of the United States was and continues to be an expression of the dominant Anglo-Saxon immigrants who held power in this country by 1800. *Ethnocentrism* is the view that the attitudes, behaviors and way of life of one group are more valuable than those of other cultures and should be uncritically and unquestioningly accepted. Other cultures are seen as less advanced, less correct, and less moral. Ethnocentrism in American schools and society hinders the celebration of the rich diversity of our heritage.

For many years, Americans have clung to the ideal of the "melting pot," the belief that people of diverse ethnic groups who came to the United States would eventually lose their distinctive characteristics and be assimilated into the dominant Anglo-Saxon mainstream of society. It was the responsibility of schools to facilitate this process as indicated in the Goals of the Common School:

> Everywhere these people tend to settle in groups or settlements and to set up here their national manners, customs and observances. Our task is to break up these groups of settlements, to assimilate and amalgamate these people as part of our American race, and to implant in their children, as far as can be done, the Anglo-Saxon conception of righteousness, law and order, and popular government, and to awaken in them a reverence for our democratic institutions and for those things in our national life which we as a people hold to be of abiding worth. (Cubberly, 1909, pp. 15–16)

▲ The tapestry of American society is woven from the threads of many ethnic groups. *Courtesy Webster University.*

Those of European descent have largely been assimilated into the Anglo-Saxon ideal, but even within these groups there has been resistance. Many people of Moslem, Orthodox Jewish, Polish, Italian, Hispanic, Asian, and African descent reject the Anglo-Saxon ideal and continue to emphasize their own ethnic heritages. Some educators and policy makers believe assimilation is still the appropriate role of schools. In a study of a desegregated elementary school, Ray Rist (1978) found that the purpose was to make African-American students more like white children. "Black children came off the bus to a setting where the goal was to make them invisible." (p. 244) Robert Green (1978) explains that the intention is "to educate Blacks to the point where their unfortunate stigma of blackness fades away. This will occur as a result of exposing black students to the majority values so that they may . . . be absorbed into a culture based upon white middle-class values and biases" (p. 11). Rist advocates, instead, a move toward cultural pluralism in American schools and society.

Cultural pluralism is the belief that social groups can preserve their distinct cultures and peacefully coexist in the same society. It encourages respect for the rights of all groups and fosters appreciation of their various cultures, histories, and contributions to the whole.

In schools, cultural pluralism requires valuing and accommodating students' diverse learning styles. Rita Dunn and Shirley Griggs (1988) define *learning style* as a "biologically and developmentally imposed set of characteristics that makes the same teaching method wonderful for some and terrible for others" (p. 3). For example, African-Americans, Native Americans, and Hispanic-Americans are usually group-oriented and tend to have difficulty learning in highly individualistic, competitive classrooms (Ramirez & Casteñada, 1974; Hale-Benson, 1986). They usually prefer working collaboratively, using cooperative learning strategies rather than working alone (Slavin, 1983; Cohen, 1986).

Characteristics of African-American Learners

1. African-American students learn best through observation and modeling of the activity, not by being told.

2. African-American learners have a high energy level and need a variety of tasks and much movement.

3. African-American learners function best if the material is contextualized, thus providing it a relationship with time and place.

4. African-American learners prefer process material and they learn through kinesthetic activities (writing, physical games, role playing); visual images (photographs, charts); auditory (records, music), interactive (group discussion) and haptic strategies (drawing, painting, sculpturing); and finally through print-oriented approaches (reading assignments).

5. African-American children prefer to demonstrate their knowledge in practical ways rather to demonstrate it on tests. They are always and foremost performers.

6. African-American children are highly creative and imaginative and demonstrate excellent physical coordination, which suggests that art and physical education must become integrated aspects of the cognitive; not just frills.

7. African-American children are vivacious, expressive, and excited by engaging in verbal dueling even if with the teacher.

8. African-American children demonstrate a thinking style which might best label them as parallel processors . . . and intuitive thinkers.

Adapted from Barbara J. Shade, "Engaging the Battle for African-American Minds," A Commissioned Paper for the Charles Moody Research Institute First Annual Research Roundtable, 18th Annual Conference of the National Alliance of Black School Educators in Dallas, Texas, November 1990.

James Banks (1988) contends that schools must not only adopt new teaching and learning strategies, the curriculum must become multiethnic to reflect the history, culture, and experiences of diverse ethnic groups. The first attempts at multicultural or multiethnic programs have been criticized as "tourist curricula" because they focused largely on ethnic holidays and special events. Ethnic groups were presented in superficial and stereotypic ways. Mexicans were portrayed wearing sombreros and riding burros, and the people of the Netherlands were pictured wearing wooden shoes. At Thanksgiving, Native Americans were studied alongside Pilgrims without appreciating their various cultures or understanding their subsequent subjugation and genocide.

In addition to accurately depicting ethnic groups, multiethnic education now includes an emphasis on overcoming stereotypes, prejudice, and discrimination. *Stereotypes* are standardized mental images of members of a group representing oversimplified and often inaccurate opinions or judgments. Stereotypes perpetuate *prejudice*, which is defined as learned attitudes, values, and beliefs that motivate discriminatory behavior. *Discrimination* is a pattern of actions which advances the interests, privileges, and power of one group over another and guarantees inequalities (Feigin & Feigin, 1978).

James Banks (1988) has developed a typology of six stages of ethnicity that offers valuable direction to teachers implementing a multiethnic curriculum. Each student could be characterized by one of the six stages. The goal would be to enable the learner to move to a higher stage. At Stage 1 (Ethnic Psychological Cavity), a student has low self-esteem and a negative view of her own ethnic group. In Stage 2 (Ethnic Encapsulation), other groups are considered enemies and racists. At Stage 3 (Ethnic Identity Clarification), pride in the student's own ethnic group develops that is not dependent on hatred or fear of other groups. By Stage 4 (Biethnicity), children are able to participate comfortably in two cultures, as is often true of people of color living in a predominantly white society. At Stage 5 (Multiethnicity and Reflective Nationalism), students have progressed so that they can function competently within several ethnic groups in their society. By Stage 6 (Globalism and Global Competency), learners have developed the abilities and sensitivities to work well within many ethnic groups in their own nation and beyond.

▲ The school curriculum must become multiethnic to reflect the history, culture and experiences of diverse ethnic groups. *Courtesy Francis Howell (Missouri) School District.*

Critics of multicultural and multiethnic curriculum projects argue that the emphasis on differences is a divisive force which separates rather than unifies American society. Pluralism, they contend, actually encourages ethnocentric attitudes and polarization of ethnic groups.

The dynamic tension between unity and diversity is ever present in American society and schools. Some may settle for uniformity when the real goal is unity. Uniformity and diversity are mutually exclusive, while unity and diversity are complementary goals. The challenge to teachers and schools is to nurture the richness of diversity while simultaneously fostering a shared "American culture." The challenge to our nation is to continue building a just and equitable pluralistic society.

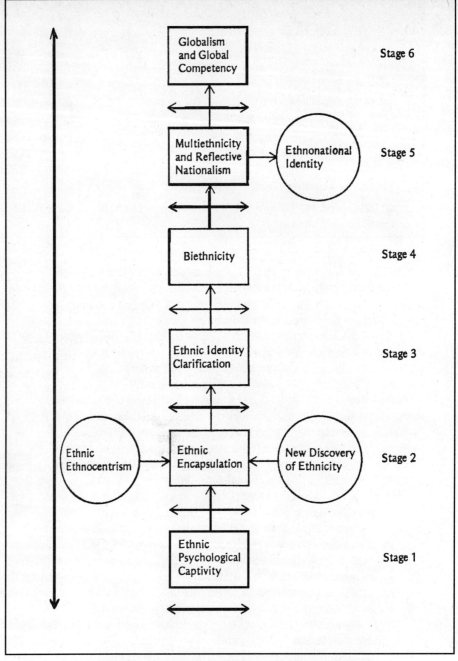

▲ The Stages of Ethnicity: A Typology. *Courtesy James A. Banks,*
Multiethnic Education: Theory and Practice, Boston: Allyn and Bacon (1981) 135.

Gender

Boys and girls are raised differently in American society. The gender of an infant is a powerful influence on the choices that will be made for and by the individual throughout life. Decisions about names, colors and styles of clothing and surroundings, education, occupations, hobbies, and life-styles are largely based on gender.

This is not limited to the United States. The organization of every society depends on gender, and every culture has developed processes to socialize individuals into sex roles. Carol Gilligan (1982) cites research that indicates that gender identity is firmly defined in both girls and boys at age three, while Nancy Romer (1981) suggests that sex roles are established by age six. At any rate, there is strong evidence to support the view that when they begin elementary school, children already "think of themselves as members of their own sex, behave in sex-typical ways, want to be like members of their own sex, and feel emotionally committed to this point of view" (Romer, 1981, p. 50).

Although every society allocates roles on the basis of gender, there is considerable diversity among cultures in the nature and flexibility of assigned roles. For example, Margaret Meade (1949) found that both men and women of the Mundugumor tribe were hostile and cruel. She described both females and males of the Arapesh as compassionate, peaceful, and cooperative. In the Tchambuli tribe, men were submissive and emotionally dependent while women were dominating and detached. From her ethnographic research, Meade concluded that there are no universal attitudes nor behaviors that define "male" or "female."

Clyde Kluckhohn (1953) disagrees. He cites achievement and self-reliance as universal male traits and contends that men control the military and politics in all societies. S. B. Ortner (1974) contends that in all known cultures, the work of men is more highly valued than the work of women regardless of the nature of the work.

Biological differences between females and males are universal. These physical differences provide the basis for the assignment of gender roles such as child-bearing and breast-feeding. The distribution of roles, however, has gone far beyond reproduction. The division of labor along gender lines has generally allocated domestic and nurturing tasks to females and leadership, public, and production roles to males.

Which characteristics of males and females are genetically determined and which are culturally determined is not clear. Scientists have documented physical, structural, and hormonal differences between the sexes. But there is inadequate evidence to support the view that cognitive, affective, personality, and social differences between males and females are biologically determined.

The fact that there are differences between the sexes is indisputable. Injustices arise,

▲ Critics of multiethnic curriculum projects argue that they are a divisive force in American society. *Courtesy Kirkwood (Missouri) School District.*

however, when one gender group is considered to be more worthy or valuable than the other. Consider the Orthodox Jewish prayer: "Blessed art Thou O Lord our God, King of the Universe, that I was not born a woman." Sexism, according to Casey Miller and Kate Swift (1977), is the "pervasive ideology that sees females as inferior beings" (p. 128). Sexism views males and females as fundamentally different. Men are superior and have the natural right to dominate women.

The selection of social roles based on gender is not in itself unjust. However, when individuals find the roles traditionally available to them to be narrow, rigid, confining, or oppressive, society must reconsider the unexamined assumptions transmitted by the family, school, religious institutions, and the media.

Charol Shakeshaft (personal communication, 1992) and her associates have examined elementary children's views of gender roles. Children were asked to imagine how they would feel if they woke up tomorrow as members of the opposite sex. Girls responses typically included the words, "I would get to." Boys frequently mentioned

▲ The challenge of teachers is to nurture the richness of diversity while simultaneously fostering a shared "American culture." *Courtesy Null Elementary, Saint Charles (Missouri) Public Schools.*

suicide. Shakeshaft's research offers evidence that elementary-age children perceive that boys have a greater number or a higher quality of options available to them than do girls.

Next to the family, schools are one of the most powerful socializing agents in American society. The relationships between teachers and students is central in the development of gender identity.

Myra and David Sadker (1982) report several studies that focus on teacher-student relationships. Results indicate that beginning in preschool, teachers give more attention to boys than girls. Teachers are also more likely to have lengthy conversations with male students. Boys more often "grab" the teacher's attention than girls do. Teachers give male and female students different feedback. Their response to male students was generally specific, forceful, and effective. Feedback to girls, however, was usually vague and bland. The Sadkers conclude that girls go through schools without adequate feedback to know when or why they have failed or succeeded. Classrooms may be unfriendly environments to girls because their words and actions seem unimportant. This results in girls' disengagement with schools and lowered self-esteem.

Other teacher behaviors may be important in establishing gender role distinctions. When teachers ask a female student to water plants and a male student to carry books, we reinforce gender stereotypes. Organizing students according to gender for seating, lining up, and forming teams may seem to be a quick and harmless way to divide the class into two nearly equal groups, but such practices reinforce gender distinctions. We would never think of asking Jews to form one line and Catholics another. Nor would teachers today require that African-American students sit on one side of the classroom and white students on the other. Yet, we have unquestioningly perpetuated the polarization of gender groups in elementary classrooms.

Sadker and Sadker's (1982) study of public school textbooks indicated that curriculum materials also contribute to sexism. Males are typically portrayed in positions of prestige as being strong, courageous, clever, adventurous, active, and competitive. Females are generally presented in subservient roles as dependent, passive, fearful, obedient, domestic, and concerned with their physical appearance. Textbook images such as these help both boys and girls accept the notion of male superiority.

The Sadkers also found that females were largely invisible in schoolbooks. Stories about boys outnumbered those about girls by a ratio of five to two. Adult males were main characters of stories three times more than women. Biographies were six times more likely to be written about men. Even animal and fantasy stories more often featured male characters. Girls and boys, thereby, learn that females are less important than males because the experience of females is not reflected in the official knowledge presented in schools.

Although much of gender research in schools has focused on experiences of females, Patricia Sexton's (1969) classic study examines the experiences of boys. Because most teachers are women, Sexton argues that female values predominate in elementary schools. "Proper behavior" takes on a feminine definition. Value conflicts occur when boys find difficulty adjusting to female views of appropriate behavior. Other studies indicate that boys are more likely than girls to experience academic failure in school, to be assigned to special education and remedial programs, to be referred to the principal because of discipline problems, and to receive harsher punishments as a result.

As teachers confront our own gender biases, examine gender stereotypes in curriculum materials, and challenge our students to reconsider their own and society's views of gender roles, we offer greater opportunities to both males and females. Gender equity requires more than women and men receiving equal pay for the same job. It means more than men gaining acceptance as nurses or women being hired as plumbers. Gender equity empowers both women and men to define themselves as sensitive, strong, nurturing, brave, gentle, or adventurous.

Activities to Promote Gender Equity

- Invite men and women in non-traditional careers to speak to your class about their choices, challenges, and successes.

- Ask students to examine the index of their social studies textbook in order to make a list of all the women and a list of all the men included in the text. Ask children which list is longer. As a class, formulate hypotheses to explain why members of one gender group are predominant. On another day, repeat the activity with another textbook (science, math, etc.) and compare results.

- Assign students to find newspaper or magazine pictures of people at work. Be sure to include photographs of men and women in nontraditional occupations such as male flight attendants or females in the military. Discuss reasons some careers are dominated by members of one gender group and ways this might change in the future.

- Replicate Charol Shakeshaft's study of children's views of gender roles. Ask them to do a free write describing how they would feel if they awake tomorrow morning as members of the opposite sex. Ask volunteers to read their paragraphs to the class.

- Read a fiction book to the class changing the gender identity of the central character. Discuss the impact of the change on the story.

- Compare roles of women and men at different times in American history or their roles in other cultures today. Explore reasons for similarities and differences.

Special Education

Educating children with disabilities presents a special challenge to teachers and schools concerned with equity, access, and justice. Handicapped children generally did not have access to schooling until the 19th century, when they were sent to private or state schools designed especially for them. During the 20th century, physicians, psychologists, sociologists, and educators lobbied against the segregation of handicapped individuals in schools and society. Public schools responded by providing special programs for students with disabilities.

During the 1970s, Congress passed two laws that dramatically changed the education of special learners. The Vocational Rehabilitation Act of 1973 protects the civil rights of handicapped persons. It prohibits discrimination against individuals with disabilities in the workplace and in educational programs that receive federal aid. *Disabilities* were defined as health conditions or physical impairments that limited individuals' capabilities to function in essential life activities for extended time periods. The Vocational Rehabilitation Act also required that all activities be accessible to handicapped participants, which resulted in the removal of barriers in architecture and transportation.

The Education for All Handicapped Children Act, also knows as Public Law 94-142, was approved by Congress in 1975. This law requires special education services for the disabled, including medical evaluation, physical and occupational therapy, counseling, speech pathology and audiology, and psychological services. P. L. 94-142 is a long and complicated piece of legislation that mandates:

1. A free and appropriate public education for handicapped individuals between the ages of 3 and 21. Districts are required to seek out and identify handicapped children.

2. An Individualized Education Program (IEP) for each handicapped child developed by a collaborative team of parents or guardians, teachers, and administrators.

3. The formulation of due process procedures to protect children from inappropriate evaluation, classification, and placement.

4. The completion of a comprehensive evaluation involving multiple instruments and procedures before placing a child in any special education program. Evaluation mechanisms must be designed for assessment of specific handicaps and must not discriminate on the basis of race, culture, or language.

5. The education of handicapped children in the least restrictive environments possible. This requirement has encouraged mainstreaming of handicapped students in classrooms with nonhandicapped youngsters.

It is likely that all elementary teachers will have one or more children with various types and degrees of handicaps mainstreamed in their classrooms for one or more subjects each day. How to meet the needs of these children depends largely on the handicapping conditions. A student with a hearing impairment, a child in a wheelchair, and a youngster with Down's Syndrome require different accommodations.

It is not only important for social studies educators to meet the educational needs of special learners in their classrooms, it is also important to address issues of *handicapism*, which has been defined by Robert Bogan and Douglas Biklen (1977) as "a set of assumptions and practices that promote the differential and unequal treatment of people because of apparent or assumed physical, mental, or behavioral differences" (p. 14). The attitudes of others and the attitudes of the handicapped toward themselves may be even more confining than the disability itself. Democratic classroom arrangements, including collaborative learning strategies may be the most successful strategy for full inclusion of students with disabilities in elementary and middle school classrooms.

▲ An important task of the social studies is to address handicapism. *Photo by Claudia Burris. Courtesy Webster University.*

The issue of handicapism remains largely unaddressed in the elementary school curriculum (Shaver & Curtis, 1981). Individuals with disabilities are an invisible minority in textbooks and other instructional materials. Teachers must devise strategies to include fully the handicapped and handicapism in the social studies curriculum.

Using Cooperative Learning to Facilitate Mainstreaming in the Social Studies

- Choose academic and social learning objectives that are appropriate for the students' grade and skill level.
- Explain assignment objectives and procedures explicitly and completely.
- Describe to students the social-cooperative skills on which they will be evaluated.
- Start with small groups working on discrete, easy-to-evaluate tasks.
- Publicly value group diversity and full participation.
- Monitor and reinforce group collaborative processes as well as individual behavior and accomplishment.
- Attend to the physical arrangement and sound level of the classroom.
- Periodically hold plenary class meetings.
- Establish written guidelines and norms for group work that clearly define suitable behavior.
- Employ cooperative learning for an appreciable amount of time.
- Adapt cooperative learning strategies to your needs and style of teaching.

Adapted from "Using Cooperative Learning to Facilitate Mainstreaming in the Social Studies," Howard Margolis, Patrick P. McCabe, and Elliot Schwartz, *Social Education*, February 1990, 111-114.

Child Abuse, Drug Abuse, and AIDS

Child abuse, AIDS, and drug abuse are also important social justice issues that impact the lives of children in elementary classrooms. The social studies curriculum offers opportunities to devote serious attention to these concerns.

Child abuse, also called the battered-child syndrome, was until recently shrouded in secrecy. Congress enacted the Child Abuse and Prevention Act in 1974 which offers a legal definition of child abuse:

> The physical or mental injury, sexual abuse, negligent treatment, or maltreatment of a child under the age of eighteen by a person who is responsible for the child's welfare under circumstances which indicate that the child's health or welfare is harmed or threatened thereby. (Quoted in Beezer, 1985, p. 435)

Abuse and neglect impact children's physical, emotional, and psychological development in many ways including their ability to learn in school. Educators in all 50 states are required by law to report suspected cases of abuse. Teachers must inform themselves regarding potential signs of abuse and procedures for reporting suspected abuse.

In addition to reporting, teachers must create classroom climates and relationships that offer safety and stability to abused children. These children need consistency, affirmation, and supportive relationships with adults who offer structure and opportunities to feel successful and in control of their own lives. They need honest praise, concrete rewards, and positive ways to feel ownership of their own learning (Distad, 1987).

The National Committee for Prevention of Child Abuse has compiled the following list of signs of abuse. Abuse is more likely when more than one symptom is apparent.

- Repeated injuries such as bruises, welts, and burns. When questioned, parents may give unlikely explanations or deny that anything is wrong
- Neglected appearance. The child seems poorly nourished or inadequately clothed, is repeatedly left alone, or wanders at all hours.
- Disruptive behavior. The child constantly repeats negative behavior and is very aggressive.
- Passive, withdrawn behavior. The child is overly shy and friendless.
- "Supercritical" parents. Parents are harshly critical of their children or remain extremely isolated from the school and community. Attempts at friendly contact may be resented and distrusted.

(From "Abused Responsibility" *Teacher Magazine*, Nov. 1989, 69.)

Drug abuse was once considered an issue for secondary teachers to address. It is necessary for elementary teachers to confront the fact that drug abuse has become a problem among elementary-age youngsters. The National Institute on Alcohol Abuse and Alcoholism (NIAAA) developed a kindergarten through 12th grade curriculum, *Here's Looking at You, Two,* which has become a model for other drug prevention curricula. It offered:

1. Information—to introduce youth to the basic facts about physiological, psychological, and sociological implications of drug and alcohol use, and to teach them how to gather information about alcohol and drugs; to distinguish between reliable and unreliable, and relevant and irrelevant information.

2. Analysis—to help youngsters identify and define problems; gather information; brainstorm alternatives; predict consequences associated with different choices and behaviors; identify analysis factors such as attitudes, values, feelings, emotions, pressures from peers and families, risk levels and habits; develop action plans on the basis of these analyses and evaluate the appropriateness of their actions.

3. Coping skills—to help students gain skills in identifying sources of stress in their lives; to recognize when they are stressed and its effects on them; to identify mechanisms for coping with stress and determining consequences of the coping behaviors.

4. Self-concept—to help young people increase their self-awareness by helping them identify what is important to them in their lives; to help them recognize their feelings and know how to express them by explaining how they feel about themselves and identifying their various roles and activities, as well as increasing positive self-concepts so that students can identify their own personal strengths and weaknesses and develop skills in selecting and practicing changed behaviors. (National Institute on Alcohol Abuse and Alcoholism, 1979)

▲ Drug education has become part of the elementary school curriculum.
Courtesy Webster University.

The issue of AIDS is often considered as part of sex education which is included in the health or science curriculum. It is also appropriate to consider AIDS in the social studies curriculum especially in regards to family and gender roles, as well as issues of prejudice and discrimination. It is interesting to note that more states require AIDS education than sex education.

The federal *Objectives for the Nation* (Department of Health and Human Services, 1986) suggested preventive measures for the spread of AIDS that included education about sexually transmitted diseases for all school children before and during the high-risk adolescent years. The major goal of the Centers for Disease Control guidelines for AIDS education is to prevent transmission of the HIV virus. The guidelines indicate specific facts appropriate for the various age levels. Early elementary children should learn that AIDS cannot be transmitted through casual contact. Older elementary students should be taught about viruses, transmission, risks, and behavioral aspects of the disease. AIDS education at every level must also focus on the just and compassionate treatment of individuals with AIDS.

SUMMARY

The central focus of this chapter has been issues of social justice in the elementary classroom and their relationship to the ideals that guide our nation. The social studies are a vital force in the development of children's values and behaviors. Democratic elementary and middle school classrooms offer youngsters the challenge of translating the often repeated ideal "liberty and justice for all" into action.

QUESTIONS

1. Identify how you fit into a system of social stratification.

2. Cite an example from your school experience in which students were segregated on the basis of ability or social class.

3. Do you agree that specific ethnic groups have specific learning styles?

4. What do you believe should be the goals of multiethnic education?

5. How do you reflect traditional gender stereotypes and attitudes in your everyday thinking?

6. Cite an example in which you observed a failure by a school to accommodate the needs of a handicapped person.

7. What role, if any, do you believe schools should play in AIDS education?

8. What role, if any, should teachers play in drug education?

9. There are over 100 language groups in Los Angeles public schools. What problems would you encounter in dealing with multiethnic education in the Los Angeles system?

10. What should be the basis of multiethnic education in school districts that are predominantly one skin color or ethnic group?

ACTIVITIES

1. Conduct a study regarding your college or university's goals and programs in multiethnic education.

2. Survey several local school districts regarding their multiethnic education programs.

3. Visit a school or facility that deals predominantly with visually or auditorially impaired people. Interview staff regarding

their ideas of how these teachers effectively work with their students.

4. Interview staff at a drug rehabilitation center regarding the school's role in drug education.

5. Interview parents from several ethnic groups regarding what they seek in schools regarding multiethnicity.

On the first day of the new school year, all teachers in one private school received the following note from their principal:

Dear Teacher:
I am a survivor of a concentration camp. My eyes have seen what no man should witness:
Gas chambers built by *Learned* engineers.
Children poisoned by *Educated* physicians.
Infants killed by *Trained* nurses.
Women and babies shot and burned by *High School and College Graduates*.
So, I am suspicious of education.
My request is: help our children become human. Your efforts must never produce learned monsters, skilled psychopaths, educated Eichmanns. Reading, writing, arithmetic are important only if they serve to make our children more humane.
Education must prepare people not just to earn a living, but to live a life.

READING

Affirmative Action in the Classroom: What Would It Mean?
by Roberta Woolever

We are all aware of the meaning of the term "affirmative action" when it is applied to the hiring and promoting of women and minorities in the workforce. In higher education, affirmative action has meant admitting minorities and women to educational opportunities traditionally denied to them. The intent of affirmative action is to make up for the injustices of the past by what may be described as temporary and morally defensible injustices in the present. An awareness of the temporary nature of affirmative action is critical to an acceptance of it. Once women and minorities have secured their rightful place in society, then affirmative action will no longer be required or just. At that point in history, justice will be possible and real for all people regardless of race, sex, ethnic origin, religion, handicap, and/or native language.

Affirmative action implies unequal treatment. The use of such action to achieve equality may at first seem to present a paradox. How can unequal treatment result in equality of opportunity? The answer lies in the temporary nature of an affirmative action program. An affirmative action program begins because there has been unequal treatment in the past. The affirmative action plan also promotes unequal treatment *but in the opposite direction*. The focus in affirmative action is on the goal to be achieved: equality. Once that objective has been reached, then all individuals should be treated equally.

The notion of different treatment for different students, to achieve desired educational outcomes, is not new. The widely accepted practice of individualized instruction is based upon the recognition that students differ in abilities, needs, and interests. Such differences are viewed as normal and inevitable. Moreover, they are considered by both teachers and parents to be a legitimate basis for differentiation of instruction to achieve equality of opportunity to succeed in school and society.

Students also vary in a number of other dimensions, such as sex, race, ethnic background, language spoken at home, and family socio-economic level. These variables, like reading skills and IQ, have been found to be related to success in school. However, most teachers do not say that they differentiate instruction on the basis of these group characteristic variables. On the contrary, it is not unusual to hear teachers say with pride that they treat "boys and girls" or "blacks and whites" *just the same*.

Does the equal treatment of all students, regardless of group-characteristics variables such as sex and race, actually help each and every student to develop her or his capabilities to the fullest? The remainder of this article will attempt to answer this question, focusing on one variable— sex—as a possible basis for differential instruction.

Stereotypes and Documented Sex Differences

Despite what teachers may say, there is much evidence that they do not, in fact, treat boys and girls the same. Sears and Feldman (1966) discovered that elementary teachers interacted more with boys than with girls in four main categories of teaching behavior: approval, instruction, listening to the student, and disapproval. Another study by Ricks and Pyke (1973) also found that more teachers, especially female teachers, preferred male students than preferred female students.

What kinds of comments do teachers make about male and female students? Males are frequently referred to as "outspoken," "active," "open," and "honest." Females "listen," "follow directions," and "don't cause discipline problems." A teacher's preference for one gender or the other is usually based on perceived group differences.

Most teachers are fully aware of the commitment of the *profession* to the avoidance of sexism or discrimination on the basis of sex, but teachers are also members of the larger society and have learned the societal beliefs that males differ from females on a wide variety of attributes beyond the obvious physical ones. It has been documented again and again that Americans, regardless of age, sex, religious or political preference, or level of educational attainment, share a common set of beliefs about the characteristics of males and females. For example, it is widely believed that males are more aggressive, more interested in mathematics and science, more logical, more independent, more active, more dominant, less neat, less emotional, and less gentle than are females (e.g., Broverman, Vogel, Broverman, Clarkson and Rosenkrantz, 1972).

Such beliefs, about how males and females differ with respect to personality traits, are usually referred to as *sex-role stereotypes.* Teachers, like other well-educated members of society, know that stereotypes do not hold true for all individual members of a group; but many stereotypes may no even be true for *most* members of the group being characterized. Stereotypes may be thought of as bits of folklore which have evolved over time and have been taught to succeeding generations by both formal and informal institutions (e.g., family, church, peers, school). While sex-role stereotypes are pervasive, consistent, and persistent over time in the folklore of the culture, they are not the result of scientific investigation. That is, they are most accurately classified as myths, rather than as knowledge about how males and females differ.

The single most valuable resource addressing the question of empirically established differences between the sexes in terms of intellect, achievement and social behavior is provided by Maccoby and Jacklin's *The Psychology of Sex Differences* (1974). In this single volume, psychologists Eleanor Maccoby and Carol Jacklin provide a systematic review and analysis of over 1,400 research studies published since 1965. On the basis of their review of the literature, the authors conclude that, of all the commonly held stereotypes about how males and females differ, only four beliefs are, in fact, supported by scientific investigations: (1) girls, on the average, have greater verbal ability than boys;[1] (2) boys, on the average, excel in visual-spatial ability;[2] (3) boys, on the average, excel in mathematical ability;[3] and (4) males, on the average, are more aggressive. They also conclude that some beliefs are still open to question; either there is too little scientific evidence to permit a decision, or there are inconclusive findings regarding whether some beliefs about sex differences are myths or realities. Differences still open to question are: tactile sensitivity; fear, timidity, and anxiety; activity level; competitiveness; dominance; compliance; and nurturance and "maternal" behavior. Maccoby and Jacklin found *no* scientific evidence to back up the validity of the following stereotypes: (1) girls are more "social" than boys; (2) girls are more "suggestible" than boys; (3) girls have lower self-esteem; (4) girls are better at role learning and simple repetitive tasks; boys are better at tasks that require higher-level cognitive processing and the inhibition of previously learned responses; (5) boys are more "analytic"; (6) girls are more affected by heredity; boys are more affected by environment; (7) girls lack achievement motivation; and (8) girls are auditory; boys are visual.

Individualizing on the Basis of Documented Differences

At this point, it appears that the unequal treatment of boys and girls engaged in school activities related to the four documented sex differences (i.e., verbal ability, visual-spatial ability, mathematical

---

[1]Maccoby and Jacklin (1974) note that while girls' verbal abilities develop more rapidly in the early years, the sexes are very similar from preschool to early adolescence. It is only at age 11 that the sexes begin to diverge; females then exhibit increasingly superior verbal skills through high school and possibly beyond.

[2]Male superiority in visual-spatial tasks first become evident in adolescence and continues into adulthood, according to Maccoby and Jacklin (1974).

[3]As for verbal and visual-spatial skills, this documented sex difference does not occur until age 12–13; beginning at this age, boys tend to increase their mathematical skills faster than do girls. (Maccoby and Jacklin, 1974).

ability, and aggression) would be a valuable extension of the notion of individualized instruction. For example, given that girls excel in verbal skills, then perhaps reading instruction should be started earlier for girls; and girls should be provided with "enrichment" courses through the high school level (or, conversely, boys should start later and be provided with "remedial" courses).

But there is a serious flaw in this logic. Research shows that girls *on the average* have more verbal skills than boys *on the average*. *All* girls do no have greater verbal abilities than *all* boys. Thus, the most obvious course of action, for the teacher who is committed to promoting the fullest development of each individual, is to test each individual student (to determine readiness to read, need for enrichment, etc.) and to provide instruction and materials at the appropriate level. However, given an awareness of the literature on documented sex differences, the teacher should not be surprised if she or he finds that the sexes are disproportionally represented in the various reading or language arts groups.

The documented difference in aggression (which has a physiological basis) suggests a different type of consideration. Most psychologists and human relations experts agree that it is the *assertive* person, as contrasted to the aggressive or passive individual, who is more likely to succeed in business and personal relationships. Teachers who strive to provide their students with opportunities to learn and practice assertive behavior may expect to find that, *in general*, more boys will need to be helped to become assertive by becoming less aggressive, while, *in general*, girls will need to be encouraged to be assertive by becoming less passive. Note that the goal—to become assertive—is the same for both sexes; but the approach to achieving the goal may differ for boys and girls, given the documented group difference. Again, the most enlightened policy is to treat each student as an individual: the aggressive child, be that child a boy or girl, is helped to become less aggressive, while the passive child, regardless of sex, should be encouraged to develop techniques for asserting himself or herself.

In summary, while a few of the commonly shared beliefs about sex differences have been verified by scientific inquiry, most of them have proved to be erroneous and, therefore, should not be used by teachers as a basis on which to differentiate instruction. Further, even the documented differences are only true *on the average* and do not hold for all members of either the male or female group. Thus, before individualizing instruction in any aspect of the school curriculum, the teacher should assess the needs, interests, and abilities of each student, and then proceed to plan and instruct on the basis of verified individual (not group) differences.

Affirmative Action in the Classroom

Societal myths about what people—as males and females—can and cannot become are hard to unlearn; but teachers who are aware of the possible differential effects of schooling on females and males can take steps to avoid discriminating on the basis of sex. Moreover, they can take an active role in structuring activities designed to communicate and promote role expectations based on individual, not group, differences.

The Checklist which follows can be used by teachers to change sex-stereotyped attitudes and behaviors in the classroom. The Checklist also includes activities which can make students more fully aware of the multiple life-roles they can play, both now and in the future. Results from two large-scale affirmative action programs indicate that when teachers engage in activities similar to those suggested by the Checklist, there is a reduction in students' sex-stereotyped attitudes and an expanded view of what they can become. Guttentag and Bray (1976) found that after exposure to an affirmative action program, elementary-school students in kindergarten and fifth grade were more susceptible to positive attitudinal changes than were ninth-grade students. Woolever (1976, 1977) also found that younger pupils, in an affirmative action program involving 76 classrooms, were more amendable to changing their sex-stereotyped attitudes than were older students. Students in kindergarten through second grade experienced the greatest positive attitudinal changes, followed by students in grades three through four, then by pupils in grades five through six.

How many of the following action questions can you answer in the affirmative?

Checklist for Elementary Teachers

1. Do you avoid asking your students to line up *by sex* (other than perhaps to go to the bathroom)?
2. Do both boys and girls do *all* classroom maintenance jobs equally?
3. Do both boys and girls take classroom leadership roles on an equal basis?
4. Are both boys and girls *encouraged* and allowed to run A-V equipment?
5. Do you avoid dividing up your class into teams by sex for group projects, spelling bees, relay races, team sports, etc.?
6. Do you consistently avoid use of the generic words *man, men,* and *he* when you really mean to communicate *men* and *women, humans,* or *people?*
7. Have you *reeducated* yourself in the area of the history of women in the United States by taking women studies courses or by reading one or more recent books on the topic?
8. Do you *supplement* the textbooks, especially in social studies, so that your students learn about the history and contributions of women?
9. Do you occasionally show films or filmstrips about famous women, non-stereotyped careers for women, men in non-stereotyped professions (poet, dancer), or sex discrimination?
10. Have you ever played (and discussed) any part of the record or film, "Free to Be You and Me"?
11. Do you frequently read non-stereotyped books or stories to your class? (For example: a book which shows a boy who cries or a girl who is adventurous, or a story which shows an adult with a non-stereotyped job or interests.)
12. Do you frequently show and discuss pictures from magazines, newspapers, or commercial picture sets of men or women (boys and girls) in nontraditional occupations or roles?
13. Do you occasionally put up bulletin boards (or other displays) which show females and/or males in non-stereotyped roles or careers? (For example: a woman doctor or firefighter, or a man primary teacher or secretary.)
14. Have you had any outside speakers come in and tell about their non-stereotyped career or hobby?
15. Have you taken a field trip to see workers in nontraditional jobs? (For example: visited a female garage mechanic or bank executive or male nurse at work.)
16. Do you occasionally initiate general classroom discussions (not related to a specific film, book, etc.) about: (a) jobs that can be done by either men or women, (b) famous women in history, (c) the women's rights movement, (d) sex discrimination, and (e) myths about sex differences?
17. Do you often have classroom discussions spontaneously as a result of: (a) a child's sexist comment or behavior, (b) a sex-biased story in a basal reader, (c) a section in a social studies text which ignored or misrepresented the contribution of women, (d) a *"sexist"* film/filmstrip or TV program, (e) a sexist or stereotyped character or episode in a *"fun"* book which you were reading to your class?
18. Do you resist having different expectations for your male and female students which are based on group stereotypes? (For example: do you expect most girls to like science and mathematics and most boys to like poetry and art, etc.?)

19. Do you *actively* work to help the boys and girls in your classroom learn to get along and co-operate with one another? (For example: do you assign boys and girls to work together on small group projects? If you hear boys putting down girls as a group, do you challenge the students' negative statements and/or behavior?)

20. Do you believe that, *and act as if,* it is part of your job to help all of your students, both male and female, to expand their view of what boys and girls are like and what each is capable of becoming? (For example: do you help boys to realize that they may one day be husbands and fathers, and do you help girls to realize that many of them will work outside the home for a large proportion of their adult lives?)

Total Possible Score: 20

References

Broverman, I., Vogel, S., Broverman, D., Clarkson, F., and Rosenkrantz, P. Sex-role stereotypes: A current appraisal. *Journal of Social Issues,* 1972, 29, 59–78.

Guttentag, M., and Bray, H. *Undoing sex stereotypes: research and resources for educators.* New York: McGraw-Hill, 1976.

Maccoby, E., and Jacklin, C. *The psychology of sex differences.* Stanford: Stanford University Press, 1974.

Ricks, F., and Pyke, S. Teacher perceptions and attitudes that foster or maintain sex role differences. *Interchange,* 1973, 4, 26–33.

Sears, P., and Feldman, D. Teacher interactions with boys and with girls. *National Elementary Principal,* 1966, 46, 30–35.

Woolever, R. *Expanding elementary pupils' occupational and social role perceptions: An examination of teacher attitudes and behavior and pupil attitude change.* Unpublished doctoral dissertation, University of Washington, 1976.

Woolever, R. *Expanding elementary pupils' occupational and social role perceptions: An innovative federal project.* Chapel Hill, N.C.: University of North Carolina, 1977. (ERIC Document Reproduction Service No. ED 133 249.)

Roberta Woolever is an Assistant Professor in the School of Education, Division of Curriculum and Instruction, University of North Carolina at Chapel Hill.

(Courtesy © *National Council for the Social Studies.* Used with permission.)

QUESTIONS ON READING

1. Which of the stereotypes cited in this article are present in your thinking?

2. Cite examples from your school experience in which teachers displayed bias.

3. What would you find mot difficult in implementing affirmative action for boys and girls? What would be easiest?

LESSON PLANS

Donna Carillo

Objective: To help children in grades 1 through 3 be more emphathetic and understanding of siblings who have special needs.

Rationale: Children raised with siblings who have special needs may respond negatively or positively to the situation. These lessons are designed to foster positive attitudes towards siblings with special needs.

Activities:

1. Teacher shows children a picture of her own family, including a sister who is mentally retarded. Teacher talks about the importance of confidentiality. She then reads from Nancy McConnell's *Difference and Alike,* which introduces young children to the idea of being different.

2. Teacher uses two puppets to lead a discussion about how the puppets differ. Do differences make one better or worse than the other?

3. Teacher presents a time capsule made from a paper towel tube using foil. Each child is asked to write on a piece of paper about a special time they spent with a sibling. Several of these are placed in the time capsule. The child then selects one of the pieces of paper and discusses it with the class. Children with siblings participate in the discussion.

4. Teacher and class read *Our Brother Has Down's Syndrome,* by Cairo S. It is a story about the joys and difficulties of being the sibling of a child with Down's Syndrome.

   • Teacher shows an episode from *Life Goes On* in which Corky wins a medal at the Special Olympics. Class discussion follows.

5. Teacher initiates a Simon Says game in which everyone gets a turn to ask classmates to do a physical task. Following the game students discuss how some things were easy or hard to do. Teacher asks if brothers and sisters also have similar strengths and weaknesses.

6. Students are asked to pick up small objects with their hands. Later, a plastic band is placed around their elbows making it difficult to straighten their arms while picking up objects. A physical therapist presents a demonstration of how she aids children with physical handicaps. The physical therapist teaches children games to play with siblings who have difficulty with motor coordination.

7. Children are asked to complete, "A time I really felt proud of my brother or sister was . . ."

8. Teacher passes out card entitled, "Helpful Hints When Meeting Friends with Disabilities," which contains examples such as:

   • It's OK to offer help, but first ask the person if he or she wants help.

   • It's OK to ask people about their disabilities, but it's also OK not to ask.

   • It's OK to ask people who have speech problems to repeat what they say if you didn't understand the first time.

   • Don't speak loudly to blind people; their hearing is OK.

9. Teacher brings a "Dear Abby" mailbox and encourages children to write anonymous letters discussing situations about brothers and sisters who have disabilities.

Molly Zoth   Middle School
Objectives: Participants will identify women artists who have made significant contributions to art and how they overcame societal prejudices.

Activities:

Anticipatory Set: Participants will:
- List on the board all artists they consider famous.
- Discuss stereotypes of gender-related occupations and list on the board.

Input & Modeling: Participants will:
- View a slide collection of women's artwork, such as teacher resource kits available at local art museums.
- Consult several books on women artists.

Check for Understanding and Guided Practice: Participants will:
- List four examples of women artists who overcame male prejudices in their society and then find artwork created by these four women.
- Practice discussing information about these women and the societies in which they lived.
- Make an outline for presentation or to write a paper.
- Create visual aids to enhance the presentation such as posters, slides, charts, or info-graphics.
- Participate in classroom discussions of traditional male and female roles through the ages.

Independent Practice: Participants will:
- Present the report.
- Gather feedback from classmates.

Closure: Participants will:
- Request that classmates ask at least one question about any aspect of the report that is still not clear.

Evaluation: Class will:
- Write at least two ideas learned from the report.

Barbara Stein   3rd Grade Level
Objective: To create a healthy class environment by educating children concerning the dangers of prejudice.

Rationale: Children can appreciate and understand the need for diversity and why prejudiced behavior hinders the right of each person to be a unique individual.

Activities:

1. Have students create an animal mask using geometric shapes provided by the teacher. Children march around room wearing the mask and dancing to music. Teacher asks:
   - How does it feel to wear someone else's face? What do you like best about it? Least?
   - Did you feel different about your friends while they were wearing their masks?

2. Teacher hands out following poem:

Everybody Says

Everybody says,
I look just like my mother.
Everybody says,
I'm the image of Aunt Bee
Everybody says,
My nose is like my father's
But, I want to look like ME!"

From *Pepito's Story*

Students give reaction to the poem by telling how it relates to their own lives and how they feel when people compare them to parents or relatives.

Students cut out pictures of important people from magazines and newspapers and place them in a collage. A mirror is placed in center of collage. Teacher asks: "Who is the most important person in this collage?"

3. Class makes list of words that hurt people's feelings. They discuss why the words hurt them.

- Students color two puppets. Class discusses: "Would you like the puppet for a friend? What does the puppet like to do best? How are you like or not like a puppet?"
- Students put on a puppet show in which two puppets have an argument, then agree to become friends.

4. Students are asked to complete the following statement: "You can't play because . . . " Class discussion follows about how a person feels when others say that to them.

- Students divided into two teams. "Yes" team plans a strategy to convince "No" team to take a dare. "No" team plans a strategy to refuse the dare. Students switch sides. Class discusses times when they felt pressure to take a dre and go against their own feelings and beliefs.

5. Teacher brings in tray with artichokes and asks students to sample them. Students share feelings about eating the strange food. Discuss other times they have prejudged a food by its outward appearance.

- Class discussion on times individuals have judged other children on outward appearances. Class makes a list of words children who were judged must have felt when others prejudged them.

6. Guest speaker is a grocer who sells products from many cultures. Grocer brings some sample items for students to taste.

- Class collects pictures of foods from many cultures and displays them.
- Children are asked to bring interesting foods their family eats. Class has food fest.

7. Class reads several versions of the Cinderella story.

Vasilisa the Beautiful from Russia.
Yen-Shen: A Cinderella Story from China.
In the Land of the Small Dragon from Vietnam.

After reading stories class designs costumes based on what characters wrote in the stories. Class discussion on how people in different nations can express the same idea in different ways.

Bibliography:

Hirsh, Marilyn, *Potato Pancakes All Around,* Bonim Books, N.Y. 1978.
Kerr, J. *When Hitler Stole the Pink Rabbit,* Dell Pub. N.Y. 1980.
Kraus, Robert, *Leo the Late Bloomer,* Wind Mill Press.

Pamela M. Bertani   Grade 6
Objective: Sharing information with EMH children concerning issues of sexual abuse.

Rationale: EMH students, along with other children, require knowledge about sexual abuse and ways to handle this problem if it should occur.

Activities:

1. Teacher sends home a letter to parents explaining the nature of the lessons on sexual abuse. Parents are requested to sign a form consenting to their child's participation in learning this information.

   - Teacher takes pictures of children demonstrating "good touch" situations.

   - Teacher introduces idea of "type of touch" by reading stories such as *Something Happened to Me* or *The Standoffs*. In small groups students make list of examples of "good" and "bad" touch. Examples of good touch are: hug from grandma, handshake, or pat on back. Examples of bad touch are: bite, slap, hit by student in a fight. For students who can not read very well, these ideas are conveyed through means of pictures.

2. Teacher places chair in front of room. Students are asked to touch the chair in different ways—hug, kiss, tickle, etc. As one student demonstrates, other students are asked for which type of touch would they like to trade places with the chair if the touch was given by a friend.

   - Teacher sends home a color sheet showing examples of good touch. Children share the sheet with parents and talk about good touch.

3. Teacher shows film *Child Molestation: When to Say No.* Students in small groups discuss the film and make a list of key ideas. Show film again and stop it at key points and ask each group to give examples of other ways the problem could be handled.

   - Students practice ways to say "No" by using animal or people shapes made out of cardboard. A stick or pencil is taped to cardboard. Two students stand behind a sheet with a light behind them so class sees shadows. Each pair enacts a skit about a situation in which the issue of saying "no" comes up.

4. Teacher discusses ways to say "no" that are polite but firm. Examples are: "My mom won't let me" or "It's against the law." Teacher discusses nonverbal messages to send by use of a look or tone of voice.

   - Class discusses "bad" touches. Students put word on one side of a card and on reverse draw a picture.

   - Class discusses the idea of a "stranger." Teacher and class list "what if situations." After class discussion, students take home examples to discuss with parents.

5. Teacher discusses what is meant by a "sexual assault." Teacher discusses importance of remembering all you can about someone who tries to bother you.

   - Students make up situations that might involve sexual abuse and discuss how to handle it.

6. Teacher shows film *No More Secrets* and stops it every so often to discuss key issues or ask students how they might handle the situation.

   • In small groups, students brainstorm key ideas learned from the film.

   • Teacher role plays situations with puppets and allows each group to discuss how to handle the situation.

   • Class discusses prevention skills. This involves discussing how to assert one's boundaries, and how to handle potential touching problems. Class discusses when it would be hardest to say "no."

7. Teacher shows film *What Do You Tell?* Film stopped at key points to engage students in discussion.

Bibliography:

Champlin, J. and Champlin, C. *Puppets and the Mentally Retarded Student,* Special Literature, 1981.

Palmer, Pat, *Liking Myself,* Impact Pub. San Luis Obispo, 1982.

Plummer, C. A., *Preventing Sexual Abuse,* Holmes Beach, Florida, Learning Publications, Inc. 1984.

Sweet, Phyllis *Something Happened to Me,* ED-U Press, 1981.

Wheat, Patty, *The Standoffs,* Parents Anonymous, Torrance, 1980.

No More Secrets, (16 mm film) ODN Prod. NY (212) 431-8923.

Who Do You Tell (16 mm film)

REFERENCES

Anyon, J. (1980). Social class and the hidden agenda of work. *Journal of Education, 162,* 67–92.

Banks, J. (1988). *Multiethnic education: Theory and practice* (2nd ed.). Boston: Allyn & Bacon.

Beezer, B. (1985, February). Reporting child abuse and neglect: Your responsibility and your protection. *Phi Delta Kappan, 66,* p. 434–36.

Bogdan, R., & Biklen, D. (1977, March). Handicapism. *Social Policy, 7,* p. 14–19.

Borko, H., & Eisenhart. (1986). Students' conceptions of reading and their reading experience in school. *Elementary School Journal, 86,* 589–612.

Cohen, E. G. (1986). *Designing groupwork: Strategies for heterogeneous classrooms.* New York: Teachers College Press.

Cubberly, E. P. (1909). *Changing conceptions of education.* Boston: Houghton Mifflin.

Department of Health and Human Services, Division of HIV/AIDS. (1986). *Objectives for the nation.* Washington, DC: HHS.

Distad, L. (1987). A personal legacy. *Phi Delta Kappan, 68,* 744–745.

Dobzhansky, T. (1962). *Mankind evolving: The evolution of the human species.* New Haven, CT: Yale University Press.

Dunn, R., & Griggs, S. A. (1988). *Learning styles: Quiet revolution in American schools.* Reston, VA: National Association of Secondary School Principals.

Feigin, J. R., & Feigin, C. B. (1978). *Discrimination American style.* Englewood Cliffs, NJ: Prentice Hall.

Fine, M. (1986). Why urban adolescents drop into and out of public high school. *Teachers College Record, 87,* 393–409.

Gilligan, C. (1982). *In a different voice.* Cambridge: Harvard University Press.

Grant, L., & Rothenberg, J. (1986). The social enhancement of ability differences: Teacher-student interactions in first and second grade reading groups. *Elementary School Journal, 87,* 29–50.

Green, R. (1978, August). [Review of *The invisible children: School integration in American society.*] *Harvard Education Review, 48,* 11, p. 410–14.

Hale-Benson, J. E. *Black children: Their roots, culture, and learning styles.* Baltimore: Johns Hopkins University Press.

Jefferson, T. (1967). *Bill for the More General Diffusion of Knowledge.* Excerpted from David Tyack (Ed.) *Turning Points in American Educational History.* p. 110–14. Waltham, Ma: Blairdell Publishing Company.

Kluckhohn, C. (1953). Universal categories of culture. In A. L. Kroeber (Ed.), *Anthropology today* (pp. 507–523). Chicago: University of Chicago Press.

Kozal, J. (1991). *Savage inequalities: Children in American schools.* New York: Crown.

Meade, M. (1949). *Male and female.* New York: William Morrow.

Miller, C., & Swift, K. (1977). *Words and women.* New York: anchor.

Murdock, G. P. (1967). *The Ethnographic Atlas.* Pittsburgh: University of Pittsburgh Press.

National Institute on Alcohol Abuse and Alcoholism. (1979). *Here's looking at you two: A K–12 drug and alcohol curriculum.* Washington, DC: NIAAA.

Ortiz, F. I. (1988). Hispanic-American children's experiences in classrooms: A comparison between Hispanic and non-Hispanic children. In L. Weis (Ed.), *Race, class, and gender in American education* (pp. 63–87). Albany: State University of New York Press.

Ortner, S. B. (1974). Is female to male as nature is to culture? In M. Z. Rosaldo and L. Lamphere (Eds.), *Women, culture and society.* Stanford: Stanford University Press.

Ramirez, M., and Casteñada, A. (1974). *Cultural democracy, biocognitive development and education.* New York: Academic Press.

Reimer, E. (1971). *School is dead: Alternatives in education.* New York: Doubleday.

Rist, R. (1978). *The invisible children: School integration in American society.* Cambridge: Harvard University Press.

Romer, N. (1981). *The sex role cycle.* Old Westbury, NY: Feminist Press.

Sadker, M., & Sadker, D. (1982). *Sex equity handbook for schools.* New York: Longman.

Sadker, M. & Sadker, D. (1985, March). Sexism in the schoolroom of the '80s. *Psychology Today,* p. 52–57.

Sexton, P. (1969). *The feminized male: Classrooms, white collars, and the decline of manliness.* New York: Random House.

Shaver, J., & Curtis, C. (1981, March). Handicapism: Another challenge for social studies. *Social Education, 45,* (3), 208–211.

Slavin, R. E. (1983). *Cooperative learning.* New York: Longman.

Volverde, S. A. (1987). A comparative study of Hispanic dropouts and graduates: Why do some leave early and some finish? *Education and Urban Society, 19,* 311–320.

Glossary

Ability grouping is placing students in specific groups based upon some criteria of ability to learn.

Accountability refers to being held responsible for one's actions in the educative process and the extent of student learning.

Action research is a form of self-reflection undertaken by participants in social situations to improve the rationality and justice of their own practices and understanding of those practices.

Affective domain refers to learning associated with feelings, attitudes, and values.

Afrocentricism seeks to emphasize the significant historical, cultural, literary, and scientific developments originating within the African continent.

Analytical thinking is the process of subjecting materials to the scientific method of analysis.

Assertive discipline is a process of behavior modification originating in the teacher's goals and aspirations for student behavior.

Assessment is the process of gauging the quality and quantity of learning.

Authoritarian education is a teacher-dominated setting in which students have limited power to establish learning goals or procedures.

Behavioral objective is a statement depicting goals to be taught in terms of how they will be demonstrated in human behavior.

Behavioral modification is a strategy of shaping behavior by reinforcing desirable responses and ignoring undesirable ones.

Bloom's Taxonomy refers to a widely used taxonomy of educational objectives formulated by Benjamin Bloom and his associates.

Certification is a set of requirements established by state agencies to determine who is qualified to teach or administer in public schools.

Child-centered is the view that each child contains a capacity to learn, to be caring, and to function with mature attitudes and values.

Class meetings are sessions in which students and teacher collaboratively plan class activities.

Classification is the act of grouping, clustering, or categorizing.

Cognitive domain refers to academic or intellectual learning.

Collaborative learning is a process of group investigation and cooperation in the pursuit of learning tasks.

Committee of Ten Report, issued in 1893, emphasized the need for an academic foundation in elementary and secondary education.

Community involvement is an educational thrust to involve students with the everyday issues of their own communities and to play a role in improving the quality of life in those settings as well as involve community members in the life of schools.

Concept is a learnable, idea, skill, attitude, equation, or principle.

Corporal punishment is physical contact inflicting pain taken by school authorities against students, such as paddling or spanking.

Creativity is the act of uncovering new patterns within existing data leading to originality of thinking.

Critical thinking is an active process involving a number of denotable mental operations such as induction, deduction, reasoning, sequencing, classification, and the definition of relationships.

Culture of school refers to the values, belief systems, and norms found in a particular school or school system.

Cultural literacy is the belief that a common set of knowledge about one's culture exists and should be taught.

Curriculum is the process of pedagogy including the selection and organization of what is to be taught.

Curriculum guide describes learning objectives and material to be studied at various grade levels and within different subject areas and ways they should be taught.

Discovery learning is an approach to curriculum in which teachers organize materials to allow students to formulate hypotheses, gather data, and assess their hypotheses.

Divergent thinking entails formulating hypotheses regarding possible alternatives.

Equity in education is the concept that every student is afforded an equal opportunity to fulfill his or her innate capacities.

Enrichment is supplementary educational experiences and materials provided students beyond the norm of the existing curriculum.

Environmental education is learning about the interdependence of physical, economic, political, and social factors as they impact planet Earth and the need for conservation of resources.

Expository learning is learning that occurs from the general to the specific, from rule to example.

Extrinsic motivation is doing something because it is required or in expectation of a reward from an outside source.

Gender-role expectations is the belief or assumption that men and women have distinctive human capacities.

Gifted education refers to educational programs provided to students identified as possessing high intellectual capacity.

Global education refers to efforts to incorporate within the curriculum a more complex understanding of the worldwide human community.

Hidden or implicit curriculum refers to behavior, attitudes, and values taught in schools that often assume greater importance than the formal curriculum.

Humanistic education emphasizes values, attitudes, and learning geared to meet the needs of students and develop positive self-concept.

Information age refers to the exponential growth in data due to the emergence of advanced technology such as computers.

Individual education plan (IEP) is a written plan of education designed to meet the needs or concerns of an individual student with special needs.

Individualized instruction is organized in order to meet the needs of individual students.

Indoctrination is the process of imposing values, information, and attitudes upon people in an authoritarian manner.

In-service education is learning geared to meet the needs of practicing teachers who seek further education.

Integrated learning is an educational approach that unifies a number of academic fields of study into one focus or topic.

Intrinsic motivation is a stimulation for learning arising from within the individual apart from any external reward system.

Law-related education refers to teaching students about law, the legal processes, and the legal system.

Learning disability is a disorder in one or more of the basic psychological processes involved in understanding or in using spoken or written language which manifests itself in difficulty in learning.

Learning strategies are approaches used by students to enhance comprehension of material being studied.

Lesson plan is a teacher's plan of instruction which includes goals and instructional methodologies.

Madeline Hunter Model refers to a format of lesson design based upon instructional ideas developed by Dr. Madeline Hunter.

Mainstreaming enables students legally identified as handicapped to be educated within regular classroom settings.

Mastery learning is a process employing criterion-based objectives, flexible time, and opportunities for students to use their learning style in mastering the material being studied.

Metacognition is thinking about how one thinks.

Middle schools are educational institutions designed to meet the needs of the pre-adolescent student. It ordinarily includes some combination of grades five through eight.

Mnemonic is the process by which people memorize or remember information by utilizing various strategies including visualization, letter patterns, diagrams, or imagery.

Modeling is the process of behaving or setting an example that one intends for others to emulate.

Moral development refers to stages of ethical reasoning.

Multiculturalism emphasizes the historical, cultural, literary, religious, and scientific accomplishments of people of diverse backgrounds and the need to present the diverse story of human development as well as the common factors that bind humans.

Nonverbal communication is communicating without use of words.

Open education is a model of education emphasizing student interest areas, collaborative learning, and active engagement of students in planning and pursuing the learning process.

Peer mediators assist their peers in peaceful resolution of school-based conflicts.

Portfolio is a collection of student materials that plays a role in determining their mastery of course objectives and provides evidence of student learning.

Pseudowriting is a process in which students locate and copy or paraphrase information.

Psychomotor domain is that aspect of human learning involving use of motor skills.

Rhetorical questions are those without an intended answer.

Role playing is a communicative process requiring the participants to understand the feelings, emotions, and attributes of other people in new situations.

Scope refers to a range of substantive content, values, skills, and learner experiences that is included within the social studies curriculum.

Self-concept is the image held by an individual about his or her personal worth.

Sequence is the order in which social studies components appear within the curriculum.

Simulation is an action or tool that imitates a process, concept, or situation.

Social efficiency is a philosophy emphasizing the importance of schools teaching students practical skills that can immediately be applied in life or the workplace.

Spiral curriculum is a process in which ideas are taught at varying levels of complexity through-out the total social studies curriculum.

Synthetics is a process of joining together different and apparently irrelevant elements or ideas to create a new entity.

Tracking is ability grouping that assigns students to continuing academic levels based upon criteria such as standardized testing or teacher recommendations.

Underachievers are students who consistently perform below their expected ability level.

Unit is a curriculum plan of action for a one- to two-week period centered around a major theme.

Values education refers to teaching about human attitudes in making moral choices.

Wait-time is the time after a teacher asks a question before a student is asked to respond.

Index